P9-DXN-931

To
Victoria and Jonathan
Barbara, Jonathan, and Adam

PERGAMON INTERNATIONAL LIBRARY
of Science, Technology, Engineering and Social Studies

*The 1000-volume original paperback library in aid of education,
industrial training and the enjoyment of leisure*

Publisher: Robert Maxwell, M.C.

Behavioral Assessment

(PGPS - 65)

THE PERGAMON TEXTBOOK
INSPECTION COPY SERVICE

An inspection copy of any book published in the Pergamon International Library
will gladly be sent to academic staff without obligation for their consideration for
course adoption or recommendation. Copies may be retained for a period of 60 days
from receipt and returned if not suitable. When a particular title is adopted or
recommended for adoption for class use and the recommendation results in a sale
of 12 or more copies, the inspection copy may be retained with our compliments.
The Publishers will be pleased to receive suggestions for revised editions and new
titles to be published in this important International Library.

Pergamon Titles of Related Interest

Hersen/Barlow SINGLE CASE EXPERIMENTAL DESIGNS: Strategies for Studying Behavior Change
Kanfer/Goldstein HELPING PEOPLE CHANGE: A Textbook of Methods, Second Edition
Karoly/Kanfer SELF-MANAGEMENT AND BEHAVIOR CHANGE: From Theory to Practice
Sarbin/Mancuso SCHIZOPHRENIA — MEDICAL DIAGNOSIS OR MORAL VERDICT?
Walker CLINICAL PRACTICE OF PSYCHOLOGY: A Guide for Mental Health Professionals

Related Journals*

Addictive Behaviors
Analysis and Intervention in Developmental Disabilities
Behavioral Assessment
Journal of Behavior Therapy and Experimental Psychiatry
Physiology and Behavior

*Free specimen copies available upon request.

91821

Behavioral Assessment

a practical handbook
Second Edition

ST. PATRICK'S SEMINARY LIBRARY
MENLO PARK, CALIFORNIA
94025
DISCARD

Edited by
Michel Hersen
University of Pittsburgh School of Medicine
Alan S. Bellack
University of Pittsburgh

Pergamon Press
New York   Oxford   Toronto   Sydney   Paris   Frankfurt

RC
489
B4
B4354
1981

Pergamon Press Offices:

U.S.A.	Pergamon Press Inc.. Maxwell House. Fairview Park. Elmsford. New York 10523. U.S.A.
U.K.	Pergamon Press Ltd.. Headington Hill Hall. Oxford OX3 0BW. England
CANADA	Pergamon Press Canada Ltd.. Suite 104. 150 Consumers Road. Willowdale. Ontario M2J 1P9. Canada
AUSTRALIA	Pergamon Press (Aust.) Pty. Ltd.. P.O. Box 544. Potts Point. NSW 2011. Australia
FRANCE	Pergamon Press SARL. 24 rue des Ecoles. 75240 Paris. Cedex 05. France
FEDERAL REPUBLIC OF GERMANY	Pergamon Press GmbH. Hammerweg 6. Postfach 1305. 6242 Kronberg/Taunus. Federal Republic of Germany

Copyright © 1981 Pergamon Press Inc.

Library of Congress Cataloging in Publication Data
Main entry under title:

Behavioral assessment.

  (Pergamon general psychology series ; v. 65)
  Includes bibliographies and indexes.
  1. Behavior therapy. 2. Mental illness--
Diagnosis. I. Hersen, Michel. II. Bellack, Alan S.
III. series. [DNLM: 1. Behavior therapy.
2. Mental disorders--Diagnosis. WM 420 B4179]
RC489.B4354   1981   616.89'142   81-970
ISBN 0-08-025956-1   AACR2
ISBN 0-08-025955-3 (pbk.)

*All Rights reserved. No part of this publication may be reproduced,
stored in a retrieval system or transmitted in any form or by any means:
electronic. electrostatic. magnetic tape, mechanical, photocopying,
recording or otherwise, without permission in writing from the
publishers.*

Printed in the United States of America

Contents

Preface to Second Edition

Since publication of the first edition, the field of behavioral assessment has burgeoned and undergone refinement and enhancement. First, several new journals in the area have been founded. One in 1977, *Behavior Modification,* deals with behavioral assessment and modification. Two others *(Behavioral Assessment; Journal of Behavioral Assessment)* both founded in 1979, specifically are concerned with publication of articles that cover various aspects of behavioral assessment. It is clear that behavioral assessment has made its impact on clinical psychology, psychiatry, education, and behavioral medicine. In our view, developments in behavioral assessment have even influenced those colleagues and students in the field who do not share out theoretical persuasion.

Most important, however, are the newer theoretical and empirical currents in behavioral assessment. Greater precision of thinking and experimentation has characterized this field since we undertook to edit the first edition. This has been reflected by concerns with parametric issues such as reliability and validity. Gone is the initial untested clinical bravado of the behavioral assessors in favor of more scientifically obtained and carefully delineated assessment strategies. In the last few years the "baby" has been "retrieved for the bath water" casually cast away. There has been growing recognition that psychometricians of the past did have something to say, and that certain features of traditional psychometric principles could be blended with behavioral assessment in an improved amalgam. We believe that many of the chapters in this volume reflect these trends in the behavioral assessment enterprise.

Using the feedback received on the first edition, we have made a number of changes in organization and content. *Indeed, with the exception of three chapters, all of the material is new.* And, in these three chapters (3, 8, and 10) there has been considerable revision. The book is organized into three *Parts:* I *Fundamental Issues,* II *Assessment Strategies,* and III *Evaluation for Treatment Planning.* In contrast to the first edition, we now have a chapter dealing with psychometric considerations, accord greater theoretical and methodological attention to the specifics of behavioral observation (Chapter 4), and have divided the evaluation of children into outpatient and inpatient settings. Furthermore, for heuristic purposes we asked contributors for Part III *(Evaluation for Treatment Planning)* to provide actual case descriptions to illustrate how behavioral assessment is accomplished for that specific disorder. We felt this would enhance readability and provide necessary clinical material for students.

As in the first edition, many individuals have contributed to this volume. First, we again thank the contributors for articulating their thoughts about their sub-specialties. Second, we would like to acknowledge the encouragement we have received from Jerome B. Frank at Pergamon Press. And third, we are grateful to Mary Newell, Lauretta Guerin, Jan Twomey, and Harry Sherick for their technical assistance.

Michel Hersen
Alan S. Bellack

Part I:
Fundamental Issues

Chapter 1
Nature of Behavioral Assessment

Rosemery O. Nelson and
Steven C. Hayes

INTRODUCTION

Behavioral assessment is the identification and measurement of meaningful response units and their controlling variables (both environmental and organismic) for the purposes of understanding and altering human behavior. This chapter describes the theoretical assumptions underlying behavioral assessment, its goals and techniques, and methods of evaluating the quality of behavioral assessment devices and data. Finally, some directives for future research and practice are suggested.

While behavioral assessment has a long past, it has a short history. During behavior therapy's first 50 years, treatment, intervention, and independent variables were understandably of primary concern. Experimental design, methodology, dependent variables, and other behavioral assessment topics were considered, but merely as necessary adjuncts to treatment issues. Only when ample evidence of treatment effectiveness began to accumulate were assessment questions meaningful in themselves. For example, behavioral researchers and clinicians began to wonder: Are these appropriate behaviors to alter? Are these valid and reliable ways of measuring behavior? Can these changes be attributed to the intervention? How can assessment enhance treatment effectiveness?

Thus, behavioral assessment has only lately become a field of study in its own right. The number of recent publications in behavioral assessment serve witness to its emergence: books by Barlow (1981),

3

Ciminero, Calhoun, and Adams (1977), Cone and Hawkins (1977), Haynes (1978), Haynes and Wilson (1979), Hersen and Bellack (1976),. Keefe, Kopel, and Gordon (1978), Mash and Terdal (1976, 1981); and journals entitled *Behavioral Assessment* (Pergamon and the Association for Advancement of Behavior Therapy) and *Journal of Behavioral Assessment* (Plenum). Indeed, this present revision of Hersen and Bellack's book (1976) is evidence of the growth of behavioral assessment which accompanied its identification as a nuclear field of study.

THEORETICAL ASSUMPTIONS UNDERLYING BEHAVIORAL ASSESSMENT

A Comparison of Behavioral Assessment with Traditional Assessment

At times it may be difficult to distinguish between behavioral and traditional approaches to assessment because the differences do *not* lie in techniques used. In fact, the two approaches share several assessment devices (e.g., role-playing, interviews, questionnaires, and standardized tests). The differences lie rather in the assumptions of the two approaches and in the implications of these assumptions (see also Hartmann, Roper, & Bradford, 1979).

Traditional views typically emphasize personologism; that is, psychopathology is thought to result from relatively stable intraorganismic (usually intrapsychic) variables. Hence, during assessment behavior or appearance is interpreted as a *sign* of these underlying variables (Goldfried & Kent, 1972; Goodenough, 1949). The focus of assessment is on what the person *has* (Mischel, 1968). Since the causes of behavior are believed to lie within the person, the assessment situation is not emphasized. Rather, the nature and quality of the assessment device *per se* is considered to be most important. Since these internal causes of behavior are thought to be stable, assessment techniques can be evaluated by their psychometric or structural properties. In psychometrics, a score on an assessment device is assumed to reflect both the "true" score (the "ideal" measurement of the underlying variable) and measurement error. Consistency in measurement across time (test-retest reliability), across test items (split-half reliability), or across assessment devices (concurrent or predictive validity) is considered to be the hallmark of a good assessment technique, because it indicates that more of the true score is being measured instead of the randomly distributed measurement error.

The assumptions of behavioral assessment stand in contrast to these assumptions of traditional assessment. Indeed, at one time (perhaps in reaction to personologism) many behaviorists held a situational position which seemed to attribute behavior almost exclusively to immediate environmental variables. Most modern behaviorists have adopted an interactionist view (Bowers, 1973; Ekehammer, 1974; Mischel, 1968, 1973) that behavior is a function of both current environmental and organismic variables (such as one's physiological state and learning history). Because of the importance assigned to immediate environmental variables, the assessment situation is viewed as crucial in providing an opportunity to generate the behavior of interest. The assessment situation is considered to be as important as the assessment device. Behavior is viewed as a sample of responding in that particular assessment situation (Goldfried & Kent, 1972; Goodenough, 1949). Inferences to other situations, even the criterion situation of the natural environment, are made only with caution. The focus of assessment is on what the person *does* rather than on what he or she *has* (Mischel, 1968). A score on an assessment device is usually assumed to reflect both the "true" behavior and measurement error. But since behavior is seen to be the result of changing environmental conditions, *consistency* in measurement across time, items, or devices cannot be the sole (or even the major) criterion of good behavioral assessment devices. This is so because inconsistency may reflect actual changes in behavior rather than measurement error. Therefore, the quality of behavioral assessment must be evaluated in terms of its accuracy and functional utility. Of prime importance is the question, does this assessment function to increase our understanding of behavior or to improve our treatment of this client? Thus, while traditional and behavioral assessors share some of the same assessment techniques, their assumptions and resultant implications differ.

SORC (Stimulus-Organism-Response-Consequences)

Many of the variables which should be considered during a thorough behavioral assessment are summarized in the convenient acronym SORC or Stimulus-Organism-Response-Consequences (Goldfried & Sprafkin, 1976). The response is the target behavior (i.e., the problematic behavior that has been identified for modification). The other SORC components represent the controlling variables of which this response is a function. In the spirit of interactionism, both immediate environmental and organismic controlling variables are considered to be important. The immediate environmental variables are represented as S, the stimuli which precede the target behavior, and C, the consequences which follow the target behavior. The organismic variables are represented as O and include both physiological state and past learning. Each of these SORC components is described in detail below.

Stimuli. It has been widely documented that behavior is usually situation-specific (Mischel, 1968; Peterson, 1968). In other words, the behavior of an individual depends in large part on the immediate stimulus situation. Thus, an exhibitionist may exhibit himself only when a particular constellation of stimulus events occur (for example, it is evening, nothing else is planned, the person goes to the local library, an attractive woman appears among the book shelves) or a child may be noncompliant only when one particular parent or one particular teacher issues commands.

Evidence for situation specificity is generally provided by two different methodologies. In one type, the same subjects' responses are correlated across different situations. Evidence for situation specificity is found in relatively low correlations across situations. For example, a classic study by Hartshorne and May (1928) correlated children's "honesty responses" in the home, party games, athletic contests, and classroom tests. The overall correlations between situations was low; the more dissimilar the situations, the lower the correlation. In a second type of methodology, researchers calculate the proportion of the variance which can be accounted for by subjects, situations, and their interaction, typically by using an analysis of variance. For example, with aggressive boys in six different situations (e.g., breakfast, structured games, arts, and crafts), Rausch, Dittman, and Taylor (1959) found that more variance was accounted for by the individual x situation interaction than by either main effect of individual or of situation.

Several theoretical explanations have been posited for situation specificity. On the one hand, situation-specific responding has been accounted for by the individual's learning history during which environmental stimuli assume discriminative properties (via stimulus discrimination or generalization) and assume reinforcing properties (via secondary reinforcement). This is thought to produce the individual's unique pattern of situation-specific responding (Staats, 1975). On the other hand, a more cognitive account of situation specificity has been offered. It includes organism variables, such as "construction competencies" or "encoding strategies and personal constructs" (Mischel, 1973), by which an individual interprets environmental stimuli to produce an idiosyncratic pattern of situation-specific responding. Regardless of the theoretical explanation, there is general agreement among behaviorists that behavior is generally situation specific.

Situation specificity has a least three implications for behavioral assessment. The first is that the clinician must assess not only a client's problematic responses, but also the specific stimulus situations in which these responses are likely to occur. For example, it may be important in the treatment of an alcoholic to determine the specific situations in which problem drinking is likely to occur. The measurement of the environment presents a critical challenge to behavioral assessment (McReynolds, 1979; Moos, 1973). This challenge is twofold: (a) how can the environment be quantified?, and (b) how can it be organized into behaviorally meaningful (i.e., functional) units? Behavioral assessors have generally focused on quantification of the response in terms of frequency, duration, or intensity. Situations, however, are usually evaluated in a more qualitative fashion; for example, the laboratory is "different" from the home, or role-playing with Peer 1 is "similar" to role-playing with Peer 2. Occasionally, more precise quantitative measurement of environmental stimuli occurs: for example, the number of feet between the subject and the snake during a behavioral avoidance test for a snake phobic, or the decibel readings produced by different intensities of thunder during a behavioral avoidance test for a storm phobic. Quantification of dimensions of the stimulus situation is important because it sets the stage for organizing the environment into behaviorally meaningful units. This is critical in evaluating whether or not the crucial (i.e., functional) aspects of the assessment situation are the same or different from those aspects of the natural environment.

A second implication of situation specificity is that assessment devices cannot evaluate a problematic response in isolation. The assessment device must incorporate critical parts of the stimulus situation that are likely to generate the response of interest. For example, if the client's target behavior is sexual, the assessment device must include sexual stimuli.

A third implication is that the process of behavioral assessment must be compatible with situation specificity. Typically, assessment occurs to determine how the client behaves in the natural environment before, during, or after treatment. Unfortunately, the assessment situation may differ radically from the natural environment. This is clearly evident when assessment occurs in the clinic by means of interviewing or role-playing. It can also occur, however, even when observations are made in the natural environment; the assessment procedure itself will often alter the natural environment sufficiently to alter responding. Kazdin (1979a) has labeled the dilemma produced by situation specificity as "the two-edged sword of behavioral assessment." On one hand, behavioral assessors pay homage to situation specificity by including specific situations within the assessment procedure and by attempting to determine the idiosyncratic situations producing the client's problematic responses. On the other hand, an overly strict interpretation of situation specificity makes assessment nearly impossible since the assessment situation is not identical to the criterion situation in the natural environment. Possible solutions to this dilemma include the use of unobtrusive assessment methods in the natural environment or the use of informants (Kazdin, 1979a, 1979b). Further, as more knowledge is developed on the quantification and analysis of stimuli, behavioral assessors may be able to maximize the functional similarity of the assessment situation and the natural environment.

Organism. In accordance with interactionism, behavior is best viewed as a function of both immediate environmental and organism variables. Organism variables are those individual differences the client brings to the current environmental situation. These differences are produced by more remote environmental influences such as past learning, by genetic variables, and by current physiology. Identification of organism variables is helpful in understanding how the person's problems developed. For example, current strange behaviors might be better understood in light of a familial history of schizophrenia or a diagnosed organic brain syndrome. Sometimes, identification of organism variables is directly useful in designing treatment. A familial history of schizophrenia, in addition to present schizophrenic behavior, might suggest that phenothiazines be included in the treatment regimen. In one of our cases, for example, a child was referred because of stealing at school. Interviews and observations revealed that the stolen goods were always food or money to buy food, and that her foster parents provided little to eat at home. Identification of this physiological variable of hunger suggested an alternative foster placement to treat her "stealing."
    Examination of past learning history is also helpful in understanding the client's present behavioral repertoire and in predicting the probability of treatment success. For example, it is generally held that the probability of treatment success is greater for sexual deviants who have had some history of heterosexual experience than for those who have not (Feldman & MacCulloch, 1965), despite similarity in current behavior patterns. Occasionally, knowledge of past learning history may be important in determining current environmental variables which may be used in subsequent treatment. For example, Wolpe (1958) reports the case of an anxious client who revealed an incident from his past in which he had been both sexually attracted and repulsed by a woman with whom he had intercourse. Since the room lights were off, only the dark outlines of objects were visible. This bit of history helped to determine that his pervasive anxiety worsened around sexual stimuli and dark, heavy objects.

Response. Another assumption of behavioral assessment is that topographically distinct responses can covary or even be members of the same response class. Physically different behaviors may be controlled by some or all of the same environmental contingencies. Response covariations can be studied at the level of either the individual or the group. As an example of the former, Wahler (1975) examined the behavioral repertoires of two boys in home and school settings. Each boy displayed a unique but stable (three years) set of covarying responses which differed at home and in school. As an example of the latter the supportive literature of specific diagnostic classifications stands. In the third edition of the Diagnostic and Statistical Manual of Mental Disorders (American Psychiatric Association, 1980), to cite one instance, the diagnosis of major depressive episode is given to an adult based on the following response covariation: dysphoric mood or loss of interest or pleasure in all or almost all usual activities and pastimes; poor appetite or significant weight loss (when not dieting) or increased appetite or significant weight gain; insomnia or hypersomnia; psychomotor agitation or retardation; loss of interest or pleasure in usual activities or decrease in sexual drive; loss of energy, fatigue; feelings of worthlessness, self-reproach, or excessive or inappropriate guilt; complaints or evidence of diminished ability to think or concentrate or indecisiveness; and recurrent thoughts of death, suicidal ideation, wishes to be dead, or suicide attempt. Evidence exists for the actual covariation of many of these behavioral characteristics (Beck, Rush, Shaw, & Emery, 1980). While such responses may covary for a group of depressed individuals, this exact response covariation may not be characteristic of a particular depressed individual. Indeed, many of the problems with previous diagnostic systems stem from this. For example, in an often-cited study, Zigler and Phillips (1961) found little relation between a patient's diagnostic category and his or her specific behaviors.

At times, topographically different responses may be controlled by identical contingencies and thus be conceptualized as members of the same response class. This presents a challenge to behavioral assessment because it requires that behavior be assessed according to specified stimulus, organism, and consequence units. For example, a child may show a wide variety of attention getting behavior in a classroom. Changes in the strength of this response class may well be missed if enough members of the class are not assessed or recognized as part of the overall class.

Discovery of individual or group response covariation is not only interesting at a conceptual level, but may also be useful in treatment.

In a sample of eight children, Wahler and Moore (1975) found aggressive behavior and solitary play activity to be negatively correlated. In a subsequent study (Wahler & Fox, 1980), solitary toy play was the target behavior for four oppositional aggressive boys, resulting in reduced oppositional behavior.

The above discussion deals with covariation among physically different behaviors. Another assumption of behavioral assessment is that within a similar behavior or behavioral construct the specific mode or type of response must be assessed (e.g., motoric, cognitive, and physiological indicants of fear). Early behaviorists generally limited their study of behavior to overt motor responses. Most contemporary behaviorists consider all forms of organismic activity to be "behavior." Thus, behavioral assessment includes the measurement of overt motor, cognitive-verbal, and physiological-emotional behavior. Although these three types of behavior may covary, such covariation cannot be assumed (Lang, 1968). In fact, when simultaneous measurements are taken from all three response systems, the correlations are often only moderate among measures thought to be "aspects" of the same "overall behavior" (Bandura, Blanchard, & Ritter, 1969; Hartshorne & May, 1928; Lang & Lazovik, 1963; Risley & Hart, 1968). Inconsistent relationships among the three response systems are found not only in baseline measurements, but also during treatment. For example, different relationships between heart rate and behavior change occurred in phobics exposed to the same treatment of reinforced practice (Leitenberg, Agras, Butz, & Wincze, 1971), and different relationships among heart rate, behavior change, and questionnaire measures occurred in phobics treated by one of several fear-reduction techniques (Odom, Nelson, & Wein, 1978).

The implication of inconsistencies among the triple response system for behavioral assessment is that a thorough assessment will often require examination of each of the response systems thought to be important before, during, and after treatment. Usually, all three types of behavior must be assessed. This strategy is frequently used in the assessment of phobias, for example, where motoric avoidance, verbal ratings of fear, and physiological measures are simultaneously taken in the context of the behavioral avoidance test (Borkovec, Weerts, & Bernstein, 1977).

Not only are relationships frequently inconsistent across different response systems, but many are also inconsistent among different measures taken from the same response system. Different measures of change in obesity status produced by weight loss treatment, for example, are imperfectly correlated (Rogers, Mahoney, Mahoney, Straw, & Kenigsberg, 1980). An implication for behavioral assessment is that multiple aspects of a response often merit measurement, in addition to the commonly measured response frequency or rate. In the assessment of smoking, for example, Frederiksen, Martin, and Webster (1979) advocate assessment of the substance smoked and the topography of consumption, in addition to smoking rate.

While the common belief among behaviorists is that responding across the three response systems is frequently inconsistent, Cone (1979) speculates that the inconsistency may be due in part to a methodological artifact. Cone (1979) argues that a system by method confound has often recurred in past research on the triple response system. That is, self-report methods are used to assess cognitive content but direct observation methods are used to assess motor or physiological content. Cone proposes that if only method were varied (e.g., direct observation of a person perspiring during a behavioral avoidance test versus self-report of perspiring) more consistent relationships may be obtained across the three response systems. Indeed, when subjects are asked to report what they would do and then are asked to perform those tasks, the correlations between self-report and overt behavior are often very high (Bandura & Adams, 1977; McReynolds & Stegman, 1976). Further research may determine the conditions under which the response systems are consistent or inconsistent; but for current clinical purposes, consistency should not be assumed, and hence measurement in all response systems of importance should occur.

Consequences. Consequent stimuli are those environmental events which occur contingently after a response to influence its frequency. The assessment goal is to identify the short-term and long-term consequences which surround both the target and competing behavior. For example, if the target is an inappropriate behavior that requires deceleration, both the positive consequences maintaining the problematic response and the negative consequences that make the response a problem should be assessed. In terms of Mowrer's neurotic paradox (1950), abnormal behaviors may be both "self-perpetuating" (have positive consequences) and "self-defeating" (have negative consequences). Given the gradient of reinforcement, short term positive consequences may often be more powerful than long-term negative consequences. In addition, consequences surrounding alternative behaviors should be known. Assessment of this consequential matrix may allow the therapist to select among various alternative treatment strategies, such as cueing the client to these long term negative consequences; helping the client to obtain the same rewards (e.g., obtaining attention in more socially desirable ways); training incompatible behavior; or punishing the inappropriate behavior directly. Often, the assessment goal is not only to identify

existing consequences but also to locate potentially effective consequences. For example, in training a child in self-help skills, the determination of effective reinforcers may be critical.

Temporal Stability

Situation specificity is generally investigated by considering a cross-
section of an individual's behavior across different situations within a
relatively brief period of time. Temporal stability is generally investigated by considering a longitudinal section of an individual's behavior
in similar situations.

   While behavior is usually found to be situation specific, it is often
longitudinally consistent. One reason for temporal stability is that the
person may live in a fairly stable environment, with repetitive discriminative, eliciting, and reinforcing stimuli (Mischel, 1968). Indeed, preschool children were found to exhibit stable behavior patterns over a
4-month interval, but only within assessment situations; across situations, behavioral patterns showed variability even from day-to-day
(Rose, Blank, & Spalter, 1975). Relatedly, it has been claimed that
the stability in children's IQ scores over years may be due to the stability of home environmental variables (Hanson, 1975). Besides repetitive situations, other reasons offered for the temporal consistency of
behavior include the following: intermittent reinforcement contributes
to the durability of behavior (Mischel, 1968); the person's learned cognitive encoding strategies may remain constant (Mischel, 1968, 1973);
physiological needs continue over time as do stable behavior patterns
to fill these needs; the person's gender and physical appearance remain
somewhat constant, serving as a stable discriminative stimulus to others
(Staats, 1971); current behavioral repertoires set limits on situations
to which one is exposed, additional responses that one is capable of
making, and available rewards (Staats, 1971, 1975).

   Thus, temporal consistency should not be surprising to the behavioral
assessor. If, however, some of these apparent causes of temporal stability are altered, inconsistency in responding should be expected.

Nomothetic Principles and Idiographic Application

It has been a behavioral tradition to focus on the individual subject or
client. An empirical clinical science, however, demands general principles which are universally applicable. Therefore, it seems advantageous to search in behavioral assessment for nomothetic or general

principles which can then be utilized in an idiographic or individualized manner.

One nomothetic principle is represented in the SORC model, presented above—behavior is a function of immediate environmental and organismic variables. While specific responses and their controlling variables may take infinite forms, the general principle is nonetheless useful in guiding our assessment procedures.

Another nomethetic principle is that there are common patterns of response covariation. The existence of such "syndromes" forms the basis of most classification or diagnostic systems. For example, in the third edition of the Diagnostic and Statistical Manual of Mental Disorders (DSM-III) (American Psychiatric Association, 1980), "each of the mental disorders is conceptualized as a clinically significant behavioral or psychological syndrome or pattern. . . . [Introduction to DSM-III, p. 6]." These patterns of response covariation are useful in suggesting behaviors, in addition to the presenting problem, which should be examined in an individual client. Such covarying responses may become target behaviors for modification and may help to confirm the presence of a particular pattern or syndrome.

Identified nomothetic patterns often allow for a good deal of idiographic variability as well. For example, the diagnostic criteria for generalized anxiety disorder includes generalized, persistent anxiety, continuous for at least one month, manifested by symptoms from three of the following four classes of behavior: (1) motor tension (shakiness, trembling, fidgeting, muscle aches); (2) autonomic hyperactivity (sweating, clammy hands, dry mouth, dizziness); (3) apprehensive expectation (anxiety, worry, fear); and (4) vigilance and scanning (hyperattentiveness resulting in distractibility, insomnia, impatience).

Of course, it is an empirical question whether such response covariation exists and whether particular identified patterns should weigh heavily in making treatment decisions. The exact sources for these identified syndromes or patterns are not specified in the DSM-III manual, although other classification systems (especially International Classification of Diseases, ninth edition, p. 3) mention field trials and "relevant research studies are mentioned."

Several behavioral classification schemes have been proposed which also assume nomothetic response covariations (Adams, Doster, & Calhoun, 1977; Cautela & Upper, 1975; Dengrove, 1972; Ferster, 1967; Suinn, 1970). It would seem, however, that DSM-III holds certain advantages for behavioral assessors as a general classification scheme. For example, DSM-III might help behaviorists to communicate with a professional world that is largely nonbehavioral. Such communication is useful in administrative record-keeping, satisfying third-party payers, writing grant proposals, preparing journal articles, referring clients, and as an entry into the psychological and psychiatric literature. It is also important that the field trials for DSM-III produced respectable reliability figures (expressed as Kappa, which corrects for chance agreement). A 1978 draft of DSM-III was used in Phase I of the field trials, whereas the revised 1980 DSM-III was used in Phase II. For adult clients, Kappa is .68 for Phase I (n = 339) and .72 for Phase II (n = 331). For child clients, Kappa is .68 for Phase I (n = 71) and .52 for Phase II (n = 55) (DSM-III, pp. 470–471).

Nomothetic patterns are useful in suggesting responses which should be investigated in addition to the presenting problem. Moreover, since nomothetic response patterns may be controlled by nomothetic categories of controlling variables (as suggested by research in abnormal psychology), a pattern of response covariation may suggest controlling variables to investigate with a particular client. For example, a depressive pattern of behavior may suggest both immediate environmental controlling variables (e.g., sudden environmental changes or loss of reinforcers) and organismic controlling variables (e.g., familial history of manic-depressive psychosis or an inadequate repertoire of social skills to obtain or maintain sufficient reinforcers or a longstanding history of irrational cognitive responses). Although research in abnormal psychology provides nomothetic suggestions of possible controlling variables, it should be understood that the goal of behavioral assessment is always to determine the controlling variables unique to an individual client.

Finally, a pattern of response covariation might not only suggest other target behaviors and typical controlling variables, but an effective treatment program. For example, clinical research indicates that a depressed client may respond to a structured program of increasingly pleasant activities, to social skills training, to modification of irrational cognitions, and/or to antidepressant medication. An anxious client may respond to relaxation training, modeling, or to exposure treatments. Once again, however, one must keep in mind that while such clinical research may suggest effective intervention programs, the goal of behavioral assessment is to design an intervention program tailored to an individual client.

GOALS OR PURPOSES OF BEHAVIORAL ASSESSMENT

Within the context of the theoretical assumptions outlined above, behavioral assessment has four major goals or purposes: (1) to identify the target behavior(s) and appropriate method of measurement; (2) to determine the environmental and organismic controlling variables, (3) to select an intervention strategy that has a high probability of success; and (4) to evaluate the effectiveness of that intervention. Each of these goals is elaborated below.

As these goals are elaborated, it should be recognized that behavioral assessment may be conducted on either an individual or programmatic level (Hawkins, 1979). While all four goals may be applicable to the assessment of an individual, the treatment program in program evaluation may have been selected by someone other than the assessor and may, in fact, have already been implemented. In summative program evaluation (where emphasis is on the outcome of the program) only the first and fourth goals may be applicable: that is, selecting the behaviors to be measured, the methods of measurement, and a means of evaluating treatment program effectiveness. In formative program evaluation (where emphasis is on improving the program) it may also be important to determine the controlling variables so that they can be used in formulating program improvement. For an overview of behavioral assessment and program evaluation, see Hawkins, Fremouw, and Reitz (in press); for examples of program evaluation as related to behavioral assessment, see Filipczak, Archer, Neale, and Winett (1979) and Schnelle, Kirchner, Galbaugh, Domash, Carr, and Larson (1979).

Identification of the Target Behavior(s)

The specific target behaviors that are selected involve a value judgement by both the therapist and client (Meyerson & Hayes, 1978). A large number of philosophical and empirical guidelines have been proposed. However, to influence this value judgment, many of which were previously summarized by Nelson and Hayes (1979). Among the philosophical guidelines are: (1) behavior should be altered if it is dangerous to the client or to others in the environment; (2) target behaviors should be selected which maximize the client's reinforcers (Krasner, 1969); (3) behaviors which are desirable and can be increased in frequency should be selected rather than undesirable behaviors which must be decreased (Goldiamond, 1974; McFall, 1976; (4) target behaviors should maximize the flexibility of the client's repertoire to achieve long term individual and social benefits (Meyerson & Hayes, 1978); and (5) optimal not average levels of performance should be sought (Foster & Ritchey, 1979; Van Houten, 1979). Among the empirical guidelines are: (1) the collection of normative data (Hartmann et al., 1979; Kazdin, 1977; Nelson & Bowles, 1975); (2) the use of task analysis and of developmental norms (Hawkins, 1975); (3) subjective ratings by community volunteers regarding which behaviors and rates thereof are important (Wolf, 1978); (4) a behavioral-analytic model in which target

situations are identified, possible responses are enumerated and evaluated, and measurement items and their scoring are determined (Goldfried & D'Zurilla, 1969, with exemplars by Mathews, Whang, & Fawcett, 1980, in the assessment of occupational skills, and by Perri &
Richards, 1979, in the assessment of heterosocial skills); (5) the known
groups method (McFall, 1976) by which specific behaviors are identified
that differentiate two established groups; (6) a components analysis in
which different response parameters are experimentally manipulated and
their relative effects empirically determined (Mullinix & Galassi, 1981);
(7) regression equations to determine which specific behaviors best predict to important criteria (Cobb, 1972; Kupke, Hobbs, & Cheney,
1979); and (8) experimental intervention in which it is shown that intervening with target "a" produces greater change in an important
global measure that intervening with target "b" (Kupke, Calhoun, &
Hobbs, 1979).

If several socially desirable target behaviors have been identified, a
remaining question is where intervention should begin. As previously
summarized by Nelson and Hayes (1979), several guidelines have been
offered: (1) alter the most irritating behavior first (Tharp & Wetzel,
1969); (2) alter a behavior that is relatively easy to change first
(O'Leary, 1972); (3) alter behaviors that will produce therapeutically
beneficial response generalization (e.g., Hay, Hay, & Nelson, 1977);
and (4) when responses exist as part of a longer chain, first alter the
responses at the beginning of the chain (Angle, Hay, Hay, & Ellinwood,
1977).

Determine Controlling Variables

After selecting the target behavior(s), the next step in behavioral assessment is to determine the organismic and environmental variables
that control the occurrence of the target behavior(s). As discussed earlier, the nature of the target behavior frequently suggests nomothetic
categories of controlling variables which merit further idiographic assessment. For example, if a client displays typical schizophrenic responses, it would be advisable to assess familial history of schizophrenia
and the client's history of social interactions.

Sometimes, assessment will result in organismic or environmental
variables that cannot be altered. Discovery of Down's syndrome or an
organic brain syndrome may caution that treatment results will have
limits. Other unalterable controlling variables can suggest specific interventions that are relatively successful. A familial history of schizophrenia and a longstanding pattern of social withdrawal, along with
schizophrenic responses, may suggest the use of phenothiazines and

social skills training. A major environmental loss (even though it cannot be reconstituted), coupled with depressive responses, may suggest intervention aimed at increasing pleasant events and social skills while decreasing unpleasant events and irrational cognitions (Beck et al., 1980, Lewinsohn, 1974).

At other times, assessment will result in organismic or environmental variables which can be altered. The basic philosophy here is that if a problematic response is to be changed, its controlling variables must be altered. Organismic variables that can be modified include: fatigue, hunger, visual or auditory acuity, health and appearance, obesity, and hygiene. Examples of modifying antecedent stimuli to effect response change include alterations of seating patterns to change the social interactions among hospitalized psychiatric patients (Holahan, 1972) and reductions in the number of child commands issued by mothers (Peed, Roberts, & Forehand, 1977). Examples of modifying consequent stimuli to bring about response change include cases from behavioral medicine, such as changing contingencies for bedtime asthmatic attacks so that such attacks were ignored and lack of coughing was rewarded (Neisworth & Moore, 1972); and from parent management training, such as decreasing maternal criticisms of children and increasing the frequency and range of maternal social reinforcement (Peed et al., 1977).

While it is generally believed that identification of controlling variables enhances treatment success, it has not been *demonstrated* that such identification is required in *each* case (Haynes, 1979; O'Leary, 1972). In other words, the "treatment validity" of the functional analysis has not been experimentally verified (Nelson & Hayes, 1979). It may be feasible, for example, to implement a package treatment for each depressed client rather than spending the hours required to perform an individualized assessment and to design an individualized treatment.

Selecting Treatment Strategy

The nature of the target behavior may provide nomothetic suggestions for alternative treatment strategies that have a high probability of success. The assessor, however, then usually determines which specific treatment will be likely to be effective with a particular client. Guidelines about treatment choice have generally taken two forms. The first is choosing treatment based on the specific responses exhibited by a client (perhaps within a syndrome or pattern of responses). For example, treatment of phobias may differ if the client displays cognitive misinformation or conditioned anxiety (Wolpe, 1977); treatment of sexual deviations may differ if the client fails to display appropriate sexual arousal, heterosocial skills, or gender appropriate behavior, in addition

to displaying deviant sexual arousal (Barlow & Abel, 1976); and treatment of social skills may differ if the client displays conditioned anxiety, a skills deficit, or irrational cognitions (Curran, 1977; Marzillier
& Winter, 1978). A second guideline is to use identified controlling
variables to determine appropriate treatment. For example, biofeedback
may be appropriate only with other adjunct techniques for the treatment
of faulty autonomic responses, depending on the variables controlling
these responses (Evans, 1977); and the treatment of headaches may be
determined by an analysis of the function served by the headaches
(Norton & Nielson, 1977).

Evaluating Treatment Outcome

After the first three goals of behavioral assessment have been accomplished (i.e., the target behavior selected, the controlling variables
identified, and a treatment plan designed) the last assessment goal begins evaluation of the success of the treatment program. Two elements
are critical to this evaluation: selection of an appropriate evaluative
design and selection of practical dependent measures, as previously
summarized by Nelson and Barlow (1981).

While group experimental designs and related statistical analyses are
useful in many circumstances, single subject designs are usually more
useful to evaluate effectiveness for either an individual or a program.
The most frequently used evaluation in the clinical setting is the A-B
design (where A stands for baseline and B stands for intervention).
Repeated measures obtained during baseline and intervention permit
change to be assessed. However, such case studies have little internal
validity. That is, the cause of the changes cannot usually be attributed
with any certainty to the treatment because alternative explanations are
not systematically ruled out. Nonetheless, many clinicians may be satisfied with empirical evidence that improvement has indeed occurred.
Many single-subject designs with greater internal validity are described
by Hersen and Barlow (1976). One of these is the reversal or withdrawal
design, represented by A-B-A-B, in which treatment is systematically
implemented but at different points in time with either different target
behaviors, different settings, or different subjects. With both the with-
and because of ethical concerns in withdrawing an effective treatment,
the multiple baseline design is more popular than the reversal in clinical
settings. In the multiple baseline design, the same treatment must be
implemented by at different points in time with either different target
behaviors, different settings, or different subjects. With both the withdrawal and multiple baseline designs, internal validity is obtained by
demonstrating that improvements occurred each time but only when

treatment was implemented. Improvements may then be attributed to the intervention with some certainty, since it is unlikely that another efficacious event covaried with each treatment implementation. A new single-subject design permits the effectiveness of two or more interventions to be compared within one client or program. In the alternating treatments design, two (or more) interventions are implemented during different (usually somewhat random) blocks of time (Barlow & Hayes, 1979; Kazdin & Hartmann, 1978). Internal validity is present if the two (or more) treatments produce *consistent* differences in effectiveness because it is unlikely that an extraneous efficacious factor covaried with each treatment implementation.

A great variety of dependent measures can be successfully used in the clinical environment to evaluate treatment effectiveness. A few examples may delineate the range of techniques available. Therapists may have clients fill out the same self-report questionnaire at weekly or biweekly intervals. Self-report of idiosyncratic items may be obtained by using a card-sort procedure in which stimulus items are written on index cards and then rated or sorted at regular intervals. The client may keep quantitative records of frequency, duration, or self-ratings, or use a diary format in which significant events are entered into a notebook or a structured form. The client may be directly observed, either in the natural setting by mediators or in the clinic. In the clinic, the therapist can quantify specific behaviors as they occur or do so subsequently from audio or video tapes. Relatedly, the same contrived setting can be presented regularly to the client and repeated physiological or observational data taken. Indirect measures like archival data or permanent product data may be used. Because these measures assess different aspects of the client's behavior and hence do not necessarily produce consistent findings, the use of multiple dependent measures is often advisable.

TECHNIQUES OF BEHAVIORAL ASSESSMENT

Since the techniques of behavioral assessment are described fully in other chapters of this volume, they are mentioned only briefly here. A useful schema for categorizing behavioral assessment techniques has been developed by Cone (1978): *direct* assessment methods include observation in naturalistic situations, or in analogue situations, and self-monitoring; *indirect* assessment methods include interviews, self-report, and rating by others. In addition to the present volume, more information about these techniques is available: on observation in naturalistic situations (Foster & Cone, 1980; Haynes, 1978; Haynes & Wilson, 1979; Kent & Foster, 1977; Wildman & Erickson, 1977); on observations in analogue situations (Haynes, 1978; Haynes & Wilson, 1979; McFall, 1977a; Nay, 1977); on self-monitoring (Haynes & Wilson, 1979; Kazdin, 1974; McFall, 1977b; Nelson, 1977); on interviews (Haynes, 1978; Haynes & Wilson, 1979; Linehan, 1977; Meyer, Liddill, & Lyons, 1977; Morganstern, 1976; Nelson & Barlow, 1981); on self-report measures (Bellack & Hersen, 1977; Haynes, 1978; Haynes & Wilson, 1979; Tasto, 1977); and on ratings by others (Walls, Werner, Bacon, & Zane, 1977). Other assessment techniques include the use of instrumentation to assess physiological responses (Epstein, 1976; Geer, 1977; Haynes, 1978; Haynes & Wilson, 1979; Kallman & Feuerstein, 1977; Lang, 1977); the use of intelligence or achievement tests to assess particular types of cognitive responses (Nelson, 1981); and the use of permanent products or archival records to assess behavioral by-products (Kazdin, 1979b).

In selecting from these behavioral assessment techniques, three general considerations (other than quality or convenience of the method) should be kept in mind. First, different techniques are often required depending upon the stage of assessment. The process of behavioral assessment can be conceptualized as a funnel (Hawkins, 1979; Peterson, 1968). At the wide mouth of the funnel, screening procedures may be employed to determine which persons would profit from treatment. Since a large number of people usually undergo screening, these procedures should be relatively inexpensive in terms of both cost and time. For example, Foster and Ritchey (1979) and Greenwood, Walker, Todd, and Hops (1979) theoretically and empirically examined the use of a relatively inexpensive screening device—peer judgments—to predict children's observed social withdrawal. Once the client has been selected, a broad range of information should be gathered. The client's functioning in many life areas is considered until suitable target behaviors are selected. Interviewing, self-report questionnaires, ratings by others, and self-monitoring may be techniques particularly appropriate for this broad assessment. Eventually, the assessment funnel narrows and more specific information is sought: a) the variables controlling the target behaviors are determined; b) a treatment is selected and c) changes in the target behavior produced by this treatment are evaluated. At this more specific stage, techniques may include observations in naturalistic or analogue situations, self-report questionnaires, self-monitoring, physiological measurement, intelligence or achievement testing, or behavioral by-products.

A second consideration in determining the specific technique is that different behavioral assessment procedures assess different aspects of the triple response system. Overt motor responses are generally assessed by observations in naturalistic or analogue situations, by self-monitoring, or by ratings by others. Cognitive verbal responses are generally assessed by interviews, self-report questionnaires, self-monitoring, or intelligence and achievement tests. Physiological-emotional responses are generally assessed by physiological recordings or sometimes by direct observation. Since consistency across the three response systems cannot be assumed, a thorough behavioral assessment requires evaluation of all the response systems of interest. Hence, several different assessment techniques must frequently be employed. The different techniques, expectedly, do not necessarily produce the same information. For example, when interviewing, role-playing, questionnaires, and self-rating during role-playing were used to assess the social skills of 50 subjects, the techniques produced significantly different social skills ratings, with higher ratings produced by the first two techniques than by the latter two (Nelson, Hayes, Felton, & Jarrett, 1979). The point is that no one assessment technique produces "true" information, but rather different assessment techniques produce different information for different purposes.

A third consideration in selecting among assessment techniques is the situation specificity of behavior. The assessment device must include the specific situation that is likely to generate the response of interest. The situation is readily included in direct observation of behavior in the natural environment by trained observers, mediators, or self-recorders; observations are timed to occur when the specific situation and target responses occur. For example, familial interactions were observed in two rooms of the home just prior to dinner with the contraints of no visitors, television, or telephone (Jones, Reid, & Patterson, 1975). The stimulus situation is arranged to occur in direct observations of behavior in analogue or contrived situations. The best known examples of analogue situations include the behavioral avoidance test in which the phobic object is presented *in vivo* (Lang & Lazovik, 1963) or by slides (Burchardt & Levis, 1977), the presentation of sexual stimuli while sexual arousal is measured physiologically (Barlow, 1977), and the presentation of social stimuli to assess heterosocial skills (Perri & Richards, 1979) or assertiveness (Galassi & Galassi, 1976). The stimulus situation is also included in many self-report questionnaires, for example, the Fear Survey Schedule (Wolpe & Lang, 1964), and in intelligence or achievement testing. Care must be taken by the interviewer to include specific situations in questions posed to the interviewee if situation-specific information is to be generated.

Discussed above were deliberate attempts to include the stimulus situation with the assessment technique so that the response of interest is produced. Research has also shown that other situational factors un-wittingly influence the responses displayed during assessment. Perfor-mance on the behavioral avoidance test has been shown to be influenced by the demand placed on the subject to remain in the phobic situation (Miller & Bernstein, 1972), whether the source of instructions is from a live experimenter or from a tape-recorder (Bernstein & Nietzel, 1973), and by the housing provided the fear-producing organism (Lick & Un-ger, 1975). As another example, performance during role-playing as-sessing assertiveness has been shown to be influenced by the mode of stimulus presentation and number of required subject responses (Galassi & Galassi, 1976), and by situational knowledge of the specific type of required assertive behavior, knowledge of criteria for effective as-sertive behavior, and instructions on how to act (Westefeld, Galassi, & Galassi, 1980). Since such situational variations cannot be avoided, the assessor must be aware that consistency in clients' behaviors across different assessment procedures cannot be assumed and that the relative importance of these situationally produced variations must be deter-mined.

Finally, not only is the client's behavior subject to situational influ-ences, but so is the assessor's. This topic has been most carefully re-searched when the assessor assumes the role of observer. It has been shown that observational data can be influenced by the observers' awareness that interobserver agreement is being assessed, by the cal-culation procedures used to determine agreement, and by the feedback provided on the collected observational data (Kent & Foster, 1977). Influences on the assessor while using other assessment techniques have thus far received less attention, but many techniques (e.g., interviewing, testing) obviously allow room for such influences.

EVALUATIONS OF THE QUALITY OF BEHAVIORAL ASSESSMENT

Critical to the use of any assessment device is a method for determining the likely quality of the data obtained. The most popular current strategy for evaluating this is the use of psychometric procedures. For example, the concurrent validity of role-playing has been examined by comparing data obtained through role-playing with data obtained through contrived situations in the natural environment (e.g., Bellack, Hersen, & Lamparski, 1979); the concurrent validity of a self-report measure of heterosocial anxiety, the Situation Questionnaire, has been examined by comparing it against a role-played interaction (Heimberg, Harrison,

Montgomery, Madsen, & Sherfey, 1980); and the test-retest reliability and concurrent validity of several physiological measures of
women's sexual arousal have been examined across two measurement
sessions (Henson, Rubin, & Henson, 1979).

The various types of reliability and validity have been categorized
more systematically within generalizability theory (Cronbach, Gleser,
Nanda, & Rajaratnam, 1972), which relabels the types of reliability and
validity into universes of generalization (e.g., across scorer, item, time,
setting, or method). Generalizability procedures have also been used
with behavioral assessment techniques. In a study by Jones et al. (1975),
the following universes of generalization were examined: subjects (13
referred deviant boys and 17 normal control boys), observers (2), and
occasions (observations were made on two different days of the baseline
period). When the observational data for the deviant boys were subjected
to an analysis of variance, the subjects factor and the subjects by occasions interaction accounted for most of the variance. A similar pattern
emerged for normal boys, with more variance accounted for by the
subjects by occasions interaction, and less by the subjects main effect.
In neither case did the main effect for observer or interactions with the
observer factor reach significance, permitting generalization across the
universe of observers. Similar generalizability across observers was
found by Coates and Thoresen (1978). With the response of social skills,
universes of generalization which have been examined include method
of assessment, assessment items, judges who provided social skills ratings, and responses of skill versus anxiety (Curran, Monti, Corriveau,
Hay, Hagerman, Zwick, & Farrell, 1980; Farrell, Mariotto, Conger,
Curran, & Wallander, 1979). It has also been suggested that generalizability theory is applicable to single-subject designs in addition to the
group designs exemplified above (Strossen, Coates, & Thoresen, 1979).

While these psychometric and generalizability procedures may be
applicable to data generated by behavioral assessment techniques, the
assumptions underlying these procedures do not often apply. These
evaluation procedures evolved from trait theory; consistent data are the
hallmark of a good assessment device since it is assumed that more of
the enduring consistent trait is being measured. As described earlier,
however, it is an assumption of behavioral assessment that behavior
is not necessarily enduring and consistent, but instead may be change-
able. Therefore, inconsistency in measurement may be produced by
actual changes in behavior and not by an imprecise behavioral assessment technique (Nelson, Hay, & Hay, 1977). In fact, when behavioral
assessors find inconsistent responding, it is often attributed to behavior
changes rather than the assessment device. For example, inconsistent

sexual responses found by Henson et al. (1979) were attributed not to poor assessment, but to changing organismic variables such as hormone level, or to changing situational variables, such as placement of the measuring device. The assumption that a good assessment device produces consistent responding also creates practical problems for behavioral assessment where the goal is frequently to identify *differential* controlling variables (Nelson et al., 1977). Consistent responding across questionnaire items or role-playing scenes would be of little practical utility. Finally, even if particular studies conclude consistency across specific techniques or specific situations, such conclusions are unlikely to be nomothetic. During other assessment occasions, if any aspects of the techniques or situations were to vary, outcomes might well be different.

Despite recognition of these arguments, counter-arguments have been proposed that psychometric or generalizability procedures, if not assumptions, are applicable to behavioral assessment (Cone, 1977; Jones, 1977), and that certain types of validity are useful in behavioral assessment (Hartmann et al., 1979). It may be true that evaluation of some structural components of behavioral assessment devices is important. For example, it is important that test items have content validity or adequately sample the population of interest, as exemplified in the development of role-playing tests for heterosocial skills (Perri & Richards, 1979) and employment skills (Mathews et al., 1980). Similarly, if the behavior is somehow "captured" so that it cannot change (e.g., through the use of videotapes or scripts consistently used by actors), then consistent responding across observers or interviewers would be of interest. A structural quality that comes close to being a reasonable measure of the quality of behavioral assessment is accuracy. If it can be shown that there is a close correspondence between the data yielded by an assessment device and reality, then one could claim that this device is valid. Unfortunately, assessment of accuracy is often difficult or impossible because it requires an independent knowledge of what exists. Further, a device can be accurate but useless. Nevertheless, future work on assessment of accuracy may contain real value to behavioral assessment.

While such evaluations of the structure of behavioral assessment tools may be useful, an equally if not more important question is the *function* served by behavioral assessment. At least two of these functions seem critical: 1) the function of the procedure or experiment in increasing understanding of behavior (termed conceptual validity) and 2) the function of behavioral assessment in improving treatment outcome (termed treatment validity) (Nelson & Hayes, 1979). Conceptual validity cannot be measured in a quantitative fashion; it only becomes apparent with the passage of time as more and more general and conceptually consistent principles of behavior evolve. A distinction made by Bijou, Peterson, and Ault (1968) between descriptive and experimental studies may be useful here. Descriptive studies describe an existing state of affairs: for example, responses which covary, relationship between data produced by role-playing versus the natural environment, the behavioral differences between happily and unhappily married couples. Experimental studies ask *why* these phenomena occur. The conceptual validity of behavioral assessment requires both thorough descriptions and experimental analyses of assessment issues.

Treatment validity can be demonstrated experimentally by showing that a particular behavioral assessment led to a better treatment than would have occurred without it. Any experiment with internal validity tests treatment validity in a primitive fashion by demonstrating that the identified independent variable produced change. Better tests of treatment validity require a *comparison* between using the results of a particular behavioral assessment and not using the results, as further elaborated below.

FUTURE DIRECTIONS

Treatment Validity

While the relationship between behavioral assessment and treatment has traditionally been acclaimed (Goldfried & Pomeranz, 1968), there is a need to demonstrate experimentally that specific methods of behavioral assessment actually lead to better treatment. Treatment validity can be determined for each step of behavioral assessment. For example, in order to determine the treatment validity of the selection of a specific target behavior, researchers have shown that contingency contracting for solitary toy play was more effective in reducing aggressive and oppositional behaviors than contingency contracting for social play (Wahler & Fox, 1980). Training males in personal attention during conversation produced higher ratings of female attraction than training males in another conversational skill of minimal encouragement (Kupke, Calhoun, & Hobbs, 1979). The treatment validity of the functional analysis of depression is now being investigated in our laboratory in a Master's thesis by Robin Jarrett. One-half of the depressed female subjects are receiving treatment idiographically designed for them based on pretreatment assessment, while the other half are yoked, receiving the same treatment but not designed specifically for them. The treatment validity of treatment selection based on subject classification has also been assessed occasionally. One study showed that subjects classified by an electroencephalographic evaluation as idiopathic insomniacs improved more on objective sleep measures with tension-release relaxation than subjects classified as pseudoinsomniacs (Borkovec, Grayson, O'Brien, & Weerts, 1979). Another study showed that subjects who evidenced a specific speech anxiety improved with desensitization, while subjects who evidenced a generalized social anxiety improved with more cognitively oriented insight treatments, although a post hoc analysis revealed this interaction (Meichenbaum, Gilmore, & Fedoravicius, 1971). Treatment validity could also be investigated by within-subject designs, especially the alternating treatment design (Barlow & Hayes, 1979; Kazdin & Hartmann, 1978), in which the results of different behavioral assessment findings (target behavior, functional analysis, subject classification, treatment, etc.) could be compared. In one such case in our laboratory, it has been shown, contrary to expectation, that an alternation of systematic desensitization and social skills training within one subject led to greater improvements in social anxiety scores following social skills training and greater improvements in role playing following desensitization. While it is highly unlikely that this is a general finding, it still points out that our assessment decisions must be tested with data, not just logic. It can probably be said that any assessment device or conceptualization claiming to have applied value should be considered unproven until its treatment validity is experimentally demonstrated. Unfortunately, by this standard the applied value of virtually all of behavioral assessment is still "unproven."

Transition from Nomothetic Principles to Idiographic Application

While suggestions for covarying responses, controlling variables, and treatment strategies may be provided at a nomothetic level, the transition to idiographic application is in need of research. Currently, the transition is all too often made by means of "clinical judgment." While clinical judgment may be effective, it is not sufficient for an empirical clinical science which requires general principles or verbal rules to summarize and guide clinical activities.

A first attempt to specify the transition from nomothetic principles to idiographic application was in the area of diagnosis. The decision-making process used by the clinician to move from a nomothetic classification schema to an individualized diagnosis of a particular client was delineated either through computer programs or through decision trees. Information based on the Current and Past Psychopathology Scales (Endicott & Spitzer, 1972) was utilized by a computer program called

DIAGNO II (Spitzer & Endicott, 1969) to produce a DSM-II diagnosis (Diagnostic and Statistical Manual of Mental Disorders, American Psychiatric Association, second edition, 1968). Similarly, information based on the Present State Examination (Wing, Birley, Cooper et al., 1967) was utilized by a computer program called CATEGO (Wing, Cooper, & Sartorius, 1974) to result in a diagnosis. For DSM-II, Nathan (1967) elaborated decision-making rules which the clinician could follow in reaching a diagnosis. Similarly, Appendix A of DSM-III contains decision trees to guide the clinician in reaching an individualized diagnosis.

Behavioral assessors have been even less sophisticated in specifying the procedures comprising clinical judgment by which nomothetic principles are used idiographically. In the selection of target behaviors, for example, specific rules are needed by which all clinicians would select the same target behaviors for a particular client. One strategy for producing these rules has two stages: first, evidence that the clinical judgments of behavioral assessors produce consistent outcomes and second, specification of the rules by which these outcomes are generated. Unfortunately, current evidence suggests that behavioral assessors do not agree on target behaviors, even at the primitive nonscientific level of clinical judgment. When the same four clients were interviewed by the same four interviewers, agreement was reached only on the overall *number* of areas identified as problems for a client, but not on *specific* problem areas and items (Hay, Hay, Angle, & Nelson, 1979). When a sample of behavioral clinicians was provided protocols of child cases, the average agreement on the first priority target for intervention was 39 percent (Wilson & Evans, in press). A second, more inductive strategy would be to conduct treatment validity studies of target behavior selection in specific populations. The empirically derived rules from these studies (e.g., when you have a client displaying this pattern, treatment outcome is enhanced best by treating this specific behavior) could then guide clinical decision making. Unfortunately, virtually no data of these sort currently exist. Much work remains to be done to produce general rules by which target behaviors are selected.

Another goal is to specify rules by which controlling variables are determined. Again, two strategies suggest themselves. The first would be to determine the rules that clinicians actually use consistently. A current study in our laboratory (a Master's thesis by Jeffrey Felton) investigates the reliability of the functional analysis. The same three clients are interviewed by six assessors whose task is to identify environmental and organismic controlling variables for specified target behaviors. Reliable clinical judgments may lead to specification on verbal rules by which these judgments are reached. A second strategy (which does not require this initial reliability) is to conduct treatment validity studies of various methods of functional analysis. Any resultant successful rules could then guide the clinician.

Finally, rules or procedures are needed for clinicians to determine which nomothetically suggested treatment procedure is most likely to succeed with a particular client. More headway has been made in this transition from nomothetic suggestions to idiographic applications than in the other assessment areas noted above. Various assessment devices have been shown to predict success of certain treatment techniques: physiological recordings from an electroencephalograph were demonstrated to predict the success of relaxation training with insomniacs (Borkovec et al., 1979); questionnaires predicted success of treatment of Raynaud's disease (Surwit, Bradner, Fenton, & Pilon, 1979) and of dysmenorrhea (Chesney & Tasto, 1975), and population characteristics of alcoholics predicted success of a controlled drinking treatment Vogler, Weissbach, & Compton, 1977). Of course, a great deal more research must be conducted to guide clinicians to the most effective treatment for the range of specific disorders likely to be seen by the clinician.

Evolution of Behavioral Assessment in Treatment Settings

As a recent President of the Association for Advancement of Behavior Therapy, Barlow (1980) urged greater participation of practicing clinicians in meaningful clinical research. To facilitate this goal, behavioral assessment must be made more useful through the development and dissemination of practical single subject designs and dependent variables. In response to a survey, 43.8 percent of 257 respondents reported that behavioral assessment strategies were impractical in applied settings (Wade, Baker, & Hartmann, 1979). Much of our current research underscores this impression with repeated concern over lack of generalization across situations, responses, assessment techniques, and emphasis on seemingly esoteric topics such as alternative ways to calculate interobserver agreement. Instead of emphasizing the imprecision and inaccuracy of our assessment devices, a more relevant question for applied settings would be: is the information gained through assessment *sufficiently* accurate to be useful in selecting target behavior, determining controlling variables, choosing intervention strategies, and evaluating intervention outcome? A criterion against which assessment tools and issues should be evaluated is its *utility* in applied settings.

While promulgation of useful assessment techniques might encourage more clinicians to attempt behavioral assessment and perhaps on-line clinical research, a related need is the evolution of procedures to enhance compliance (e.g., Levy, 1977). All too often, clinicians who do ask clients to self-record or ask confederates to report on client activities become discouraged by lack of compliance with these requests. More data could be produced by currently available assessment methods if these methods were indeed used.

SUMMARY

Behavioral assessment is the identification and measurement of meaningful response units and their controlling variables (both environmental and organismic) for the purpose of understanding and altering human behavior. The theoretical assumptions of behavioral assessment are contrasted with those of traditional assessment as emphasizing situation-specific samples of behavior (overt motor, cognitive verbal, and physiological emotional). The variables to consider during behavioral assessment are summarized by the SORC acronym (Goldfried & Sprafkin, 1976) of Stimulus-Organism-Response-Consequence. In the spirit of interactionism, both immediate environmental (antecedent and consequent stimuli) and organismic (physiological and past learning) variables are deemed important. While behavioral assessment is always conducted at an idiographic or individualized level, certain nomothetic principles are applicable, such as SORC, response patterns labeled by DSM-III, temporal stability of responding, categories of controlling variables for particular responses suggested by abnormal psychology, and effective treatment for particular responses suggested by clinical research.

Within the framework of these theoretical assumptions, the four goals of behavioral assessment are: (1) to identify the target behavior(s) and appropriate method of measurement; (2) to determine environmental and organismic controlling variables; (3) to select an intervention strategy that has a high probability of success; and (4) to evaluate the effectiveness of that intervention. The techniques of behavioral assessment include: observation in naturalistic or analogue situations, self-monitoring, interviews, self-reports, ratings by others, use of instrumentation to measure physiological responses, intelligence or achievement tests, and permanent product or archival data. While static or structural evaluations of the quality of behavioral assessment based on psychometrics or generalizability theory may sometimes be useful, the quality of behavioral assessment should also be judged by its accuracy and functional utility. The critical question is, does this assessment help increase our understanding of behavior (conceptual validity) and our ability to alter it therapeutically (treatment validity)? Three future directions are outlined: more experiments examining treatment validity, the development of more specific guidelines to move from the level of nomothetic principles to idiographic applications, and the evolution of more practical dependent variables and single subject designs so that behavioral assessment can enhance clinical research in applied settings.

REFERENCES

Adams, H. E., Doster, J. A., & Calhoun, K. S. A psychologically based system of response classification. In A. R. Ciminero, K. S. Calhoun, & H. E. Adams (Eds.), *Handbook of behavioral assessment*. New York: Wiley, 1977.

American Psychiatric Association. *Diagnostic and statistical manual of mental disorders*. (2nd ed.) Washington, D.C.: American Psychiatric Association, 1968.

American Psychiatric Association. *Diagnostic and statistical manual of mental disorders*. (3rd ed.) Washington, D.C.: American Psychiatric Association, 1980.

Angle, H. V., Hay, L. R., Hay, W. M., & Ellinwood, E. H. Computer assisted behavioral assessment. In J. D. Cone & R. P. Hawkins (Eds.), *Behavioral assessment: New directions in clinical psychology*. New York: Brunner/Mazel, 1977.

Bandura, A., & Adams, N. E. Analysis of self-efficacy theory of behavioral change. *Cognitive Therapy and Research*, 1977, *1*, 287–310.

Bandura, A., Blanchard, E. B., & Ritter, B. Relative efficacy of desensitization and modeling approaches for inducing behavioral, affective, and attitudinal changes. *Journal of Personality and Social Psychology*, 1969, *13*, 173–199.

Barlow, D. H. Assessment of sexual behavior. In A. R. Ciminero, K. S. Calhoun, & H. E. Adams (Eds.), *Handbook of behavioral assessment*. New York: Wiley, 1977.

Barlow, D. H. Behavior therapy: The next decade. *Behavior Therapy*, 1980, *11*, 315-328.

Barlow, D.H. (Ed.) *Behavioral assessment of adult disorders*. New York: Guilford Press.

Barlow, D. H. (Ed.) *Behavioral assessment of adult disorders*. New York: Guilford Press 1981.

Barlow, D. H., & Abel, G. G. Sexual deviation. In W. E. Craighead, A. E. Kazdin, & M. J. Mahoney (Eds.), *Behavior modification: Principles, issues, and applications*. Boston: Houghton Mifflin, 1976.

Barlow, D. H., & Mayes, S. C. Alternating treatments design: One strategy for comparing the effects of two treatments in a single subject. *Journal of Applied Behavior Analysis*, 1979, *12*, 199-210.

Beck, A. T., Rush, A. J., Shaw, B. E., & Emery, G. *Cognitive therapy of depression*. New York: Guilford Press, 1980.

Bellack, A. S., & Hersen, M. Self-report inventories in behavioral assessment. In J. D. Cone & R. P. Hawkins (Eds.), *Behavioral assessment: New directions in clinical psychology*. New York: Brunner/Mazel, 1977.

Bellack, A. S., Hersen, M., & Lamparski, D. Role-playing tests for assessing social skills: Are they valid? Are they useful? *Journal of Consulting and Clinical Psychology*, 1979, *47*, 335–342.

Bernstein, D. A., & Nietzel, M. T. Procedural variation in behavioral avoidance tests. *Journal of Consulting and Clinical Psychology*, 1973, *41*, 165–174.

Bijou, S. W., Peterson, R. F., & Ault, M. H. A method to integrate descriptive and experimental field studies at the level of data and empirical concepts. *Journal of Applied Behavior Analysis*, 1968, *1*, 175–191.

Borkovec, T. D., Grayson, J. B., O'Brien, G. T., & Weerts, T. C. Relaxation treatment of pseudoinsomnia and idiopathic insomnia: An electroencephalographic evaluation. *Journal of Applied Behavior Analysis,* 1979, *12,* 37–54.

Borkovec, T. D., Weerts, T. C., & Bernstein, D. A. Assessment of anxiety. In A. R. Ciminero, K. S. Calhoun, & H. E. Adams (Eds.), *Handbook of behavioral assessment.* New York: Wiley, 1977.

Bowers, K. S. Situationism in psychology: An analysis and a critique. *Psychological Review,* 1973, *80,* 307-336.

Burchardt, C. J., & Levis, D. J. The utility of presenting slides of phobic stimulus in the context of the behavioral avoidance procedure. *Behavior Therapy,* 1977, *8,* 340–346.

Cautela, J. R., & Upper, D. The process of individual behavior therapy. In M. Hersen, R. M. Eisler, & P. M. Miller (Eds.), *Progress in behavior modification,* Vol. 1. New York: Academic Press, 1975.

Chesney, M. A., & Tasto, D. L. The effectiveness of behavior modification with spasmodic and congestive dysmenorrhea. *Behaviour Research and Therapy,* 1975, *13,* 245–253.

Ciminero, A. R., Calhoun, K. S., & Adams, H. E. (Eds.) *Handbook of behavioral assessment.* New York: Wiley, 1977.

Coates, T. J., & Thoresen, C. E. Using generalizability theory in behavioral observation. *Behavior Therapy,* 1978, *9,* 605–613.

Cobb, J. A. The relationship of discrete classroom behaviors to fourth-grade academic achievement. *Journal of Educational Psychology,* 1972, *63,* 74–80.

Cone, J. D. The relevance of reliability and validity for behavioral assessment. *Behavior Therapy,* 1977, *8,* 411–426.

Cone, J. D. The Behavioral Assessment Grid (BAG): A conceptual framework and a taxonomy. *Behavior Therapy,* 1978, *9,* 882–888.

Cone, J. D. Confounded comparisons in triple response mode assessment research. *Behavioral Assessment,* 1979, *1,* 85–95.

Cone, J. D., & Hawkins, R. P. (Eds.) *Behavioral assessment: New directions in clinical psychology.* New York: Brunner/Mazel, 1977.

Cronbach, L. J., Gleser, G. C., Nanda, H., & Rajaratnam, N. *The dependability of behavioral measurements: Theory of generalizability for scores and profiles.* New York: Wiley, 1972.

Curran, J. P. Skills training as an approach to the treatment of heterosexual-social anxiety: A review. *Psychological Bulletin,* 1977, *84,* 140–157.

Curran, J. P., Monti, P. M., Corriveau, D. P., Hay, L. R., Hagerman, S., & Zwick, W. R., & Farrell, A. D. The generalizability of procedures for assessing social skills and social anxiety in a psychiatric population. *Behavioral Assessment,* 1980, *4,* 389-401.

Dengrove, E. Practical behavioral diagnosis. In A. A. Lazarus (Ed.), *Clinical behavior therapy.* New York: Brunner/Mazel, 1972.

Ekehammer, B. Interactionism in personality from a historical perspective. *Psychological Bulletin,* 1974, *81,* 1026-1048.

Endicott, J., & Spitzer, R. L. Current and past psychopathology scales (CAPPS). *Archives of General Psychiatry,* 1972, *27,* 678-687.

Epstein, L. H. Psychophysiological measurement in assessment. In M. Hersen & A. S. Bellack (Eds.), *Behavioral assessment: A practical handbook.* New York: Pergamon, 1976.

Evans, M. B. Biofeedback training: Some clinical considerations. *Behavior Therapy,* 1977, *8,* 101–103.

Farrell, A. D., Mariotto, M. J., Conger, A. J., Curran, J. P., & Wallander, J. L. Self-ratings and judges' ratings of heterosexual social anxiety and skill: A generalizability study. *Journal of Consulting and Clinical Psychology,* 1979, *47,* 164–175.

Feldman, M. P., & MacCulloch, M. J. The application of anticipatory avoidance learning to the treatment of homosexuality: I. Theory, technique, and preliminary results.
Behaviour Research and Therapy, 1965, *3*, 165–183.

Ferster, C. B. Classification of behavioral pathology. In L. Krasner & L. P. Ullmann
(Eds.), *Research in behavior modification*. New York: Holt, Rinehart, & Winston,
1967.

Filipczak, J., Archer, M. B., Neale, M. S., & Winett, R. A. Issues in multivariate
assessment in a large-scale behavioral program. *Journal of Applied Behavior Analysis*,
1979, *12*, 593–613.

Foster, S. L., & Cone, J. D. Current issues in direct observation. *Behavioral Assessment*,
1980, *2*, 313-338.

Foster, S. L., & Ritchey, W. L. Issues in the assessment of social competence in
children. *Journal of Applied Behavior Analysis*, 1979, *12*, 625–638.

Frederiksen, L. W., Martin, J. E., & Webster, J. S. Assessment of smoking behavior.
Journal of Applied Behavior Analysis, 1979, *12*, 653–664.

Galassi, M. D., & Galassi, J. P. The effects of role-playing variations on the assessment
of assertive behavior. *Behavior Therapy*, 1976, *7*, 343–347.

Geer, J. H. Sexual functioning: Some data and speculations on psychophysiological
assessment. In J. D. Cone & R. P. Hawkins (Eds.), *Behavioral assessment: New
directions in clinical psychology*. New York: Brunner/Mazel, 1977.

Goldfried, M. R., & D'Zurilla, T. J. A behavioral-analytic model for assessing competence. In C. D. Spielberger (Ed.), *Current topics in clinical and community psychology*. Vol. 1. New York: Academic Press, 1969.

Goldfried, M. R., & Kent, R. N. Traditional versus behavioral assessment: A comparison of methodological and theoretical assumptions. *Psychological Bulletin*, 1972,
77, 409–420.

Goldfried, M. R., & Pomeranz, D. M. Role of assessment in behavior modification.
Psychological Reports, 1968, *23*, 75–87.

Goldfried, M. R., & Sprafkin, J. N. Behavioral personality assessment. In J. T. Spence,
R. C. Carson, & J. W. Thibaut (Eds.), *Behavioral approaches to therapy*. Morristown,
N.J.: General Learning Press, 1976.

Goldiamond, I. Toward a constructional approach to social problems: Ethical and con-
stitutional issues raised by applied behavior analysis. *Behaviorism*, 1974, *2*, 1–85.

Goodenough, F. L. *Mental Testing*. New York: Holt, Rinehart, & Winston, 1949.

Greenwood, C. R., Walker, H. M., Todd, N. M., & Hops, H. Selecting a cost-effective
screening measure for the assessment of preschool social withdrawal. *Journal of
Applied Behavior Analysis*, 1979, *12*, 639–652.

Hanson, R. A. Consistency and stability of home environmental measures related to
IQ. *Child Development*, 1975, *46*, 470–480.

Hartmann, D. P., Roper, B. L., & Bradford, D. C. Some relationships between behavioral and traditional assessment. *Journal of Behavioral Assessment*, 1979, *1*, 3–
21.

Hartshorne, H., & May, M. A. *Studies in the nature of character: Vol. I, Studies in
deceit*. New York: Macmillan, 1928.

Hawkins, R. P. Who decided that was the problem? Two stages of responsibility for
applied behavior analysts. In W. S. Wood (Ed.), *Issues in evaluating behavior modification*. Champaign, Ill.: Research Press, 1975.

Hawkins, R. P. The functions of assessment: Implications for selection and development
of deyices for assessing repertoires in clinical, educational, and other settings. *Journal
of Applied Behavior Analysis*, 1979, *12*, 501–516.

Hawkins, R. P., Fremouw, W. J., & Reitz, A. L. A model for use in designing or
describing evaluations of mental health or educational intervention programs. *Behavioral Assessment*, in press.

Hay, W. M., Hay, L. R., Angle, H. V., & Nelson, R. O. The reliability of problem identification in the behavioral interview. *Behavioral Assessment*, 1979, *1*, 107–118.

Hay, W. M., Hay, L. R., & Nelson, R. O. Direct and collateral changes in on-task and academic behavior resulting from on-task versus academic contingencies. *Behavior Therapy*, 1977, *8*, 431–441.

Haynes, S. N. *Principles of behavioral assessment*. New York: Gardner Press, 1978.

Haynes, S. N. Behavioral variance, individual differences, and trait theory in a behavioral construct system: A reappraisal. *Behavioral Assessment*, 1979, *1*, 41–49.

Haynes, S. N., & Wilson, C. C. *Recent advances in behavioral assessment*. San Francisco: Jossey-Bass, 1979.

Heimberg, R. G., Harrison, D. F., Montgomery, D., Madsen, C. H., & Sherfey, J. A. Psychometric and behavioral analysis of a social anxiety questionnaire: The Situation Questionnaire. *Behavioral Assessment*, 1980, *4*, 403-415.

Henson, D. E., Rubin, H. B., & Henson, C. Analysis of the consistency of objective measures of sexual arousal in women. *Journal of Applied Behavior Analysis*, 1979, *12*, 701–711.

Hersen, M., & Barlow, D. H. *Single case experimental designs: Strategies for studying behavior change*. New York: Pergamon, 1976.

Hersen, M., & Bellack, A. S. (Eds,). *Behavioral assessment: A practical handbook*. New York: Peragamon, 1976.

Holahan, C. Seating patterns and patient behavior in an experimental day-room. *Journal of Abnormal Psychology*, 1972, *80*, 115–124.

Jones, R. R. Conceptual vs. analytic uses of generalizability theory in behavioral assessment. In J. D. Cone & R. P. Hawkins (Eds.), *Behavioral assessment: New directions in clinical psychology*. New York: Brunner/Mazel, 1977.

Jones, R. R., Reid, J. B., & Patterson, G. R. Naturalistic observation in clinical assessment. In P. McReynolds (Ed.), *Advance in psychological assessment*. Vol. 3. San Francisco: Jossey-Bass, 1975.

Kallman, W. M., & Feuerstein, M. Psychophysiological procedures. In A. R. Ciminero, K. S. Calhoun, & H. E. Adams (Eds.), *Handbook of behavioral assessment*. New York: Wiley, 1977.

Kazdin, A. E. Reactive self-monitoring: The effects of response desirability, goal setting, and feedback, *Journal of Consulting and Clinical Psychology*, 1974, *42*, 404-416.

Kazdin, A. E. Assessing the clinical or applied importance of behavior change through social validation. *Behavior Modification*, 1977, *1*, 427–452.

Kazdin, A. E. Situational specificity: The two-edged sword of behavioral assessment. *Behavioral Assessment*, 1979, *1*, 57–75. (a)

Kazdin, A. E. Unobtrusive measures in behavioral assessment. *Journal of Applied Behavior Analysis*, 1979, *12*, 713–724. (b)

Kazdin, A. E., & Hartmann, D. P. The simultaneous-treatment design. *Behavior Therapy*, 1978, *9*, 912–922.

Keefe, F. J., Lopel, S. A., & Gordon, S. B. *A practical guide to behavioral assessment*. New York: Springer, 1978.

Kent, R. N., & Foster, S. L. Direct observation procedures: Methodological issues in naturalistic settings. In A. R. Ciminero, K. S. Calhoun, & H. E. Adams (Eds.), *Handbook of behavioral assessment*. New York: Wiley, 1977.

Krasner, L. Behavior modification—values and training: The perspective of a psychologist. In C. M. Franks (Ed.), *Behavior Therapy: Appraisal and status*. New York: McGraw-Hill, 1969.

Kupke, T. E., Calhoun, K. S., & Hobbs, S. A. Selection of heterosocial skills. II. Experimental validity. *Behavior Therapy*, 1979, *10*, 336–346.

Kupke, T. E., Hobbs, S. A., & Cheney, T. H. Selection of heterosocial skills. I.

Criterion-related validity. *Behavior Therapy,* 1979, *10,* 327–335.

Lang, P. J. Fear reduction and fear behavior: Problems in treating a construct. In J. M. Schlien (Ed.), *Research in psychotherapy: Vol. 3.* Washington, D.C.: American Psychological Association, 1968.

Lang, P. J. Physiological assessment of anxiety and fear. In J. D. Cone & R. P. Hawkins (Eds.), *Behavioral assessment: New directions in clinical psychology.* New York: Brunner/Mazel, 1977.

Lang, P. J., & Lazovik, A. D. Experimental desensitization of a phobia. *Journal of Abnormal and Social Psychology,* 1963, *66,* 519–525.

Leitenberg, H., Agras, W. S., Butz, R., & Wincze, J. Relationship between heart rate and behavioral change during the treatment of phobias. *Journal of Abnormal Psychology,* 1971, *78,* 59–68.

Levy, R. L. Relationship of an overt commitment to task compliance in behavior therapy. *Journal of Behavior Therapy and Experimental Psychiatry,* 1977, *8,* 25–29.

Lewinsohn, P. M. Clinical and theoretical aspects of depression. In K. S. Calhoun, H. E. Adams, & K. M. Mitchell (Eds.), *Innovative treatment methods in psychopathology.* New York: Wiley, 1974.

Lick, J. R., & Unger, T. External validity of laboratory fear assessment: Implications from two case studies. *Journal of Consulting and Clinical Psychology,* 1975, *43,* 864–866.

Linehan, M. M. Issues in behavioral interviewing. In J. D. Cone & R. P. Hawkins (Eds.), *Behavioral assessment: New directions in clinical psychology.* New York: Brunner/Mazel, 1977.

Marzillier, J. S., & Winter, K. Success and failure in social skills training: Individual differences. *Behaviour Research and Therapy,* 1978, *16,* 67–84.

Mash, E. J., & Terdal, L. G. (Eds.) *Behavior therapy assessment.* New York: Springer, 1976.

Mash, E., & Terdal, L. (Eds.) *Behavioral assessment of childhood disorders.* New York: Guilford Press, 1980.

Mathews, R. M., Whang, P. L., & Fawcett, S. B. Development and validation of an occupational skills assessment instrument. *Behavioral Assessment,* 1980, *2,* 71–85.

McFall, R. M. Behavioral training: A skill-acquisition approach to clinical problems. In J. T. Spence, R. C. Carson, & J. W. Thibaut (Eds.), *Behavioral approaches to therapy.* Morristown, N.J.: General Learning Press, 1976.

McFall, R. M. Analogue methods in behavioral assessment: Issues and prospects. In J. D. Cone & R. P. Hawkins (Eds.), *Behavioral assessment: New directions in clinical psychology.* New York: Brunner/Mazel, 1977. (a)

McFall, R. M. Parameters of self-monitoring. In R. B. Stuart (Ed.), *Behavioral self-management: Strategies, techniques, and outcomes.* New York: Brunner/Mazel, 1977. (b).

McReynolds, P. The case for interactional assessment. *Behavioral Assessment,* 1979, *1,* 237–247.

McReynolds, W. T., & Stegman, R. Sayer versus sign. *Behavior Therapy,* 1976, *7,* 704–705.

Meichenbaum, D. H., Gilmore, J. B., & Fedoravicius, A. Group insight versus group desensitization in treating speech anxiety. *Journal of Consulting and Clinical Psychology,* 1971, *36,* 410–421.

Meyer, V., Liddell, A., & Lyons, M. Behavioral interviews. In A. R. Ciminero, K. S. Calhoun, & H. E. Adams (Eds.), *Handbook of behavioral assessment.* New York: Wiley, 1977.

Miller, B. V., & Bernstein, D. A. Instructional demand in a behavioral avoidance test for claustrophobic fears. *Journal of Abnormal Psychology,* 1972, *80,* 206–210.

Mischel, W. *Personality and assessment.* New York: Wiley, 1968.

Mischel, W. Toward a cognitive social learning reconceptualization of personality. *Psychological Review*, 1973, *80*, 252–283.

Moos, R. H. Conceptualizations of human environments. *American Psychologist*, 1973, *28*, 652–665.

Morganstern, K. P. Behavioral interviewing: The initial stages of assessment. In M. Hersen & A. S. Bellack (Eds.), *Behavioral assessment: A practical handbook*. New York: Pergamon, 1976.

Mowrer, O. H. *Learning theory and personality dynamics*. New York: Ronald Press, 1950.

Mullinix, S. D., & Galassi, J. P. Deriving the content on social skills training with a verbal response components approach. *Behavioral Assessment*, 1981, *3*, 55-66.

Myerson, W. A., & Hayes, S. C. Controlling the clinician for the clients' benefit. In e.g., *Behaviorism and ethics*. Kalamazoo, Michigan: Behaviordelia, 1978.

Nathan, P. E. *Cues, decisions, diagnoses*. New York: Academic Press, 1967.

Nay, W. R. Analogue measures. In A. R. Ciminero, K. S. Calhoun, & H. E. Adams (Eds.), *Handbook of behavioral assessment*. New York: Wiley, 1977.

Neisworth, J. T. & Moore, F. Operant treatment of asthmatic responding with the parent as therapist: *Behavior Therapy*, 1972, *3*, 95-99.

Nelson, R. O. Assessment and therapeutic function of self-monitoring. In M. Hersen, R. M. Eisler, & P. M. Miller (Eds.), *Progress in behavior modification*. Vol. 5. New York: Academic Press, 1977.

Nelson, R. O. The use of intelligence tests within behavioral assessment. *Behavioral Assessment*, 1980, *2*, 417-423.

Nelson, R. O., & Barlow, D. H. Behavioral assessment: Basic strategies and initial procedures. In D. H. Barlow (Ed.), *Behavioral assessment of adult disorders*. New York: Guilford Press, 1981.

Nelson, R. O., & Bowles, P. E. The best of two worlds—observations with norms. *Journal of School Psychology*, 1975, *13*, 3–9.

Nelson, R. O., Hay, L. R., & Hay, W. M. Comments on Cone's "The relevance of reliability and validity for behavioral assessment." *Behavior Therapy*, 1977, *8*, 427–430.

Nelson, R. O., & Hayes, S. C. Some current dimensions of behavioral assessment. *Behavior Assessment*, 1979, *1*, 1–16.

Nelson, R. O., Hayes, S. C., Felton, J. L., & Jarrett, R. B. A comparison of the data produced by different behavioral assessment techniques. Paper presented at the meeting of the Association for Advancement of Behavior Therapy, San Francisco, December, 1979.

Norton, G. R., & Nielson, W. R. Headaches: The importance of consequent events. *Behavior Therapy*, 1977, *8*, 504–506.

Odom, J. V., Nelson, R. O., & Wein, K. S. The differential effectiveness of five treatment procedures on three response systems in a snake phobia analogue study. *Behavior Therapy*, 1978, *9*, 936–942.

O'Leary, K. D. The assessment of psychopathology in children. In H. C. Quay and J. S. Werry (Eds.), *Psychopathological disorders of children*. New York: Wiley, 1972.

Peed, S., Roberts, M., & Forehand, R. Evaluation of the effectiveness of a standardized parent training program in altering the interaction of mothers and their noncompliant children. *Behavior Modification*, 1977, *1*, 323–350.

Perri, M. G., & Richards, C. S. Assessment of heterosocial skills in male college students. *Behavior Modification*, 1979 *3*, 337-354.

Peterson, D. R. *The clinical study of social behavior*. New York: Appleton-Century-Crofts, 1968.

Raush, H. L., Dittmann, A. T., & Taylor, T. J. Person, setting, and change in social interaction. *Human Relations*, 1959, *12*, 361–378.

Risley, T. R., & Hart, B. Developing correspondence between the non-verbal and verbal behavior of preschool children. *Journal of Applied Behavior Analysis*, 1968, *1*, 267–281.

Rogers, T., Mahoney, M. J., Mahoney, B. K., Straw, M. K., & Kenigsberg, M. I. Clinical assessment of obesity: An empirical evaluation of diverse techniques. *Behavioral Assessment*, 1980, *2*, 161–181.

Rose, S. A., Blank, M., & Spalter, I. Situational specificity of behavior in young children. *Child Development*, 1975, *46*, 464–469.

Schnelle, J. F., Kirchner, R. E., Galbaugh, F., Domash, M., Carr, A., & Larson, L. Program evaluation research: An experimental cost-effectiveness analysis of an armed robbery intervention program. *Journal of Applied Behavior Analysis*, 1979, *12*, 615–623.

Spitzer, R. L., & Endicott, J. DIAGNO II: Further developments in a computer program for psychiatric diagnosis. *American Journal of Psychiatry*, 1969, *125*, 12–21.

Staats, A. W. *Child learning, intelligence, and personality.* New York: Harper & Row, 1971.

Staats, A. W. *Social behaviorism.* Homewood, Illinois: Dorsey Press, 1975.

Strossen, R. J., Coates, T. J., & Thoresen, C. E. Extending generalizability theory to single-subject designs. *Behavior Therapy*, 1979, *10*, 606-614.

Suinn, R. M. (Ed.) *Fundamentals of behavior pathology.* New York: Wiley, 1970.

Surwit, R. S., Bradner, M. N., Fenton, C. H., & Pilon, R. N. Individual differences in response to the behavioral treatment of Raynaud's disease. *Journal of Consulting and Clinical Psychology*, 1979, *47*, 363–367.

Tasto, D. L. Self-report schedules and inventories. In A. R. Ciminero, K. S. Calhoun, & H. E. Adams (Eds.), *Handbook of behavioral assessment.* New York: Wiley, 1977.

Tharp, R. G., & Wetzel, R. J. *Behavior modification in the natural environment.* New York: Academic Press, 1969.

Van Houten, R. Social validation: The evolution of standards of competency for target behaviors. *Journal of Applied Behavior Analysis*, 1979, *12*, 581–591.

Vogler, R. E., Weissbach, T. A., & Compton, J. V. Learning techniques for alcohol abuse. *Behaviour Research and Therapy*, 1977, *15*, 31–38.

Wade, T. C., Baker, T. B., & Hartmann, D. P. Behavior therapists' self-reported views and practices. *The Behavior Therapist*, 1979, *2*(1), 3–6.

Wahler, R. G. Some structural aspects of deviant child behavior. *Journal of Applied Behavior Analysis*, 1975, *8*, 27–42.

Wahler, R. G., & Fox, J. J. Solitary toy play and time out: A family treatment package for children with aggressive and oppositional behavior. *Journal of Applied Behavior Analysis*, 1980, *13*, 23-39.

Wahler, R. G., Moore, D. R. School-home behavior change procedures in a high-risk community. Paper presented at the meeting of the Association for Advancement of Behavior Therapy, San Francisco, December 1975.

Walls, R. T., Werner, T. J., Bacon, A., & Zane, T. Behavior checklists. In J. D. Cone & R. P. Hawkins (Eds.), *Behavioral assessment: New directions in clinical psychology.* New York: Brunner/Mazel, 1977.

Westefeld, J. S., Galassi, J. P., & Galassi, M. D. Effects of role-playing instructions on assertive behavior: A methodological study. *Behavior Therapy*, 1980, *11*, 271–277.

Wildman, B. G., & Erickson, M. T. Methodological problems in behavioral observation. In J. D. Cone and R. P. Hawkins (Eds.), *Behavioral assessment: New directions in clinical psychology.* New York: Brunner/Mazel, 1977.

Wilson, F. E., & Evans, I. M. Goal specification and the reliability of target-behavior selection in behavioral assessment. *Behavioral Assessment,* in press.

Wing, J. K., Birley, J. L. T., Cooper, J. E., Graham, P., & Isaacs, A. D. Reliability of a procedure for measuring and classifying present psychiatric state. *British Journal of Psychiatry,* 1967, *113,* 499–515.

Wing, J. K., Cooper, J. E., & Sartorius, N. *The measurement and classification of psychiatric symptoms.* Cambridge: Cambridge University Press, 1974.

Wolf, M. M. Social validity: The case for subjective measurement or how applied behavior analysis is finding its heart. *Journal of Applied Behavior Analysis,* 1978, *11,* 203–214.

Wolpe, J. *Psychotherapy by reciprocal inhibition.* Stanford: Stanford University Press, 1958.

Wolpe, J. Inadequate behavior analysis: The Achilles heel of outcome research in behavior therapy. *Journal of Behavior Therapy and Experimental Psychiatry,* 1977, *8,* 1–3.

Wolpe, J., & Lang, P. A fear survey schedule for use in behavior therapy. *Behaviour Research and Therapy,* 1964, *2,* 27–30.

Zigler, E., & Phillips, L. Psychiatric diagnosis and sympomatology. *Journal of Abnormal and Social Psychology,* 1961, *63,* 69–75.

Chapter 2
Psychometric Considerations

John D. Cone

By the standards employed in some other areas of psychological research, it can be charged that much behavior modification research data is subject to observer bias, observee reactivity, fakability, demand characteristics, response sets, and decay in instrumentation. In addition, the accuracy, reliability, and validity of the data used is often unknown or inadequately established [Johnson & Bolstad, 1973, p. 8].

In reading through the various chapters in Hersen and Bellack (1976), I was struck more by the primitive stage of research in certain areas of behavioral assessment than I was by startling new developments. In some respects, by comparison to the traditional psychometric literature we have a long way to go . . . Where are the factor analytic studies, item analysis, split half and test-retest reliability determinations? Where are the large sample cross-validity studies? [Leitenberg, 1978, p. 138]

We must pay attention to problems and issues discussed by our psychometric brethren and develop a better degree of sophistication in our assessment procedures [Curran, 1978, p. 137].

It is the thesis of the present paper that the concepts of reliability and validity used in traditional assessment are applicable to behavioral assessment as well [Cone, 1977, p. 411].

These opening quotes reflect two concerns common among behavioral assessors today: (a) the relatively primitive state of our methodology, and (b) the possibility that classical psychometric procedures can be used to elevate it to a higher level of sophistication. The present chapter will examine the applicability of classical psychometric procedures to behavioral assessment. Some of those most frequently used will be analyzed and evaluated in terms of the information they can provide about the adequacy of behavioral assessment procedures. It will be shown that the conceptual-philosophical basis of classical psychometrics is so different from a radical behavioral assessment that psychometric procedures are actually of limited value to behavioral assessors. Alternative approaches to evaluating the adequacy of assessment measures will be proposed and ways of implementing them suggested.

THE BASIS FOR CONCERN WITH MEASUREMENT ADEQUACY

There are clinical as well as research-based reasons for concern with the trustworthiness of the data produced by our assessment devices. Important decisions about clients must not be significantly influenced by random error or factors which might lead to atypical performance on a particular assessment occasion. As Cronbach (1970) has noted, erroneous decisions resulting from faulty measurement can irreparably harm an individual client or the larger community. Similarly, in the research use of assessment procedures, accurate measurement is essential for appropriate conclusions concerning relationships among variables.

Concern with the adequacy of behavioral assessment procedures and the accuracy of the data produced by them has led some of us to appeal to traditional psychometrics in the hope of preventing the proliferation of unsound measures. In describing the spread of projective techniques in the 1940s, Goldfried (1977) lamented the unfortunate tendency of history to repeat itself and warned that a plethora of poorly constructed measures could easily dot the behavioral assessment landscape if insufficient attention is given to their psychometic characteristics.

Once any measure appears in the literature, it becomes capable of developing its own momentum. If a behavioral assessment procedure is clearly specified and easily administered, researchers and clinicians are likely to use it. At this point it becomes a ''frequently used'' behavioral assessment procedure, thereby justifying its use by assessors in the future. It then only requires a factor analysis—and perhaps a short form—to provide it with a completely independent life of its own [Goldfried, 1977, p. 4].

In recognizing the importance of accurate assessment and witnessing the ease with which inadequate measures can be developed and rapidly disseminated, behavioral assessors are justifiably concerned with the quality of their own devices. In searching for ways to establish that quality, it is reasonable to turn to something familiar, i.e., the concepts and procedures of classical psychometric test theory.

CLASSICAL PSYCHOMETRIC PROCEDURES AND WHAT THEY TELL US

Occasionally the familiar is not always as helpful as it first appears. In this section a brief discussion of the conceptual basis for classical psychometric procedures will be followed by a description of some of those most frequently used. Information provided by each procedure will be contrasted with information required by behavioral assessors and discrepancies noted.

Conceptual Bases for Psychometric Procedures

As eloquently traced by Johnston and Pennypacker (1980), classical psychometric test theory has its origins in the study of measurement error by Legendre in the early 1800s. Legendre developed a mathematical procedure for producing the best single value representing a physical characteristic from a series of such values which show variability. The mathematics of probability theory enables us to estimate a "true" score from a measure of the dispersion or variability of the series of values. Later, Adolphe Quetelet used demonstrated variability to *define* "latent entities or characteristics" (Johnston & Pennypacker, 1980). Thus, variability in natural phenomena is observed and described, and this variation is used as a basis for defining phenomena into existence.

It remained for Francis Galton to synthesize the ideas of Quetelet with those of Gustav Fechner, who had created units of measurement from observed variability in judgments of stimulus intensity. This synthesis led to the origins of mental abilities measurement and was to have a profound influence on the measurement of all kinds of differences between individuals. Galton created the concept of intelligence by assuming that mental abilities are normally distributed in the human population and suggesting an equal interval scale along which scores on various mental tests would be distributed. The subsequent work of Binet and others involved creating measures that showed variability across different individuals in terms of various academically relevant performances. As Johnston and Pennypacker noted, since this variability was distributed consistently with the normal law of error (as Galton suggested was necessary for tests of mental ability), it was natural to assume the tests thus derived were, indeed, measures of mental ability.

It is not difficult to complete the connection between these early undertakings and contemporary trait-based psychological assessment.

Nor is it difficult to see that the armamentarium of psychometric procedures developed during the early part of the 1900s is clearly predicated on the view that important psychological processes can be defined in terms of variation in scores on measures of them. Thus, a phenomenon is conceptualized, a measure is developed, and the measure is administered to a group of people. The significance of the phenomenon is supported if there is some variability in scores on the measure, and this variability simultaneously provides the basis for establishing the adequacy of the measuring instrument itself.

Nearly all subsequent efforts to demonstrate the quality of the instrument resolve to questions about the variability of the scores it produces. Also, most classical psychometric procedures and concepts deal with different ways of analyzing that variability. For example, issues of reliability have to do with the extent to which differences between scores are unchanged across time, subsets of items within the measure, alternate forms of the same measure, and so on. Issues of validity have to do with the relationships between variability on one measure and variability on another. If scores for a group of people retain their relative positions in distributions from two different measures, we say one is predictable from the other and that the validity of each is enhanced by the strength of the relationship. A closer look at some important psychometric procedures and what they tell us should make these points clearer.

Reliability

The most basic consideration in classical measurement theory is the consistency with which a thing is measured. While consistency is generally considered under the rubric of "reliability," over the years the different uses of reliability have been anything but consistent. Unfortunately, it is beyond the scope of this chapter to discuss the fascinating story of reliability in detail, but some of the traditional, more prosaic uses of the concept will be reviewed. The customary view of reliability as the superordinate concept in establishing the adequacy of measuring devices will be adopted. In a later section behavioral alternatives to classical psychometrics will be presented and it will be shown that reliability is not the superordinate concept.

Without getting into epistemological issues about the nature of reliability (these will also be discussed later), it can be said that in most forms the consistency of two sets of scores obtained on the same measure for the same group of persons is examined. The most basic type of reliability deals with consistency of scoring, a subject to which we now turn.

Interscorer reliability. Before any significance can be attached to a score, it is necessary to know how consistently it represents what the subject did to produce it. If the subject made marks on a true-false, paper-and-pencil, self-report measure, these marks must be converted to scores of some type. To the extent that the conversion by one scorer duplicates that of another we say the measure has been scored reliably, and we can now examine relationships into which the scores may enter. The extent to which scores do not depend on the scorer is the index of interscorer reliability when self-report is the method of interest. Interrater and interobserver reliabilities are the counterparts, respectively, when ratings by others and direct observation methods are being used.

As with most classic forms of reliability and validity, interscorer reliability is normally computed by correlating scores between scorers across a group of people who have been assessed with the measure. The resulting coefficient reflects the extent different scorers alter the group members' positions relative to one another. For example, a high correlation tells us, in general, that a person who is one standard deviation above the mean in Scorer A's distribution is one standard deviation above the mean in Scorer B's distribution as well.

It is interesting to note that, while conventional wisdom claims interscorer reliability as critical to other forms of reliability and validity, this is less a necessity than a simple convenience. What is critical is not so much whether two people agree on their scores, but whether either one or both is measuring something consistently. If they agree, consistency can be assumed. If they do not, it is still the case that either or both may be scoring consistently. Consistency is a necessary but not a sufficient condition for interscorer/rater/observer reliability. As long as a particular scorer is consistent, it is possible for his/her scores to enter into relationships with other variables. It is inconvenient to build a science of behavior on such relationships, of course, but it is possible nevertheless. This is less of a problem in clinical assessment. It is conceivable that scores of a particular clinician are consistently related to significant criteria and that decisions based on them will allow appropriate decisions for individual clients. The question of interscorer agreement is more complicated than it initially appears, and more will be said about its meaning in a later section.

Temporal consistency. Temporal consistency or test-retest reliability is an important characteristic of any measure assumed to reflect an enduring psychological attribute. Scores on the measure are obtained at two different points in time for a single group of persons, and the consistency of the variability in their scores is noted. To the extent that each person occupies the same position relative to others in both distributions of scores, it may be assumed that the measure is temporally stable. Note that the demonstration of temporal consistency requires variability in scores (i.e., differences between individuals). Though not addressed in the previous section, this is also a requirement of interscorer reliability. Temporal consistency measures the consistency of this variability (or these differences) over some period of time. In other words, the procedure, like all classical psychometric procedures, relies on consistency in the differences between individuals to demonstrate the adequacy of the measure being evaluated.

Of course, the degree of inter-individual consistency over time required of a measure depends on one's interpretation of the attribute or construct being assessed. All individual differences are not hypothesized to remain stable, as recent studies of the trait-state distinction have shown (e.g., Spielberger, Gorsuch, & Lushene, 1970; Zuckerman, 1977; 1979). Whether evidence for temporal stability is interpreted as supporting or refuting the theory underlying a particular construct, however, it is still assessed in terms of differences between individuals on a measure of it. The value of such information for behavioral assessors will be discussed in a later section.

Internal consistency. Most assessment devices require multiple responses, combined in some way to produce a score. If the device is consistently measuring the same characteristic, it is reasonable to expect some relationship among the different responses produced. Internal consistency concepts have been most thoroughly developed and applied with self-report methods (see Cronbach, 1970; Horst, 1966; Wiggins, 1973). Here various statistical indices reflect the extent to which responses on different subsets of items are related. The best known of these procedures involve correlations among odd-even splits (e.g., split-half reliability), and the average correlation resulting from all possible splits (e.g., Kuder-Richardson formulas).

A high degree of internal consistency assessed in these ways tells us that an individual occupies the same position relative to others on each of the item subsets. Thus, regardless of which portion of the total items is used, the same information is provided about the respondent. The requirement of a high degree of internal consistency is conceptually intuitive, since it leads to clearer interpretations of what the measure is tapping. Imagine the difficulty of using a thermometer that measured temperature at some points along its scale but humidity or atmospheric pressure at others!

Internal consistency requirements extend to other methods of assessment as well as self-reports and have been recently applied to direct observation methods. For example, Johnson and Bolstad (1973) and Patterson (1974) reported data showing correlations among directly observed behavior over the odd and even days of a baseline period. Gottman (1978) discussed factor analytic and discriminant function procedures for examining the composition of items making up various direct observation coding systems.

Recent work of Gottman (1978; 1979) and others (e.g., Kent, O'Leary, Coletti, & Drabman, reported in Kent & Foster, 1977) has highlighted an alternative way of looking at internal consistency. While it has typically dealt with the formulation of classes of topographically similar responses, these authors suggest the possibility of what might be referred to as functional internal consistency. Thus, behaviors (responses, "items") are grouped according to the effects they produce. For example, observed pupil behaviors shown to be correlated with teacher ratings of disruptiveness would be grouped into a single category (response class, "scale") labeled "student deviant," regardless of their topographic similarity. The examination of internal consistency in terms of functional equivalence of component responses will undoubtedly occur more often as the use of direct observation methods continues to increase. The application of functional internal consistency concepts to other assessment methods also awaits exploration. For example, while the psychometric procedures for estimating the internal consistency of self-report measures have been extended to direct observation measures, the application of response class concepts to self-report methodology has not yet occurred. The notion of functional internal consistency may have implications for self-report measures that should be explored as well.

This brief discussion of classical reliability concepts has been intended as a review of precisely what we know when we have found interscorer, temporal, and internal consistency estimates for an assessment device. Before discussing the usefulness of this knowledge for behavioral assessors, a similar review of the major classical validity concepts will be provided.

Validity

While reliability is typically concerned with relations among scores on the same device, validity deals with relationships between scores on different devices (Campbell & Fiske, 1959). Numerous of different validity concepts have been developed over the years, and space does not permit each to be treated here. In the next few sections only the major types of validity will be discussed.

Content validity. Classical psychometric test theory has not dealt with the question of content validity and it will be treated only briefly here. When the items included in a measure adequately represent the domain the user wants the measure to cover, it is said to have content validity. For thorough discussions of the term from a traditional perspective, see Anastasi (1968), Cronbach (1970), or Gulliksen (1950). Linehan (1980) has recently treated content validity from a behavioral point of view.

Content validity has generally been of more concern to achievement test developers and users than to persons concerned with aptitude and/ or personality assessment. This is primarily because performance on achievement tests is *the* behavior of interest (or at least a direct sampling of it), and a review of the test's content provides useful information about what is actually being measured. When aptitude or underlying personality traits are being assessed, test performance is important only as an indirect indicator of status on the relevant underlying dimension. Surveying the content of the measure merely provides information regarding the developer's interpretation of the trait and its manifestations. However, such information is not particularly useful in determining whether the test is a good measure of that trait.

Unlike other forms of reliability and validity, there is no content validity coefficient, though at least one attempt has been made to quantify the concept (Lawshe, 1975). Generally, the adequacy of a measure's content (i.e., its representativeness) must come from a systematic inspection of what is included in the measure and a comparison with the user's understanding of the behavior universe that is being assessed. Content validity may be built into a measure from the beginning by defining and systematically mapping the universe to be represented (e.g., Anastasi, 1968; Goldfried & D'Zurilla, 1969; McFall, 1977; Mathews, Whang, & Fawcett, 1980). The success of these efforts is supported by empirical evidence of the measure's subsequent usefulness.

Construct validity. When there is no single, agreed-upon operational index of what it is a test measures, as when hypothetical constructs are being assessed, it is necessary to resort to construct validation. The construct thought to underly test performance receives validation to the extent that test scores enter relationships predicted by the theory in which the construct is embedded. This form of validity has been of great interest to trait-oriented personality assessors (see Bechtoldt,

1959; Campbell, 1960; Cronbach & Meehl, 1955;), and has recently been examined by behavioral assessors as well (see, Haynes, 1978; Jones, Reid, & Patterson, 1975).

As typically pursued, construct validity involves correlations of scores on one measure with those on others. A relationship between scores is predicted on the basis of a theoretical understanding of the relationship between the variables believed to underly performance on the measures. According to Haynes, "We would predict that depressed compared to nondepressed individuals would manifest a lower rate of social initiation behaviors . . . [Haynes, 1978, p. 178]." The construct "depression" is thought to be related to that of "social initiation" in the manner suggested. Whether it is will be tested by correlating scores between measures presumed to reflect depression on the one hand, and social initiation on the other.

Construct validity proceeds most clearly when there is independent evidence of the theoretical utility of the construct and the appropriateness of the measure being used to tap it. That is, if we have evidence of the value of depression in some theoretical network or other, and also know that scores on our measure of depression have been shown to behave appropriately (i.e., relate to other measures in ways predicted from the theory), then its correlation (or lack thereof) with a measure of social initiation can be interpreted fairly easily. The job is complicated when neither the theory supporting the construct (i.e., depression), nor the presumed measure of it have received previous independent verification. In such a case, failure to find the predicted correlation puts the investigator squarely on the horns of a negative evidence dilemma. Either the theory underlying the construct is faulty, the measure of the construct is no good, or there are problems with both. Of course, it is also possible that the same difficulties underly the construct and measure being related in the present case. That is, neither social initiation nor our measure of it may have received independent verification.

It is nearly impossible to avoid the dual validation of construct and measure in the early stages of theory building and testing. As empirical support is developed for either the construct, the measure, or both, the results of later research become more easily interpretable. If it has been shown, for example, that depression is a relatively stable characteristic, then a measure of it should show temporal consistency. If it does not, the subsequent overhaul is more likely to be focused on the measure than the construct.

The concept and process of construct validity are based in a hypothetico-deductive approach to understanding and assessing human behavior which is characteristic of trait-based views of assessment. As will be shown later, such a general to specific type of reasoning is inappropriate to behavioral assessment, and constructs and construct validity are of no utility for it.

Criterion-related validity. While construct validity has been of greatest importance to personality theorists, the related concept of criterion-related validity has been of greater concern to practicing clinicians. To be sure, the practice of relating scores on different measures is basic to construct validity. But the examination of such relationships from a theoretically neutral, practically-oriented perspective is more often termed criterion-related validity.

The process of relating scores on a particular measure to outcome in therapy is an example of the procedures involved in criterion-related validity. Relating scores on selection measures to subsequent employee performance is another. In each, differences between a group of clients or employees on one measure are related to their differences on others. As with all interindividual, difference-based psychometric procedures, validity is established to the extent that the persons assessed retain their relative positions on the measures being related.

Criterion-related validity is of great importance to behavioral and nonbehaviorally-oriented clinicians alike. As a later section will show, however, the approach taken by behavioral assessors for establishing criterion-related validity for their measures needs to be considerably different from the interindividual, difference-based approach used almost exclusively heretofore.

Miscellaneous forms of validity. Content, construct, and criterion-related validity comprise the most important and widely examined forms of validity in traditional clinical assessment. There are numerous other forms of validity which deserve brief mention before moving on.

Convergent validity describes the extent to which different measures of the same thing are correlated. Especially important in the validation of constructs and their measures, convergent validity has usually involved relationships between different methods of assessing a trait or construct (Campbell & Fiske, 1959). For example, ratings by others of anxiety manifested in a public speaking situation would be correlated with self-reported anxiety in the same situation.

Discriminant validity shows the extent to which a measure is independent of or uncorrelated with things it is not supposed to measure (Cambell & Fiske, 1959). For example, a measure of ethnocentrism should not be highly correlated with years of education (Adorno, Frenkel-Brunswik, Levinson, & Sanford, 1950). That is, variables thought to be irrelevant to the measurement of particular characteristics should

be shown to be uncorrelated with them. Thus, in the behavioral assessment arena, measures of social skills should be shown to be more
than new scales for measuring social desirability (Kiecolt & McGrath,
1979). They should be expected to bear *some* relationship with measures
of social desirability, while not being so highly correlated that they are
interchangeable with them. With respect to traditional, trait-oriented modes
of assessment, Campbell (1960)) made important recommendations regarding discriminant validity which merit the attention of behavioral
assessors as well.

It should be noted that the conventional use of the term "discriminant
validity" does not refer to the extent that a measure accurately discriminates between groups known to differ on a particular characteristic.
Showing significant differences on the Social Anxiety and Distress Scale
(Watson & Friend, 1969) between groups of socially effective and ineffective persons is not discriminant validity as the term is usually employed. Such a differentiation certainly supports the validity of the
scale, but is perhaps better referred to as the known groups approach
to test validation (Bellack, 1979) or as a measure of the scale's discriminative efficiency (Wiggins, 1973).

Incremental validity (Sechrest, 1963) is an index of the improvement
in prediction made possible by the addition of a particular measure to
an already existing battery of assessment devices or prediction procedures. The term might also apply to any improvement in the magnitude
of the relationship between two variables which was effected by a
change in the method of measuring one of them. For example, relatively
expensive behaviorally anchored rating scales (BARS) might be compared with simple numerical ratings of the behaviors to determine
whether increased correlations with relevant criteria attend the use of
the BARS (e.g., Borman, 1979; Smith & Kendall, 1963). The magnitude
of any improvement would be a measure of the incremental validity of
the BARS.

Finally, the relatively new concept of treatment validity represents
how a measure enhances the outcome of a particular intervention (Nelson & Hayes, 1979). The evaluation of a measure's treatment validity
would be a complex undertaking if taken seriously, and it is not expected
that any single numerical index would ever represent this form of validity. It is likely that measures will have different degrees of treatment
validity depending on the behaviors, the subject, the treatment options,
and the way the effects will be measured. Despite this complexity, treatment validity is likely to receive increased attention as human service
provision becomes more accountable and as the relative contributions
of all aspects of the service delivery process come under closer scrutiny.

Summary

Starting with their underlying conceptual basis, the most familiar psychometric procedures have been reviewed. Since variability has historically been used to define human behavioral characteristics, it is important that measures of these characteristics produce differences between persons assessed by them. Once such variability has been established, the adequacy of the measure can be demonstrated by examining the interindividual differences in numerous ways. The many forms of reliability have been represented in terms of the consistency of these differences when generated by alternate ways of looking at data from the same measuring instrument. Likewise, construct and criterion-related validity were represented in terms of the consistency of interindividual differences between measures of two or more separate variables.

The point was made that behavioral and all other assessors need to be concerned with the adequacy of their measures. Afraid of the proliferation of unsound procedures, it is understandable that behavioral assessors have looked to classical psychometric concepts for help. Nonetheless, throughout this discussion it was hinted that these concepts may be inappropriate for an approach to assessment which is based on a radically different view of behavior. However, before showing why this is the case, attention must be given to one more psychometric perspective.

GENERALIZABILITY THEORY

Concerned with the "conceptual compartmentalization of 'types' of [reliability and] validity" (Dunnette & Borman, 1979), some behavioral assessors (e.g., Cone, 1977; Curran, Monti, Corriveau, Hay, Hagerman, Zwick, & Farrell, in press; Jones, Reid, & Patterson, 1975) have argued for consideration of the conceptually more consistent, more parsimonious generalizability theory of Cronbach and his colleagues (Cronbach, Gleser, Nanda, & Rajaratnam, 1972). Proponents of generalizability theory argue that the various forms of reliability and validity are simply different ways in which data from a measure can be generalized. Thus, if data generated by one scorer match those of a second, they are generalizable across the two scorers. In other words, the data do not depend on the specific scorers that provide them.

As noted by Cronbach et al., all observations can be generalized to a number of operationally definable universes. Therefore, in the previous example our calculation of interscorer reliability reflects an interest in generalizing to a universe of scorers. Similarly, the calculation of coefficients of internal consistency reflects an interest in generalizing across a universe of items or scale content. If items on one-half of a measure correlate highly with those on the other, we say our scores do not depend on which of the items we use. We have defined a universe of scale content, sampled from it, and shown that our samples are comparably representative of that universe.

Cone (1977) has identified six *universes of generalizability* likely to be of particular interest to behavioral assessors: scorer, item, time, setting, method, and dimension. In addition to the scorer and item universes, concern with time and setting reflect the behavioral assessor's interest in generalizing scores to times and places other than those in which the assessment occurs. For example, direct observation of family interaction is typically carried out during a very small portion of all available times or occasions of measurement (see Eyberg & Johnson, 1974; Patterson, 1971, 1974; Reid, 1978). The users of such procedures generally assume some generalizability to times unobserved and occasionally even test for them (e.g., Johnson, Christensen, & Bellamy, 1976).

Another type of temporal generalizability of interest to behavioral assessors has to do with the stability of responses over time. Here the question is not whether the assessment occasions are representative of a universe at all possible times, but whether responses observed during them will persist and manifest comparable frequencies at later times. This type of temporal generalizability is of extreme importance to behavioral assessors and will be discussed more thoroughly in a subsequent section.

Setting generalizability deals with the extent to which assessment data depend on the particular circumstances in which they are obtained. Are social interactions of second graders in structured play situations comparable to those observed on the playground during recess or in the neighborhood after school? Temporal generalizability is a prerequisite to setting generalizability since assessments in different settings are, of necessity, separated in time. Generalization over settings will also be discussed more thoroughly in a later section.

Generalizability across methods deals with the extent to which assessment information depends upon the method used to obtain it. As mentioned earlier, it has been customary to refer to this form of generalizability as convergent validity (Campbell & Fiske, 1959). There are practical as well as theoretical reasons for investigating the comparability of data from alternative assessment methods, and the implications of cross-method generalizability and the need for its evaluation by behavioral assessors have recently been examined (Cone, 1979; Cone & Foster, in press). Briefly, the examination of relationships among behaviors requires demonstration that these relationships are due to more than the fortuitous use of a common method of assessment; such relationships should generally not depend on how they are assessed. Of course, some behaviors (e.g., private events) can be assessed with only a single method (e.g., self-report), making it difficult to sort out potential content-method confounds in resulting correlations.

Generalizability over dimensions represents the extent to which different behaviors of a common response repertoire are related. Dimensions are used here to suggest larger or more general behaviors than typically indexed by items. Indeed, aggregates of items forming scales or response classes are related to other such aggregates in studying generalizability over dimensions. For example, disruptive classroom behavior might be related to academic performance (e.g., Ayllon & Roberts, 1974; Ferritor, Buckholdt, Hamblin, & Smith, 1972).

Generalizability theory has been positively received by behavioral assessors who have shown its applicability to the assessment of family interaction (Jones, Reid, & Patterson, 1975), social skills (Curran et al., in press; Farrell, Mariotto, Conger, Curran, & Wallander, 1979), overeating (Coates & Thoresen, 1978), and the behavior of institutionalized psychiatric clients and staff (Mariotto & Paul, 1975). In spite of this warm reception, it is not clear that generalizability theory has that much direct relevance to behavioral assessment. Jones (1977) distinguished between the conceptual contributions of generalizability theory on the one hand, and its analytical contributions on the other, pointing out that the interindividual differences basis for the analytical procedures limits their applicability to the study of differences within individuals over time. The limitations of its analytical procedures notwithstanding, Jones suggested the conceptual aspects of generalizability theory might still be of value to the field. Recently, Hartmann, Roper, and Bradford (1979) noted that "the usefulness of generalizability theory to single-subject research remains to be demonstrated [p. 15]."

Though Strossen, Coates, and Thoresen (1979) present data which seem to contradict the Hartmann et al. statement, it is probably safe to say (at least at the present time) that despite the initial enthusiasm of a number of researchers (e.g., Cone, 1977; Jones, Reid, & Patterson, 1975), generalizability theory has not proven to be the answer to behavioral assessment's quest for satisfactory ways of evaluating the adequacy of its measures. In the next section it will be argued that a truly behavioral view of assessment is based on an approach to the study of behavior so radically different from the customary individual differences model that a correspondingly different approach must be taken in evaluating the adequacy of behavioral assessment procedures.

THE BEHAVIORAL ASSESSMENT ALTERNATIVE

A Conceptual Basis for the Behavioral View

As noted in the beginning of this chapter, the individual differences assessment movement is founded on the use of demonstrated variability to define phenomena into existence. Using the mathematics of probability theory to estimate "true" scores from measures of variability, it was just a small step to defining characteristics or traits in terms of this variability. As described by Johnston and Pennypacker (1980):

> The use of procedures wherein the phenomena being measured and/ or the units of measurement are defined in terms of variability characterizing a set of otherwise direct observations seems peculiar to psychology and the other social sciences. This difference is perhaps the most fundamental one between the natural and social sciences [pp. 64-65].

From the individual differences or psychometric perspective, observed variability in performance is assumed to be reflective of differences on an underlying dimension, trait, or characteristic. For example, if we observe persons known to have comparable levels of interpersonal skills and find them to perform quite differently in contexts involving the opposite sex, we might attribute the differences to heterosocial anxiety. The validity of this supposition will derive from a literature dealing with heterosocial anxiety and correlates thereof, or from empirical tests we develop specifically to examine our explanation.

In pursuing our own empirical test, it will be necessary to find an existing measure of heterosocial anxiety or build one ourselves. Whatever route, it will be necessary for the resulting measure to show differences between subjects assessed by it. This is clearly the case since the construct or trait is being invoked to explain differences we have already observed in the performance of our subjects in interpersonal situations. As previously noted, once variability is produced on our measure of the construct, it then becomes possible to explore the adequacy of the measure in terms of various questions about that variability, i.e., whether it is stable over time, across sets of items, whether it relates to variability on other measures in expected ways, and so on.

From a behavioral perspective, based on a natural science point of view, variability in observed performance is interpreted quite differently. Instead of defining phenomena, variability is used as a "window through which to observe the workings of basic controlling relationships [Johnston & Pennypacker, 1980, p. 70]." More fundamentally, however, the subject matter of the behavioral assessor taking a natural science point of view is behavior itself, and behavior can be defined as:

> that portion of the organism's interaction with its environment that is characterized by detectable displacement in space through time of some part of the organism and which results in a measurable change in at least one aspect of the environment [Johnston & Pennypacker, 1980, p. 48].

When defined in this way behavior can be seen to have "many of the characteristics of matter in motion, and the same principles of measurement are applicable [Johnston & Pennypacker, 1980, p. 73]."

The principles of measurement in the natural sciences require counting phenomena in terms of units which are standard and absolute, and do not depend for their definition on variability in the subject matter being studied. In the physical sciences standard units exist for measuring distance, mass, and time. Various combinations of these define additional units such as velocity and density. As Johnston and Pennypacker have noted, these units of measurement have anchors in natural phenomena. For example, time and length can be defined in terms of certain wavelengths of light and "atomic vibrational phenomena."

Once it is accepted that behavior is comparable to matter in motion, then measurement principles worked out for matter can be applied to behavior as well. Such dimensional characteristics of behavior as frequency, latency, duration, and intensity (force) can all be assessed in terms of the same absolute and standard units employed with other forms of matter.

Implications for Assessment and the Evaluation of Assessment Methods

If we accept the view that behavior is comparable to other forms of matter, our assessment activities consist of obtaining information about one or more dimensional quantities of interest. We develop ways of generating this information and evaluating them in terms of the accuracy with which they portray it.

As noted elsewhere (Cone, 1978), we are concerned with assessing facts about behavior which are more or less independently verifiable. That is, we want to know: (a) whether a behavior occurs; (b) whether it occurs repeatedly; (c) whether it occurs in more than one setting; (d) whether it can be measured in more than one way; and (e) whether it is systematically related to the occurrence of other behavior(s).

Whatever dimensional quantity we select to observe, the significance we attach to the values obtained derives from comparing them with some relatively absolute standard of effective performance. In this regard, behavioral assessment is criterion-referenced (Livingston, 1977). This perspective is in sharp contrast to the traditional practice of assigning significance to scores based on comparison with the average or normal performance of a group of persons. For example, in assessing the effectiveness of several opening gambits used in approaching opposite-sexed strangers, McFall (1977) had confederates ask the strangers to rate the gambit. Those rated as highly effective would presumably become part of the repertoire taught heterosocially inept clients. In assessing clients on such skills, their responses would be compared with what was effective during the development of the measure. There would be no need to compare the client's score against the typical performance of a group of normal or "healthy" persons. Indeed, it is hard to see how such a comparison would produce information of much value to the clinician planning and evaluating a particular intervention strategy.

To summarize, behavioral assessors taking a natural science point of view are concerned with determining certain verifiable facts about behavior. Moreover, their interpretation of the information obtained in relation to these facts rests on comparisons against relatively absolute levels of effective performance.

In obtaining their information, behavioral assessors, like their traditional counterparts, must rely on a set of methods, the adequacy of which must be established independently. In behavioral assessment the most important feature of an assessment device is its accuracy, i.e., its sensitivity to the facts about behavior it is being used to discover. For example, a measure of disruptive classroom activity such as getting out of one's seat, talking without permission, and throwing spitballs will be adequate to the extent that it reflects the occurrence of these behaviors accurately. At least, the measure will be adequate for assessing the occurrence and, perhaps, repeated occurrence of the behaviors. Its adequacy for detecting occurrence in other settings and relationships with other behaviors would require its accuracy or sensitivity to these questions also be demonstrated.

In the following sections the general concept of accuracy will be discussed and the types of accuracy important to behavioral assessors described. Procedures for demonstrating the various types of accuracy will also be suggested.

Measurement Accuracy: General Considerations

A student gets out of his seat; a husband says "I love you" to his wife; a speaker trembles and perspires before a large audience. Most of us would agree that the occurrence or nonoccurrence of these behaviors can be established relatively clearly, given appropriately designed assessment procedures. If we are interested in whether clients perform any of these behaviors, we should use assessment devices shown to be sensitive to their occurrence. That is, we will want to use measures which accurately reflect occurrence-nonoccurrence values of these activities.

The situation facing the behavioral assessor is similar to that confronting a biologist interested in examining the structure of a particular cell. The microscope used must be sufficiently accurate to detect the structure that actually exists. Therefore, before examining the cell, the biologist typically knows the power and resolution of the microscope and is confident that it is providing a true picture of what is there. This is so because the accuracy of the particular microscope has previously been determined and the limits of that accuracy are known.

The pre-eminent characteristic of measuring devices in the biological sciences is their accuracy in detecting the qualities of the phenomena they are being used to study. A perfectly analogous case exists in the study of behavior. The most important aspect of the measures we use to assess responding is their accuracy, i.e., their sensitivity to what is true about the behavior in question.

Moreover, the establishment of accuracy is a prior requirement to the use of the measure in determining something about behavior. If we are interested in how frequently clients make positive self-referent comments in therapy sessions, we must assess it with a procedure already proven sensitive to the occurrence of self-referent statements of similar clients, in similar contexts, when used in similar ways. This is in contrast to the typical practice of developing a measure *de nouveau* and using it to assess and report certain characteristics of behavior without ever having shown whether the measure is even sensitive to such characteristics. Data are usually reported on the attributes of the measure (e.g., its consistency across multiple scorers, its temporal stability), simultaneously with data on the characteristics of the particular behavior being observed. In some cases the same data are involved in establishing the adequacy of the measure and providing information on the behavior being assessed. Conclusions that responses are relatively enduring over time and a measure temporally stable because it reflects this endurance, exemplify this point. Failure to find temporal generalizability in the absence of prior demonstrations of the measure's sensitivity to such generalizability creates the same negative evidence dilemma referred to earlier. Is it the measure or the behavior?

It should be noted that the common practice of reporting interobserver agreement data for direct observation coding systems developed specifically for a particular study does not exemplify the problem being

discussed. In the cases where agreement is low, it is generally regarded
as appropriate to draw conclusions about the behavior being studied.
Here, agreement between observers is required *before* information is
gathered about the behavior itself.

Requirements of Measurement Accuracy for Common Questions about Behavior

As previously suggested, the five most frequently sought kinds of information about a given response are: (a) its occurrence, (b) its repeated
occurrence, (c) its occurrence in different settings, (d) its measurability
by different assessment methods, and (e) its relation to other responses.
These five kinds of information define the major accuracy requirements
for any measuring device—at least to the extent that it is used to provide
data in all five areas. A behavioral assessment device may be termed
adequate for use with particular behaviors to the extent that it has been
previously shown to reflect these five important characteristics accurately.

To illustrate these points further and provide preliminary suggestions
as to how one might establish the adequacy of a device in this sense,
let us consider a direct observation coding system designed for assessing
positive verbal interchanges between spouses. Much of the material in
this section closely parallels that found in Cone (1978) and Cone and
Foster (in press).

Having defined "positive verbal interchange" for purposes of the
particular assessment, the investigator either develops procedures for
assessing it *de nouveau* or an already existing device is accepted and
used. In either case, information must be produced (or available) relating to the measure's suitability for the purposes intended.

To show that the measure is accurate for detecting occurrence and
repeated occurrence of positive verbal interchanges, several procedures
could be used. It is necessary in each to compare data generated by
the measure with independent, incontrovertible sources of information
about the same behavior. For example, a scripted interaction between
professional actors/actresses might have been written to include positive
verbal interchanges at a rate of .05 per minute. Comparisons of tape
recordings against the written script verify its faithful portrayal by the
performers. The direct observation coding system in question might then
be compared with the tape recording of the performance and deemed
accurate if it reveals what is already known about positive verbal interchanges.

This method is comparable to those reported in literature comparing
different types of direct observation coding systems (Powell, Martindale, Kulp, Martindale, & Bauman, 1977; Powell & Rockinson, 1978;

Repp, Roberts, Slack, Repp, & Berkler, 1976). In the Powell et al. (1977) study, for example, an adult male produced "in-seat behavior" to match instructions to be in his seat "6 min, 15 min, and 24 min [p. 325]" of 15, 30-minute sessions. Thus, for five sessions the behavior was programmed for 20 percent occurrence; for five more it was programmed for 50 percent occurrence, and for five more, 80 percent. Various ways of using interval direct observation systems were then compared in terms of their sensitivity for reflecting what was already known about the behavior.

Similarly, Borman (1979) recently studied the accuracy of ratings-by-others by having actors portray the job of recruiting interviewer or manager in a business/industrial setting. Scripts were carefully prepared to reflect pre-set levels of performance on several different dimensions. Fourteen expert judges then viewed and rated videotapes of the actors' performances. Composites of the experts' ratings subsequently served as criteria against which the accuracy of novice raters could be compared. Accuracy was used as one of the criteria for evaluating the adequacy of several different types of rating scale format, much in the manner of the studies by Powell et al. (1977), Repp et al. (1976), and others just mentioned. Thus, the importance of measurement accuracy has recently been recognized in other contexts as well as behavioral assessment. Of course, there are differences between the approach being suggested for behavioral assessors and that taken by Borman (1978, 1979) and others in the performance appraisal area of industrial/organizational psychology. Interested readers are referred to Cone (1980) for a more thorough discussion of some of these differences.

In establishing the accuracy of a behavioral assessment device it is necessary to have: (a) clearly spelled out rules/procedures for using the device, and (b) an incontrovertible index against which data from its use can be compared. The rules must be generated by the developers of the measure and must indicate precisely how it was used in the original conditions from which accuracy data were derived. In order for our aforementioned investigators to accept the accuracy information provided by the purveyors of an already existing system for observing positive verbal interchanges, they must have technologically complete information about the original calibrating conditions. This will permit them to compare these conditions with their own anticipated uses. Such a comparison is critical if original accuracy is to be generalized to uses planned by the investigators.

Of course, regardless of who generates the accuracy data it will be necessary for subsequent users to conform to the calibrating conditions. Otherwise, it would be inappropriate to assume that the measure is still faithfully reflecting the objective features of the behavior being assessed. At present, consistency of use data are most often the result

of computing agreement measures between independent observers, raters, or scorers. These data can be used as some indication that derivation condition rules are being followed, but they offer no positive
proof that this is the case. The finding of disagreement alerts the investigator to check further, but the converse does not assure that the
observers are using the measure in ways consistent with the calibrating
conditions. It merely shows that they are using it consistently between
themselves. Nonetheless, the use of a calibrator observer in the manner
of Patterson (1971; Patterson, Cobb, & Ray, 1973) and others (De-Mas-
ter, Reid, & Twentyman, 1977; Eyberg & Johnson, 1974) comes close
to providing the necessary documentation for generalizing original accuracy data to present applications. The well-documented reactivity of the
agreement check process (see Romanczyk, Kent, Diament, & O'Leary,
1973; Taplin & Reid, 1973) argues for keeping such checks as unobtrusive as possible, however.

The discussion to this point has dealt with only the accuracy of a
measure for answering the first two questions about positive verbal interchanges between spouses, i.e., their occurrence and their repeata-
bility. The same basic logic applies to showing the measure's adequacy
for assessing this behavior in different settings. That is, an incontrovertible index of the behavior's occurrence in multiple settings would
be developed and data from the measure compared against it. High
correspondence would demonstrate accuracy, and meeting the appropriate assumptions (e.g., comparability of application and derivation
settings, consistent adherence to the rules/procedures of use, and so on)
would permit generalizing that accuracy from derivation to application
conditions.

For positive verbal interchanges, two settings of obvious importance
for measure accuracy would be the therapist's office and the couple's
home. In order to assess this correspondence, it is necessary to have
a measure which accurately reflects positive verbal interchanges in both
environments. This form of accuracy should have been assessed prior
to and independently of its use to answer questions about the cross-
setting generalizability of the behaviors in the present case.

Similarly, whether or not a behavior is measurable by more than one
method requires the prior demonstration of the correspondence of data
on some incontrovertible criterion when assessed by the method of interest and at least one other. The requirement that behaviors be measurable in more than one way has practical as well as theoretical bases.
Practically, the less expensive of two equally accurate measures will
be preferred, other things being equal. For example, self-report or self-
monitored data on positive verbal interchanges would be preferred over
direct observation measures. Theoretically, the almost inevitable reactive influence of the measure on behaviors assessed with it requires

that relationships between behaviors prove to be more than the fortuitous effect of a common measuring method. Campbell and Fiske (1959) illustrated this requirement for trait measures years ago, and the logic appears sound when applied to behavior measures as well (Cone, 1979).

Thus, the last two facts most often sought about behaviors (i.e., their measurability in multiple ways and their relationship to other behaviors) require two comparable forms of measurement accuracy that are inextricably combined. To examine interbehavior relationships, more than one assessment method is necessary, and those methods must have been shown to be individually accurate for each of the behaviors being related. The measures must also have proven to be sensitive to known relationships among the behaviors in original, accuracy derivation conditions. If these requirements are met, it follows that a relationship must exist between the measures themselves.

Accuracy, Reliability, and Validity

It is important to note that accuracy is not fully equivalent to reliability in either traditional or behavioral uses of the latter term. Accuracy is meant to describe how faithfully a measure represents objective topographic features of a behavior of interest. Reliability has been used in numerous ways in both traditional and behavioral literatures, but for the present it means the consistency with which repeated observations of the same phenomenon yield equivalent information.

Using these respective definitions of accuracy and reliability, it can be seen that accurate measures must be reliable, but that the latter term implies nothing about the former. Repeated observations of the same behavior may consistently yield inaccurate information. The nonequivalence of accuracy and reliability with respect to direct observation assessment has been appreciated for some time (e.g., Gewirtz & Gewirtz, 1969; Johnson & Bolstad, 1973; Kazdin, 1973). Two observers may agree with one another (i.e., observe consistently) but both may have drifted away from control by objective, topographic features of the behavior in question. It is not possible for each observer to be controlled by the objective, topographic features of the behavior in question and not agree with one another, however. It is this relationship that defines the superordinate status of accuracy.

The term validity might also be considered in a comparative sense. It is customary in traditional, trait-oriented assessment to view reliability as establishing upper limits for validity, so that an unreliable measure cannot be highly valid. This is logically the case since reliability is commonly represented as the ratio of true to observed score variances, the latter of which is increased to the extent that error enters the measurement process. Since error is considered to be random and thus uncorrelated over successive occasions or between different measures, its presence reduces the magnitude of validity coefficients.

If by validity we mean the relationships between observed behavior and some other variable(s), an accurate measure may or may not be valid, and a measure may be valid but not accurate. One only has to consider the example of an observer who systematically attributes higher frequencies of heterosocially effective responses to physically more attractive subjects. Subsequent correlations across subjects show high positive relationships between these responses and judgments of social effectiveness by confederates with whom the subjects have interacted. The "moderator" in this case is physical attractiveness, and the "apparent" validity of our measure of heterosocial skills is due to observers and confederates being similarly affected by it, rather than objective features of the behaviors observed.

To summarize, an accurate measure must be by definition reliable, but the converse is not required; a measure may be valid but not accurate. A measure may be reliable and valid or reliable and not valid, but it cannot be valid if it is not reliable.

Behavioral versus Psychometric Concepts of Reliability

As previously suggested, reliability as classically conceived involves a ratio of "true" score variance to observed score variance. The typical formula relating the three is:

$$r_{11} = \frac{\sigma_t^2}{\sigma_x^2}$$

where r_{11} is reliability and σ_x^2 is a composite of σ_t^2 ("true" score variance) and σ_e^2 (error variance). As Wiggins (1973, p. 283) has observed, "when observational procedures are completely random, no component of the true score is involved, and the reliability of observation is zero. When random error is totally absent form observation, $\sigma_x^2 = \sigma_t^2$, and the associated reliability is 1.00."

It is not uncommon to find σ_x^2 broken down in different ways as well. For example, Landy and Farr (1980) recently explained the variance in performance reflected by ratings-by-others as composed of true performance, rater bias, and error. Thus,

$$\sigma_P^2 = \sigma_t^2 + \sigma_B^2 + \sigma_e^2$$

The partialing of observed score variance into different composites can, of course, continue *ad infinitum*.

A behavioral interpretation of this partialing process would be that it merely reflects the isolation of different variables influencing the scores obtained on assessment devices. While it may be reasonable and even useful to represent observations in terms of notation like $\sigma_x^2 = \sigma_a^2 + \sigma_b^2 + \ldots + \sigma_z^2$, the terms σ_t^2 and σ_e^2 or true and error variance, respectively, have no clear place in a behavioral conceptualization. The "true" score is one which accurately reflects behavior, i.e., is maximally controlled by objective, topographic features of the response itself. Error is just a blanket way of referring to a host of "don't knows, none of which are random. Indeed, the term "random" is really a pseudonym for "haven't found out yet" from a behavioral perspective, since all behavior is lawful whether we know the precise controlling variables or not.

Pursuing this logic further leads to a mathematical definition of accuracy in terms of a ratio of actual behavior to a score reflective of that behavior on a particular assessment device. Thus,

$$A = \frac{\sigma_B^2}{\sigma_x^2}$$

where σ_B^2 is the variance in actual behavior and σ_x^2 is the variance in scores presumably reflective of that behavior. The denominator can be subdivided into numerous components in a manner analogous to observed scores in classical reliability theory. That is, $\sigma_x^2 = \sigma_B^2 + \sigma_c^2 + \ldots \sigma_z^2$, where $\sigma_c^2 \ldots \sigma_z^2$ represent contributions to our observations which are additional to those made by the behavior itself. From such an equation it is immediately apparent that a measure will be maximally accurate if its scores are determined solely by objective features of the behavior.

This mathematization of the definition of accuracy is not meant to launch a whole set of statistical procedures for evaluating and demonstrating the various types of accuracy needed by behavioral assessment devices. Rather, it is intended as a conceptual tool for understanding a behavioral alternative to traditional psychometrics. In the sections that follow some analytical tools for establishing accuracy will be suggested.

Calculating and Representing Different Types of Measurement Accuracy

The preceding sections have described the requirements for measurement accuracy of five different types and provided a mathematical conceptualization of the term. Thus far nothing has been said about just how such accuracy might be calculated and/or represented to potential users of a measure. While there are undoubtedly sophisticated mathematical procedures which could be derived from the basic accuracy formula just mentioned, it seems preferable to avoid such complexity, at least in the early stages of the evaluation of the usefulness of accuracy concepts. As mentioned in an earlier paper (Cone, 1978), it is possible to calculate the different types of accuracy just discussed in terms of simple percentage measures, and to represent them graphically in ways already familiar to behavioral assessors. In fact, many of the procedures suggested for calculating interobserver agreement [see Berk (1979) for a review] can be used for calculating and representing accuracy as well. After all, accuracy merely represents the agreement between data produced with a measure and some incontrovertible index of the behavior in question. If, for example, positive verbal interchanges were scripted to occur at a mean rate of .05 per minute, but at varying rates over sessions, accuracy would merely be the percentage agreement between observed and scripted rates. The graphic procedures recently suggested by Birkimer and Brown (1979) for portraying interobserver agreement could just as easily be used for representing accuracy.

Simple agreement percentages will probably suffice for calculating the accuracy of a measure with respect to occurrence and repeated occurrence of behaviors. When accuracy deals with the sensitivity of the measure to the same behavior in different settings, to relationships between behaviors, or to relationships between different measures of the same behavior, the calculation would involve juxtaposing two or more individual accuracy measures. For example, accuracy of a device for assessing the cross-setting generalizability of a behavior would first require the separate calculation of its accuracy in each setting. Thus,

$$A_1 = \frac{Ag_1}{Ag_1 + D_1}$$

where A_1 = accuracy in Setting 1, Ag_1 = agreement between observed and actual frequencies of the behavior in Setting 1, and D_1 = disagreements between observed and actual frequencies. Repeating the calculation for behavior observed in Setting 2 provides A_2. The accuracy of the measure for assessing cross-setting generalizability then becomes

$$A_{cs} = \frac{Ag_1 + Ag_2}{Ag_1 + Ag_2 + D_1 + D_2}$$

Calculations of the measure's sensitivity to behavior-behavior relationships and to multiple ways of assessing the same behavior would proceed similarly.

Accuracy of Methods other than Direct Observations

Though the discussion to this point has been restricted to direct observation assessment methods, it can be applied with some qualification to other methods as well. The important restriction is that these methods be designed to assess objective, observable dimensional quantities of behavior. At the present time accuracy concepts have not been sufficiently developed to permit their application to private events.

The other major assessment methods include interviews, self-reports, ratings-by-others, and self-observation (or self-monitoring). Descriptions of these methods have been provided elsewhere (Cone, 1977; 1978; Cone & Hawkins, 1977) and will not be repeated here. When using any of them to assess overt observable behavior, it is possible to evaluate their adequacy in terms of the accuracy concepts just discussed. Thus, self-reports of reactions to strangers of the opposite sex are subject to verification. Ratings-by-others of the frequency of positive physical contact between mothers and their handicapped children can be similarly verified for accuracy. Indeed, the applicability of accuracy concepts to these methods was implied in the preceding discussion of cross-method generalizability.

SUMMARY AND CONCLUSIONS

The original invitation from the editors of this volume was for the preparation of a chapter dealing with psychometric considerations in behavioral assessment. Their openness to alternatives is evidenced by their willingness to publish a chapter considerably at odds with classical psychometric approaches to establishing measurement adequacy.

An effort has been made throughout this chapter to show that the assessment of behavior requires a radically different paradigm than the assessment of traits and hypothetical constructs. A context was established for this argument by reviewing the major psychometric procedures for evaluating the quality of assessment devices. Their conceptual basis in interindividual differences was described and later contrasted with that of behavioral procedures which rests in intraindividual differences. The newer, conceptually more elegant notions of generalizability theory were examined and shown to be inappropriate for behavioral assessment because of a comparable basis in differences between individuals. The evaluation of measurement adequacy in terms of characteristics of these differences (i.e., their temporal consistency, generalizability over setting, and so on) was repeatedly shown to be irrelevant to an assessment discipline concerned with characteristics of behavior in individual persons.

The most important attribute of any behavioral assessment device is its sensitivity to objective, dimensional quantities of the response(s) being measured, i.e., its accuracy. Accuracy was contrasted with psychometric concepts of reliability and validity, and with a behavioral view of reliability in terms of consistent representation of some feature of a behavior over multiple assessments. It was pointed out that accuracy requires reliability in this sense, but that the accuracy-reliability relationship is not symmetrical. It was noted further that, while validity requires reliability, there is no apparent relationship between validity and accuracy. Thus, reliable and valid measures may not be accurate.

Requirements of measurement accuracy were outlined for five common questions about behavior: (a) its occurrence, (b) its repeated occurrence, (c) its occurrence in more than one setting, (d) its measurability by more than one method, and (e) its relationship to other behaviors. Ways of calculating and representing the accuracy of a measure for the assessment of each of these questions were suggested and were shown to draw heavily on current procedures for calculating and representing interobserver agreement.

Finally, it was emphasized that the superordinance of accuracy applies to all methods in behavioral assessment when overt, objectively verifiable responses are being assessed. The relevance of accuracy to the assessment of private behaviors has not yet been analyzed extensively.

This chapter argues that it is time for behavioral assessors to adopt a paradigm more suitable to behavior as a subject matter and to reject concepts belonging to a radically different paradigm developed for a completely different subject matter altogether. The present state of the discipline is similar to the field of clincial psychology at the time applied behavior analysis broke away and established itself independently. While unlikely, it would not be surprising to see a similar separatist movement erupt in behavioral assessment, with radical behavioral assessors forming their own clearly identifiable discipline or subdiscipline within the overall framework of the study of behavior study from a natural science perspective.

REFERENCES

Adorno, T. W., Frenkel-Brunswik, E., Levinson, D. J., & Sanford, R. N. *The authoritarian personality*. New York: Harper & Low, 1950.
Anastasi, A. *Psychological testing* (3d ed.) London: The MacMillan Co., 1968.
Ayllon, T., & Roberts, M. D. Eliminating discipline problems by strengthening academic performance. *Journal of Applied Behavior Analysis*, 1974, *7*, 71–76.
Bechtoldt, H. Construct validity: A critique. *American Psychologist*, 1959, *14*, 619–629.

Bellack, A. S. A critical appraisal of strategies for assessing social skill. *Behavioral Assessment*, 1979, *1*, 157–176.

Berk, R. Generalizability of behavior observations: A clarification of interobserver agreement and interobserver reliability. *American Journal of Mental Deficiency*, 1979, *83*, 460–472.

Birkimer, J. C., & Brown, J. H. A graphical judgmental aid which summarizes obtained and chance reliability data and helps assess the believability of experimental effects. *Journal of Applied Behavior Analysis*, 1979, *12*, 523–533.

Borman, W. C. Exploring upper limits of reliability and validity in job performance ratings. *Journal of Applied Psychology*, 1978, *63*, 135–144.

Borman, W. C. Format and training effects on rating accuracy and rater errors. *Journal of Applied Psychology*, 1979, *64*, 410–421.

Campbell, D. T. Recommendations for APA test standards regarding construct, trait, and discriminant validity. *American Psychologist*, 1960, *15*, 546–553.

Campbell, D. T., & Fiske, D. W. Convergent and discriminant validation by the multitrait-multimethod matrix. *Psychological Bulletin*, 1959, *56*, 81–105.

Coates, T. J., & Thoresen, C. E. Using generalizability theory in behavioral observations. *Behavior Therapy*, 1978, *9*, 605–613.

Cone, J. D. The relevance of reliability and validity for behavioral assessment. *Behavior Therapy*, 1977, *8*, 411-426.

Cone, J. D. Truth and sensitivity in behavioral assessment. Paper presented at the meeting of the Association for the Advancement of Behavior Therapy, Chicago, November 1978.

Cone, J. D. Confounded comparisons in triple response mode assessment research. *Behavioral Assessment*, 1979, *1*, 85-95.

Cone, J. D. Inductive behavioral assessment. Paper presented at the meeting of the Southeastern Psychological Association, New Orleans, March 1979.

Cone, J. D. The overlapping worlds of behavioral assessment and performance appraisal. Paper presented at the First Annual Scientist-Practitioner Conference in Industrial/Organizational Psychology, Virginia Beach, VA, April 1980.

Cone, J. D., & Foster, S. L. Direct observation in clinical psychology. In P. C. Kendall, & J. N. Butcher (Eds.), *Handbook of research methods in clinical psychology*. New York: Wiley (in press).

Cone, J. D., & Hawkins, R. P. *Behavioral assessment: New directions in clinical psychology*. New York: Brunner/Mazel, 1977.

Cronbach, L. J. *Essentials of psychological testing*. (3d ed.) New York: Harper & Row, 1970.

Cronbach, L. J., Gleser, G. C., Nanda, H., & Rajaratnam, N. *The dependability of behavioral measures*. New York: Wiley, 1972.

Cronbach, L. J., & Meehl, P. E. Construct validity in psychological tests. *Psychological Bulletin*, 1955, *52*, 281–302.

Curran, J. P. Review of *Annual review of behavior therapy: Theory and practice*. (4th ed.) *Behavior Modification*, 1978, *2*, 135-137.

Curran, J. P., Monti, P. M., Corriveau, D. P., Hay, L. R., Hagerman, S., Zwick, W. R., & Farrell, A. D. The generalizability of a procedure for assessing social skills and social anxiety in a psychiatric population. *Behavioral Assessment*, in press.

DeMaster, B., Reid, J., & Twentyman, C. The effects of different amounts of feedback on observer's reliability. *Behavior Therapy*, 1977, *8*, 317–329.

Dunnette, M. D., & Borman, W. C. Personnel selection and classification systems. *Annual Review of Psychology*, 1979, *30*, 477–525.

Eyberg, S. M., & Johnson, S. M. Multiple assessment of behavior modification with families: Effects of contingency contracting and order of treated problems. *Journal of Consulting and Clinical Psychology,* 1974, *42,* 594-606.

Farrell, A. D., Mariotto, M. J., Conger, A. J., Curran, J. P., & Wallander, J. L. Self and judges' ratings of heterosexual-social anxiety and skill: A generalizability study. *Journal of Consulting and Clinical Psychology, 1979, 47,* 164–175.

Ferritor, D. E., Buckholdt, D., Hamblin, R. L., & Smith, L. The noneffects of contingent reinforcement for attending behavior on work accomplished. *Journal of Applied Behavior Analysis,* 1972, *5,* 7–17.

Gewirtz, H. B., & Gewirtz, J. L. Caretaking settings, background events and child-rearing environments: Some preliminary trends. In B. M. Foss (Ed.), *Determinants of infant behavior, Vol. IV.* London: Methuen & Co., 1969.

Goldfried, M. R. Behavioral assessment in perspective. In J. D. Cone & R. P. Hawkins (Eds.), *Behavioral assessment: New directions in clinical psychology.* New York: Brunner/Mazel, 1977.

Goldfried, M. R., & D'Zurilla, T. J. A behavioral-analytic model for assessing competence. In C. D. Speilberger (Ed.), *Current topics in clinical and community psychology.* New York: Academic Press, 1969.

Gottman, J. M. Nonsequential data analysis techniques in observational research. In G. P. Sackett (Ed.), *Observing behavior: Vol. II.: Data collection and analysis methods.* Baltimore, MD: University Park Press, 1978, pp. 45–61.

Gottman, J. M. *Marital interaction: Experimental investigations.* New York: Academic Press, 1979.

Gulliksen, H. *Theory of mental tests.* New York: John Wiley, 1950.

Hartmann, D. P., Roper, B. L., & Bradford, D. C. Some relationships between behavioral and traditional assessment. *Journal of Behavioral Assessment,* 1979, *1,* 3–21.

Haynes, S. N. *Principles of behavioral assessment.* New York: Gardner Press, 1978.

Hersen, M., & Bellack, A. S. *Behavioral assessment: A practical handbook.* New York: Pergamon Press, 1976.

Horst, P. *Psychological measurement and prediction.* Belmont, CA: Wadsworth Publishing Co., 1966.

Johnson, S. M., & Bolstad, O. D. Methodological issues in naturalistic observation: Some problems and solutions for field research. In L. A. Hamerlynck, L. C. Handy, & E. J. Mash (Eds.), *Behavior change: Methodology, concepts, and practice.* Champaign, IL: Research Press, 1973.

Johnson, S. M., Christensen, A., & Bellamy, G. T. Evaluation of family intervention through unobtrusive audio recordings: Experiences in "bugging" children. *Journal of Applied Behavior Analysis,* 1976, *9,* 213-219.

Johnston, J. M., & Pennypacker, H. S. *Strategies and tactics of human behavioral research.* Hillsdale, NJ: Lawrence Erlbaum Associates, 1980.

Jones, R. R. Conceptual vs. analytic uses of generalizability theory in behavioral assessment. In J. D. Cone & R. P. Hawkins (Eds.), *Behavioral assessment: New directions in clinical psychology.* New York: Brunner/Mazel, 1977.

Jones, R. R., Reid, J. B., & Patterson, G. R. Naturalistic observation clinical assessment. In P. McReynolds (Ed.), *Advances in psychological assessment* (Vol. 3). San Francisco: Jossey-Bass, Inc., 1975.

Kazdin, A. E. Methodological and assessment considerations in evaluating reinforcement programs in applied settings. *Journal of Applied Behavior Analysis,* 1973, *6,* 517-531.

Kent, R. N., O'Leary, K. D., Coletti, G., & Drabman, R. S. Increasing the validity of an observational code: An empirical methodology. Unpublished paper, State

University of New York at Stony Brook, 1975.

Kiecolt, J., & McGrath, E. Social desirability responding in the measurement of assertive behavior. *Journal of Consulting and Clinical Psychology,* 1979, *47,* 640–642.

Landy, F. J., & Farr, J. L. Performance rating. *Psychological Bulletin,* 1980, *87,* 72–107.

Lawshe, C. H. A quantitative approach to content validity. *Personnel Psychology,* 1975, *28,* 563–575.

Leitenberg, H. Review of *Behavioral assessment: A practical handbook., Behavior Modification,* 1978, *2,* 137–139.

Linehan, M. M. Content validity: Its relevance to behavioral assessment. *Behavioral Assessment,* 1980, *2,* 147–159.

Livingston, S. A. Psychometric techniques for criterion-referenced testing and behavioral assessment. In J. D. Cone & R. P. Hawkins (Eds.), *Behavioral assessment: New directions in clinical psychology.* New York: Brunner/Mazel, 1977.

Mariotto, M. J., & Paul, G. L. Persons versus situations in the real-life functioning of chronically institutionalized mental patients. *Journal of Abnormal Psychology,* 1975, *84,* 483-493.

Mathews, R. M., Whang, P. L., & Fawcett, S. B. Development and validation of an occupational skills assessment instrument. *Behavioral Assessment,* 1980, *2,* 71–85.

McFall, R. M. Analogue methods in behavioral assessment: Issues and prospects. In J. D. Cone & R. P. Hawkins (Eds.), *Behavioral assessment: New directions in clinical psychology.* New York: Brunner/Mazel, 1977.

Nelson, R. O., & Hayes, S. C. Some current dimensions of behavioral assessment. *Behavioral Assessment,* 1979, *1,* 1–16.

Patterson, G. R. Behavioral intervention procedures in the classroom and in the home. In A. E. Bergin & S. Garfield (Eds.), *Handbook of psychotherapy and behavior change.* New York: Wiley, 1971.

Patterson, G. R. Interventions for boys with conduct problems: Multiple settings, treatments, and criteria. *Journal of Consulting and Clinical Psychology,* 1974, *12,* 471-481.

Patterson, G. R., Cobb, J. A., & Ray, R. S. A social engineering technology for retraining the families of aggressive boys. In H. E. Adams & I. P. Unikel (Eds.). *Issues and trends in behavior therapy.* Springfield, IL: Charles C. Thomas, 1973.

Powell, J., Martindale, B., Kulp, S., Martindale, A., & Bauman, R. Taking a closer look: Time sampling and measurement error. *Journal of Applied Behavior Analysis,* 1977, *10,*tt 325-332.

Powell, J., & Rockinson, R. On the inability of interval time sampling to reflect frequency of occurrence data. *Journal of Applied Behavior Analysis,* 1978, *11,* 531–532.

Reid, J. B. Study of drinking in natural settings. In G. A. Marlatt & P. E. Nathan (Eds.), *Behavioral approaches to alchoholism.* New Brunswick, NJ: Rutgers Center of Alcohol Studies, 1978, pp. 58-74.

Repp, A. C., Roberts, D. M., Slack, D. J., Repp, C. R., & Berkler, M. S. A comparison of frequency, interval, and time-sampling methods of data collection. *Journal of Applied Behavior Analysis,* 1976, *9,* 501–508.

Romanczyk, R. G., Kent, R. N., Diament, C., & O'Leary, K. D. Measuring the reliability of observational data: A reactive process. *Journal of Applied Behavior Analysis,* 1973, *6,* 175-186.

Sechrest, L. Incremental validity: A recommendation. *Educational and Psychological Measurement,* 1963, *23,* 153–158.

Smith, P. C., & Kendall, L. M. Retranslation of expectations: An approach to the construction of unambiguous anchors for rating scales. *Journal of Applied Psychology,*

1963, *47*, 149–155.

Spielberger, C. D., Gorsuch, R. L., & Lushene, R. E. *Manual for the State Trait Anxiety Inventory.* Palo-Alto, Calif: Counseling Psychologists Press, 1970.

Strossen, R. J., Coates, T. J., & Thoresen, C. E. Extending generalizability theory to single-subject designs. *Behavior Therapy,* 1979, *10*, 606–614.

Taplin, P. S., & Reid, J. B. Effects of instructional set and experimenter influence on observer reliability. *Child Development,* 1973, *44*, 547–554.

Watson, D., & Friend, R. Measurement of social-evaluative anxiety. *Journal of Consulting and Clinical Psychology,* 1969, *33*, 448–457.

Wiggins, J. S. *Personality and prediction: Principles of personality assessment.* Reading, Mass.: Addison-Wesley, 1973.

Zuckerman, M. Development of a situation-specific trait-state test for the prediction and measurement of affective responses. *Journal of Consulting and Clinical Psychology,* 1977, *45*, 513–523.

Zuckerman, M. Traits, states, situations, and uncertainty. *Journal of Behavioral Assessment,* 1979, *1*, 43–54.

Part II:
Assessment Strategies

Chapter 3
Behavioral Interviewing

Kenneth P. Morganstern
and Helen E. Tevlin*

INTRODUCTION

The initial publication of this chapter noted the absence in the behavioral literature of specific techniques and guidelines for accurately and completely defining target problems. While students are often encouraged to read overviews of multifaceted assessment schema (e.g., Kanfer & Saslow, 1969), the *manner* in which the necessary information is obtained is often unclear. While the process of assessment may be relatively straightforward once the specific target behaviors are *known,* inexperienced therapists may be uncertain how to determine what the problem *is.*

Although we have witnessed a remarkable surge of interest in behavioral assessment in the last few years (Adams [ed.], 1979; Ciminero, Calhoun, & Adams, 1977; Cone & Hawkins, 1977; Hersen & Bellack, 1976; Mash & Terdal, 1976), the interview itself, during which the therapist elicits information that determines the ultimate target problems to be assessed, has been generally ignored. A few recent reports (Linehan, 1977; Meyer, Liddell, & Lyons, 1977) have discussed the general nature of the interview, as well as methodological and research issues. The purpose of this chapter is to provide a framework for clinicians during the initial stages of assessment and to elaborate upon a number of practical issues and procedures in behavioral interviewing.

*The authors acknowledge Anthony Biglan, W. Edward Craighead, Edward Lichtenstein, and Elizabeth Steinbock for their helpful suggestions and comments during the preparation of the initial manuscript.

This chapter is divided into two sections. The first part discusses several important issues in behavioral interviewing. These include: goals of assessment (including a review of the major multifaceted assessment schema), ethical considerations, and the role of relationship variables. The second section focuses primarily on a few selected methods and procedures employed in the behavioral interview, with a number of clinical illustrations presented. While assessment often requires information from a variety of sources (including the client's family, employers, friends, co-workers, etc.), the major emphasis in this chapter is on the information provided by the individual client.

One of the major goals of the present paper is to provide some practical suggestions for the new or inexperienced clinician. It is essential to note, however, that while the methods of behavioral treatment enjoy considerable empirical support, research on the effects of interview procedures are noticeably absent. The techniques and guidelines that are presented in this chapter, therefore, need to be considered cautiously. While the suggestion for future research in this area is, perhaps, obvious, it is nevertheless important that every component of the entire therapeutic process be empirically validated.

BEHAVIORAL INTERVIEWING: ISSUES

Goals of Assessment

From the first contact between therapist and client, behavioral interviewing must be intimately tied to the ultimate goals of assessment. The answer to the question, often asked by students, "What do I need to know about the client?" should be, "*Everything* that is relevant to the development of effective, efficient, and durable treatment interventions." And from an ethical (and economical) consideration, one could add, "And no more." Ideally, every question asked by the therapist (or for that matter, anything that occurs during the therapy situation) should have a purpose, the major one being to gain a thorough functional analysis of the problematic behavior. This analysis establishes the precise covariations between changes in stimulus conditions and changes in selected behaviors (Mischel, 1971); that is, it defines the "ABC's (*a*ntecedents, *b*ehaviors, and *c*onsequences) of behavior control [O'Leary & Wilson, 1975, p. 25]." Such an analysis is an important challenge to criticisms that behavioral approaches are superficial and narrow. It reduces the possibility that treatments will be ineffective or that new maladaptive responses will appear after the removal of a particular problem. While it is important to avoid the tautology that behavior therapy "successes" are the result of thorough analyses while "failures" are the product of inadequate ones (Kazdin, 1973), most behaviorists would agree with Lazarus' (1973) statement that "faulty problem identification (inadequate assessment) is probably the greatest impediment to successful therapy [p. 407]."

A complete functional analysis of problematic behavior often goes beyond first appearances in therapy (Goldfried, 1977; Goldfried & Davison, 1976; Mahoney, Kazdin, & Lesswing, 1974). The "bridge phobia" described by Lazarus (1971a) is a well known example. In this case, the client originally complained of a fear of crossing bridges. Further exploration revealed considerable anxiety and uncertainty in regard to work, competence, obligations, and achievements. In particular, the client was acutely sensitive to his mother's pejorative statements that "he would never amount to anything." What was actually being avoided was not only a bridge, but also a new work situation across the bridge, and in turn, the potential criticisms of himself and his mother. Desensitization was, in fact, successfully employed, but it was primarily directed at the real or imaginal critical statements of the client's mother. Such cases are commonplace in the clinic: the obese individual who avoids work or heterosexual encounters by being overweight (Mahoney et al., 1974) or the anxious client who receives social reinforcement for certain fears. In some instances, a complete assessment may reveal that a specific technique is inappropriate because of certain idiosyncracies of the client (Morganstern, 1974), or indicate that treatment is impossible without substantial changes in the client's environment.

A final caution is important. In their desire to be thorough, clinicians need not, and should not, move toward the other extreme and attempt to assess everything in the background and present situation of their clients. Often, much of the information gathered by traditional therapists is unnecessary. Peterson (1968), for example, estimated that three-fourths of the material usually covered in interviews could probably be eliminated "with no loss whatever to the patient (since) only rarely do the conventional data have anything to do with treatment [p. 119]." Not only is such practice inefficient, it also raises an ethical question regarding the legitimacy of inquiry into diverse aspects of a client's life, however interesting they may be to the therapist or the client himself, when such content is irrelevant to treatment.

Multifaceted Assessment Schema

It is clear that a thorough assessment is essential to ensure maximal treatment efficacy. Although many of the early reports of behaviorists were criticized for inadequate assessement (Goldfried & Pomeranz, 1968), a number of broad-spectrum, multifaceted assessment guidelines have been proposed in recent years. This section briefly reviews a few of the major schema that have been proposed. Peterson (1968), one of the most outspoken critics of traditional assessment procedures in the late 1960s, described an overview of the entire interview strategy that included a scanning operation, extended inquiry, periodic reappraisal, and, ideally, a final phase that involved a follow-up study. He suggested that the content of the interview focus on two broad sets of variables: (a) the definition, severity, and generality of the problem (including the client's own view of his behavior) and (b) the determinants of the target behavior (e.g., the conditions which intensify or alleviate the problem, perceived antecedents, consequences, and the client's own suggested changes).

Goldfried (Goldfried & Pomeranz, 1968; Goldfried & Sprafkin, 1974; Goldfried, 1977) outlined four major classes of variables in any assessment process, employing the acronym SORC: (a) the antecedent *s*ituational variables; (b) *o*rganismic variables (psychological and physiological): (c) the overt maladaptive behavior itself. i.e., response dimensions, and (d) the consequent changes in the environment. Goldfried has noted that the target behavior selected in many behavioral reports is often oversimplified, and has underscored the importance of organismic variables, especially cognitive sets, perceptions, mediation responses, and cues.

In probably the most extensive assessment scheme, Kanfer and Saslow (1969) described an approach that incorporated variables from both the client's current situation and past history. They emphasized, however, that historical information is relevant only to the extent that it facilitates the description of current problematic behaviors and future therapeutic interventions. In order to accomplish this task, Kanfer and Saslow suggested examination of each of the following areas: (1) analysis of the problem situation (including behavioral excesses, deficits, and assets); (2) clarification of the problem situation that maintains the targeted behaviors; (3) a motivational analysis; (4) a developmental analysis (including biological, sociological, and behavioral spheres); (5) a self-control analysis; (6) an analysis of social relationships; and (7) an analysis of the social-cultural-physical environment. A noteworthy contribution of Kanfer and Saslow's outline is the inclusion of an assessment of the client's strengths, assets, skills, and talents.

Wolpe (1969) provided an assessment guideline that comprises four main areas of the client's life: (a) familial experiences during childhood, including information about influential "significant others" (friends, parents, siblings, etc.) and an exploration of the individual's religious background when relevant; (b) school experiences and employment history; (c) sexual history and current sexual functioning; and (d) current social relationships.

Stuart (1970) outlined an assessment system that begins with the precise specification of problematic behaviors, followed by the identification of four classes of antecedent stimuli (instructional, discriminative, potentiating, and facilitating) and four classes of consequent events (positive reinforcement, punishment, extinction, and negative reinforcement). In addition, Stuart suggested that assessment strategies describe acceptable behaviors as fully as maladaptive responses because more powerful techniques are available for increasing desired behaviors than for decreasing undesirable ones.

Lazarus (1971b), noting the "relapse" of many of his clients, suggested the need for a multimodal behavior therapy approach in order to ensure thorough assessment. Assessment explores the modalities deemed essential by Lazarus (1973), the first letters of each forming the acronym *BASIC ID: B*ehavior; *A*ffect (e.g., joy, anxiety, anger); *S*ensation (e.g., muscle tension); *I*magery (positive or negative); *C*ognition (e.g., insights, ideas, philosophies); *I*nterpersonal relationships and *D*rugs (the need, if any, for medication). Such an assessment is initiated, however, only *after* assessing the broad environmental realities of the client's life, including cultural and socioeconomic factors (Lazarus, 1976). An innovation that deserves consideration is the suggestion by Lazarus (1973) to assess anticipated areas of stress (perhaps through imaginal rehearsal) that the client is likely to experience at some future point. Finally, Lazarus (1976) has suggested that inquiry into modalities omitted by the client in his descriptions of problems is likely to yield crucial assessment information.

Mischel (1973), whose classic work on assessment in 1968 challenged every major assumption of traditional trait approaches to personality, is consistent with most behaviorists in his emphasis on the importance of specific environmental events in behavior control. He has proposed, however, a second class of variables, "person variables," involving a number of cognitive social learning factors. Such person variables are believed to develop from each individual's unique social learning history and influence or mediate the way in which environmental conditions affect behavior. The specific person variables that Mischel suggested include: (a) cognitive and behavioral construction competencies; (b) encoding strategies and personal constructs; (c) behavior-outcome and stimulus-outcome expectancies; (d) subjective stimulus values; and (e) self-regulatory systems and plans.

Meichenbaum (1976) proposed an approach to assessment that underscored the critical role that cognitions (appraisals, attributions, expectations, self-evaluations) and images play in target problems. According to this "cognitive-behavior modification" approach, the basic task of the clinician is to determine the client's internal dialogue and the extent to which these self-statements (or the omission of such self-statements) interfere with the client's behavioral repertoire.

Meyer et al. (1977) suggested that in addition to assessing the nature of the presenting complaints and the maintaining variables in the client's recent history, it is often necessary to include an assessment of the client's past history in order to more fully understand the attitudes and value systems which underlie more generalized and complex presenting problems. Meyer and his colleagues also advocate an assessment of the client's general and specific strengths and assets, including a thorough analysis of the biological and social systems in which the client functions successfully, previous attempts at controlling the maladaptive behaviors, and how reliant the client is on others for reinforcement and feedback.

Finally, Angle and his colleagues (Angle, Hay, Hay, & Ellinwood, 1977; Angle, Ellinwood, Hay, Johnsen, & Hay, 1977) described a computer assisted system for a comprehensive behavioral assessment based on the broad outline of Kanfer and Saslow (1969). In this program, problematic behaviors are first indentified across a broad spectrum of 26 problem areas (e.g., marriage, sex, child rearing, employment, assertion, sleep, and tension), and are then clarified through a series of in-depth computer interviews.

In sum, a variety of broad, multifaceted assessment guidelines have been proposed within recent years. Although some of the approaches suggest additional areas that warrant exploration, all of them share the common emphasis on the specification of the "ABC's" of behavior control. It is important to note, however, that such comprehensive outlines as suggested by Lazarus or Kanfer and Saslow, while applicable in some cases, may be unnecessary for many individuals. The identification, for example, of a client's strengths or the description of his learning history is often irrelevant for treatment planning. Multifaceted behavioral assessment, therefore, must always be guided by the principle of parsimony (Stuart, 1970).

Ethical Issues

Behavior therapy, characterized by empirically validated procedures for *client-stated objectives*, has considerably tempered Halleck's (1971) observation that therapists are never politically or ethically neutral.

Nevertheless, several critical ethical considerations, particularly during the initial stages of assessment, remain. Important questions central to those issues involve: the determination of the client's goals; the degree of therapist-influence on the selection of these objectives; and the decision to "accept" the goals of the client and intervene, or refuse treatment. An additional ethical issue, regarding the client's right to minimal intrusion has previously been discussed. In general, the arguments presented here assume the individual to be an adult volunteer in a non-institutionalized setting; however, many of the remarks may be equally applicable to clients not sharing these criteria. Questions concerning children or institutionalized individuals, while important, are beyond the scope of the present chapter (see McNamara, 1978; Wexler, 1973).

It has been emphasized that behavior therapy "is a system of principles and not a system of ethics [Bandura, 1969, p. 87]. "In addition, the focus of treatment is the client's, not the therapist's, goals. However, it is the rare individual who refers himself to therapy with his problems and future objectives clearly crystallized. Far more often, the client's needs and wants become clearer as he talks to the practitioner (Halleck, 1971), and thus the goals, desires, and values of the therapist are an inescapable reality in influencing both the interview process and the end product of assessment. Recently, behaviorists have been called to task in relation to the target behaviors selected for institutionalized clients (Wexler, 1973) and school children (Winett & Winkler, 1972). The same issues are relevant to adult out-patients. The case of homosexuality provides an excellent example of the implicit (and often explicit) value judgments of therapists that influence the determination of the client's goals. Despite the fact that homosexuality is no longer included in the Diagnostic and Statistical Manual, most therapists, including behaviorists, "regard homosexual behavior and attitudes to be undesirable, sometimes pathological, and at any rate in need of change towards a heterosexual orientation [Davison, 1974, p. 4]." It is difficult to imagine such biases not entering into the assessment process in some, perhaps, subtle ways. Consider, for example, the decision made by Fensterheim (1972) to offer behavior therapy to a client who happened to be homosexual but who emphatically stated that he did not desire to change his sexual orientation:

I do agree to confine the treatment to the specific target symptoms as best I can. However I also state that I will present for their consideration a plan for the treatment of homosexuality. All I ask is that I be permitted a brief time to present a possible treatment plan and that the client listen to it [pp. 25–26].

Although Fensterheim goes on to emphasize that there is no attempt to "sell" treatment of homosexuality to the client, there is an implicit assumption in the therapeutic suggestion that the individual *should,* in fact, change. While Fensterheim's decision to accept the client's original objective for treatment is a highly commendable one, it should be clear that additional suggestions on the part of the therapist to modify these objectives may constitute very powerful influences on the client.

Ethical issues also become complicated when the therapist must decide whether it is ethically responsible to accept the *client's* initially stated goals. The choice to deny particular treatment requests is obvious in certain stereotypic example, (e.g., the anxious murderer seeking desensitization to feel better about killing, or the housewife who similarly desires desensitization so that she is no longer anxious when anticipating her husband's beatings). It is also unlikely that practitioners would immediately accept a client's request to eliminate masturbation and proceed to treat the "problem." The therapist would almost certainly offer information to the individual in an attempt to reeducate him. Or desensitization might be instituted to reduce the anxiety associated with masturbation.

More often, however, the ethical implications are considerably more subtle, as in the case of homosexuality, when therapists are far more likely to consider the behavior as problematic and to intervene accordingly. The very existence of a variety of techniques to change sexual orientation not only encourages their use, but may also condone the current societal prejudice concerning such behavior (Davison, 1974). While the resolution of such ethical problems may be exceedingly difficult, therapists need to be aware of the implications of "accepting" the client's goals when to do so explicitly reinforces the social *status quo* and may, in fact, impede social change. Winett and Winkler (1972) emphasize this point in their criticism of target behaviors that have often been selected for disruptive school children. In a similar fashion, Davison (1974) has suggested critical examination of the target behaviors involved in *any* anxiety-reduction procedure:

> Should we reduce anxiety, or should we perhaps address ourselves to the problematic educational system which can contribute to the kind of test anxiety we desensitize? . . . Why do we engage in assertion training for people who are taken advantage of by an unfeeling society rather than attempt to persuade the offenders that their sometimes unkind actions cause others grief? [p. 3]

It would seem apparent, then, that behaviorists cannot separate themselves entirely from the important ethical and societal implications that are involved in any assessment and treatment intervention.

Related ethical questions involve situations where the client insists on a technique that the practitioner has evidence is ineffective, when a specific "problem" may be beyond the realm of psychotherapy, or when a thorough assessment reveals that the person is unable or unwilling to change the contingencies that control the target behavior. It is the *responsible* practitioner who, after careful assessment, concludes that he cannot effectively treat the individual *unless* certain environmental conditions are considered, whether that means including the spouse in treatment, or involves the extensive rearrangement of contingencies, Kanfer (1975) has remarked that behavior therapy need not adopt a "Statue of Liberty" (Give me your tired, your poor") philosophy. That is, behaviorists need to accept their limitations and realize they cannot treat everybody, whether due to the fact that effective procedures may not exist for a specific problem, or the "environmental realities" of the individual contraindicate treatment efficacy for a given target behavior.

Clients often come to therapy with a variety of expectations about what treatment will be like. Many of them request specific techniques such as hypnosis, bioenergetics, psychoanalysis, yoga, dream interpretation, past life regressions, and a host of other treatments. While it is probably sound clinical practice to incorporate some of those procedures which the client feels will be most helpful, since expectancy of therapeutic gain undoubtedly accounts for some portion of the outcome variance (see Lick & Bootzin, 1975), the ethically responsible therapist must assess and communicate to the client the likelihood of success with any of these procedures. In many cases, the practitioner will refuse to adopt a particular method, either because he is unfamiliar with the technique or because there is no evidence that such a procedure is effective (especially when other, empirically-tested treatments are available). Even in situations in which the client is in complete agreement with the therapist, both in respect to the assessment of the problem and the intervention planned, it is still the responsibility of the therapist to communicate to the individual the probabilities of success with a given technique (Biglan, 1975), the "emotional cost" of such a procedure (Morganstern, 1973), and the availability of alternative treatments.

In sum, behaviorists need to examine and be acutely aware of several ethical considerations and value judgments that are continually made. Whereas social learning principles may be relatively free of such biases, the interview and assessment process is not. In the final analysis, behavior therapy has little to apologize for, particularly when compared to other schools of therapy. The emphasis given to functional analyses, specification of goals, and objective measurement of process and outcome, fosters accountability on the part of behavioral practitioners (Davison, 1974).

Interviewer-Client Relationship Variables

It is often assumed that behaviorists are cold, mechanistic, uncaring laboratory technicians with little regard for the "therapeutic relationship." On numerous occasions, students and clients have indicated surprise that the behavioral clinicians they have seen or heard (or have been treated by) have been concerned, understanding, warm, and "human." Such surprise is not limited to laypersons. Klein, Dittman, Parloff, and Gill (1969) noted that the behavior therapy they observed for 5 days was characterized by "experienced clinicians" who were seen as confident and skillful, and made "very effective use of the patient-therapist relationship to establish a context in which the specific behavioral techniques can be utilized most effectively [p. 265]." Apparently the stereotype of the "misanthropic behaviorist" is popular enough to compel some authors to caution the "would-be practitioner who chooses to be a behavior therapist because he finds it difficult to put clients at ease, through using a more traditional approach . . . to rethink his professional goals [Rimm & Masters, 1974, p. 35]." Lazarus (1971a) has suggested, "If a person does not possess genuine compassion for the plight of his patients and have a strong desire to diminish their suffering, it would be a boon to psychotherapy if he would enter some other field of endeavor [p. 56]." While such statements may appear to be obvious (and perhaps even surprising that they have to be made), they raise a number of important questions that need to be considered. For example, *do* we want to communicate to professionals and trainees that behavioral techniques, well-validated and seemingly simple, may be instituted *without* regard to "therapist" or "relationship" variables? Or *do* such variables relate to the completeness and accuracy of information obtained during interview and assessment and, more importantly, to treatment outcome? Which variables are important and how do we know? Finally, are we then forced into the awkward position of advocating a variety of suggestions to students with preciously little support for them?

There is considerable agreement that a variety of therapist behaviors relate to the openness, accuracy, and content of interviews (see Carkhuff, 1969a, 1969b, Cormier & Cormier, 1979; Goldstein, 1975; Gordon, 1970; Kanfer, 1968; Krasner, 1962; Marsden, 1971; Matarazzo, 1965; Salzinger, 1959; Truax & Carkhuff, 1967; Truax & Mitchell, 1971). Within the behavioral literature, Peterson (1968) has remarked that:

The nature of the transaction . . . between interviewer and client
. . . [is] of utmost importance in determining the amount and quality
of information gained [and] a sense of [the interviewer's] interest on
the part of the client probably has much to do with the extent and
the accuracy of the information he provides [p. 123].

Rimm and Masters (1974) have noted that an atmosphere of warmth
and acceptance will facilitate the goal of assessment (i.e., to obtain
considerable information from the client). Further, these authors point
out that, "no therapy can succeed if the client perceives his therapist
as cold and indifferent and, therefore, drops out of treatment [p. 35]."
While one cannot question the logic that therapy cannot proceed without
the client, it is unclear whether it is the therapist characteristics of
"coldness" and "indifference" that drive the client away. Similarly,
there is no substantial evidence that therapist variables affect the accuracy and completeness of assessment information to the degree that
treatment outcome is impaired. Moreover, it is uncertain what combination of behaviors the clinician should have in his repertoire, since
no practitioner could possibly possess the several dozen laudatory characteristics of the "ideal therapist" that have been variously proposed
(Krasner, 1963). While it could be argued by some that such variables
as empathy, warmth, and genuineness have been shown to relate to
interview content (by increasing, for example, self-exploration and self-
disclosure) and, in turn, to treatment outcome in traditional therapy
(see Cormier & Cormier, 1979; Cozby, 1973), the generalizability of
this research to an empirically oriented behavioral approach (with radically different criteria for defining process and outcome measures) is
questionable. This is not to suggest that such variables as empathy,
warmth, genuineness, openness, honesty, etc. are *unimportant* in behavioral interviewing. On the contrary, it is strongly felt by the authors
that under most circumstances certain relationship variables will facilitate assessment and enhance treatment outcome. The point, however,
is that very little is known about the effects of particular therapist characteristics on assessment information, continuance in therapy, compliance, and outcome measures *in behavior therapy*. Along these lines,
it is interesting to note Bandura's (1969) challenge to the distinction
made between "specific" and "nonspecific" influences in therapy:

It is difficult to conceive of nonspecific influence in social interchanges. Each expression by one person elicits some type of response from the other participant, which inevitably creates a specific reinforcement contingency that has a specific effect on the
immediately preceding behavior [p. 77].

While it is beyond the scope of this chapter to discuss the relationship of therapist variables and treatment outcome in behavior therapy (see Kanfer & Goldstein, 1975; Wilson & Evans, 1978), it should be noted that behaviorists have long acknowledged that social reinforcement assumes a role of major importance in the modification and maintenance of behavior (Bandura, 1969). It is important to remember, however, that *no* therapist characteristic(s) can be expected to be effective across all clients under all circumstances. Even Truax (Truax & Mitchell, 1971), who concluded that "the personality of the therapist is more important than his techniques [p. 341]," cautioned that high levels of warmth or accurate empathy could be totally inappropriate with certain clients.

In sum, effective behavioral outcome depends on thorough and accurate assessment, continuance in therapy compliance with therapeutic intervention, as well as the treatment methods themselves. How client-therapist relationship variables affect each of these is, as yet, an unanswered, but empirical question.

BEHAVIORAL INTERVIEWING: METHODS AND PROCEDURES

While it is evident that a number of behavioral procedures need more detailed and explicit description to facilitate their use by practitioners, behaviorists, in general, have been quite responsive in disseminating the necessary information and guidelines for *treatment*. Many journal articles contain complete procedures for specific interventions or authors furnish them upon request. Simplified texts of the "how-to" variety have been available for a number of years. Manuals are also available for relaxation, desensitization, and the treatment of obesity, alcoholism, smoking, self-control, and many other problem areas, and there are movies, tapes, and records providing therapists with adequate descriptions of treatment methods. In contrast, practical guidelines for behavioral *assessment,* and especially behavioral interviewing, have only recently appeared. A few sources provide examples of behavioral interviews, particularly the initial session (Fensterheim, 1972; Goldfried & Davison, 1976; Lazarus, 1971a; Meyer et al., 1977; Peterson, 1968; Rimm & Masters, 1974; Wolpe, 1969, 1970). The reader is also referred to the classic texts of Menninger (1952) and Sullivan (1954) and more recently, the works of Gorden (1969) and Cormier and Cormier (1979), which all provide valuable information that may be useful to the behavioral clinician.

As previously discussed, the ultimate goal of assessment is an accurate functional analysis of the problematic behaviors, the environmental contingencies of those behaviors, the resources available to the individual, and any other information that is necessary in arriving at effective treatment decisions. With this objective as the focal point of interviewing, the remainder of this section outlines a number of possible procedures, questions, and problems encountered in this process. While obvious, perhaps, it is important to note that there are many avenues to obtain the same end product. Thus, one should view the following "techniques" and issues as only a few of the many conceivable strategies that may be employed. In addition, it should not be inferred that all of these procedures are always applicable or that any particular sequence must be rigidly followed. Finally, as emphasized before, how each of these methods relate to the essential variables of assessment, commitment, and treatment efficacy is a question of future empirical research.

Starting the Interview

The first session is often of critical importance. Several decisions need to be made, not the least of which concerns whether or not the client (and the therapist) wishes to continue. Both the client and the therapist will be (and should be) asking the questions: Does the therapist understand what the problem is? What can be gained from therapy? What are the probabilities that such outcomes will be reached? Are there alternative procedures that are as effective, more efficient, less risky, etc.? In addition, the client will undoubtedly be concerned about the therapeutic relationship (i.e., Does the therapist care about me? Will treatment be a pleasant or aversive process and, even, does the therapist like me?).

Students awaiting their first contact with clients ask numerous questions about getting the interview started. They are often concerned with introductions, seating arrangements, whether they should remain silent until the client has spoken or if it is better for them to make some opening statements, and if so, what they should say. While anything but the most nondirective approach will shape and bias the interview to some degree, there are a number of advantages in having the therapist make some sort of introductory remarks. Such an opening statement is likely to reduce some of the client's initial anxiety about what to say and expect. In almost every case, something is already known about the client. Often, the person has already been through one or more intake evaluations, has been referred with some accompanying statement, or has communicated something about the nature of the problem on the telephone in setting up an appointment. Therefore, some introduction briefly summarizing what is already known about the client is usually desirable. For example:

Therapist: Dr. Gordon, whom you spoke with last week, has told me
              that you are having some difficulties since your recent di-
              vorce. From what I understand, you are depressed much
              of the time and are finding it hard to make some career
              decisions. Apart from that, I really don't know much more
              about you. What I would like us to do today is to understand
              more fully what your problems and concerns are and what
              has brought you to seek therapy at this particular time. Can
              you tell me how you see the problem?

This brief summary statement communicates to the client that the therapist has taken the time to speak to the referral source, read the case
material that is available, or simply remembers the initial telephone
conversation. In addition, the simple invitation to elaborate upon his
problems provides the client with a framework from which to start and
some initial expectations about the purpose of the interview. The latter
is not as obvious as it sounds, considering the many myths and misconceptions about psychotherapy. Some individuals, for example, may
expect to be tested, answer long questionnaires, or to lie on a couch
and free associate. Still others may enter the first session with little
notion of what will be expected of them and may experience considerable anxiety in response to ambiguous clues about where to begin.
   With such a minimal stimulus as this opening statement, a great many
clients will begin to relate, often in very specific detail, the reasons
they seek treatment. Others, however, have considerable difficulty getting started (for example, they become tearful, stammer, or wring their
hands in silence) apparently inhibited by the interview situation itself.
Clients may be embarrassed about sharing intimate feelings with a
stranger, worry that their problems are not important enough to merit
therapy or "the doctor's time," or are afraid that once they reveal their
true concerns, they will be labelled "crazy" or will even be institutionalized. Some intervention to reduce the client's current anxiety may
be necessary before a meaningful assessment of the presenting problem
can proceed. Often, encouraging the client to discuss his fears about
the interview, reassuring him that other people also find it hard to begin,
or providing him information about confidentiality (especially if the
interviewer is tape recording the session) will enable the client to continue with more comfort. For those clients who are unresponsive and
distracted by high levels of anxiety, breathing and brief relaxation exercises may be required. Finally, therapeutic attention to the client's
initial distress communicates caring and respect for his feeling and can
enhance therapeutic expectancy.

When clients begin to describe the reasons why they seek treatment, it is useful, within limits, to simply listen and allow them to "tell their story." The decision to seek professional counseling is rarely an immediate, spur-of-the-moment step. The client has most likely considered his problems over and over, with facts, thoughts, and feelings weighed and ordered. Just as it is often unsettling to have prepared at length for an important exam and not be tested when one arrives, so it is probably quite frustrating for the client to have carefully thought out his present difficulties and then not have a chance to share them.

This is not to imply that the therapist adopt a nondirective attitude, following the client wherever, and for as long as, he leads. Certainly, carefully considered questions are essential to both direct and clarify what is being said. Just listening to a client present his "autobiography" session after session is unnecessary, inefficient, and ineffectual.

Listening, then, would seem to be an essential skill of the interviewer. Interrupting with premature questions or clarifications of misconceptions may inhibit the client from relating certain information. It is possible for the therapist to distort what the client is saying since the therapist may actually prompt and shape inaccurate or partially accurate verbal statements by the client to coincide with the interviewer's initial perception of the problem. Annon (1974) provides some excellent examples of how this may occur in the assessment of sexual problems. For example, a client's statements, "I've been a homosexual for 10 years" or "I'm not easily aroused" might immediately elicit reassuring comments or detailed inquiry on the part of the therapist, when the problems may lie elsewhere. In a similar fashion, middle class interviewers may react inappropriately to such emotionally charged words as rape, abortion, incest, etc., when in reality, the client experiences no "problem" in these areas. Listening focuses on the problems of the client, not the preconceptions of the therapist.

During these first stages of behavioral assessment (and to a lesser extent throughout the course of therapy), a case can be made for the *selective* use of empathic statements, such as reflection and paraphrasing. One does not have to accept Rogers' deterministic notion of "self-actualization," nor believe in the need or utility of "unconditional positive regard" to effectively make use of reflective procedures. A number of behavior therapists have explicitly suggested such techniques (e.g., Lazarus, 1971a; Peterson, 1968; Rimm & Masters, 1979) and the general use of reflective statements is apparent in most observations of behavioral assessments. When reflecting, the therapist communicates to the client that he has heard and understood the message. Expanding upon Rogers' use of the word, one does not have to limit the reflections to feelings, since the content of such messages may be as, or more, important than the effect. Needless to say, the behavioral clinician cannot effectively intervene until he understands fully and accurately what the problem is. Training in reflection and paraphrasing, therefore, forces the therapist to listen and focus on what the client is saying. These techniques, in combination with direct questioning, probes, and provisional restatements (Peterson, 1968), may facilitate assessment in a number of ways. First, the experience of being heard and understood may be extremely positive for many individuals, reinforcing them to continue to go into further detail. While good questions serve this purpose to some degree, reflective statements, at times, may communicate this message better. In addition, the therapist who is perceived as understanding may be a potent source of social reinforcement for the client. Finally, reflective remarks and restatements are often necessary to validate for the interviewer what is being said. In the following example, a number of these techniques are illustrated:

Therapist: You say that you are very jealous a lot of the time and this upsets you a great deal.

Client: Well, I know it's stupid for me to feel that way, but I am hurt when I even *think* of Mike with another woman.

Therapist: You don't want to feel jealous but you do.

Client: I know that's not the way a "liberated" woman should be.

Therapist: What is your idea of how a liberated woman should feel?

Client: I don't know. In many ways I feel I've changed so much in the last year. I really don't believe you have the right to own another person—and yet, when it happens to me, I really feel hurt. I'm such a hypocrite!

Therapist: You're unhappy because you are not responding the way you would really like to?

Client: I'm not sure of the person I want to be.

Therapist: So there's really "double jeopardy." When Mike is with someone else it really hurts you. And, then when you feel jealous, you criticize yourself for being that way.

Client: Yes. I guess I lose both ways.

In the above example, the reflective statements communicated to the client that she was being understood and helped her specify what she was experiencing. The final synthesis integrated the various feelings she was expressing, and the validation at the end indicated that the therapist was, indeed, accurate. Quite often, however, the process is not as straightforward. In the example below, the reflections and questions are, at first, somewhat off track. The therapist eventually narrows in on what the client is saying:

Client: Whenever my boss asks to see me, I almost start shaking, wondering what I've done wrong.

Therapist: The anticipation of criticism really makes you anxious?

Client: Well, it's not really that. I'm scared of what might happen.

Therapist: What might happen?

Client: I don't know what will happen, that's it.

Therapist: So it's the suspense that makes you feel uncomfortable.

Client: No, not the suspense—I keep saying to myself that if he starts chewing me out I'm going to let him have it.

Therapist: How would you let him have it?

Client: Well, what I *think* I'm going to do is argue right back at him—or even quit right there.

Therapist: And what *do* you do?

Client: Nothing!

Therapist: Nothing?

Client: I never do anything. I just stand there while he's talking and never say a word.

Therapist: What really makes you shake, as you say, is feeling a great deal of anger and not being able to express it.

Client: Yeah. And the one I'm really mad at is myself for being such a patsy all the time.

Therapist: What do you think would happen if you really did argue with your boss?

Client: He'd probably respect me a lot more than someone who's too scared to defend himself.

Therapist: You're really afraid to challenge your boss' criticism. But when you think about it, you become angry at yourself for not being assertive.

Client: Yes.

It should be evident that reflective comments are not novel techniques. In most conversations, there is a continual exchange of information with feedback that the information has been received and understood. The intention here is not to suggest that reflection be the sole, or even major, assessment procedure on the part of the therapist. Often reflection is useful to keep assessment flowing smoothly, to validate the conclusions of the therapist, or simply to acknowledge that the client is being understood. However, it must be repeatedly emphasized that the goals of assessment are quite clear, underscoring the need for specific questions and direct behavioral measures. Thus, the *extensive* use of non-directive procedures may be, at best, inappropriate for behavioral interviewing (Suinn, 1974). At worst, it can be "as extremely hostile act to refuse to answer a direct and reasonable request or to withhold information from patients . . . [Marquis, 1972, p. 44]." Finally, suggesting the selective use of reflective methods during the initial stages of the interview does not imply that such procedures are advocated as treatment techniques. Reflection is probably insufficient for the client presenting problems of anxiety, stuttering, sexual dysfunction, or the vast majority of other target behaviors for which the individual desires change. Noteworthy in this regard is Haley's (1969) inclusion of "be reflective" in his satirical article outlining "The Five B's Which Guarantee Dynamic Failure."

Preparing the Client for Assessment

While the goals of assessment are quite clear to the interviewer, clients are not always aware that "an assessment" is taking place, what this process entails, or that such information will influence later treatment decisions. In contrast to many traditional forms of psychotherapy, where little distinction is made between assessment and treatment, behaviorists take for granted that active intervention won't begin before a detailed and individualized assessment is completed. Such a "delay" may be surprising or frustrating to the client who expects treatment to begin in the initial session (especially in situations when baseline data are necessary). A brief introduction, therefore, *preparing* the client for the assessment process is useful early in the initial session. For example:

Therapist: Now that I understand more of the reasons that you are coming for therapy, we will be exploring in the next ses-sions(s) these concerns in more detail. I need to learn as much as possible about each of your concerns and how you'd like things to be different so that together we can make some decisions about therapy. How does this sound to you?

This introduction communicates to the client that more complete information about his problems is required before treatment can begin. In addition, it communicates that therapy, rather than a magical elixir dispensed to a passive client irrespective of his individual needs and desires, will be a cooperative process requiring the client's active participation in providing assessment information and, eventually, treatment planning.

More importantly, the invitation to the client to react to the therapist's overview introduces the notion that therapy, even at the initial stages of assessment, will be of a contractual nature. While in most instances treatment proceeds smoothly from assessment, the client should be made aware that his only commitment at this point is for an assessment of his problems and goals. That is, the client is prepared at the outset that treatment is not necessarily automatic and that a decision about treatment can be made *only* at the later stages of assessment, when client and therapist have sufficient information to make the most appropriate choice regarding disposition, be it intervention, referral, or postponement of treatment.

Specification of the Problem

Quite often the client can specify in exacting detail the nature of his problems and with the help of the therapist provide the necessary data concerning both antecedent and consequent conditions. Many times, however, the client is unable to explain what is wrong. It is in these cases that the inexperienced therapist may encounter much difficulty. There are several ways to facilitate the narrowing process. Since the decision to seek professional services is frequently related to some events that have recently occurred in the client's life, questions centering around the reasons that brought the client to treatment can be extremely useful. Often there have been recent changes such as a new job, marriage, divorce, moving, or other situations that may have radically shifted. In addition, the client may have recently had a number of unfortunate experiences such as being fired, rejected at a party, a fight with a spouse, or a death in the family. Finally, in many cases, the "problem" may have been defined by someone else. That is, the recommendation to go for treatment may have come from the client's spouse, parents, or friends, and information regarding the reasons for such referrals may be quite helpful. Such an analysis of the "labeling" process may, thus, provide valuable information, although questions concerning "who is the client" and "to whom is the problem disturbing" must be considered.

Once the problem area has been broadly defined, a thorough behavioral analysis is derived: a careful description of the behavior itself, as well as the antecedent and consequent variables is elicited. Even in situations in which the client reports that he is depressed *all* of the time, or *always* anxious, or a failure at *everything,* careful questions may delimit the problem considerably. A person who reports that he is depressed all of the time almost certainly can think of circumstances when he is more depressed than others. Detailing certain activities, certain places, and certain people also serve to specify the problem more clearly. The client may also be able to relate experiences in the past, or imagine future situations in which the "depressions" may be better or worse. Similarly, the individual who reports a global, undifferentiated fear of traveling, for example, will almost certainly be able to identify situations in which the fear is somewhat attenuated because of the time of day, number of people present, presence of companions, familiarity with the route, type of transportation, etc.

In many cases, the interview material may be supplemented with observation in the natural setting or behavioral measurement during the interview process. Tracking the frequency of certain behaviors may help the client more narrowly define the problem behavior and the circumstances surrounding it even when he has previously been unable to specify those variables. Behavior therapists, therefore, often ask their clients to carry around a diary in which frequency, duration, time, and other circumstances surrounding the target behaviors are carefully recorded. As O'Leary and Wilson (1975) have noted, most clients present themselves as "trait theorists" with descriptions such as "uptight," "lazy," "passive-agressive," etc. A focused functional analysis with behavioral referents of the problem (using both the client's self-report during the interview and the tracked behavior), is probably one of the most essential activities of behavioral assessment. It is quite likely that the behavioral monitoring *itself* may be a "therapeutic" process, communicating to the client that he or she does not suffer from a deep-seated disease or some enduring underlying personality trait. Rather, the emphasis is on discrete behaviors, emitted at specific times with certain frequencies and intensities, and once these behaviors are changed, there is no longer a "problem."

A behavioral analysis also minimizes the possibility that certain self-reported feelings will be misinterpreted. Literally hundreds of commonly used words may imply very different things for different people. It is, therefore, a mistake for the therapist to assume that he or she knows what the client is talking about without any operational referents. It is quite illuminating, for example, to ask a class of students to define in one sentence what they mean by the words "anxiety" or "depression" or "assertive." Even in a group of professional counselors there is often a diverse array of meanings attached to these "feelings" or "states." In sum, it is sound advice for clinicians to "be ignorant" when it comes to understanding what a client means by such words as uptight, heavy, angry, together, spaced-out, freaky, dependent, mellow, passive, etc. The following examples illustrate, first, the acceptance without further exploration of several poorly-defined terms used by the

client; and second, a more careful analysis of these self-reported feelings:

Client: When I'm in such heavy situations, I just get real uptight.
Therapist: What makes you uptight?
Client: Well, the whole thing. Everybody kind of hanging out and
             running around. I can't seem to get it together with any-
             body, so I guess I freak out.
Therapist: And then what happens?
Cleint: I usually go home and go to sleep. But I'm usually pretty
             bummed out.
Therapist: Are you saying that you don't fit in with these people and
             that's what makes you feel bummed out?
Client: Well, I don't know. These are my friends, I guess—but it
             never seems to work out.

In this example, the therapist may have no idea what the client is talking about.
Furthermore, there is certainly no way of knowing whether any inferences are
accurate or not. While at first glance it may appear that the therapist who does
not understand such terminology is hopelessly naive, such "naivete" is probably
essential in order to understand exactly what the client is saying:

Client: When I'm in such heavy situations, I just get real uptight. You
             know, I just can't make it, so I kind of drop out.
Therapist: When you say that you're uptight in these situations, what does
             that mean for you?
Client: Well, uptight, you know. Tense.
Therapist: You mean your muscles get tense?
Client: My neck gets very sore—and I get a headache lots of times.
Therapist: What else happens?
Client: Well, either because of my neck or my headache, I start sweating
             a lot.
Therapist: When you say you're uptight you are really experiencing it phys-
             ically. What are you thinking when this happens? What thoughts
             are going through your head?
Client: I'm thinking, man, you really are paranoid. You just can't relax
             in any situation. You really are a loser. And then I want to get out
             of there fast . . .

In this example, the interviewer has clarified the word "uptight." Although we
all have some idea of what this word means, there is much variation in its usage
depending on the individual. The client in this case was able to point to some
very definite physiological changes that accompanied this feeling. In addition,

there were a number of self-verbalizations (which would have required further elaboration and behavioral reference) as well as resultant avoidance behaviors. The therapist would have then proceeded in getting a good behavioral analysis of what the "heavy" situations were in the client's life and to what he was referring when he said he "couldn't make it." Although such questions may initially seem to the client to be evidence of a lack of therapist understanding, it is quickly communicated to the client that this inquiry is essential for maximal understanding of the problem. Care must be taken, however, to elicit the necessary information without insulting or punishing the client for using his own words.

The need for specific, operational terminology is especially well-illustrated in the area of sexual assessment, particularly since discussion of this material may be associated with a great deal of discomfort and embarrassment for the client and even the therapist. Annon (1974) has discussed the merits of using technical descriptions versus the street language that is commonly used, and indicates that a compromise between the two is sometimes the best strategy. Whatever the language, an exact understanding on the part of both the therapist and the client is important. Thus, the expressions "doing it" or "down there" may be so vague as to provide very little information to the interviewer. Even the use of precisely defined terms must be validated to insure that both individuals understand what is being communicated. Annon also noted that some clients did not know what the word circumcision meant, or exactly where the clitoris was located; intervention in these cases might be doomed to fail unless such questions are clarified. In dealing with very sensitive topics, therapists as well as clients may be shaped into vague explanations and descriptions, depending on their own comfort with such terminology. The direct, straightforward discussion and questioning on the part of the interviewer communicates to the client that it is quite acceptable to talk about such issues. The therapist who models vague and euphemistic language may reinforce the client's belief that such topics should not be discussed and that it is better *not* to deal openly with these problems.

Redefinition of Problems

In a sense, the assessment process with its demand for a functional analysis and clear, operationalized behavioral referents, is a reinterpretation of the client's problem into a social-learning framework. An important question is whether the same ethical objections that are raised about such redefinitions in insight-oriented therapies (Bandura, 1969) cannot also be raised concerning behavioral assessment. It is important to note, however, that behavioral assessment, unlike insight-oriented approaches, redefines neither the client's problems nor his *goals* in terms of *unmeasureable* hypothetical constructs.

Within a behavioral assessment, it is useful and ethically responsible for the interviewer to explicitly redefine the client's statements within a behavioral framework. Even from the very beginning, it is essential that the clinician not reinforce the client's inappropriate self-explanations, be they psychodynamic notions, trait theories, or existential analyses. This is not to suggest that the clinician attempt to attack or antagonize his client by demanding well thought out operational definitions for everything the client says. The interviewer can, however, continually point out different ways of conceptualizing the problem. In sum, the therapist is both modeling and shaping a behavioral language and, at times, directly restating what the client has said in social-learning terms. This "reinterpretation" process communicates to the client that he is not "crazy," "paranoid," or "lacking in self-control," and may be therapeutic in its own right. The client will hopefully begin to see his problems as specific behaviors emitted under specific circumstances, with well-defined psychological principles explaining their development and maintenance. The example below illustrates a few ways in which a client's statements are either questioned or "reinterpreted":

Client:	I know I must be pretty neurotic.
Therapist:	Can you tell me what you mean by neurotic?
Client:	Someone who panics everytime she's alone and even cries when her husband leaves for work must be pretty crazy. Isn't that neurotic?
Therapist:	I don't see that as either crazy or neurotic. Practically everything we do is based on experiences that we have had. Apparently at some time you learned to be very anxious when you were alone. That fear now is very disruptive in your life and you'd like to change how you react.
Client:	But most people don't act that way. Why is that?
Therapist:	More than likely, most people have not had the same experiences with being alone as you described; but if they had, undoubtedly they would feel much the same way as you.
Client:	But if I know this, why don't things change? I keep saying to myself that I'll be okay if I'm alone and that nothing bad is going to happen. But when my husband starts to leave, I panic and burst into tears.
Therapist:	What happens when you cry?
Client:	I feel terrible. I feel like a helpless little girl.
Therapist:	What does your husband do?

Client: He's always very understanding. I don't know how he puts
               up with me, but he is so considerate. When I've really been
               panicked he sits and talks with me until I've calmed down
               and even tells me to go buy myself a present.
Therapist: So even though it is really painful for you, in a sense you
               get "rewarded" for reacting so intensely.

The therapist in this case refused to accept the client's self-labels of crazy or
neurotic. In addition, in very simple terms, the interviewer pointed out how
the intense reactions might be reinforced. Finally, the brief explanation of the
client's problems in terms of learning theory should be noted. Although the
interviewer's attitudes and orientation are implicitly communicated to the client
via the types of questions asked, the explanations offered, and the areas explored, an *explicit* restatement of the problem in social-learning terms at some
time early in assessment may also be desirable. It should be empahsized, however, that the presentation of a social-learning model may be quite unexpected
by the client. It is useful, therefore, to continually assess the reactions that the
client may have to any analysis, interpretation, or conceptualization that the
interviewer offers. Lazarus (1971a), in fact, has suggested that every comment
made by the therapist be followed with the question, "What do you think about
(or, how do you feel about) what I have just said? [p. 61]" Although it is
unnecessary to follow each statement with such a question, it is important to
gauge whether or not the client understands or agrees with what is being communicated.

Toward a Broad Assessment

While the possession of certain professional credentials does not give
an interviewer license to explore *anything* in a client's life, the need
for a thorough analysis is obvious. Not only must the therapist assess
in great detail the specific presenting problems, he or she must also
gain an understanding of how these problems have generalized and affected other areas in the client's life. In addition, a complete assessment
forestalls the introduction of treatment strategies that are inappropriate
or likely to fail. Thus, modifying a child's behavior in therapy without
intervening in the home environment and changing the important controlling variables may be pointless. Similarly, assessing a client's
aggressive behaviors and providing techniques to reduce or eliminate
them without also assessing whether or not the client has other behaviors
in his repertoire which can be equally reinforced is, at best, a sloppy
and inefficient method of treatment.

   A good analysis of the problematic behavior not only allows the interviewer to get a very specific understanding of the client's presenting

difficulties, but also lends itself to a logical continuation into more broadly defined areas. A motivation analysis, for example, or explorations into the client's social relationships and the social, cultural, and physical environment may all be important, not only in defining the problem (and all the controlling variables), but also in assessing both the resources available to the client and what limitations must be considered in treatment (Kanfer & Saslow, 1969). A variety of multifaceted assessment outlines have already been reviewed, and the reader is referred to those sources for more detailed guidelines. It should be noted that a behavioral assessment rarely includes a complete life history of the client, since the past is considered relevant *only to the extent* that it affects the present. Some demographic data, of course, is essential to evaluate much of what the client reports. For example, career indecision may be viewed quite differently by both the therapist and the client depending on whether the individual is 19 or 39. Similarly, lack of employment may be related to an entirely different set of circumstances for the uneducated, unskilled client than for the person with a college degree.

Closing the Interview

A sufficient amount of time at the end of the initial interview(s) should be allowed for the therapist to provide the client with a summary of the information that has already been obtained, an explanation of additional data that is needed, and a reasonable estimate of the likelihood of successful intervention. A good summary communicates to the client that he has been understood and provides him with a behavioral framework to view his problems. Although the therapist has offered such "redefinition" throughout the interview, it is desirable to reiterate many of these statements at the end of the session, integrating all of the material that has been covered. Caution must be taken to insure that this explanation is neither condescending nor too technical for the client to comprehend.

Quite often, additional information is necessary before any treatment decisions can be made, and the client should know what areas need further delineation and what he can do to facilitate the process. Sometimes he may be asked to track certain behaviors, seek out information from others, or simply spend some time thinking about problems that he has had difficulty clarifying.

Even though assessment may be incomplete at this stage, clients should be provided with information concerning possible intervention strategies, length of treatment, and the financial and emotional cost of therapy. Most importantly, it should be clearly communicated to the client that he has a choice in every decision that is made.

While the majority of clients may feel reassured that mutual treatment decisions will be based on a thorough assessment, others may have entirely different expectations and hopes for therapy or the roles of client and therapist. A discussion of the client's expectations can help clarify certain misconceptions and may even enhance positive expectancy about therapy. It is crucial at this point that clinicians be able to respond to the variety of criticisms and "ethical" challenges that have been directed towards behavior therapy. The behaviorist must be comfortable in dealing with the issues of freedom, control, superficiality, etc. that are commonly raised (see Bandura, 1969; Davison & Stuart, 1975; Mahoney et al., 1974 for good summaries of these arguments). Such a "strategic" invitation to the client to openly air his objections and doubts will more likely lead to the establishment of trust and increase the client's initial receptivity and motivation for therapy.

At the end of the initial interview(s), the therapist (or client) may conclude that behavior therapy is inappropriate. The client may present problems and goals for which there is no available treatment, he may not accept a behavioral explanation or treatment plan for his difficulties, or the objectives may be unacceptable to the therapist because of certain ethical or practical reasons. In such instances, the clinician may decide that appropriate referral is in the client's best interests.

Finally, when the joint decision is made to continue therapy, the client should be offered as much encouragement as is reasonably possible. As obvious as this may appear, trainees often neglect to communicate any hope to the individual, or take the other extreme and make unrealistic promises that are doomed to fail. Unlike most traditional approaches, behavior therapy has considerable empirical support for a variety of treatments. Both therapist and client have a legitimate basis for optimism.

SUMMARY

In contrast to the extensive literature on behavioral treatment procedures, and more recently, assessment strategies, guidelines for interviewing techniques have been relatively neglected. This chapter has elaborated upon a number of issues and procedures in behavioral interviewing in order to provide a framework for clinicians during the initial stages of assessment.

Four major issues, interrelated to some degree, were discussed. First, the goals of assessment were specified, since every activity within the interview process is ultimately tied to such objectives. The basic task for the clinician is to obtain as complete a behavioral analysis as possible in order to develop effective, efficient, and durable treatment interventions. At the same time, there is an avoidance of gathering material that is unnecessary for such a task and which may overstep the ethical boundaries of legitimate inquiry when a wide range of the client's life history is explored.

Second, several multifaceted assessment schema were reviewed. Although some suggested a number of new and different areas in which information might be useful, all of them emphasized that the major focus of assessment is on the antecedents, behavior, and consequences of targeted problems.

Third, two major ethical considerations were discussed: the degree of therapist influence on the determination of the client's objectives; and the decision to accept the client's goals and intervene, or to refuse treatment when certain ethical responsibilities are violated.

The fourth issue concerned the interviewer-client relationship in behavioral interviewing. It was concluded that certain relationship variables probably facilitate and enhance treatment outcome, although the absence of any empirical support for this conclusion was noted and the need for extensive research in the area underscored.

The second section of this chapter outlined a number of procedures and techniques available to the clinician during the early stages of assessment. Methods were proposed for starting the initial interview, preparing the client for the assessment process, specification of target behaviors, redefinition of the problem, and, finally, closing the interview.

REFERENCES

Adams, H. E. (Ed.) *Journal of Behavioral Assessment,* 1979.

Angle, H. V., Ellinwood, E. H., Hay, W. M., Johnsen, T., & Hay, L. R. Computer-aided interviewing in comprehensive behavioral assessment. *Behavior Therapy,* 1977, *8,* 747–754.

Angle, H. V., Hay, L. R., Hay, W. M., & Ellinwood, E. H. Computer assisted behavioral assessment. In J. D. Cone & R. P. Hawkins (Eds.), *Behavioral assessment: New directions in clinical psychology.* New York: Brunner/Mazel, 1977.

Annon, J. S. *The behavioral treatment of sexual problems* Vol. 1. *Brief therapy.* Honolulu: Kapiolani Health Services, 1974.

Bandura, A. *Principles of behavior modification.* New York: Holt, Rinehart and Winston, 1969.

Biglan, A. Personal communication, July, 1975.

Carkhuff, R. *Helping and human relations.* Vol. 1. *Selection and training.* New York: Holt, Rinehart and Winston, 1969. (a)

Carkhuff, R. *Helping and human relations.* Vol. 2. *Practice and Research.* New York: Holt, Rinehart and Winston, 1969. (b)

Ciminero, A. R., Calhoun, K. S., & Adams, H. E. (Eds.) *Handbook of behavioral assessment.* New York: Wiley, 1977.

Cone, J. D., & Hawkins, R. P. (Eds.) *Behavioral assessment: New directions in clinical psychology.* New York: Brunner/Mazel, 1977.

Cormier, W. H., & Cormier, L. S. *Interviewing strategies for helpers: A guide to assessment, treatment, and evaluation.* Monterey: Brooks/Cole, 1979.

Cozby, P. C. Self-disclosure: A literature review. *Psychological Bulletin,* 1973, *79,* 73–91.

Davison, G. C. *Homosexuality: The ethical challenge.* Presidential address presented at the meeting of the Association for Advancement of Behavior Therapy, Chicago, November 1974.

Davison, G. C., & Stuart, R. B. Behavior therapy and civil liberties. *American Psychologist,* 1975, *30,* 755–763.

Fensterheim, H. The initial interview. In A. A. Lazarus (Ed.), *Clinical behavior therapy.* New York: Brunner/Mazel, 1972.

Goldfried, M. R. Behavioral assessment in perspective. In J D. Cone & R. P. Hawkins (Eds.), *Behavioral assessment: New directions in clinical psychology.* New York: Brunner/Mazel, 1977.

Goldfried, M. R., & Davison, G. C. *Clinical behavior therapy.* New York: Holt, Rinehart and Winston, 1976.

Goldfried, M. R., & Pomeranz, D. Role of assessment in behavior modification. *Psychological Reports,* 1968, *23,* 75–87.

Goldfried, M. R., & Sprafkin, J. N. *Behavioral personality assessment.* Morristown, N.J.: General Learning Press, 1974.

Goldstein, A. P. Relationship-enhancement methods. In F. H. Kanfer & A. P. Goldstein (Eds.), *Helping people change.* New York: Pergamon Press, 1975.

Gorden, R. L. *Interviewing: Strategy, techniques, and tactics.* Homewood, Ill.: Dorsey Press, 1969.

Gordon, T. *Parent effectiveness training.* New York: Wyden, 1970.

Haley, J. The art of being a failure as a therapist. *American Journal of Orthopsychiatry,* 1969, *39,* 691–695.

Halleck. S. L. *The politics of therapy.* New York: Science House, 1971.

Hersen, M., & Bellack, A. S., (Eds.), *Behavioral assessment: A practical handbook.* New York: Pergamon Press, 1976.

Kanfer, F. H. Verbal conditioning: A review on its current status. In T. R. Dixon & D. L. Horton (Eds.), *Verbal behavior and general behavior theory.* Englewood Cliffs, N. J.: Prentice-Hall, 1968.

Kanfer, F. H., & Goldstein, A. P. (Eds.), *Helping people change.* New York: Pergamon Press, 1975.

Kanfer, F. H., & Saslow, G. Behavioral diagnosis. In C. M. Franks (Ed.), *Behavior therapy: Appraisal and status.* New York: McGraw-Hill, 1969.

Kazdin, A. E. The failure of some patients to respond to token programs. *Journal of Behavior Therapy and Experimental Psychiatry,* 1973, *4,* 7–14.

Klein, M. H., Dittman, A. T., Parloff, M. B., & Gill, M. M. Behavior therapy: Observations and reflections. *Journal of Consulting and Clinical Psychology,* 1969, *33,* 259–266.

Krasner, L. The psychotherapist as a social reinforcement machine. In H. H. Strupp & L. Luborsky (Eds.), *Research in psychotherapy.* Vol. 2. Washington, D. C.: American Psychological Association, 1962.

Krasner, L. *The therapist as a social reinforcer: Man or machine.* Paper presented at the meeting of the American Psychological Association, Philadelphia, September 1963.

Lazarus, A. A. *Behavior therapy and beyond.* New York: McGraw-Hill, 1971. (a)

Lazarus, A. A. Notes on behavior therapy, the problem of relapse and some tentative solutions. *Psychotherapy,* 1971, *8,* 192–196. (b)

Lazarus, A. A. Multimodal behavior therapy: Treating the "BASIC ID." *The Journal of Nervous and Mental Disease,* 1973, *156,* 404–411.

Lazarus, A. A. *Multimodal behavior therapy.* New York: Springer, 1976.

Lick, J., & Bootzin, R. Expectancy factors in the treatment of fear: Methodological and theoretical issues. *Psychological Bulletin,* 1975, *82,* 917–931.

Linehan, M. M. Issues in behavioral interviewing. In J. D. Cone & R. P. Hawkins (Eds.), *Behavioral assessment: New directions in clinical psychology.* New York: Brunner/Mazel, 1977.

Mahoney, M. J., Kazdin, A. E., & Lesswing, N. J. Behavior modification: Delusion or deliverance. In C. M. Franks & G. T. Wilson (Eds.), *Annual review of behavior therapy: Theory & practice.* Vol. 2. New York: Brunner/Mazel, 1974.

Marquis, J. N. An expedient model for behavior therapy. In A. A. Lazarus (Ed.), *Clinical behavior therapy.* New York: Brunner/Mazel, 1974.

Marsden, G. Content analysis studies of psychotherapy: 1954 through 1968. In A. E. Bergin & S. L. Garfield (Eds.), *Handbook of psychotherapy and behavior change: An empirical analysis.* New York: Wiley, 1971.

Mash, E. J., & Terdal, L. G. *Behavior therapy assessment: Diagnosis, design, & evaluation.* New York: Springer, 1976.

Matarazzo, J. D. The interview. In B. B. Wolman (Ed.), *Handbook of clinical psychology.* New York: McGraw-Hill, 1965.

McNamara, J. R. Socioethical considerations in behavior therapy reserach and practice. *Behavior Modification,* 1978, *2, 3–23.*

Meichenbaum, D. A cognitive-behavior modification approach to assessment. In M. Hersen & A. S. Bellack (Eds.), *Behavioral assessment: A practical handbook.* New York: Pergamon Press, 1976.

Menninger, K. A. *A manual for psychiatric case study.* New York: Grune & Stratton, 1952.

Meyer, V., Liddel, A., & Lyons, M. Behavioral interviews. In A. R. Ciminero, K. S. Calhoun, & H. E. Adams (Eds.), *Handbook of behavioral assessment.* New York: Wiley, 1977.

Mischel, W. *Personality and assessment.* New York: Wiley, 1968.

Mischel, W. *Introduction to personality.* New York: Holt, Rinehart and Winston, 1971.

Mischel, W. Toward a cognitive social learning reconceptualization of personality. *Psychological Review,* 1973, *80,* 252–283.

Morganstern, K. P. Implosive therapy and flooding procedures: A critical review. *Psychological Bulletin,* 1973, *79,* 318–334.

Morganstern, K. P. Cigarette smoke as a noxious stimulus in self-managed aversion therapy for compulsive eating: Technique and case illustration. *Behavior Therapy,* 1974, *5,* 255–260.

Morganstern, K. P. Behavioral interviewing: The initial stages of assessment. In M. Hersen & A. S. Bellack (Eds.), *Behavioral assessment: A practical handbook.* New York: Pergamon Press, 1976.

O'Leary, K. D., & Wilson, G. T. *Behavior therapy: Application and outcome.* Englewood Cliffs, N. J.: Prentice-Hall, 1975.

Peterson, D. R. *The clincial study of social behavior.* New York: Appleton-Century-Crofts, 1968.

Rimm, D. C., & Masters, J. C. *Behavior therapy: Techniques and empirical findings.* New York: Academic Press, 1974.

Rimm, D. C., & Masters, J. C. *Behavior therapy: Techniques and empirical findings.* (2nd ed.) New York: Academic Press, 1979.

Salzinger, K. Experimental manipulation of verbal behavior: A review. *Journal of General Psychology,* 1959, *61,* 65–94.

Stuart, R. B. *Trick or treatment: How and when psychotherapy fails.* Champaign, Ill.: Research Press, 1970.

Suinn, R. M. Training undergraduate students as community behavior modification consultants. *Journal of Counseling Psychology,* 1974, *21,* 71–77.

Sullivan, H. S. *The psychiatric interview.* New York: Norton, 1954.

Truax, C. B., & Carkhuff, R. *Toward effective counseling and psychotherapy: Training and practice.* Chicago: Aldine, 1967.

Truax, C. B., & Mitchell, K. M. Research on certain therapist interpersonal skills in relation to process and outcome. In A. E. Bergin & S. L. Garfield (Eds.), *Handbook of psychotherapy and behavior change: An empirical analysis.* New York: Wiley 1971.

Wexler, D. B. Token and taboo: Behavior modification, token economies, and the law. In C. M. Franks & G. T. Wilson (Eds.), *Annual review of behavior therapy: Theory & practice.* Vol. 2. New York: Brunner/Mazel, 1974. (Reprinted form *California Law Review,* 1973, *61.*)

Wilson, G. T., & Evans, I. M. Adult behavior therapy and the client-therapist relationship. In C. M. Franks & G. T. Wilson (Eds.), *Annual review of behavior therapy: Theory & Practice.* Vol. 4. New York: Brunner/Mazel, 1978.

Winett, R. A., & Winkler, R. C. Current behavior modification in the classroom: Be still, be quiet, be docile. *Journal of Applied Behavior Analysis,* 1972, *5,* 499–504.

Wolpe, J. *The practice of behavior therapy.* New York: Pergamon Press, 1969.

Wolpe, J. Transcript on initial interview in a case of depression. *Journal of Behavior Therapy and Experimental Psychiatry,* 1970, *1,* 71–78.

Chapter 4
Behavioral Observation

Alan E. Kazdin

INTRODUCTION

Assessment of overt performance is a distinguishing feature of behavioral assessment. Overt performance, especially when measured in the situation in which behavior usually occurs, is considered to be a direct measure of client dysfunction. By assessing actual performance, the investigator samples behaviors that are to be focused upon in treatment. Hence, minimal inferences need to be made about the relationship between the measure used to assess performance and actual client behavior. Of course, assessment of overt behavior is only one facet of *behavioral assessment,* as that term has been used (e.g., Ciminero, Calhoun, & Adams, 1977; Goldfried & Kent, 1972; Nelson & Hayes, 1979). Other response modalities including cognitive, emotive, and psychophysiological events, in addition to overt motor behavior, need to be assessed. Indeed, behavior assessment is characterized by comprehensive assessment of multiple response modalities.

The purpose of the present chapter is to discuss the assessment of overt behavior as one facet of behavioral assessment. Specifically discussed are the prerequisites for observing overt performance, alternative assessment strategies, the conditions under which assessment can be obtained and current issues that need to be considered when obtaining and evaluating measures of overt performance, and future areas of research.

PREASSESSMENT CONSIDERATIONS

The actual assessment of overt performance reflects the completion of several tasks. These prior tasks are extremely important and determine the extent to which the assessment procedures can be carried out. The

101

major prerequisite for observing performance is defining the behavior that is to be assessed, i.e., the target behavior.

Defining the Target Behavior

Identification of the target behavior is deceptively simple. Clinical problems are typically described to professionals in general and global terms inadequate for beginning behavioral observations. People are concerned with such general concepts as depression, aggressiveness, introversion, social withdrawal, and others, none of which is sufficiently concrete to begin observations. Each of these terms might be defined in an indefinite number of ways but target behaviors need to be defined explicitly so that they can actually be observed, measured, and agreed upon by persons administering the intervention. The global term needs to be translated into observable acts that occur at specific times.

the clinical problem in behavioral terms, difficulties may arise in proceeding to the concrete behavioral observational system. After obtaining the specific terms that identify the target behaviors, the response usually has to be defined even further. For example, a behavior problem child in the home may be described as not following instructions or hitting a sibling. These concrete behavioral referents move one much closer to actually conducting observations, but additional work remains in obtaining a definition of the response that is to be assessed.

For behavioral observations, a response definition should meet three criteria: objectivity, clarity, and completeness (Hawkins & Dobes, 1975). To be *objective,* the definition should refer to observable characteristics of behavior or environmental events. Definitions should not refer to inner states of the individual such as aggressiveness or emotional disturbance. To be *clear,* the definition should be so unambiguous that it could be read, repeated, and paraphrased by observers. Reading the definition should provide a sufficient basis for beginning actual observations. To be complete, the boundary conditions of the definition must be delineated so that the responses to be included and excluded are enumerated.

Developing a definition that is complete often creates the greatest problem because decision rules are needed to specify how behavior should be scored. If the range of responses included in the definition is not described carefully, observers have to infer whether the response has occurred. For example, a simple greeting response such as waving one's hand to greet someone may serve as the target behavior (Stokes, Baer, & Jackson, 1974). In most instances, when a person's hand is fully extended and moving back and forth, there is no difficulty in agreeing that the person was waving. However, ambiguous instances may require judgments on the part of observers. A child might move his or her hand once (rather than back and forth) while the arm is not extended, or may not move the arm at all, but simply move all fingers on one hand up and down (in the way that infants often learn to say good-bye). These latter responses are instances of waving in everyday life because we can often see others reciprocate with similar greetings. For assessment purposes, the response definition must specify whether these and related variations would be scored as waving.

Behavior modification programs have reported clear behavioral definitions which were developed from global and imprecise terms. For example, the treatment focus of one program was on aggressiveness of a 12-year-old institutionalized retarded girl (Repp & Deitz, 1974). The specific behaviors included biting, hitting, scratching, and kicking others. In a program conducted in a psychiatric hospital, the focus was on poor communication skills of a schizophrenic patient (Fichter, Wallace, Liberman, & Davis, 1976). The conversational behaviors included speaking loud enough so another person could hear (from about 10 feet away) and speaking for a specified amount of time. These examples illustrate how clear behavioral definitions can be derived from general terms which may have diverse meanings to different individuals.

Focus of Assessment

Assessment invariably focuses on the behaviors of interest. The purpose of assessing the target behavior is to examine how and how often the behavior is performed and to provide a basis for evaluating subsequent changes that occur with treatment. Although the target behavior serves as the main impetus for observation, several other behaviors may be assessed, depending upon the goals of the program.

Quite often alteration of one behavior has impact on several others. For example, changing one social behavior (e.g., approaching other persons) may affect other social behaviors (e.g., talking to others) (Buell, Stoddard, Harris, & Baer, 1968). Altering one behavior may be associated with changes in several others, even when the interrelationships among the behaviors are not obvious. For example, in one report, decreasing a child's inappropriate talking at school was associated with increases in social behavior and disruptive behavior, and decreases in attentive behavior in a group and the use of certain toys (Sajwaj, Twardosz, & Burke, 1972). Topographically distinct behaviors sometimes go together or "cluster" across settings and over time for a given person (Wahler, 1975). Thus, change in one behavior may be associated with changes in other behaviors as well. Often the investigator may wish to alter several behaviors, but constraints on implementation of treatment may dictate focusing on only one or two. In such cases it may be useful to observe several behaviors that ultimately will need treatment to examine whether initial changes for one of the behaviors extends to others.

Assessing the occurrence of target behaviors may exclude considerable information that is useful in treatment. The target response may be associated with various antecedent and consequent events. It is important to observe these events for two reasons. First, many behaviors seen in treatment are problems only in relation to particular events that occur in the environment. For example, the appropriateness of a person's social response may be determined by the antecedent responses of others. Classification of the response may require consideration of antecedent conditions. Second, assessment of antecedent and consequent events may be required to evaluate the impact or lack of impact of treatment. For example, a behavioral program for a child in the home may rely upon parental approval. Observation of child behavior may reveal no improvements. In such cases, it is essential to have additional information regarding parent behavior to assess whether approval was delivered at all or correctly. Changes in the program very much depend upon the information concerning parent behavior.

In general, assessment often extends beyond the target behavior. Antecedent and consequent events that may influence behavior are important to observe as well. These antecedent and consequent events usually are the behaviors of other persons such as parents, teachers, and ward staff who are in daily contact with the client. The overt behaviors of these persons may need to be monitored as part of a larger program designed to improve client performance.

STRATEGIES OF ASSESSMENT

Assessment of overt behavior can be accomplished in different ways. In most cases, behaviors are assessed on the basis of discrete response occurrences or the amount of time that the response occurs. However, several different types of measures are available.

Frequency Measures

Frequency counts require simply tallying the number of times the behavior occurs in a given period of time. This measure is referred to as *response rate* (frequency of the response divided by time). Measures of response rate are particularly useful when the target response is discrete and when the response takes a relatively constant amount of time whenever it is performed. A discrete response has a clearly delineated beginning and end, so that separate instances of the response can be counted. Ongoing behaviors, such as smiling, sitting in one's seat, lying down, and talking, are difficult to record simply by counting because each response may occur for different amounts of time.

Frequency measures have been used for a variety of behaviors. For example, in a program for an autistic child, frequency measures were used to assess the number of times the child engaged in social responses such as saying "hello" or sharing a toy or object with someone and the number of self-stimulatory behaviors such as rocking or repetitive pulling of clothing (Russo & Koegel, 1977). With hospitalized psychiatric patients, one program assessed the frequency that patients engaged in intolerable acts, such as assaulting someone or setting fires and social behaviors such as initiating conversation or responding to someone else (Frederiksen, Jenkins, Foy, & Eisler, 1976).

A frequency measure has several desirable features for use in applied settings. *First,* frequency of a response is relatively simple to score for individuals working in natural settings. Keeping a tally of behavior usually is all that is required. *Second,* frequency measures readily reflect changes over time. *Third,* and related to the above, frequency expresses the amount of behavior performed. In many cases, the goal of the program is to increase or decrease the number of times a certain behavior occurs.

Discrete Categorization

Often it is very useful to classify responses into discrete categories such as correct-incorrect, performed-not-performed, or appropriate-inappropriate. In many ways, discrete categorization is like a frequency measure because it is used for behaviors that have a clear beginning and end and a constant duration, yet there are at least two important differences. With a frequency measure, performances of a particular behavior are tallied. The focus is on a single response, and the number of times the behavior may occur is theoretically unlimited. Discrete categorization is used to measure whether or not several different behaviors may have occurred, and there is only a limited number of opportunities to perform the response.

Discrete categories have been used to assess behavior in many behavioral programs. For example, Neef, Iwata, and Page (1978) trained mentally retarded and physically handicapped young adults to ride the bus in the community. Several different behaviors related to finding the bus, boarding it, and leaving the bus were included in a checklist and classified as performed correctly or incorrectly. The effect of training was evaluated on the number of steps performed correctly. Similarly, in a camp setting, the cabin-cleaning behaviors of emotionally disturbed boys were evaluated using discrete categorization (Peacock, Lyman, & Rickard, 1978). Tasks such as placing coats on hooks, making beds, having no objects on the bed, putting toothbrushing materials away, and other specific acts were categorized as completed or not to evaluate the effects of the program.

Discrete categorization is very easy to use because it requires listing a number of behaviors and checking off whether they were performed. The behaviors may consist of several different steps that all relate to completion of a task, such as developing dressing or grooming behaviors in retarded children. However, the behaviors need not be related to each other. For example, room-cleaning behaviors are not necessarily related in the sense that doing one correctly (making one's bed) may be unrelated to another (cleaning up dishes). Hence, discrete categorization is a very flexible method of observation which allows one to assess all sorts of behaviors independently of whether they are necessarily related to each other.

Number of Clients

Occasionally, the effectiveness of interventions is evaluated on the basis of the number of clients who perform a response. This measure usually is used in group situations, such as a classroom or psychiatric hospital where the purpose is to increase the overall performance of a particular behavior, i.e., coming to an activity on time, completing homework, or speaking up in a group. Once the desired behavior is defined, observations consist of noting how many participants in the group have performed the response.

Several programs have evaluated the impact of treatment on the number of people who are affected. For example, one program increased the extent that senior citizens participated in a community meal program that provided low-cost nutritious meals (Bunck & Iwata, 1978). The program was evaluated on the number of new participants from the community who sought out the meals. In a large institution for the retarded, a program was designed to increase the number of residents who were included in a toilet training program that staff were supposed to implement (Greene, Willis, Levy, & Bailey, 1978). The program focused upon increasing the frequency with which staff put the residents through the training procedure, but was evaluated on the number of clients participating each day.

The number of individuals who perform a response is very useful when the explicit goal of the program is to increase performance in a large group of subjects. A problem with the measure in many treatment programs is that it does not provide information about performance of a particular individual. The number of people who perform a response may be increased in an institution or society at large. However, performance of any particular individual may be sporadic or very low. One really does not know how a particular individual is affected. This information may or may not be important depending upon the goals of the program.

Interval Recording

A frequent strategy of measuring behavior is based upon units of time rather than discrete response units. Behavior is recorded during short time intervals for the total time that it is observed. With interval recording, behavior is observed for a single block of time (e.g., 30 minutes) once per day. A block of time is divided into a series of short intervals (10 or 15 seconds), and the behavior of the client is observed during each of them. The target behavior is scored as having occurred or not occurred during each interval. If a discrete behavior, such as hitting someone, occurs one or more times in a single interval, the response is scored as having occurred. Several response occurrences within an interval are not counted separately. If the behavior is ongoing with an unclear beginning or end, such as talking, playing, and sitting, or occurs for a long period of time, it is scored during each interval in which it is occurring.

Interval recording for a single block of time has been used in many programs. For example, one program focused upon several inappropriate child behaviors (e.g., roughhousing, touching objects, playing with merchandise) that occurred during shopping trips with parents (Clark et al., 1977, Exp. 3). Observers followed the family in the store to record whether the inappropriate behaviors occurred during consecutive 15-second intervals. Interval assessment was also used in a program to develop conversational skills in delinquent girls (Minkin et al., 1976). Observations were made of whether appropriate conversational behaviors occurred (asking questions of another person and making comments that indicated understanding or agreement with what the other person said) during 10-second intervals while the youths conversed.

A variation of interval recording is referred to as *time-sampling*. This variation uses the interval method but the observations are conducted for brief periods at different times, rather than in a single block of time.

As an illustration, psychiatric patients participating in a hospital reinforcement program were evaluated with time-sampling procedures
(Paul & Lentz, 1977). Patients were observed each hour, and an observer looked at the patient for a two-second interval. At the end of
the interval, the observer recorded the presence or absence of several
behaviors related to social interaction, activities, self-care, and other
responses. The procedure was continued throughout the day, sampling
one interval at a time. The advantage of time sampling is that the observations represent performance over the entire day.

   There are significant features of interval recording which make it a
widely adopted strategy. *First,* interval assessment is very flexible because virtually any behavior can be recorded. The presence of absence
of a response during a time interval applies to any measurable response.
Whether a response is discrete and unvarying in duration, continuous,
or sporadic, it can be classified as occurring or not occurring during
any time period. Second, the observations resulting from interval recording can be easily converted into a percentage. The number of intervals that the response is scored as occurring can be divided by the
total number of intervals observed. This ratio, multiplied by 100, yields
a percentage of intervals that the response is performed. A percentage
is easily communicated to others by noting that a certain behavior occurs
a specific percentage of time (intervals).

Duration

Another time-based method of observation is duration or amount of time
that the response is performed. This method is particularly useful for
ongoing responses that are continuous rather than discrete acts or responses of extremely short duration. Programs that attempt to increase
or decrease the length of time a response is performed might profit from
a duration method. For example, duration has been used to assess the
amount of time that a claustrophobic patient spent sitting voluntarily
in a small room (Leitenberg, Agras, Thompson, & Wright, 1968) and
the time delinquent boys spent returning from school and errands (Phillips, 1968).

   Another measure based upon duration is not how long the response
is performed, but how long it takes for the client to begin the response.
The amount of elapsed time between a cue and the response is referred
to as *latency.* For example, in one program designed to improve compliance with instructions, response latency was used to evaluate treatment (Fjellstedt & Sulzer-Azaroff, 1973). Compliance with instructions
became much more rapid over the course of the program.

Duration and latency are often fairly simple measures to implement and require starting and stopping a stopwatch or noting the time of response performance. However, the onset and termination of the response must be carefully defined. Use of response duration or latency is restricted to situations where these characteristics of behavior are of major concern. Although programs occasionally are designed to increase time dimensions of a particular behavior (e.g., duration of study time), the focus usually emphasizes other performance characteristics measured with one of the other assessment strategies.

Selection of an Assessment Strategy

One of the above assessment methods is commonly used for behavioral observations. Occasionally, other measures might be used because they provide direct measures of behavior that are of obvious importance. For example, treatments for obesity or cigarette smoking commonly evaluate intervention effects by simply looking at client weight in pounds or the number of cigarettes smoked. In other programs, the specific behavior may lend itself to a measure unique to the investigation. For example, interventions designed to reduce energy consumption can monitor gas or electric meters or look at a car's odometer to record whether home or car use of energy has changed.

In most situations, the investigator needs to develop an assessment procedure based upon one of the methods mentioned above. Some behaviors may lend themselves well to frequency counts or categorization because they are discrete, such as the number of profane words used, or the number of toileting or eating responses; others are suited to interval recording such as reading, working, or sitting; and still others are suited to duration such as time spent studying, crying, or getting dressed. Target behaviors usually can be assessed in more than one way, so there is no single strategy that must be adopted.

Although many different measures can be used in a given program, the measure finally selected may be dictated by the purpose of the program. Different measures sometimes have slightly different goals. For example, consider two behavioral programs that focused upon increasing toothbrushing, a seemingly simple response which can be assessed in many different ways. In one of the programs, the *number of individuals* who brushed their teeth in a boys' summer camp was observed (Lattal, 1969). The boys knew how to brush their teeth and an incentive system increased their performance of the response. In another program that increased toothbrushing, the clients were mentally retarded residents at a state hospital (Horner & Keilitz, 1975). The residents were unable

to brush their teeth at the beginning of the program, so the many behaviors involved in toothbrushing were developed. *Discrete categorization* was used to assess toothbrushing, and each component step of
the behavior (wetting the brush, removing the cap, applying the toothpaste, and so on) was scored as performed or not performed. The percent
of steps correctly completed measured the effects of training. Although
both of the above investigations assessed toothbrushing, the different
methods reflect slightly different goals, namely getting children who
can brush to do so or training the response in individual residents who
did not know how to perform the response.

CONDITIONS OF ASSESSMENT

Aside from the strategies to assess behavior, observations may vary
markedly in how they are obtained. The present discussion addresses
the range of conditions under which overt behaviors are often assessed.

Naturalistic versus Contrived Observations

Naturalistic observation in the present context refers to observing performance without intervening or structuring the situation for the client.
Ongoing performance is observed as it normally occurs, and the situation
is not intentionally altered merely to obtain the observations or to evoke
certain types of overt behavior. For example, observations of interaction
among children at school during a free-play period would be considered
naturalistic in the sense that an ordinary activity was observed during
the school day (Hauserman, Walen, & Behling, 1973). Similarly, observation of obese and nonobese persons eating in a restaurant would
constitute assessment under naturalistic conditions (Gaul, Craighead,
& Mahoney, 1975).

Although direct observation of performance as it normally occurs is
very useful, naturalistic observation often is not possible or feasible.
Many of the behaviors of interest are not easily observed because they
are of low frequency, require special precipitating conditions, or are
prohibitive to assess in view of available resources. Situations are often
contrived to evoke responses so that the target behavior can be assessed.
For example, to assess affectionate behavior (e.g., smiling and laughing
with a child, using affectionate words, providing affectionate physical
contact) among staff of a day-care facility, Twardosz, Schwartz, Fox,
and Cunningham (1979) instructed some staff to behave affectionately
to obtain a measure of the desired behaviors. Purely naturalistic observation may not have resulted in a sufficiently frequent sample of the
desired behaviors.

Perhaps the most familiar use of contrived situations for behavioral observation consists of techniques used to measure anxiety (Bernstein, 1973). Persons are placed in a contrived situation, sometimes referred to as a *behavioral avoidance test,* in which they are required to interact in increasingly intimate contact or proximity with a feared object (e.g., snakes). The behavioral tasks may include such items as entering the room where the feared object is located, walking up to the object, touching it, and so on. The assessment procedures are obviously contrived because a client ordinarily is unlikely to encounter the feared stimulus in such a prearranged or carefully calibrated set of tasks. The client is also fully aware that the tasks are presented for assessment purposes in safe situations.

Performance under conditions that simulate or reflect the responses in which the client's behavior is problematic provides information that would be too difficult to obtain under naturalistic conditions. Also, when several persons need to be assessed, as in treatment outcome research, the assessment conditions need to be standardized. Because the testing conditions are standardized, comparisons across subjects and within subjects over time can be readily interpreted.

Clinic versus Natural Settings

The previous discussion examined how the situation is structured to obtain behavioral observations, namely in naturalistic or contrived conditions. Another dimension that distinguishes behavioral observations is where the assessment is conducted. Observations can be obtained in the clinic or laboratory setting or in the natural environment. In addition, the behavior can be observed in natural situations or a contrived situation can be arranged.

Ideally, direct observations are made in the natural setting where the clients normally function. Such observations may be especially likely to reflect performance that the client has identified as problematic. Naturalistic situations might include the community, job location, classroom, home, and institutions. For example, in one investigation an adult male who was extremely anxious and deficient in verbal skills was trained to speak in an organized and fluent fashion (Hollandsworth, Glazeski, & Dressel, 1978). Observations were made in the natural environment to examine the client's verbal skills after treatment. Specifically, observers were sent to the store where the client worked and posed as shoppers and observations of interactions with customers were sampled directly.

Often, behavioral observations are made in the homes of those under treatment. For example, to treat marital discord or conduct problem children and their families, observers may assess family interaction directly in the home (Patterson, 1974; Patterson, Hops, & Weiss, 1975). Restrictions may be placed on the family such as having them remain in one or a few rooms, not spend time on the phone, or refrain from watching television to help standardize the conditions of assessment. The assessment is in a naturalistic setting even though the actual circumstances of assessment are slightly contrived, i.e., structured in such a way that the situation probably departs from ordinary conditions.

Assessment in naturalistic settings raises obvious problems. A variety of practical issues often present major obstacles, such as the cost required for conducting observations and reliability checks, ensuring and maintaining standardization of the assessment conditions, and so on. Clinic and laboratory settings have been heavily relied upon because of the convenience and standardization of assessment conditions afforded by these settings. In the vast majority of clinic observations, contrived situations are used, such as those illustrated earlier. When clients come to the clinic, it is difficult to observe direct samples of performance that are not under somewhat structured, simulated, or contrived conditions.

Obtrusive versus Unobtrusive Assessment

Independently of whether the measures are obtained under contrived or naturalistic conditions and in clinic or natural settings, observations of overt behavior may differ in whether they are *obtrusive*, i.e., whether the subjects are aware that their behaviors are assessed. Obtrusiveness of an assessment procedure may be a matter of degree, so that subjects may be aware of assessment generally and know that they are being observed, but be uncertain of the target behaviors, and so on. The potential issue with obtrusive assessment is that it may be *reactive*, i.e., the assessment procedure may influence the subject's performance.

Observations of overt performance may vary in the extent to which they are conducted under obtrusive or unobtrusive conditions. In many investigations that utilize direct observations, performance is assessed under obtrusive conditions. For example, observation of behavior problem children in the home or the clinic are conducted in situations where families are aware that they are being observed. Similarly, clients who are seen for treatment of anxiety-based problems usually are fully aware that their behavior is assessed where avoidance behavior is calibrated under contrived conditions.

Occasionally, observations are conducted under *un*obtrusive assessment conditions (Kazdin, 1979a, 1979d). For example, Bellack, Hersen, and Lamparski (1979) evaluated social skills of college students by placing them in a situation with a confederate. The situation was contrived to appear as if the subject and confederate had to sit together during a "scheduling mix-up." The confederate socially interacted with the subject who presumably was unaware of the assessment procedures. The interaction was videotaped for later observation of such measures as eye contact, duration of responding, smiles, and other measures. As another example, McFall and Marston (1970) phoned subjects who completed an assertion training program. The caller posed as a magazine salesperson and completed a prearranged sequence of requests designed to elicit assertive behavior. Because the phone call was under the guise of selling magazines, it is highly likely that the persons were unaware their behaviors were being assessed.

Unobtrusive behavioral observations are reported relatively infrequently. In many situations clients may not know all the details of assessment but are partially aware that they are being evaluated (e.g., children in a classroom study). However, completely withholding information about the assessment procedures raises special ethical problems that often preclude the use of unobtrusive measures based upon direct observations of overt performance.

General Comments

The conditions under which behavioral observations are obtained may vary markedly. The dimensions that distinguish behavioral observations discussed above do not exhaust all of the possibilities. Moreover, for purposes of presentation, the conditions of assessment were discussed as either contrived *or* naturalistic, in clinic *or* natural settings, and as obtrusive *or* unobtrusive. Actually, these characteristics vary along continua. For example, many clinic situations may approximate or very much attempt to approximate the natural settings. As an illustration, alcohol consumption of hospitalized alcoholics is often measured by observing patients as they drink in a simulated bar in the hospital. The bar is in a clinic setting, yet the conditions closely resemble the physical environment in which drinking often takes place.

The range of conditions under which behavioral observations can be obtained provides many options for the investigator. When the strategies for assessment (e.g., frequency, interval observations) are added, the diversity of observational practices is even more impressive. Thus, for a given behavior several options for direct behavioral observation are available. An interesting issue yet to be fully addressed in behavioral assessment is the interrelationship among alternative measures that can be used for particular behaviors.

ISSUES IN THE ASSESSMENT OF OVERT PERFORMANCE

Discussion of the alternative observational strategies and conditions of assessment may imply that measuring overt behavior is a relatively straightforward enterprise. Actually, several issues arise regarding how the measures are obtained, the extent to which the measures represent performance of the client, and interpretation of the measure.

Interobserver Agreement

Requirements for Overt Behavioral Assessment. Traditional assessment devices have included several standardized procedures in the form of questionnaires, inventories, checklists, and interviews. With standardized measures, psychometric investigations have examined the extent to which measures are used consistently among different investigators and examiners. However, direct measures of overt behavior are rarely standardized. The measures often are improvised to take into account individual performance characteristics of the client. Target behaviors are defined, an assessment strategy is selected, conditions of assessment are specified, and observers begin to record behavior. An obvious issue is how consistently observers record the responses. Assessment of consistency among observers is referred to as *interobserver agreement* or *reliability*. Independently of the assessment strategy, it is essential for observers to agree on the response.

Assessment of interobserver agreement is important for at least two reasons. First, assessment is useful only to the extent that it can be obtained with some degree of consistency since this is a prerequisite for obtaining a clear pattern of performance of the client. Inconsistent measurement introduces variation in the data as a function of the observers and assessment procedures. If variation is large, a systematic pattern of client performance may be obscured. High interobserver agreement minimizes the variability due to who actually observes performance. *Second,* interobserver agreement is important because it serves as a partial check of how well the target behavior is defined. If observers can readily agree on client performance, this suggests that the behavior is well defined, and those who need to identify the behaviors for purposes of intervention (e.g., parents, teachers) should be able to intervene more readily.

To assess interobserver agreement, periodic checking is required over the course of assessment. Typically, two or more observers independently observe and record performance on several occasions to check interobserver agreement. Constant checks are required to ensure that the extent of agreement is maintained over the course of the assessment. Periodic retraining of observers over the course of assessment, in addition to constant checking of agreement can help sustain consistency in completing observations.[1]

Special Considerations. Research over the last several years has demonstrated that assessment of interobserver agreement may be complicated by a variety of sources of artifact and bias (Kazdin, 1977a; Kent & Foster, 1977). One identified problem pertains to the definitions of behaviors that observers employ. When observers are initially trained to record behavior, they are likely to adhere to the intended definitions of them. Once observers master the definition, it is often assumed that they continue to apply the same definition and to record behavior accurately. However, evidence suggests that observers "drift" or gradually depart from the original definitions over time (Kent, Kanowitz, O'Leary, & Cheiken, 1977; Kent, O'Leary, Diament, & Dietz, 1974). For example, if observers record talking out in a class of students, the criterion for scoring the behavior may gradually change over time from the original definition. Whispers or brief vocalizations may be scored differently over time. The threshold for the observers to score the behavior may change.

To ensure that observers adhere to consistent definitions over time, many investigators conduct periodic training of observers throughout the assessment period. Observers may meet as a group, rate behavior in the situation or from video tapes, and receive feedback on the accuracy of the observations. The feedback conveys how correctly observers invoke the definitions for scoring behavior and helps reduce drift from the original behavioral codes (DeMaster, Reid, & Twentyman, 1977).

Another problem pertains to how checks of interobserver agreement are conducted. A major factor that may influence interobserver agreement is whether observers know that their agreement is being checked. When observers are aware that reliability is being assessed, they tend to show higher agreement than when they are led to believe their agreement is not under scrutiny (e.g., Kent et al., 1974, 1977). Also, knowledge that reliability is being assessed may even influence the behaviors that observers record. In some studies, observers have recorded less

---

[1] A major issue regarding reliability of observational data pertains to the methods of computing interobserver agreement. Several options are available, depending upon the assessment strategy that has been selected and characteristics of the data. The computation of interjudgement agreement is beyond the scope of the present paper and has been carefully elaborated in several other sources (see for example, *Journal of Applied Behavior Analysis,* 1977, *10* (1) for a series of papers).

disruptive child behavior when they were aware that their agreement was checked than when they were unaware (Reid, 1970; Romanczyk, Kent, Diament, & O'Leary, 1973.).

It is important to make the conditions of assessment consistent on days that reliability is and is not assessed. It may be useful to convey that all observations are being checked, so that the data obtained on days with actual reliability assessment will not differ from nonchecked days. Since observers tend to be more accurate when they believe their agreement is assessed, keeping them aware and informed of frequent reliability checks might be advantageous, even on days when no checks are made (Reid, 1970; Taplin & Reid, 1973).

In general, the interpretability of measures of overt performance depend on the evidence regarding interobserver agreement. In addition, the specific conditions under which agreement is obtained, as highlighted above, are important to specify as well. Data on client performance are not simply a function of what the client does, but depend upon several facets of observer agreement and how that agreement is assessed and estimated.

Situational Specificity

An underlying assumption of most measurement techniques is that the measures provide a sample of behavior that reflect important areas of performance beyond the testing situation. The main interest usually is not in the specific content of the measure, but in the construct or larger areas of performance that the measure samples. For example, self-report measures are important in part because the responses reflect a larger domain of behavior which extends well beyond the specific test items and endorsements completed by the client. However, there is an inferential leap from the client's report of various responses to the actual performance which these responses putatively reflect. Responses to assessment inventories, particularly self-report measures, cannot, of course, automatically be accepted at face value. The responses may or may not reflect actual performance in everyday life.

Assessment of overt behavior has been considered as a distinct methodological advance because performance is measured directly. If overt behaviors are sampled directly, the inferential leap from test performance to actual behavior is narrowed or even possibly eliminated. Unfortunately, direct observations of overt performance do not necessarily reflect actual performance in everyday situations. Performance tends to be specific to the situations and conditions under which it is assessed, a phenomenon commonly referred to as *situational specificity*.

Hence, direct observation of behavior may not necessarily reflect performance outside of the special conditions under which assessment has been conducted (Mischel, 1968; Kazdin, 1979c).

Overt performance is a direct function of several variables, such as the information, context, and cues provided to the client. For example, several studies that assess fear have shown that instructions encouraging subjects to approach the feared stimulus lead to greater levels of approach behavior than those which exclude such encouragement (Bernstein, 1973; Borkovec, 1973; Kazdin, 1973). The setting in which the performance is assessed when either perceived different by the subject or actually different may dictate the performance that is obtained. For example, Bernstein and Nietzel (1973) found that greater fear was evinced by subjects assessed in the "clinic" setting than those assessed in the "laboratory" setting. In the context of child behavior, differences in behavior across settings was examined by Wahler (1975), who measured several behaviors at school and at home. In each setting, children evinced "cluster" of behavior (i.e., responses that tended to covary within a particular setting), but the clusters in one setting differed from those in another. Thus, different conclusions might be reached from direct observations of performance of a particular behavior in one setting rather than another.

Finally, the obtrusiveness of overt behavioral assessment may influence performance. As noted earlier, when subjects are aware that their behaviors are being assessed, their performance may change. Subjects frequently perform differently on similar measures depending upon whether they are aware or unaware that their behavior is being assessed (Johnson, Christensen, & Bellamy, 1976; Roberts & Renzaglia, 1965). For example, Bellack et al. (1979) assessed heterosocial skills of male and female college students and found only low to moderate correlations between similar behaviors assessed across obtrusive and unobtrusive assessment conditions.

The above research suggests that direct samples of overt behavior may be specific to the assessment situations, and that observations obtained under one set of conditions need not necessarily reflect performance in other situations. As noted earlier, assessment can vary along several dimensions, such as whether observations are obtained under naturalistic versus contrived conditions, in clinic versus natural settings, and under obtrusive or unobtrusive assessment conditions. The extent to which performance under one set of conditions extends to similar behaviors under other conditions remains to be investigated.

Much of behavioral assessment is conducted under conditions that depart considerably from the situation to which the investigator wishes to generalize. Assessment may include different conditions that depart from everyday situations. The generality of results from one set of conditions to another may be tenuous. For example, Martin, Johnson, Johansson, and Wahl (1976) examined the relationship between parents' responses toward children under contrived conditions in the clinic and observations at home. Little or no relationship was found in parental responses under these different assessment conditions. In some instances negative correlations were found, suggesting an inverse relationship between clinic performance and performance in the home setting.

In general, direct observations of overt performance add considerably to an assessment battery that might otherwise be restricted to paper and pencil inventories, self-report measures, ratings by significant others, and psychophysiological responses. However, assessment of overt performance does not *ipso facto* provide samples of behavior that necessarily represent performance beyond a relatively restricted set of conditions.

Interpretation of Observational Data

A major advantage of many traditional assessment techniques is that a particular person's score conveys where he or she falls with respect to the larger population. Normative samples (''norms'') have been obtained for many psychological tests and inventories to provide the basis for interpreting test performance. A potential problem with measures of overt behavior is that a person's performance is difficult to interpret or place within the larger context of his or her peers. Of course, in principle the measures of overt performance do not preclude normalization samples; however, such samples have only rarely been assessed. Therefore, unless performance on the measure of overt behavior is so extreme that a behavior is never or virtually never performed (e.g., severe social withdrawal), or is performed excessively (e.g., overeating), the client's standing on the measure may be difficult to interpret.

For many overt behaviors assessed in treatment, it would be useful to have normative data. Among the many uses of such information, normative data could serve as a basis for identifying clients whose behaviors warrant treatment and provide a basis for evaluating the extent to which treatment produced an important change (see Hartmann, Roper, & Bradford, 1979). Recently, the notion of *social validation* has been proposed and refers to consideration of the social context for examining the behaviors focused upon in treatment, the acceptability of the treatment techniques, and the magnitude of treatment effects (Wolf, 1978). For present purposes, aspects of social validation that are especially germane are the use of data from the social context to determine the need for treatment and to evaluate the extent to which changes produced in the client are clinically important (Kazdin, 1977b).

Important information about the focus of treatment and the magnitude of treatment effects can be obtained by comparing the performance of the client with his or her peers. The client's peers include persons who are similar to the subject on demographic variables but who are believed to differ in the target behavior. Specifically, the client's behavior is observed becuse he or she has been identified as in need of treatment. The peers are observed because they are believed to be performing well or at least adequately with respect to the target behavior. Presumably if the performance of the client departs considerably from peers before treatment, credence is lent to the behavioral measures. It is quite possible that the behaviors of the client would not depart from peers, in which case either the critical behaviors have not been observed or some features of the measurement system (e.g., interobserver agreement) require futher improvements.

The collection of normative data is also useful for examining the magnitude of treatment effects. If treatment is highly effective, observations of overt performance would be expected to show that the client's behavior falls within the normative range. Although there is no agreed upon "normative range," one might expect to find that the client's performance after treatment approaches or surpasses the mean level of the normative group (e.g., $\pm$ 1 standard deviation). Normative data have been used in several studies using measures of overt performance to evaluate the extent to which treatment has produced clinically important changes. The magnitude of change has been evaluated with normative data in treatment studies for children with social withdrawal and conduct problems, adults who are unassertive, and mentally retarded persons with self-care deficits (e.g., Azrin & Armstrong, 1973; Kazdin, 1979b; Patterson, 1974; Walker & Hops, 1976).

Since the use of normative data to clarify the meaning of observational data has yet to receive widespread use, performance on various measures of overt behavior are not always readily interpretable. Intervention programs can show that the client's performance on a particular measure is low or high and that treatment results in changes in the obviously appropriate direction (e.g., decrease in episodes of enuresis or aggressive acts; increase in exercise or school attendance). Many behavioral interventions focus on extreme behaviors, so that normative data are not required to identify the problem. However, even here normative data on overt behavior may be of considerable value in evaluating the magnitude of treatment effects.

FUTURE CONSIDERATIONS

Since the routine collection of observational data in treatment research is a relatively recent development, fundamental questions remain regarding the problems and methods of observational assessment and the meaning of performance-based data. Future research is likely to proceed along several lines to develop performance-based assessment techniques. In particular, two general lines of research seem to be important.

To begin with, several issues need to be addressed pertaining to the interrelationship among alternative measures of overt performance. Since behavioral assessment has embraced the view that assessment needs to incorporate multiple modalities or response channels, research often includes measures based upon self-report, overt performance, and psychophysiology. Although assessment of different modalities is important, one should not ignore within modality variation among alternative measures. For measures of overt performance for example, a great deal of research is needed to elaborate the interrelationship among alternative measures of the "same" or similar responses. As highlighted earlier, the need exists to evaluate the conditions under which overt performance is assessed and the impact of these conditions on generality of the results beyond the assessment situation. Hopefully, future research will address the interrelationships among alternative methods of overt behavioral assessment and the conditions under which assessment is obtained.

A second line of inquiry that may increase in the future pertains to the interrelationship of various measures of overt performance and other measures including self-report, ratings of others, and psychophysiological responses. Rachman and Hodgson (1974; Hodgson & Rachman, 1974) have suggested that over the course of treatment, changes in client performance among multiple measures may not correspond, i.e., are *desynchronous*. The lack of correspondence among measures and the rate of change among alternative measures raises important theoretical and practical questions that should receive systematic attention in future research.

A related issue that has recently prompted research is the relationship between measures of overt performance in the client and reactions or evaluations of other persons in contact with the client. Although an important consideration in treatment is altering overt performance, it may also be important to assess how differently others in the environment evaluate the client as a result of behavior change. For example, investigators have recently examined the extent to which changes in the social behaviors of delinquent youths are evaluated by people in everyday situations who are likely to have contact with them (e.g., Maloney et al., 1976; Minkin et al., 1976). In future research, it is likely that additional attention will be devoted to examining the relationship between behavior change and how clients are perceived by others in everyday life. Such research will further elaborate the social impact that current treatments have on client functioning (Kazdin, 1977b; Wolf, 1978).

SUMMARY

The present chapter has focused on assessment of overt performance, often considered the salient characteristic of behavioral assessment. Assessment of overt performance involves several steps. First, the target behaviors need to be carefully defined so that objective, clear, and complete definitions are provided. Second, the assessment strategy needs to be specified. Major strategies are based upon frequency, discrete categorization, number of clients, interval recording, or duration. Finally, the conditions of assessment need to be defined. Major dimensions that distinguish assessment conditions include naturalistic versus contrived observations, clinic versus natural settings, and obtrusive versus unobtrusive assessment.

Several issues were discussed regarding the assessment of overt behavior. Major issues include the requirement of assessing interobserver agreement and problems that arise in obtaining estimates of agreement, the situational specificity of overt performance, and the use of normative data to identify clients whose behaviors warrant treatment and to evaluate the magnitude of treatment effects. Finally, future directions were discussed, including the interrelationships among alternative measures of overt performance and among measures of overt performance with measures from other modalities. Assessment of overt performance has made major contributions to treatment evaluation by extending the information about client change. However, in the process many questions have been raised that warrant attention in their own right.

REFERENCES

Azrin, H. H., & Armstrong, P. M. The "mini-meal"—a method for teaching eating skills to the profoundly retarded. *Mental Retardation,* 1973, *11,* 9–13.

Bellack, A. S., Hersen, M., & Lamparski, D. Role-play tests for assessing social skills: Are thy valid? Are they useful? *Journal of Consulting and Clinical Psychology,* 1979, *47,* 335–342.

Bernstein, D. A. Behavioral fear assessment: Anxiety or artifact? In H. Adams & I. P. Unikel (Eds.), *Issues and trends in behavior therapy.* Springfield, Illinois: Charles C. Thomas, 1973.

Bernstein, D. A., & Nietzel, M. T. Procedural variation in behavioral avoidance tests. *Journal of Consulting and Clinical Psychology*, 1973, *41*, 165–174.

Borkovec, T. D. The effects on instructional suggestion and physiological cues on analogue fear. *Behavior Therapy*, 1973, *4*, 185–192.

Buell, J., Stoddard, P., Harris, F., & Baer, D. M. Collateral social development accompanying reinforcement of outdoor play in a preschool child. *Journal of Applied Behavior Analysis*, 1968, *1*, 167–173.

Bunck, T. J., & Iwata, B. A. Increasing senior citizen participation in a community-based nutritious meal program. *Journal of Applied Behavior Analysis*, 1978, *11*, 75–86.

Ciminero, A. R., Calhoun, K. S., & Adams, H. E. (Eds.) *Handbook of behavioral assessment.* New York: Wiley, 1977.

Clark, H. B., Greene, B. F., Macrae, J. W., McNees, M. P., Davis, J. L., & Risley, T. R. A parent advice package for family shopping trips: Development and evaluation. *Journal of Applied Behavior Analysis*, 1977, *10*, 605–624.

DeMaster, B., Reid, J., & Twentyman, C. The effects of different amounts of feedback on observer's reliability. *Behavior Therapy*, 1977, *8*, 317–329.

Fichter, M. M., Wallace, C. J., Liberman, R. P., & Davis, J. R. Improving social interaction in a chronic psychotic using discriminated avoidance ("nagging"): Experimental analysis and generalization. *Journal of Applied Behavior Analysis*, 1976, *9*, 377–386.

Fjellstedt, N., & Sulzer-Azaroff, B. Reducing the latency of a child's responding to instructions by means of a token system. *Journal of Applied Behavior Analysis*, 1973, *6*, 125–130.

Frederiksen, L. W., Jenkins, J. O., Foy, D. W., & Eisler, R. M. Social skills training to modify abusive verbal outbursts in adults. *Journal of Applied Behavior Analysis*, 1976, *9*, 117–125.

Gaul, D. J., Craighead, W. E., & Mahoney, M J. Relationship between eating rates and obesity. *Journal of Consulting and Clinical Psychology*, 1975, *43*, 123–125.

Goldfried, M. R., & Kent, R. N. Traditional vs. behavioral personality assessment: A comparison of methodological and theoretical assumptions. *Psychological Bulletin*, 1972, *77*, 409–420.

Greene, B. F., Willis, B. S., Levy, R., & Bailey, J. S. Measuring client gains from staff-implemented programs. *Journal of Applied Behavior Analysis*, 1978, *11*, 395–412.

Hartmann, D. P., Roper, B. L., & Bradford, D. C. Some relationships between behavioral and traditional assessment. *Journal of Behavioral Assessment*, 1979, *1*, 3–21.

Hauserman, N., Water, S. R. & Behling, M. Reinforced racial integration in the first grade: A study in generalization. *Journal of Applied Behavior Analysis*, 1973, *6*, 193–200.

Hawkins, R. P., & Dobes, R. W. Behavioral definitions in applied behavior analysis: Explicit or implicit. In B. C. Etzel, J. M. LeBlanc, & D. M. Baer (Eds.), *New developments in behavioral research: Theory, methods, and applications. In honor of Sidney W. Bijou.* Hillsdale, New Jersey: Lawrence Erlbaum Associates, 1975.

Hodgson, R., & Rachman, S. II. Desynchrony in measures of fear. *Behaviour Research and Therapy*, 1974, *12*, 319–326.

Hollandsworth, J. G., Glazeski, R. C., & Dressel, M. E. Use of social-skills training in the treatment of extreme anxiety and deficient verbal skills in the job-interview setting. *Journal of Applied Behavior Analysis*, 1978, *11*, 259–269.

Horner, R. D., & Keilitz, I. Training mentally retarded adolescents to brush their teeth. *Journal of Applied Behavior Analysis*, 1975, *8*, 301–309.

Johnson, S. M., Christensen, A., & Bellamy, G. T. Evaluation of family intervention through unobtrusive audio recordings: Experience in "bugging" children. *Journal of Applied Behavior Analysis,* 1976, *9,* 213–219.

Kazdin, A. E. The effect of suggestion and pretesting on avoidance reduction in fearful college students. *Journal of Behavior Therapy and Experimental Psychiatry,* 1973, *4,* 213–221.

Kazdin, A. E. Artifact, bias, and complexity of assessment: The ABC's of reliability. *Journal of Applied Behavior Analysis,* 1977, *10,* 141–150.(a)

Kazdin, A. E. Assessing the clinical or applied significance of behavior change through social validation. *Behavior Modification,* 1977, *1,* 427–452.(b)

Kazdin, A. E. Direct observations as unobtrusive measures in treatment evaluation. *New Directions for Methodology of Behavioral Science,* 1979, *1,* 19–31.(a)

Kazdin, A. E. Imagery elaboration and self-efficacy in the covert modeling treatment of assertive behavior. *Journal of Consulting and Clinical Psychology,* 1979, *47,* 725–733.(b)

Kazdin, A. E. Situational specificity: The two-edged sword of behavioral assessment. *Behavioral Assessment,* 1979, *1,* 57–75.(c)

Kazdin, A. E. Unobtrusive measures in behavioral assessment. *Journal of Applied Behavior Analysis,* 1979, *12,* 713–724.(d)

Kent, R. N., & Foster, S. L. Direct observational procedures: Methodological issues in naturalistic settings. In A. R. Ciminero, K. S. Calhoun, & H. E. Adams (Eds.), *Handbook of behavioral assessment.* New York: Wiley, 1977.

Kent, R. N., O'Leary, K. D., Diament, C., & Dietz, A. Expectation biases in observational evaluation of therapeutic change. *Journal of Consulting and Clinical Psychology,* 1974, *42,* 774–780.

Lattal, K. A. Contingency management of toothbrushing behavior in a summer camp for children. *Journal of Applied Behavior Analysis,* 1969, *2,* 195–198.

Leitenberg, H., Agras, W. S., Thompson, L. D., & Wright, D. E. Feedback in behavior modification: An experimental analysis in two phobic cases. *Journal of Applied Behavior Analysis,* 1968, *1,* 131–137.

Maloney, D. M., Harper, T. M., Braukmann, C. J., Fixsen, D. L., Phillips, E. L., & Wolf, M. M. Teaching conversation-related skills to predelinquent girls. *Journal of Applied Behavior Analysis,* 1976, *9,* 371.

Martin, S., Johnson, S. M., Johansson, S., & Wahl, G. The comparability of behavioral data in laboratory and natural settings. In E. Mash, L. Hamerlynck, & L. Handy (Eds.), *Behavior modification and families.* New York: Brunner/Mazel, 1976.

McFall, R. M., & Marston, A. R. An experimental investigation of behavior rehearsal in assertive training. *Journal of Abnormal Psychology,* 1970, *76,* 295–303.

Michel, W. *Personality and assessment,* New York: Wiley, 1968.

Minkin, N., Braukmann, C. J., Minkin, B. L., Timbers, G. D., Timbers, B. J., Fixsen, D. L. Phillips, E. L., & Wolf, M. M. The social validation and training of conversational skills. *Journal of Applied Behavior Analysis,* 1976, *9,* 127–139.

Neef, N. A., Iwata, B. A., & Page, T. J. Public transportation training: *In vivo* versus classroom instruction. *Journal of Applied Behavior Analysis,* 1978, *11,* 331–344.

Nelson, R. O., & Hayes, S. C. Some current dimensions of behavioral assessment. *Behavioral Assessment,* 1979, *1,* 1–16.

Patterson, G. R. Interventions for boys with conduct problems: Multiple settings, treatments, and criteria. *Journal of Consulting and Clinical Psychology,* 1974, *42,* 471–481.

Patterson, G. R., Hops, H., & Weiss, R. L. Interpersonal skills training for couples in early stages of conflict. *Journal of Marriage and the Family,* 1975, *37,* 295–304.

Paul, G. L., & Lentz, R. J. *Psychosocial treatment of chronic mental patients: Milieu versus social-learning programs.* Cambridge, Massachusetts: Harvard University Press, 1977.

Peacock, R., Lyman, R. D., & Rickard, H. C. Correspondence between self-report and observer-report as a function of task difficulty. *Behavior Therapy,* 1978, *9,* 578–583.

Phillips, E. L. Achievement Place: Token reinforcement procedures in a home-style reha-bilitation setting for "pre-delinquent" boys. *Journal of applied behavior Analysis,* 1968, *1,* 213–223.

Rachman, S., & Hodgson, R. I. Synchrony and desynchrony in fear and avoidance. *Behaviour Research and Therapy,* 1974, *12,* 311–318.

Reid, J. B. Reliability assessment of observation data: A possible methodological prob-lem. *Child Development,* 1970, *41,* 1143–1150.

Repp, A. C., & Deitz, S. M. Reducing aggressive and self-injurious behavior of in-stitutionalized retarded children through reinforcement of other behaviors. *Journal of Applied Behavior Analysis,* 1974, *7,* 313–325.

Roberts, R. R., & Renzaglia, G. A. The influence of tape recording on counseling. *Journal of Counsleing Psychology,* 1965, *12,* 10–16.

Romanczyk, R. G., Kent, R. N., Diament, C., & O'Leary, K. D. Measuring the re-liability of observational data: A reactive process. *Journal of Applied Behavior Anal-ysis,* 1973, *6,* 175–184.

Russo, D. C., & Koegel, R. L. A method for integrating an autistic child into a normal public school classroom. *Journal of Applied Behavior Analysis,* 1977, *10,* 579–590.

Sajwaj, T., Twardosz, S., & Burke, M. Side effects of extinction procedures in a re-medial preschool. *Journal of Applied Behavior Analysis,* 1972, *5,* 163–175.

Stokes, T. F., Baer, D. M., & Jackson, R. L. Programming the generalization of a greeting response in four retarded children. *Journal of Applied Behavior Analysis,* 1974, *7,* 599–610.

Taplin, P. S., & Reid, J. B. Effects of instructional set and experimenter influence on observer reliability. *Child Development,* 1973, *44,* 547–554.

Twardosz, S., Schwartz, S., Fox, J., & Cunningham, J. L. Development and evaluation of a system to measure affectionate behavior. *Behavioral Assessment,* 1979, *1,* 177–190.

Wahler, R. G. Some structural aspects of deviant child behavior. *Journal of Applied Behavior Analysis,* 1975, *8,* 27–42.

Walker, H. M., & Hops, H. Use of normative peer data as a standard for evaluating classroom treatment effects. *Journal of Applied Behavior Analysis,* 1976, *9,* 159–168.

Wolf, M. M. Social validity: The case for subjective measurement of how applied be-havior analysis is finding its heart. *Journal of Applied Behavior Analysis,* 1978, *11,* 203—214.

Chapter 5
Self-Report and the Assessment of Cognitive Functions*

Steven D. Hollon
and
Kelly M. Bemis

In no case may we interpret an action as the outcome of the exercise of a higher psychical faculty, if it can be interpreted as the outcome of the exercise of one which stands lower in psychological scale [Lloyd Morgan, 1894].

Nature is notoriously prodigal; why should we interpret only parsimoniously? [Boring, 1950, p. 475].

It is reasonable to conclude that many of the phenomena of learning experiments cannot economically be described in simple stimulus-response terms. The theorist who would attempt to do so must concede that the covert responses have behavioral laws different from those governing overt responses: such a conclusion results in a loss of the logic of the stimulus-response approach [Hinde, 1970, pp. 591-592].

*Preparation of this chapter was supported, in part, by PHS Grant 1R01MH32209-01 to the senior author, the University of Minnesota, and the Medical Education and Research Foundation Grant #6287, Department of Psychiatry, St. Paul-Ramsey Medical Center, St. Paul, Minnesota. We would like to thank Judy Garber for her comments on an earlier version of this manuscript, and the several colleagues, particularly Lyn Abramson, Aaron Beck, and Philip Kendall, with whom we have discussed and debated many of the issues we have attempted to address. We would also like to thank Mary Jones for her secretarial assistance in the preparation of this manuscript.

INTRODUCTION

Basic Questions

In this chapter, we will be concerned with the assessment of cognition. Several questions can be raised about this endeavor:

1. *What are we trying to assess?* What do we mean when we say cognition? What distinguishes cognition from other types of phenomena? What are the components of this phenomenon with which we need to be concerned?
2. *Why are we trying to assess cognition?* What are the purposes of cognitive assessment? Why is it important to incorporate cognitive assessment (as opposed to the assessment of noncognitive phenomena) to meet these purposes? What can we learn about the role of cognition in the etiology, maintenance, and, perhaps, reduction of psychopatholoy?
3. *How are we to assess cognition?* What are the ways in which we are to go about assessing cognition? What tools can we use? What are the procedures to follow? What are the errors to avoid?
4. *Where are we to assess cognitions?* Under what circumstances and in which contexts is assessment most meaningful? Does the nature of the setting color the quality of the assessment? If so, can we develop procedures which compensate for various pragmatic constraints?
5. *When are we to assess cognition?* At what temporal point is assessment most meaningful? Do basic processes underlying the phenomenon dictate the optimal temporal strategies?

In this chapter, we address each of these questions, although not necessarily in the specific order listed. We begin with a discussion of the reasons for an interest in cognitive assessment, then move on to the remaining issues. Our intent is to provide an overview of the process of cognitive assessment that outlines the various procedures which have been developed, while addressing the conceptual and methodological problems inherent in those procedures.

The title of this chapter, "Self-Report and the Assessment of Cognitive Functions," represents an intentional misnomer. Self-report and cognitive function have been linked to one another by association, not necessity. Self-report entails a method of data collection; cognitive function is a phenomenon or set of phenomena inferred to exist (and/or occur) on the basis of the observation of events. A phenomenon inferred to exist on the basis of observations generated by a methodology should not be equated with that methodology. While our knowledge of a process may be based on a given methodology, the existence of the phenomenon is not dependent on the validity of that set of operations.

We will target our discussion to those cognitive processes of greatest interest to scientists and practitioners interested in behavior change. Thus, we will be less interested in basic cognitive processes (e.g., learning, memory information processes, etc.) than in the role such processes play in inducing, maintaining, and alleviating psychopathology. In all events, our basic emphasis will be on the assessment of these processes.

WHY ASSESS COGNITIONS?

What Goals are to be Met?

Kendall and Korgeski (1979) have outlined some of the purposes to be served by cognitive assessment. In brief, these include: (1) an interest in the processes and contents of the phenomenon itself; (2) an interest in clarifying what role, if any, such cognitions play in the etiology or maintenance of psychopathology; (3) an interest in ascertaining whether those change strategies that allegedly work by means of altering cognitive content and process actually do so by changing those contents and processes; and (4) an interest in determining whether those procedures seen as involving the manipulation of cognition are adequately implemented. Thus, accurate cognitive assessment is necessary whether one is interested in cognition as a phenomenon in and of itself (dependent variable), as a mechanism in those processes producing either inductive or reductive change in other phenomena of interest (intervening variable), or as a manipulation check for an experimental or clinical intervention (independent variable). In any of these events, our interest may extend to either basic psychopathological or treatment outcome research. As we shall describe, the purposes for which we intend our assessment may help guide our selection of the means.

How Does Assessing Cognitions Help Reach These Goals?

Cognition assessment is a notoriously risky endeavour. Given our inability to directly observe another person's cognitions, and given that we are generally interested in their content, we are dependent on indirect means of observation subject to inaccuracy and reactivity. Why, then, bother to assess cognition?

As Mahoney (1977a) has argued, the return of an interest in such alleged phenomena is motivated by their hypothesized role as more than epiphenomenal mediators of important human processes. Mahoney considers four assertions to be the essence of a cognitive-learning perspective:

1. The human organism responds primarily to cognitive representations of its environments rather than to those environments per se.
2. These cognitive representations are functionally related to the processes and parameters of learning.
3. Most human learning is cognitively mediated.
4. Thoughts, feelings, and behaviors are causally interactive [pp. 7–8].

Mahoney then infers several predictions from these propositions:

1. If the model is valid, then such constructs as beliefs or expectancies should be better predictors of human behavior than external variables; that is, when there is a discrepancy between a person's cognitions and reality (as externally defined), the former should account for more of his 'experiential variance' than the latter, and a combined prediction should be better yet.
2. Each class of events (i.e., cognitions and behaviors) can be said to be causal of the other; events at one point in time in one class can play a role in determining the nature of events at a later point in time in the other class. Causality is said to be interactive between classes (although unidirectional over time), a relationship called *reciprocal determinism* by Bandura (1978).

Since these two predictions are subject to verification, they are testable. Attention to presumably cognitive processes can be said to increase our capacity to predict (account for) variability in important, directly observable, noncognitive phenomena. These same processes, if manipulated, can cause variance in the latter noncognitive phenomena. Evidence speaking to these predictions has been reviewed extensively elsewhere (e.g., Bandura, 1969; Brewer, 1974; Grings, 1973; Hollon Kendall, 1979; Mahoney, 1974; Meichenbaum, 1977), and will not be addressed in this chapter. For our purposes, it is sufficient to note that cognitive processes can be hypothesized to be more than epiphenomena and subject to the adequacy of assessment methodologies, can be subjected to potential empirical verification. Whatever its outcome, such an effort is clearly within the bounds of an empirical behavioral science. We recognize that it is not necessary to accept a proposition as being valid in order to conduct a test of that proposition. What is necessary is that operations for the assessment of key conceptual units in that proposition be available. Our intent is to highlight major operating factors which facilitate or hinder the generation of evidence relevant to those predictions.

Cognition and Behavioral Models of Psychopathology

We assume, though it has never been proven, that variance in the etiology of psychopathology has its roots in the differential experiences of organisms. In one classical conditioning model of phobia acquisition, for example, phobic anxiety is viewed as a conditioned response (CR) stemming from the unfortunate, possibly coincidental, pairing of an initially neutral to-be-conditioned stimulus (CS) with a *universally* noxious unconditioned stimulus (UCS) (e.g., Wolpe, 1978). Similarly, some operant theories of depression view this condition as being the consequence of an environment in which reinforcements (S*'s) are too infrequent to support appropriate behaviors (R's) (see Ferster, 1973). The emphasis is on variance across the experienced environments to which essentially equivalent organisms are exposed.

Yet, is it not possible at least in some instances, that it is the variance in the nature of the *organism* which is most powerfully related to the development or (in the context of therapy) the reduction of psychopathology? We clearly have one example in the incidence of bipolar affective disorders, in which carefully controlled monozygotic/dizygotic twin inheritance studies have pointed to a strong genetic predisposition (see Bertelson, Harvald, & Hauge, 1977). We are unaware of any current behavioral (i.e., environmentally-focused) theory of mania which can account for these findings. Once we acknowledge that the locus of a disorder may reside, at least in part or at times, with processes occurring within the organism, the issue then becomes one of defining the nature of those processes.

There are at least two ways in which cognitive processes may play a role in the etiology and/or maintenance of psychopathology. First, there may be basic dysfunctions in biochemistry, acquired or inherited, which manifest themselves, at least in part, as aberrations in information processing. Such a model is clearly the current dominant model of the etiology of schizophrenia. A more subtle variation on this theme might well involve an overly arousable nervous system that, when confronted with a given noxious stimulus, is more likely than the typical nervous system to develop a strong, negative reaction, thus leading to a greater capacity for aversive conditioning.

The second type of role need not involve basic dysfunction in the biochemical basis of information processing. Rather, an organism with a nervous system functioning normally might well learn certain propositions that are: (1) the erroneous consequence of the misperception or misinterpretation of a situation; (2) inappropriately generalized to other situations; or (3) inaccurately combined with other cognitions and altered in such a fashion as to produce new cognitions (insights) which are inaccurate or dysfunctional. Even such a staunch behaviorist as Wolpe (1978) argues that such errors in thinking occur *and* can lead to the development of psychopathological states, although he argues that such etiologies are rare, subsumed by the same functional alterations in the control nervous system as experienced environmental events, and are ultimately remediated most readily by classical conditioning procedures.

As a direct clinical example, one of the authors (Hollon) once worked with a 40-year-old male client exhibiting primary impotence. A major source of his anxiety surrounding attempted intercourse came from a misunderstanding of which partner would experience pain, tissue damage, and bleeding as a consequence of his or her *first* heterosexual experience. As typified by this example, the errors are essentially ones of information processing. Such cognitive processes would ultimately be biochemically mediated, but the biochemical system could well be essentially well-functioning.

There is little doubt that various types of psychopathology, or at least, some components of those various psychopathologies, can be induced by means of environmental manipulations. Examples include Watson and Rayner's induction of phobic anxiety in Little Albert (Watson & Rayner, 1920), or depression following events (such as loss of a loved one or incarceration) which presumably limit access to desirable reinforcers (see Averill, 1968). But, as Davison and Neale (1978) point out, demonstrating that a causal relationship *can* exist does not prove that it actually occurs in nature. This error in logic, labeled *affirming the consequent,* becomes particularly untenable when pushed to the extreme of arguing that a demonstrated causal relationship is the *sole* causal relationship.

What has all this to do with cognitive assessment? Such arguments play an obvious role in attempting to justify cognitive models of psychopathology, thereby increasing the importance of assessing cognition. While being able to generate a plausible account does not prove a case, it does encourage researchers to test that formulation. While less obvious, it may potentially be more critical to recognize that cognitive factors have played a role in our earlier attempts to generate observations of behavioral and/or environmental events. In several instances, we may well have misconstrued variance in cognitive processes as variance in behaviors and/or environmental events.

One example will suffice. Lewinsohn and colleagues have conducted a program of research over the past decade in which they have sought to relate variance in pleasant (and, later, unpleasant) environmental events to variance in syndrome depression (see Lewinsohn, 1975; Lewinsohn & Graf, 1973; Lewinsohn & Libet, 1972). The problem with this program of research is that the investigators have relied on variations of the Pleasant Events Schedule (PES: MacPhillamy & Lewinsohn, 1971), a self-report instrument on which subjects were asked to retrospectively endorse the events that they had experienced over a given period of time. Given the absence of appropriate validational studies, we do not know whether subjects were reporting events that had occurred, or events *remembered* to have occurred. Studies that controlled for the actual occurrence of events have provided clear evidence of a negative distortion in the recall of events in depressed subjects (e.g., Evans & Hollon, 1979; Lishman, 1972; Lloyd & Lishman, 1975). While Lewinsohn and colleagues' program has been an extremely productive one, it remains possible that they have overestimated the role of environmental events in the etiology and/or maintenance of depression by relying on an assessment strategy which may well confound the occurrence of events with subjective (potentially cognitive) biasing factors.

WHAT DO WE ASSESS?

Basic Definitions

At this point, it is important to define several key concepts. *Cognition,* as defined by the American College Dictionary (Barnhart, 1947), can be defined as either "The act or process of knowing; perception," or the "product of such a process." Since this dual definition is both serviceable and informative, we do not feel compelled to alter it. Such a definition is informative because it points to what we regard as a critical distinction between process and content. We will argue in a later section that much of the literature regarding the difficulties of securing accurate self-report of cognition from humans (see Nisbett & Wilson, 1977) has focused on process: i.e., people being asked to introspect and discern what steps in information processing have occurred. We believe the products or contents are far more accessible to introspection, and therefore more amenable to valid self-report.

Conscious, as defined by the same dictionary, means to be "awake to one's own existence, sensations, cognitions, etc.; endowed with consciousness . . . (or) . . . inwardly sensible or awake to something.

. . ." In behavioral terms, being conscious of *"something,"* with respect to cognition, can be redefined as the self-observation of a presumably covert process. We are not wholly satisfied with the standard term "self-statements," because we think that some very important cognitive content may be more evocative of visual, tactile, olfactory, or gustatory sensations. We concur with the radical behaviorists that, at the present there appears to be no direct way of observing whether or not cognition actually occurs. But, as Mahoney (1974; 1977a) points out, the sciences frequently deal with unobservable (but not unmeasurable) phenomena. It would seem that processes and products of cognition can be as reasonably inferred to exist on the basis of *universal* self-report and crude indications of biochemical-electrical activity (e.g., Penfield, 1969; Penfield & Perot, 1963; Penfield & Roberts, 1959), as can the occurrence of dreams on the basis of self-report and correlated REM activity. The problem, from the point of view of assessment, is not "does cognition occur?," but rather, "can the process and/or products be validly assessed?" From the theoretical viewpoint, the question is "do variations in cognition influence subsequent events in a way not wholly predictable from the immediate, preceding environment?" From the point of view of therapy, the question is "does attention to inducing change in cognition produce greater changes in processes of interest than nonattention to producing such changes in cognition?"

It is not critical that a radical behaviorist could describe some sequence of events by relying soley on concepts and processes derived from operant or classical theory. Such a task could be as readily accomplished as having a biochemist describe that same sequence of events in strictly biochemical terms. Compelling as those efforts may seem to be, such reductionistic efforts are *always* logically possible. The capacity to generate an explanation does not prove the merit of that explanation. We opened with the well known quote from Lloyd Morgan regarding parsimony because, in essence, it is such a widely invoked canon. There is no empirical law which holds that nature is parsimonious. In historical context, Morgan's canon was put forward to counter the excesses of animal behavior theorists such as Romanese, who ascribed a fantastic array of motivations and strategies to account for observed variations in behavior. If cognitive processes follow the same sets of laws and principles as other classes of behaviors, then the greatest risk we run is a semantic one; we can be reductionistic or nonreductionistic, treating cognition as an intervening variable. To the extent that cognitive processes follow somewhat different sets of laws, or follow the same sets of laws in different ways or on different schedules, then we run the risk of limiting the predictive and manipulative capacities of our behavioral science by excluding them from consideration. Ultimately, the goal of science is not to be parsimonious, but to increase understanding. We might conclude this section by pointing out that the same New World Collegiate Dictionary defines parsimony as "extreme or excessive frugality."

Accessibility: Process versus Content

Nisbett and Wilson (1977) have argued that humans are not particularly adept at reporting their own cognitive processes. The authors argue that:

1. People often cannot report accurately on the effects of particular stimuli on higher order, inference-based responses . . . .

2. When reporting the effects of stimuli, people may not interrogate a memory of the cognitive processes that operated on the stimuli; instead, they may base their reports on implicit, *a priori* theories about causal connection between stimulus and response. . . .

3. Subjective reports about higher mental processes are sometimes correct, but even the instances of correct report are not due to direct introspective awareness. Instead, they are due to the incidentally correct employment of *a priori* causal theories [p. 233].

Citing evidence from various social-psychological paradigms, the authors point out that subjects have frequently been unable to verbally report cognitive processes presumed by investigators to mediate "stimuli → cognitive processes → evaluative and motivational state change → behavior change" chains. For example, subjects given inadequate justification for taking shock learned more quickly and showed lower GSR responsivity to shock than did adequate justification subjects, but those former subjects did not report the shocks to be "less painful" (Zimbardo, Cohen, Weisenberg, Dworkin, & Firestone, 1969). Similarly, Nisbett and Wilson found that subjects were consistently unable to detect the role that left-to-right position preference played in their evaluation of articles of clothing.

If correct, what are the implications of such an argument for cognitive theories of psychopathology and behavior change? It would be premature to again relegate cognition and cognitive mediators to the role of epiphenomena. First, Nisbett and Wilson accept the tacit assumption that the cognitive processes in question are "for the most part verbal, conscious ones [p. 234]." Thus, failure to observe reportable difference in the process of cognition is regarded as embarrassing to cognitive-mediational theories. Yet, it would be a mistake to equate cognition with "that which can be introspected." Important variations in information processing may well be assessable by means other than subjective introspection (see, for example, Kihlstrom & Nasby, 1981), and these variations may well be meaningfully related to variations in subsequent behavior and affect. If Nisbitt and Wilson's point is that introspection can often be misleading or inadequate (and this appears to be their major point), then we can only concur. Introspection may often prove inadequate for some assessment purposes, yet these methodological limitations do not rule out a possible mediational role for cognition. However, even when introspection is an adequate methodology, evidence must be available from other means to suggest the operation of such central processing.

Second, Nisbett and Wilson draw a distinction between the processes and contents of cognition which we regard as particularly critical. In brief, the authors suggest that individuals are much more accurate in reporting the *contents* (products) of their cognitive activity (e.g. the beliefs, expectations, attributions, preferences, evaluations, etc.), than they are the *processes* they follow in making them. Thus, a subject may be quite capable of telling you that he/she anticipates having a 30 percent chance of succeeding on a given task but quite incapable of describing the steps involved in generating that expectation.

Cognitive approaches to psychopathology and therapy have been concerned with both products and processes. Beck (1967), for example, describes both specific beliefs (products) typically verbalized by depressed patients, (e.g., "I am a failure," "I'm a loser," "Nothing I do ever works out," "Things are hopeless,") and some of the idiosyncratic distorting processes (selective abstraction, arbitrary inference, magnification, etc.) which may describe how these beliefs are induced and/or maintained. Our experience suggests that depressed clients have a differential ability to recognize products as opposed to processes. The product-content statements are frequently verbalized, often spontaneously, and are readily recognized. Further, such statements are generally accepted as being not only representative of private events in conscious awareness, but as mirroring external reality. The process statements, on the other hand, are almost never verbalized or recognized as operating. They may even be rejected when pointed out by the clinician and require repeated evidential confirmation before being accepted as more or less accurate descriptors of the patient's cognitive processes. In short, patients can generally access products-contents and frequently misconstrue them as being "facts." Yet they are typically incapable of introspection regarding process.

We would anticipate that cognitive assessment efforts incorporating introspection will prove most satisfying when the targets are products-contents in nature, and least satisfying when processes are targeted. Efforts at discerning process may require inference based on observed variation between differential input-output sequences. In the latter event, the burden of proof will fall quite heavily on the behavioral scientist to provide operational assessment procedures which will make it possible to contrast central (cognitively-mediated) and peripheral (noncognitively-mediated) models of information processing.

Covert Self-Talk or Something Different?

Recent texts on behavioral interventions frequently refer to self-statements or covert verbalizations when referring to the alleged *contents* of cognition (e.g., Craighead, Kazdin, & Mahoney, 1976; Goldfried & Davison, 1976; Mahoney, 1974). What do these terms mean, and why are they preferred to such standard lay terms as "thought" or "cognition?"

The answer, of course, is that the latter terms have been rejected as being mentalistic and implying the existence of a phenomenon which has never been directly observed by one individual as occurring in another. As an exercise in semantic relabeling, such efforts appear relatively harmless. We do observe speech,[2] and referring to thinking in others as "covert verbalizations" or "self-statements" probably reduces arousal for the nonradical behaviorist. But do we lose anything in the process?

Turning again to our American College Dictionary, we find (to) *think* defined as: "to form or conceive in the mind; have in the mind as an idea, conception, or the like; to turn over in the mind; meditate; ponder; *to hold as an opinion; believe; suppose.*" These references to "mind" are sufficient to make even a cognitive-behaviorist shudder; but, on the whole, we could translate the first several components of the definition(s) into acceptable neurophysiologic or overtly verbalized correlates. What we could not do is directly translate the final components of the definition, "to hold as an opinion; believe; suppose," into those same correlates. A self-statement or covert verbalization may encompass some of the alleged properties of a privately monitored "thought"; it is "observed" to occur, and it has temporal, topographical, and semantic referents. What it need not encompass is any substantive estimate of the probability that the statement is valid. All thoughts are not "believed," nor are all covert verbalizations or self-statements. It is *critical* to ascertain the degree to which the subject would ascribe validity to the covert verbalization, self-statement, thought, cognition, or whatever the alleged phenomenon is labelled. One of the characteristics of these phenomena is that they may or may not be taken as an accurate indication of some type of empirically defined reality. To focus only on the alleged occurrence/nonoccurrence of these "events" is insufficient. One of the special characteristics of all phenomena that are propositional in nature (that is, symbolic representations of relationships between "things"), be they overt verbalizations, the products of certain motoric acts (such as written or typed statements), or alleged covert "whatevers," is that some estimate can be generated of how well these products validly represent reality. We need not, and indeed cannot, do this for an *act*, per se. We do not speak (or think) of a physical motion as being more or less "true"; nor do we speak of an external event (e.g., rain falling to the ground) as being true. But, whenever we are concerned with representational systems, those where signs and symbols are manipulated to convey meaning, then we can speak of the validity or reality of that representation.

In assessing covert phenomena, we typically want to concern ourselves with their occurrence or nonoccurrence (that is their status as events in time and place), their meaning (referents within whatever representational system has been adopted), and their validity (both subjective and objective). So long as we do not lose sight of these three requirements as a consequence of our relabeling, then we have no problem with interchangeably using such terms as covert verbalization, self-statement, cognition, or thought. Methodological-behaviorists can use the first two terms to refer to the inferred phenomena, cognitivists can use the last two terms to refer to the inferred phenomena, and radical behaviorists can continue to refuse to infer anything, except that others actually "observe" something.

Level of Assessment: Surface versus Deep Structures

Linguists frequently discriminate between *surface* versus *deep* structure or semantic space (Lindsay & Norman, 1977). Surface structure represents what is directly observable to at least someone: the spoken sentence, the overt self-statement, the covert self-statement. Deep structure refers to the meanings that underlie these observable referents. Our methodologies may or may not provide us with representative samples of surface structures with regard to cognitive events, but our theories often require analysis at a "deeper" level. Few modern cognitivists are interested in precisely what is said or thought, so much as in precisely what is meant. It is frequently difficult to ascertain the latter without some recourse to inference. Most typically, the major inference involved is that any two individuals in a given culture share major components of their respective propositional networks (that is, the systems of meaning, or referents, attributed to any given word set). In some cases, however, this may not be so. Therapists, for example, may come to attribute certain meanings to a given surface structure (e.g.,

"Depression may be, in part, hereditary"), which may be followed by a very different decoding by a client (e.g., "I may be responsible for my children's future misery by virtue of passing on 'bad' genes.")

Is it possible for a person to process information as if he/she holds one set of "deep structures," yet not recognize or even repudiate those structures? We think that this might be so. This would mean that an individual would reliably process input across different situations in such a way as to yield idiosyncratic contents/products which were similar to one another, yet be unaware of the propositional transformation rules that best describe the ways in which this input was transformed.

For example, take an individual who, when confronted with a spouse reading the newpaper at breakfast, a child saying "I hate you" after being reprimanded for running in the street, co-workers who eat lunch separately, and neighbors who throw a dinner party without offering an invitation, responds with hurt feelings and the belief that "nobody loves me." This person may have other available information suggesting that this belief is not true, or, at least, not totally true, but he or she appears to process each of these events as if believing the proposition, "Unless everyone loves me all the time, and gives me an indication in their every action, then no one loves me."

Our experience has been that clients are far more likely to report the first type of thought ("nobody loves me") in a variety of situations, and that they are more likely to accept its validity than they are likely to report the occurrence, or accept the validity, of the second.

In a sense, surface and deep structures are analogous to the distinction between spoken or written communications and the rules of grammar describing the procedures followed in generating those communications. While many of us can produce relatively well-formed sentences, few of us can generate (or even recognize) the rules we follow in producing them. Do we actually hold those rules in memory as propositions accessible to introspection? Are those rules part of the contents/products of cognition? Possibly, but we are inclined to doubt that this is true. More likely, these "rules" describe processes which influence information processing without themselves ever being directly coded into representational format. Are they cognitive, in the traditional sense? This is likely, though not necessarily so. Reflex arcs function as if the stove were recognized as hot and the organism cognizes that it is adaptive to remove its hand from the stove. We think it is conceivable that some or all of the "as if" propositional transformations acting to mediate input-output relationships occur outside of conscious awareness.

Ellis and colleagues (1962; Ellis & Grieger, 1978) have described sets of "irrational beliefs" and Beck (1976) has described "underlying assumptions" which appear to represent deep, "as if," transformational rules (e.g., "I must be perfect," "Everyone must love or approve of me"). While such propositions might receive differential endorsement, we would be surprised if they were spontaneously produced by clients and/or subjects. Such propositional statements might well be operative in a descriptive sense, without really being represented in a phenomenal sense. If so, this would make them very difficult to assess by means of introspection.

Beck also talks in terms of automatic thoughts, defined as phenomenally experienced propositional statements, or shards of statements. As defined, this term probably refers to the same class of events indicated by such terms as "self-statements" or "covert verbalizations." These phenomena appear to represent surface structure propositions with the first level of meaning ascribed. As such, they are likely to be both endorsed and produced. Many of our efforts at cognitive assessment might be facilitated by specifying the level of cognition to which one is referring, and selecting a format for assessment most compatible with that level of cognition. Our guess is that "deeper" structures are more likely to be endorsed than produced spontaneously, and that such endorsement is more likely to reflect acceptance of content validity than recognition of previous occurrence.

Conscious versus Nonconscious Cognition

Shevrin and Dickman (1980) reviewed evidence strongly suggestive of information processing (cognition) outside of consicious awareness. Based on evidence drawn from studies of selective attention, subliminal perception, and certain selected visual phenomena (e.g., retinal image stabilization, binocular rivalry, and backward masking), the authors drew three conclusions.:

1. The initial stages in the cognitive processing of all stimuli occur without conscious awareness.
2. Initial states are psychological in nature (i.e., they are similar in nature to common descriptions of conscious information processing such as perception, judgment, thought, affect, motivation, etc., *and* they are correlated with biochemical/electrical events in the central nervous system), have an active effect on subsequent thought and action, and differ in terms of their principles of action from conscious processing.
3. Consciousness (awareness) of any stimulus occurs later in time than nonconscious processes, and, in some events, may not occur at all.

Particularly intriguing is the suggestion that such nonconscious cognitive processes can influence autonomic nervous system arousal before they stimulate conscious awareness of their occurrence. Dixon (1971) has proposed a particularly intriguing neurophysiological model which argues that classical afferent fibers transmit information that influences both autonomic nervous system arousal and, perhaps, the nonspecific reticular system. Only when the latter system is activated does the subject become consciously cognizant of the stimuli; hence, it is possible to be activated autonomically before, and perhaps without, conscious awareness of the stimulus. According to this model, afferent connections to autonomic arousal systems transmit both more rapidly and more reliably than connections engaging systems which mediate consciousness.

In these terms, Zajonc's recent evaluation of the interrelationship between event, affect, and cognition (Zajonc, 1980), in which he argues that affective processing occurs temporally prior to cognitive processing, can be seen to be compatible if we recognize that Zajonc equates cognition with consciousness. His use of the term "pre-cognitive" is probably a dysfunctional misnomer in this case. Afferent information processing, as described by Shevrin and Dickman or Dixon, is no less cognitive because it occurs prior to or in the absence of stimulation of those nervous system processes that mediate the experience of awareness. If correct, however, these theories argue for the occurrence of cognitive processes that are more than epiphenomenal and that occur either prior to or without accompanying awareness. In essence, awareness of a stimulus may not be necessary for it to influence subsequent affect, cognition, and action.

Is such a proposition embarrassing to cognitive theories of psychopathology? In some respects, yes. If a cognitive theory of psychopathology argues that cognitive processes preceding affective states must be conscious and readily accessible, then Zajonc's conclusions, if correct, would seem to contradict such arguments. If cognition is defined as biochemical/electrical activity in the central nervous system amenable to alteration on the basis of prior conscious cognition, then such theories are less likely to be embarrassed. The issue actually involves the nature of the relationship between conscious cognitive and affective and/or motoric processes. If conscious cognitive activity can alter the nature of subsequent nonconscious processes, then cognitive theories of therapy are not compromised, though they would need to be reorganized.

Further, if we distinguish between cognitive theories of psychopathology and cognitive theories of therapy, then the question is not whether cognition, conscious or nonconscious, *typically* plays a role in the initial etiology or maintenance of psychopathology. Rather, the question becomes one of whether the manipulation of such processes (with conscious processes the most readily accessible) *can* influence subsequent cognition, feeling, or action. For theoretical purposes we need to be clear as to whether we are referring to accessible or inaccessible cognitive processes and whether we are referring to what typically happens or to what could be made to happen. For therapeutic purposes, we need only be concerned with what *could* happen, since some human agent can perform manipulations to increase the probability that something does occur.

Our quarrel with dynamic theories of psychopathology or therapy lies not with the existence or nonexistence of nonconscious cognitive processes. We must admit that the current cognitive psychological literature is persuasive; it appears to us that the nonconscious cognitive "pig does fly." Our concern lies with the degree of causal power ascribed to such processes vis-a-vis affect, conscious cognition, and motoric behavior, and most particularly with the absence of causal impact on such processes ascribed to life experiences and organismic activities after the time of early childhood. The postulation of a set of nonconscious cognitive processes is not unique to Freud, but insistence on such processes being relatively fixed from early childhood, yet almost totally decisive with regard to subsequent feeling, thinking, and action is axiomatic in Freudian thinking. We think that such dynamic models have unnecessarily elevated processes which may play a large role in determining relatively inconsequential events (e.g., slips-of-the-tongue, dream content, the emergence of spontaneous content into awareness) to the status of processes which play a large role in determining major events (e.g., motoric behaviors, guided attention, maintenance of affective states). The issue in causal terms is which set of processes is the iceberg, and which the tip. We would argue for a relatively minor role for the nonconscious processes, pointing for support to the fact that therapies based on nondynamic models can produce change much more rapidly than those based on dynamic theories. In summary, we would argue that such nonconscious cognitive processes do occur, but may be of relatively little importance, relative to more readily observable or accessible processes.

Reliance on Retrospective Report

Loftus and Loftus (1980) reviewed evidence regarding the processes associated with memorial recall which should give pause to anyone attempting to base his or her assessment on recollections of past events. In brief, the authors address the question of whether any information, once processed, is ever actually lost from central storage. This hypothesized permanence, labeled the "video tape recorder" hypothesis, was found to be the most common view of memorial processes, even more among psychologists than the lay public. This model appears largely based on observations suggesting that a variety of procedures such as hypnosis, free association, and most strikingly, electrical stimulation of the cortex (see Penfield, 1969; Penfield & Perot, 1963; Penfield & Roberts, 1959), as well as spontaneous recall, appear to promote the recall of memories previously unrecoverable (i.e., forgotten).

Pitted against this view is the hypothesis of loss or change in the material stored in the memory. Old information could be lost (supplemented by nothing), paralleled (coexisting with new constructions of old events), or substituted (altered so as to conform with such new constructions).

Reviewed evidence strongly suggests that the reported hypnotic, free association or electrical stimulation phenomena involved constructed cognitions heavily influenced by current cases and contexts, rather than literal triggerings of bona fide perceptions of past experiences. Such "video tape recordings" were likely to involve the recollection of perceptions taken from perspectives not physically possible (e.g., one woman, under electrical cortical stimulation, recalled watching herself go through labor and delivery, but from a vantage point across the room from which she could "see" her own face). Further, experimental studies involving hypnosis or free association found that recollections incorporating false cues supplied by the experimenter were readily generated (e.g., Putnam, 1979).

On the whole, the authors concluded that these various classes of recollections were most likely current reconstructions of past events colored by cues and conditions operating at the time of recall. Most critically, the evidence frequently favored the *substitution* mechanism. Under experimental conditions, current cues prompted inaccurate recall of earlier events. Further, subjects were unable to recall those past events accurately, even under high monetary incentive conditions. These findings suggested that, in at least some instances, subjects, recollections of past events were so altered by subsequent information that the altered construction was accepted and reported uncritically as the "true" construction of the earlier events.

If these conclusions are correct, they have important implications. Not only must recall of past thoughts or thought processes be considered suspect, but recall of past events, actions, and affects may also be "colored" by current cues and contexts. Further, such factors clearly work on the reconstruction processes of outside observers, just as they clearly influence self-reports. The major distinction between reports of cognition and reports of external events and/or behaviors may reside less in the probability of distortion than in our capacity to detect distortion. In any event, the greater the reliance on retrospective reconstruction, regardless of respondent or target to be assessed, the greater the likelihood of inaccurate recall.

Functional Analysis—A Cognitive Taxonomy

Contents. We start with the assumption that cognitive contents are the end products of various information processing chains. Frequently, though not always, these contents are accessible to conscious introspection and are propositional in nature, expressing relationships between a subject and a predicate. Typically, such propositional contents mimic auditory (especially verbal) stimulation. Some propositional contents may mimic other sensory channels (e.g., imagining a mathematical equation), and other types of sensory experiences are, of course, reported, sometimes as a "visual" image, or a "tactile-like" experience, or a "gustatory-like" experience, or an "olfactory-like" experience.

Can we meaningfully subdivide the various classes of propositional contents which have been of interest to cognitivists? Table 5.1 represents an effort to develop such a taxonomy.

We will restrict our attention largely to propositional content, that is, beliefs. Any propositional representation essentially consists of two or more "things"(X and Y) and the perceived relationship between them. In our taxonomy, attributions, attributes, and expectations are all examples of beliefs. Under this system, an *attribution of causality*

Table 5.1. Cognitive Taxonomy: Classes of Propositional Representations

Propositions (Beliefs):	X acts on, or is related to Y; or subject (S), predicate (action or relationship), object (S*)
Attribution:	X causes Y; $S^d \rightarrow S^*$
Attribute:	X is an aspect of Y; $S^d \Sigma S^D$
Expectation:	X predicts Y; $P(S^*/S) \neq (P(S^*/\bar{S})$
Intention:	X intends to do Y; $S^d \underset{\rightarrow}{Int} S^* (S^* = R)$
Value:	X values Y; $S^d \underset{\rightarrow}{Val} S^*$
Self-concept:	$X_1 \ldots X_n$ are aspects of Y = self; $S_1^d \ldots S_n^d \Sigma S^D (S^D = self)$
Self-esteem:	X values Y (Y = self); $S^d Val S^D = self)$

can be seen as a propositional statement in which some stimulus X (S^d = X) is said to have caused (relationship = →) some other stimulus event Y (S^* = Y). For example, to say that an individual lost his/her job because of incompetent performance is to make a causal attribution: incompetent performance (X) led to (→) job loss (Y). An *attribute* stimulus (S^d = X) is said to be a component or characteristic of some other more encompassing stimulus (S^D = Y). Continuing with our example, we might say that incompetence (X) is an attribute of (Σ) that individual (Y). An *expectation* can be seen as a prediction, or differential perceived probability ($P_1 \neq \bar{P}_1$), that some stimulus condition (S^* = Y) will occur in the future. In some cases, the basis for that prediction, the predictor stimulus (S^d = X), is specified. To finish our example, we might predict that our sample individual will have future trouble holding a job.

Using this notational system, we can largely describe the universe of contents typically of interest under the various rubrics currently in use: "self-statements," "automatic thoughts," "irrational beliefs," "coping cognitions." We can expand our taxonomy profitably if we add several additional concepts. *Intention* (Int$\overrightarrow{~}$R), is one example, that strictly speaking, contains some agent as the subject, the act (R = Y) as the object, and the intention to commit the act (Int) as the same relationship. *Value* is a second example which indicates that the same agent (S^d = X) ascribes worth (Val) to some second stimulus (S^* = Y).

Self-statements have been typically defined as overt or covert "statements" made by an agent *to* himself or herself. There is no necessary requirement about the nature of the content. *Self-referential* comments, in this system, are statements made by an individual about himself or herself. *Self-concept,* that stalwart of traditional approaches to psychology, can be defined as the set of propositional beliefs held regarding one's own attributes. *Self-esteem* can be defined similarly as the set of value statements applied by an individual to himself or herself.

By carefully defining the subject, object, predicate, and relationship involved, it is possible to meaningfully define the nature of the propositional statements involved. Can differential variations in classes of content be meaningfully related to variations in psychopathology? Beck (1963; 1967) has systematically described negative self-attribution systems and future expectations in depression. Schwartz and Gottman (1976) have pointed to the presence of predictions of negative outcomes, rather than the absence of knowledge regarding appropriate behaviors, as best differentiating nonassertive from assertive individuals. Garner and Bemis (1981) have identified strong value assignments to thinness and personal self-control in anorexia. In some instances, it may be the absence of appropriate mediators that is decisive, as in the apparent deficit in covert mediators noted by Kendall and Finch (1979) in impulsive children. It may prove possible to correlate differential deficits, excesses, or aberrations in specific content categories to specific classes of pyschopathology. Further, it may prove that problems in one specific class of contents are relevant to the onset of a disorder, but that alteration in a different class of contents may prove most powerful in affecting treatment-related reduction in that psychopathology (see Hollon & Garber, 1980).

While we have focused on propositional content, we do not mean to exclude other classes of cognition from consideration. Imagery (see Tower & Singer, 1981) provides an example of reported cognitive experience that "mimics" a distinctly different sensory channel. We would regard the assessment of imagery as an equally cognitive task, although one with its own inherent conceptual and methodological difficulties. Typically, a great deal more information is conveyed in any given image or visual perception than is carried via auditory or verbal channels during the same time span (perhaps this is the basis for the saying, "One picture is worth a thousand words"). Assessing and reporting that information necessarily results in a loss of information. We are struck by the somewhat *more frequent* attempts to assess physical characteristics of imagery (e.g., vividness, duration) than has been the case for ruminatory cognition. Ultimately, we would presume that the three dimensions described earlier; occurrence/nonoccurrence, meaning, and perceived validity of the information contained in the imagery experiences, will prove of greater interest to psychopathologists and therapists than its physical attributes.

Processes. Cognitive processes are defined as those patterns followed in information processing. Such patterns may be more critical than any specific content produced, although they frequently must be inferred from systematic variations in cognitive content. Abramson, Seligman, and colleagues (see Abramson, Garber, & Seligman, 1980; Abramson, Seligman, & Teasdale, 1978) have argued that dysfunctional attributional styles play a central role in the etiology of depression, and Beck (1976) has described several categories of errors in information processing, including, selective abstraction, arbitrary inference, all-or-none thinking, and magnification. Cognitive styles (e.g., Butler & Meichenbaum, 1980) and cognitive strategies (e.g., Spivac & Shure, 1974) represent higher order cognitive processes receiving increasing attention. In these programs of research, emphasis is on the way information is processed, rather than the specific content of any given cognition. While fewer assessment strategies have been clearly delineated for cognitive processes, some, like Seligman et al.'s Attributional Styles Questionnaire (ASQ: Seligman, Abramson, Semmel, & von Bayer, 1979), the Matching Familiar Figures Test (MFF): Kagan, 1966), or the Sky (1950) chance-skill apparatus for expectancy-formation assessment, as modified by Rotter, Liverant, and Crowne (1961), approach this level of assessment.

Cognitive-behavioral functional relationships. We can divide the world into several classes of events: *stimulus* events (S^d's), which are largely external events but potentially include internal events; *responses* (R's), defined as motoric behaviors; *cognitions* (Cog's), defined as covert information processing events as described in the preceding section; and *affective* or *autonomic* events (Aff/Auto's), defined as feeling states or autonomic nervous system arousal functions. Further, we can talk about functional relationships between these classes of events. Figure 5.1, adapted from Hollon and Kendall (1979), presents these basic topographical components. We can ask,*"What is affected and how?"* Clearly, events can only influence one another in a temporally linear fashion; an event at Time 2 cannot influence an event at Time 1. All events, except motoric responses, are seen as being causally correlated over time. Thus, stimuli at Time 1 may influence the occurrence and nature of stimuli at Time 2; similarly for cognitions from Times 1 to 2, and affective/autonomic processes from Times 1 to 2. Stimuli are capable of influencing the occurrence and nature of cognition, but cognition is not seen as being capable of directly impacting on external events. Thus, causal influences over time for either stimuli or cognitions include causal autocorrelations, but causal influences between stimuli and cognitions operate only from the former to the latter. These causal influences are seen as occurring through traditional associationistic and perceptual processes (Neisser, 1967). It is important to note that consequences or current motivations are not necessary for stimuli to influence cognitions, although as we shall see later, anticipated consequent and motivational processes may influence the relationship between stimuli and cognitions.

Motoric responses are seen as causally influencing the occurrence of subsequent stimulus events, but motoric responses are not shown as causally autocorrelated over time, nor are stimuli shown as directly causal to motoric behavior. We have not drawn these relationships because we believe that they have been so overemphasized that they dominate some forms of the more radical behavioral approaches to psychology. We might label these latter behavioral approaches "decorticated behaviorism." We would acknowledge that, in some instances, behavioral sequences may be so highly automated that, within any highly practiced sequence, individual actions appear causally autocorrelated. This is the process described by Vygotsky (1962) and Meichenbaum (1974), and is analogous to the apparently automated, nonmediated response sequences that an individual can emit, even in the absence of external cues or, apparently, internal mediation. Driving a standard

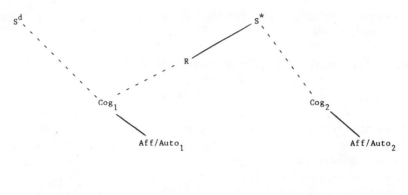

KEY:

S: Stimuli
- S^d = discriminative stimuli
- S^* = outcome or consequent stimuli important to the organism

Cog: Cognition
- includes beliefs, attributions and expectations;
- Cog 1 = especially emphasizes expectations
- Cog 2 = especially emphasizes attributions

Aff/Auto: Affective and autonomic process
- includes mood states (feelings), but also includes autonomic nervous system processes

R: Response
- motoric behavior

Fig. 5.1. A cognitive-behavioral functional analysis.

transmission car or fingering guitar chords with or without an instrument are frequently cited examples. Similarly, some stimuli produce nearly instantaneous, reflexive motoric responses (touching a hot stove elicits reflexive removal behavior). Of course, this has been described as the classic Sherrington reflex arc (Sherrington, 1960), and clearly occurs across all animal species with nervous systems. We would not dispute the existence of such processes, but would prefer not to attempt to erect a complete theory of human behavior on elaborations of these processes.

Affective/autonomic processes are seen as accessible only to cognitive mediation (Grings, 1973) or prior affective/autonomic processes, although the same type of nonmediated, overlearned responses are seen as possible as with motoric responses. Prior affective/autonomic processes may well influence the occurence and nature of cognitive events (see Kihlstorm & Nasby, 1980).

When the various processes are allowed to interact over time, the possible lines of causal influence are shown in figure 5.1. Note that we now have a highly complex systems, one which makes specific predictions about particular causal paths, but will allow some major classes of events to both cause, and be caused by, other processes.

As we have discussed elsewhere (Hollon & Garber, 1980), different classes of cognitions may be differentially involved at different points and in different processes (acquisition versus maintenance versus treatment-related reversal). Specifically, expectations typically refer to events which have yet to occur: they are predictions. They may refer to predictions regarding subsequent stimulus events, given certain cues $[P(S*/S^d)]$, or to subsequent events given certain behaviors $[P(S*/R)]$. Bandura (1977) has described these two classes of expectations as outcome expectancies and efficacy expectancies.

Attributions typically refer to events that have already occurred, or characteristics already in existence. Thus, an *attribution of causality* typically involves an ascription of causal status to a variable for an event *that has already occurred*. An anticipation that the variable will continue to exercise a causal influence is a belief, while the prediction of a given outcome is occurrence in the future, as a consequence of the operation of that causal factor, is an expectation. The recent reformulation of the learned helplessness model (Abramson et al., 1978) has argued for a central role for attributional processes in the acquisition of depressive cognitive sets. In a sense, learned helplessness/depression is seen as resulting from the mistaken attribution of failure (S*) to behavioral inadequacy (R) in figure 5.1, with the attribution occurring at point Cog 2. The expectation at Cog 1 might have been a relatively nondepressed one. However, once the unfortunate misattribution has occurred, it has a malignant influence on subsequent beliefs and expectational processes. In subsequent situations, expectations at Cog 1 (Situation 2) are likely to be depressive in nature. Abramson et al. refer to this as the stability component of attributions, but it appears that once an individual considers the probable impact of a stable causal factor on subsequent outcomes, he/she is forming an expectation.

These distinctions represent more than simple exercises in semantics. For the purposes of the cognitive-behavioral analyst, it becomes critical to retain some degree of clarity when attempting to assess and integrate the complex interaction of processes presented by any given client. The clinician will want to know not only what types of effects his or her client experiences, but also what situations preceded and followed those experiences, what cognitions may have mediated or been influenced by those states, and what the subsequent behaviors were. Different classes of cognitions may be of interest at different points in the functional chain. Cognitions are rarely of interest in and of themselves, but because of the functional relationships in which they are presumably embedded. Assessment procedures need to be tailored to fit the special requirements of the questions being asked.

Similarly, motoric behavioral, cognitive, and affective/autonomic processes are seen as potentially obeying different types of laws. Motoric behaviors appear to be largely under consequent control. The acquisition, nature, and occurrence of this class of events appears to be largely a function of the nature of events following the occurrence of a response (Skinner, 1953). Affective/autonomic processes appear to be largely under antecedent control (Wolpe, 1978). Cognition seems to be capable of operating on either basis. Associative processes appear to be typically under antecedent control. It is very difficult to obey the request not to think about something, for example, even if strong contingencies are in effect. If the reader doubts this observation, try *not to think about an ice cream sundae*. Of course, it makes sense to design an organism so that it considers possible dangers in the world, even if the consequences of such consideration entails the generation of unpleasant affective states. An organism that could readily block attention to potentially dangerous situations would be unlikely to live for very long. However, there also appear to be instances in which organisms can select to think about certain topics. This capacity, and perhaps the capacity to exercise control over sequential information processing, appears to be largely under consequent control. We "associate" because we are "wired" to do so, we reason because we learn to do so, and we develop preferred strategies for reasoning because it is to our advantage to do so.

HOW ARE COGNITIONS ASSESSED?

Major Issues

If we accept (or, at least for the moment, choose not to reject) the argument that the effort to assess cognition is a legitimate enterprise, how are we to go about the task? We can readily see a host of potential threats to the validity of the assessment process, assuming that there is something to validly assess. Some of these threats are shared with other domains of measurement; others are relatively unique to cognitive assessment. In the sections to follow, we present an overview of a model for assessing cognition paying specific attention to the universe of threats to that endeavour.

Accuracy. Cognitive assessment typically involves self-report, or at the very least, inference based on observations subsequently correlated with self-report. How are we to know whether such reports are *accurate?* That is, are observers really reporting what has occurred?

At this time there is no direct answer to this question, given our current technical limitations. We rely on the construct utility of cognitive analysis to maintain our interest in the role such processes may play. Nonetheless, even granting an interest in those processes, how are we to proceed to study a process directly "observable" only by the organism allegedly experiencing the phenomenon?

We may derive some guidelines from our knowledge of other efforts at behavioral assessment. Particularly useful are the bodies of information associated with self-monitoring (see Kazdin, 1974; Mahoney, 1977b; McFall, 1977; Nelson, 1977) and *in vivo* cognitive-behavioral assessment (see Hollon & Kendall, 1981). Evaluation of the various factors known to affect the accuracy of self-monitoring of observable events may well serve to promote our understanding of those factors influencing the report of covert processes.

Nelson's review is particularly useful in this regard. She notes that several factors can influence the probable accuracy of the report: the *valence* of the target (does the subject value and/or anticipate positive consequences for a given report?), the *nature* of the target (product or process), the *reinforcement* provided for (or intrinsic to) monitoring (is the observation process itself reinforced?), the *temporal schedules* followed, (concurrent or retrospective), the nature of *concurrent activities* (is the subject required to engage in additional, distracting activities?), and *training* in monitoring procedures. It is important to distinguish between errors and dissimulations; in the former case, the subject simply misperceives or misreports; while in the latter the subject's report is in direct contradiction to his or her observation. In a later section we describe a model of the cognitive self-monitoring process designed to provide a framework for integrating these various guidelines into maximally accurate procedures of operation. With no direct check on the accuracy of the self-observation, the cognitive-behavioral scientist is ultimately at the mercy of the respondent. The unannounced spot-check, a favorite procedure for ensuring observer attention and accuracy in the behavioral literature, is by definition unavailable in cognitive assessment.

Reactivity. Reactivity is the tendency for a phenomenon to change as a consequence of obtrusive monitoring. In a sense, reactivity can be seen as a threat to the external validity of an observation (see below), for while the phenomenon may have been accurately observed, its occurrence was determined in part by the special conditions imposed by the assessment context. Such an observation may not be representative of the nature and occurrence of the phenomenon in nonmonitored, real-world situations.

Elsewhere (Hollon & Kendall, 1981) we have suggested that covert cognitive events may obey different laws from voluntary motoric events. Cognition, we argue, can operate either as a respondent or an operant behavior, much as breathing. Given a compelling external or internal stimulus, it is almost impossible to avoid entertaining certain thoughts, even if their consequences are undesirable. Nonetheless, it is possible to direct one's attention in a manner likely to maximize gains and minimize losses. Whether or not such processes occur outside of volitional awareness is controversial, such a processing "screen" keyed to affective consequences would conform descriptively to the psychodynamic notion of repression (Shevrin & Dickman, 1980).

Whatever the nature of the processes discovered, it is apparent that self-monitoring must always be obtrusive. However, some methods may produce less reactivity than others. Thought-listing or production (see Kendall & Hollon, 1981), in which the subject is asked to recall cognitions spontaneously, may be less reactive with regard to content than endorsement methods that provide "cognitions" and ask the subject to recognize specific experienced thoughts. By judiciously selecting tools and procedures, it may prove possible to minimize reactivity.

Temporal Stability. There is good reason to believe that human beings do not necessarily produce the same contents, nor follow the same processes to produce those cognitions across time. This potential for temporal instability is one reason why we have elsewhere (Hollon & Kendall, 1981) argued against the assumption of *cognitive intransience*. This latter assumption is the postulate that people think the same things in the same ways, at all assessment points at all times. From the standpoint of assessment, such an assumption can be fatal. The burden of proof always falls on the assessor to demonstrate, for instance, that a retrospectively recalled attribution of job loss to bad luck was indeed the attribution made at the time the job was actually lost. While we frequently rely on retrospective report for convenience sake, we should always be wary of doing so, since we may be misled by current recollections of prior events.

Situational Stability. Potential lack of situational stability is the second reason why we are uncomfortable with the assumption of cognitive intransience. Do people's beliefs vary across situations? We think that they might. Many rational beings who do not believe in supernatural influences are likely to assign a slightly higher probability to their occurrence when asked to walk through a graveyard at night. Similarly, Beck (1976) has described an increase in cognitions about the potential dangers (i.e., expectations) associated with elevators as he walked an elevator-phobic client out of the consulting room and down the hall toward an elevator. We have witnessed similar spontaneous shifts in cognitive content and processes when anorexics were confronted by desirable foodstuffs, bulimics were prevented from vomiting after eating, or agoraphobics were instructed to self-present imaginal scenes of feared situations. This is a phenomenon which we have observed so frequently and across so many disparate types of psychopathological processes, that we frankly regard the traditional clinical notion that neurotic reactions are irrational as a misconstrual based on *faulty assessment*. When assessed in the quiet and safety of the consulting room, graveyards, elevators, or any other pertinent stimuli are simply not as likely to be viewed as dangerous. When assessed *in vivo*, however, different cognitive contents and processes are elicited. Without being concerned about whether such beliefs mediate arousal (or whether peripherally conditioned arousal mediates the emergence of such beliefs), it is appropriate to point out that the adequacy, and especially the generalizability, of the cognitive assessment may be determined by the context in which that assessment takes place.

A Model for Measurement

We present in this section an overview of the cognitive assessment process. In fact, we think that this model can be extended to any assessment context and for any assessment purpose, but we shall limit our comments to those situations in which the targets of interest are cognitive in nature.

As shown in figure 5.2, it is possible to distinguish between the organism (Actor) experiencing the event (S^d) and the organism (Observer) who monitors that event. In this schemata, the initial event is typically some cognition engaged in by the Actor. If we were concerned about a more general assessment model, the event could be a motoric action (R), autonomic/affective process (Aff/Auto), or external event (S^d).

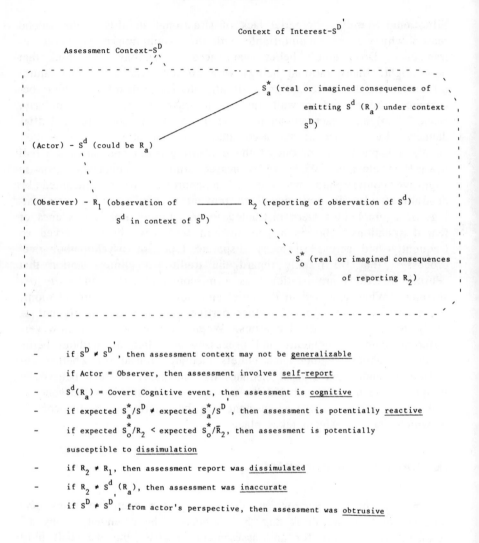

Fig. 5.2. An overview of the assessment process from a behavioral perspective.

The same event serves as the discriminative stimulus (S^d) for the Observer. The observation of this event is a response in itself (R_1), one engaged in by the observer.

Making an observation (R_1) and reporting an observation (R_2) are not necessarily the same events. Typically, the initial observation (R_1) is actually a covert cognitive event, while the second response (R_2) involves some type of motoric action; e.g., speaking, writing, signalling, etc.

Consequent reinforcement effects (S*'s) may enter at either of two points. Frequently, the nature and occurrence of the initial events (S^d) for the actor may be influenced by the real and/or anticipated consequences of the event (S_a^*). As we described previously, we think that cognitive events often occur more frequently as reactions to antecedent events than in response to probable consequences, but at least some classes of cognitions (e.g., attentional deployment, sequential reasoning, intentional problem-solving) fall largely under consequent control.

More important for our purposes are consequent reinforcement effects (S_o^*) on the observer. Both observational (R_1) and reporting responses (R_2) may be influenced by the real and/or perceived consequences. (We have drawn in only one set of consequent reinforcements, S_o^*'s, although those events influencing R_1 are not necessarily the same as those influencing R_2).

Now that we have our basic model laid out, we can draw several distinctions. When the event in question is cognitive in nature, then our assessment process is one of *cognitive assessment*. When Actor and Observer are the same individual, the assessment procedure involves *self-report*. As we have noted, most efforts at cognitive assessment involve self-report, but the initial alleged cognitive event (S^d), the observation (R_1), and/or the report of that observation (R_2) are not the same events. Recognition of this nonequivalence can be extremely important. While we cannot directly observe someone else's cognition (given current limits on our technology), we can often minimize the probability of distortion in the report of that event by maximizing the perceived reinforcement for valid self-report. How can this be done? In truth, it cannot, but reinforcements can be provided for careful attention at R_1, and extraneous reinforcements for dissimulation at R_2 can be minimized. Finally, efforts can be made to accentuate the perceived intrinsic motivation for accuracy.

Some investigators have adopted indirect methods to attempt cognitive assessments. Diener and Dweck (1978), for example, have asked subjects to think out loud while they work on a task. This verbal production is then tape recorded. Verbal production, then, becomes the trigger event (S^d) from which the researcher attempts to infer the subject's cognitions.

What other properties can we derive from the model? We have encircled the entire paradigm in an overall context (S^D). To the extent that the assessment context S^D is equivalent to the situations of interest ($S^{D'}$), then assessment is likely to be generalizable. Less obvious, to the extent that reinforcement effects (S_a^*/S^D) in the assessment are dissimilar to reinforcement effects in the situation of interest ($S_a^*/S^{D'}$), then the potential for consequent mediated *reactivity* exists.

This is not the only set of circumstances that may produce reactivity. Any assessment situation (S^D) perceived by the subject as being an assessment situation is, of course, an instance of *obtrusive assessment*, and potentially reactive. In this system, whenever the report is not isomorphic with the observation ($R_2 \neq R_1$), we can label the report *dissimulated;* when the report is not isomorphic with the event ($R_2 \neq S^d$), then the assessment is said to be inaccurate.

Threats to the Validity of Assessment

In the assessment process, there are several classes of threats which can be discriminated from one another. Cook and Campbell (1979) have described an elegant taxonomy of both types of validity and threats to the validity of conclusions drawn from empirical trials. We draw heavily on their discussion below.

Threats to the *internal validity* of any assessment relate to the accuracy of an observation. When we say "X was observed under Y conditions," there are a host of ways our statement could have been incorrect. "X" may well not have been present and our observer(s) may have been in error or dissimulating.

A second major class of threats relate to the *external validity*, or *generalizability*, of an observation. This occurs when we say "X was observed under Y conditions, and that tells us that X likely occurs under Y' conditions." We may well have observed X accurately under Y conditions, but that observation, although internally valid, may not generalize to Y' conditions. Using this definition, we can see that reactivity is a threat to external validity when some phenomenon (X) occurs and is accurately observed in an assessment situation (Y) which is unrepresentative of the occurrence of X in the real world situation Y''s.

The third major type of threat lies in the *construct* validity of an observation. We may accurately observe a phenomenon we call X in the assessment context Y, and we validly generalize our observation to the real world conditions of interest Y', but may be wrong in labeling our phenomenon X. In essence, we have misconstrued or mislabeled the nature of the observed phenomenon, although the internal and external validities of our observation are intact. If we were observing studying behavior in a child in a classroom, we might note the times that he or she sat at a desk looking at a text. We might use the consensus across multiple observers to estimate the internal validity of our observation and might even utilize some form of unobtrusive measurement system (a concealed camera or one-way mirror) to reduce the discrepancies between the assessment context and the context to which we wished to generalize. Nonetheless, our target child might as readily be daydreaming as studying, and we would incorrectly identify our X phenomenon.

Cognitive assessment frequently involves self-report of the processes and products of cognition. There are different methodologies available and each has its strength and limitations. The strength of behavioral assessment has always been in the extent of the effort to sample X directly in the context of greatest interest, Y'. Preferably, this is done so as to minimize reactivity, and is typically best accomplished by keeping the assessment process unobtrusive.

Referring again to figure 5.2, the essential phenomenon observed, S^d (or X), can either be an event not involving an organism or an organismic activity (R or response). If the latter, then we immediately must decide whether our actor organism and our observer organism are to be the same or different. In the first instance, of course, we are dealing with self-report; in the second, external observation.

For the observer, the observational process begins with R_1, the observation of S^d. There are a host of errors that can occur at R_1, any of which will reduce the accuracy or internal validity of the observation. The observer may be attending to something else, may be fatigued, stupid, etc. Assuming that an observation is made, it must be reported by the observer. If there are strong, real or imagined consequences for various types of reports, the observer may alter his or her report so as to maximize his or her gains. Reported R_2 will not be congruent with observed R_1, resulting in damage to the internal validity (accuracy) of the observation, as reported. This process could be labeled falsification or lying.

So far, we have operated with a given context, S^D. To the extent that S^D is similar to the context of interest, Y', and the actor is unaffected by the assessment process, we can increment the external validity of our assessments.

The standard self-report questionnaire typically samples the phenomenon of interest (X) out of the context and at a time other than when the phenomenon of interest occurs. In most instances, this means that we attempt to measure cognitive products in a way such that Y and Y' are maximally dissimilar. Further, actor and observor are typically one and the same, making unobtrusive measurement virtually impossible and maximizing the risk that various real and imagined consequences will alter the nature of the reported observation.

CURRENT MEASUREMENT METHODS

A variety of general methods and specific measures have been developed for the assessment of cognitions. To provide an estimate of the frequency with which cognitive assessment procedures are incorporated into clinical and experimental studies appearing in the cognitive literature, the two most recent complete volumes of *Cognitive Therapy and Research* were reviewed. The 86 reports published in the journal during 1978 and 1979 were scanned for the inclusion of three types of cognitive assessment: (1) manipulation checks on cognitive intervention procedures, (2) cognitive devices used as change measures, and (3) attempts to collect and/or evaluate subjects' cognitions in any form. While recognizing that none of these types of cognitive assessment was indicated or desirable in many of the articles surveyed, we were impressed by the number of other papers that omitted cognitive assessments where they might have contributed significantly to the obtained results.

Under the first category of assessment types, we found 11 studies[3] that incorporated manipulation checks of cognitive procedures into the experimental design. Generally, these took the form of asking subjects in cognitive imagery or self-instructional cells to report what they had thought about during the experimental period, as a means of evaluating whether subjects had complied with instructions to concentrate on particular kinds of cognitive content. Nine other studies in which such manipulation checks would have been desirable failed to include them.[4] Within the second category, only six reports were found to include a cognitive device in the pre-post battery of change measures,[5] although in our judgment at least 14 other investigations would have been enhanced by the inclusion of such a measure.[6] The form of cognitive assessment most often represented among the articles reviewed was some kind of effort to collect cognitions from subjects in at least one of the experimental conditions—this occurred in 18 instances.[7] These attempts to gather cognitive data varied widely in scope and sophistication, ranging from an analysis of scores obtained on standardized cognitive measures, to a simple notation to the effect that "the patient was asked to keep track of his negative thoughts." Several other papers employed additional types of cognitive assessment as dependent variables in the experimental procedure; these included the use of a chance-skill task to evaluate expectancies (Donovan & O'Leary, 1979), an attribution task (Oliver & Williams, 1979), and a method for evaluating the presence of schemata through the recall of personal adjectives (Davis, 1979a, 1979b). In general, however, both this survey and a broader review of the literature have impressed us with the fact that cognitive assessment is by no means routine practice even within the selective field of cognitive therapy research.

A number of systems have been developed to classify the kinds of cognitive measurement methods that do exist (see Kendall & Hollon,

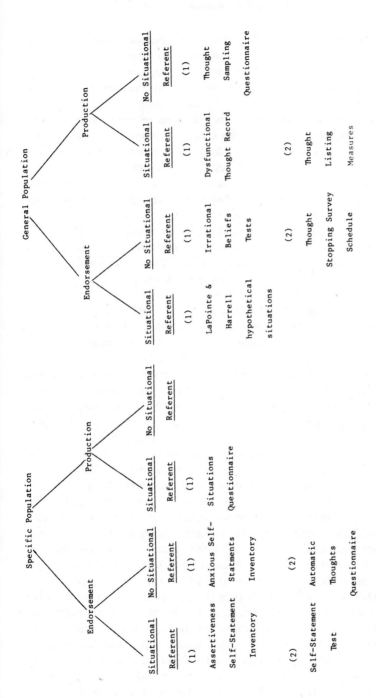

Fig. 5.3. A taxonomy of current cognitive assessment devices.

1981; Kendall & Korgeski, 1979). We offer another system for conceptualizing cognitive assessment techniques in figure 5.3—not with
the assumption that it provides a comprehensive or definitive taxonomy,
but simply to highlight various dimensions of assessment devices that
investigators may have practical reasons for delineating.

The primary division in figure 5.3 is intended to emphasize the distinction between measures designed for specific groups of subjects (such
as depressed or socially anxious individuals) and more generic measures
that can be used with less selected populations, such as either normal
or general psychiatric groups. The distinction between these categories
is not absolute; for example, the Automatic Thoughts Questionnaire
(Hollon & Kendall, 1980), listed as a "specific population" measure
because it was designed for and validated with depressed individuals,
may also be used to investigate negative cognitions associated with
disorders other than depression. Moreover, at least in current usage if
not by necessity, some kinds of "general population" methods are often
used preferentially to study certain types of individuals. For example,
the Dysfunctional Thought Record (Beck et al., 1979) has been most
often employed with depressed and anxious patients, while random sampling methods such as the Thought Sampling Questionnaire (Klinger,
1978) have been used almost exclusively with normals.

The basis for the distinction between endorsement and production
methods is whether the *content* of the cognitions being assessed is provided by the examiner or the subject. In endorsement methods, the
experimenter or clinician furnishes the subject with specific thoughts
that he or she may rate on dimensions such as frequency of occurrence
or degree of belief. Examples include the Irrational Beliefs Test (Jones,
1968) and the Dysfunctional Attitude Scale (Weissman & Beck, 1978),
in which subjects are provided with lists of statements expressing an
outlook believed to be associated with maladjustment and asked to indicate their agreement or disagreement with these statements. In production methods, the source of the reported thoughts is the subject,
whether or not the examiner has provided stimulus material such as
imagined scenes to elicit these cognitions. Examples include the Dysfunctional Thought Record (Beck et al., 1979; Ellis & Grieger, 1977;
Goldfried & Davison, 1976) which requires clients to generate their own
charts of the sequence of situations, beliefs, and affects they experience
in daily living, and the various forms of thought listing (see Bruch,
1978; Cacioppo et al., 1979), in which subjects are asked to report all
the cognitions of which they were aware during the last five or ten
minutes. Several essentially "production" methods have "endorsement" components. Klinger's Thought Sampling Questionnaire (Klinger, 1978; Klinger et al., 1979) asks subjects to rate the thoughts they

experienced just prior to a random signal on a variety of scales presented in inventory form. However, this measure remains a "production" method in which the questionnaire format simply serves as a technique for imposing a desired structure on subjects' idiosyncratic styles of reporting their own content.

The final distinction in figure 5.3 is between measures that include a clear situational referent and those that do not. The former designation indicates that an assessment device is intended to elicit cognitions associated with a particular situation, rather than a sample of thoughts across time in a variety of situations. An example of the former would be Schwartz and Gottman's Assertiveness Self-Statement Inventory (1976), in which subjects report the frequency of various kinds of self-statements they experienced during a role-play exercise. The second type may be represented by the Automatic Thoughts Questionnaire (Hollon & Kendall, 1980) which asks subjects to rate how often they have experienced specific negative cognitions over the past week. The differentiation between these two approaches does not imply that stimulus conditions are of no interest in measures that lack specific situational referents, but simply that the instrument is not keyed to thoughts occurring in a *particular* situation. Measures with no situational referents ask subjects the question, "What do you think about?"; while measures with situational referents ask, "What do you think about *when* you are. . .?"

The dimensions that we have identified for the classification of cognitive assessment devices certainly do not exhaust the possibilities for distinguishing between different kinds of measures. Other dimensions along which measures might be meaningfully divided, or further subdivided along with other dimensions, including the following:

1. *Retrospective/Concurrent.* Some measures ask subjects to report on thoughts they have experienced in the past or "in general," (Automatic Thoughts Questionnaire, Dysfunctional Attitude Scale, Irrational Beliefs Test), while others require subjects to supply thoughts they have *just* experienced (Assertiveness Self-Statement Inventory, Thought Sampling Questionnaire, thought listing measures). The distinction does not imply a dichotomy, but suggests relative position along a temporal continuum. Very few measures approach being truly "concurrent" with the cognitions being assessed; most often, the "concurrent" designation refers to methods like thought listing that are actually "briefly retrospective." Methodologies requesting subjects to "think out loud" while engaged in some activity (see Diener & Dweck, 1978) probably come closest to approximating concurrent report.

2. *In vivo/in vitro*. The familiar distinction between assessments made
   in real-life situations and those made during laboratory or consulting
   room procedures may also be applied to cognitive measures. While
   overlapping with the "situational referent/no situational referent"
   boundary discussed above, the two dimensions are not isomorphic;
   thought sampling is one technique that is used to collect subjects'
   real-life cognitions without being restricted to a particular situation
   or setting.
3. *Sample/sign*. Cognitive measures may be designed to determine the
   conscious content of a subject's thoughts (Automatic Thoughts Questionnaire, Self-Statements Test) or to assess the presumed deeper
   structure of his or her cognitive system, whether or not the subject
   actually "thinks" in such terms until required to do so by the assessment process (Dysfunctional Attitude Scale, Irrational Beliefs
   Test, Hopelesness Scale). To some extent, the distinction between
   sample and sign concerns the level of inference involved in extrap-
   olating from the subject's self-report to the presumed meaning of
   his or her statements, and is related to the difference between automatic thoughts and underlying assumptions delineated by Beck
   (Beck et al., 1979; Hollon & Beck, 1979).
4. *All cognitions/selected cognitions*. Endorsement methods are always
   designed to assess a limited number of specific thoughts; production
   methods may require subjects to report all the cognitions experienced
   during a specified time period (thought listing measures, random
   sampling measures) or only selected cognitions of interest (Dysfunctional Thought Record and other self-monitoring variants).

A variety of cognitive assessment methods employed with general populations are charted in Table 5.2, while a number of instruments designed for use with specific populations are presented in Table 5.3.
Only a handful of measures have achieved wide currency even within
the cognitive literature. It is not always evident that these few have
earned their distinction on the basis of any merit other than their availability.

SUMMARY

We have now reviewed various aspects of the why, what, where, when,
and how of cognitive assessment. We have attempted to provide a taxonomy of the types of phenomena likely to be of interest to cognitive
assessors, and a model for that assessment process. A variety of scales

and instruments are currently available, many of recent vintage. Increasing attention is being paid to the methods followed for optimal assessment.

Several points appear to be of major importance:

1. Adequate assessment procedures are necessary to test theories. One need not accept the validity of cognitive models to have an interest in assessing cognition.
2. Several distinctions can be made regarding the nature of the cognitive phenomena of interest. Are we concerned with products-contents or processes? Are we interested in phenomena accessible to introspection (conscious), or phenomena relatively inaccessible to introspection (nonconscious)? Are we interested in "surface" or "deep" structures? While these distinctions may prove somewhat redundant, it is likely that different assessment strategies will be required.
3. Various aspects of these cognitive phenomena may be differentially important for any given question of interest. Are we concerned, for example, with whether or not a specific cognition occurred (occurrence/nonoccurrence), with what it means to the individual (meaning), or with how strongly it is believed (subjective validity)? Different assessment devices tend to ask different questions about the cognitions they assess.
4. It may prove useful to develop a taxonomy of cognitive content. We have attempted such a taxonomy, one which discriminates between attribution of causality, attributes, expectations, values, and intentions. We have focused largely on propositional content, which is most frequently experienced as auditory-like rumination, but recognize that other types of contents and modalities may be of interest. Even within the limited domain encompassed by our taxonomy, it is apparent that different cognitions are likely to be differentially involved in different types of disorders or differentially involved in the causal chains leading to etiology versus intervention. It may prove useful to attempt to place the cognitive processes we assess in a temporal and functional context with other phenomena of interest, such as external events, affective and autonomic processes, and motoric behavior. It is not enough to assess cognitions; rather, we must have some theoretically based notion of where in the stream of ongoing external and organismic events we wish to aim our assessment efforts.
6. Methodological issues involve more than simple questions regarding "which scale" to use. Relevant questions concern the effects of temporal and situational variants on the validity of the assessment process. What risks are incurred to the internal, external, and con-

Table 5.2. Cognitive Assessment Methods Used with General Populations

Method	Source	Target	Format	Examples of Use	
Inventories					
Irrational Beliefs Test (IBT)	Jones, 1968	Irrational beliefs presumably related to neuroticism and maladaptive behavior	Endorsement—pencil and paper	Craighead et al., 1979: Derry & Stone, 1979: Goldfried & Sobocinski, 1975: Hamberger & Lohr, 1980: Nelson, 1977: Sutton-Simon & Goldfried, 1979:	social approval assertiveness anxiety anger depression psychiatric outpatients public speaking
Thought Stopping Survey Schedule (TSSS)	Cautela & Upper, 1976	Thoughts presumably related to depression, anxiety, and other maladpative behavior	Endorsement—pencil and paper	Trexler & Karst, 1972:	
Self-Monitoring Dysfunctional Thought Record (DTR)	See Beck, Rush, Shaw, & Emery, 1979; Ellis & Grieger, 1977; Goldfried & Davison, 1976	Selected cognitions, with associated situations, affect, behavior	Production—pencil and paper	Beck & Emery, 1979: Beck et al., 1978, 1980: Emery & Fox, 1981 Hollon, 1981 Khatami & Rush, 1976:	anxiety, phobias depression alcoholism pansituational anxiety chronic pain
Assorted forms	See Goldfried & Davison, 1976; Ellis & Grieger, 1978; Maultsby, 1975	Selected cognitions or selected cognitions, situation, affects	Production—pencil and paper	Linehan, 1979: Mahoney, 1971: Marlatt, 1979: Novaco, 1977, 1979: Sims & Lazarus, 1973:	assertiveness obsessiveness, depression alcoholism anger mania

Table 5.2. (continued)

Method Inventories	Source	Target	Format	Examples of Use	
Thought listing	Brock, 1967; Greenwald, 1968	Self-statements during specific time period—often experimental period	Production—pencil and paper or recording	Avia & Kanfer, 1980: Bruch, 1978: Cacioppo et al., 1979: Cacioppo & Petty, in press: Diener & Dweck, 1978: Girodo & Wood, 1979: Hollandsworth et al., 1979:	pain tolerance test anxiety social anxiety social anxiety learned helplessness pain tolerance test anxiety
Random sampling		Cognitions preceding random signal	Production—pencil and paper or recording	Foulkes et al., 1966: Hurlburt, 1976: Hurlburt & Spipprelle, 1978: Klinger, 1978: Klinger et al., 1979: Larson & Csikzentmikalyi, in press:	normal adult relaxed condition normal adult anxiety normal adult normal adult adolescents

Table 5.3. Cognitive Assessment Measures Designed for Specific Populations

Population	Measure	Source	Target	Format	Specific Information
Depressed	Attributional Styles Questionnaire (ASQ)	Seligman, Abramson, Semmel, & Von Bayer, 1979	Attributional styles	Production—pencil and paper	12 hypothetical situation vignettes (6 positive, 6 negative outcomes) with 1 open-ended attribution question and 4 ratings on 7-point scales (internality-externality, stability globality, and importance) for each vignette
	Automatic Thoughts Questionnaire (ATQ)	Hollon & Kendall, 1980	Self-statements associated with depression	Endorsement—pencil & paper	30 Items: frequency of and degree of belief in depressive self-statements
Depressed	Cognitive Response Test (CRT)	Watkins & Rush, in press	Cognitions associated with depression	Production—pencil and paper	36 item free response; completion of stem sentences
	Dysfunctional Attitude Scale (DAS)	Weissman & Beck, 1978	Idiosyncratic cognitions associated with depression	Endorsement—pencil and paper	40 items; 2 parallel forms; Agree/disagree with attitude statements
	Hopelessness Scale (HS)	Beck, Weissman, Lester, & Trexler, 1974	Negative expectancies of self and future	Endorsement—pencil and paper	20 items; true-false statements of negative expectancies

Table 5.3. (continued)

Population	Measure	Source	Target	Format	Specific Information
Depressed	Story Completion Test	Hammen & Krantz, 1976	Depressive biases in the interpretation and evaluation of hypothetical event	Endorsement—pencil and paper	6 hypothetical situation vignettes, each followed by 3 or 4 multiple choice endorsement questions
Anxious, phobic	Anxious Self-Statements Inventory	Kendall & Hollon, 1979	Self-statements associated with anxiety	Endorsement—pencil and paper	33 items; frequency of anxious self-statements
	Situations Questionnaire	Sutton-Simon & Goldfried, 1979	Self-statements associated with social situations heights, and neutral situations	Production—pencil and paper	14 situations with open-ended questions
Nonassertive	Assertiveness Self-Statement Inventory (ASSI)	Schwartz & Gottman, 1976	Self-statements during situations calling for assertiveness	Endorsement—pencil and paper	34 Items; frequency of statements adaptive/maladaptive to assertive behavior in role-play situations
Medical	Self-Statement Inventory (SSI)	Kendall et al., 1979	Self-statements associated with undergoing cardiac catheterization	Endorsement—pencil and paper	20 items; statements adaptive/maladaptive to coping with stressful medical procedure

struct validities of our assessment effort when we select any specific
set of operations? How can we minimize inaccuracy and reactivity, or
even detect their occurrence? We have attempted to generate a functional analysis of the assessment context to facilitate addressing these
issues.

7. Finally, several assessment devices are now available, most of recent
vintage. Relatively little is known about their psychometric properties and perhaps even less about how variations in the ways these
scales are used influence the answers they produce. Endorsement
format questionnaires, generally without situational referents, appear
to be the modal tool developed in the context of laboratory-based
studies, while production-format tools appear to be found in clinical
contexts. Ultimately, we will need to develop and integrate an understanding of what types of tools may prove most serviceable for
different kinds of purposes.

At present, interest in cognitive assessment is increasing. New tools
are available, and more will probably be forthcoming. We do not feel
compelled to call for more research; that will probably follow. But we
do feel compelled to call for studies designed to facilitate our understanding of the cognitive assessment context.

NOTES

1. We will follow Bowers (1972) convention and indicate any event with "importance"
   to an organism as an S*. This more general rubric encompasses both reinforcing
   (S^r) and punishing (S^p) stimuli. Potentially informative events will continue to be
   designated with the conventional symbol for discriminative stimuli (S^d), and motoric
   responses will be designated with the conventional symbol for a response (R).
2. It is interesting that while most of us see, we *never* observe anyone else's "sight."
   We hear their self-reports, observe the presumed influence of "seeing" on their
   behavior, and can even monitor its neurophysiological correlates; but we can not
   observe its occurrence directly. It is interesting that the radical behaviorist will infer
   that (some) organisms "see" but not that they "think." The evidential bases and epis-
   temologies involved in each case are identical.
3. The 11 studies with manipulation checks were Bruch, 1978; Derry and Stone, 1979;
   Dunn, 1979; Girodo and Stein, 1978; Girodo and Wood, 1979; Glogower, Fremouw,
   and McCroskey, 1978; Grayson and Borkovec, 1978; Hodges, McCaulay, Ryan, and
   Strosahl, 1979; LaPointe and Harrell, 1978; Shelton and Mahoney, 1978; Worthington, 1978.
4. The nine studies that could have used manipulation checks were Carmody, 1978; Catanese, Rosenthal, and Kelley, 1979; Cradock, Cotler, and Jason, 1978; Jenni and
   Wollersheim, 1979; Myers, Schleser, Cooke, and Cuvillier, 1979; Norton, MacLean, and
   Wachna, 1978.
5. The six studies with pre-post change measures were Bruch, 1978; Derry and Stone, 1979;
   Dunn, 1979; Hurlburt and Sipprelle, 1978; Shelton and Mahoney, 1978; and Worthington, 1978.

6. The 14 studies that could have used pre-post change measures were: Carmody, 1978; Catanese et al., 1979; Dunkel and Glaros, 1978; Girodo and Wood, 1979; Glogower et⁻ al., 1978; Grayson and Borkovec, 1978; Harrell and Beiman, 1978; Hodges et al., 1979; Hussian and Lawrence, 1978; Jenni and Wollersheim, 1979; Myers et al., 1979; Norton et al., 1978; Shahar and Jaffe, 1978; Tesser, Leone, and Clary, 1978.

7. The 18 studies that used some form of collection of cognitions were: Alden and Safran, 1978; Bruch, 1978; Cacioppo et al., 1979; Derry and Stone, 1979; Dunn, 1979; Girodo and Stein, 1978; Girodo and Wood, 1979; Glogower et al., 1978; Hammen, 1978; Harrell and Beiman, 1978; Hollandsworth et al., 1979; Hurlburt and Sipprelle, 1978; Hussian and Lawrence, 1978; LaPointe and Harrell, 1978; Shelton and Mahoney, 1978; Sutton-Simon and Goldfried, 1979; Tesser et al., 1978; and Worthington, 1978.

REFERENCES

Abramson, L. Y., Garber, J., & Seligman, M. E. P. Learned helplessness in humans: An attributional analysis. In J. Garber & M. E. P. Seligman (Eds.), *Human helplessness: Theory and applications*. New York: Academic Press, 1980.

Abramson, L. Y., Seligman, M. E. P., & Teasdale, J. D. Learned helplessness in humans: Critique and reformulation. *Journal of Abnormal Psychology*, 1978, *87* 49–74.

Alden, L., & Safran, J. Irrational beliefs and nonassertive behavior. *Cognitive Therapy and Research*, 1978, *2*, 357–364.

Averill, J. R. Grief: Its nature and significance. *Psychological Bulletin*, 1968, *70*, 721–749.

Avia, M. D., & Kanfer, F. H. Coping with aversive stimulation: The effects of training in a self-managment context. *Cognitive Therapy and Research*, 1980, *4*, 73–82.

Bandura, A. *Principles of behavior modification*. New York: Holt, Rinehart, & Winston, 1969.

Bandura, A. Self-efficacy: Toward a unifying theory of behavioral change. *Psychological Review*, 1977, *84*, 191–215.

Bandura, A. The self system in reciprocal determinism. *American Psychologist*, 1978, *33*, 344–358.

Bandura, A., Adams, N. E., Hardy, A. B., & Howells, G. N. Tests of the generality of self-efficacy theory. *Cognitive Therapy and Research*, 1980, *4*, 39–66.

Barnhart, C. L. (Ed.) *The American college dictionary*. New York: Random House, 1947.

Beck, A. T. Thinking and depression. *Archives of General Psychiatry*, 1963, *9*, 324–333.

Beck, A. T. *Depression: Clinical, experimental, and theoretical aspects*. New York: Harper & Row, 1967.

Beck, A. T. Cognitive therapy: Nature and relation to behavior therapy. *Behavior therapy*, 1970, *1*, 184–200.

Beck, A. T. *Cognitive therapy and the emotional disorders*. New York: International Universities Press, 1976.

Beck, A. T., & Emery, G. *Cognitive therapy of anxiety*. Philadelphia: Center for Cognitive Therapy, 1979.

Beck, A. T., Rush, A. J., Shaw, B. F., & Emery, G. *Cognitive therapy of depression: A treatment manual*. New York: Guilford Press, 1979.

Beck, A. T., Weissman, A., Lester, D., & Trexler, L. The measurement of pessimism: The hopelessness scale. *Journal of Consulting and Clinical Psychology*, 1974, *42*, 861–865.

Bertelsen, A., Harvald, B., & Hauge, M. A Danish twin study of manic-depressive disorders. *British Journal of Psychiatry*, 1977, *130*, 330–351.

Boring, E. G. *A history of experimental psychology*. (2nd ed.) New York: Appleton-Century-Crofts, 1950.

Bower, G. H. Contacts of cognitive psychology with social learning theory. *Cognitive Therapy and Research*, 1978, *2*, 123–146.

Brewer, W. F. There is no convincing evidence for operant or classical conditioning in adult humans. In W. E. Weimer & D. S. Palermo (Eds.), *Cognition and the symbolic processes*. Hillsdale, New Jersey: Erlbaum, 1974.

Brock, T. C. Communication discrepancy and intent to persuade as determinants of counterargument production. *Journal of Experimental Social Psychology*, 1967, *3*, 269–309.

Bruch, M. A. Type of cognitive modeling, initiation of modeled tactics, and modification of test anxiety. *Cognitive Therapy and Research*, 1978, *2*, 147–164.

Butler, L., & Meichenbaum, D. The assessment of interpersonal problem-solving skills. In P. C. Kendall & S. D. Hollon (Eds.), *Assessment strategies for cognitive-behavioral interventions*. New York: Academic Press, 1981.

Cacioppo, J. T., Glass, C. R., & Merluzzi, T. V. Self-statements and self-evaluations: A cognitive-response analysis of heterosocial anxiety. *Cognitive Therapy and Research*, 1979, *3*, 249–262.

Cacioppo, J. T., & Petty, R. E. The effects of message repetition and position on cognitive response, recall, and persuasion. *Journal of Personality and Social Psychology*, 1979, *37*, 97–109.

Carmody, T. P. Rational-emotive, self-instructional, and behavioral assertion training: Facilitating maintenance. *Cognitive Therapy and Research*. 1978, *2*, 241–253.

Catanese, R. A., Rosenthal, T. L., & Kelley, J. E. Strange bedfellows: Reward punishment, and impersonal distraction strategies in treating dysphoria. *Cognitive therapy and Research*, 1979, *3*, 299–306.

Cautela, J., & Upper, D. The Behavioral Inventory Battery: The use of self-report measures in behavioral analysis and therapy. In M. Hersen & A. S. Bellack (Eds.), *Behavioral assessment: A practical handbook*. New York: Pergamon Press, 1976.

Colby, K. M. *Artificial paranoia: A computer simulation of paranoid processes*. New York: Pergamon Press, 1975.

Cook, T. D., & Campbell, D. T. *Quasi-experimentation: Design and analysis issues for field settings*. Chicago: Rand McNally, 1979.

Cradock, C., Cotler, S., & Jason, L. A. Primary prevention: Immunization of children for speech anxiety. *Cognitive Therapy and Research*, 1978, *2*, 389–396.

Craighead, W. E., Kazdin, A. E., & Mahoney, M. J. *Behavior modification: Principles, issues, and applications*. Boston: Houghton Mifflin, 1976.

Craighead, W. E., Kimball, W. H., & Rehak, P. J. Mood changes, physiological responses, and self-statements during social rejection imagery. *Journal of Consulting and Clinical Psychology*, 1979, *47*, 385–396.

Davis, H. Self-reference and the encoding of personal information in depression. *Cognitive Therapy and Research*, 1979, *3*, 97–110.(a)

Davis, H. The self-schema and subjective organization of personal information in depression. *Cognitive Therapy and Research*, 1979, *3*, 415–425.(b)

Davison, G. C., & Neale, J. M. *Abnormal psychology: An experimental clinical approach*. (2nd ed.) New York: Wiley, 1978.

Derry, P. A., & Stone, G. L. Effects of cognitive-adjunct treatments on assertiveness. *Cognitive Therapy and Research*, 1979, *3*, 213–221.

Diener, C., & Dweck, C. An analysis of learned helplessness: Continuous changes in performance strategy and achievement cognitions following failure. *Journal of Personality and Social Psychology*, 1978, *36*, 451–462.

Dixon, F. *Subliminal perception: The nature of a controversy*. London: McGraw-Hill, 1971.

Donovan, D. M., & O'Leary, M. R. Depression, hypomania, and expectation of future success among alcoholics. *Cognitive Therapy and Research*, 1979, *3*, 141–154.

Dunkel, L. D., & Glaros, A. G. Comparison of self-instructional and stimulus control treatments of obesity. *Cognitive Therapy and Research*, 1978, *2*, 75–78.

Dunn, R. J. Cognitive modification with depression-prone psychiatric partients. *Cognitive Therapy and Research*, 1979, *3*, 307–318.

Ellis, A. *Reason and emotion in psychotherapy*. New York: Stuart, 1962.

Ellis, A., & Grieger, R. The present and future of RET. In A. Ellis & R. Grieger (Eds.), *Handbook of rational-emotive therapy*. New York: Springer, 1977.

Emery, G., & Fox, S. Cognitive therapy of alcohol dependency. In G. Emery, S. D. Hollon, & R. C. Bedrosian (Eds.), *New directions in cognitive therapy: A casebook*. New York: Guilford Press, 1981.

Evans, M. D., & Hollon, S. D. *Immediate versus delayed mood self-monitoring in depression*. Paper presented at the Annual Meeting of the Association for Advancement of Behavior Therapy, San Francisco, California, December 1979.

Ferster, C. B. A functional analysis of depression. *American Psychologist*, 1973, *28*, 857–870.

Foulkes, D., Spear, P. S., & Symonds, J. D. Individual differences in mental activity at sleep onset. *Journal of Abnormal Psychology*, 1966, *71*, 280–286.

Garner, D. M., & Bemis, K. M. A. cognitive-behavioral approach to anorexia nervosa. *Cognitive Therapy and Research*, 1981.

Girodo, M., & Stein, S. J. Self-talk and the work of worrying in confronting a stressor. *Cognitive Therapy and Research*, 1978, *2*, 305–307.

Girodo, M., & Wood, D. Talking yourself out of pain: The importance of believing that you can. *Cognitive Therapy and Research*, 1979, *3*, 23–34.

Glogower, F. D., Fremouw, W. J., & McCroskey, J. C. A component analysis of cognitive restructuring. *Cognitive Therapy and Research*, 1978, *2*, 209–224.

Goldfried, M. R., & Davison, G. C. *Clinical behavior therapy*. New York: Holt, Rinehart, and Winston, 1976.

Goldfried, M. R., & Sobocinski, D. Effect of irrational beliefs on emotional arousal. *Journal of Consulting and Clinical Psychology*, 1975, *43*, 504–510.

Grayson, J. B., & Borkovec, T. D. The effects of expectancy and imagined response to phobic stimuli on fear reduction. *Cognitive Therapy and Research*, 1978, *2*, 11–24.

Greenwald, A. G. Cognitive learning, cognitive response to persuasion, and attitude change. In A. G. Greenwald, T. C. Brock, & T. M. Ostrom (Eds.), *Psychological foundations of attitudes*. New York: Academic Press, 1968.

Grings, W. W. The role of consciousness and cognition in autonomic behavior change. In F. J. McGuigan, & R. A. Schoonover (Eds.), *The psycho-physiology of thinking*. New York: Academic Press, 1973.

Hamberger, K., & Lohr, J. M. Rational resstructuring for anger control: A quasi-experimental case study. *Cognitive Therapy and Research*, 1980, *4*, 99–102.

Hammen, C. L. Depression, distortion, and life stress in college students. *Cognitive Therapy and Research*, 1978, *2*, 189–192.

Hammen, C. L., & Krantz, S. Effect of success and failure on depressive cognitions. *Journal of Abnormal Psychology,* 1976, *85,* 577–586.

Harrell, T. H., & Beiman, I. Cognitive-behavioral treatment of the irritable colon syndrome. *Cognitive Therapy and Research,* 1978, *2,* 371–375.

Hinde, R. A. *Animal behaviors: A synthesis of ethology and comparative psychology.* (2nd ed.) New York: McGraw-Hill, 1970.

Hodges, W. F., McCaulay, M., Ryan, V. L., & Strosahl, K. Coping imagery, systematic desensitization, and self-concept change. *Cognitive Therapy and Research,* 1979, *3,* 181–192.

Hollandsworth, J. G., Jr., Glazeski, R. C., Kirkland, K., Jones, G. E., & Van Norman, L. R. An analysis of the nature and effects of test anxiety: Cognitive, behavioral, and physiological components. *Cognitive Therapy and Research,* 1979, *3,* 165–180.

Hollon, S. D. Cognitive-behavioral interventions for drug-induced anxiety states. In G. Emery, S. D. Hollon, & R. C. Bedrosian (Eds.), *New directions in cognitive therapy, A casebook.* New York: Guilford Press, 1981.

Hollon, S. D., & Beck, A. T. Cognitive therapy of depression. In P. C. Kendall & S. D. Hollon (Eds.), *Cognitive-behavioral interventions: Theory, research, and procedures.* New York: Academic Press, 1979.

Hollon, S. D., & Garber, J. An expectancy-based model for change in the treatment of depression. In J. Garber & M. E. P. Seligman (Eds.), *Human helplessness: Theory and applications.* New York: Academic Press, 1980.

Hollon, S. D., & Kendall, P. C. Cognitive-behavioral interventions: Theory and procedure. In P. C. Kendall & S. D. Hollon (Eds.), *Cognitive-behavioral interventions: Theory, research, and procedures.* New York: Academic Press, 1979.

Hollon, S. D., & Kendall, P. C. *In vivo* assessment techniques for cognitive-behavioral strategies. In P. C. Kendall & S. D. Hollon (Eds.), *Assessment strategies for cognitive-behavioral interventions.* New York: Academic Press, 1981.

Hollon, S. D., & Kendall, P. C. Cognitive self-statements in depression: Development of an automatic thoughts questionnaire. *Cognitive Therapy and Research,* 1980, *4,* 383–395.

Hurlburt, R. T. Random sampling of cognitions and behavior. *Journal of Research in Personality,* 1979, *13,* 103–111.

Hurlburt, R. T., & Sipprelle, C. N. Random sampling of cognitions in alleviating anxiety attacks. *Cognitive Therapy and Research,* 1978, *2,* 165–169.

Hussian, R. A., & Lawrence, P. S. The reduction of test, state, and trait anxiety by test-specific and generalized stress inoculation training. *Cognitive Therapy and Research,* 1978, *2,* 25–37.

Jenni, M. A., & Wollersheim, J. P. Cognitive therapy, stress management training, and the type A behavior pattern. *Cognitive Therapy and Research,* 1979, *3,* 61–73.

Jones, R. A. *A factored measure of Ellis' irrational belief system with personality and maladjustment correlates.* Unpublished doctoral dissertation, Texas Technological College, 1968.

Kagan, J. Reflection-impulsivity: The generality and dynamics of conceptual tempo. *Journal of Abnormal Psychology,* 1966, *71,* 17–24.

Kanfer, F. H., & Phillips, J. S. *Learning foundations of behavior therapy.* New York: Wiley, 1970.

Kazdin, A. E. Covert modeling, model similarity, and reduction of avoidance behavior. *Behavior Therapy,* 1974, *5,* 325–340.(a)

Kazdin, A. E. Self-monitoring and behavior change. In M. J. Mahoney & C. E. Thoresen (Eds.), *Self-control: Power to the person.* Monterey, California: Brooks-Cole, 1974.(b)

Kazdin, A. E. Covert modeling, imagery assessment, and assertive behavior. *Journal of Consulting and Clinical Psychiatry,* 1975, *43,* 716–724.

Kendall, P. C., & Finch, A. J. Developing nonimpulsive behavior in children: Cognitive-behavioral strategies for self-control. In P. C. Kendall, & S. D. Hollon (Eds.), *Cognitive-behavioral interventions: Theory, research, and procedures.* New York: Academic Press, 1979.

Kendall, P. C., & Hollon, S. D. *Development and validation of an anxious self-statements inventory.* Manuscript in preparation, University of Minnesota, 1979.

Kendall, P. C., & Hollon, S. D. Assessment of self-statements. In P. C. Kendall & S. D. Hollon (Eds.), *Assessment strategies for cognitive-behavioral interventions.* New York: Academic Press, 1981.

Kendall, P. C. & Korgeski, G. P. Assessment and cognitive-behavioral interventions. *Cognitive Therapy and Research,* 1979, *3*, 1–22.

Kendall, P. C., Williams, L., Pechacek, T. F., Graham, L. G., Shisslak, C. S., & Herzoff, N. Cognitive-behavioral and patient education interventions in cardiac catheterization procedures: The Palo Alto medical psychology project. *Journal of Consulting and Clinical Psychology,* 1979, *47*, 49–58.

Khatami, M., & Rush, A. J. *A pilot study of the treatment of outpatients with chronic pain: Symptom control, stimulus control and social system interaction.* Paper presented at the Annual Meeting of the Association for the Advancement of Behavior Therapy, New York, 1976.

Kihlstrom, J., & Nasby, W. Cognitive tasks in clinical assessment: An exercise in applied psychology. In P. C. Kendall & S. D. Hollon (Eds.), *Assessment strategies for cognitive-behavioral interventions.* New York: Academic Press, 1981.

Klinger, E. Modes of normal conscious flow. In K. S. Pope & J. L. Singer (Eds.), *The stream of consciousness: Scientific investigations into the flow of human experience.* New York: Plenum, 1978.

Klinger, E., Barta, S. G., & Maxeiner, M. E. Current concerns: Assessing therapeutically relevant motivation. In P. C. Kendall & S. D. Hollon (Eds.), *Assessment strategies for cognitive-behavioral interventions.* New York: Academic Press, 1981.

Krantz, S., & Hammen, C. *Assessment of cognitive bias in depression.* Manuscript in preparation, University of California, Los Angeles.

LaPointe, K. A., & Harrell, T. H. Thoughts and feelings: Correlational relationships and cross-situational consistency. *Cognitive Therapy and Research,* 1978, *2*, 311–322.

Larson, R. & Csikszentmikalyi, M. Experiential correlates of time alone in adolescence. *Journal of Personality,* in press.

Lewinsohn, P. M. Engagement in pleasant activities and depression level. *Journal of Psychology,* 1975, *84*, 729–731.

Lewinsohn, P. M., & Graf, M. Pleasant activities and depression. *Journal of Consulting and Clinical Psychology,* 1973, *41*, 261–286.

Lewinsohn, P. M., & Libet, J. Pleasant events, activity schedules, and depressions. *Journal of Abnormal Psychology,* 1972, *79*, 291–295.

Lindsay, P. H., & Norman, D. A. *Human information processing.* New York: Academic Press, 1977.

Linehan, M. Structured cognitive-behavioral treatment of assertion problems. In P. C. Kendall & S. D. Hollon (Eds.), *Cognitive-behavioral interventions: Theory, research, and procedures.* New York: Academic Press, 1979.

Lishman, W. A. Selective factors in memory: II. Affective disorders. *Psychological Medicine,* 1972, *2*, 248–253.

Lloyd, G. G., & Lishman, W. A. Effects of depression on the speed of recall of pleasant and unpleasant experiences. *Psychological Medicine,* 1975, *5*, 173–180.

Loftus, E. F., & Loftus, G. R. On the permanence of stored information in the human brain. *American Psychologist,* 1980, *35*, 409–420.

MacPhillamy, D., & Lewinsohn, P. M. *The Pleasant Events Schedule*. Unpublished manuscript, University of Oregon, 1971.

Mahoney, M. J. The self-management of covert behavior: A case study. *Behavior Therapy*, 1971, *2*, 575–578.

Mahoney, M. J. *Cognition and behavior modification*. Cambridge, Massachusettes: Ballinger, 1974.

Mahoney, M. J. Reflections on the cognitive-learning trend in psychotherapy. *American Psychologist*. 1977, *32*, 5–13.

Mahoney, M. J. Some applied issues in self-monitoring. In J. D. Cone & R. P. Hawkins (Eds.), *Behavioral assessment: New directions in clinical psychology*. New York: Brunner/Mazel, 1977.

Marlatt, G. A. Alcohol use and problem drinking. In P. C. Kendall & S. D. Hollon (Eds.), *Cognitive-behavioral interventions: Theory, research, and procedures*. New York: Academic Press, 1979.

Maultsby, M. C., Jr. *Help yourself to happiness*. New York: Institute for Rational Living, 1975.

McFall, R. M. Parameters of self-monitoring. In R. B. Stuart (Ed.), *Behavioral self-management*. New York: Brunner/Mazel, 1977.

McFall, R. M., & Hammen, C. L. Motivation, structure, and self-monitoring: Role of nonspecific factors in smoking reduction. *Journal of Consulting and Clinical Psychology*. 1971, *37*, 80–86.

Meichenbaum, D. *Cognitive behavior modification*. Morristown, New Jersey: General Learning Press, 1974.

Meichenbaum, D. *Cognitive-behavior modification: An integrative approach*. New York: Plenum, 1977.

Morgan, C. L. *An introduction to comparative psychology*. London: Scott, 1894.

Myers, A. W., Schleser, R., Cooke, C. J., & Cuvillier, C. Cognitive contributions to the development of gymnastics skills. *Cognitive Therapy and Research*, 1979, *3*, 75–85.

Neisser, U. *Cognitive psychology*. New York: Appleton-Century-Crofts, 1967.

Nelson, R. E. Irrational beliefs and depression. *Journal of Consulting and Clinical Psychology*, 1977, *45*, 1190–1191.

Nelson, R. O. Methodological issues in assessment via self-monitoring. In J. D. Cone & R. P. Hawkins (Eds.), *Behavioral assessment: New directions in clinical psychology*. New York: Brunner/Mazel, 1977.

Nisbett, R. E., & Wilson, T. D. Telling more than we can know: Verbal reports on mental processes. *Psychological Review*, 1977, *84*, 231–259.

Norton, G. R., MacLean, L., & Wachna, E. The use of cognitive desensitization and self-directed mastery training for treating stage fright. *Cognitive Therapy and Research*, 1978, *2*, 61–64.

Novaco, R. W. Stress inoculation: A cognitive therapy for anger and its application to a case of depression. *Journal of Consulting and Clinical Psychiatry*, 1977, *45*, 600–608.

Novaco, R. W. The cognitive regulation of anger and stress. In P. C. Kendall & S. D. Hollon (Eds.), *Cognitive-behavioral interventions: Theory, research, and practice*. New York: Academic Press, 1979.

Oliver, J. M., & Williams, G. The psychology of depression as revealed by attribution of causality in college students. *Cognitive Therapy and Research*, 1979, *3*, 355–360.

Osgood, C. E. *Method and theory in experimental psychology*. New York: Oxford University Press, 1953.

Penfield, W. Consciousness, memory, and man's conditioned reflexes. In K. Pribram (Ed.), *On the biology of learning*. New York: Harcourt, Brace and World, 1969.

Penfield, W., & Perot, P. The brain's record of auditory and visual experience. *Brain*, 1963, *86*, 595–696.

Penfield, W., & Roberts, L. *Speech and brain mechanisms*. Princeton: Princeton University Press, 1959.

Putnam, B. Hyposis and distortions in eyewitness memory. *International Journal of Clinical and Experimental Hypnosis*, 1979, *27* 437–448.

Rotter, J. B., Liverant, S., & Crowne, D. P. The growth and extinction of expectancies in chance-controlled and skilled tasks. *Journal of Psychology*, 1961, *52*, 161–177.

Schwartz, R., & Gottman, J. M. Toward a task analysis of assertive behavior. *Journal of Consulting and Clinical Psychology*, 1976, *44*, 910–920.

Seligman, M. E. P., Abramson, L. Y., Semmel, A., & von Bayer, C. Depressive attributional style. *Journal of Abnormal Psychology*, 1979, *88*, 242–247.

Shahar, A., & Jaffe, Y. Behavior and cognitive therapy in the treatment of vaginismus: A case study. *Cognitive Therapy and Research*, 1978, *2*, 57–60.

Shelton, T. D., & Mahoney, M. J. The content and effect of "psyching up" strategies in weight lifters. *Cognitive Therapy and Research*, 1978, *2*, 275–284.

Sherrington, C. S. *Integrative action of the nervous system*. New Haven: Yale University Press, 1906.

Shevrin, H., & Dickman, S. The psychological unconscious: A necessary assumption for all psychological theory? *American Psychologist*, 1980, *35*, 421–434.

Sims, G. K., & Lazarus, A. A. The use of random auditing stimulation in the treatment of a manic-depressive patient. *Behavior Therapy*, 1973, *4*, 128–133.

Skinner, B. F. *Science and human behavior*. New York: Macmillan, 1953.

Sky, A. W. An apparatus for frustration task. *Australian Journal of Psychology*, 1950, *2*, 116–120.

Spivack, G., & Shure, M. *Social adjustment of young children: A cognitive approach to solving real-life problems*. San Francisco: Jossey-Bass, 1974.

Sutton-Simon, K., & Goldried, M. R. Faulty thinking patterns in two types of anxiety. *Cognitive Therapy and Research*, 1979, *3*, 193–203.

Tesser, A., Leone, C., & Clary, E. G. Affect control: Process constraints versus catharsis. *Cognitive Therapy and Research*, 1978, *2*, 265–274.

Tower, R. B., & Singer, J. L. The measurement of imagery: How can it be clinically useful? In P. C. Kendall & S. D. Hollon (Eds.), *Assessment strategies for cognitive-behavioral interventions*. New York: Academic Press, 1981.

Trexler, L. D., & Karst, T. O. Rational-emotive therapy, placebo, and no treatments effects on public-speaking anxiety. *Journal of Abnormal Psychology*, 1972, *79*, 60–67.

Vygotsky, L. *Thought and language*. New York: Wiley, 1962.

Watkins, J. T., & Rush, A. J. *The Cognitive Response Test*. Paper presented at the Annual Meeting of the Association for Advancement of Behavior Therapy, Chicago, November 1978.

Watson, J. B., & Rayner, R. Conditioned emotional reactions. *Journal of Experimental Pscyhology*, 1920, *3*, 1–14.

Weissman, A. N., & Beck, A. T. *Development and utilization of the Dysfunctional Attitude Scale*. Paper presented at the Annual Meeting of the Association for the Advancement of Behavior Therapy, Chicago, 1978.

Wolpe, J. Cognition and causation in human behavior and its therapy. *American Psychologist*, 1978, *33*, 437–446.

Worthington, E. L., Jr. The effects of imagery content, choice of imagery content, and self-verbalization on the self-control of pain. *Cognitive Therapy and Research*, 1978, *2*, 225–240.

Zajonc, R. B. Feeling and thinking: Preferences need no inferences. *American Psychologist,* 1980, *35*, 151–175.

Zimbardo, P. G., Cohen, A., Weisenberg, M., Dworkin, L., & Firestone, I. The control of experimental pain. In P. G. Zimbardo (Ed.), *The cognitive control of motivation.* Glenview, Illinois: Scott, Foresman, 1969.

Chapter 6
Psychophysiological Assessment

William J. Ray & James M. Raczynski

INTRODUCTION

Although we think of the application of psychophysiological measures for the assessment and evaluation of behavioral change and psychotherapeutic process as a recent development, the conceptualization underlying these applications dates back to at least the time of Plato. Plato, in a tripartate organizational system, connected the head with rational thought, the lower spinal cord with the instincts, and the heart as the seat of emotions. In one sense, we pay homage to this system even today when we record heart rate hoping to find a measure of emotional activity. As has been discussed by Mesulam and Perry (1972), the use of psychophysiological measures as a means of assessment also dates back to the time of the early Greeks. Erasistratos, who was a physician during the time of Alexander, assessed an apparent physiological disorder through an early technique we would today refer to as lie detection. Galen, a second century A.D. physician who is often seen as the father of modern physiology, used heart rate change as a measure of emotional involvement. In one particular case where a woman had developed insomnia, Galen began to compare various stimuli until the woman showed physiological changes in response to a particular one. Through this procedure Galen demonstrated a physiological reaction to the name of a certain male dancer and concluded that the insomnia was produced by being in love. Early psychophysiological approaches were not limited to the Western world, as demonstrated by the work of Ibn Sina, a tenth century A.D. Persian, who used physiological reactions to determine psychological factors in health much in the same manner as Galen had earlier.

The promise of psychophysiological assessment was first conceptualized as engendering the possibility of discovering physiological
marker variables that could be used to delineate traditional psychological
constructs. That is, researchers sought to find objective and easily recorded physiological measures, such as heart rate or electrodermal activity, that could be used to differentiate such psychological states as
arousal and anxiety as well as traditional diagnostic groupings such as
depression and schizophrenia. From this interest the attempt to use
psychophysiological measures to assess and evaluate behavioral change
and psychotherapy has developed. In a process manner, it was hoped
that physiological changes could be utilized as an indicant of outcome
for the more difficult to quantify measures of subjective change and
would thus prove valuable as a psychotherapeutic evaluation technique
(see Lacey, 1959). In other therapeutic intervention techniques such as
biofeedback, the psychophysiological measure often served as the focus
for therapy and as an important indicant of progress (see Ray, Raczynski, Rogers, & Kimball, 1979). For example, progress in relaxation
training might be linked to a reduction in the activity of a certain set
of muscles, such as the frontalis. Finally, strides are being made in
the use of psychophysiological measures as a means of examining physiological patterning and the interrelationships between autonomic and
central nervous system events, and cognitive and overt behaviors.

In this chapter, we will discuss: (1) how psychophysiological measures are recorded; (2) concepts related to interpretation of psychophysiological measurements; (3) some of the ways in which psychophysiological measures have been used in the assessment and evaluation of
psychological processes; and (4) future considerations in the use of
psychophysiological measurements.

EQUIPMENT FOR PSYCHOPHYSIOLOGICAL
ASSESSMENT

One could perform psychophysiological assessment without any equipment other than one's own ability to observe and sense changes in another's body. Pulse rate could be measured by counting the pulses at
any one of the arteries of the body. A measure of autonomic activity
could also be determined by feeling the palms to notice the amount of
sweating that has taken place, such as before one gives an important
speech. One could likewise notice pupillary changes as another person
reacts to varying stimuli. These types of measurement have been used
for thousands of years and are still in use today, as exemplified by the
physician listening to the heart of the patient with a stethoscope or by

the salesman watching the person's reaction as new merchandise is brought forth. Although assessments performed in this manner may be useful and even accurate, it is difficult to quantify and compare objectively measurements on different occasions under varying conditions. Psychophysiologists have thus sought methods that record the various psychophysiological measures. In this section of the chapter we will discuss how psychophysiological signals are recorded, the equipment necessary for these recordings, and some of the more important measures used in assessment and research. Parts of this discussion will rely on information discussed in greater detail in *Psychophysiological Recordings* (R. M. Stern, Ray, & Davis, 1980).

When one makes any movement or even thinks about one, bioelectrical activity from the affected muscle can be recorded. This bioelectrical activity results from biochemical changes and may be recorded from the surface of the skin. In order to record this electrical activity, two small metal disks called electrodes are placed in contact with the surface of the skin. Electrodes are used to record any electrical activity resulting from biochemical changes within the body. This includes not only muscle activity (EMG), but also the activity of the cardiac muscle or heart (EKG), the electrical activity found on the scalp (EEG), electrical activity resulting from changes in the gastrointestinal tract (EGG), and activity resulting from eye movement (EOG).

From a technical standpoint, electrodes are much more than simple connections to the skin from which bioelectrical activity can be recorded (Cromwell, Weibell, Pfeiffer, & Usselmann, 1973). Electrodes aid in converting ionic potential generated by muscle and other cells into electrical potentials that can be measured. For technical reasons (Lykken, 1959), the most common electrodes today are made of silver-silver chloride (Ag-AgCl) disks encased in a plastic housing. The electrode itself does not actually touch the skin but is slightly recessed in a plastic casing; skin contact is made through a paste or jelly-like substance capable of conducting electrical activity. Most commercially available silver/silver-chloride electrodes and electrode pastes are of high quality and will serve adequately for psychophysiological assessment. However, additional considerations regarding proper electrode selection and placement and appropriate electrolytes may be found in introductory (see R. M. Stern, Ray, & Davis, 1980) and more advanced texts in psychophysiology (see Brown, 1967; Venables & Martin, 1967), as well as in biomedical instrumentation references (see Cromwell, Anditti, Weibell, Pfeiffer, Steele, & Labok, 1976; Geddes, 1972).

The one extremely important concern in making bioelectrical recordings is proper skin preparation. Without proper skin preparation and electrode placement, the bioelectrical signal will not only be reduced in amplitude, but will contain unwanted artifact. Since the outer layer of skin is composed mainly of dead cells, dirt, and oils, these must be removed by rubbing the skin with an abrasive pad or with an electrolyte containing a mild abrasive, and cleaning the skin with alcohol. Once the two electrodes are positioned by using adhesive collars and an electrolyte, the electrical connection can be checked through the use of an impedance meter or ohmeter. Generally, impedance or resistance levels below 10,000 ohms are considered acceptable.

Although we have presented a general description of electrode connection, the specific choice of electrodes and electrode paste is related to the particular measure that is being recorded. Signals of large amplitude, such as heart activity, can be recorded with minimal effort; small signals, such as EEG, require greater care and a lower impedance for high quality recordings to be made. Once the electrical activity is recorded from the surface of the skin, the next step requires that the signal be amplified and/or conditioned by a polygraph so that it can be evaluated and quantified.

Polygraph

The main component of a psychophysiological recording system is a polygraph. A polygraph is nothing more than a device for conditioning, amplifying, and reproducing psychophysiological signals from various response systems. In the same way that a stereo amplifier is actually made up of two separate amplifiers, one for each stereo channel, a polygraph is composed of anywhere from two to 32 separate amplifiers, each capable of reproducing a specific type of psychophysiological signal. Conceptually, a polygraph can be divided into three main components: (1) a signal conditioner or coupler; (2) a preamplifier and amplifier; and (3) a device for displaying the signal.

Couplers. A coupler is designed to condition the signal coming from the subject. Some couplers change the form of the signal in order to meet the requirements of the preamplifier. Others contain specialized circuits for use with transducers that record blood pressure, respiration, skin resistance, and so forth. In addition, some couplers perform selective filtering or compute rate measures, as in the case of heart rate.

Amplifiers. The signal goes from the coupler to the preamplifier, which increases its magnitude to a level that can be accepted by the power amplifier. The power amplifier in turn multiplies the signal until it is of sufficient potential to drive the writer units, interface with a computer, and/or control some type of display. The output of most polygraph amplifiers is around one volt. This means that a bioelectrical signal such as EEG, which is in the micro-volt range (one-millionth of a volt), requires amplification of a million times before it can be output to the pen or writer unit of a polygraph.

Due to the large amplification factor in psychophysiological research, it is often necessary to use filters to remove unwanted electrical activity or interference that is also amplified by the polygraph. Filtering often takes place in the amplification section of the polygraph, although some couplers also contain filters. Lowpass filters allow only frequencies *below* a certain frequency to pass, whereas highpass filters allow only frequencies *above* a certain frequency to pass. A highpass and a lowpass filter may also be combined to only allow the passing of certain frequency ranges, as is done for alpha waves of the EEG (in the 8 to 12 Hz. range). Notch filters may also be set at certain frequencies such as at 60 Hz., for filtering out electrical interference from normal wall current.

Conceptually, psychophysiologists speak of two types of amplifiers: AC and DC amplifiers. AC amplifiers are designed to reproduce *changes* in a bioelectrical signal without remaining absolutely faithful to the slow changes in the bioelectrical potential difference between the electrodes connected to the person. The DC amplifier, on the other hand, faithfully reproduces slow-changing potentials. Practically, this means that a psychophysiologist uses a DC amplifier for such slow-changing measures as temperature, skin potential, and CNV (a slow-changing potential recorded from the brain), and an AC amplifier for more rapidly changing potentials such as heart activity, EEG, and EMG (muscle potentials). Through the use of a time-constant, the AC amplifier basically filters out the DC or slow-moving component; the shorter the time constant, the less low frequency or slow-moving component will be displayed.

Displays. The most common device for displaying the electrical signal is a pen-writing unit that traces the physiological signal on paper. As useful as visual inspection may be, today new forms of data reduction make paper recorders less necessary as many psychophysiological laboratories now connect the polygraph either directly (''on-line'') or indirectly (''off-line'') to a digital computer. On-line means that the computer is being used to analyze the data at the same time that it is being collected. In order to accomplish this, the physiological signal is sent from the power amplifier of the polygraph to the A-to-D (analogue to digital) converter section of the computer, where the analogue or continuous physiological signal is changed into a discontinuous or discrete set of numbers. The computer can then perform numerical calculations on these numbers. ''Off-line'' refers to collecting the physiological signal on some type of recording device, such as an FM tape recorder, for *later* analysis at a time when the subject is not connected to the equipment. It should be noted that physiological signals must be recorded on a special type of tape recorder (an FM tape recorder) since normal voice recorders (AM tape recorders) cannot faithfully reproduce frequencies below 50 to 100 hz. With this brief introduction to the equipment necessary for psychophysiological recordings, we can now turn to the measures themselves.

PSYCHOPHYSIOLOGICAL MEASURES

General Organization of the Nervous System

The terminology of the nervous system reflects an anatomical organizing principle. The *central nervous system* (CNS) is composed of all cells within the bony enclosure of the spinal cord and skull, whereas the *peripheral nervous system* includes those neurons outside of these structures. The CNS is subdivided into the brain and spinal cord, with each of these structures further divided along anatomical lines. The peripheral nervous system is also divided into two main parts: the *somatic* system and the *autonomic* system. Whereas the somatic system is concerned with adjustment between the external world and the organism, the autonomic system deals with internal regulation of the organism. The autonomic nervous system (ANS) is further divided into two parts, depending upon where the neurons originate along the spinal cord: the *sympathetic* division is within the thoracic and lumbar sections of the spinal cord; the *parasympathetic* division originates in the cranial and sacral regions.

The autonomic nervous system and its interaction with the central nervous system has been of particular interest to psychologists because of its important role in the experience of emotion. In general, the sympathetic division activates the body, whereas the parasympathetic division conserves the resources of the body and helps to return physiological functioning to a state of equilibrium. For example, increases in heart rate, sweating, vasoconstriciton of the peripheral blood vessels, and stimulation of the sphincters (bladder and intestine) are all controlled in part by the sympathetic nervous system. The parasympathetic system, on the other hand, decreases heart rate, controls erection of the genitalia, stimulates the peristalsis of the gastrointestinal tract, increases tearing and salvation, and has little effect on the peripheral vasculature. In general, the sympathetic system acts more diffusely whereas the parasympathetic system is capable of independent actions in each of its parts.

Cardiovascular System

The cardiovascular system produces three major measures of interest to behavioral scientists. They are: (1) heart rate, (2) blood pressure, and (3) vasomotor activity.

Heart rate. The heart contracts following an impulse from specialized cells in the heart, referred to as pacemaker cells, contained in the sinoatrial node (S-A node). This initial impulse results in the contraction of the atrium and then the ventricles, which produce the distribution of blood first to the lungs and then to the body. The depolarization of the ventricles results in the characteristic spike (QRS complex) of bioelectrical potential that can be recorded from the surface of the skin. In order to record the depolarization of the atrium and ventricles, one need only place two electrodes on the skin, one on each side of the heart. This signal coming from the surface of the skin is approximately 1 millivolt (1/1000 of a volt) in size, with a frequency of around 1 hz. (one per second). Thus, the equipment must be able to amplify the signal at least 1000 times, and the activity is generally recorded with an AC amplifier, which produces less drift in the electrical signal on paper.

There are two common ways in which heartbeat data are reported: heart rate (HR) and inter-beat-interval (IBI). Heart rate is measured in units of the number of beats per time period, usually minutes. Most polygraphs also have a special coupler referred to as a cardiotachometer to electronically determine heart rate. Inter-beat-interval, on the other hand, is determined by recording the amount of time between each heartbeat. While many researchers previously determined this measure from the polygraph records, more and more researchers today use computers in quantifying this measure. Although heart rate and inter-beat-interval are highly related, there can be problems when one measure is converted into another for purposes of analysis (see Khachaturian, Kerr, Kruger, & Schachter, 1972).

F. K. Graham (1978) has also suggested that the measure and the time units should be carefully considered to produce statistically unbiased means. For example, one has the choice of recording either the first twelve *beats* following a stimulus or the first twelve *seconds* following a stimulus. To complicate matters, each of these choices may be recorded either in beats per minute or in inter-beat-intervals, and depending on the study, these four possible combinations may actually produce different results using the same set of subjects. Although complicated, the matter of heart rate or IBI measurement need not be difficult if the researcher carefully considers the type of question being asked and the most appropriate measure to answer it.

Blood pressure. The maximal blood pressure or systolic blood pressure occurs when the ventrical of the heart contracts. The subsequent relaxation of the ventricle is associated with the period when blood pressure is at a minimum, the diastolic blood pressure. Blood pressure is reported as systolic over diastolic with the standard unit of measurement being millimeters of mercury (mm-Hg.). The so-called normal blood pressure is said to be about 120/80 mm–Hg., although such factors as age, diet, posture, and weight are important to consider (Brobeck, 1973).

The most common measuring device for blood pressure involves a sphygmomanometer and a stethoscope, the device used by most physicians in this country. The cuff is placed around the person's arm and then inflated to cut off all arterial blood flow. As the pressure in the cuff is reduced, tapping sounds (Korotkoff sounds) are heard in the stethoscope, placed over the brachial artery below the cuff, as blood begins to flow again. The point at which the first sound is heard is referred to as systolic blood pressure. As pressure in the cuff is reduced further, the sounds change through a series of well described stages (see Brobeck, 1973) until no sound is heard. The measurement at this point is considered the diastolic blood pressure.

Polygraph couplers have been designed to produce a permanent record by replacing the stethoscope with a microphone whose output is displayed on the polygraph tracing superimposed over the pressure record as the cuff is deflated. Problems emerge in quantifying these data, however, as a visual judgment must be made regarding the first and last sounds as they appear on the chart paper, and the inflation and deflation of the cuff itself may be a strong stimulus for the subject. There is also a limit to the number of blood pressure recordings that can be taken during any one session, and repeated measures may actually artificially alter readings through tissue changes. Finally, large variations may be seen in individuals' readings during a session (Tursky, 1974b). Hence, using blood pressure as an assessment device should be approached with caution.

Vasomotor activity. Vasomotor changes are often experienced as cold hands or feet, when someone is about to take an exam or meet an important person. The opposite reaction, blushing, is also commonly experienced during emotional arousal. There are two commonly used measures of vasomotor activity: blood volume and pulse volume.

Blood volume reflects slow changes in the amount of blood in the arm, finger, leg, or toe, whereas pulse volume is a more rapid change reflecting both the contraction of the heart as well as peripheral changes. Blood volume measurements are made with the transducer connected to a DC amplifier whereas pulse volume measurements use an AC amplifier.

The most popular method for recording blood volume and pulse volume is with a photoelectric plethysmograph. A photoelectric plethysmograph consists of a light source in the infrared range and a photodetector. Depending on the particular photoelectric pletysmograph, the light is either measured as it passes through the tissue (more blood equals less light passing through) or as it bounces off the blood (the detector is on the same side as the light source).

While the recording of vascular activity is relatively simple, the interpretation and accurate quantification of this measure is a difficult task. Since many factors such as room temperature, variation in skin characteristics, difficulty of exact placement from person to person and on the same person at different occasions, and even variations in the intensity of the light source make absolute vasomotor measurement impossible and complicate relative ones. (See Cook, 1974 for a more detailed discussion of factors that influence vasomotor activity.)

Muscle Activity. Muscular activity has played a predominant role in behavioral assessment. It has been used both as an assessment measure for discussing such constructs as anxiety and relaxation (e.g., Jacobson, 1938) and as a treatment modality when fed back to the person in clinical biofeedback (see Ray, Raczynski, Rogers, & Kimball, 1979). The most common technique for recording muscular activity is the EMG (electromyogram), which is the result of action potentials spreading over the skeletal muscle cells following neural stimulation. With increased stimulation and the resultant activity or tension, numerous motor units begin to fire. However, the EMG is most representative during tension but less so during the actual movements (Lippold, 1952).

Muscle activity is recorded from the surface of the skin in much the same way as heart rate activity, but there are some important considerations that should be noted when making EMG recordings. First, both electrodes should be over the same muscle or muscle group. To illustrate this point, C. M. Davis, Brickett, Stern, and Kimball (1978) have noted that most biofeedback researchers record frontalis activity from placements over the two different frontalis muscles. This produces unnecessary artifacts in the recording and not a true representation of EMG activity. Second, the electrodes, when possible, should be on a line parallel with the muscle fibers. Third, the length between the electrodes will determine whether they are recording the activity of single motor units (1-2 cm. between them) or a general index of muscle tension. However, even with careful placements, activity from other muscles nearby may also be picked up. Thus, to claim that one is recording from *only* a certain muscle is impossible with surface electrodes.

Since EMG activity can range from a few microvolts to the millivolt range, the amplifier settings depend on the type of activity with which one is concerned. For example, bioelectrical activity generated from a subject imagining that an activity is being performed would be much less than that generated from voluntary contraction of a muscle group. The frequency of muscle activity may likewise range from a few hertz or over 1000 hz., although most of the single power is between 10 and 150 hz. It should be noted that polygraph pen units rarely function accurately above 75 hz.; if only a general tension level is desired this should pose little problem.

Most behavioral researchers quantify EMG activity through the use of an integrator unit. This device, supplied by many polygraph companies, summates the amount of EMG activity over time and can be used to determine the amount of muscle tension during various phases of an experimental session.

Electrodermal Activity. Electrodermal activity has been used for assessment since the beginning of this century when Carl Jung used GSR as a measure of emotional reactivity to a set of stimulus words (Jung, 1907). There are two major methods for measuring electrodermal activity, both dating back to the 1800s. The first method passes a current through the skin from an external source and measures the changes in resistance of the skin to this current. Today the reciprocal of resistance, skin conductance, is usually recorded for a number of reasons (see R. M. Stern, Ray & Davis, 1980). The second method, referred to as skin potential, does not use an external current but measures the electrical activity at the surface of the skin.

Skin conductance, skin resistance, and skin potential may all be examined in regard to specific stimuli, the general basal level, or changes which cannot be attributed to a specific stimulus. Changes to specific stimuli are referred to as responses, measures of the general basal level are called tonic measures, and responses to unknown stimuli are considered spontaneous activity.

The most common measure used in behavioral assessment, and the measure which should be used, is that of skin conductance. Skin conductance is usually recorded from the palmar surface of the hands. If a bipolar placement is to be used, the electrode sites on the hand are cleaned but not abraded; with monopolar recording the inactive site (usually on the arm) is abraded. Skin conductance responses are recorded using a special coupler that imposes a small constant voltage across the two electrodes.

While this measure, like vascular activity, is relatively easy to record, the quantification of skin conductance is a complex matter and may involve quantification of response amplitudes, frequency of spontaneous responses, as well as certain aspects of the responses themselves (see Edelberg, 1967, for a more complete discussion). In addition, Venables and Christie (1973) have reported a number of factors that may influence skin conductance responses, including such subject factors as age, sex, race, and stage of the menstrual cycle, and such environmental factors as temperature, humidity, time of day, day of week, and season of the year.

Respiration. Depending on the degree of a person's inhalation, autonomic activity such as vasoconstriction in the finger, an increase followed by a decrease in heart rate, and an increase in skin conductance may occur (R. M. Stern & Anschel, 1968). Since these effects may be confounds, respiration rate is often recorded as a control for artifact. Respiration rate may also be used as a measure in and of itself, such as in measuring respiratory changes during sleep (Timmons, Salamy, & Kamiya, 1972), although this and other applications have only been rarely examined.

The most common polygraphic measure of respiration uses a strain gauge placed on the subject's stomach or chest. The strain gauge is simply a thin plastic tube filled with mercury which has a small current passed through it as a part of a special bridge circuit from the respiration coupler in the polygraph. With respiratory changes and consequent changes in the length of the tube, changes in resistance occur and may be recorded.

Other Psychophysiological Measures

There are numerous other psychophysiological measures that can be used for assessment purposes. There are such measures as the electrical activity recorded from the scalp (either evoked potentials or EEG); electrical activity recorded from the gastrointestinal system; eye movement and pupil size; and specialized sexual measures. Because of the complexity in recording these measures, they are not included in this review. However, other books may be consulted for a discussion of these measures (e.g., Brown, 1967; Venables & Martin, 1967; R. M. Stern, Ray, & Davis, 1980).

CONCEPTS RELATED TO THE INTERPRETATION OF PSYCHOPHYSIOLOGICAL ASSESSMENT AND RESEARCH

At the present time, there is no one theoretical orientation that unites psychophysiological assessment and research. However, numerous research programs throughout this century have developed certain principles or concepts which apply to psychophysiological studies. In this section, we will acquaint you briefly with some of the more important ones. For a more in depth discussion, Sternbach (1966), and Greenfield and Sternbach (1972) should be consulted.

Law of Initial Values

The law of initial values was first formally presented by Wilder (1967). In general, as pre-stimulus levels increase, responses to stimulation have been found to decrease. To illustrate this point, consider a subject who is late for your experiment and runs over to your building and up the stairs to the laboratory. When heart rate electrodes are attached and this subject is presented with a stimulus that usually increases heart rate, heart rate activity might not increase and, in some cases, might actually decrease. Most psychophysiologists conceptualize the law of initial values as resulting from a given individual's physiological limits. It is assumed that heart rate will vary only between certain limits as a result of the normal negative feedback mechanisms of the body. From a practical standpoint, this means that pre-stimulus levels must be taken into account when calculating heart rate change scores. In conceptual terms, this also means that a change from a heart rate of 120 to 125 represents a different amount of effort on the part of the organism than a change from 60 to 65 beats per minute, although both changes are an absolute five beats per minute. When correcting for the law of initial values with heart rate, skin resistance, blood pressure or other measures, one of two common techniques is used. The first is to use Lacey's autonomic liability score (Lacey, 1956), a form of residualized gain scored (see Cronbach & Furby, 1970). The second is an analysis of covariance as applied to psychophysiological data (Benjamin, 1967).

Homeostasis

Homeostasis is best understood as part of general systems theory. The homeostatic state is the state of equilibrium that is maintained through a negative feedback loop. For example, when you set a thermostat at

65°, the heating system will be cut off once the temperature goes above this setting. The body has also been conceptualized in this manner as can be illustrated through sweating. As the temperature of the body is increased, negative feedback mechanisms produce sweating until the temperature is returned to a homeostatic state. It has been similarly suggested that there is a normal return to equilibrium after an anxiety-producing event.

The concept of homeostatis was first introduced by Claude Bernard and made popular by Walter Cannon in his book, *The Wisdom of the Body* (1939). Cannon basically suggested that the body is capable of regulating itself without any conscious control. Some recent conceptualizations in biofeedback suggest that physiological disorders are the result of a break-down in the homeostatic mechanisms, and that biofeedback may offer an external means of reestablishing normal homeostatic processes. Likewise, some psychophysiologists suggest that homeostatic mechanisms are the basis of the law of initial values.

Habituation

Habituation is the process by which the physiological responses diminish upon continued presentation of the stimulus. It may be generally stated that habituation will be slower the greater the intensity of stimulation, the more unique the stimulus, and the more complex the stimulus (see F. K. Graham, 1973).

Orienting and Defensive Responses

Pavlov (1927) noticed that previously conditioned dogs did not show conditioning in the presence of a novel stimulus. He described this process as a reflex present in men and animals which responds immediately to the slightest changes in the environment. This process is now called the orienting response (OR) or the "what is it?" response. Lynn (1966) has summarized the orienting response as follows: (1) an increase in sensitivity of sense organs; (2) body orientation toward sound (turning head, etc.); (3) increase in muscle tone with decrease in irrelevant motor activity; (4) pattern of EEG activation (faster frequency, lower amplitude); (5) vasoconstriction in the periphery (limbs) and vasodilation in the head; (6) skin conductance increase; (7) after initial delay, respiration shows amplitude increase and frequency decrease; and (8) heart rate slows.

Understanding the orienting response prevents a researcher from confusing initial OR reactions to the first few stimuli that might be displayed in a series with the physiological response to the stimuli themselves. Since it is often difficult to differentiate which psychophysiological responses are to the stimuli themselves and which represent orienting responses, the beginning stimuli are often disregarded in psychophysiological research, especially in those cases where the stimuli are novel to the subject.

Whereas the OR represents an attention to a novel stimulus, the defensive response (DR) is thought to represent a turning away from painful and intense stimuli. The DR also habituates much slower than the OR. The psychophysiological reactions of the two are similar except that vasomotor activity in the head shows constriction in a DR while heart rate shows an increase in the DR (see Sokolov, 1963, 1965). The other psychophysiological responses are similar to those discussed by Lynn (1966) in relation to the OR.

THE THEORETICAL RELATIONSHIP BETWEEN PHYSIOLOGICAL VARIABLES AND PSYCHOLOGICAL CONSTRUCTS

A great emphasis of early psychophysiological research was directed to the search for physiological correlates of psychological constructs. One of the more important constructs in this search was that of activation (also called arousal), which has often been seen as a general determinate of emotionality. The general construct of activation can be traced back to Cannon (1915) and his emphasis on a general state of arousal that would lead to "fight or flight" behavior. Since the time of Cannon, research has been directed in one of two directions. The first direction is a more cortical one in which activation, and in turn emotionality, are thought to be related to specific structures in either the brain stem or neocortex. This particular direction, although important theoretically, has had little direct effect on behavioral assessment work. The second direction is exemplified by the work of Duffy (1962, 1972), Malmo (1959), Lindsley (1951, 1952) and others. This approach has viewed arousal as a unidirectional continuum with the degree of arousal being related to some index of performance. Duffy (1957) hypothesized an inverted U-shaped curve, with the best performance being associated with medium states of arousal, and the poorest performance associated with either minimal or extreme arousal. Measures such as heart rate, EEG, and muscle tension were all related to performance in this manner.

Lacey (1967) suggested that this view of arousal is too simple and ignores the complexity of the phenomenon. In turn, he suggested that in order to understand the construct of arousal one must differentiate between cortical, autonomic, or behavioral arousal. As Borkovec (1976) and Davidson and Schwartz (1976) have recently reported, it is possible to show arousal in one area (e.g., cognitive) and not in another (e.g., somatic). Lacey further suggested that even among autonomic variables, it is possible to have a patterning inconsistent with a uni-directional arousal continuum: it is quite possible to find a situation that produces an increase in skin conductance and muscle tension but a decrease in heart rate and respiration rate.

In an excellent review of the application of psychophysiological measures to the evaluation of psychotherapy process and outcome, Lacey (1959) suggests that there are at least four situations that must be considered when performing psychophysiological assessment.

1. Intra-stressor stereotypy is descriptive of the case where an individual in response to a certain kind of stimuli gives a reproducible pattern.
2. Inter-stressor stereotypy occurs when a pattern obtained with one stressor is also found using different stressors.
3. Situational stereotypy, on the other hand, is found when different patterns of response occur with different task demands. For example, Darrow (1929) suggested that "sensory" stimuli (those not requiring thinking) would be associated with heart rate decreases, whereas "ideational" stimuli would be associated with an increase in heart rate.
4. Finally, symptom specificity describes the case where a stressor will produce one type of psychophysiological problem (e.g., headaches) in one person and produce another problem (e.g., heart palpitations) in someone else (see Malmo & Shagass, 1949).

Although one might want to conclude at this moment that psychophysiological approaches are too complex and should be ignored, neither Lacey in his 1959 review, nor the present authors would consider this conclusion warranted. In fact, a brief review of the areas in which psychophysiology has contributed to behavioral assessment dispels this notion.

REVIEW OF PSYCHOPHYSIOLOGICAL ASSESSMENT APPLICATIONS

As this chapter has noted, psychophysiology has long existed as a discipline within itself and has also received increased interest relatively

recently from those endeavoring to utilize psychophysiological methodologies with behavioral disorders. As such, two distinct but not
mutually exclusive forms of literature have emerged. The first and older
of these literatures has developed from the traditional psychophysiologists who were, and are, individuals of different conceptual orientations bound by common methodologies. They include not only a few
clinical psychologists, but also persons from experimental, physiological, and medical, as well as psychophysiological backgrounds (Sternbach, 1966). As such, the literature has examined questions concerning
the relationships between physiological activity and abnormal psychological processes. In addition, psychophysiologists have also considered
relationships between abnormal physiological activity and psychological
events and between normal variations in both physiological activity and
psychological events. The second and later attempt to develop literature
has emerged as a subset of the previous work. Behavioral clinical psychologists, bound by a common conceptual basis, have sought to examine physiological activity as one of the tripartite response systems.
Thus, an examination of physiological activity became an aspect of
behavioral assessment in "the identification of meaningful response
units and their controlling variables (both current environmental and
organismic) for the purposes of understanding and altering human behavior'' (Nelson & Hayes, 1979, p. 491).

In the discussions of the role of physiological measures in behavioral
assessment, emphasis was initially placed on the relationships between
physiological events and abnormal behavior. Psychophysiological assessment procedures were quickly adopted by behaviorally-oriented clinical psychologists in areas where there was a strong hypothesized physiological component, such as in the study of anxiety (e.g., Lang, 1971;
Mathews, 1971) and sexual disorders (e.g., Bancroft, 1971). However,
this represents a very limited view of behavioral assessment in general
(see Nelson & Hayes, 1979) and of the potential utility of psychophysiological assessment procedures. Indeed, behavioral assessment targets
are expanding into areas of normal variations in persons' functioning
(see Nelson & Hayes, 1979) and of the potential utility of psychophysiological assessment procedures. Indeed, behavioral assessment targets
erature of psychophysiologists emerges as important in providing a base
for this expansion of behavioral assessment procedures.

For an appreciation of the manner in which psychophysiological methodologies have been applied to assessment, the interested reader is referred to books dealing with general psychophysiological relationships
(Andreassi, 1980; Fowles, 1975; Greenfield & Sternbach, 1972; Prokasy

& Raskin, 1973; Venables & Christie, 1975) and emotions (Grings & Dawson, 1978; S. Schacter, 1971). For a more in-depth review of specific psychophysiological assessment measures, works discussing electrodermal activity (Edelberg, 1972; J. A. Stern & Janes, 1973), cardiovascular activity (Gunn, Wolf, Block, & Person, 1972), plethysmography (Ackner, 1956), electromyography (I. B. Goldstein, 1972), pupillometrics (Hess, 1972), and salivation (Brown, 1970) should be consulted. Various electrocortical assessment measures have been reviewed frequently and include examinations of general activity (Andreassi, 1980; Shagass, Gershon, & Friedhoff, 1977; Zubin & Shagass, 1969), coherence and asymmetry measures (Thatcher & Maisel, 1979), visual and auditory evoked responses (Begleiter, 1979; Callaway, 1975; Perry & Childers, 1969), and event-related slow electrocortical potentials such as the contingent negative variation (CNV), postimperative negative variation (PINV), and other readiness potentials (Dongier, Dubrovsky, & Engelsmann, 1977; Karlin, 1970; Tecce, 1971). In addition, reviews of the psychophysiological effects of specific tasks, such as the cold pressor task (Lovallo, 1975) and conditioning (Martin, 1975), may be further consulted.

In classifying the areas in which psychophysiological methodologies are, or may be, of utility in behavioral assessment, three divisions emerge. *First* is the area which has been considered by previous reviews, where investigators have attempted to delineate the particualr physiological accompaniments of psychological constructs. *Second* is an area where psychophysiological assessment methodologies are being employed in the area of psychophysiological disorders and behavioral medicine. This area thus includes disorders in which assessments of physiological function are used with psychophysiological disorders, e.g., when the blood pressure of hypertensives is taken or electromyographic levels of tension headache sufferers are assessed. While one may believe that the physiological cannot be separated from the psychological (D. T. Graham, 1971) and that all medicine and psychology should be considered to be behavioral medicine (Schwartz, 1978), a distinction must be made between cases where this assessment is purely for obtaining medical information and those in which the physiological assessment is considered within a broader context of behavioral assessment. The former cases are not considered examples of behavioral assessment and will not be covered in this review. This second area also includes applications in which physiological assessment may be utilized in measuring compliance and topographical features of such responses as smoking and weight control problems. The *third* area to be considered is where physiological assessment is used to assess the relationship between normal ranges of both physiological activity and cognitive and behavioral events.

Traditional Applications with Clinical Disorders

Psychophysiological methodologies have been applied in the assessment of psychotic disorders, anxiety, depression, and psychopathy. Recent areas of investigation have also included the psychophysiology of learning disabled and hyperactive children, and attempts have been made to examine the psychophysiological effects of psychotherapy itself.

Psychoses. Psychotic disorders have generated one of the largest literatures dealing with psychophysiological assessment. Various EEG measures have been extensively reviewed and have included general EEG activity during awake states (Alexander, 1972; Andreassi, 1980; Ax, 1962; Buchsbaum, 1977a, 1977b; L. Goldstein & Sugarman, 1969; Heath, 1977; Itil, 1977; Shagass, 1977b; Venables, 1975) and during sleep (Feinberg & Evarts, 1969). Various event-related potentials have been reviewed to auditory and visual stimuli (Shagass, 1977a, 1977b, 1979 (and in regard to late positive components and slow potentials (Roth, 1977; Tecce, 1971). Asymmetrical EEG activity has been considered in a review by Alpert and Martz (1977), and work with bilateral electrodermal activity has been reviewed in an attempt to relate these effects to lateralized central nervous system activity (Venables, 1977). Investigations examining various autonomic measures of psychotic persons have also been reviewed. These have included examinations of electrodermal activity (Depue & Fowles, 1973; Jordan, 1974; J. A. Stern & Janes, 1973; Zahn, 1977), electromyographic activity (Goode, Meltzer, Crayton, & Mazura, 1977), and electrooculographic activity (Holzman & Levy, 1977). Psychophysiological measures have also been examined in identifying high risk children (see Friedman, Frosch, & Erlenmeyer-Kimling, 1979; Venables, 1977). In general, these reviews suggest that psychophysiological measures are of value in assessing psychotic disorders and in revealing data of conceptual significance.

Anxiety. Anxiety is another disorder frequently investigated with psychophysiological methodologies, and these investigations have generated a fair number of review articles. The autonomic concomitants of anxiety have been discussed in several general reviews (Lader, 1975; Lader & Noble, 1975; Lader & Wing, 1966; Lang, 1977) and in a review of electromyograpahic activity (I. B. Goldstein, 1972). The effects of systematic desensitization upon autonomic measures has been reviewed by Mathews (1971). The occurrence of adrenalin effects (Breggin, 1964) and of psychophysiological differentiation of orienting and defensive responses among anxious persons (Froehlich, 1978) has also been discussed. Finally, electrocortical measures of anxiety have been reviewed (Froehlich, 1978; Tecce, 1971), and the potential for differentiating between somatic and cognitive forms of anxiety based on electrocortical measures has been discussed (Davidson, 1978). These reviews suggest that no one psychophysiological measure may be used as an index of anxiety. However, multiple measures may be of utility in evaluating the contribtuion of the physiological system to anxiety (see Borkovec, 1976).

Depression. Pscyhophysiological investigations of depressed persons have been infrequently undertaken (see Raczynski & Craighead, 1980). Most EEG studies of depressed persons have been reported with what have been described as psychotic depressions and are contained within reviews of psychotic disorders. However, electocortical studies of depressed persons while asleep have been reviewed (Feinberg & Evarts, 1969; Mendels & Chernick, 1975). Several reviews of autonomic measures of depressed individuals have also appeared (Lader, 1975; Lader & Noble, 1975; Raczynski & Craighead, 1980), along with specific autonomic measures, such as salivation (Brown, 1970). In general, these reviews suggest that while autonomic measures may be altered during depression, the direction and extent of change may be related more to the presence or absence of anxiety or agitation-retardation than to the degree of depression (see Raczynski & Craighead, 1980).

Psychopathy. Hare (1970, 1971, 1975a, 1975b) has generated a number of review articles dealing with the psychophysiology of psychopathic persons. Additional reviews may be found by S. Schacter (1971), S. Schacter and Latane (1964), and J. A. Stern and Janes (1973). Finally, electrocortical measures of the contingent negative variation of psychopaths may be found (Tecce, 1971), and a recent review by Fowles (1980) of heart rate and electrodermal activity suggests an arousal model for psychopathy. Taken together, these reviews suggest that psychopaths differ in certain psychophysiological aspects from normal persons.

Learning disabled and hyperactive children. Two recent reviews have emerged dealing with the psychophysiology of hyperactive children (Satterfield, Cantwell, & Satterfield, 1974) and with the relationship between event-related potentials and reading disability (Preston, 1979). Studies are also beginning to emerge suggesting that event-related potentials of hyperactive children might serve as predictors of improvement (see Halliday, Rosenthal, Naylor, & Callaway, 1976). While this area of application of psychophysiological assessment methodologies suffers from a paucity of research, results appear promising and suggest that further research be conducted.

Psychotherapy. While there have been attempts to examine psychophysiological activity during psychotherapy, only a very few attempts have been made to summarize this literature. I. B. Goldstein (1972) has discussed electromyographic activity during psychotherapy, and Lacey (1959) reviewed the available psychophysiological literature. Nonetheless, psychophysiological methodologies may provide a valuable source of data for examining the process of psychotherapy.

APPLICATIONS WITH PSYCHOPHYSIOLOGICAL DISORDERS AND BEHAVIORAL MEDICINE PROCEDURES

Psychophysiological assessment procedures have been utilized in the assessment of sexual disorders, neurological problems, mental retardation, pain, and drug addictions among others. In addition, psychophysiological methodologies are playing an ever-increasing role in the assessment and treatment of other psychophysiological disorders.

Sexual disorders. Bancroft (1971) reviewed the early literature concerning psychophysiological applications with sexual disorders. Heiman (1978) and Geer (1977) have since expanded upon this review, and Karacan and colleagues (Karacan, 1978; Karacan, Salis, & Williams, 1978) have reviewed the promising data concerning the utility of psychophysiological procedures in the assessment and differential diagnosis of impotence. Taken togther, the psychophysiological evaluation of sexual disorders appears to be a valuable form of behavioral assessment in understanding the behavior and its underlying physiological basis.

Neurological disorders. EEG measures have, of course, been frequently applied in the assessment of neurological disorders. The literature has been reviewed for the use of auditory evoked potentials (Cracco, 1979), the contingent negative variation (Tecce, 1971), EEG activity during sleep (Feinberg & Evarts, 1969), and subcortical potentials (Heath, 1977). Recently, evidence has been reported (Pace, Molfese, Schmidt, Mikula, & Ciano, 1979) to suggest that physiological assessment may be of utility in the differential neuropsychological assessment of aphasic and non-aphasic disorders. Finally, J. A. Stern and Janes (1973) have reviewed the literature concerning the relationship between autonomic activity and brain damage. While these forms of physiological assessment may be conceptualized as purely medical, they may prove valuable in the behavioral assessment of neurologically impaired and nonimpaired functions and provide a guideline for behavioral interventions.

Mental retardation. As with neurological disorders, the relationships between impairment of function and event-related EEG potentials (see Galbraith, Squires, Altair, & Gliddon, 1979) and autonomic measures (see J. A. Stern & Janes, 1973) have been discussed. Again, this form of behavioral assessment may prove to be of utility in the understanding and altering of human behavior.

Pain. The relationship between psychophysiological activity and pain has been considered by several reviewers (Melzack & Wall, 1975; S. Schacter, 1971; Sternbach, 1974) and regarding electrical stimulation by Tursky (1974a). In addition, several recent articles dealing with the psychophysiological treatment of different types of pain suggest the potential of psychophysiological assessment procedures in the cases of low back pain (e.g., Nouwen & Solinger, 1979), anginal pain (e.g. Hartman, 1979), chronic pain due to causalgia (Blanchard, 1979), as well as pain due to tension and migraine headaches and temporomandibular joint dysfunction (see Ray, Raczynski, Rogers, & Kimball, 1979). The available data suggest that psychophysiological assessment procedures may be valuable in the behavioral assessment of the physiological basis of pain and in the assessment of topographical features of the disorder.

Drug addictions. The utility of psychophysiological assessment of pharmacological effects has been reviewed (Stroebel, 1972). Recent psychophysiological studies have also investigated the psychophysiological effects of such drugs as marijuana (e.g., Naliboff, Rickles, Cohen, & Naimark, 1976) and the psychophysiological reactivity of drug abusers (e.g., Prystav, 1975). The effects of chronic alcohol use have also been reviewed for evoked potentials (Dustman, Snyder, Callner, & Beck, 1979; Porjesz & Begleiter, 1979). Continued investigation of the effects of drug use and of the psychophysiological activity of drug users may aid in our understanding of the relationship between the physiological system and the behavior of drug abusers.

Other applications. Other recent applications of psychophysiological assessment methodologies with psychophysiological disorders and behavioral medicine procedures have appeared. For example, Doerr, Follette, Scribner, and Eisdorfer (1980) have suggested that psychophysiological measures may be important in the assessment of renal dialysis patients. Continued investigation of potential autonomic indices of renal failure may contribute to the behavioral assessment of renal patients and the understanding and altering of the relationship between their disorder and their behavior. Similarly, psychophysiological methodologies may contribute to the assessment of stuttering, for example, where elevated levels of electromyographic activity have been noted in the involved musculature (see Stroemer, 1979).

Finally, the role of psychophysiology in the behavioral assessment of self-control disorders, such as smoking and weight control, should not be overlooked. For example, electrocortical activity of smokers has been examined (Knott & Venables, 1979) and may contribute to our understanding of smoking behavior. The potential for physiological assessment procedures in the measuring of compliance and outcome should be considered (see Frederiksen, Martin, & Webster, 1979). In obesity research, the need for metabolic assessment and the assessment of arousal has been stressed (Wooley, Wooley, & Dyrenforth, 1979) and may only be met adequately by the inclusion of psychophysiological indices within a behavioral assessment package.

Applications with the Assessment of Normal Variations in Activity

Psychophysiological assessment has been examined in relation to cognitive porcesses, various personality factors, emotion, sleep, sexual arousal, deception, aging, and a variety of other organismic and environmental influences. While these applications have rarely been considered within discussions of behavioral assessment (see Epstein, 1976; Lang, 1971), they are important for two reasons. First, these psychophysiological applications have yielded a substantial literature from which a better understanding of normal behavior may be obtained. Second, these investigations have identified factors which must be considered as a broad contextual base from which any psychophysiological relationship must be appreciated. Environmental and organismic effects have been revealed which must be accounted for before other hypotheses for obtained effects may be entertained.

Cognitive processes. The effects of attention, arousal, information processing, performance, motivation, achievement, and learning have been the source of a number of review articles. Most of these reviews have focused on various electrocortical measures, such as the evoked-potentials and contingent negative variation (Donchin, 1979; I. B. Goldstein, 1972; John, 1967; Naatanen, 1975; Ritter, 1979; Shagass, 1972; Tecce, 1972). However, autonomic activity has also been considered as associated with achievement (Shapiro & Schwartz, 1970) and motivation (Ax, Lloyd, Gorham, Lootens, & Robinson, 1978).

Personality factors. The relationship between various personality factors and psychophysiological measures has been discussed in several reviews of the literature (Alexander, 1972; Edelberg, 1972 Eysenck, 1968; Rusinov, 1970; J. A. Stern & Janes, 1973) and has even been considered in the development of specific psychosomatic disorders (D. T. Graham, 1962, 1972). Other reviews have considered more specific personality constructs such as introversion and extraversion (Gray, 1970, 1972; Shagass & Canter, 1972), ego strength (Roessler, 1973), and relationship, personal development, and system factors (Kiritz & Moos, 1974). While this body of research suffers from the problems associated with traditional personality assessment (see Goldfried & Kent, 1972), the available research does suggest that differences in psychophysiological responses exist between individuals who differ in self-report and behavioral measures.

Emotion. Psychophysiological differentiation between different emotions has been attempted and discussed in a number of reviews (e.g., Lang, Rice & Sternbach, 1972; Pribram, 1967; S. Schacter, 1971; Shcwartz, 1978). Although much is known about the psychophysiology of disorders of affect, and data suggest some complex relationships between emotion and psychophysiological responding, research is still evolving concerning the psychophysiology of emotions, as in the case of the response of the facial musculature during emotion (e.g., Schwartz, Ahern, & Brown, 1979; Schwartz, Brown, & Ahern, 1980).

Sleep. The associations between psychophysiological measures and sleep have been addressed by several general reviews (Johnson, 1970, 1975; Snyder & Scott, 1972). Other reviews have discussed the relationship between sleep and various measures such as electrodermal activity (Edelberg, 1972), electrocortical activity (Feinberg & Evarts, 1969), and electromyographic activity (I. B. Goldstein, 1972). The effects of sleep deprivation (Naitoh, 1975) and of the hypnagogic state (D. L. Schacter, 1976) have also been considered.

Sexual arousal. The psychophysiological effects of normal sexual arousal have been discussed by a number of reviewers (Bancroft, 1971; Heiman, 1977; Masters & Johnson, 1966; R. M. Stern, Farr, & Ray, 1975; Zuckerman, 1972). While the finding that physiological changes occur during sexual arousal is not surprising, this research has been important in delineating normal responses and the relationship of physiological responses to cognitive activity.

Deception. The detection of deception has been the target of numerous psychophysiological investigations. This work has been recently reviewed for laboratory studies (Podlesney & Raskin, 1977) and field investigations (Raskin, Barland, & Podlesney, 1977). Other reviews may also be found (Andreassi, 1980; Barland & Raskin, 1973; Lykken, 1974; Orne, Thackray, & Paskewitz, 1972).

Aging. The psychophysiological effects of aging have been studied most frequently from an electrocortical standpoint. An excellent review of brain electrical activity and behavior relationships over the life span may be found in Woodruff (1978). Significant changes have been found during aging in evoked potentials (Dustman, Snyder, Callner, & Beck, 1979; Perry & Childers, 1969; Shagass, 1972), the contingent negative variation (Shagass, 1972; Tecce, 1971), and in electrocortical activity during sleep (Feinberg & Evarts, 1969). Electrodermal changes during aging have also been discussed by Edelberg (1972). The most recent summary of all this literature, however, has been presented by Marsh and Thompson (1977).

Other organismic variations. A variety of organismic variables have been discussed by reviewers as affecting psychophysiological measures. These include effects from sex differences (e.g., Edelberg, 1972; Perry & Childers, 1969; Shagass, 1972), women's menstrual cycles (Bell, Christie, & Venables, 1975), socio-cultural differences (Shapiro & Schwartz, 1970), racial and ethnic differences (Christie & Todd, 1975), and circadian rhythm effects (Mefferd, 1975). Obviously, psychophysiological measures provide a rich source of information for the behavioral assessment of these variations, while these relationships serve, at least partially to delimit the sources of variance with psychophysiological measures.

Environmental influences. Another substantial source of variance in psychophysiological activity is environmental effects. Mefferd (1975) has discussed the effects upon physiological measures of temperature, humidity, barometric pressure, weather fronts, wind speed, amount of sunshine, and geomagnetic activity. Additional sources of variance may be found, not only in the time of the year, but in the day of the week (Christie, 1975) and the time of the quarter for students (Fisher & Winkel, 1979).

FUTURE CONSIDERATIONS AND SUMMARY

As this chapter has noted, behavioral assessment uses of psychophysiological methodologies began with disorders in which there were evident links between the behavior being assessed and the physiological measure examined. From this beginning, the utility of these methodologies was quickly realized in initial assessments as with sexual behaviors (Bancroft, 1971), as outcome measures in the assessment of procedures such as systematic desensitization (Mathews, 1971), and in the assessment and modification of psychophysiological disorders (see Ray, Raczynski, Rogers, & Kimball, 1979). Thus, psychophysiology was first considered in behavioral assessment as simply a methodology—a means of assessing and predicting outcome, either by examining the change in a psychophysiological measure associated with a particular psychological construct or by examining the change in a particular psychophysiological disorder itself, such as hypertension. More recently, the theoretical sophistication of the area has increased as psychologists have recognized incidents of low correlation between physiological activity and cognitive and motoric events (Lang, 1971). Following the direction of Lacey (1959), researchers have begun to examine the interrelationships of cognitive, motoric, and autonomic events, as in cases of anxiety (see Borkovec, 1976) and insomnia (see Borkovec, 1979). To use the terminology of Schwartz (1978), psychophysiology is moving toward a position in behavioral assessment where it is considered a *mechanism,* as strides are made to examine the interrelationships between various systems. While advances are still to be realized in the utility of psychophysiology as both a method and a means of assessing outcome, the main focus of future directions will be in terms of considering psychophysiology as a way of understanding the interrelationships between behavioral, cognitive, cortical, and autonomic changes.

While psychophysiological methods are fairly well defined, some advances are still to be realized in the use of innovative means of monitoring the physiology of individuals. For example, the use of portable automated methods for the in vivo recording of blood pressure (see Schneider, 1968) might aid in the understanding of normal blood pressure parameters and would be of value in determining the topography of changes in blood pressure levels of hypertensive persons. Even newer methods, such as the use of pulse wave velocity measures (Steptoe, Smulyan, & Gribbin, 1976), might further aid in this endeavor. Finally, as the behavioral medicine movement results in further collaboration between psychologists and medical personnel, psychophysiological applications of medical technology might increase in areas such as the use of thermographic recordings in the assessment of temperature patterning (Schwartz, 1978) and of computerized axial tomography and brain blood flow methodologies in the examination of cortical functioning.

Gains are also to be realized in the use of psychophysiological measures to assess outcome. Weight control serves as a prime example of an area in which physiological measures might be applied in the assessment of metabolic changes and autonomic arousal patterns. Other application might include such areas as smoking, renal dialysis, stuttering, and learning disabled and hyperactive children.

In addition to considering innovative methods and areas for assessing outcome, future methodologies must follow the lead of early psychophysiologists such as Darrow (1943), R. C. Davis (1957), and Lacey (1959) in considering the psychophysiological patterning of responses within different individuals and under different conditions (see Schwartz, 1978; Sternbach, Alexander, & Greenfield, 1969). Such concepts as the autonomic balance between sympathetic and parasympathetic branches of the autonomic nervous system (Wenger, 1966), as well as intro-stressor stereotypy, inter-stressor stereotypy, and situational stereotypy thus emerge as important in understanding the relationship between physiological activity in different individuals and situations.

This examination of response patterning has already been extended to cases in which lateralization effects have been noted. For example, Gruzelier and Venables (1973, 1974) have reported differences in the electrodermal activity of the two hands for schizophrenic and depressed populations. Lateralized electrodermal findings have also been reported by Myslobodsky and Horesh (1978) for depressed persons and by Hare (1978) for a psychopathic population. Similarly, lateralized findings have been found for hand temperature in test-anxious subjects (McCann & Papsdorf, 1979) and in normal subjects during visual stimulation (van Houten & Chemtobolo, 1979), results which suggest lateralization effects in the peripheral vasculature. Lateralization of activity in psychophysiological measures has even been found in the facial musculature (Schwartz, Ahern, & Brown, 1980). While autonomic events from one side of the body may correlate highly with contralateral measures (Bull & Gale, 1975), these results obviously suggest that researchers should consider the patterning of psychophysiological activity and exert caution in generalizing from unilateral electrodermal, electromyographic, temperature, and plethysmographic responses to the person as a whole.

At a broader level, these data suggest that efforts must be made to understand the mechanisms by which the patterning of both autonomic and central nervous system responses are related to cognitive and behavioral events. While several attempts have been made to relate lateralized autonomic activity to cognitive events (Diekhoff, Garland, Dansereau, & Walker, 1978; Ketterer & Smith, 1977; Lacroix & Comper, 1979; Myslobodsky & Rattok, 1975, 1977) and to different behavior disorders (e.g., Flor-Henry, 1976), few consistent relationships have emerged. Yet, these interrelationships may prove to be of value for both assessment and conceptual purposes (see Galin, 1974).

As well as understanding how patterned psychophysiological activity, both central and autonomic, is related to cognitive and overt events, the way that cognitive and overt behaviors are related to patterned physiological activity should also be a future focus of research. While most contemporary theories of emotion acknowledge the influence of physiological responses (see Grings & Dawson, 1978), the particular mechanisms by which specific patterned atuonomic events influence central nervous system activity as well as cognitions and behaviors have yet to be clarified. For example, the Laceys (Lacey & Lacey, 1970) have proposed that cardiovascular activity is part of an active negative feedback mechanism with electrocortical and cognitive activity and with overt behavior influences. The clarification of such possible relationships will be a great aid in understanding the mechanisms of interrelationships between cognitive, behavioral, central nervous stysem and autonomic nervous system activities.

In summary, psychophysiological assessment involves methodologies that rely on sometimes complex instrumentation that may exert reactive effects upon individuals being assessed, resulting in data that at times may present interpretation difficulties. Yet, psychophysiological behavioral assessment has demonstrated utility in providing some objective measures of outcome and as a source of data for examining interrelationships between cognitive, motoric, CNS, and autonomic events. The future should bring an expansion of applications and some possible methodological innovations. Perhaps more importantly, though, future considerations should include an examination of patterned ANS and CNS concomitants of cognitive and overt behaviors and a focus on the mechanisms of interrelationships between these systems.

REFERENCES

Ackner, B. Emotions and the peripheral vasomotor system. A review of previous work. *Journal of Psychosomatic Research*, 1956, *1*, 3–20.
Alexander, A. A. Psychophysiological concepts of psychopathology. In N. S. Greenfield & R. A. Sternbach (Eds.), *Handbook of psychophysiology*. New York: Holt, Rinehart and Winston, 1972.

Alpert, M., & Martz, M. J. Cognitive views of schizophrenia in light of recent studies of brain asymmetry. In C. Shagass, S. Gershon, & A. J. Friedhoff (Eds.), *Psychopathology and brain dysfunction.* New York: Raven Press, 1977.

Andreassi, J. L. *Psychophysiology: Human behavior and physiological responses.* New York: Oxford University Press, 1980.

Ax, A. F. Psychophysiological methodology for the study of schizophrenia. In R. Roessler & N. S. Greenfield (Eds.), *Physiological correlates of psychological disorder.* Madison: Univeristy of Wisconsin Press, 1962.

Ax, A. F., Lloyd R., Gorham, J. C. Lootens, A. M., & Robinson, R. Autonomic learning: A measure of motivation. *Motivation and Emotion,* 1978, *2,* 213–242.

Bancroft, J. The application of psychophysiological measures to the assessment-modification of sexual behavior. *Behaviour Research and Therapy,* 1971, *8* 119–130.

Barland, G. H., & Raskin, D. C. Detection of deception. In W. F. Prokasy & D. C. Raskin (Eds.), *Electrodermal activity in psychological research.* New York: Academic Press, 1973.

Begleiter, H. (Ed.) *Evoked brain potentials and behavior.* New York: Plenum, 1979.

Bell, B., Christie, M. J., & Venables, P. H. Psychophysiology of the menstrual cycle. In P. H. Venables & M. J. Christie (Eds.), *Research in psychophysiology.* New York: Wiley, 1975.

Benjamin, L. S. Facts and artifacts in using analysis of covariance to "undo" the law of initial values. *Psychophysiology,* 1967, *4,* 187–206.

Blanchard, E. B. The use of temperature biofeedback in the treatment of chronic pain due to causalgia. *Biofeedback and Self-Regulation,* 1979, *4,* 183–188.

Borkovec, T. D. Physiological and cognitive process in the regulation of anxiety. In G. E. Schwartz & D. Shapiro (Eds.), *Consciousness and self-regulation.* Vol. 1. New York: Plenum, 1976.

Borkovec, T. D. Pseudo (experimental)—insomnia and idiopathic (objective) insomnia: Theoretical and therapeutic issues. *Advances in Behavior Research and Therapy,* 1979, *2,* 27–55.

Breggin, P. R. The psychophysiology of anxiety with a review of the literature concerning adrenaline. *Journal of Nervous and Mental Diseases,* 1964, *139,* 558–568.

Brobeck, J. R. (Ed.) *Best and Taylor's physiological basis of medical practice.* Baltimore: Williams & Wilkins, 1973.

Brown, C. C. *Methods in psychophysiology.* Baltimore: Williams and Wilkins, 1967.

Brown, C. C. The parotid puzzle: A review of the literature on human salivation and its application to psychophysiology. *Psychophysiology,* 1970, *7,* 66–85.

Buchsbaum, M. S. Psychophysiology and schizophrenia. *Schizophrenia Bulletin,* 1977, *3,* 7–14. (a)

Buchsbaum, M. S. The middle evoked response components and schizophrenia. *Schizophrenia Bulletin,* 1977, *3,* 93–104. (b)

Bull, R. H. C., & Gale, M. A. Electrodermal activity recorded concomitantly from the subject's two hands. *Psychophysiology,* 1975, *12,* 94–97.

Callaway, E. *Brain electrical potentials and individual psychological differences.* New York: Grune & Stratton, 1975.

Cannon, W. B. *The wisdom of the body* (2nd ed.) New York: Norton, 1939.

Christie, M. J. The psychosocial environment and precursors of disease. In P. H. Venables & M. J. Christie (Eds.), *Research in psychophysiology.* New York: Wiley, 1975.

Christie, M. J., & Todd, J. L. Experimenter-subject-situational interactions. In P. H. Venables & M. J. Christie (Eds.), *Research in psychophysiology.* New York: Wiley 1975.

Cook, M. R. Psychophysiology of peripheral vascular change. In P. Obrist, A. H. Black,

J. Brener, & L. DiCara (Eds.), *Cardiovascular psychophysiology.* Chicago: Aldine, 1974.

Cracco, R. Q. Evoked potentials in patients with neurological disorders. In H. Begleiter (Ed.), *Evoked brain potentials and behavior.* New York: Plenum, 1979.

Cromwell, L., Arditti, M., Weibell, F. J., Pfeiffer, E. A., Steele, B., & Labok, J. *Medical instrumentation for health care.* Englewood Cliffs, N.J.: Prentice-Hall, 1976.

Cromwell, L., Weibell, F. J., Pfeiffer, E. A., & Usselmann, L. B. *Biomedical instrumentation and measurements.* Englewood Cliffs, N.J.: Prentice-Hall, 1973.

Cronbach, I. J., & Furby, L. How should we measure "change"—or should we? *Psychological Bulletin,* 1970, *74,* 68–80.

Darrow, C. W. Differences in the physiological reactions to sensory and ideational stimuli. *Psychological Bulletin,* 1929, *26,* 185–201.

Darrow, C. W. Physiological and clinical tests of autonomic function and autonomic balance. *Physiological Reviews,* 1943, *23,* 1–36.

Davidson, R. J. Specificity and patterning in biobehavioral systems. *American Psychologist,* 1978, *33,* 430–436.

Davidson, R. J., & Schwartz, G. E. The psychobiology of relaxation and related states: A multi-process theory. In D. I. Mostofsky (Ed.), *Behavior control and modification of physiological activity.* Englewood Cliffs, N.J.: Prentice-Hall, 1976.

Davis, C. M., Brickett, P., Stern, R. M. & Kimball, W. H. Tension in the two frontles: Electrode placement and artifact in the recording of forehead EMG. *Psychophysiology,* 1978, *15,* 591–593.

Davis, R. C. Response patterns. *Transactions of the New York Academy of Sciences,* 1957, *19.* 731–739.

Depue, R. A., & Fowles, D.C. Electrodermal activity as an index of arousal in schizophrenics, *Psychological Bulletin,* 1973, *79,* 233–238.

Deickhoff, G. M., Garland, J., Dansereau, D. F., & Walker, C. A. Muscle tension, skin conductance, and finger pulse volume: Asymmetries as a function of cognitive demands. *Acta Psycholoigca,* 1978, *42,* 83–93.

Doerr, H. O., Follette, W., Scribner, B. H., & Eisdorfer, C. Electrodermal response dysfunction in patients on maintenance renal dialysis. *Psychophysiology,* 1980, *17,* 83–86.

Donchin, E. Event-related brain potentials: A tool in the study of human information processing. In H. Begleiter (Ed.), *Evoked brain potentials and behavior.* New York: Plenum, 1979.

Dongier, M., Dubrovsky, B., & Engelsmann, F. Event-related slow potentials in psychiatry. In C. Shagass, S. Gershon, & A. J. Friedhoff (Eds.), *Psychopathology and brain dysfunction.* New York: Raven Press, 1977.

Duffy, E. The psychological significance of the concept of "arousal" or "activation." *Psychological Review,* 1957, *64,* 265–275.

Duffy, E. *Activation and behavior.* New York: Wiley, 1962.

Duffy, E. A. Activation. In N. S. Greenfield & R. A. Sternbach (Eds.), *Handbook of psychophysiology.* New York: Holt, Rinehart & Winston, 1972.

Dustman, R. E., Snyder, W. W., Callner, D. A., & Beck, E. C. The evoked response as a measure of cerebral dysfunction. In H. Begleiter (Ed.), *Evoked brain potentials and behavior.* New York: Plenum, 1979,

Edelberg, R. Electrical properties of the skin. In C. C. Brown (Ed.), *Methods in psychophysiology.* Baltimore: Williams & Wilkins, 1967.

Edelberg, R. Electrical activity of the skin. In N. S. Greenfield & R. A. Sternbach (Eds.), *Handbook of psychophysiology.* New York: Holt, Rinehart & Winston, 1972.

Epstein, L. H. Psychophysiological measurement in assessment. In M. Hersen & A.

S. Bellack (Eds.), *Behavioral assessment: A practical handbook*. New York: Pergamon Press, 1976.

Eysenck, H. J. *The biological basis of personality*. Springfield: Thomas, 1968.

Feinberg, I., & Evarts, E. V. Some implications of sleep research for psychiatry. In J. Zubin & C. Shagass (Eds.), *Neurobiological aspects of psychopathology*. New York: Grune & Stratton, 1969.

Fisher, L. E., & Winkel, M. H. Time of quarter effect: An uncontrolled variable in electrodermal research. *Psychophysiology*, 1979, *16*, 158–163.

Flor-Henry, P. Lateralized temporal-limbic dysfunction and psychopathology. *Annals of the New York Academy of Sciences*, 1976, *280*, 777–795.

Fowles, D. C. (Ed.) *Clinical applications of psychophysiology*. New York: Columbia University Press, 1975.

Fowles, D. C. The three arousal model: Implications of Gray's two-factor learning theory for heart rate, electrodermal activity, and psychopathy. *Psychophysiology*, 1980, *17*, 87–104.

Frederiksen, L. W., Martin, J. E., & Webster, J. S. Assessment of smoking behavior. *Journal of Applied Behavior Analysis*, 1979, *12*, 653–664.

Friedman, D., Frosch, A., & Erlenemeyer-Kimling, L. Auditory evoked potentials in children at high risk for schizophrenia. In H. Begleiter (Ed.), *Evoked brain potentials and behavior*. New York: Plenum, 1979.

Froehlich, W. D. Stress, anxiety, and the control of attention: A psychophysiological approach. In C. D. Spielberger & I. G. Sarason (Eds.), *Stress and anxiety*. Vol. 5. Washington: Wiley, 1978.

Galbraith, G. C., Squires, N., Altair, D., & Gliddon, J. B. Electrophysiological assessments in mentally retarded individuals: From brainstem to cortex. In H. Begleiter (Ed.), *Evoked brain potentials and behavior*. New York: Plenum, 1979.

Galin, D. Implication for psychiatry of left and right cerebral specialization. *Archives of General Psychiatry*, 1974, *31*, 572–583.

Geddes, L. A. *Electrodes and the measurement of bioelectric events*. New York: Wiley-Interscience, 1972.

Geer, J. H. Sexual functioning: Some data and speculations on psychophysiological assessment. In J. D. Cone & R. P. Hawkins (Eds.), *Behavioral assessment: New directions in clinical psychology*. New York: Bruner/Mazel, 1977.

Goldfried, M. R., & Kent, R. N. Traditional versus behavioral assessment. A comparison of methodological and theoretical assumptions. *Psychological Bulletin*, 1972, *77*, 409–420.

Goldstein, I. B. Electromyography. In N. S. Greenfield & R. A. Sternbach (Eds.), *Handbook of psychophysiology*. New York: Holt, Rinehart & Winston, 1972.

Goldstein, L., & Sugerman, A. A. EEG correlates of psychopathology. In J. Zubin & C. Shagass (Eds.), *Neurobiological aspects of psychopathology*. New York: Grune & Stratton, 1969.

Goode, D. J., Meltzer, H. Y., Crayton, J. W., & Mazura, T. A. Physiologic abnormalities of the neuromuscular system in schizophrenia. *Schizophrenia Bulletin*, 1977, *3*, 121–139.

Graham, D. T. Some research on psychophysiologic specificity and its relation to psychosomatic disease. In R. Roessler & N. S. Greenfield (Eds.), *Physiological correlates of physiological disorder*. Madison: University of Wisconsin Press, 1962.

Graham, D. T. Psychophysiology and medicine. *Psychophysiology*, 1971, *8*, 121–131.

Graham, D. T. Psychosomatic medicine. In N. S. Greenfield & R. A. Sternbach (Eds.), *Handbook of psychophysiology*. New York: Holt, Rinehart & Winston, 1972.

Graham, F. K. Habituation and distribution of responses innervated by the autonomic nervous system. In H.U.S. Peeke & M. J. Herz (Eds.), *Habituation: Vol. 1, Behavioral studies*. New York: Academic Press, 1973.

Graham, F. K. Constraints on measuring heart rate and period sequentially through real and cardiac time. *Psychophysiology*, 1978, *15*, 492–495.

Gray, J. A. The psychophysiological basis of introversion-extraversion. *Behaviour Research and Therapy*, 1970, *8*, 249–266.

Gray, J. A. The psychophysiological nature of introversion-extraversion: A modification of Eysenck's theory. In V. D. Nebylitsyn & J. A. Gray (Eds.) *Biological bases of individual behavior*. New York: Academic Press, 1972.

Greenfield, N. S., & Sternbach, R. A. (Eds.) *Handbook of psychophysiology*. New York: Holt, Rinehart and Winston, 1972.

Grings, W. W., & Dawson, M. E. *Emotions and bodily responses: A psychophysiological approach*. New York: Academic Press, 1978.

Gruzelier, J. H., & Venables, P. H. Skin conductance responses to tones with and without attentional significance in schizophrenic and nonschizophrenic psychiatric patients. *Neuropsychologia*, 1973, *11*, 221–230.

Gruzelier, J., & Venables, P. Bimodality and lateral asymmetry of skin conductance orienting activity in schizophrenics: Replication and evidence of lateral asymmetry in patients with depression and disorders of personality. *Biological Psychiatry*, 1974, *8*, 55–73.

Gunn, C. G., Wolf, S., Block, R. T., & Person, R. J. Psychophysiology of the cardiovascular system. In N. S. Greenfield & R. A. Sternbach (Eds.), *Handbook of psychophysiology*. New York: Holt, Rinehart & Winston, 1972.

Halliday, R., Rosenthal, J. H., Naylor, H., & Callaway, E. Averaged evoked potential predicators of clinical improvement in hyperactive children treated with methylphenidate: An initial study and replication *Psychophysiology*, 1976, *13*, 429–440.

Hare, R. D. *Psychopathy: Theory and research*. New York: *Wiley*, 1970.

Hare, R. D. Psychopathic behavior: Some recent theory and research. In H. Adams & W. Boardman (Eds.), *Advances in experimental clinical psychology*. New York: Pergamon Press, 1971.

Hare, R. D. Psychopathy. In P. H. Venables & M. J. Christie (Eds.), *Research in psychophysiology*. New York: Wiley, 1975, (a)

Hare, R. D. Psychophysiological studies of psychopathy. In D. C. Fowles (Ed.), *Clinical applications of psychophysiology*. New York: Columbia University Press, 1975. (b)

Hare, R. D. Psychopathy and electrodermal responses to nonsignal stimulation. *Biological Psychology*, 1978, *6*, 237–246.

Hartman, C. H. Response of anginal pain to hand warning. *Biofeedback and Self-Regulation*, 1979, *4*, 355–357.

Heath, R. G. Subcortical brain function correlates of psychopathology and epilepsy. In C. Shagass, S. Gershon, & A. J. Friedhoff (Eds.), *Psychopathology and brain dysfunction*. New York: Raven Press, 1977.

Heiman, J. R. A psychophysiological exploration of sexual arousal patterns in females and males. *Psychophysiology*, 1977, *14*, 266–274.

Heiman, J. R. Uses of psychophysiology in the assessment and treatment of sexual dysfunction. In J. LoPiccolo & L. LoPiccolo (Eds.), *Handbook of sex therapy*. New York: Plenum, 1978.

Hess, E. H. Pupillometrics: A method of studying mental, emotional, and sensory processes. In N. S. Greenfield & R. A. Sternbach (Eds.), *Handbook of psychophysiology*. New York: Holt, Rinehart & Winston, 1972.

Holzman, P. S., & Levy, D. L. Smooth pursuit eye movements and functional psychoses; A review. *Schizophrenia Bulletin*, 1977, *3*, 15–27.

van Houten, W. H., & Chemtolo, C . *Lateralized differences in temperature and in the skin's electrical activity in response to visual stimulation.* Paper presented at the meeting of the Biofeedback Society of America, San Diego, February 1979.

Itil, T. M. Qualitative and quantitative EEG findings in schizophrenia. *Schizophrenia Bulletin,* 1977, *3,* 61–79.

Jacobson, E. *Progressive relaxation.* Chicago: University of Chicago Press, 1938.

John, E. R. *Mechanisms of memory.* New York: Academic Press, 1967.

Johnson, L. C. A psychophysiology for all states. *Psychophysiology,* 1970, *6,* 501–516.

Johnson, L. C. Sleep. In P. H. Venables & M. J. Christie (Eds.), *Research in psychophysiology.* New York: Wiley, 1975.

Jordan, L. S. Electrodermal activity in schizophrenics: Further considerations, *Psychological Bulletin,* 1974, *81,* 85–91.

Jung, C. G. On psychophysical relations of the associative experiment. *Journal of Abnormal Psychology,* 1907, *7,* 247–255.

Karacan, I. Advances in the psychophysiological evaluation of male erectile impotence. In J. LoPiccolo & L. LoPiccolo (Eds), *Handbook of sex therapy.* New York: Plenum, 1978.

Karacan, I., Salis, P. J., & Williams, R. L. The role of the sleep laboratory in diagnosis and treatment of impotence. In R. L. Williams & I. Karacan (Eds.), *Sleep disorders: Diagnosis and treatment.* New York: Wiley, 1978.

Karlin, L. Cognition, preparation, and sensory-evoked potentials. *Psychological Bulletin,* 1970, *73,* 122–136.

Ketterer, M. W., & Smith, B. D. Bilateral electrodermal activity, lateralized cerebral processing and sex. *Psychophysiology,* 1977, *14,* 513–516.

Khachaturian, Z. S., Kerr, J., Kruger, R., & Schachter, J. A methodological note: Comparison between period and rate data in studies of cardiac function. *Psychophysiology,* 1972, *9,* 539–545.

Kiritz, S., & Moos, R. H. Physiological effects of social environments. *Psychosomatic Medicine,* 1974, *36,* 96–114.

Knott, V. J., & Venables, P. H. EEG alpha correlates of non-smokers, smokers, and smoking deprivation. *Psychophysiology,* 1977, *14,* 150–156.

Lacey, J. I, The evaluation of autonomic responses: Towards a general solution. *Annals of the New York Academy of Science,* 1956, *67,* 123–163.

Lacey, J. I, Psychophysiological approaches to the evaluation of psychotherapeutic process and outcome. In E. A. Rubinstein & M. B. Parloff (Eds.), *Research in psychotherapy.* Washington, D.C.: National Publishing Co., 1959.

Lacey, J. I. Somatic response patterning and stress: Some revisions of activation theory. In M. H. Appley & R. Trumbull (Eds), *Psychological stress.* New York: Appleton-Century-Crofts, 1967.

Lacey, J. I., & Lacey, B. C. Some autonomic-central nervous system interrelationships. In P. Black (Ed.), *Physiological correlates of emotion.* New York: Academic Press, 1970.

Lacroix, J. M., & Comper, P. Lateralization in the electrodermal system as a function of cognitive/hemispheric manipulations. *Psychophysiology,* 1979, *16,* 116–129.

Lader, M. The psychophysiology of anxious and depressed patients. In D. C. Fowles (Ed.), *Clinical applications of psychophysiology.* New York: Columbia University Press, 1975.

Lader, M. H., & Noble, P. The affective disorders. In P. H. Venables & M. J. Christie (Eds.), *Research in psychophysiology.* New York: Wiley, 1975.

Lader, M. H., & Wing, L. *Physiological measures, sedative drugs, and morbid anxiety.*

New York: Oxford University Press, 1966.

Lang, P. The application of psychopyhsiological methods to the study of psychotherapy and behavior modification. In A. E. Bergin & S. L. Garfield (Eds), *Handbook of psychotherapy and behavior change: An experimental analysis.* New York: Wiley, 1971.

Lang, P. J. Physiological assessment of anxiety and fear. In J. D. Cone & R. P. Hawkins (Eds.), *Behavioral assessment: New directions in clinical psychology.* New York: Brunner/Mazel, 1977.

Lang, P. J. Rice, D. G., & Sternbach, R. A. The psychophysiology of emotion. In N. S. Greenfield & R. A. Sternbach (Eds.), *Handbook of psychophysiology.* New York: Holt, Rinehart & Winston, 1972.

Lindsley, D. B. Emotion. In S. S. Stevens (Ed.), *Handbook of experimental psychology.* New York: Wiley, 1951.

Lindsley, D. B. Psychological phenomena and the electroencephalogram. *EEG and Clinical Neurophysiology,* 1952, *4,* 443–456.

Lippold, O. C. J. The relations between integrated action potentials in a human muscle and its isometric tension. *Journal of Physiology,* 1952, *117,* 492–499.

Lovallo, W. The cold pressor test and autonomic function: A review and integration. *Psychophysiology,* 1975, *12,* 268–282.

Lykken, D. T. Properties of electrodes used in electrodermal measurement. *Journal of Comparative and Physiological Psychology,* 1959, *52,* 629–634.

Lykken, D. T. Psychology and the lie detection industry. *American Psychologist,* 1974, *29,* 725–739.

Lynn, R. *Attention, arousal and the orientation reaction.* Oxford: Pergamon, 1966.

Malmo, R. B. Activation: A neuropsychological dimension. *Psychological Review,* 1959, *66,* 367–386.

Malmo, R. B., & Shagass, C. Physiologic study of symptom neurosis in psychiatric patients under stress. *Psychosomatic Medicine,* 1949, *11,* 25–29.

Marsh, G. R., & Thompson, L. W. Psychophysiology of aging. In J. E. Birren & K. W. Schaie (Eds.), *Handbook of the psychology of aging.* New York: Van Nostrand Reinhold, 1977.

Martin, I. Psychophysiology and conditioning. In P. H. Venables & M. J. Christie (Eds.), *Research in psychophysiology.* New York: Wiley, 1975.

Masters, W. H., & Johnson, V. E. *Human sexual response.* Boston: Little, Brown, 1966.

Mathews, A. M. Psychophysiological approaches to the investigation of desensitization and related procedures. *Psychological Bulletin,* 1971, *76,* 73–91.

McCann, B. S., & Papsdorf, J. D. *Bilateral hand temperature, test anxiety and anagram solution stress.* Paper presented at the meeting of the Biofeedback Society of America, San Diego, February 1979.

Mefferd, R. B. Some experimental implications of change. In P. H. Venables & M. J. Christie (Eds.), *Research in psychophysiology.* New York: Wiley, 1975.

Melzack, R., & Wall, P. D. Psychophysiology of pain. In M. Weisenberg (Ed.), *Pain: Clinical and experimental perspectives.* St. Louis: Mosby, 1975.

Mendels, J., & Chernick, D. A. Psychophysiological studies of sleep in depressed patients: An overview. In D. C. Fowles (Ed.), *Clinical applications of psychophysiology.* New York: Columbia University Press, 1975.

Mesulam, M., & Perry, J. The diagnosis of love-sickness: Experimental psychophysiology without the polygraph. *Psychophysiology,* 1972, *9,* 546–551.

Myslobodsky, M. S., & Horesh, N. Bilateral electrodermal activity in depressive patients. *Biological Psychology,* 1978, *6,* 111–120.

Myslobodsky, M. S., & Rattok, J. Asymmetry of electrodermal activity in man. *Bulletin of the Psychonomic Society*, 1975, *6*, 501–502.

Myslobodsky, M. S., & Rattok, J. Bilateral electrodermal activity in waking man. *Acta Psychologica*, 1977, *41*, 273–282.

Naatanen, R. Selective attention and evoked potentials in humans—A critical review. *Biological Psychology*, 1975, *2*, 237–307.

Naitoh, P. Sleep deprivation in humans. In P. H. Venables & M. J. Christie (Eds.), *Research in psychophysiology*. New York: Wiley, 1975.

Naliboff, B. D., Rickles, W. H., Cohen, M. J., & Naimark, R. S. Interactions of marijuana and induced stress: Forearm blood flow, heart rate, and skin conductance. *Psychophysiology*, 1976, *13*, 517–522.

Nelson, R. O., & Hayes, S. C. The nature of behavioral assessment: A commentary. *Journal of Applied Behavior Analysis*, 1979, *12*, 491–500.

Nouwen, A., & Solinger, J. W. The effectiveness of EMG biofeedback training in low back pain. *Biofeedback and Self-Regulation*, 1979, *4*, 103–111.

Orne, M. T., Thackray, R. I., & Paskewitz, D. A. On the detection of deception. In N. S. Greenfield & R. A. Sternbach (Eds.), *Handbook of psychophysiology*. New York: Holt, Rinehart & Winston, 1972.

Pace, S. A., Molfese, D. L., Schmidt, A. L., Mikula, W., & Ciano, C. Relationships between behavioral and electrocortical responses of aphasic and non-aphasic brain-damaged adults to semantic materials. In H. Begleiter (Ed.), *Evoked brain potentials and behavior*. New York: Plenum, 1979.

Pavlov, I. P. *Conditional reflexes: An investigation of the cerebral cortex*. London: Oxford University Press, 1927.

Perry, N. W., & Childers, D. G. *The human visual evoked response: Methods and theory*. Springfield: C. C. Thomas, 1969.

Podlesney, J. A., & Raskin, D. C. Physiological measures and the detection of deception. *Psychological Bulletin*, 1977, *84*, 782–799.

Porjesz, B., & Begleiter, H. Visual evoked potentials and brain dysfunction in chronic alcoholics. In H. Begieiter (Ed.), *Evoked brain potentials and behavior*. New York: Plenum, 1979.

Preston, M. S. The use of evoked response procedures in studies of reading disability. In H. Begleiter (Ed.), *Evoked brain potentials and behavior*. New York: Plenum, 1979.

Pribram, K. H. The new neurology and the biology of emotion: A structural approach. *American Psychologist*, 1967, *22*, 830–838.

Prokasy, W. F., & Raskin, D. C. (Eds.) *Electrodermal activity in psychological research*. New York: Academic Press, 1973.

Prystav, G. H. Autonomic responsivity to sensory stimulation in drug addicts. *Psychophysiology*, 1975, *12*, 170–178.

Raczynski, J. M., & Craighead, W. E. *A review of the autonomic activity of depressed persons*. Unpublished manuscript, 1980.

Raskin, D. C., Barland, G. H., & Podlesney, J. A. Validity and reliability of detection of deception. *Polygraph*, 1977, *6*, 1–39.

Ray, W. J., Raczynski, J. M., Rogers, T., & Kimball, W. H. *Evaluation of clinical biofeedback*. New York: Plenum, 1979.

Ritter, W. Cognition and the brain. In H. Begleiter (Ed.), *Evoked brain potentials and behavior*. New York: Plenum, 1979.

Roessler, R. Personality, psychophysiology, and performance. *Psychophysiology*, 1973, *10*, 315–325.

Roth, W. T. Late event-related potentials and psychopathology. *Schizophrenia Bulletin*, 1977, *3*, 105–120.

Rusinov, V. S. (Ed.) *Electrophysiology of the central nervous system.* New York: Plenum, 1970.

Satterfield, J. H., Cantwell, D. P., & Satterfield, B. T. Psychophysiology of the hyperactive child syndrome. *Archives of Child Psychiatry,* 1974, *31,* 839–844.

Schachter, D. L. The hypnagogic state: A critical review of the literature. *Psychological Bulletin,* 1976, *83,* 452–481.

Schacter, S. *Emotion, obesity, and crime.* New York: Academic Press, 1971.

Schacter, S., & Latane, B. Crime, cognition and the autonomic nervous system. In M. R. Jones (Ed.), *Nebraska symposium on motivation.* Lincoln: University of Nebraska Press, 1964.

Schneider, R. A. A fully automatic portable blood pressure recorder. *Journal of Applied Physiology,* 1968, *24,* 115–118.

Schwartz, G. E. Psychobiological foundations of psychotherapy and behavior change. In S. L. Garfield & A. E. Bergin (Eds.), *Handbook of psychotherapy and behavior change: An empirical analysis.* (2nd ed.) New York: Wiley, 1978.

Schwartz, G. E., Ahern, G. L., & Brown, S. L. Lateralized facial muscle response to positive and negative emotional stimuli, *Psychophysiology,* 1979, *16,* 561–571.

Schwartz, G. E., Brown, S. L., & Ahern, G. L. Facial muscle patterning and subjective experience during affective imagery: Sex differences. *Psychophysiology,* 1980, *17,* 75–82.

Shagass, C. Electrical activity of the brain. In N. S. Greenfield & R. A. Sternbach (Eds.), *Handbook of psychophysiology.* New York: Holt, Rinehart & Winston, 1972.

Shagass, C. Early evoked potentials. *Schizophrenia Bulletin,* 1977, *3,* 89–92. (a)

Shagass, C. Twisted thoughts, twisted brain waves? In C. Shagass, S. Gershon, & A. J. Friedhoff (Eds.), *Psychopathology and brain dsyfunction.* New York: Raven Press, 1977. (b)

Shagass, C. Sensory evoked potentials in psychosis. In H. Begleiter (Ed.), *Evoked brain potentials and behavior.* New York: Plenum, 1979.

Shagass, C., & Canter, A. Cerebral evoked responses and personality. In V. D. Nebylitsyn & J. A. Gray (Eds.), *Biological bases of individual behavior.* New York: Academic Press, 1972.

Shagass, C., Gershon, S., & Friedhoff, A. J. (Eds.) *Psychopathology and brain dysfunction.* New York: Raven Press, 1977.

Shapiro, D., & Schwartz, G. E. Psychophysiological contributions to social psychology. *Annual Review of Psychology,* 1970, *21,* 87–112.

Snyder, F., & Scott, J. The psychophysiology of sleep. In N. S. Greenfield & R. A. Sternbach (Eds.), *Handbook of psychophysiology.* New York: Holt, Rinehart & Winston, 1972.

Sokolov, E. N. *Perception and the conditioned reflex.* New York: MacMillan, 1963.

Sokolov, E. N. The orienting reflex, its structure and mechanisms. In L. G. Veronin, A. N. Leontrev, A. R. Luria, E. N. Sokolov, & O. S. Vinogradova (Eds.), *Orienting reflex and exploratory behaviour.* Washington, D.C.: American Institute of Biological Sciences, 1965.

Steptoe, A., Smulyan, H., & Gribbin, B. Pulse wave velocity and blood pressure change: Calibration and applications, *Psychophysiology,* 1976, *17,* 488–493.

Stern, J. A., & Janes, C. L. Personality and psychopathology. In W. F. Prokasy & D. C. Raskin (Eds.), *Electrodermal activity in psychological research.* New York: Academic Press, 1973.

Stern, R. M., & Anschel, C. Deep inspirations as stimuli for responses for the autonomic nervous system. *Psychophysiology,* 1968, *5,* 132–141.

Stern, R. M., Farr, J. H., & Ray, W. J. Pleasure. In P. H. Venables & M. J. Christie

(Eds.), *Research in psychophysiology*. New York: Wiley, 1975.

Stern, R. M., Ray, W. J., & Davis, C. M. *Psychophysiological recording*. New York: Oxford University Press, 1980.

Sternbach, R. A. *Principles of psychophysiology*. New York: Academic Press, 1966.

Sternbach, R. A. *Pain patients: Traits and treatment*. New York: Academic Press, 1974.

Sternbach, R. A., Alexander, A. A., & Greenfield, N. S. Autonomic and somatic reactivity in relation to psychopathology. In J. Zubin & C. Shagass (Eds.), *Neurobiological aspects of psychopathology*. New York: Grune & Stratton, 1969.

Stroebel, C. F. Psychophysiological pharmacology. In N. S. Greenfield & R. A. Sternbach (Eds.), *Handbook of psychophysiology*. New York: Holt, Rinehart & Winston, 1972.

Stromer, J. M. Some comments on "Biofeedback in the treatment of psychophysiologic disorders: Stuttering." *Biofeedback and Self-Regulation*, 1979, *4*, 383–385.

Tecce, J. J. Contingent negative variation and individual differences. *Archives of General Psychiatry*, 1971, *24*, 1–16.

Tecce, J. J. Contingent negative variation (CNV) and psychological processes in man. *Psychological Bulletin*, 1972, *77*, 73–108.

Thatcher, R. W., & Maisel, E. B. Functional landscapes of the brain: An electrotopographic perspective. In J. Begleiter (Ed.), *Evoked brain potentials and behavior*. New York: Plenum, 1979.

Timmons, B., Salamy, J., & Kamiya, J. Abdominal-thoracic respiratory movements and level of arousal. *Psychonomic Science*, 1972, *27*, 173–175.

Tursky, B. Physical, physiological, and psychological factors that affect pain reaction to electrical shock. *Psychophysiology*, 1974, *11*, 95–112. (a)

Tursky, B. The indirect recording of human blood pressure. In P. Obrist, A. H. Black, J. Brener, & L. DiCara (Eds.), *Cardiovascular psychophysiology*. Chicago: Aldine, 1974. (b)

Venables, P. H. Psychophysiological studies of schizophrenic pathology. In P. H. Venables & M. J. Christies (Eds.), *Research in psychophysiology*. New York: Wiley, 1975.

Venables, P. H. The electrodermal psychophysiology of schizophrenics and children at risk for schizophrenia: Controversies and developments. *Schizophrenia Bulletin*, 1977, *3*, 28–48.

Venables, P. H., & Christie, M. H. Mechanisms, instrumentation, recording techniques and quantification of responses. In W. F. Prokasy & D. C. Raskin (Eds.), *Electrodermal activity in psychological research*. New York: Academic Press, 1973.

Venables, P. H., & Christie, M. J. (Eds.) *Research in psychophysiology*. New York: Wiley, 1975.

Venables, P. H., & Martin, I. *A manual of psychophysiological methods*. Amsterdam: North-Hollands, 1967.

Wenger, M. A. Studies of autonomic balance: A summary. *Psychophysiology*, 1966, *2*, 173–186.

Wilder, J. *Stimulus and response: The law of initial value*. Bristol: Wright, 1967.

Woodruff, D. S. Brain electrical activity and behavior relationships over the life span. In P. Baltes (Ed.), *Life span development and behavior*. Vol. 1 New York: Academic Press, 1978.

Wooley, S. C., Wooley, O. W., & Dyrenforth, S. R. Theoretical, practical, and social issues in behavioral treatment of obesity. *Journal of Applied Behavior Analysis*, 1979, *12*, 3–25.

Zahn, T. P. Autonomic nervous system characteristics possibly related to a genetic predisposition to schizophrenia. *Schizophrenia Bulletin*, 1977, *3*, 49–60.

Zubin, J., & Shagass, C. (Eds.) *Neurobiological aspects of psychopathology.* New York: Grune & Stratton, 1969.

Zuckerman, M. Physiological measures of sexual arousal in the human. In N. S. Greenfield & R. A. Sternbach (Eds.), *Handbook of psychophysiology.* New York: Holt, Rinehart & Winston, 1972.

Part III:
Evaluation for Treatment Planning

Chapter 7

Assessment of Anxiety and Fear

Michael T. Nietzel

and

Douglas A. Bernstein

INTRODUCTION

In his *Pensées*, Pascal listed inconstancy, boredom, and anxiety as the state of man. As psychologists, we might want to expand this list somewhat, but the fact remains that anxiety and fears are probably the most numerous and significant clinical phenomena treated by modern therapists. In this chapter we focus on the assessment of anxiety and fears, beginning with some discussion of how these constructs are typically conceptualized. We should stipulate at the outset that we make no distinction between the terms "anxiety" and ."fear." We are aware of a conventional differentiation which regards *anxiety* as a generalized type of emotional distress and *fear* as an aversive emotion elicited by some particular stimulus class. However, this distinction is not particularly useful to the social learning theorist, who attempts to analyze all behavior as a function of specific eliciting and reinforcing stimuli.

Anxiety is one of psychology's central concepts. From a research perspective it has been reliably related to perceptual abilities, performance proficiency, learning, memory, cognition and sexual responsivity. Every major theory of personality and psychopathology has emphasized anxiety as a necessary explanatory concept. According to Borkovec, Weerts, and Bernstein (1977):

"Anxiety" entered the psychological lexicon as the English transla-
tion of Freud's *Angst*, a word he used to describe the negative affect and physiological arousal that is analogous to the consequence
of having food stuck in one's throat (McReynolds, in press; Sarbin,
1964, 1968). Although Freud never specifically defined the unique
identifying characteristics of *Angst*, the construct was nevertheless
emphasized in his theory of the development of behavior and behavior disorder. Consequently, psychology and psychiatry were faced
with the task of measuring and modifying a vague, ill-defined, and
metaphorical variable that, over time, was reified (Sarbin, 1964) into
a "thing" assumed to be of vital importance in the understanding of
human behavior. It is important to note that, in the reification
process, anxiety developed a "multiple personality." It has been
viewed as transient emotional/physiological behavior (i.e., "He is
anxious today"), a dispositional trait ("She is an anxious person"),
and a cause or explanation of behavior (i.e., "He overeats because
of anxiety"; "Her seductiveness is a defense against anxiety") [p.
367–368].

Over the past 50 years research on the construct of anxiety has been
prolific. Prior to the ascendency of social learning approaches in recent
years, Cattell and Scheier (1961) identified over 120 instruments that
measured some aspect of anxiety. The advent of the social learning
approach to clinical research and practice resulted in a host of new
anxiety measures, many of which we will discuss later. Social learning
theorists contributed a new approach to the construct itself, which was
responsive to criticisms that "anxiety" had become a vague, poorly
defined concept that had failed to promote satisfying theoretical or practical advances.

Before discussing specific techniques for anxiety measurement, it is
important to describe four distinguishing dimensions of the social learning conceptualization of anxiety.

1. *Anxiety is not a trait or personality characteristic which is internal
   to an individual.* One of the most durable and consensual assumptions of social learning theory is that behavior is related to
   the specific stimulus setting in which it occurs. Because of this
   notion, behavioral approaches to anxiety measurement place a
   premium on clearly identifying the environmental conditions in
   which a person responds fearfully and on objectively quantifying
   these responses. Although behaviorists still employ self-report instruments, the use of psychological tests to measure a global,
   generalized personality construct is minimized. The traditional

reliance on what have been called *trait anxiety* tests has given way to the construction of *state anxiety* measures that attempt to establish relationships between anxiety and variations in (internal and external) environmental conditions (Bernstein & Nietzel, 1980). As with a behaviorally based assessment of any clinical target, two tasks are essential in anxiety assessment: first, specify the external and cognitive stimuli that prompt distress, and second, identify the contingencies that serve to maintain that distress. Consistent with this perspective, evaluations of various social-learning approaches to anxiety concentrate on reliably measurable changes in the targeted components of anxiety as they are assessed before and after an intervention.

2. *Anxiety can be acquired through different learning mechanisms.* The most common manner by which anxiety and fears are developed is through associative learning, in which formerly neutral stimuli take on stressful dimensions because of their direct and/ or vicarious association (conditioning) with aversive stimuli [discussions of the limitations of strict associative learning views of fear are provided by Öhman (1979) and Seligman (1971)]. Anxiety of this type is usually called *conditioned*. It comprises the classic type of fear which is usually irrational, inappropriate, maladaptive, and stubbornly resistant to verbal exhortations and exercise of "will power." The person who reacts with panic in small, enclosed spaces, but who feels embarrassed by the "silliness" of this extreme, uncontrollable response provides a common example.

Anxiety may also develop as a result of real environmental dangers or behavioral deficits. In such instances, anxiety is often called *reactive*. Fears of this type are realistic reactions to objectives stresses in punishing situations. A student whose fear of a final examination is a consequence of failing to study the course material is suffering reactive anxiety. This problem also is common in interpersonal-evaluative situations, where persons with minimal conversational and other skills may suffer rejection or insult and become very fearful of social encounters as a consequence.

Therapists must be sensitive to the presence of reactive aspects of anxiety in their clients. Carefully conducted interviews and selected role-played interactions are often effective in differentiating between conditioned and reactive anxiety. If a reactive componenet is present, training in requisite social, sexual, study, or other skills is required prior to or in association with anxiety-reducing interventions. (See Chapters 9 & 12 of this volume.)

3. *Anxiety consists of multiple response components.* The term *anxiety* refers to a complex, multichannel pattern of behavior that occurs

in response to externally (environmentally) and internally (cognitively) produced stimuli. Such behavior is manifest in three response systems or channels. The first is the *self-report channel,* also referred to as the subjective channel. In this dimension, an individual may indicate informally ("I was terrified") or formally (through psychological test scores) the amount of anxiety experienced. Although behaviorists have had a tendency to be critical of the validity and utility of self-report measures (Mischel, 1968), subjective-verbal reports are very important because they are our only access to the feelings of *dread* and *helplessness* with which clients must live and struggle.

The second anxiety measurement channel is the *physiological* (also termed visceral or somatic), focusing particularly on the responsiveness of the sympathetic portion of the autonomic nervous system (see Paul & Bernstein, 1973). Anxiety in this channel is revealed by changes in such arousal indices as galvanic skin response, blood pressure, heart rate, muscular tension, respiration rate, temperature, and the like. Physiological assessments of anxiety are plagued by many technical problems that make accurate, unbiased measurement quite difficult. Body movement, temperature and weight, diet, cognitive activity, and drug use are just a few of the subject factors that may affect physiological measures. Characteristics of the physical environment (lighting, temperature, humidity), attachment of electrodes, habituation, and a variety of procedural variations can also influence electro-physiological assessments. Furthermore, it is almost always advisable to measure anxiety through more than one index of physiological activity since arousal for each individual may appear in different patterns and at different temporal rates. Often, different physiological measures correlate surprisingly poorly with one another (Haynes, 1978).

The third response channel involves *motor* or *overt behavior.* Paul and Bernstein (1973) subdivided this channel into *direct* and *indirect* measures. Direct assessments involve measures of overt, behavioral consequences of physiological arousal. Recording the frequency or intensity of behavioral disruptions (e.g., stuttering, trembling, pacing, tremors) during stressful activities, such as giving a speech or approaching a feared object, are examples of direct behavioral measures. Indirect behavioral assessment involves observation of escape and/or avoidance of anxiety-eliciting stimuli. These direct and indirect observations are usually coded and quantified on some type of rating scale. Both types of behavioral assessment are subject to artifactual influences especially the category of events known as demand characteristics (Bernstein & Nietzel, 1973, 1974, 1977; Blom & Craighead, 1974; Rosenthal, Kelly, & Hung, 1976). Despite such limitations, however, behavioral measures have been the most emphasized assessment component when evaluating social-learning interventions for anxiety.

    4. *Anxiety response channels are not highly correlated.* Problems in measuring anxiety are further complicated by the common finding that the three anxiety channels do not correlate well with one another (Lacey, 1967; Lang, 1968, 1971, 1977). An individual who is anxious in a particular stimulus setting may show strong reactivity in only one channel; in self-report, for example, but not in physiological or motor activity. This characteristic of anxiety indices is known as *response fractionation* (Haynes, 1978), *asynchrony* (Lick & Katkin, 1976), or *desynchrony* (Hodgson & Rachman, 1974), and is a very reliable finding in the anxiety assessment literature.

Response desynchrony is due in part to the fact that the display of anxiety in each channel is a function not only of the eliciting stimulus, but many other variables as well. A male college student may experience extreme physiological arousal and behavioral disruption whenever he interacts with a female, but because he does not want to appear foolish, he may deny feeling any discomfort. On the other hand, a person may report strong anxiety in relation to dentistry and show clear autonomic responses when in a dentist's chair, but reveal little or no overt avoidance behavior because of the anticipated positive consequences of receiving relief from a toothache (Kleinknecht & Bernstein, 1978).

Thus, when anxiety becomes a clinical problem, the client's presenting complaints may involve clearly recognized and defined "symptoms" in one or more of the three anxiety response systems. Desynchrony of anxiety channels requires not only multi-method assessment (Nay, 1979), but also suggests the need for multiple-component treatments. Lang (1977) has proposed in this regard that

> The behavior therapeutic enterprise should be a vigorous multi-system program. That is to say, the patient who shows social performance deficits, the physiology of anxiety and also reports a feeling of dread or helplessness would most likely respond to a program which included the direct modification of each of these behavior sets [p. 181].

In developing intervention procedures applicable to anxiety, social-learning therapists have originated treatments which are appropriate to one or more of the three anxiety channels. For example, systematic desensitization is intended to reduce physiological turbulence and maladaptive cognitions to the point where more appropriate behaviors can occur. Treatments like rational emotive therapy and other types of cognitive behavior therapy emphasize the need to modify the maladaptive language (self-statements) that is associated with emotional problems. Finally, modeling, guided interaction, and skill training focus on developing or disinhibiting behaviors and thoughts that can reduce anxiety.

PSYCHOPHYSIOLOGICAL MEASURES

Psychological study of emotions has long struggled with the relationship between patterns of visceral, subjective, and behavioral responsiveness. For example, William James (1884) proposed that verbal accounts of the emotions were determined by initial reactivity in the physiological and behavioral channels. Cannon's (1915) formulation was more purely physiological and stressed lower brain structures as a common activating agent for the other parameters of emotional responding. More recently, Schachter (1964) has emphasized visceral arousal as a substrate of emotion, with the subjective nature determined by subjects' interpretations of the environmental cues present during the arousal. There may be other views as well (see Arnold, 1960).

Whatever our theoretical view of physiology's contribution to aversive emotional states, it is clear that anxiety-related clinical problems entail significant physiological activation, and that behavioral interventions (e.g., systematic desensitization, biofeedback) often aim to modify the physiological components of aversive emotional states. For these reasons it is important to review the physiological indices most often monitored in assessments of anxiety and fear.

Psychophysiological (or electrophysiological) measurements can serve important diagnostic functions when applied as part of a comprehensive, preintervention assessment. They may also pinpoint etiological factors and suggest the most appropriate treatments to be applied to a given anxiety reaction. In practice, however, sophisticated physiological measurement has been more characteristic of the laboratory researcher than the working clinician. Reasons for this imbalance include the expense of the measurement technology, inconvenience, the need to be skilled in principles of electronics and physiology, and the realization that physiological measures are very sensitive to instrument errors and artifactual contamination.

Recent advances in telemetric technology (Rugh & Schwitzgebel, 1977), and self-monitoring of physiology (Bell & Schwartz, 1975) have enabled physiological assessments to occur in natural environments, but the controlled laboratory is still the most common setting for *accurate* electrophysiological assessment.

Haynes (1978) describes the usual physiological measurement procedure as follows:

> Typically, a client is seated in an environmentally controlled room and electrodes and transducers are attached. An adaptation period usually precedes measurement. This period allows the subject to adjust to the new surroundings and is associated with decreases in the level of arousal and variability of psychophysiological measures. Following the adaptation period, the client is usually presented with audio or visual stimuli, exposed to intervention procedures or instructed to engage in various activities. The client's physiological responses to these stimuli and procedures are monitored. In some cases, the client may be presented with intervention manipulations prior to or between test stimuli (e.g., desensitization or relaxation training prior to presentation of feared stimuli) [p. 346].

Readers interested in thorough discussions of the utilization and methodology of electrophysiological assessment should consult excellent reviews by Borkovec and Sides (in press), Haynes (1978), Greenfield and Sternbach (1972), Mathews, (1971), and Venables and Martin (1967). For our present purposes, we will only discuss those methods most often used as indices of fear and anxiety: electromyographic, cardiovascular, and electrodermal measures.

Electromyography

Technique. When skeletal muscles contract, electrical activity is generated. The measurement of this activity is called electromyography or EMG. It is possible to infer the level of muscular tension by measuring electrical activity in a contracting muscle or muscle group. (See Goldstein, 1972 or Haynes, 1978, for more complete presentations of the technique and logic of EMG recording.)

EMG levels are usually recorded from electrodes placed on a carefully prepared skin surface at the site of a muscle group. Signals from the electrodes are then fed to an amplifier, where they are increased until they can be monitored visually on some type of polygraph, meter, or scope. Interpretation of the signal may be further aided by integration techniques that allow the user to grade the raw electrical activity data over a certain period of time. EMG recordings have been taken from several muscle sites, but the most common location is the frontalis muscle (across the forehead) because it is believed to be sensitive to general or nonspecific tension and arousal.

Examples. Frontalis EMG is often monitored in clients suffering from muscle-contraction headaches (Epstein & Abel, 1977) and in clients being treated with biofeedback, desensitization, and relaxation training. To the extent that anxiety is mediated in part by muscular tension (e.g., Paul & Bernstein, 1973), EMG should be responsive to exposures of fear-eliciting stimuli.

There are data which indicate the utility of EMG as an index of anxiety. For example, Haynes (1978) reports unpublished data (McGowan, Haynes, & Wilson, 1977) on subjects who listened to tape-recorded descriptions of scenes they had previously indicated to be anxiety-arousing (e.g., being in an accident). EMG and cardiovascular measures were collected before, during, and after presentations of the scenes, and were also used to assess the effects of relaxation training administered to the subjects. Although the relaxation intervention did not affect various cardiovascular measures, it was associated with reduced frontalis EMG response to the stressful stimuli. Other research on EMG as an outcome measure has been mixed. For example, Brandt (1973), Reinking and Kohl (1975), and Schandler and Grings (1976) found that EMG measures differentiated progressive relaxation from a variety of control conditions in reducing EMG, but Israel and Beiman (1977), Paul and Trimble (1970) and Russell, Sipich and Kripe (1976) did not.

Of course, EMG can also be monitored as subjects are confronted with *in vivo* fear stimuli, as in behavioral avoidance tests, role-playing tasks, or as they engage in fear imagery (see Lang, 1977). This type of assessment has both diagnostic and outcome implications since it can be conducted before, during and after treatment.

Issues in interpretation. Although EMG levels are apparently sensitive to general arousal, they are particularly subject to the fractionation problem mentioned earlier. EMG not only demonstrates low correlations with other physiological measures, but frontalis EMG levels often do not correlate well with EMG monitored from different muscle sites. For this reason, reliance on single-site EMG as a valid measure of physiological activation would be hazardous.

Cardiovascular measures

Technique. Cardiovascular measures are the most frequently utilized index of physiological arousal in anxiety research. Among the several indications available, measures of heart rate, blood pressure, and peripheral blood flow are the most popular.

Heart rate has been the most often selected cardiovascular index of fear. It is measured by a cardiotachometer, which can continuously track the time interval between successive heartbeats before, during, and after presentations of aversive stimuli. Although heart rate data are subject to nonthreat parameters of fear stimuli and therefore require appropriate control procedures (e.g., Borkovec, Weerts, & Bernstein, 1977), heart rate is less sensitive than most other visceral responses to measurement artifacts and is monitored relatively easily. While it is generally assumed that exposure to a stressor produces heart rate acceleration, this may be an overly simplified view (Lacey, 1967). Some subjects may show heart rate *deceleration* to certain stimuli they fear. Deceleration is often indicative of the orienting response that occurs when a person pays attention to the introduction of a new stimulus. While acceleration is the usual reaction to a stressful stimulus, individual differences such as repression-sensitization might reverse this prototype.

Systolic and diastolic blood pressure are additional cardiovascular activities that are measured in anxiety research. Although several factors influence blood pressure, its utility as a measure of fear is based on its involvement in sympathetic activity in the autonomic system. Because systolic blood pressure is more sensitive to short-term environmental changes, it is usually a better measure than diastolic blood pressure for detecting reactivity to stressful stimuli. The greatest difficulty with blood pressure as a measure of arousal is that unless highly sophisticated equipment is available, a rather long interval between measures is required (see Haynes, 1978, for discussion of other technical problems).

Reactions to stress may also be revealed by changes in blood flow through peripheral arterioles since such changes are a result of sympathetic reactivity. Measures of this type include strain gauges and plethysmography that assess blood volume of tissue and monitoring of skin surface temperatures through the use of various temperature sensors. Blood volume is often measured as part of an overall assessment of sexual preferences and performance (e.g., Quinsey, Chaplin, & Carrigan, 1979). Skin temperature is a useful indicator for conditions such as Raynaud's disease. Although peripherial blood flow is responsive to environmental changes, it has not been used frequently as a fear index.

Examples. Early examples of heart rate assessments in the anxiety treatment literature are provided by Paul's (1966) classic study on fear of public speaking, and Lang, Melamed, and Hart's (1970) investigation of automated desensitization. A very well-designed experiment by Borkovec. Stone, O'Brien, and Kaloupek (1974) reveals the utility of heart rate data in the assessment of social-evaluative anxiety.

In this study, males who either were or were not socially anxious were required to perform on two interaction tasks conducted two to three weeks apart. Heart rate data were collected from the time subjects were informed that they would be asked to interact with a female until the interaction was completed.

At the very beginning of the first session, highly anxious subjects averaged about 11 beats/minute higher than their low anxiety counterparts. Both groups showed a 20 beat/minute increase from the time the female confederate entered the room to the start of actual interaction. During the second task, low and high anxiety participants produced essentially equivalent heart rate increases in the anticipatory period. These data show the advantage of a response like heart rate that can be monitored continuously, but they also reveal the importance of conditions that could differentiate effects due to stress from those produced by the perceptual and behavioral activity that such interaction tasks demand.

A very interesting use of heart rate is provided by Lang's (1977) research on the effects of different parameters of fear imagery. The basic methodology was to give groups of phobic subjects different types of "scripts" or instructions that specify the content of images to be visualized. Scripts may consist of *stimulus propositions* which simply describe properties of the feared stimuli, or *response propositions* which describe the verbal, behavioral, and somatic responses of the subject when confronted with the stressor. Heart rate can be monitored during presentation of scripts, as the subject actually visualizes the scene, and during "recovery" or subsequent relaxation periods. Among the interesting results from this project is the finding that stimulus plus response propositions usually produce more heart rate activity than stimulus propositions alone. A possible outgrowth of this research is a system of imagery profiles which would classify subjects according to the type of imagery associated wtih indices of anxiety and fear. Ultimately, different types of treatment might be indicated for patients with certain types of imagery profiles.

Heart rate and blood pressure also are often included in the evaluation of tension-reduction techniques like relaxation training (see Shoemaker & Tasto, 1975).

Issues in interpretation. Heart rate appears to be the cardiovascular index of choice within the research literature on anxiety. This preference is primarily justified by its capacity to be monitored continuously and by the fact that it is, relative to other physiological measures, reasonably error-free. However, caution in the use of heart rate as a measure of anxiety is warranted on two counts. First, it is sensitive to motor and perceptual activities, which are often confounded with stress in many assessment tasks. Second, the direction of heart rate change will not be identical for all subjects, thereby requiring the researcher-clinician to consider individual differences in the response tendencies of their participants.

Electrodermal measures

Techniques. Electrodermal activity is measured by placing electrodes on the skin and passing a slight electric current between them. Several types of electrodermal response are available. The most common in fear research are skin conductance and its reciprocal, skin resistance. Changes in conductance and resistance can then be displayed on a polygraph or meter (see Edelberg, 1972, 1973; Katkin, 1975; Prokasky & Raskin, 1973).

Conductance and resistance are influenced by sweat glands innervated by the autonomic nervous system. Increases in sweating will be reflected by decreased resistance (increased conductance) to the electrical flow between the skin electrodes. A typical procedure for assessing skin conductance changes as a stress response would involve the following steps: (a) determine the basal or resting level of skin conductance (often measured from the palm of the hand), (b) present the fear stimulus either "live," pictorally, or through imagery, (c) measure the maximal increase in palmer skin conductance following stimulus presentation, and (d) compute the difference in conductance experienced before and after stimulation.

Changes that occur after presentation of a stimulus are called *evoked responses*. Changes in skin conductance may also occur without any specific stimulus presentations. These changes are known as *spontaneous* or *nonspecific fluctuations,* and although they are usually less pronounced than evoked responses, they are believed to be a relatively valid measure of anxiety. In an extensive research program, Katkin (1966, 1975; Lick & Katkin, 1976) has shown that spontaneous electrodermal fluctuations are reliably related to induced stress, even though they fail to show any meaningful relationship to verbal reports of anxiety.

Examples. Electrodermal measures have been used extensively in laboratory evaluations of behavioral treatments such as desensitization (see Katkin & Deitz, 1975, for an excellent review). Several studies (e.g., Lehrer, 1977; Schandler & Grings, 1976) have found greater electrodermal changes associated with relaxation training than with control procedures; others (e.g., Davidson & Hiebert, 1971; Paul & Trimble, 1970) have not found relaxation training effects on skin conductance measures.

Several studies have demonstrated that electrodermal activity can differentiate phobics' responses to feared objects from their responses to nonfeared objects, and that phobics can be discriminated from non-phobics on the basis of skin conductance or resistance changes (Craig, 1968; Geer, 1966; Wilson, 1967). Electrodermal measures have also shown a concurrent relationship with other measures of arousal, although this relationship is not as replicable as one would hope (see Haynes, 1978).

Issues in interpretation. Electrodermal measures have much to recommend them as a component of a comprehensive clinical assessment of anxiety. Lick and Katkin (1976) endorse the use of spontaneous electrodermal activity on the grounds that it is easily scored, technically undemanding, and economical. Electrodermal measures are influenced by procedural variations and environmental intrusions and are therefore by no means completely free of artifact. But for the clinician looking for a middle ground between the burdens of psychophysiological techniques and the disadvantages of omitting such measures altogether, electrodermal assessment may provide an acceptable compromise.

BEHAVIORAL MEASURES

The preference for overt behavioral measures of anxiety by social learning theorists is illustrated by several conspicuous themes in the literature. A primary sign is that discrepancies among the three anxiety assessment channels are often resolved by concentrating on the behavioral data as the "real" phenomena and relegating self-report and physiological results to secondary, almost epiphenomenal, roles. Demotion of subjective and visceral data is quite apparent in much of the outcome literature. Accompanying this "seeing is believing" attitude is the conviction that samples of behavior represent the most direct, error-free, scientific assessment channel available. This confidence in the reliability and validity of behavioral observation is difficult to reconcile with some of the data on observation (e.g., Cone, 1977; Kent, Diament, Dietz, & O'Leary, 1974) and has been challenged by clinicians who are less sanguine about a behavioral emphasis (e.g., Korchin, 1976).

Direct measures

The clinician interested in direct behavioral measures may either observe the overt effects of physiological activation and emotional distress on motor functioning or look for the interference effects of arousal on ongoing performance. Examples in the first category would include heavy breathing, tremors, moistening/biting lips, facial grimaces, pacing, perspiration. Interference effects might involve stammering, impaired recall, reduced motor dexterity and speech blocks.

One of the best known illustrations of the observation of overt behavioral manifestations of anxiety is provided in Paul's (1966) Timed Behavioral Checklist (TBCL). The TBCL includes 20 behaviors thought to be directly related to physiological activation (e.g., pacing, extraneous limb movements). Observers using the TBCL are trained to record the occurrence of each of these behaviors during specific time intervals (often around 30 seconds). Occurrences of each behavior can then be summed over all intervals and represented as an index of overt anxiety. Interrater reliabilities on the TBCL can be quite high (Paul, 1966 reported an average of .95), and it has been used in a variety of anxiety studies (e.g., Bernstein & Nietzel, 1974; Borkovec, Stone, O'Brien, & Kaloupek, 1974).

Several overt behavioral measures concentrate on disruptions of speech as a direct index of anxiety. Perhaps the most widely used of these methods is Mahl's (1956) *speech disturbance ratio.* This measure is computed by dividing the number of speech dysfluencies (corrections, "ah's," "uh's," mispronunciations, incomplete words, etc.) by the total number of word productions. Percentage of silent time is also computed as a measure of arousal. Mahl's indices show good interrater reliabilities and test-retest stability. Borkovec, Fleischmann, and Caputo (1973) reported that non-ah speech disturbances increased in association with stress produced by a social interaction task.

Direct behavioral measures may also focus upon the general effectiveness and efficiency of other ongoing behaviors that should be related to anxiety. Monitoring the academic performance of test-anxious clients before and after a clinical intervention (Allen, 1971) and observing the recovery and recuperation efforts of patients undergoing stressful medical procedures illustrate this approach.

There are several reasons why no single, direct behavioral measure of anxiety would be an entirely acceptable index. First, because less than maximum degrees of arousal are usually involved, only the effects on an individual's most responsive systems are usually observed. Second, the level of task difficulty and the amount of previous practice at the observed activity will interact in determining the extensiveness of behavioral disruption. Finally, as with any behavior, performance is influenced by many other variables besides affect and physiological responsiveness.

Indirect measures

Indirect behavioral measures are concerned with the observation of secondary behavioral effects of anxiety reactions. They rest on the assumption that escalating anxiety will be accompanied by behaviors that have reduced the anxiety reaction in the past, either by avoiding or escaping arousing stimuli or by being incompatible with anxiety.

Observation in the natural environment. Indirect assessments can be conducted in the natural environment. As our case example (see pp. 236-239) indicates, a claustrophobic can be watched as (s)he enters and remains in closed, restrictive places. This approach is akin to "free operant" measurement, where a person's relative frequency of avoidance or interaction with a particular stimulus is monitored. Indirect assessments in the natural environment are time consuming and subject to some special ethical problems. Other difficulties include the fact that the very act of observation itself can affect the person being observed. This quality of observation, known as *reactivity,* can be partly circumvented through the planful use of unobtrusive measures and/or third party "informers" (Lick & Katkin, 1976).

Behavioral Avoidance Tests. The most common form of indirect behavioral measure is the behavioral avoidance test (BAT). In this method, a fear-eliciting stimulus is placed in a standardized environment, and a person is instructed to approach the stimulus and engage in progressively more intimate or bold interactions with it. The logic of the BAT is that the more intense the anxiety elicited, the earlier in the approach sequence the person will initiate avoidance or escape from the provocative stimulus.

Within the behavior therapy literature, analogue research on anxiety reduction procedures has become associated with a fairly standard overall approach. After a variety of initial recruitment strategies, individuals are selected for participation on the basis of some behavioral avoidance test that involves engaging in a feared activity (e.g., speechmaking, snake-touching). Subjects are then assigned (randomly or after matching) to one of several groups (e.g., a treatment-of-interest group, alternative-treatment or treatment component group, a placebo-control group, or a no-contact control group), and their posttreatment improvement is assessed by a BAT posttest procedurally similar or identical to the pretest. The rationale is that elimination of anxiety will be reflected in logical changes in certain specifically observed behaviors.

Lang and Lazovik (1963) were the first to report the use of a standard BAT in a therapy outcome study. Their procedure consisted of requesting individuals who reported fear of snakes to enter a room containing a caged, harmless snake. Subjects were informed that the purpose of the test was to assess their feelings toward snakes. While each subject remained at the door of the test room, the experimenter moved toward the cage, opened the top, and then invited the subject to approach, touch, and hold the snake. The experimenter repeated each invitation once if the subject did not immediately comply. The subject's behavior was scored on a 3-point scale which corresponded to discrete look, touch, hold criteria.

While the Lang and Lazovik procedures have served as a prototype for later analogue researchers, several procedural variations have been introduced into BAT administration. These include type of subject (required "subject-pool" participants vs. volunteers), mode of instructional presentation (live, taped, or written), timing of instructions ("one-shot" pre-BAT presentation, vs. progressive presentation augmented by written instructions which the subject takes to the BAT), nature of instructions ("approach as close as you can" versus "do only what is comfortable for you"), criterion behavior (a certain proximity from the target object, touching the object, or holding the object), and experimenter behavior in the test situation (experimenter present versus absent; experimenter modeling approach versus no modeled approach).

Researchers' interest in the BAT has resulted in a sizable literature on this technique's validity and reliability, and several problems have became apparent. As Paul and Bernstein (1973) note:

All the problems of the potential lack of validity of self-report measures as a response system under direct voluntary control also apply to the observational assessment of secondary behaviors. Thus, in mild or moderate degrees of anxiety, the situational context of assessment, the level of demand for approach behavior, and the perceived positive or negative consequences for a given degree of approach may be more potent motivating factors in determining secondary motoric behaviors than the degree of anxiety experienced. These motoric behaviors may further interact with other individual characteristics (tolerance for distress, knowledge and experience in interacting with the stimuli involved, prior cultural experience) relatively independently of anxiety level [p. 9].

It is now obvious that while "anxiety" (as determined by a person's history of direct and vicarious contact with a feared object or situation) may determine general behavioral tendencies on a BAT, the degree of avoidance actually displayed within these broad limits can be viewed as a direct function of method variance, social cues, demand characteristics and payoffs transmitted explicitly and implicitly to a subject in the measurement situation (Bandura, Blanchard, & Ritter, 1969; Bernstein, 1973, 1974; Bernstein & Nietzel, 1973, 1974; Borkovec, 1973; Kazdin, 1973; Lick & Unger, 1975; Smith, Diener, & Beaman,

1974; Tryon & Tryon, 1974). These findings have obvious implications for the design of future research on fear assessment, but it is important to recognize that they also represent an extension and confirmation of results supporting the pervasive influence of situational-demand factors on many clinical phenomena (Bernstein & Nietzel, 1977).

We wish to underscore the importance of exploring the degree to which all targets of behavioral assessment are vulnerable to bias via unprogrammed factors. Evidence accumulating along these lines currently indicates that demand cues can significantly alter behavioral measures of social skills (Nietzel & Bernstein, 1976; Rodriguez, Nietzel, & Berzins, 1980), speech anxiety (Blom & Craighead, 1974), and claustrophobia (Miller & Bernstein, 1972), but that interpersonal anxiety may be relatively unaffected (Borkovec, Stone, O'Brien, & Kaloupek, 1974).

Role-playing tests. While BATs are used primarily to assess fear elicited by some specific stimulus, role-playing tests are employed to measure anxiety generated by situations involving social interaction. They usually involve the creation of a make-believe situation in which the person to be assessed is asked to respond in his or her typical way. Role-playing has been an element in several types of therapy for many years, but it is only since the late 1960s that it has become a part of the clinical assessment of anxiety.

Occasionally, the procedures are simple and structured, as in the Situation Test (ST) developed by Rehm and Marston (1968) to explore college males' social skills. In the ST, the client sits with a person of the opposite sex and listens to a tape recorded description of the scene to be role-played. The woman (an assistant to the clinician) then reads a question or statement such as "What would you like to do now?" or "I thought that was a lousy movie," and the client is asked to respond as if the situation were real. In the Social Behavior Situations Test (SBT: Twentyman & McFall, 1975), social situations are also created via tape recording, but the client listens alone. The tape may contain material such as: "You are on a break at your job. You see a girl who is about your age at the canteen. She works in another part of the store and consequently you don't know her very well. You would like to talk to her. What would you say? [Twentyman & McFall, 1975, p. 386]." After hearing the tape, the client is asked to act as if he were actually in the situation and to carry on an interaction over an intercom with a female assistant in the next room. In both the ST and SBT, client's behaviors are coded and judged for anxiety, response latency, speech dysfluencies, overall adequacy, and other variables.

Taped stimuli have been commonly used to assess the social competency and assertiveness of college students (e.g., Arkowitz, Lichtenstein, McGovern, & Hines, 1975; MacDonald, 1978; McFall & Marston, 1970). Clients' responses to these situations are usually recorded and then rated for overall assertiveness, response latency, dysfluency, response duration, and other related factors. Situations of a similar type have also been included on tapes developed for use with psychiatric inpatients (e.g., Goldsmith & McFall, 1975; Goldstein, Martens, Hubben, VanBelle, Schaaf, Wiersma, & Goedhart, 1973).

There is even a tape that "talks back." In order to assess the firmness and generality of clients' assertion skills (especially involving refusal of unreasonable requests), McFall and Lillesand (1971) used an Extended Interaction Test in which the clients' refusal to submit to a demand was met with gradually escalating insistence on the part of a taped antagonist. Presumably, a person who can withstand repeated requests is more assertive than one who "caves in" after an initial attempt at refusal (Nietzel, Martorano, & Melnick, 1977).

One clinical advantage of role-playing tests is that they permit the simultaneous assessment of reactive and conditioned contributions to an anxiety reaction. The sequential use of different types of role-playing tests within a clinical interview can provide information about whether a client has failed to acquire the requisite behaviors for skillful social performance and is anxious as a consequence, or whether the performance of available skills is inhibited by conditioned anxiety, among other factors (Nietzel & Bernstein, 1976). Clients possessing performance deficits could then be assigned to treatments designed to remove inhibitions, while those with impoverished repertoires could be exposed to skill-building experiences instead of, or as a prelude to techniques aimed at disinhibition.

SELF-REPORT MEASURES

Social learning approaches to assessment have been very critical of self-report measures. Common among the litany of behaviorists' objections to self-reports has been deficiencies of reliability and validity, contamination by faking and bias, low correlations with concurrent behavioral and physiological measures, and error associated with such response sets as acquiescence and social desirability (Bellack & Hersen, 1977; Mischel, 1968). Despite all these limitations, self-reports are the only means assessors have to learn about the cognitive, subjective components of fear experienced by their clients. Behaviorists are increasingly realizing that a wholesale rejection of self-report instruments would be premature and result in a rather limited conception of anxiety. The error of omitting subjective data on anxiety is no less problematic than overemphasizing it.

In this section we discuss four categories of self-report measures: questionnaires or surveys about the intensity of certain fears, ratings of elicited anxiety, self-monitoring, and interviews.

Questionnaires and surveys

There are many self-report instruments requiring respondents to indicate presence and intensity of their fear in relation to various stimuli. One type of questionnaire asks subjects to rate a wide variety of fear stimuli (high places, closed places, dogs, snakes, strangers); others concentrate on a particular stimulus class (e.g., dentistry), but contain several items representing different parameters of the situation. Ratings are usually made on 5- or 7-point Likert scales.

The best known questionnaire that covers a diversity of commonly feared stimuli is the Fear Survey Schedule (FSS). Geer's (1965) version contains 51 items; Wolpe and Lang (1964) developed a 120-item FSS; and Braun and Reynolds (1969) report a 100-item form. Fear Survey Schedules are generally used either to prescreen large samples of subjects for inclusion in a study on some shared fear or to monitor changes in fears other than the one(s) targeted for clinical intervention.

Hersen's (1973) review of such surveys concludes that they possess adequate test-retest stability, internal consistency, and concurrent validity with other self-report scales. However, correlations with physiological and behavioral indices have most often been disappointing. The major reason for this last deficiency is the simple fact that Fear Survey Schedules do not provide specific descriptions of the stimulus items. Correlations between overt behavior and subjective ratings improve when the self-report stimuli are worded with a degree of specificity that matches the stimuli encountered in an overt behavioral test (Lick & Sushinsky, 1975).

FSS formats have also been used to assess in more depth a selected, specific fear. Among these scales, Suinn's (1969) Test Anxiety Behavior Scale and Watson and Friend's (1969) Social Avoidance and Distress Scale are probably the best known. These scales show psychometric properties that are similar to their more general counterparts.

Ratings of elicited anxiety

Prior to and/or immediately following actual or imagined exposure to a feared stimulus, subjects can be asked to rate the degree of their subjective discomfort. This type of self-report permits a more specific rating of anxiety in the critical, fear-eliciting situation itself. Ratings of this sort are actually examples of very focused measures of state anxiety.

Walk's (1956) Fear Thermometer (FT) is one of the most frequently used scales in this category. The Wolpe and Lazarus (1966) subjective units of disturbance (SUD) scale is another common example. The FT usually involves asking a subject to rate on a 10-point scale (1 = completely calm, 10 = absolute terror) the amount of anxiety experienced during approach or exposure to the feared stimulus. The SUD Scale ranges from 1–100. The major advantages of such scales is the ease and quickness with which they can be applied to virtually any type of fear. Their psychometric properties appear adequate, although they are obviously subject to deliberate distortions by raters.

Less obvious measures of current anxiety are available in the form of Husek and Alexander's (1963) Anxiety Differential (AD) and Zuckerman's (1960) Affect Adjective Check List (AACL). The AD consists of 23 bipolar-adjective scales (tight-loose, wet-dry) on which subjects rate various concepts ("me," "fingers"). These concepts were selected empirically and with the purpose of minimizing falsification. The AD has been used in several anxiety-analogue studies (Bernstein & Nietzel, 1974; Paul, 1966) and has proven able to distinguish changes in situational anxiety (e.g., Kleinknecht & Bernstein, 1978).

The AACL is composed of a list of adjectives that describe various emotions and moods. Subjects can check any of 11 "anxiety-plus" adjectives (e.g., shaky) or 10 "anxiety-minus" adjectives (e.g., cheerful) to describe how they generally feel ("general" form) and how they feel in the immediate situation ("today" form). The AACL is sensitive to induced stress, but because it has not been used in behaviorally oriented research as often as AD-type instruments, less is known about its concurrent validity.

Self-monitoring

Self-monitoring is an increasingly popular form of behavioral assessment (Mahoney, 1977; Nelson, 1977; Thoresen & Mahoney, 1974; Zimmerman, 1975). It involves having a person observe the occurrence of certain aspects of his/her own behavior and keep a record of these observations. A popular form of self-monitoring is to ask a client to keep a diary of how often some problem behavior (e.g., nail biting) occurs, in what stimulus contexts it occurs, how long its duration is, and what the consequences of its occurrence are. Such diary records can later serve as a dependent measure in the assessment of how successful an intervention for nail biting has been.

One of the most important methodological issues in self-monitoring is the extent to which the act of self-observation itself affects the behavior being monitored. As we previously indicated, this phenomenon is known as *reactivity*. Because clinicians are concerned about the accuracy of self-monitoring, reactivity is a threat to valid assessment. However, reactivity can also serve therapeutic purposes, since in some cases it causes positive behaviors to become more frequent and negative behaviors to become less frequent (Kazdin, 1974).

Although self-monitoring can be used to measure either overt or covert events, it has not been employed very often with fear targets. Anxiety may be a particularly difficult class of response to self-monitor because the crucial behavioral and physiological changes are often fleeting and subtle. In addition, high levels of arousal are disruptive and may interfere with accurate self-observation.

Twentyman and McFall (1975) requested that shy males record their social interactions with women for a week. Compared to a group of confident collegians, shy males interacted with fewer women for shorter periods. Following an intervention consisting of behavioral rehearsal, modeling, and coaching, they showed improvement on several measures of frequency and duration of heterosexual interaction when compared to untreated controls. These differences were paralleled by other self-report, observational, and physiological changes in anxiety.

The value of self-monitoring in a multi-channel approach to anxiety assessment rests on its capacity to focus on specific target events as they occur in the client's "real world." As such, self-monitoring extends the data collection process to tap the natural flow of problem behavior while providing fine-grain information on the topography, frequency, and consequences of that behavior. Data from self-observation can be used to order the items in a desensitization hierarchy, indicate skill deficits that may be contributing to social anxiety, assess characteristics of stimulus settings that are most stressful for a given client, evaluate the immediate effects of therapeutic interventions, and measure the generalizability and durability of post-treatment reductions in anxiety.

Interviews

One of the most efficient methods for learning about a person's experiences is simply to ask him or her about them. This type of inquiry usually takes place in a clinical interview which, among other purposes, is usually aimed at determining the nature of the client's problems and how to best solve them. Excellent discussions of the theory and practice of interviewing from a social learning perspective can be found in Fensterheim (1972), Kanfer and Saslow (1969), Linehan (1977), Meyer, Liddell, and Lyons (1977), Peterson (1968), Rimm and Masters (1979), and Wolpe (1973).

For any clinical problem, including anxiety, the interview is probably the most indispensable element in a complete assessment enterprise. A properly conducted preintervention interview will enable the clinician to assess the specific manifestations of a client's anxiety, the situations in which it most often occurs, the consequences of its appearance, the circumstances which constrain or exacerbate it, and its history, current intensity, and prognosis. Interviews can be conducted at any time during or after treatment, thereby allowing an up-to-date description and understanding of changes in crucial behaviors.

The emphasis of any behavioral interview is on specifying as many of the functional or controlling dimensions of a problem as possible. Questions usually concentrate on *what* a client does, and *when, where,* and under what *circumstances* various activities occur. With respect to anxiety and fear, the clinician will normally inquire about the following factors (Haynes, 1978):

1. What is the client's specific complaint? It is important to determine what a client means by ''anxiety'' and to distinguish it from other aversive emotional states such as depression and anger. The therapist will usually try to translate vague concepts into clear behavioral descriptions.
2. What events follow the experience of anxiety? The therapist looks for the consequences of being anxious. Anxiety can *sometimes* be reduced by altering maladaptive reinforcement contingencies that may be present.
3. What are the cues that precede anxiety? The therapist will need to know the triggering stimuli for anxiety in order to help the client modify it. Adequate assessment of stimulus-control is especially important in planning treatments that will have a generalized effect on targeted fears.
4. What historical and developmental factors have contributed to anxiety? Are there special conditions that have tended to precipitate anxiety? Have there been methods that have previously proven successful in alleviating the client's problem?
5. Are there special client strengths or weaknesses that the therapist must consider in designing a treatment program? It is also important to determine whether the client's customary environment presents special demands that will maintain anxiety reactions unless they are modified in some way.

A CASE STUDY

Now that we have considered the multichannel nature of the anxiety construct and examined various anxiety assessment techniques, it may be helpful to illustrate the way in which clinicians might go about integrating assessment and treatment in a representative case.

A typical example is provided by a case study recently reported by Speltz and Bernstein (1979). The client was a 48-year-old accountant who came to a university psychology department for help with claustrophobia. Mr. V reported a fear of small, closed places which had become increasingly extreme and debilitating over a period of more than 30 years. The client reported that his fear began when he suffered a severe attack of asthma while in a crawl-space under his home. The situations that reportedly provoked extreme anxiety reactions at the time of referral included being in elevators, sleeping bags, boats, travel trailers, and shower stalls. Being under bed covers produced similar discomfort, and the client reported "panic" reactions to any form of breathing restriction (e.g., having a scarf over his mouth, using nose plugs, wearing a mask), even when the rest of his body was unconfined.

Mr. V's fear was causing considerable day-to-day discomfort, including loss of certain leisure activities (e.g., camping) and inability to do some household jobs (e.g., working under furniture, a car, or the house), but there were two additional and more immediate problems which had prompted him to seek help. First, his inability to wear an oxygen mask had forced him to resign from a volunteer firefighting organization. Second, Mr. V and his physician felt that his claustrophobia was at least partly responsible for a hypertensive condition which was severe enough to require regular medication.

The assessment process began with two interviews designed to: (a) establish rapport, (b) outline the general nature of Mr. V's presenting problems, (c) obtain a broad picture of his history and current living situation, his level of functioning, his strengths and weaknesses (à la Kanfer & Saslow, 1969), and (d) develop a more detailed functional analysis of the claustrophobia that would be set against the backdrop of the client's overall life situation.

The idea was to learn not just about the fear that brought Mr. V for help, but to try to put that fear in some perspective. The questions in the clinicians' mind at this time were of the following type: Is the claustrophobia the client's only (or main) problem? How does the problem affect those around him? To what extent are there environmental or other rewards for maintaining the problem? What effect will resolution of the problem have on the client's life and on those with whom he interacts? Is the presenting problem part of a larger problem or set of problems that might make attention to it irrelevant or insignificant? What personal and environmental assets can the client utilize in attempting to deal with the problems to be addressed?

At the conclusion of the first two interviews, the therapists were satisfied that Mr. V was a person whose developmental history, current life situation, and general functioning were essentially unremarkable. The history of his fear revealed a clear pattern of increasing response intensity and broader eliciting stimulus generalization. There was no reason to suspect that other, more subtle, etiological or maintenance factors were significant for understanding and modifying the problem. Data which might have suggested the need for further assessment of the existence of such factors would have included: (a) sudden onset of the fear in the absence of a precipitating event; (b) a history or current manifestations of other forms of maladaptive behavior; (c) the existence of current stress coming from the client's marriage, or occupation; or (d) observation during interviews and subsequent assessment or treatment sessions of verbal and nonverbal behaviors which appeared overly dependent, bizarre, or manipulative.

Given the absence of more fundamental problems, the interview phase of assessment ultimately focused upon two categories of fear stimuli (i.e., body restriction and breathing restriction) and four contextual variables. The latter included: (a) the size of the area in which restriction occurred; (b) the amount of illumination present; (c) body position (i.e., standing vs. lying down); and (d) the extent to which the client could control restriction. Mr. V's most intense anxiety reactions invariably occurred while in a passive, recumbent position in small, poorly illuminated enclosures.

These interview data guided selection of stimulus situations in which the client's anxiety responses could be directly observed. The observation phase of assessment was designed not only to confirm prior verbal reports, but to provide a supplementary pretherapy baseline against which to measure progress following treatment.

The client's reactions to body restriction were assessed by asking him to sit on a chair inside a 2.5 ft. x 4 ft. x 5 ft. wooden box with an interior lined in black muslin. This chamber was described by those who initially pretested it as being as "dark as an ape's armpit in a coalmine at midnight." After only 31 seconds in this test chamber, the client spontaneously emerged, evidencing distress, agitation, and profuse perspiration.

After a rest interval of several minutes, the client's response to breathing restriction was assessed by asking him to put on a standard firefighter's oxygen mask which included a clear plastic face plate which covered the eyes, nose and mouth. The client became very uncom-

fortable as soon as the mask was in place and he removed it after only
eight seconds.

One of the observational assessment issues that concerned the therapists in this case was that demand characteristics for fearfulness could
have exaggerated the client's responses to the test chamber and the
oxygen mask (Bernstein, 1973). A potential remedy would have been
to use "high demand" instructions (Bernstein & Nietzel, 1973) that
set up strong pressure for fearlessness or tolerance of anxiety. Clients
who behave fearfully under such circumstances are less likely to em-
bellish their responses, but in this case "high-demand" procedures were
ruled out because of the potential dangers inherent in overstressing an
already hypertensive individual.

Interview and observational data collected initially were used to guide
construction of a graded hierarchy of stimulus situations to be used in
a participant modeling program. This program, described in more detail
by Speltz and Bernstein (1979), consisted of: (a) demonstration by the
therapist of how to handle each step in the stimulus hierarchy, and
(b) use of response induction aids and prompts to facilitate the client's
ability to tolerate each step without discomfort.

Assessment continued throughout the 13 weeks of participant modeling, not only through observing the client's overt response to each
hierarchy step, but also through collection of continuous self-reports
about discomfort and discussion of responses to previously problematic
stimulus situations occurring outside the treatment room. These type
of assessment data provided valuable guidance to the therapists in deciding when to move ahead in the hierarchy and when to stop and subdivide a particular step into easier components. Continuing assessment
also provided important information about a fearful stimulus situation
which the client had not mentioned during initial discussions. After two
treatment sessions, Mr. V mentioned that he had just cancelled a dental
appointment because he typically "panicked" when the dentist placed
a rubber dam in his mouth. The stimulus hierarchy was elaborated to
incorporate this specific situation.

Following successful completion of all hierarchy steps as well as
mastery of additional tasks assigned as homework, treatment was terminated. Posttreatment assessments consisted of: (a) self-reports by the client
about his (now comfortable) response to previously distressing stimuli in
the natural environment, and (b) repetition of the test-chamber and oxygen mask tasks (both of which were tolerated without any discomfort).

A longer-term follow-up interview took place three months after treatment, where the client reported no difficulty in any restriction situations
(including a dental appointment) and a reduction in blood pressure to

a point where medication was no longer deemed necessary by his physician.

Thirty months later, the client was again interviewed and readministered the test-chamber and oxygen mask tasks. As before, no discomfort was reported or observed, and the client was proud to say that he had returned to duty as a volunteer firefighter.

SUMMARY AND FUTURE DIRECTIONS

Anxiety is one of the most significant problems faced by contemporary clinicians. It is a familiar, but complex construct that can be assessed by self-reports, physiological measures, and observation of overt behavior, each of which may or may not correlate well with one another. Behaviorally-oriented clinicians view this multifaceted construct not so much as a trait or personality characteristic, but as a set of behaviors that have been learned, sometimes adaptively, but often with problematic consequences. Behavioral treatments in turn, are focused upon helping clients "unlearn" maladaptive anxiety reactions and replace those unwanted reactions with new or previously suppressed responses which are more comfortable and functional.

The clinical assessment of anxiety preceding such treatment is aimed primarily at a functional understanding of the development and maintenance of a given client's anxiety and at guiding selection of those treatment procedures most likely to produce desired changes. As is true of other clinicians, the behaviorally-oriented assessor seeks to learn about anxiety through some combination of interviews, tests, physiological measures, and observations of client's overt behavior.

In this chapter we have reviewed representative examples of the behavioral assessment methods available in each of these anxiety measurement "channels," and have illustrated the way in which combinations of these can be employed before, during, and after treatment to: (a) understand a client's problem, (b) plan treatment, (c) keep track of progress, and (d) measure long-term success.

Advances in the assessment of anxiety are anticipated in three areas. First, post-intervention and follow-up assessments need to achieve the level of completeness and sophistication currently possessed by preintervention methods. Preintervention assessments often reveal better quantification and control than assessments after treatment. A second and related consideration is that researchers and clinicians alike need to be more sensitive to the issue of ecological validity. A premium should be placed on developing behavioral, self-report, and physiological measures that tap anxiety as it occurs in naturalistic settings.

Finally, the clinicians should begin to benefit from the increasing sophistication of anxiety assessment as practiced in the research laboratory. Researchers are becoming better able to identify the multiple determinants of anxiety reactions. Of particular importance is the ability to separate the influence of anxiety-eliciting stimuli from artifactual influences, such as social contingencies, situational cues, voluntary distortion, and observer unreliability. The role of individual differences in all three channels, particularly the physiological, is also becoming better understood. Ultimately, the clinician's task of functionally analyzing the crucial contributions to a client's anxiety will be facilitated by laboratory discoveries that permit valid measurement of all the components of fear responses.

REFERENCES

Allen, G. J. The effectiveness of study counseling and desensitization in alleviating test anxiety in college students. *Journal of Abnormal Psychology*, 1971, *77*, 282–289.

Arkowitz, H., Lichtenstein, E., McGovern, K., & Hines, P. The behavioral assessment of social competence in males. *Behavior Therapy*, 1975, *6*, 3–13.

Arnold, M. B. *Emotion and Personality*. Vol. 2. New York: Columbia University Press, 1960.

Bandura, A., Blanchard, E. B., & Ritter, B. The relative efficacy of desensitization and modeling approaches for inducing behavioral, affective and attitudinal changes. *Journal of Personality and Social Psychology*, 1967, *5*, 16–23.

Bell, I. R., & Schwartz, G. E. Voluntary control and reactivity of human heart rate. *Psychophysiology*, 1975, *12*, 339–348.

Bellack, A. S., & Hersen, M. Self-report inventories in behavioral assessment. In J. D. Cone & R. P. Hawkins (Eds.), *Behavioral assessment: New directions in clinical psychology*. New York: Brunner/Mazel Publishers, 1977.

Bernstein, D. A. Behavioral fear assessment: Anxiety or artifact? In H. Adams & P. Unikel (Eds.), *Issues and trends in behavior therapy*. Springfield: C. C. Thomas, 1973.

Bernstein, D. A. Manipulation of avoidance behavior as a function of increased or decreased demand on repeated behavioral tests. *Journal of Consulting and Clinical Psychology*, 1974, *42*, 896–900.

Bernstein, D. A., & Nietzel, M. T. Procedural variation in behavioral avoidance tests. *Journal of Consulting and Clinical Psychology*, 1973, *41*, 165–174.

Bernstein, D. A., & Nietzel, M. T. Behavioral avoidance tests: The effects of demand characteristics and repeated measures on two types of subjects. *Behavior Therapy*, 1974, *5*, 183–192.

Bernstein, D. A., & Nietzel, M. T. Demand characteristics in behavior modification: A natural history of a "nuisance." In M. Hersen, R. M. Eisler, & P. M. Miller, (Eds.), *Progress in behavior modification*. Vol. 4 New York: Academic Press, 1977.

Bernstein, D. A., & Nietzel, M. T. *Introduction to clinical psychology*. New York: McGraw-Hill, 1980.

Blom, B. E., & Craighead, W. E. The effects of situational and instructional demand on indices of speech anxiety. *Journal of Abnormal Psychology*, 1974, *83*, 667–674.

Borkovec, T. D., Fleischmann, D. J., & Caputo, J. A. The measurement of anxiety in an analogue social situation. *Journal of Consulting and Clinical Psychology*, 1973, *41*, 157–161.

Borkovec, T. D. The effects of instructional suggestion and physiological cues on analogue fear. *Behavior Therapy*, 1973, *4*, 185–192.

Borkovec, T. D., & Sides, J. K. Critical procedural variables related to the physiological effects of progressive relaxation: A review. *Behavior Therapy*, in press.

Borkovec, T. D., Stone, N. M., O'Brien, G. T., & Kaloupek, D. G. Evaluation of a clinically relevant target behavior for analogue outcome research. *Behavior Therapy*, 1974, *5*, 504–514.

Borkovec, T. D., Weerts, T. C., & Bernstein, D. A. Assessment of anxiety. In A. R. Ciminero, K. S. Calhoun, & H. E. Adams (Eds.), *Handbook of behavioral assessment*. New York: Wiley, 1977.

Brandt, K. The effects of relaxation training with analog HR feedback on basal levels of arousal and response to aversive tones in groups selected according to Fear Survey scores. *Psychophysiology*, 1973, *11*, 242. (Abstract)

Braun, P. R., & Reynolds, D. N. A factor analysis of a 100-item fear survey inventory. *Behaviour Research and Therapy*, 1969, *7*, 399–402.

Cannon, W. B. *Bodily changes in pain, hunger, fear, and rage*. New York: Appleton-Century-Crofts, 1915.

Cattell, R. B., & Scheier, I. H. *Neuroticism and anxiety*. New York: Ronald Press, 1961.

Cone, J. D. The relevance of reliability and validity for behavioral assessment. *Behavior Therapy*, 1977, *8*, 411–426.

Craig, K. D. Physiological arousal as a function of imagined, vicarious, and direct stress experiences. *Journal of Abnormal Psychology*, 1968, *73*, 513–520.

Davidson, P. O., & Hiebert, S. F. Relaxation training, relaxation instruction, and repeated exposure to a stressor film. *Journal of Abnormal Psychology*, 1971, *78*, 154–159.

Edelberg, R. Electrodermal recovery rate, goal-orientation, and aversion. *Psychophysiology*, 1972, *9*, 512–520.

Edelberg, R. Mechanisms of electrodermal adaptations for locomotion, manipulation or defense. In E. Stellar & J. M. Sprague (Eds.), *Progress in physiological psychology*. Vol. 5. New York: Academic Press, 1973.

Endler, N. S., Hunt, J. McV., & Rosenstein, A. J. An S-R inventory of anxiousness. *Psychological Monographs: General and Applied*, 1962, *76*, No. 536.

Epstein, L. H., & Abel, G. G. An analysis of biofeedback training effects for tension headache patients. *Behavior Therapy*, 1977, *8*, 37–47.

Fensterheim, H. The initial interview. In A. A. Lazarus (Ed.), *Clinical behavior therapy*. New York: Brunner/Mazel, 1972, 22–40.

Geer, J. H. The development of a scale to measure fear. *Behaviour Research and Therapy*, 1965, *3*, 45–53.

Geer, J. H. Fear and autonomic arousal. *Journal of Abnormal Psychology*, 1966, *71*, 253–255.

Goldsmith, J. B., & McFall, R. M. Development and evaluation of an interpersonal skill-training program for psychiatric inpatients. *Journal of Abnormal Psychology*, 1975, *84*, 51–58.

Goldstein, A. P., Martens, J., Hubben, J., VanBelle, H. A., Schaaf, W., Wiersman, H., & Goedhart, A. The use of modeling to increase independent behavior. *Behaviour Research and Therapy*, 1973, *11*, 31–42.

Goldstein, I. B. Electromyography: A measure of skeletal muscle response. In N. S. Greenfield & R. A. Sternbach (Eds.), *Handbook of psychophysiology*. New York: Holt, Rinehart, & Winston, Inc., 1972.

Greenfield, N.S., Sternbach, R.A. : *Handbook of Psychophysiology*. New York: Holt, Rinehart, & Winston, Inc., 1972.

Haynes, S. N. *Principles of behavioral assessment*. New York: Gardner Press, Inc., 1978.

Hersen, M. Self-assessment of fear. *Behavior Therapy*, 1973, *4*, 241–257.

Hodgson, R., & Rachman, S. Desynchrony in measures of fear. *Behaviour Research and Therapy*, 1974, *2*, 319–326.

Husek, T. R., & Alexander, S. The effectiveness of the Anxiety Differential in examination stress situations. *Educational and Psychological Measurement*, 1963, *23*, 309–318.

Israel, E., & Beiman, I. Live versus recorded relaxation training: A controlled investigation. *Behavior Therapy*, 1977, *8*, 251–254.

Kanfer, F. H., & Saslow, G. Behavioral diagnosis. In C. M. Franks (Ed.), *Behavior therapy: Appraisal and status*. New York: McGraw-Hill, 1969.

Katkin, E. S. The relationship between a measure of transitory anxiety and spontaneous autonomic activity. *Journal of Abnormal Psychology*, 1966, *71*, 142–146.

Katkin, E. S. Electrodermal lability: A psychophysiological analysis of individual differences in response to stress. In I. G. Sarason & C. D. Speilberger (Eds.), *Stress and anxiety*. Washington, D.C.: Hemisphere Publishing Company, 1975.

Katkin, E. S., & Deitz, S. R. Systematic desensitization. In W. F. Prokasy & D. Raskin (Eds.), *Electrodermal activity and psychological research*. New York: Academic Press, 1973.

Kazdin, A. E. Reactive self-monitoring: The effects of response desirability, goal setting, and feedback. *Journal of Consulting and Clinical Psychology*, 1974, *42*, 704–716.

Kent, R. N., Diament, C., Dietz, A., & O'Leary, K. D. Expectation biases in observational evaluation of therapeutic change. *Journal of Consulting and Clinical Psychology*, 1974, *42*, 774–780.

Kleinknecht, R. A., & Bernstein, D. A. The assessment of dental fear. *Behavior Therapy*, 1978, *9*, 626–634.

Korchin, S. J. *Modern clinical psychology: Principles of intervention in the clinic and community*. New York: Basic Books, Inc., 1976.

Lacey, J. I. Somatic response patterning and stress: Some revisions of activation theory. In M. H. Appley & R. Trumball (Eds.), *Psychological stress*. New York: Appleton-Century-Crofts, 1967.

Lang, P. J. Fear reduction and fear behavior: Problems in treating a construct. In J. M. Shlien (Ed.), *Research in psychotherapy*. Washington, D.C.: American Psychological Association, 1968.

Lang, P. J. The application of psychophysiological methods to the study of psychotherapy and behavior modification. In A. E. Bergin & S. L. Garfield (Eds.), *Handbook of psychotherapy and behavior change: An empirical analysis*. New York: Wiley, 1971.

Lang, P. J. Physiological assessment of anxiety and fear. In J. D. Cone & R. P. Hawkins (Eds.), *Behavioral assessment: New directions in clinical psychology*. New York: Brunner/Mazel Publishers, 1977, 178–195.

Lang, P. J., & Lazovik, A. D. Experimental desensitization of a phobia. *Journal of Abnormal and Social Psychology*, 1963, *66*, 519–525.

Lang, P. J., Melamed, B. G., & Hart, H. A psychophysiological analysis of fear modification using an automated desensitization procedure. *Journal of Abnormal Psychology,* 1970, *76,* 220–234.

Lehrer, P. M. The physiological effects of relaxation in anxiety neurotic patients and the physiological effects of relaxation and alpha feedback in "normal" subjects. *Psychophysiology,* 1977, *14,* 93. (Abstract)

Lick, J. R., & Katkin, E. S. Assessment of anxiety and fear. In M. Hersen & A. S. Bellack (Eds.), *Behavioral Assessment: A practical handbook.* New York: Pergamon Press, 1976.

Lick, J. R., & Sushinsky, L. Specificity of fear survey schedule items and the prediction of avoidance behavior. Unpublished manuscript, State University of New York at Buffalo, 1975.

Lick, J. R., & Unger, T. External validity of laboratory fear assessment: Implications from two case studies. *Journal of Consulting and Clinical Psychology,* 1975, *43,* 864–866.

Linehan, M. M. Issues in behavioral interviewing. In J. D. Cone & R. P. Hawkins (Eds.), *Behavioral assessment: New directions in clinical psychology.* New York: Brunner/Mazel Publishers, 1977.

Mahl, G. F. Disturbances and silences in patient's speech in psychotherapy. *Journal of Abnormal and Social Psychology,* 1956, *53,* 1–15.

Mahoney, M. J. Some applied issues in self-monitoring. In J. D. Cone & R. P. Hawkins (Eds.), *Behavioral Assessment.* New York: Brunner/Mazel, 1977.

Mandler, G., Mandler, J. M., & Uviller, E. T. Autonomic feedback: The perception of autonomic activity. *Journal of Abnormal and Social Psychology,* 1958, *56,* 367–373.

Mathews, A. Psychophysiological approaches to the investigation of desensitization and related procedures. *Psychological Bulletin,* 1971, *76,* 73–91.

McFall, R. M., & Marston, A. R. An experimental investigation of behavioral rehearsal and assertive training. *Journal of Abnormal Psychology,* 1971, *76,* 295–303.

McFall, R. M., & Lillesand, D. B. Behavior rehearsal with modeling and coaching in assertion training. *Journal of Abnormal Psychology,* 1971, *77,* 313–323.

McGowan, W. T., Haynes, S. N., & Wilson, C. Frontalis EMG feedback: Cardiovascular correlates and effect on stress. Unpublished manuscript, 1977.

McReynolds, W. T. Anxiety as a fear: A behavioral approach to one emotion. In M. Zuckerman & C. D. Spielberger (Eds.), *Emotions and anxiety: New concepts, methods, and applications.* Potomac, Md.: Lawrence Erlbaum, in press.

Meyer, V., Liddell, A., & Lyons, M. Behavioral interviews. In A. R. Ciminero, K. S. Calhoun, & H. E. Adams (Eds.), *Handbook of behavioral assessment.* New York: Wiley, 1977.

Miller, B. V., & Bernstein, D. A. Instructional demand in a behavioral avoidance test for claustrophobic fear. *Journal of Abnormal Psychology,* 1972, *80,* 206–210.

Mischel, W. *Personality and assessment.* New York: Wiley, 1968.

Nay, W. R. *Multimethod clinical assessment.* New York: Gardner Press, 1979.

Nelson, R. O. Methodological issues in assessment via self monitoring. In J. D. Cone & R. P. Hawkins (Eds.), *Behavioral assessment: new directions in clinical psychology,* New York: Brunner/Mazel, 1977.

Nietzel, M. T., & Bernstein, D. A. The effects of instructionally-mediated demand on the behavioral assessment of assertiveness. *Journal of Consulting and Clinical Psychology,* 1976, *44,* 500.

Nietzel, M. T., Martorano, R., & Melnick, J. The effects of covert modeling with and without reply training on the development and generalization of assertive responses. *Behavior Therapy,* 1977, *8,* 183–192.

Öhman, A. Fear relevance, autonomic conditioning, and phobias: A laboratory model. In P. Sjoden, S. Bates, & W. S. Dockens (Eds.), *Trends in behavior therapy.* New York: Academic Press, 1979.

Paul, G. L. *Insight vs. desensitization in psychotherapy.* Stanford, Calif.: Stanford University Press, 1966.

Paul, G. L., & Bernstein, D. A. *Anxiety and clinical problems: Systematic desensitization and related techniques.* New York: General Learning Press, 1973.

Paul, G. L., & Trimble, R. W. Recorded vs. "live" relaxation training and hypnotic suggestion: Comparative effectiveness for reducing physiological arousal and inhibiting stress response. *Behavior Therapy,* 1970, *1,* 285–302.

Peterson, D. R. *The clinical study of social behavior.* New York: Appelton-Century-Crofts, 1968.

Prokasy, W. R., & Raskin, D. C. (Eds.), *Electrodermal activity in psychological research.* New York: Academic Press, 1973.

Quinsey, V. L., Chaplin, T. C., & Carrigan, W. F. Sexual preferences among incestuous and nonincestuous child molesters. *Behavior Therapy,* 1979, *10,* 562–565.

Rehm, L. P., & Marston, A. R. Reduction of social anxiety through modification of self-reinforcement: An instigation therapy technique. *Journal of Consulting and Clinical Psychology,* 1968, *32,* 565–574.

Reinking, R. H., & Kohl, M. L. Effects of various forms of relaxation training on physiological and self-report measures of relaxation. *Journal of Consulting and Clinical Psychology,* 1975, *43,* 595–600.

Rimm, D. C., & Masters, J. C. *Behavior therapy: Techniques and empirical findings* (2nd ed.) New York: Academic Press, 1979.

Rodriguez, R., Nietzel, M. T., & Berzins, J. I. Sex role orientation and assertiveness among female college students. *Behavior Therapy,* 1980, *11,* 353–366.

Rosenthal, T. L., Kelley, J. E., & Hung, J. Social influence attempts in therapy situations. Paper presented at Meeting of Association for Advancement of Behavior Therapy, New York, 1976.

Rugh, J. D., & Schwitzgebel, R. L. Instrumentation for behavioral assessment. In A. R. Ciminero, K. S. Calhoun, & H. E. Adams (Eds.), *Handbook of behavioral assessment.* New York: Wiley, 1977.

Russell, R., Sipich, J., & Knipe, J. Progressive relaxation training: A procedural note. *Behavior Therapy,* 1976, *7,* 566–567.

Sarbin, T. R. Anxiety: Reification of a metaphor. *Archives of General Psychiatry,* 1964, *10,* 630–633.

Sarbin, T. R. Ontology recapitulates philology: The mythic nature of anxiety. *American Psychologist,* 1968, *23,* 411–418.

Schachter, S. The interaction of cognitive and physiological determinants of emotional state. In L. Berkowitz (Ed.), *Advances in experimental social psychology.* Vol. 1. New York: Academic Press, 1964.

Schandler, S. L., & Grings, W. W. An examination of methods for producing relaxation during short-term laboratory sessions. *Behaviour Research and Therapy,* 1976, *14,* 419–426.

Seligman, M. E. P. Phobias and preparedness. *Behavior Therapy,* 1971, *2,* 307–321.

Shoemaker, J., & Tasto, D. Effects of muscle relaxation on blood pressure of essential hypertensives. *Behaviour Research and Therapy,* 1975, *13,* 29–43.

Smith, R. E., Diener, E., & Beaman, A. L. Demand characteristics and the behavioral avoidance measure of fear in behavior therapy and analogue research. *Behavior Therapy,* 1974, *5,* 172–182.

Speltz, M. L., & Bernstein, D. A. Participant modeling in claustrophobia. *Journal of Behavior Therapy and Experimental Psychiatry*, 1979, *10*, 251–255.

Suinn, R. The STABS, a measure of test anxiety for behavior therapy. Normative data. *Behaviour Research and Therapy*, 1969, *7*, 335–339.

Thoreson, C. E., & Mahoney, M. J.: *Behavioral self-control*. New York: Holt, Rinehart, & Winston, 1974.

Tryon, W. W., & Tryon, G. S. *Desensitization and demand characteristics*. Unpublished manuscript, Fordham University, 1974.

Twentyman, C. T., & McFall, R. M. Behavioral training of social skills in shy males. *Journal of Consulting and Clinical Psychology*, 1975, *43*, 384–395.

Venables, D. H., & Martin, I. *A manual of psychophysiological methods*. New York: Wiley, 1967.

Walk, R. D. Self-ratings of fear in a fear-invoking situation. *Journal of Abnormal and Social Psychology*, 1956, *52*, 171–178.

Watson, D., & Friend, R. Measurement of social-evaluative anxiety. *Journal of Consulting and Clinical Psychology*, 1969, *33*, 448–457.

Wilson, G. T. GSR responses to fear-related stimuli. *Perceptual and Motor Skills*, 1967, *24*, 401–402.

Wolpe, J., & Lang, P. J. A fear survey schedule for use in behavior therapy. *Behaviour Research and Therapy*, 1964, *2*, 27–30.

Wolpe, J., & Lazarus, A. A. *Behavior therapy techniques*. New York: Pergamon Press, 1966.

Wolpe, J. *The practice of behavior therapy* (2nd ed.) New York: Pergamon Press, 1973.

Zimmerman, J. If it's what's inside that counts, why not count it? I: Self-recording of feelings and treatment by self-implosion. *Psychological Record*, 1975, *25*, 3–16.

Zuckerman, M. The development of an affective adjective checklist for the measurement of anxiety. *Journal of Consulting Psychology*, 1960, *24*, 457–462.

Chapter 8
Assessment of Depression*

Lynn P. Rehm

INTRODUCTION

Only recently have behaviorally oriented clinicians and researchers turned their attention to the problems of depression. After a delayed start there has been a tremendous growth of interest in the area in the last few years. Theoretical models, case reports, outcome studies, and experimental psychopathology studies have proliferated in the journals. A great diversity of approaches to the topic are represented in these published studies.

This diversity reflects some of the basic problems inherent in the conceptualization of depression, especially from a behavioral perspective. Depression is a heterogeneous and amorphous syndrome of complaints. It is generally considered pervasive in its influence, but is elusive in its identifying signs and symptoms. Many of the models behaviorists found useful in attacking other forms of psychopathology (notably anxiety), do not carry over well when applied to depression. This has forced behaviorists to make a variety of assumptions about the nature of the disorder.

Before it is possible even to approach the topic of depression assessment, it will be necessary to address the problems inherent in the construct of depression.

Heterogeneity of the Construct

The disorder of depression is considered a syndrome. While sad affect may also be a "symptom" of other disorders (see Mendels, 1968), a

* Writing of this chapter was supported in part by National Institute of Mental Health grant MH 34204 to the author.

diagnosis depends on the existence of a correlated constellation of behavioral excesses and deficits. Many symptoms are included in the depressive syndrome. While there is general agreement among clinicians about the nature and existence of the syndrome, the specific symptom lists vary from one authority to another (e.g., Beck, 1972; Lewinsohn, Biglan, & Ziess, 1976; Mendels, 1970; Woodruff, Goodwin, & Guze, 1974).

Given the lack of consistency of these lists, the question arises as to whether there are necessary or sufficient conditions (symptoms) for a diagnosis of depression. Many of the symptoms in the typical list are not exclusive to depression. For instance, Harrow, Colbert, Detre, and Bakeman (1966) found that only 11 of 24 hypothetically differential symptoms discriminated between depressed and schizophreneic patients in state hospitals. It is also difficult to find single symptoms that are universally ascribed to depression. Even sad affect may not be necessary if one considers the possibility of "masked" or "smiling" depressions. In a discussion of the problem in the context of assessment, Levitt and Lubin (1975) present a list of 54 symptoms, which are each included on at least two of a group of 16 depression scales. Only the symptom of "self-devaluation" was represented on all 16 scales. Clinical descriptions of some apathetic depressed patients suggest that this symptom may not be necessary for depression (e.g., Beck, 1972). The problem is further complicated by the fact that some classes of symptoms may be bidirectional. For example, sleep disturbances may include excessive or deficient sleep, and eating disturbances can include weight loss or weight gain. Thus, there may be no single symptom that is either necessary or sufficient. The coexistence of a number of the symptoms in the syndrome is necessary for the diagnosis.

One way of attempting to bring greater homogeneity to the study of depression has been by separating out subtypes of depression in various ways. Many categorization schemas have been suggested. The American Psychiatric Association's last *Diagnostic and Statistical Manual of Mental Disorders* (DSM-II; 1968) listed three depressive diagnoses under Psychotic Disorders (Schizophrenia, schizo-affective type, depressed; Involutional melancholia; and Manic-Depressive illness, depressed type), one depressive diagnosis under Psychoneurotic Disorders (Depressive Neurosis), and one depressive diagnosis under Personality disorders (Cyclothymic personality). Involutional melancholia has been dropped from the DSM-III, with the rationale that it is indistinguishable from other depression except for age of onset. A frequently cited dichotomous typology in the research literature is the distinction between endogenous and reative depressions (e.g., Mendels & Cochrane, 1968). The typology is based on inferred etiology but also assumes some differences in symptomatology (i.e., a greater predominance of somatic symptoms in depression). Winokur (1973) suggested a classification schema consisting of: (1) normal grief, (2) secondary depression, in which depression occurs with other non-affective pathology, and (3) primary affective disorders. The latter category is further divided into unipolar versus bipolar depressions (Perris, 1966; 1968; 1969; 1971). In bipolar depression, episodes of mania or hypomania alternate with depressive episodes. In unipolar depressions, only episodes of depression are seen. Some differences in symptomatology differentiate the two. For example, unipolars more frequently show initial insomnia whereas bipolars show more frequent middle-early-morning awakening; bipolars more frequently show retardation while unipolars may be agitated. Differential response to drugs has also been found to support this value of the dichotomy. The unipolar-bipolar distinction has largely supplanted the endogenous-reactive distinction as a focus of research, and it has been incorporated into DSM-III.

It is notable that none of the standardized methods for assessing depression acknowledges subtypes of depression. They do not provide differentiating subscales nor specify a subtype of depression for which it is targeted.

Behavioral Perspectives

The phenomena of depression have been particulary difficult to account for from a behavioral perspective. Some of the problems are highlighted by a comparison with a behavioral approach to the phenomena of anxiety. Behavior therapy made progress with anxiety by assuming that it was a response to relatively specific situations or stimuli. Depression is assumed to be pervasive across situations in its manisfestation and is expressed in changes in many response systems. As opposed to the sampling of stimulus situations in many anxiety assessment techniques, assessment techniques for depression tend to evaluate response systems widely. The pervasiveness of depression also pertains to a temporal dimension, since it is assumed to occur in episodes measurable in weeks or months. While there is considerable evidence for day-to-day variation in mood as a function of concurrent events (Grosscup & Lewinsohn, 1980; Lewinsohn & Libet, 1972; Rehm, 1978; Lewinsohn & Graf, 1973), syndromal depression is an effect over a longer time span. Anxiety quite often occurs in situational attacks measurable in minutes! Intraindividual comparisons in depression are commonly made to premorbid baseline states that are usually not directly observable. Intraindividual comparisons in anxiety can be made by observations of individuals in the presence or absence of anxiety-provoking stimuli. Depression instruments must deal both with the response generality and the time frame of depressive symptoms.

Models of depression, behavioral or otherwise, have dealt with the heterogeneity and pervasiveness of depression by assuming that it has a central or core symptom, and that all other symptoms follow as consequences or elaborations of the core deficit. The core symptoms tend to be deficits of some generality. This kind of assumption is unusual for behavioral models, where the ideal is to measure directly the behavioral target of the intervention. With depression, the intervention is aimed at a core deficit, which may or may not be directly assessed, and the larger outcome is assessed in terms of the multiple behaviors of syndromal depression.

Many core deficits have been hypothesized. Lowered rate of activity is seen as the primary datum of depression by Ferster (1973). Lewinsohn (1974, 1976) and his colleagues have developed methods for identifying and increasing mood related activity. Anhedonia is hypothesized by Lewinsohn, Biglan, and Zeiss (1976) to be based on anxiety, and desensitization is used to increase enjoyment potential. Several cases of treating depression with desensitization or its variants, such as flooding, have been reported (see Rehm & Kornblith, 1979). Social skills in various forms have been hypothesized as the core deficits in depression. Wolpe (1979), arguing that anxiety is the basis for neurotic depression, recommends assertion training for certain cases. Lewinsohn, Weinstein, and Alper (1970) conducted group therapy focusing on deficits in communications skills of depressed subjects within groups. Several reports of social skill training have appeared in the literature (see Rehm & Kornblith, 1979). Other variations on this theme include problem-solving deficits (e.g., Caple & Blechman, 1976; Shipley & Fazio, 1973) and marital communication problems (e.g., Lewinsohn & Atwood, 1969; McLean & Hakstian, 1979; McLean, Ogston, & Grauer, 1973). Cognitive distortion has been hypothesized by Beck (1972, 1976) as the core deficit in depression, and distorted beliefs are cited by Ellis (1962). Seligman's theory (Seligman, 1974, 1975) postulates the construct of learned helplessness as central to depression. Elsewhere, I (Rehm, 1977) have proposed a model postulating deficits in self-control to account for the phenomena of depression. This model differs from the others in that it postulates multiple deficits relating to specific depressive phenomena. One of the recent trends in the assessment of depression has been the development of instruments to measure hypothetical core deficits directly.

Symptom Content

In order to compare and evaluate depression assessment instruments, it is necessary to begin with a standard list of depressive behaviors. It should be clear from the preceding discussion that any such list must necessarily be somewhat arbitrary. A list is necessary, however, in order to compare and assess how instruments cover the relevant dimensions of depression. In order to resolve some of the difficulties inherent in establishing such a list, I have opted for establishing two separate ones. The first list includes broad categories of symptomatology applicable to most forms of psychopathology. The second is made up of a few specific symptoms most frequently cited as central to a syndrome of depression. The first list is as follows:

Verbal-cognitive symptoms of depression. This label is one that has been used in the behavioral literature (e.g., Lang, 1969) to denote those symptoms expressed primarily through verbalizations or observations of the cognitive processes of the individual. For purposes of discussing the psychopathology of depression, this category can be broken down into two major subcategories. These are: (1) sad affect, and (2) cognitive distortions. Sad affect is essentially depression as a symptom. It is that state people describe as depressed, sad, blue, low, down, unhappy, dispairing, etc. It might also include the absence of emotions usually believed incompatible with depression: for instance, joy, elation, happiness, etc. The syndrome of depression is sometimes held to include affects which are differentiated from depression, including anxiety, hostility, frustration, and irritability. Cognitive distortion in depression includes a variety of attitudes and beliefs about oneself and the world. Beck (1972) identifies the cognitive triad of a negative view of self, world, and future as essential features of depression. Other symptoms included would be pessimism, hopelessness, helplessness, low self-esteem, and guilt.

Overt-motor behavioral symptoms of depression. This category includes those symptoms of depression that are manifest in the individual's observable overt-motor behavior. These may include behavioral excesses which involve an acceleration or increased frequency and behavioral deficits involving deceleration or decreased frequency. Behavioral excesses in depression include such observables as sad demeanor, hanging of the head, crying, lack of eye contact, wringing of the hands, and at times, agitation. Suicide behavior might also be classed as a behavioral excess. Behavioral deficits include psychomotor retardation, decreases in work and recreational activities, and disturbances in sleep, eating behavior, and sexual behavior.

Somatic symptoms of depression. Somatic symptoms include those bodily complaints and physical disorders frequently manifest in depression, including such typical complaints as excessive fatigue, constipation, loss of appetite, diffuse pain, and troubled breathing. Also in this category are those somatic symptoms that could be physically assessed. This would include. for example, physiological changes, such as alterations in facial muscle tension or patterns of EEG sleep recordings associated with depression. Biochemical assays might also be included here.

Interpersonal symptoms of depression. Although this category has not been a part of the traditional symptomatology of depression, theory and research evidence is increasingly pointing to the importance of social interactions as a possible locus of depressive disorder. In interpersonal behavior, depressed persons have variously been described as dependent, demanding, manipulative, negative, hostile, complaining, or withdrawn. Research on life situations (e.g., Brown, Bhrolchain, & Harris, 1975), recent life events of major magnitude (e.g., Holmes & Rahe, 1967), and minor life events (MacPhillamy & Lewinsohn, 1971) suggests that interpersonal and social stresses may be an important contributant to the onset and maintenance of depression. Alternatively, depression may yield stressful disturbances in interpersonal relationships.

A fifth major category could potentially be added to this list. History or course of the disorder is symptomatically important in establishing differential diagnosis in depression. The frequency and nature of shifts or swings in mood differentiates between unipolar and bipolar depression and between episodic, intermittent, and chronic forms. Therapy outcome assessment is usually cross-sectional in nature so that these considerations are probably more important for pretest assessment in establishing a diagnosis and perhaps for follow-up assessment in tracing the course of the disorder after therapy.

Depressive signs

The above list consists of broad categories applicable to psychopathology generally. In depression, certain disturbances in critical areas of life are usually considered necessary and sufficient conditions for a diagnosis. These criterion symptoms include the so-called neurovegetative signs. A working list of these signs would include: (1) sleep disturbances, including difficulty getting to sleep, frequent awakening, early morning awakening, and hypersomnia; (2) eating disturbances, including weight loss or gain and loss of appetite; (3) sexual disturbances, including decreased frequency of sexual behavior, diminished interest, and diminished capacity; (4) work disturbance, including decreased productivity, increased effortfulness, fatigability, and lack of motivation; (5) suicidal behavior, including attempts, gestures, threats, plans, and ruminations.

In reviewing instruments for assessing depression, the contents can be compared as to the relative weight given to verbal-cognitive (affect and cognition), behavioral, somatic, and interpersonal symptomatology. An ideal instrument would include items that would specifically assess each of these areas and each of the salient depressive signs. It is important to note that the neurovegetative signs could be assessed in multiple symptom categories. For instance, work disturbance could be assessed in terms of overt behavior (i.e., performance deficits), verbal-cognitive behavior (i.e., a loss of interest), somatic behavior (i.e., fatigability), or interpersonal behavior (i.e., inability to get along with coworkers). Thus, both lists seem to be essential for evaluating assessment instruments.

ASSESSMENT FORMATS

Several types of assessment modalities will be reviewed below. These include: (1) self-report; (2) clinician rating scales; (3) direct observational methods; and (4) significant other evaluations. In addition, methods for assessing core symptoms of depression will also be discussed.

The review will concentrate on the most popular methods employed in research and clinical settings, along with some promising methods which have the potential for filling certain gaps in the assessment armamentarium. Certain instruments that measure constructs related but not central to the concept of depression (e.g., suicidality) have been omitted as beyond the scope of the review. The review will attempt to describe each instrument, including its content, format and rationale, examine its psychometric properties, and evaluate its potential contribution to clinical and research assessment.

The latter distinction is made since the needs of clinicians and researchers may be different in terms of assessment methods. Both need to categorize individuals, predict future behavior, and measure severity of the disorder, but clinicians need to categorize clients into classes that help to conceptualize the problem and shape detailed inquiry.

Such categorizations are ideally reliable and communicable to others. The categorization schema should aid in prediction. What will be the natural course of this type of disorder? Will it respond to this or that therapy strategy? Severity may also have treatment implications, as well as being a gauge of therapy progress. Researchers need to categorize subjects reliably in order to enhance the comparability of studies conducted in different settings. Prediction of differential course or response to treatment is an increasingly important focus of research. Valid assessment of severity is essential to any study of variables hypothesized to influence a disorder. Both clinicians and researchers have decisions to make among instruments based on practicality and purpose.

Self-Report Depression Scales

Self-report has been the traditional format for assessing depression. Many instruments have been published and employed in research reports. Levitt and Lubin (1975), for example, list 23 self-report scales. Many of these are not well developed psychometrically and have been used in only a few studies. One of the problems in depression research has been the lack of comparability among studies because so many different scales have been used. Only those scales that have achieved some popularity will be reviewed here.

Beck Depression Inventory. Although originally conceived as a clinician administered scale, the Beck Depression Inventory (BDI) (Beck, 1972; Beck, Ward, Mendelson, Mock, & Erbaugh, 1961) is now used almost exclusively as a self-report instrument. Its 21 items consist of a series of ordered statements relating to a particular symptom of depression. The subjects indicate which statements describe their current state. Each statement is scaled from 0 to 3. Items and weights were derived logically. A 13-item short form is also available (Beck & Beck, 1972). The intent of the BDI was to cover the symptomatology of depression comprehensively, but it tends to emphasize cognitive content. Two items are devoted to affect (one of these to irritability), eleven to cognition, two to overt behavior, five to somatic symptoms, and one to interpersonal symptoms. All of the major signs are covered.

While no manual exists, considerable psychometric data on the BDI has accumulated. Some standardization data are available in the original report (Beck et al., 1961), and cut-off scores of 13 for screening and 21 for clinical research have been recommended (Beck & Beamesderfer, 1974). While designed for use in clinical populations, it has frequently

been used in normal populations such as college students with cut-off
scores in the 7 to 9 range. The instrument appears to be valid in this
range (see Blumberry, Oliver, & McClure, 1978).

The accumulated reliability and validity data on the scale is quite
large and beyond the scope of this chapter to fully review. Only representative data will be cited in an attempt to summarize the findings.
Beck (1972) reports Kruskal-Wallis item-total correlations of .31 to
.68 and a .93 Spearman-Brown corrected split-half reliability. Weckowicz et al. (1967) report a Kuder-Richardson -20 of .78. Test-retest
reliabilities of .75 for 23 undergraduates after one month (author's unpublished data), .74 for 31 undergraduates after 3 months (Miller &
Seligman, 1973), and .48 for 59 psychiatric patients after 3 weeks (May,
Urquhart, & Tarran, 1969) have been obtained.

Correlations reported with other self-report depression scales are generally fairly good. While Beck (1972) asserts that the BDI has excellent
discriminant validity, differentiating it from self-report of anxiety, this
can be questioned. Moderate to high correlations with anxiety have been
reported (see Papazian, unpublished), suggesting considerable method
variance. Good correlations have been found with clinician rating scales
and with a behavioral observation scale (Williams, Barlow, & Agras,
1972). The BDI is sensitive to clinical change as demonstrated in its
frequent use as an outcome measure in drug trials (see McNair, 1974)
and behavior therapy outcome studies (see Rehm & Kornblith, 1979).

In summary, the BDI is a relatively short and easily administered
instrument with a fairly solid psychometric base. While stressing cognitive symptoms, its structure allows for the possibility of systematic
item or "subscale" analyses. It has become a very popular instrument
in research and clinical practice.

CES-D. The CES-D was developed by the Center for Epidemeological
Studies of the National Institute of Mental Health. CES-D items were
derived from other self-report depression inventories and were selected
to sample the major components of depressive symptomatology. The
purpose of this scale was to measure "current level of depressive symptomatology with emphasis on the affective component, depressed mood."
Thus, it was not intended as a diagnostic instrument nor a severity instrument, but a survey of depressive symptoms that might be found in
psychiatric, medical, or general populations. Although the development
of the scale is not described in detail in the major article (Radloff,
1977), reference is made to a series of revisions in which items were
refined.

The scale is made up of 20 items, each consisting of a first person
statement of a relatively specific depressive symptom (e.g., "my sleep
was restless," "I felt sad"). Instructions ask the examinee to indicate

how often he or she has felt this way during the past week. Ratings are made on a 0 to 3 scale anchored as follows: 0—rarely or none of the time (less than one day); 1—some or a little of the time (1–2 days); 2—occasionally or a moderate amount of time (3-4 days); 3—most or all of the time (5-7 days). Sixteen items describe negative symptoms, and four are stated in a positive direction to avoid a response bias or set.

The content areas the authors tried to sample were depressed mood, feelings of guilt and worthlessness, feelings of helplessness and hopelessness, psychomotor retardation, loss of appetite, and sleep disturbance (Radloff, 1977). When viewed in terms of affect, verbal-cognitive, behavioral, somatic, and social-interpersonal symptomatology, the scale is heavily weighted in the affective area. Eight items directly tap affect (six depressive, one anxiety, one "bothered"). Four items tap other cognitive symptoms. Four items tap behavioral symptoms, and two items tap both somatic and social symptoms. One item covers each of the specific signs of sleeping, eating, and work disturbances; none refers to sexual disturbance or suicide.

The CES-D was used in a large survey study assessing psychiatric symptoms in two communities. The probability samples yielded 1173 completed interviews from a Kansas City, Missouri sample and 1673 completed interviews from a Washington County, Maryland sample. Repeat interviews were available on significant groups of subjects to assess test-retest reliability, and samples of psychiatric patients have also been reported in the literature (Craig & VanNatta 1976a, 1976b; Weissman, Prusoff, & Newberry, 1975; Weissman, Sholomskas, Pottenger, Prusoff, & Locke, 1977). Radloff (1977) presented data on the nature of the distributions of CES-D scores for the major samples and for subgroups based on various demographic variables. She notes that the scale is skewed for normals, although it appears to be symmetrical for clinical populations.

There is a fair amount of evidence that reliability and validity replicate across various normal and clinical samples (Craig & VanNatta, 1976b; Radloff, 1977; Weissman, Pottenger, Kleber, Ruben, Williams, & Thompson, 1975; Weissman, Prusoff, & Newberry, 1975). Radloff reports that, as expected for this kind of scale, the interitem correlations are relatively low, and item scale correlations are moderate. Internal consistency reliability, however, is very good. Coefficient alpha, split half, and Spearman-Brown estimates of internal consistency reliability are relatively uniform. Test-retest reliability data are available on samples with intervals of 2, 4, 6, and 8 weeks, and 3, 6, 9 and 12 months. As expected in a scale intended to assess fluctuations in mood, correlations up to eight weeks are moderate (overall test-retest correlations of .57), and correlations across months taper off to .32 for a one-year test-retest reliability. Test-retest correlations were highest for individuals who had not had intervening major life events (Radloff, 1977).

The CES-D is valid in the sense of discriminating between clinical and normal populations (Craig & VanNatta, 1976a, 1976b; Radloff, 1977; Weissman, Pottenger, Kleber, Ruben, Williams, & Thompson, 1977; Weissman, Prusoff, & Newberry, 1975). The scale also differentiates between more acutely depressed subgroups (Craig & VanNatta, 1976a, 1976b; Weissman, Pottenger, Kleber, Ruben, Williams, & Thompson, 1977; Weissman, Prusoff, & Newberry, 1975). It does not discriminate, however, between subgroups of depression, such as primary versus secondary depressives (Weissman et al., 1977). Also, at least some of the items may measure psychopathology generally rather than depression specifically (Craig & VanNatta, 1976a). Concurrent validity with other scales is generally quite good (Craig & VanNatta, 1976b; Radloff, 1977; Weissman, Pottenger, Kleber, Ruben, Williams, & Thompson, 1977; Weissman, Prusoff, & Newberry, 1975). Correlations with clinician ratings are acceptable, although there appears to be some method variance differentiating this and other self-report instruments from clinician rating scales (e.g., Weissman, Pottenger, Kleber, Ruben, Williams, & Thompson, 1977; Weissman, Prusoff, & Newberry, 1975). Weissman, Pottenger, Kleber, Ruben, Williams, and Thompson (1977) report that the CES-D changes with clinical improvement. Evidence for the discriminant validity of the CES-D is summarized by Radloff (1977) and Weissman et al. (1977). It is notable that the test does not discriminate between subtypes of depression, nor is there present evidence that it adequately discriminates depression from anxiety. This might be particularly important for the scale since it seems to have a fair amount of correlation with other measures of psychopathology.

In summary, this instrument has very good psychometric properties. It tends to stress affective symptomatolotly *per se* and is probably best suited for its original purpose: exploring relationships between depressive symptomatology and other characteristics of populations in survey samples (e.g., Radloff, 1975). The one-week time focus limits its value in assessing certain kinds of change that might be expected to occur within short periods (e.g., drug treatment effects). However, this same time focus also may be an advantage in specifying to the patient a particular objective criterion that may increase the objective validity of this self-report instrument. Since the instrument has not been widely used in clinical trials, it is not known how well it operates or relates to other instruments as an outcome measure.

Lubin Depression Adjective Check Lists. The DACL (Lubin, 1965; 1966; 1967) consists of seven alternate forms (A through G). Forms A through D contain 22 positive and 10 negative adjectives from a pool that significantly differentiated 48 depressed female psychiatric patients from 179 normal females. Forms E through G consist of 22 positive and 12 negative adjectives from a pool that differentiated 47 depressed male psychiatric patients from 100 normal males. Each form can be scored from a single template. The scoring system takes the number of positive adjectives minus the negative adjectives for a total score that attempts to minimize the bias introduced by the simple number of adjectives checked. The time frame is "today" or "in general." The content is usually in the nature of affect words, making the scale more one of mood than of syndromal depression.

A manual for the DACL is available (Lubin, 1967), and psychometric development is fairly extensive. Normative data are available for students, senior citizens, adolescent delinquents, depressed and nondepressed psychiatric samples (Lubin, 1967), and for a national sample of 3000 adults (Levitt & Lubin, 1975).

Lubin (1967) reports internal consistency reliabilities for the DACL, ranging from .79 to .88 for males and .85 to .90 for females. Split-half reliabilities ranged from .83 to .92 for normals and from .89 to .92 for patients. Intercorrelations among scales ranged from .82 to .92 for three samples. Comparable alternate form and split-half reliabilities were reported by Lubin and Himmelstein (1976), who also reported one week test-retest reliabilities of .19 for form E, .24 for form F, and .22 for form G. These low correlations are reasonable for a mood measure. Lubin (1967; Lubin, Dupre, & Lubin, 1967) found no differences among absolute scores for forms E, F, and G.

Each of the seven scales was crossvalidated on samples of 625 normals, 174 nondepressed psychiatric patients, and 128 depressed psychiatric patients. All seven scales significantly differentiated the groups. Concurrent validity in the form of correlations with other depression scales is moderate. Lubin, Horned, and Knapp (1977) report some evidence for the discriminant validity of the DACL in the form of negligible correlations with the Eysenck Personality Inventory, but Lubin (1967) reports fairly substantial correlations between forms E, F and G and the MMPI clincial scales. Lubin, Hornstra, and Love (1974) and Lubin, Dupre, and Lubin (1967) report changes in DACL scores as a function of therapeutic interventions. The DACL has been used as an outcome measure in a number of behavior therapy outcome studies (see Rehm & Kornblith, 1979). Lewinsohn (Grosscup & Lewinsohn, 1980; Lewinsohn & Graf, 1973; Lewinsohn & Libet, 1972) has used the DACL to assess daily fluctuations in mood as a correlate of daily events.

In sum, the DACL is a set of psychometrically sophisticated alternate forms for which excellent normative data are available. While perhaps most useful for assessing fluctuations in mood over brief periods, it also differentiates groups by severity of depression. It has the advantages of alternate forms to aid in frequent retesting, and is quite short and easy to administer.

MMPI-D. The MMPI-D (Hathaway & McKinley, 1951) is the most widely used psychological assessment instrument in the United States and, therefore, probably the most widely used instrument for assessing depression. Its 60 true-false items consist of 49 selected because they differentiated between a group of normals and a group of hospitalized manic-depressive, depressed patients and eleven items that distinguished between the depressed group and other psychiatric patients (Hathaway & McKinley, 1942).

The test is available in several formats (group form, step-down page or card sort) and has been translated into 30 languages. The full test takes between 45 minutes and two hours, but the MMPI-D alone can be given in five to ten minutes.

Due to the empirical nature of the scale development, there was no logical attempt to cover depressive symptomatology in a systematic fashion. Harris and Lingoes (1955) grouped the items into five logical subscales which they termed "subjective depression," "psychomotor retardation," "complaints about physical malfunctioning," "mental dullness," and "brooding." From the point of view of the content areas being used in this review, the MMPI-D has a fairly good balance between somatic (18 items) and cognitive (17 items) content. In addition, there are eight affect items (including two anxiety and three anger items), six social-interpersonal items and five behavioral symptom items. Another five items are not easily classified. In regard to the standard signs, there are three items relating to sleep disturbances, two relating to eating disturbances, one relating to work disturbances, and none relating to sexual disturbance or suicide.

A 1967 revision of the manual is available, and in addition other books such as Dahlstrom and Welsh's *An MMPI Handbook* are available as an extensive supplement to the manual. Normative data are available on a wide variety of samples.

Dahlstrom and Welsh (1960) summarize a great deal of data on the reliability of the MMPI scales. Split-half reliabilities for the MMPI-D range from .35 to .84, the median being in the low .70s. Criticisms regarding heterogeneity have already been mentioned. Test-retest reliabilities are moderate; however, Dahlstrom and Welsh argue that this is due to the scale's sensitivity to mood changes.

Since the test was empirically constructed to differentiate depressed and non-depressed groups, the MMPI-D has frequently been used to identify research populations, usually with a standard 70 T-score or greater. Correlations with other depression scales tend to be fairly good. Intercorrelations among MMPI scales, however, suggest that its discriminant validity is less than desirable. The MMPI-D has frequently been criticized for its lack of discriminant validity from anxiety (e.g., Comrey, 1957; Costello & Comrey, 1967; Mendels, Weinstein, & Cochrane, 1972). It is sensitive to change and has frequently been used as an outcome measure. McNair (1974) notes that the MMPI-D is the most frequently used instrument to assess outcome in studies of anti-depressant drugs, but criticizes it for its lack of a distinct time frame which limits its ability to differentiate over short periods of time. It has also frequently been used in behavior therapy outcome studies (see Rehm & Kornblith, 1979).

In summary, the MMPI-D is the most frequently used self-report depression instrument and has accumulated a great deal of statistical and normative background data. Despite its empirical derivation, it has fairly good coverage of a range of depressive content. The most serious shortcomings are its heterogeneity and lack of discrimination from anxiety. Its original intent was to distinguish between diagnostic subgroups. Today this is more frequently done with the MMPI by profile analysis, but screening or population definition may be an appropriate use of this instrument.

Zung Self-Rating Depression Scale. The Self-Rating Depression Scale (SDS) was devised to tap three factors: (1) pervasive affect, (2) physiological equivalence or concomitants, and (3) psychological concomitants, that were extracted from a review of factor analytic studies of depressive symptomatology. Ten items are written in a positive direction and ten in a negative direction. The examinee is asked to indicate on a four point scale how much of the time during the past week the statement was true of him or her. Answers are weighted one to four points.

Using his initial general factors, the SDS was written to include four pervasive affect questions, eight physiological disturbance questions, eight psychological disturbance questions, plus two psychomotor disturbance questions. From a comparative perspective, the SDS includes three affect items (including one on irritability), six cognition items, four overt-motor behavior items, six somatic items, and one social-in-terpersonal item. All five major signs are covered.

Although no manual exists for the SDS, the test booklet (Zung, 1974) serves partly that purpose by supplying scoring instructions and cut-off scores. While no major standardization effort has been made, Blumen-thal and Dielman (1975) summarize means for 22 separate samples. These means are generally consistent with Zung's suggested cut-off scores.

In a fairly extensive review of the literature on this instrument, I was unable to find any published reliability data, neither internal consistency nor test-retest. In general, the SDS has been found to discriminate be-tween depressed and non-depressed samples (e.g., Carroll, Fielding & Blashki, 1973; Lunghi, 1977; Marone & Lubin, 1968; Schnurr, Hoaken, & Jarrett, 1976; Zung, 1965; 1967). However, two studies (Humphrey, 1967; Zung, Richards, & Short, 1965) found that only subsets of items actually differentiated depressed individuals. In one of the few studies attempting to differentiate subtypes of depression, Raft, Spencer, Toomey, and Brogan (1977) concluded that the SDS does not differ-entiate well between primary and secondary depressions, nor was it able to discriminate depressive reactions from conversion reactions.

Concurrent validity related to correlations with other depression in-struments is good. Evidence for discriminant validity is weak. Zung (1969) reports near zero correlations with the Eysenck personality In-ventory, but Zung et al., (1965) report a correlation of .68 with the MMPI Pt scale which is quite close to the .70 correlation with the D scale. Burrows, Foenander, Davies, and Scoggins (1976) found a cor-relation of .58 between the SDS and the Taylor Manifest Anxiety Scale. It should be noted, however, that both the Pt and TMAS may have poor discriminant validity themselves.

The SDS appears to be sensitive to changes in clinical status. In a review of outcome measures in 75 clincial drug trials, McNair (1974) recommends the SDS quite highly as a sensitive instrument.

In summary, while the SDS has gained some popularity, it is not as well developed psychometrically as some of the other self-report in-struments. Standardization data have accumulated over studies, but cer-tain kinds of information are still lacking. The content distribution is fairly good, and probably the best feature is that it is relatively short and simple to administer.

Other Self-Report Scales. Several other self-report depression scales de-serve mention. In addition to the MMPI-D, other depression scales have been derived from the MMPI item pool. The most frequently used of these is the D-30 scale developed by Costello and Comrey (1967). The

D-30 was developed along with a new anxiety scale from the MMPI item pool in order to improve item homogeneity, independence of scale scores, and influence of social desirability. In comparison to the MMPI-D and the Taylor Manifest Anxiety Scale, the newly developed scales are indeed improved on all of these dimensions according to data in the original report. On the other hand, Mendels, Weinstein, and Cochrane (1972) found a correlation between these two scales of .59, which was greater than the correlation between the MMPI-D and the Taylor MAS of .40. Thus, the increased discriminant validity that was the intention of the scale was not replicated. Neufeld, Rogers, and Costello (1972) found that the D-30 appeared to be quite sensitive to therapy changes. Little other work has been done with the scale. In general, the possible advantages of the scale are probably significantly outweighted by the loss of the accumulated experience accrued by the MMPI-D. This is perhaps all the more true of other derived scales (e.g., Endicott and Jortner's (1966) D-18 scale, made up of the 18 items found to markedly differentiate depressed and mildly depressed groups at the .10 level or better).

The Profile of Mood States (POMS; McNair, Lorr, & Droppleman, 1971) is an empirically developed instrument based on factor analytic studies. It consists of 65 adjectives, each of which is rated on a five-point scale. Six scales consist of: (1) tension-anxiety; (2) depression-dejection; (3) anger-hostility; (4) vigor; (5) fatigue; and (6) confusion. Affect terms predominate the 15 items on the depression-dejection scale with a few verbal-cognitive symptoms. The standardization and psychometric development of the POMS is sophisticated, and psychometric properties are quite good. The instrument has the advantages of the additional factorially independent scales. Since its content is limited it has been used very little in the depression literature.

The SCL-90 (Derogatis, 1977) is another well developed multiple-scale instrument. Its 90 items consist of symptoms rated on a five-point scale as to how problematic they have been in the last week. Nine scales are derived: (1) somatization; (2) obsessive-compulsive; (3) interpersonal sensitivity; (4) depression; (5) anxiety; (6) hostility; (7) phobic anxiety; (8) paranoid ideation; and (9) psychoticism. The depression scale stresses cognitive and affective content, but the overal SCL-90 has good coverage of depressive symptoms and signs. There is a short form of the instrument (The Brief Symptom Inventory) and parallel rating scales to be used by expert clinicians (Hopkins Psychiatric Rating Scales) and by less expert clinical observers (SCL-90 Analog). The manual (Derogatis, 1977) presents systematic standardization and psychometric data. As yet, the SCL-90 has not been used extensively in the depression literature, but the parallel rating forms make it a good instrument for assessing various other dimensions of pathology along with depression across the assessment perspectives of self-report, clinician, and observer.

The Social Adjustment Scale in its clinician interview (Weissman & Paykel, 1974) and self-report (Weissman & Bothwell, 1976) forms also deserves mention. While designed to measure social adjustment *per se,* it was developed in the context of depression research and can probably be considered a measure of the social-interpersonal aspects of depression. The self-report form consists of 42 items, each involving the choice of choosing one of five alternate statements describing social adjustment in various roles. Psychometric properties to date appear good. The scale has the advantages of symptom coverage of social-interpersonal factors, which are only minimally covered on other scales and parallel self-report and clinicians forms.

Finally, mention should be made of the Visual Analog Scale (Aitken, 1969). The scale consists simply of a 100 mm line anchored at one end by "normal mood" and at the other by "extreme depression." The scale takes only a few seconds to fill out and is adaptable to a variety of time frames. Data available suggest that its psychometric properties are comparable to those of the more elaborate scales (e.g., Crawford, Little, & McPhail, 1973; Davies, Burrows, & Poynton, 1975; Zealley & Aitken, 1969). As a global, self-report depression scale, the Visual Analog Scale may be sufficient for many purposes.

Comment on Self-Report Depression Scales. The scales reviewed vary considerably in terms of content coverage. A balance across categories and systematic coverage are both desirable. Most of the more popular self-report depression instruments stress affective and cognitive symptoms. While it is desirable from a behavioral point of view to be able to look separately at affect, verbal-cognitive, somatic, behavioral, and social symptoms, there is some logic to including them all in a self-report measure. Depression involves distortions of experience, and the self-report of a number of specific behaviors has traditionally been seen as a part of depressive behavior. Thus, for an individual to endorse the item on the BDI, "I wake up early every day and can't get more than 5 hours sleep," should not be taken as an index of overt or physiological sleep behavior. It *should* be taken as an indication of cognitive-verbal concern and complaint about specific aspects of sleep behavior. Mode of assessment should not be confused with mode of symptom manifestation. This cognitive-verbal behavior may or may not be distorted, but in either case it is a component of depression. If overt or physiological sleep behavior is to be a specific target of intervention, it should be assessed more directly and objectively as well.

The format of the scales also differs considerably. Instruments vary in the abstractness of items, the time frame for evaluation, and the nature of endorsement (e.g., degree of agreement with, versus frequency of occurrence of the item). More specific items endorsed for frequency should better correspond to direct observation. A specific and limited time frame is important for comparisons over time (e.g., improvement from one week to the next).

The psychometric properties of the instruments offer relatively little to choose from. While they vary in sophistication of development and in amount of accumulated data, from the available data no clear superiority emerges for one versus another.

Those with more accumulated data have the advantage of comparability with prior work. For example, the MMPI has standardization data for many samples, the Beck Depression Inventory has been used frequently in psychotherapy outcome studies, and the Zung frequently in drug trials.

Ultimately, a choice among instruments must rest on its intended use. For example, global instruments with good symptoms coverage (e.g., BDI, SDS or MMPI-D) are probably best for research population defination or clinical diagnosis. The same instruments with special attention to symptom coverage may be good for outcome assessment. Frequent, repeated measures of mood variation are probably best measured by simple affect scales, such as the DACL or Visual Analog Scale. If social adjustment is important, the SAS should be added to a battery. The CES-D may be particularly appropriate in nonpsychiatric samples.

Clinician Rating Scales

Ratings by expert clinicians are frequently used as a measure of severity, extent, and type of disorder in the depression literature. The general rationale for such measures is that they are attempts to quantify and standardize expert clinical judgment.

These instruments vary considerably in format, from simple global ratings, to more complex anchored scales, to structured interviews designed to make diagnostic decisions. Such instruments are not typical of the behavior therapy literature, but are often used in the psychiatric literature, especially in evaluations of drug trials.

Clinician rating scales have the advantage of applying expert opinion in determination about depression. The clinician can decide what behavior is most relevant to a rating dimension. Clinical experience can provide a baseline for judging the severity of a particular patient's complaint and, therefore, compensate in some ways for distortion in the self-report. The clinician can evaluate the patient on abstract unfamiliar dimensions, and can conduct an inquiry which branches in different directions depending on the nature of the complaints.

The disadvantages of clinician rating scales are that they introduce their own set of potential biases into the rating process. Since most scales are scored in conjunction with an interview, there is a danger in compounding clinician and self-report biases. Items abstract enough to require expert judgment are perhaps too vague to be predictive of specific behavior. More concrete or well anchored items could probably be answered validly by self-report.

Rating scales of this type mirror a real-world process, since in clinical settings, decisions about diagnoses and severity are made by clinicians. Compared with the perspectives of self-report, direct measurement of behavior, and evaluation by a significant other, this adds a dimension of reality to an assessment battery by paralleling the evaluative perspectives which occur in clinical settings.

Hamilton Rating Scale. The Hamilton Rating Scale was developed by Max Hamilton (1960; 1967) as a method for assessing severity of depression among patients who have already been diagnosed as depressed. It consists of a survey of 17 depressive symptoms, each of which is rated on either a 3-point or a 5-point scale. Four additional symptom items are included but not scored. Minor variations in the scale occur between the published 1960 and 1967 versions. The scale is intended as a means of quantifying expert clinical judgment. Hamilton advised that all available information from interview, history, relatives, charts, observations, etc., should be taken into account when arriving at a rating on each item. Hamilton (1960) further suggests that a total score be derived from the sum of two independent ratings; if only one rater is used, the score should be doubled for comparability. No formal manual exists for the scale, but Hamilton (1967) provides a commentary for each item, suggesting general guidelines for making the ratings.

The Hamilton is intended as a survey of essential symptoms of depression. It tends to be weighted heavily with somatic complaints (eight items), with five devoted to behavioral complaints, two to cognitive complaints, and two to affect. (One of these latter items refers to anxiety and one to depression.) There are no items referring to social-interpersonal symptomatology, but all of the depressive signs are covered with one item each for eating, sex, work, and suicide, and three items for sleep disturbance.

No normative data nor cut-off scores are published as such. Means for different samples reported in the literature vary somewhat; means for psychiatric inpatients of 32.0, 42.6, 43.6 (Schwab, Bialow, & Holzer, 1967) and 29.5 (Carroll, Fielding, & Blashki, 1973) have been reported. Schnurr, Hoaken, and Jarrett (1976) report a mean of 30.6 for severe depressives and 23.9 for neurotic depressives. Outpatient means of 27.0 and 25.0 (Schwab et al., 1967) and 23.7 (Carroll, Fielding, & Blashki, 1973) have been reported. Snaith, Ahmed, Mehta, and Hamilton (1971) report a mean of 6.2 for 200 normal subjects. Apparently no internal consistency statistic has been reported to date in the published literature, but some indication of internal consistency can be gained from item-total correlations. Schwab et al. (1967) report item-whole correlations ranging from .45 to .78. Our project at the University of Pittsburgh found item-whole correlations ranging from .22 to .67. Interrater reliabilities have been reported by a number of sources and have generally been excellent (e.g., in the area of .90). Several studies have demonstrated that the Hamilton Rating Scale differentiates between clinical and normal populations: Snaith et al. (1971) demonstrated a highly significant difference between 200 normals and 100 patients. Schnurr et al. (1976) found that the Hamilton differentiated well among different depressed and nondepressed psychiatric groups, as did Weismann, Sholomskas, Pottenger, Prusoff, and Locke (1977). Carroll et al. (1973) found that the Hamilton differentiated well between inpatient day-hospital and general practice depressed patients.

A number of studies have reported concurrent validity of the Hamilton in terms of correlations with other methods. Correlations with global clinical ratings tend to be high (.84 by Bech, Gram, Dein, Jacobsen, Vitger, & Bolwig, 1975; .98 by Knesevich, Biggs, Clayton, & Ziegler, 1977). Correlations with self-report instruments have been reported in numerous sources and tend to be fairly good. For example, most tend to be .60 or better for the Beck and Zung scales.

Consistent with the original intent of the scale, the Hamilton Rating Scale appears to be sensitive to clinical change. Knesevich et al. (1977) report a correlation of .68 between Hamilton change scores and changes in a global change score. Green, Gleser, Stone, and Seifert (1975) found different score correlations between the Hamilton and the SCL-90 (r = .73) and a psychiatric evaluation form depression scale (r = .77). The Hamilton has been widely used in evaluations of clinical trials of drugs and in psychotherapy outcome studies.

To summarize, the Hamilton Rating Scale is psychometrically unsophisticated in its original development. Psychometric evidence, however, seems to be accumulating to suggest that the instrument has adequate internal consistency, excellent interrater reliability, and good concurrent validity. There are some questions about the consistency of structure of its application. Its content is heavily weighted toward somatic symptoms, which may be appropriate for its original intent in evaluating symptomatology of depressed inpatients in drug trials. But

this, however, should be noted in any application to psychotherapy
outcome for outpatients. The scale has extensive prior usage as an outcome measure and appears to be sensitive to change, but normative
information for comparison across studies is at present not very good.
Nonetheless, this instrument has achieved a central place in depression
assessment, particularly as a clinical instrument, and may continue to
serve that purpose until a better one is developed.

Schedule for Affective Disorders and Schizophrenia. The underlying rationale for the SADS is that diagnostic reliability can be enhanced by
the use of operational criteria and standardized information collection.
Toward this end, the Research Diagnostic Criteria (Feighner, Robins,
Guze, Woodruff, Winokur, & Munoz, 1972; Spitzer, Endicott, & Robins, 1975; 1978) were developed to establish standardized operational
criteria. The original purpose of the RDC was for homogeneous subject
selection in research, and much of it has been incorporated into
DSM-III. The RDC has gone through an evolutionary process of development and refinement as a function of research and clinical experience. The Spitzer, Endicott, and Robins (1978) version is much
expanded from the original Feighner et al. (1972) version. The SADS
was developed as a structured interview format for collecting standardized information to base RDC diagnostic decisions. As with the RDC,
the SADS focuses heavily on schizophrenia and affective disorders but
also has sections for closely related diagnostic categories where differential diagnoses and exclusions decisions need to be made. There
are three forms of the SADS: the SADS regular form, the SADS-L
(for lifetime) form, and SADS-C (for change). The regular SADS is
composed of two parts: part one collects information concerning the
current episode and the prior week; part two collects information concerning past episodes. SADS-L is similar to part two of the SADS, but
is organized for use with patients who are not presently ill or with
patient's relatives. The SADS-C consists of items from the regular
SADS part one collected for the past week. The purpose of the SADS-
C is to make posttest or follow-up assessments of current status.

   The SADS is somewhat unique in that the time frame of part one of
the regular form is the present episode. Thus, diagnostic decisions are
made on symptoms as they are displayed at the peak of the present
episode. Data are also collected within a past week time frame and a
lifetime time frame. In its most recent form (January 1978), the SADS
interview is 78 pages long and yields data filling 12 computer cards.
The form includes instructions to the interviewer, suggested phrasing
of questions (which can be followed up with other general and specific
questions), and rating scales to be filled out during the course of the

interview. Many items are filled out on a yes, no, or no information basis, while others are rated on three to nine point rating scales. Although the items are intended to be operational and specific, many require a fairly sophisticated knowledge of manifest psychopathology. Because of this, it is suggested that they be filled out only by professionals (psychiatrists, clinical psychologists or psychiatric social workers). Endicott and Spitzer (1978) have presented information on eight summary scales derived from the SADS: (1) depressive mood and ideation; (2) endogenous features; (3) depressive-associated features; (4) suicidal ideation and behavior; (5) anxiety; (6) manic syndrome; (7) delusions-hallucinations; and (8) formal thought disorder. Since their presentation, this list of scales has been expanded to 24, including derived Hamilton scales and replications of some of the original eight factors for current episode and past week (Endicott & Spitzer, personal communication). Scales were derived on a logical basis with reference to factor analytic studies and dimensions of importance in research. They contain items scored either as present, absent, or rated on scales of varying lengths. There is much item overlap between the subscales. Reliability and validity data for these subscales comprise the major psychometric development of an instrument which will be reviewed here. No manual exists for the SADS or its subscales, and content coverage is comprehensive by definition. In terms of standard content areas, the SADS subscales could be described as follows: Scale 1, *depressive mood and ideation,* consists of five items, one related specifically to affect and four that are cognitive. Scale 2, *endogenous features,* consists of 13 items. Seven of these refer to behavioral symptoms, four to cognitive symptoms, one to affective symptoms, and one questionable item to social interaction symptoms. Scale 3, *depressive-associated features,* consists of 17 items that are primarily behavioral symptomatology and cognition with one social item. Scale 4, *suicidal ideation and behavior,* is made up of four items concerning suicide behavior and intent. Scale 1 is intended to assess actual mood, while scale 2 is intended for features related with the concept of endogeneity. Scale 3 is intended to assess neurovegetative signs and scale 4 suicidality. There is considerable overlap among these scales, and individual items cover all of the major symptoms and signs of depression. To date, no factor analytic studies have been employed to validate the structure of these scales.

Published data on the SADS is largely limited to information coming from two samples: one from the NIMH collaborative program on the psychobiology of depression, and the other from a pilot study of 150 patients by the same four participating groups. While these samples were fairly large (104 and 150), they were insufficient for establishing norms, cut-offs, etc., and there were no data suggesting the consistency of structure of scales across subsamples, such as sex of subject. Cronbach alpha indices of internal consistency for the eight original subscales range from .47 to .97 (N = 150). With the exception of formal thought disorder (alpha = .47) and anxiety (alpha = .58), the remainder of the alphas were .79 or greater. Interrater reliabilities based on joint interviews with 150 patients ranged from interclass correlations of .82 to .99. Test-retest reliabilities based on two interviews given within a week of one another ranged from .49 to .93 based on an N of 60. Again, the formal thought disorder and anxiety scales were lowest at .49 and .67, respectively, and the remainder of the correlations were .78 or above. Concurrent validity for subscales has been established via correlations with the Katz Adjustment Scale (relative and subject forms) and with the SCL-90. Correlations with the KAS-R ranged from .23 to .58, and those for the DAS-S ranged from .34 to .46. Correlations with SCL-90 scales ranged from .15 to .68. In general, these correlations are less than desirable for similar construct scales. The construct validity of the scales has received some degree of validation in studies comparing groups that receive different RDC diagnoses on nine criterion items. Several of these comparisons are given by Endicott and Spitzer (1978; unpublished). No data have yet been offered to substantiate the sensitivity of these scales to clinical change. Endicott and Spitzer (unpublished) found that the prognostic indications of endogenous features were not supported.

While the SADS and the RDC are becoming accepted and rapidly adopted by the research community, evidence for the subscales derived from the SADS is to date relatively slight and in some instances substandard. Pending further psychometric development, it might make more sense to simply use the index of meeting RDC criteria or not for evaluation of outcome in depression psychotherapy studies. As an instrument to assess the presence or absence of syndromal depression, this instrument clearly represents the state of the art today.

Other Clinician Rating Scales. Several other clinician rating scales should be mentioned. The Raskin Three Area Rating Scale (Raskin, Schulterbrant, Reatig, & McKeon, 1969; Raskin, Schulterbrant, Reatig, & Rice, 1969) was developed as a method for selecting research subjects. Three areas, "verbal report," "behavior," and "secondary symptoms of depression" are each rated on a 5-point scale and summed. Normative and psychometric data are accumulating, and the scale may serve a variety of functions as a relatively global rating scale.

The Brief Psychiatric Rating Scale (Overall & Gorham, 1962) was originally developed to provide a rapid assessment technique of psychiatric symptoms for the purpose of evaluating change over time. Sixteen dimensions are rated on seven point scales from "not present" to "extremely severe." While the intent is a broad coverage of psychiatric symptomatology, a number of the scales are relevant to depression: (1) somatic concern, (2) anxiety, (3) emotional withdrawal, (5) guilt feelings, (9) depressed mood, (13) motor retardation, and (16) blunted affect. While these dimensions include each of the standard areas, they do not assess the specific signs of depression. A total pathology score can also be obtained by summing the 16 ratings. Scoring weights are provided for evaluating improvement in 13 specific diagnostic types, and include psychotic depressive reaction and manic-depressive, depressive type. A second set of weights is given for three major patient populations: paranoid, schizophrenic, and depressive. Despite minimal initial psychometric development, the Brief Psychiatric Rating Scale has achieved some popularity for assessing change in psychiatric and psychological outcome research. For the purpose of assessing outcome in depression studies, it is doubtful whether simple ratings on so many scales would give an unbiased estimate of generalization of improvement. The weighting systems may prove helpful in making diagnostic distinctions.

The Feelings and Concerns Checklist is made up of 47 items selected and revised on the basis of pilot work (Grinker, Miller, Sabshin, Nunn, & Nunally, 1961). Each item is rated on a 4-point scale, from 0 (not present) to 3 (markedly present). The content of the items is entirely cognitive. Five factors derived from a factor analysis of 96 depressed patients are scored separately. The factors are labeled: (1) dismal, hopeless, bad feelings, (2) projection to external events, (3) guilty feelings, (4) anxiety, and (5) clinging appeals for love. Reliability data are generally good, and the FCCL has been used in a number of psychotherapy outcome studies. Lewinsohn and his colleagues have used the instrument in several studies, primarily as a subject selection criterion. Lewinsohn and Biglan (1975) and Lewinsohn, Weinstein, and Alper (1970) also report pre-post differences on the GFCC. Padfield (1976) reported that the GFCC discriminated between treatment conditions in a psychotherapy outcome study, suggesting that the GFCC is sensitive to clinical change. This instrument had an initial development and has been used to some degree in depression research (e.g., Simon, 1966), but has not enjoyed sufficient popularity to accrue a body of additional pscyhometric support. Its cognitive content could make it useful in combination with other scales.

Mentioned under self-report instruments was the fact that there are clinician rating alternate forms of the Social Adjustment Scale (Weissman & Paykel, 1974) and the SCL-90 (i.e., the Hopkins Psychiatric rating scale; Derogatis, 1977). The Social Adjustment Scale consists of 42 items grouped within six role areas by five qualitative areas.

Social interpersonal content is most heavily weighted, but other areas of depressive behavior are included as well. Psychometric data are minimal but promising. The Hopkins Psychiatric Rating Scale consists of nine anchored rating scales paralleling the nine subscales of the SCL-90. The parallel nature of data collected from two perspectives is important for each.

Direct Observational Methods

Coding Verbal Behavior. A number of studies have focused on specific aspects of depressed verbal behavior as modification targets. Robinson and Lewinsohn (1973b) identified a slowed rate of speech as a depressive target behavior in a chronically depressed psychiatric patient. In therapy interviews, the number of words per 30-second interval was tabulated with a hand counter by an observer behind a one-way mirror. Rate of speech appeared to be a fairly stable response characteristic brought under reinforcement control. Ince (1972) used a verbal conditioning procedure to increase positive self-references over 17 therapy sessions; however, no reliability data is presented for the rating of positive self-statements. Aiken and Parker (1965) provided reinforcement contingencies for positive self-evaluation response choices to a written sentence completion task, but no reliability or validity data are presented.

Lewinsohn et al. (1968, 1970), Libet et al. (1973a,b), and Rosenberry, Weiss, and Lewinsohn (1968), have evolved a method of coding the verbal interaction behavior of individuals in group and home settings. Pursuing the general hypothesis that depression represents a deficit in social skills, these researchers have attempted to validate a series of objective measures of social skill in verbal interactions.

Rosenberry et al. (1968) selected 32 depressed and 55 nondepressed undergraduate subjects on the basis of MMPI criteria. Subjects were asked to listen to two tape recorded speakers and push a button whenever they wanted to be helpful to the speaker. Contrary to the hypothesis, no differences were found on the mean number of responses emitted by depressed and non-depressed subjects. Depressed subjects were found to respond in a less stable and predictable fashion than nondepressed subjects, although these effects reached significance for only one of the tapes.

Lewinsohn et al. (1970) selected depressed undergraduate subjects on the same MMPI criteria, along with a set derived from the Grinker Feelings and Concerns Check List factors. Five female and four male subjects were seen for 18 sessions of group therapy. Interaction data on four social skill variables were collected by two observers at each session. These variables were: (1) total amount of behavior emitted by and directed towards each individual; (2) use of positive and negative reactions by each individual; (3) interpersonal efficiency ratio, defined as the number of verbal behaviors directed toward an individual relative to the number of verbal behaviors the individual emits; and (4) range of interactions with others. Interrater reliabilities were deemed satisfactory, although figures are only given for the number of actions (r = .97) and reactions (r = .99) given by an individual. Group treatment in this study consisted of weekly feedback to subjects of their coded interpersonal data from the prior week. These data served as a basis for discussion, goal formulation, and change efforts on the part of each subject. As such, the meaning of changes on these variables is difficult to interpret, and only representative graphs of selected variables for individual subjects are presented. Pre- and post-therapy scores on the MMPI and Grinker factors suggest improvement of depression, although no statistical tests are presented.

Libet and Lewinsohn (1973) selected depressed, nondepressed "psychiatric," and normal control subjects on the basis of MMPI and Grinker interview criteria. Using a similar system, interpersonal verbal behavior was coded for two groups over a number of sessions. Interrater reliabilities ranged from .63 to .99. Depressed subjects were found to have total activity levels, although this effect was significant for only one group during its earlier sessions. Depressed subjects emitted fewer positive reactions to others, but did not differ on negative reactions. No differences were found for the interpersonal efficiency measure, and interpersonal range was found to be narrower only for depressed males. An additional measure, action latency, indicated that depressed subjects were significantly slower in responding to another's reaction.

In an elaborate and statistically sophisticated study of social skill variables in group and home observation settings, Libet et al., (1973) coded the interpersonal behavior of depressed, nondepressed "psychiatric," and normal control subjects in five self-study groups and 18 visited homes. Again, subjects were identified on the basis of MMPI and Grinker interview criteria, but included referrals and subjects solicited by newspaper ads for this study. Nineteen social skill and six criterion variables were defined in this study. Interrater reliabilities were generally good, although the authors noted that temporal stability was low for many of the variables. Situational differences between the two settings were also apparent. Depressed males in the groups were found to emit and initiate fewer questions (a functionally reinforcing event), were silent more often, and were slower in reaction response. They were also more affected by aversive reactions and elicited fewer positive reactions; results for females in the group were generally the same, but non-significant. Depressed males at home emitted fewer actions, but initiated *more*. This reversal was attributed to less participation in on-going conversations initiated by others. In addition, depressed males were more silent, slower to respond to reactions, and elicited a lower rate of positive reinforcement. Depressed females were less active, slower to respond to reactions, and elicited a lower rate of positive reinforcement. Interestingly, the authors concluded on the basis of other analysis that social skill does not seem to be evidenced by higher ratios of positive to negative reactions elicited. This ratio tended to remain constant regardless of the total number of elicited reactions. This finding may relate to the nature of the studied situations.

Lewinsohn and his colleagues have used their behavioral coding system as part of the assessment and evaluation in a series of clinical cases. As an assessment tool, the method has been used to identify problem areas which then become targets for behavioral intervention. Sample problem areas in the case studies include generally low activity level in the family (Lewinsohn et al., 1970), few initiations to the client (Lewinsohn & Atwood, 1969; Lewinsohn & Shaffer, 1971) low rates of mutual reinforcement (Lewinsohn & Shaw, 1969), and negative reactions from spouse (Lewinsohn & Shaffer, 1971). Lewinsohn and Shaffer (1971) point out that the use of home observations as a basis for assessment also provides advantages for subsequent therapy interventions by providing data that can be used as objective feedback to clients. Also, home observations focus attention on the interpersonal behavior of the client and his/her family. In two controlled studies, Johansson, Lewinsohn, and Flippo (1969) and Robinson and Lewinsohn (1973a), the content categories in Lewinsohn's coding system were used as target response classes in an interview setting. In applications of the Premack Principle, high frequency response classes were made contingent on the prior occurrence of a low frequency response class.

As described, these methods are somewhat cumbersome for most clinical uses, requiring multiple, well-trained observers in home or group settings. McLean, Ogston, and Grauer (1973) describe a simplified method based on Lewinsohn's coding system. Patient's were required to make one-half hour recordings of problem discussions with their spouses at home. These recordings were divided into 30-second intervals and coded for positive and negative initiations and reactions. Scores were calculated as proportions of interaction for both discussants. Interrater agreement ranged from 73 percent to 97 percent, with average agreement of 88 percent. Couples in the experimental group who received a behaviorally-oriented training procedure, decreased significantly in negative reactions and in negative actions and reactions on the posttest. A mixed control group did not change significantly on these measures.

Fuchs and Rehm (1977) videotaped 10-minute segments of therapist-absent interaction among groups of depressed subjects in a therapy study. The number of statements made in 10 minutes was counted as a simple assessment of verbal activity level. Interrater agreement ranged from 83 percent to 100 percent, with a mean of 87 percent. Experimental subjects increased in verbal activity level significantly more than placebo therapy controls from pre- to posttesting. Rehm, Fuchs, Roth, Kornblith, and Romano (1979) coded nine verbal and nonverbal behaviors from group therapy observations during first and last therapy sessions. Posttherapy scores, with pretherapy scores covaried, significantly differed between therapy conditions for negative self-references, negative references to others, and an overall depression rating. Rehm, Kornblith, O'Hara, Lamparski, Romano, and Volkin (in press) found therapy effects for two of eleven verbal and nonverbal behaviors coded from pre- and posttherapy interviews (expressivity and latency). Of these same measures, only loudness and latency differentiated between depressed and normal subjects (Lamparski, Rehm, O'Hara, Kornblith & Fitzgibbon, 1979).

Observations from structured interviews were also employed by Andreasen and Pfohl (1976), who found depression associated differences on dimensions of the use of power, overstatement, and achievement words. Hinchliffe, Lancashire, and Roberts (1970; 1971a, 1971b) found differences on personal references, negators, direct references, expressions of feeling, nonpersonal references, speech rate, eye contact, and gaze duration.

Coyne (1976) set up telephone interviews between depressed and nondepressed persons. He found differences in behavior codes (such as time spent talking about self versus others) and also elicited social-interpersonal evaluations of each subject from the interview partner.

Jacobson (1981) described a coding scheme used in assessing small groups. He found that certain codes discriminate better between depressed and nondepressed subjects when they are viewed in terms of conditional probabilities, rather than absolute frequencies (i.e., probability of a self-disclosure following a self-disclosure of another, rather than frequency of self-disclosure per se).

In summary, a number of different verbal behaviors have been coded in a variety of experimental conditions. Some codes appear to differentiate depressed subjects with some reliability, but failure to replicate differences in coding procedures and situation differences leaves many questions concerning the utility of coding verbal behavior as an assessment procedure. More systematic work and a standard set of codes will be required before such procedures can be adopted on a regular basis in research or clinical practice.

Coding Overt Motor Behavior. Several of the verbal behavior studies reviewed above included nonverbal codes as well (e.g., eye contact and smiling). Using an interview observation similar to the procedures carried out in the previous review, Ranelli (1978) found differences between depressed and nondepressed subjects on head nods (fewer by depressed) and head aversions (more by depressed). Waxer (1974, 1976) found posture differences, and Ekman and Friesen (1974) found differences in gestures.

Assertion skill behaviors, some of them verbal, have been assessed in two therapy studies. Rehm et al. (1979) used an audiotaped situation test and found that assertion training with depressed subjects produced greater changes in speech duration, requests for new behavior, statements of opinion, loudness, fluency, and overall assertion, in comparison with a self-control therapy. The self-control condition, however, improved on depression measures. Wells, Hersen, Bellack, and Himmelhoch (1977) found changes in a behavioral assertion test that corresponded with depression improvement in four single subject cases.

Observations of inpatients have employed direct observation measures of depressive behavior. Reisinger (1972), in a single subject reversal design study, described the use of token reinforcement and response cost to increase smiling and decrease crying behavior respectively. Careful behavioral definitions of the responses led to interrater reliabilities above 90 percent for observation periods of up to 2 hours. Token control was demonstrated and later faded.

There have been two attempts to develop scales with inpatients. Bunney and Hamburg (1963) developed a rating scale for use by nurses and psychiatrists in assessing ward behavior. Twenty-four dimensions are rated on 15-point scales with an 8-hour time frame. Subscales for depression, anger, anxiety, psychotic behaviors, somatic complaints, and physical activity can be derived. Unfortunately, reliabilities are relatively low, with intraclass rs ranging from .11 to .83 with a median of .36.

Williams, Barlow, and Agras (1972) describe the use of behavioral assessment procedures for ten depressed psychiatric inpatients. At randomly determined points during each half hour from 8 a.m. to 4 p.m., a trained observer noted the presence or absence of each of the following response classes: (1) talking, (2) smiling, (3) motor activity, (ten subclasses further define this behavior), and (4) time out of room. Interrater reliability of 96 percent was reported. An analysis of the correlations among the four behavioral measures yielded a Kendall's coefficient of concordance of .70 (P<.01). On this basis, scores were summed and treated as a single index of depression severity. Comparisons were made between the behavioral index, Beck DI, and Hamilton Rating Scale at three-day intervals during the course of the patients' hospitalizations. Mean correlations (calculated with appropriate Fisher's z-transformations) between the measures were as follows: Beck and Hamilton r = .82, Hamilton and behavioral index r = .71, Beck and behavioral index r = .67. On the basis of follow-up information for five patients, the authors suggest that the course of overt-behavioral improvement during hospitalization is more predictive of post-hospitalization improvement than either of the other instruments. Hersen, Eisler, Alford, and Agras (1973) used this behavior rating scale to assess improvement of three patients on a token economy ward. In three single-subject reversal designs, improvement on the behavior rating scale was shown to occur when patients were under token reinforcement conditions. No self-report measures were taken.

A technically sophisticated method of assessing overt-motor activity level has been employed by a group of psychiatric researchers. Kupfer, Detre, Foster, Tucker, and Delgado (1972) described an apparatus which permits 24-hour telemetric recording of activity in an inpatient setting. A miniature transmitter containing a feromagnetic ball in an inductance coil is encased in a cylinder 2.2 cm in diameter and 6.7 cm long. The transmitter is worn on a leather wrist band and has a range of 100 feet. Receivers transform the data into pulses, which are read out digitally as number of counts per minute. A reliability of 91.7 percent agreement is reported for five subjects wearing transmitters on each wrist for one hour. Kupfer, Weiss, Foster, Detre, Delgado, and McPartland (1974) reported a .73 reliability for wrist and ankle transmitters. This research has shown correlations between activity level and various sleep parameters, such as EEG movement, minutes awake, time asleep, REM time, and REM activity (Kupfer et al., 1972, 1973; Weiss, Kupfer, Foster, & Delgado, 1974). Kupfer et al. (1974) found differences between unipolar and bipolar depressives prior to drug treatment: unipolars had much higher levels of activity. No drug effects were found, but clinically improved unipolars (N = 4) decreased in activity level. This is the only study reporting relationships between the telemetered activity level and any conventional depression measure. No significant correlations were obtained with self-rating depression items on the KDS-1 (Kupfer & Detre, 1971), a general psychiatric self-report form. A correlation of .85 was found, however, with self-rated anxiety on the KDS-1 during drug treatment. This correlation is not surprising in light of the fact that a number of patients showed increased "agitation" during drug treatment. This was reflected by the anxiety rating. O'Hara and Rehm (1978) found no correlation with either anxiety or depression using simple pedometers. Further validational evidence will be needed in order to clarify relationships between retarded and agitated psychomotor activity and depression versus anxiety. Correlations between telemetered psychomotor activity and other well-validated measures of depression would be helpful. If they are to be used as standard instruments, further work is needed on any of these methods for assessing overt-motor behavior.

Activity Schedules. The use of activity schedules in depression research deserves comment, although it might be questioned whether these devices can be properly called depression assessment instruments. In general, they involve a self-recording of overt events or activities; since depression involves decreased activity, these techniques do assess it. However, since there is usually an additional assumption that some specific activities or events are particularly important as determinants of depression, occasionally the putative cause is assessed rather than depression *per se*.

The best developed instrument of this type is the MacPhillamy and Lewinsohn (1971; 1972a; 1972b; 1976) Pleasant Events Schedule (PES). The PES is based on Lewinsohn's theoretical model of depression, which accounts for depression as a lack or loss of response-contingent positive reinforcement. As such, the PES is intended to assess the amount of external positive reinforcement the individual receives. The PES consists of 320 events generated from lists of positive events elicited from 66 subjects (MacPhillamy & Lewinsohn, 1972a). A revised Form III used another 70 subjects (Lewinsohn & Graf, 1973). The instrument is used in two ways: as a retrospective report of the events of the last 30 days and as the basis for daily logs of ongoing behavior. As a retrospective instrument, subjects are first asked to indicate how frequently each item occurred within the last 30 days on a 3-point scale: 0—not happened; 1—a few (1–6 times); and 2—often (7 or more times). Subjects then go through the list a second time indicating how pleasant and enjoyable each event was or potentially would be, again using a 3-point scale: 0—not pleasant; 1—somewhat pleasant; and 2—very pleasant. Three scores are derived from these ratings: Activity Level, defined as the sum of the frequency ratings; Reinforcement Potential, defined as the sum of the pleasantness ratings; and Obtained Reinforcement, defined as the sum of the frequency and pleasantness ratings for each item. Test-retest reliabilities for 37 subjects over a 4 to 8 week span were .85, .66, and .72 for the three respective scores (MacPhillamy & Lewinsohn, 1972a, 1972b). Alpha coefficients of internal consistency were .96, .98, and .97 for the same scores. Norms for male and female college students are given by MacPhillamy et al. (1972b; 1976).

Evidence for the validity of the instrument was also presented by MacPhillamy and Lewinsohn (1974; 1976), who found that all three scores statistically differentiated between depressed individuals and both psychiatric and normal controls, defined by MMPI and Feelings and Concerns Check List factor ratings.

The entire PES has also been used by Lewinsohn and his co-workers to generate shorter lists specific to individuals. Lewinsohn and Libet (1972) and Lewinsohn and Graf (1973) selected the 160 most pleasant items for individual subjects and had them use these lists as daily activity checks for 30 days. Significant intra-individual correlations were found between number of pleasant events and mood as measured by the DACL. In the Lewinsohn et al. (1973) study, depressed subjects were found to engage in fewer pleasant events.

The use of individualized PES's in therapy has been described by Lewinsohn (1976). Schedules of 160 items derived as above were kept for 30 days by ten depressed patients. The ten items most highly correlated with mood were then selected as targets for behavior change efforts and reinforced with minutes of psychotherapy time. Target activities increased significantly more than did a set of control activities.

Ad hoc activity schedules or logs have been reported in case studies by Lewinsohn and Atwood (1969) and Rush, Khatami, and Beck (1975). The latter report employed activity schedules as a part of the therapy program. Patients' daily logs served as a basis for correcting cognitive distortions of their own behavior. In a controlled psychotherapy outcome study, Fuchs and Rehm (1978) employed an activity schedule procedure in a self-control therapy program. Using the PES as an item pool, a shortened list containing 20 classes of reinforcing behavior was constructed. Items on this list, termed the Positive Activities Schedule, were designed to emphasize the active role of the subject in producing potential reinforcement. Experimental subjects kept daily activity logs using the Positive Activities Schedule as a guide. These logs served as a basis for: (1) attempts to modify distortions of self-observation; (2) selection of target behaviors to be increased; and (3) selection of behaviors to be used as contingent self-reinforcement. In addition, this study used the PES as a pre- and posttherapy outcome measure in comparisons among the experimental group, placebo therapy, and waiting-list controls. Increases in self-reported pleasant events over the last 30 days tended to be greater for the experimental group. This effect was replicated in Rehm et al. (1979) and Rehm, Kornblith, O'Hara, Lamparski, Romano, and Volkin (in press).

278   Behavioral Assessment

More recently, an Unpleasant Events Schedule has been developed (Grosscup & Lewinsohn, 1980) that also correlates with daily mood. This finding was replicated by Rehm (1978) with a less sophisticated daily log procedure, and again by O'Hara and Rehm (1979) using similar lists.

In sum, event schedules are good examples of behavioral measures that have been subjected to careful psychometric development and analysis. The Pleasant Events Schedule has considerable promise as an instrument for use in treatment planning. Questions regarding reactivity of self-monitoring and possible depressive distortion in recall of events place a limit on these schedules as veridical measures of activity rate in depression.

Comments on Overt Behavior Assessment

Much still needs to be done before overt behavioral assessment methods can be added to a depression assessment battery on a regular basis. Generally, coding systems and other methods need further replication, pyschometric refinement, and standardization. Before these methods can be considered behavioral measures of actual depression, much more attention to breadth of content coverage will be necessary. The methods reviewed touch on most of the content areas; negative self-references, for example, are verbal-cognitive behavior; smiling or weeping is an affective behavior; activity level is an overt-motor manifestation; and Coyne's (1976) ratings by conversational partner focuses on social-interpersonal aspects of depression. No reviewed method, however, covers more than two, or perhaps three, such areas. Many areas important in depression have not been considered at all. Examples are somatic complaints or behavior associated with major depressive signs such as sleep, eating, and sexual behavior. It would be quite possible for important scales to include sleep and eating behavior. Self-recording logs could be used with outpatients. Little of the methodological advances from other areas of behavioral assessment research (e.g., obesity research measures of eating behavior) are seen in the assessment of overt behavior. Much further research is needed here.

Informant Measures

This category of instrument is included because of its potential special importance in depression assessment. Since depressed persons can be expected to distort their experience, the veridicality of certain interview aspects is in doubt. A relative or other significant informant can provide reliability checks on self-report. Such a person is likely to have a much larger sample of observation than that tapped by most of the overt-behavior assessment samples. Significant others in the depressed person's life represent a direct source of evaluation of social interpersonal problems associated with depression.

Despite the need, very little work has been done in this area. McLean, Ogston, and Grauer (1973) used an audio-taped direct sample of an interaction with spouses, but did not collect spouse evaluations. Coyne (1976) collected some ratings from strangers in his· phone call procedure. Rush, Khatami, and Beck (1975) reported having a spouse monitor specific behaviors on the part of a patient as counterevidence to distorted self-report, but this was an individually tailored procedure. No fully developed scale has appeared for significant other reports; however, one other general scale includes considerable representation of depressive content.

Katz Adjustment Scales. The Katz Adjustment Scales (Katz & Lylerly, 1963) consist of two sets of scales. Five scales are to be filled out by the subject or patient, and an additional five by a relative as an outside informant. Most work on the scales has focused on the relative or R Scales. The purpose of the Scales is to measure both psychiatric symptoms and other indices of social behavior which may be relevant to social adjustment. The Scales were developed with the intent of assessing adjustment pre- and posthospitalization. The rationale for two sets of scales is that social behavior involves both subject and social environment perceptions. The Relative Scales attempt to minimize the effects of various kinds of biasing by constructing items descriptive of behavior, rather than asking for attitudes or evaluations. The first of the Relative Scales, Form R1, consists of 127 items intended to cover symptomatology relevant to depression, anxiety, suspiciousness, belligerence and withdrawal. Each item is rated on a 4-point frequency scale from "almost never" to "almost always." In the original Katz and Lylerly article, a "several week" and a "two week" time frame were used. Hogarty (1975) reported that more recently a "three week" time frame has been employed. Form R2 is labeled "Level of Performance of Socially Expected Activities." It consists of 16 items describing typical social behaviors which are rated on a 3-point scale from "not doing" to "doing regularly." Form R3, labeled the "Level of Expectations for Performance of Social Activities," consists of the same 16 items rated on a different 3-point scale, ranging from "did not expect him to be doing" to "expected him to be doing regularly." The intention is to obtain a discrepancy reflective of the participant's degree of satisfaction or dissatisfaction with the subject's level of activity.

Form RS4, "Level of Free Time Activities," consists of 23 items covering hobbies, social and community activities, and self-improvement activities. These items are rated on a 3-point scale consisting of: (1) frequently, (2) sometimes, (3) practically never. Form R5, "Level of Satisfaction with Free Time Activities," consists of the same 23 items rated as to degree of satisfaction on a 3-point scale consisting of: (1) "satisfied with what he does here," (2) "would like to see him do more of this," and (3) "would like to see him do less."

The subject scales begin with form S1, "Symptom Discomfort," which consists of 55 items describing somatic, mood, and psychoneurotic symptoms. Responses are made on a 4-point frequency scale. Forms S2, "Level of Performance of Socially Expected Activities;" Form S9, "Level of Expectations;" Form RS4 "Level of Free Time Activities;" and Form S5, "Level of Satisfaction with Free Time Activities" are self-rating formats which are otherwise identical to the Relative forms. All items are constructed with a fairly simple vocabulary level and fairly straightforward instructions (Katz & Lyerly, 1963; Michaux, Katz, Kurland, & Gansereit, 1969). In terms of the standard content areas, roughly 29 of the 127 items of the R1 scale are descriptive of typical depressive symptomatology. Of these, the heaviest weight is on behavioral (approximately 13 items) and cognitive (approximately ten items) symptomatology. Approximately four items refer to affective symptoms and one each to somatic and interpersonal symptoms of depression. These estimates are only approximate because many additional items could be peripherally related to depression. It is interesting to note the predominance of behavioral symptoms; they have much less weight in most other scales. It is surprising that interpersonal content is not tapped more heavily, though the other subscales do so. In terms of the standard depressive signs, one item refers to sleep problems and two to suicide. There are no items for eating or sex-related problems, but scale RS4 covers certain work-related performance problems.

Normative data on a variety of psychiatric populations are available on the Katz Adjustment Scale but not always from easily obtained publications (see Hogarty, 1975). No specific cut-off scores have been established, although profiles are available for different populations.

Hogarty (1975) reported some unpublished data by Crook and Hogarty on interrater reliability for the measures. The median correlation between parents of 15 schizophrenics on the R1 symptom clusters was .71, with coefficients ranging from .33 on "nervousness" to .84 on "helplessness." Correlations on Forms R2, R4, and R5 were .85, .47, and .74 respectively. Form R3, "parental expectations," showed low correlations, although this might be expected. Katz and Lylerly (1963) present Kuder-Richardson reliabilities for two samples of schizophrenic patients. Reliabilities for 12 subscales of Form R1 for the first sample (N = 73) ranged from .61 to .87; in the second sample (N = 242) reliabilities ranged from .41 to .81.

Katz and Lylerly (1963) presented data for 15 well-adjusted and 15 poorly-adjusted ex-psychiatric patients identified by a research program involving follow-up of exhospitalized patients. All correlations were significant except for those in form S5, indicating that the self-ratings discriminate less well than the relative ratings between well- and poorly-adjusted patients. Hogarty (1975) reported on unpublished data by Katz and Lowery in which independent global rating of adjustment produced multiple rs of .70 (with R forms) to .83 (with R and S forms) in a series of multiple regression analyses.

Marsella, Sanborn, Kameoka, Shizuru, and Brennan (1975) reported correlations between a subset of depression-related items from the Katz Adjustment Scale's pool and several standard depression scales. Correlations with the MAACL ranged from .48 to .72, with the MMPI-D from .46 to .70, and with the Zung from .32 to .73. This set of items, however, is not a standard scale, but suggests that there is some covariance with depression represented within the KAS.

Hogarty, Goldberg, and Schooler (1974) found significant effects on a number of KAS variables in a study comparing drug and sociotherapy in aftercare with schizophrenic patients.

In summary, the Katz Adjustment Scales have yet to be thoroughly developed psychometrically. Most work has been done with the relative forms, particulary in terms of behavioral symptoms. There appears to be no other scale specifically designed for use by relatives or other informants that is relevant both to depressive symptomatology and social adjustment, or has any better psychometric background.

The Assessment of Core Deficits of Depression

One of the major developments in recent depression assessment research has been the construction of instruments to assess the core deficit of depression as hypothesized by new behavioral models of the disorder. MacPhillamy and Lewinsohn's (1976) Pleasant Events Schedule has already been described. Lewinsohn et al. (1976) have suggested cut-off scores for choosing between activity increase and desensitization treatment modules. Recently, an Unpleasant Events Schedule (Grosscup & Lewinsohn, 1980), an Interpersonal Events Schedule, and a Cognitive Events Schedule (cited in Zeiss, Lewinsohn, & Munoz, 1979) have been described in an attempt to provide measures specific to other therapy modules. In other programs which have hypothesized that social skills are the core deficit in depression, assessment instruments have been adopted from that research area. For example, Rehm et al. (1979) used the Wolpe-Lazarus Assertiveness Inventory (Wolpe & Lazarus, 1967) and a taped situation test, and Wells, Hersen, Bellack, and Himmelhoch (1977) used the Wolpe-Lazarus and a behavioral role-play test.

Several measures of cognitive distortion have been presented which attempt to assess deficits hypothesized by Beck (1972, 1976) as the core of the depression. Weissman (1978) developed a Dysfunctional Attitudes Scale that asks subjects how much they agree with depressive attitude statements. Hammen and Krantz (1976) developed an instrument that asks subjects to indicate which alternative reaction would be typical of them in a variety of situations. Depression and distortion of response can be scored separately.

Several methods of assessing Seligman's helplessness construct have been developed. Layden (1976) described an Attributional Scale Questionnaire that differentiates between high and low self-esteem college students. Seligman, Abramson, Semmel, and Von Baeyer (1979) have described an Attribution Styles Questionnaire that demonstrated predicted differences between depressed and nondepressed groups. A child's version of this scale, the KASTAN (Kaslow & Tanenbaum, 1978), also is available.

My colleagues and I (Fuchs & Rehm, 1977; Rehm et al., 1979; Rehm, Kornblith, O'Hara, Lamparski, Romano, & Volkin, in press) have used a Self-Control Questionnaire in conjunction with a therapy program for depression. Questionnaire scores improve with treatment. A similar instrument has been developed by Rosenbaum (1978).

Generally, these instruments are new and should be assumed experimental at this point. Much more standardization and validation data will be necessary before they are fully usable in clinical situations.

CASE DESCRIPTION

Some of the issues involved in depression assessment can be illustrated by a case example. The following case is drawn from a current research project involving a self-control behavior therapy program for depression (Rehm, 1977; in press). The program is carried out in a structured group format in which self-control deficits associated with depression are targeted over the course of ten weekly 1½-hour sessions. A more detailed description of this program can be found in Rehm (in press). Subjects for the study are recruited from the community by announcements in the news media asking for female volunteers who feel depression is a serious problem. Volunteers who are not currently in treatment are screened on BDI (≥ 20) and MMPI-D (≥ 70) criteria. Then they are given a modified SADS interview so that the resulting population can be described as manifesting a nonpsychotic, non-bipolar Major Affective Disorder. Exclusion criteria for other psychological disorders are employed.

The sample case, Ms. O. F., is a 33-year-old single woman who works as a librarian. She described episodes of depression dating back to age 22, but complained of more frequent and longer episodes in the last three years since breaking up with a boyfriend. Ms. O. F. maintains a cordial but distant relationship with both family members and work associates but has little social life. Social withdrawal was a primary complaint. She had previously sought help at a Community Mental Health Center and had consulted a psychiatrist on one occasion. He had prescribed an anti-anxiety agent which Ms. O. F. still had and took about once a week.

The SADS interview indicated complaints of initial and middle-of-the night insomnia, fatigability, anhedonia, self-criticism, concentration problems and suicidal thoughts. Pessimism, brooding, feelings of inadequacy, irritability, dependence on others, and somatic complaints were also indicated. Pretest data are shown in Table 8.1. All four of the severity scales (BDI and MMPI-D self-report scales and Hamilton and Raskin clinician ratings) are in the moderate depression range. The Self-Control Questionnaire score is about two-thirds of a standard deviation below the mean for volunteers entering the depression therapy program, indicating a low endorsement of positive self-control principles. The Pleasant Event Schedule scores indicate a very low frequency of engagement in pleasant activities, although an adequate ability to experience pleasure. This pattern fits the Lewinsohn et al. (1976) criteria for recommending a program to increase pleasant activities, a major component of the self-control therapy program.

During the course of the program, participants are told to record daily their positive activities and indicate an average mood rating for each

Table 8.1. Pre- and Posttest scores for Sample Case

Scale	Pretest	Posttest
Beck Depression Inventory	23	5
MMPI-D (T score)	96	63
Hamilton Rating Scale	21	7
Raskin Three Area Scale	9	4
Self-Control Questionnaire	4.24	5.58
Pleasant Events Schedule		
Frequency	.45	1.27
Enjoyability	1.45	1.84
F X E	1.35	2.47

Table 8.2. Sample Case Activity, Mood and Depression Measures During Therapy Program

Week	Mean Daily Activities	Mean Daily Mood	Weekly BDI-SF
1	—	—	15
2	7.9	5.6	7
3	14.4	7.4	5
4	14.2	7.8	5
5	13.9	6.4	4
6	16.0	7.1	3
7	(session missed)		
8	14.3	8.4	2
9	13.9	8.0	2
10	15.2	8.5	1

day. Such monitoring is aided by a list of positive activities categories, used as a checklist to prompt items included in the daily log. Mood is rated on a simple 11-point scale from 0 (worst mood ever) to 10 (best mood ever). In addition, subjects filled out a short-form version of the Beck Depression Inventory at the beginning of each therapy session. Average number of daily positive activities, average mood rating, and weekly Beck short-form scores are shown in Table 8.2 for the course of the therapy program.

The first three weeks of the program stressed self-monitoring of positive activities, including attention to positive activities as they occur and the awareness of a relationship between number of activities and mood. To illustrate this latter issue, participants construct simple graphs of their weekly data. These data in the sample case are shown for the first three weeks in figure 8.1.

As can be seen, a correlation is evident between mood and activity in the first three weeks; an improvement on all weekly measures is evident after the first week. This is the point at which this general rationale of modifying mood by increasing positive activities has been presented, and one week's graph of the activity and mood data has been constructed by the participants.

Scheduling activities, setting behavioral goals, and breaking goals into specific subgoal activities occur during the next three sessions. An aim is to modify self-evaluation behavior by teaching participants to set realistic self-evaluative standards and to make accurate attributions of responsibility for events. Ms. O. F. set goals of increasing outdoor physical activity and asserting herself more with colleagues at work (e.g., initiating conversations and insisting on her rights regarding work breaks). During this time period Ms. O. F. evidenced improvement.

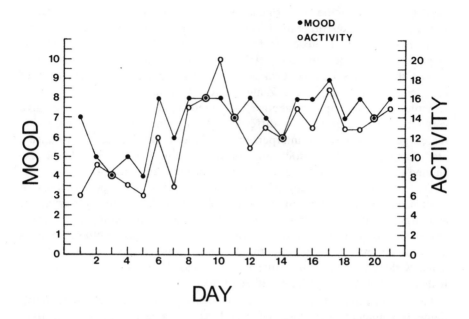

Fig. 8.1. Daily number of events and mood ratings for first three weeks of the therapy program for the sample case.

Weeks seven and eight involved teaching participants to use self-reinforcement to contingently reward their subgoal activities. Weeks nine and ten involved review and continuation of the program as a whole.

Posttest data demonstrate that positive self-control attitude on the Self-Control Questionnaire improved by more than a standard deviation. Pleasant Event Schedule scores all improved, most notably in the frequency score. Associated with these targeted changes is a general improvement on all four depression measures: All of these measures were in the normal range at posttest.

Since the therapy program in the described case is a complex package involving many procedures, it is not possible to isolate effects very specifically. (The case does illustrate the use of measures of targeted behavior along with measures of depression as a syndrome.) Changes in the targeted areas are a necessary validation of the therapy procedures.

FUTURE CONSIDERATIONS

From the perspective of behavioral measurement for clinical and research purposes, there are many problems with instruments presently available. Despite the heterogeneity of the phenomena of depression, virtually all the instruments reviewed produce a single severity score. None has developed subscales for specific sets of symptoms or subtype diagnoses. Subscales for the SADS are one development in this direction. Other scales can be broken into subscales based on the logic of their construction (e.g., the Zung Scale). Coverage of content is quite variable. When compared against one another, the reviewed scales give very different weightings to different sets of symptoms. The depression scales generally neglect interpersonal symptoms and in some instances, omit fairly basic diagnostic signs of depression. Content should be examined carefully in selecting instruments for different purposes.

The variation in content coverage also occurs across perspectives of evaluation. It is difficult to compare self-, clinician, direct observation, and significant other reports when content as well as method varies. There are some instances of parallel forms across perspective, such as the SCL-90 and its clinician-parallel rating forms, the Social Adjustment Scale with self-report and clinican forms, and the Katz Adjustment Scale with self-report and significant other forms.

Format differences also create problems in comparing instruments. Some instruments offer statements and require a response, such as true-false or degree of agreement; others ask whether a symptom is present or absent or how frequently it occurs. Time frames vary from specific periods ("this last week"), to more general designations ("recently"), to other variations ("today," or "during the present episode"). These time frames may make a considerable difference in the response and the resulting severity index of the disorder.

Given the present status of development, instrument choice should be made with an eye to specific purpose. For the clinician, differential diagnosis is aided only partially by the available instruments. Severity can be well assessed against a variety of normative populations, but most instruments do not discriminate adequately between depression and other disorders.

The greater specificity of DSM-III diagnoses, together with the use of instruments such as the SADS, offer some decision rules for more reliable categorization. Little predictive validity has been established with the usual instruments. Evaluations of specific behaviors or constructs with the new instruments that attempt to measure depression core constructs may hold more promise for prediction of response to specific treatments. Instruments chosen for the evaluation of outcome should be considered in terms of content and perspective. Content should be surveyed to assure that syndromal depression is evaluated in a program focusing on specific targets. Perspectives should be surveyed in the context of the therapy situation (i.e., has change occurred from the perspective of the clinician therapist, the patient, and the patient's significant others?).

For the researcher, population definition and description are especially important in depression, since the disorder is heterogeneous and researchers may sample very differently. Populations should be defined by using instruments from more than one perspective. To assure comparability of disorder severity with other studies in a standardized fashion, subjects should meet criteria on at least one self-report and one clinician scale. The Beck Depression Inventory, MMPI-D, and Zung Self-Rating Scale are the most popular self-report instruments for this purpose. The SADS is probably the best clinician instrument for research definition of a population. The Hamilton and Raskin scales are also popularly used for defining severity from the clinician's perspective.

Assessment for the purposes of differential treatment is an area much in need of attention by researchers. There is a need to look more generally at prediction in behavior therapy research, even in a post hoc manner. Outcome evaluation for research purposes presently necessitates a broad battery of assessment techniques to assess syndromal depression across content and perspective. Attention should be given to possible treatment by content or perspective interactions.

Future research will undoubtedly fill some of the voids in the depression assessment. We are beginning to see new instruments assessing core constructs of depression which may provide treatment selection and prediction of response. A new assessment perspective may become more feasible as physiological procedures are developed. Promising research in at least two areas may soon produce useful methods: Schwartz, Fair, Salt, Mandel, and Klerman (1976) have demonstrated EMG differences in facial muscle patterns associated with both state and trait depression; Kupfer and Foster (1972) have demonstrated that EEG measurement of REM latency differs between depressives and normals and varies with clinical status. Most interestingly, Kupfer's research suggests that drug treatment response may be predicted from EEG response well before any clinical change is seen (Kupfer, Foster, Reich, Thompson, & Weiss, 1976).

What this area ultimately needs is a systematic battery covering important subsets of symptoms in parallel fashion across perspectives. Such a battery, in conjunction with instruments assessing core constructs, could provide the necessary comparability across many dimensions for clinical and research purposes.

SUMMARY

A number of problems can be identified relating to assessment of depression from a behavioral perspective. Depression is a heterogeneous construct assessed as a syndrome including many specific behaviors. A list of categories of depressive symptoms has been suggested for the purposes of the review. These include verbal-cognitive, overt-motor, somatic, and interpersonal symptoms. Assessment instruments have been reviewed according to the perspectives of self-report, clinician rating, direct observation, and significant others. Instruments purporting to assess core deficits in depression were also reviewed briefly. Examples of the use of different assessment strategies in clinical studies were presented. Some of the deficiencies in existing instruments were pointed out and recommendations for the future were offered.

REFERENCES

Aiken, E. G., & Parker, W. H. Conditioning and generalization of positive self-evaluation in a partially structured diagnostic interview. *Psychological Reports*, 1965, *17*, 459–464.

Aitken, R. C. B. Measures of feeling using analogue scales. *Proceedings of the Royal Society of Medicine*, 1969, *62*, 989–993.

American Psychiatric Association. *DSM-II: Diagnostic and statistical manual of mental disorders*. Washington, D.C., 1968.

Andreasen, N.J.C., & Pfohl, B. Linguistic analysis of speech in affective disorders. *Archives of General Psychiatry*, 1976, *33*, 1361–1367.

Bech, P., Gram, L. F., Dein, E., Jacobsen, O., Vitger, J., & Bolwig, T. G. Quantitative rating of depressive states. *Acta Psychiatrica Scandinavica*, 1975, *51*, 161–170.

Beck, A. T. *Depression: Causes and treatment*. Philadelphia: University of Pennsylvania Press, 1972.

Beck, A. T., & Beamesderfer, A. Assessment of depression: The depression inventory. In P. Pichot (Ed.), *Psychological measurements in psychopharmacology. Modern problems in pharmacopsychiatry*. Vol. 7. Paris: Karger, Basel, 1974.

Beck, A. T., & Beck, R. W. Screening depressed patients in family practice: A rapid technique. *Postgraduate Medicine*, 1972, *52*, 81–85.

Beck, A. T., Ward, C. H., Mendelsohn, M., Mock, J., & Erbaugh, J. An inventory for measuring depression. *Archives of General Psychiatry*, 1961, *4*, 561–571.

Blumberry, W., Oliver, J. M., & McClure, J. N. Validation of the Beck Depression Inventory in a university population using psychiatric estimate as the criterion. *Journal of Consulting and Clinical Psychology*, 1978, *46*, 150–155.

Blumenthal, M., & Dielman, T. Depressive symptomatology and role function in a general population. *Archives of General Psychiatry*, 1975, *32*, 985–991.

Brown, G., Bhrolchain, M., & Harris, T. Social class and psychiatric disturbance among women in an urban population. *Sociology*, 1975, *9*, 225–254.

Bunney, W. E., & Hamburg, D. A. Methods for reliable longitudinal observation of behavior. *Archives of General Psychiatry*, 1963, *9*, 280–291.

Burrows, G. D., Foenander, G., Davies, B., & Scoggins, B. A. Rating scales as predictors of response to tricyclic antidepressants. *Australian and New Zealand Journal of Psychiatry*, 1976, *10*, 53–56.

Caple, M. A., & Blechman, E. A. *Problem solving and self-approval training with a depressed single mother: Case study*. Paper presented at the meeting of the Association for Advancement of Behavior Therapy, New York, December 4, 1976.

Carroll, B. J., Fielding, J. M., & Blashki, T. G. Depression rating scales: A critical review. *Archives of General Psychiatry*, 1973, *28*, 361–366.

Comrey, A. L. A factor analysis of items on the MMPI depression scale. *Educational and Psychological Measurement*, 1957, *17*, 578–585.

Costello, C. G., & Comrey, A. L. Scales for measuring depression and anxiety. *Journal of Psychology*, 1967, *66*, 303–313.

Coyne, J. C. Depression and the response of others. *Journal of Abnormal Psychology*, 1976, *85*, 186–193.

Craig, T. J., & VanNatta, P. A. Presence and persistence of depressive symptoms in patient and community populations. *American Journal of Psychiatry*, 1976, *133*, 1426–1429. (a)

Craig, T. J., & VanNatta, P. A. Recognition of depressed affect in hospitalized psychiatric patients. *Diseases of the Nervous System*, 1976, *37*, 561–566. (b)

Dahlstrom, W. G., & Welsh, G. S. *An MMPI handbook: A guide to use in clinical practice and research*. Minneapolis: University of Minnesota Press, 1960.

Davies, B., Burrows, G., & Poynton, C. A comparative study of four depression rating scales. *Australian and New Zealand Journal of Psychiatry*, 1975, *9*, 21–24.

Derogatis, L. R. *SCL-90 Administration, scoring and procedures manual—I*. Johns Hopkins University, 1977.

Ekman, P. & Friesen, W. V. Non-verbal behavior in psychopathology. In R. J. Friedman & M. M. Katz (Eds.), *The Psychology of depression: Contemporary theory and research*. New York: Winston-Wiley, 1974.

Ellis, A. *Reason and emotion in psychotherapy*. New York: Stuart, 1962.

Endicott, J., & Spitzer, R. L. A diagnostic interview: The Schedule for Affective Disorders and Schizophrenia. *Archives of General Psychiatry*, 1978, *35*, 837–844.

Endicott, N. A., & Jortner, S. Objective measures of depression. *Archives of General Psychiatry*, 1966, *15*, 249–255.

Feighner, J. P., Robins, E., Guze, S., Woodruff, R. A., Winokur, G., & Munoz, R. Diagnostic criteria for use in psychiatric research. *Archives of General Psychiatry*, 1972, *26*, 57–63.

Ferster, C. B. A functional analysis of depression. *American Psychologist*, 1973, *28*, 857–870.

Fuchs, C. Z., & Rehm, L. P. A self-control behavior therapy program for depression. *Journal of Consulting and Clinical Psychology*, 1977, *45*, 206–215.

Green, B. L., Gleser, G. C., Stone, W. N., & Seifert, R. F. Relationships among diverse measures of psychotherapy outcome. *Journal of Consulting and Clinical Psychology*, 1975, *43*, 689–699.

Grinker, R. R., Miller, J., Sabshin, M., Nunn, J., & Nunally, J. D. *The phenomena of depression*. New York: Harper, 1961.

Grosscup, S. J., & Lewinsohn, P. M. Unpleasant and pleasant events and mood. *Journal of Clinical Psychology*, 1980, *36*, 252–259.

Hamilton, M. A rating scale for depression. *Journal of Neurology, Neurosurgery and Psychiatry*, 1960, *23*, 56–61.

Hamilton, M. Development of a rating scale for primary depressive illness. *British Journal of School and Clinical Psychology*, 1967, *6*, 278–296.

Hammen, C. L., & Krantz, S. Effect of success and failure on depressive cognitions. *Journal of Abnormal Psychology*, 1976, *85*, 577–586.

Harris, R. E., & Lingoes, J. C. *Subscales for the MMPI: An aid to profile file interpretation*. Unpublished manuscript, The Langley Porter Neuropsychiatric Institute, 1955.

Harrow, M., Colbert, J., Detre, T., & Bakeman, R. Symptomatology and subjective experiences in current depressive states. *Archives of General Psychiatry*, 1966, *14*, 203–212.

Hathaway, S. R., & McKinley, J. C. A multiphasic personality schedule (Minnesota): III. The measurement of symptomatic depression. *Journal of Psychology*, 1942, *14*, 73–84.

Hathaway, S. R., & McKinley, J. C. *MMPI manual* (Rev. ed., 1951.) New York: The Psychological Corporation, 1951.

Hersen, M., Eisler, R. M., Alford, G. S., & Agras, W. S. Effects of token economy on neurotic depression: An experimental analysis. *Behavior Therapy*, 1973, *4*, 392–397.

Hinchcliffe, M., Lancashire, M., & Roberts, F. J. Eye contact and depression: A preliminary report. *British Journal of Psychiatry*, 1970, *117*, 571–572.

Hinchliffe, M., Lancashire, M., & Roberts, F. J. Depression: Defense mechanisms in speech. *British Journal of Psychiatry*, 1971, *118*, 471–472. (a)

Hinchliffe, M., Lancashire, M., & Roberts, F. J. A study of eye-contact changes in depressed and recovered psychiatric patients. *British Journal of Psychiatry*, 1971, *119*, 213–215. (b)

Hogarty, G. E. Informant ratings of community adjustment. In I. E. Waskow & M. B. Parloff (Eds.), *Psychotherapy change measures*. Washington, D. C.: NIMH, 1975.

Hogarty, G. E., Goldberg, S. C., & Schooler, N. R. Drug and sociotherapy in the aftercare of schizophrenic patients. III. Adjustment of nonrelapsed patients. *Archives of General Psychiatry*, 1974, *31*, 609–618.

Holmes, T. H., & Rahe, R. H. The social readjustment rating scale. *Journal of Psychosomatic Research*, 1967, *11*, 213–218.

Humphrey, M. Functional impairment in psychiatric outpatients. *British Journal of Psychiatry*, 1967, *113*, 1141–1151.

Ince, L. P. The self-concept variable in behavior therapy. *Psychotherapy: Theory, Research and Practice*, 1972, *9*, 223–225.

Jacobson, N. S. The assessment of overt behavior in depression. In L. P. Rehm, *Behavior therapy for depression: Present status and future directions*. New York: Academic Press, 1981.

Johansson, S., Lewinsohn, P. M., & Flippo, J. F. *An application of the Premack Principle to the verbal behavior of depressed subjects*. Paper presented at the Meeting of the Association for Advancement of Behavior Therapy, Washington, D. C., 1969.

Kaslow, N., & Tanenbaum, R. *KASTAN*. Unpublished manuscript, University of Pennsylvania, 1978.

Katz, M. M., & Lyerly, S. B. Methods for measuring adjustment and social behavior in the community: Rationale, description, discriminative validity and scale development. *Psychological Reports*, 1963, *13*, 503–535 (Monograph Supplement 4-V13).

Knesevich, J. W., Biggs, J. T., Clayton, P. J., & Ziegler, V. E. Validity of the Hamilton Rating Scale for Depression: *British Journal of Psychiatry*, 1977, *131*, 49–52.

Kupfer, D. J., & Detre, T. P. Development and application of the KDS-1 in inpatient and outpatient settings. *Psychological Reports*, 1971, *29*, 607–617.

Kupfer, D. J., Detre, T. P., Foster, F. G., Tucker, G. J., & Delgado, J. The application of Delgado's telemetric mobility recorder for human studies. *Behavioral Biology*, 1972, *7*, 585–590.

Kupfer, D. J., & Foster, F. G. Interval between onset of sleep as an indicator of depression. *Lancet*, 1972, *2*, 684–686.

Kupfer, D. J., & Foster, F. G. Sleep and activity in a psychotic depression. *Journal of Nervous and Mental Disease*, 1973, *156*, 341–348.

Kupfer, D. J., Foster, F. G., Reich, L., Thompson, K. S., & Weiss, B. EEG sleep changes as predictors in depression. *American Journal of Psychiatry*, 1976, *133*, 622–626.

Kupfer, D. J., Weiss, B. L., Foster, F. G., Detre, T. P., Delgado, J., & McPartland, R. Psychomotor activity in affective states. *Archives of General Psychiatry*, 1974, *30*, 765–768.

Lamparski, D. M., Rehm, L. P., O'Hara, M. W., Kornblith, S. J., & Fitzgibbon, K. *Measuring overt behavioral differences in unipolar depressed, bipolar depressed and normal subjects: A multivariate analysis.* Paper presented at the meeting of Association for Advancement of Behavior Therapy, San Francisco, California, December 13, 1979.

Lang, P. J. Fear reduction and fear behavior: Problems in treating a construct. In J. M. Shlien (Ed.), *Research in psychotherapy, III,* Washington, D. C.: APA, 1968.

Layden, M. A. *Attribution Scale Questionnaire.* Unpublished manuscript, University of Wisconsin, 1976.

Levitt, E. E., & Lubin, B. *Depression: Concepts, controversies and some new facts.* New York: Springer, 1975.

Lewinsohn, P. M. Activity schedules in treatment of depression. In J. D. Krumboltz & C. E. Thoresen (Eds.), *Counseling methods.* New York: Holt, Rinehart & Winston, 1976.

Lewinsohn, P. M. Manual of instruction for the behavior rating use for the observation of interpersonal behavior. Unpublished manuscript, University of Oregon, 1968 (revised, 1971).

Lewinsohn, P. M. A behavioral approach to depression. In R. M. Friedman & M. M. Katz (Eds.), *The Psychology of depression: Contemporary theory and research.* New York: Wiley, 1974. (a)

Lewinsohn, P. M. Clinical and theoretical aspects of depression. In K. S. Calhoun, H. E. Adams, & K. M. Mitchell (Eds.), *Innovative treatment methods of psychopathology.* New York: Wiley, 1974. (b)

Lewinsohn, P. M., & Atwood, G. E. Depression: A clinical research approach. *Psychotherapy: Theory, Research and Practice,* 1969, *6,* 166–171.

Lewinsohn, P. M., & Biglan, A. *Behavioral treatment of depression.* Paper presented at the Association for Advancement of Behavior Therapy, San Francisco, 1975.

Lewinsohn, P. M., Biglan, A., & Zeiss, A. M. Behavioral treatment of depression. In P. O. Davidson (Ed.), *The behavioral management of anxiety, depression and pain.* New York: Brunner/Mazel, 1976.

Lewinsohn, P. M., & Graf, M. Pleasant activities and depression. *Journal of Consulting and Clinical Psychology,* 1973, *41,* 261–268.

Lewinsohn, P. M., & Grosscup, S. J. *Unpleasant and pleasant events and depression.* Unpublished manuscript, 1976.

Lewinsohn, P. M., & Libet, J. Pleasant events, activity schedules and depressions. *Journal of Abnormal Psychology,* 1972, *79,* 291–295.

Lewinsohn, P. M., & Shaffer, M. The use of home observation as an integral part of the treatment of depression: Preliminary report and case studies. *Journal of Consulting and Clinical Psychology,* 1971, *37,* 87–94.

Lewinsohn, P. M., & Shaw, D. A. Feedback about interpersonal behavior as an agent of behavior change: A case study in the treatment of depression. *Psychotherapy and Psychosomatics,* 1969, *17,* 82–88.

Lewinsohn, P. M., Weinstein, M. S., & Alper, T. A behavioral approach to the group treatment of depressed persons: Methodological contribution. *Journal of Clinical Psychology,* 1970, *26,* 525–532.

Libet, J., Lewinsohn, P. M., & Javorek, F. *The construct of social skill: An empirical study of several measures on temporal stability, internal structure, validity, and structural generalizability.* Unpublished manuscript, University of Oregon, 1973.

Libet, J. M., & Lewinsohn, P. M. The concept of social skill with special reference to the behavior of depressed persons. *Journal of Consulting and Clinical Psychology,* 1973, *40,* 304–312.

Little, J. C., & McPhail, N. J. Measures of depressive mood at monthly intervals. *British Journal of Psychiatry,* 1973, *122,* 447–452.

Lubin, B. Adjective checklists for measurements of depression. *Archives of General Psychiatry,* 1965, *12,* 57–62.

Lubin, B. Fourteen brief Depression Adjective Checklists. *Archives of General Psychiatry,* 1966, *15,* 205–208.

Lubin, B. *Manual for the depression adjective check lists.* San Diego: Educational and Industrial Testing Service, 1967.

Lubin, B., Dupre, V. A., & Lubin, A. W. Comparability and sensitivity of set 2 (Lists E, F and G) of the Depression Adjective Check Lists. *Psychological Reports,* 1967, *20,* 756–758.

Lubin, B., & Himmelstein, P. Reliability of the Depression Adjective Check Lists. *Perceptual and Motor Skills,* 1976, *43,* 1037–1038.

Lubin, B., Horned, C. M., & Knapp, R. R. Scores on adjective check list, Eysenck Personality Inventory, and Depression Adjective Check List for a male prison population. *Perceptual Motor Skills,* 1977, *45,* 567–570.

Lubin, B., Hornstra, R. K., & Love, A. Course of depressive mood in a psychiatric population upon application for service and at 3- and 12 month reinterview. *Psychological Reports,* 1974, *34,* 424–426.

Lunghi, M. E. The stability of mood and social perception measures in a sample of depressed in-patients. *British Journal of Psychiatry,* 1977, *130,* 598–604.

MacPhillamy, D., & Lewinsohn, P. M. *The pleasant events schedule.* Unpublished manuscript, University of Oregon, 1971.

MacPhillamy, D. J., & Lewinsohn, P. M. The measurement of reinforcing events. Paper presented at the 80th Annual Convention of the APA, Honolulu 1972, (a).

MacPhillamy, D. J., Lewinsohn, P. M. Depression as a function of levels of desired and obtained pleasure. *Journal of Abnormal Psychology,* 1974, *83,* 651–657.

MacPhillamy, D. J., & Lewinsohn, P. M. *Manual for the pleasant events schedule.* Unpublished manuscript, University of Oregon, 1976.

MacPhillamy, D. J., & Lewinsohn, P. M. The structure of reported reinforcement. Unpublished manuscript, University of Oregon, 1972.

Marone, J., & Lubin, B. Relationship between set 2 of the depression adjective check lists (DACL) and Zung Self-rating Depression Scale (SDS). *Psychological Reports,* 1968, *22,* 333–334.

Marsella, A., Sanborn, K., Kameoka, V., Shizuru, L., & Brennan, J. Cross-validation of self-report measures of depression among normal populations of Japanese, Chinese, and Caucasian ancestry. *Journal of Clinical Psychology,* 1975, *31,* 281–287.

May, A. E., Urquhart, A., & Tarran, J. Self-evaluation of depression in various diagnostic and therapeutic groups. *Archives of General Psychiatry,* 1969, *21,* 191–194.

McLean, P. D., & Hakstain, A. R. Clinical depression: Comparative efficacy of outpatient treatments. *Journal of Consulting and Clinical Psychology,* 1979, *47,* 818—836.

McLean, P. D., Ogston, K., & Grauer, L. A behavioral approach to the treatment of depression. *Journal of Behaviour Therapy and Experimental Psychiatry,* 1973, *4,* 323–330.

McNair, D. M. Self-evaluations of antidepressants. *Psychopharmacologia,* 1974, *37,* 281–302.

McNair, D. M., Lorr, M., & Droppleman, L. F. *EITS Manual for the Profile of Mood States.* San Diego: Educational and Industrial Testing Service, 1971.

Mendels, J. Depression: The distinction between syndrome and symptom. *British Journal of Psychiatry,* 1968, *114,* 1549–1554.

Mendels, J. *Concepts of depression.* New York: Wiley, 1970.

Mendels, J., & Cochrane, C. The nosology of depression: The endogenous-reative concept. *American Journal of Psychiatry,* 1968, *124,* (May supplement), 1–11.

Mendels, J., Weinstein, N., & Cochrane, C. The relationship between depression and anxiety. *Archives of General Psychiatry,* 1972, *27,* 649–653.

Michaux, W. W., Katz, M. M., Kurland, A. A., & Gansereit, K. H. *The first year out: Mental patients after hospitalization.* Baltimore: Johns Hopkins Press, 1969.

Miller, W. R., & Seligman, M. E. P. Depression and the perceptions of reinforcement. *Journal of Abnormal Psychology,* 1973, *82,* 62–73.

Neufeld, R. J., Rogers, T. B., & Costello, C. G. Comparisons of measures of depression by the experimental investigation of single cases. *Psychological Reports,* 1972, *31,* 771–775.

O'Hara, M. W., & Rehm, L. P. *Self-monitoring, activity levels and mood in the development and maintenance of depression.* Unpublished manuscript, 1978.

Overall, J. E., & Gorham, D. R. The brief psychiatric rating scale. *Psychological Reports,* 1962, *10,* 799–812.

Padfield, M. The comparative effects of two counseling approaches on the intensity of depression among rural women of low socio-economic status. *Journal of Counseling Psychology,* 1976, *23,* 209–214.

Papazian, A. L. *The Beck depression inventory: A critical review.* Unpublished manuscript.

Perris, C. Genetic transmission of depressive psychoses. *Acta Psychiatrica Scandinavica,* 1968, *42,* (supplement no. 203), 45–52.

Perris, C. A study of bipolar (manic–depression) and unipolar recurrent depressive psychoses. *Acta Psychiatrica Scandinavica,* 1966, *42,* (supplement 194), 7–189.

Perris, C. The separation of bipolar (manic-depressive) from unipolar recurrent depressive psychoses. *Behavioral Neuropsychiatry,* 1969, *1,* 17–25.

Perris, C. Abnormality on paternal and maternal sides: Observations in bipolar (manic-depressive) and unipolar depressive psychoses. *British Journal of Psychiatry,* 1971, *118,* 207–210.

Radloff, L. Sex differences in depression: The effects of occupation and marital status. *Sex Roles,* 1975, *1,* 249–265.

Radloff, L. S. The CES-D scale: A self-report depression scale for research in the general population. *Applied Psychological Measurement,* 1977, *1,* 385–401.

Raft, D., Spencer, R. F., Toomey, T., & Brogan, D. Depression in medical outpatients: Use of the Zung scale. *Diseases of the Nervous System,* 1977, *38,* 999–1004.

Ranelli, C. J. *Nonverbal behavior and clinical depression.* Unpublished doctoral dissertation, University of Pittsburgh, 1978.

Raskin, A., Schulterbrandt, J., Reatig, N., & McKeon, J. J. Replication of factors of psychopathology in interview, ward behavior and self-report ratings of hospitalized depressives. *Journal of Nervous and Mental Disease,* 1969, *148,* 87–98.

Raskin, A., Schulterbrandt, J., Reatig, N., & Rice, C. E. Factors of psychopathology in interview, ward behavior, and self-report ratings of hospitalized depressives. *Journal of Consulting Psychology,* 1967, *31,* 270–278.

Rehm, L. P. A self-control model of depression. *Behavior Therapy,* 1977, *8,* 787–804.

Rehm, L. P. Mood, pleasant events and unpleasant events: Two pilot studies. *Journal of Consulting and Clinical Psychology,* 1978, *46,* 849–853.

Rehm, L. P. Self-control techniques for the treatment of depression. In J. F. Clarkin & H. Glazer (Eds.), *Depression: Behavioral and directive treatment strategies*. New York: Garland Press, in press.

Rehm, L. P., Fuchs, C. Z., Roth, D. M., Kornblith, S. J., & Romano, J. A comparison of self-control and social skill treatments of depression. *Behavior Therapy*, 1979, *10*, 429–442.

Rehm, L. P., & Kornblith, S. J. Behavior therapy for depression: A review of recent developments. In M. Herson, R. M. Eisler, & P. M. Miller (Eds.), *Progress in behavior modification*. Vol. 7. New York: Academic Press, 1979.

Rehm, L. P., Kornblith, S. J., O'Hara, M. W., Lamparski, D. M., Romano, J. M., & Volkin, J. An evaluation of major elements in a self-control therapy program for depression. *Behavior Modification*, in press.

Reisinger, J. J. The treatment of "anxiety-depression" via positive reinforcement and response cost. *Journal of Applied Behavior Analysis*, 1972, *5*, 125–130.

Robinson, J. C., & Lewinsohn, P. M. An experimental analysis of a technique based on the premack principle for changing the verbal behavior of depressed individuals. *Psychological Reports*, 1973, *32*, 199–210. (a)

Robinson, J. C., & Lewinsohn, P. M. Behavior modification of speech characteristics in a chronically depressed man. *Behavior Therapy*, 1973, *4*, 150–152. (b)

Rosenbaum, M. *A schedule for assessing self-control behavior: Preliminary findings*. Paper presented at the meeting of the Association for Advancement of Behavior Therapy, Chicago, November, 1978.

Rosenberry, C., Weiss, R. L., & Lewinsohn, P. M. *Frequency and skill of emitted social reinforcement in depressed and nondepressed subjects*. Unpublished manuscript, University of Oregon, 1968.

Rush, A. J., Khatami, M., & Beck, A. T. Cognitive and behavior therapy in chronic depression. *Behavior Therapy*, 1975, *6*, 398–404.

Schnurr, R., Hoaken, P. C. S., & Jarrett, F. J. Comparison of depression inventories in a clinical population. *Canadian Psychiatric Association Journal*, 1976, *21*, 473–476.

Schwab, J. J., Bialow, M. R., & Holzer, C. E. A comparison of two rating scales for depression. *Journal of Clinical Psychology*, 1967, *23*, 94–96.

Schwartz, G. E., Fair, P. L., Salt, P., Mandel, M. R., & Klerman, G. L. Facial muscle patterning to affective imagery in depressed and nondepressed subjects. *Science*, 1976, *192*, 489–491.

Seligman, M. E. P. Depression and learned helplessness. In R. J. Friedman & M. M. Katz (Eds.), *The Psychology of depression: Contemporary theory and research*. New York: Winston-Wiley, 1974.

Seligman, M. E. P. *Helplessness: On depression, development and death*. San Francisco: Freeman, 1975.

Seligman, M. E. P., Abramson, L. Y., Semmel, A., & Von Bayer, C. Depressive attributional style, *Journal of Abnormal Psychology*, 1979, *88*, 242–247.

Shipley, C. R., & Fazio, A. F. Pilot study of a treatment for psychological depression. *Journal of Abnormal Psychology*, 1973, *82*, 372–376.

Simon, J. I. A study of feelings and concerns in depressed patients. *Archives of General Psychiatry*, 1966, *15*, 506–515.

Snaith, R. P., Ahmed, S. N., Mehta, S., & Hamilton, M. Assessment of the severity of primary depressive illness. *Psychological Medicine*, 1971, *1*, 143–149.

Spitzer, R. L., Endicott, J., & Robins, E. Research diagnostic criteria. *Psychopharmalogia Bulletin*, 1975, *11*, 22–25.

Spitzer, R. L., Endicott, J., & Robins, E. Research Diagnostic Criteria: Rationale and reliability. *Archives of General Psychiatry*, 1978, *36*, 773–782.

Waxer, P. Nonverbal cues for depression. *Journal of Abnormal Psychology*, 1974, *83*, 319–322.

Waxer, P. Nonverbal cues for depth of depression: Set versus no set. *Journal of Consulting and Clinical Psychology*, 1976, *44*, 493.

Weckowicz, T. E., Muir, W., & Cropley, A. J. A factor analysis of the Beck Inventory of depression. *Journal of Consulting Psychology*, 1967, *31*, 23–28.

Weiss, B. L., Kupfer, D. J., Foster, F., & Delgado, J. Psychomotor activity, sleep, and biogenic amine metabolites in depression. *Biological Psychiatry*, 1974, *9*, 45–53.

Weissman, A. *Development and validation of the Dysfunctional Attitude Scale (DAS)*. Paper presented at the meeting of the Association for Advancement of Behavior Therapy, Chicago, November, 1978.

Weissman, M. M., & Bothwell, S. Assessment of social adjustment by patient self-report. *Archives of General Psychiatry*, 1976, *33*, 1111–1115.

Weissman, M. M., & Paykel, E. S. *The depressed woman: A study of social relationships*. Chicago: University of Chicago Press, 1974.

Weissman, M. M., Pottenger, M., Kleber, H., Ruben, H. L., Williams, D., & Thompson, W. D. Symptom patterns in primary and secondary depression. *Archives of General Psychiatry*, 1977, *34*, 854–862.

Weissman, M. M., Prusoff, B. A., & Newberry, P. *Comparison of CES-D, Zung Self-Rating Depression Scale and Beck Depression Inventory*. Progress Report, 1975.

Weismann, M. M., Sholomskas, D., Pottenger, M., Prusoff, B. A., & Locke, B. Z. Assessing depressive symptoms in five psychiatric populations: A validation study. *American Journal of Epidemiology*, 1977, *106*, 203–214.

Wells, K. C., Hersen, M., Bellack, A. S., & Himmelhoch, J. *Social skills training for unipolar depressive females*. Paper presented at the meeting of the Association for Advancement of Behavior Therapy, Atlanta, December 1977.

Williams, J. G., Barlow, D. H., & Agras, W. S. Behavioral measurement of severe depression. *Archives of General Psychiatry*, 1972, *27*, 330–333.

Winokur, G. The types of affective disorders. *Journal of Nervous and Mental Disease*, 1973, *156*, 82–96.

Wolpe, J. The experimental model and treatment of neurotic depression. *Behaviour Research and Therapy*, 1979, *17*, 555–566.

Wolpe, J., & Lazarus, A. A. *Behavior therapy techniques*. Oxford: Pergamon Press, 1967.

Woodruff, R. A. Jr., Goodwin, D. W., & Guze, S. B. *Psychiatric diagnosis*, New York: Oxford University Press, 1974.

Zealley, A. K., & Aitken, R. C. B. Measurement of mood. *Proceedings of the Royal Society of Medicine*, 1969, *62*, 993–997.

Zeiss, A. M., Lewinsohn, P. M., & Munoz, R. F. Non-specific improvement effects in depression using interpersonal, cognitive, and pleasant events focused treatments. *Journal of Consulting and Clinical Pyschology*, 1979, *47*, 427–439.

Zung, W. W. K. A self-rating depression scale. *Archives of General Psychiatry*, 1965, *12*, 63–70.

Zung, W. W. K. Factors influencing the Self-rating Depression Scale. *Archives of General Psychiatry*, 1967, *16*, 534–547.

Zung, W. W. K. A cross-cultural survey of symptoms in depression. *American Journal of Psychiatry*, 1969, *126*, 116–121.

Zung, W. W. K. *The measurement of depression*. Milwaukee: Lakeside Laboratories, 1974.

Zung, W. W. K., Richards, C. B., & Short, M. J. Self-rating depression scale in an outpatient clinic. *Archives of General Psychiatry*, 1965, *13*, 508-515.

Chapter 9
Assessment of Social Skills

Hal Arkowitz

INTRODUCTION

In the past few years, there has been a phenomenal growth of interest in the assessment and treatment of social skill problems. In addition to the appearance of numerous chapters and review articles (e.g., Arkowitz, 1977; Curran, 1977; Hersen & Bellack, 1977; Twentyman & Zimering, 1979), there have also been several major books devoted entirely to these subjects (e.g., Bellack & Hersen, 1979; Trower, Bryant, & Argyle, 1978). All that seems needed to complete the picture is a *Journal of Social Skills*. Given the proliferation of work in this area, such a possibility may soon become a reality. In a relatively short period of time, we have advanced our knowledge regarding the assessment and treatment of interpersonal difficulties quite considerably.

In this chapter, I will focus on the advances we have made in the assessment of social skills. The existence of reliable and valid assessment procedures is a prerequisite for evaluating the outcome of social skills training procedures. At a more clinical level, assessment is also crucial for effective treatment planning and selection. Some of the major issues in the assessment of social skills will be reviewed, along with some of the major methods and empirical findings emerging from this work.

Consistent with current usage by Curran and Weissberg (in press) among others, I will use the broad term "social inadequacy" throughout this chapter. The reason for this relates to conceptualizations of the nature of the problem. As clinicians, we are often faced with social inadequacy from our patients: their social lives are not satisfactory, and their social behaviors are not effective. One possible reason for this is that the patient may lack adequate social skills. In this case, the social skills deficit might primarily mediate the social inadequacy.

However, a person may be inadequate in social relationships for reasons other than a social skills deficit; they may have adequate social skills, but evaluate them overly negatively and subsequently avoid social situations. This inappropriate avoidance is also a problem and is another form of social inadequacy. In these cases, the person might have effective skills, but a negative set and unrealistic anxiety may lead to avoidance and distress. Curran and Wessberg (in press) have proposed an interesting classificatory scheme which emphasizes distinctions based on social skill deficit as opposed to social performance problems. Social performance problems can be mediated by emotional, motivational, or cognitive factors. Thus, inadequate social performance may be due to a number of factors, only one of which is a social skills deficit. In order to fully assess the reasons for the social inadequacy, we need to assess the person's social skills and anxiety, as well as cognitive and motivational factors relating to their social performance. Any or all of these might contribute significantly to social inadequacy.

It is interesting to note that there are no traditional diagnostic categories which primarily reflect social inadequacy in either DSM II or DSM III. Despite this neglect, it appears that problems relating to social inadequacy cut across a number of traditional diagnostic categories, rather than being associated with any particular one (Curran, Miller, Zwick, Monti, & Stout, 1980; Bryant, Trower, Yardley, Urbieta, & Letemandia, 1976). It may be that the relative neglect of social inadequacy by the traditional classification system has slowed progress in the assessment and treatment of such problems. It has been only relatively recently that problems relating to social inadequacy have come to be recognized as major problems in their own right.

The lack of attention to social inadequacy in the DSM system is not due to the infrequency of such problems; in fact, several survey studies have revealed that these problems are major ones for a considerable percentage of inpatients and outpatients. Argyle, Trower, and Bryant (1974) found that 28 percent of their sample of applicants for treatment at an English mental hospital were judged to be socially inadequate. (Although recent surveys using more stringent criteria have yielded somewhat lower incidence rates for social inadequacy.) Bryant et al. (1976) studied a sample of English outpatients whose diagnoses were restricted to neurotic and personality disorders. They found that 16.3 percent were judged by experts to be socially inadequate. Curran et al. (1980) studied 779 randomly selected admissions to the inpatient and day-care units of an American psychiatric hospital. Using reliable ratings of the patients' social inadequacy, Curran et al. found that approximately seven percent of this sample were socially inadequate. Although seven percent is not a dramatically high incidence rate, it exceeds those for many of the traditional categories of psychopathology. In addition, socially inadequate patients had a significantly longer stay in the hospital and functioned more poorly after hospitalization compared to other patients.

It is also possible that a lack of social skills may be a predisposing factor in the development of psychopathology. For example, there are a number of commonly encountered life situations which require new or modified social skills. The inability to deal with these situations may precipitate serious psychological problems for some individuals. Such situations include death of a loved one, divorce, geographical relocation, job change, and retirement. Without effective social skills, such stressful life situations may become precipitators of serious psychopathology.

The proper assessment of social inadequacy is also crucial to treatment planning. We need to know the situations in which the patient is inadequate, as well as relevant antecedents, consequences, and mediating cognitions. The relative contributions of social skill deficits, unrealistic social anxiety, and maladaptive cognitions about social performance also need to be assessed before we can select the best treatment strategy for an individual.

In a relatively short period of time, behavioral researchers and clinicians have learned a great deal regarding the assessment of social inadequacy. It is to this knowledge, as well as the unanswered questions in the assessment of social inadequacy to which we now turn.

MAJOR ISSUES AND QUESTIONS

Before considering the assessment procedures and associated research findings, some of the major issues and questions which confront practitioners and researchers in the area will be reviewed. These questions can be divided into two major categories: the first concerns *what* to measure; the second *how* to measure it. In this section, we will consider the broader conceptual questions of *what* to measure.

Social skill and social adequacy are elusive phenomena. It appears that most people believe they can recognize social skill when they see it, but have a difficult if not impossible time when they try to define it behaviorally. This is also true of much of the research in which general ratings of social skill or social effectiveness often can discriminate between criterion groups (e.g., assertive versus unassertive patients). However, specific behavioral measures designed to measure social skill often do not discriminate between these groups.

Part of this difficulty is a conceptual one. Workers in the area have had considerable difficulty in defining and conceptualizing social adequacy and skill. A good working definition and model of social skill still eludes us, although we now have the parameters of the issue more clearly specified than before. Rather than trying to provide a definition of social skill or adequacy, I will now turn to some of the major issues which confront us in trying to develop a viable definition of the construct of social skill.

Content vs. consequences

An important issue in such a definition relates to the degree to which we need to measure the *content* of interpersonal behaviors as opposed to the *consequences* of such behavior. By content, I am referring to the aspects of behavior which we observe and believe may contribute to effective social performance. These may be verbal behaviors, such as initiating conversations, refusing unreasonable requests, giving praise, and demonstrating appropriate degrees of self-disclosure. Other behaviors believed to contribute to social skill are nonverbal, such as eye contact, smiling, gesturing, voice volume and expressiveness. While these and other behaviors may seem reasonable as components of socially skilled behavior, we do not have any clear way of knowing whether they really are significant components of skilled performance. In this sense, definitions based on the content of behaviors are rather arbitrary. Different writers emphasize somewhat different behaviors as important in social skill. Even when we turn to the research in this area, the same question remains. For example, we may find that assertive subjects engage in certain behaviors more frequently than unassertive individuals. The problem is that we still do not know how important these behaviors are in determining effective performance. Finding that the criterion groups differ does not ensure that these are the most important differences. For example, we may find that unassertive subjects play tennis more poorly than assertive subjects. A naive content definition would lead to a definition of social skill that includes playing tennis. The point is that such observed differences may be mediated by factors other than social skill. Subassertive individuals, for example, may be more anxious and inhibited about trying competitive sports. Such a difference between assertive and unassertive individuals may be more a function of this anxiety than of any supposed lack of social skills.

Contrasting the content approach to social skills, the consequences approach emphasizes the reactions that behaviors receive from the environment, regardless of what they are. Lewinsohn is probably the best known representative of the consequences approach. Libet and Lewinsohn (1973) defined social skill as, "the ability to maximize the rate of positive reinforcement and to minimize the strength of punishment from others [p. 311]." Thus, behavior followed by positive reinforcement is considered to be socially skilled. In the consequences approach, what matters entirely are the consequences which the person receives in the situation, regardless of the content of the behaviors.

While the content approach is rather arbitrary, the consequences approach also has its limitations. For example, a person who takes a courageous but unpopular assertive position in a group would be considered unskilled. A juvenile delinquent who assaults others may be positively reinforced by his peer group, but we would be reluctant to consider such behaviors socially skilled. The consequences definition is an entirely relative one, defined by the reactions of the individual's social environment. While it is important to realize that different social environments will reinforce different behaviors, a definition of social skill based entirely on consequences seems misdirected in some respects.

Both the content and consequences of interpersonal behaviors should be taken into account in any definition of social skill. By starting with some idea of what may constitute the content of socially skilled behavior, and evaluating the consequences of those behaviors, we can get some estimate of the degree of social skill. In general, socially skilled behavior would be expected to elicit positive reinforcement more often than punishment. At a clinical level, it is important to assess both what people do and the reactions which their behavior elicits from others.

Situational specificity of social skills

A behavioral approach considers social skill to be situation-specific, rather than a broad trait consistent across different situations. Thus, a person might be socially skilled in some situations, but not in others. We need to avoid making unwarranted assumptions about a person based on our assessment of this behavior only in certain situations. A patient may appear generally socially skilled in the way he reacts in a clinical interview: engaging in appropriate self-disclosure, good eye contact, and fluent speech. Although interviewers often assume that we can make generalizations from interview behavior to other situations in the naturalistic environment, such generalizations are often quite unwarranted.

Several studies point to the situational specificity of social skills. Eisler, Hersen, Miller, and Blanchard (1975) demonstrated that psychiatric patients' responses to a role play test of assertiveness varied as a function of the sex and familiarity of the other person. Phibbs and

Arkowitz (in press) found that men and women with problems in the area of dating interaction did not have any difficulties in the area of assertiveness. Himadi, Arkowitz, Hinton, and Perl (1980) showed that dating-shy women did not have difficulties with same sex friendship interactions while dating-shy men did.

Thus, while there is a tendency to think of social skills as a cross-situational trait, we should question this assumption and assess social skills in the particular situations of interest.

Overt behaviors vs. social perception and cognition

Although until recently, most work on the assessment of social skill has focused almost exclusively on overt behaviors, there has been increasing interest in the area of cognitive and perceptual factors in social skill. Bellack (1979a) has criticized existing work on social skills assessment for its relatively exclusive emphasis on behavioral output variables while neglecting variables related to social perception. Morrison and Bellack (in press) discuss social perception as consisting of the following: knowledge of social mores; knowledge of the significance or meaning of various response cues; attention to relevant aspects of the interaction (e.g., context and responses emitted by the partner); information processing capability; and the ability to predict and evaluate interpersonal consequences. This recent interest in cognition is consistent with the relatively recent interest in cognitive mediating factors in social learning theory (e.g., Bandura, 1977).

It is possible for someone to behave unskillfully in a situation because they are unaware of the social norms or misread cues from others. In order to behave skillfully, there should be a match between the behavior and situation. If the person cannot accurately "read" relevant cues in the situation, he or she will not be able to behave skillfully regardless of the behavioral repertoire. A person who inaccurately believes that he or she has been insulted may react angrily; this may be an appropriate response to an insult, but the insult may not have actually occurred. In this case, the problem was in the social misperception rather than in the actual response. The response accurately fits the perception, but the perception did not accurately reflect the situation, leading to an inappropriate and unskilled social response. In this regard, the ability to accurately read cues from others is a particularly important and neglected area. While there are several instruments available for testing social sensitivity and perceptions of others (e.g., Ekman, Friesen, & Ellsworth, 1972; Rosenthal, Hall, DiMatteo, Rogers, & Arthur, 1979), they are fairly complex and more appropriate to research than clinical assessment. We need to assess the individual's ability to accurately "read" social situations as well as their response repertoire for dealing with the situation. Difficulties in social perception may mediate the social inadequacy.

Single responses vs. behavioral sequences

Most work on the assessment of social skill has emphasized frequency counts of various categories of verbal and nonverbal behaviors. However, simple frequency counts may obscure some very important issues relating to the timing, sequencing, and context of behaviors: issues which may determine the adequacy or skillfullness of the behavior (see Bellack, 1979a).

There are times when simple frequency counts may be quite useless and even misleading. As an example, consider the following incident which occurred with a subject in one of my experiments. The experiment involved having the male subject interact with a woman for 10 minutes while we coded several of his behaviors. The man had never met the woman before he was introduced to her in the laboratory. One category, coded "self-disclosure," was obtained by counting the number of self-disclosures during the 10-minute interaction. Since the man began his conversation with a vivid description of his recent hernia operation, he received high frequency scores. However, we might well question the appropriateness of such self-disclosure in the context of meeting a woman for the first time. From the expression on the woman's face during his description, it appeared that she was having a rather strong negative reaction to the man and his behavior. The same self-disclosure to a family member or perhaps at a later point in the interaction with the woman might have had a very different impact. Since in each case the man would receive the same score for frequency of self-disclosure, such a count neglects the context and timing of the behavior. Similarly, a person who continually smiled would receive high frequency scores for smiling, but the impact of that behavior would be different depending on whether he and his partner were talking about pleasant matters or personal tragedies. Once again, simple frequency counts obscure some very important issues in measuring social interaction through direct observation techniques. Thus, we need ways to take into account the context of the behavior and its timing. The importance of such variables was underlined by recent findings by Fischetti, Curran, and Wessberg (1977). They found that socially incompetent and competent subjects did not differ in the frequency of response, but did significantly in the timing and distribution of their responses.

The beginning of an analysis of behavior sequences has been made through the use of conditional probabilities and time-series analyses (Gottman, 1979). However, this is just a beginning. Analysis of the timing and sequence of behavior should be addressed more fully before our direct observation techniques can really capture the complexity and reciprocal nature of social interaction.

There is one other problem with simple frequency counts in measuring social skill. Implicit in such an approach is that it is better to have more of a "good" behavior (e.g., eye contact), and less of a "bad" behavior (e.g., speech disruptions). Perhaps there can be too much of a "good" thing and too little of a "bad" one. For example, someone who continually stared during a social encounter and was completely fluent without any speech disruptions, might be considered less skillful than someone with less eye contact and an average amount of speech disruption. There may be optimal levels of certain behaviors in particular situations; simple analysis of frequency counts does not take this possibility into consideration.

Social skill deficit vs. performance inhibition

Many times we are faced with people whose problems are behavioral deficits in social situations. Our assessment may reveal avoidance of social situations or very low rates of appropriate social behaviors once they are in them. We may draw the conclusion from this that the individual lacks social skills and is in need of social skill training. However, the behavioral deficit may be a function of either a performance inhibition due to anxiety *or* the lack of effective social skills in the individual's repertoire. This is an important distinction, since different treatment strategies fit these different alternatives. If the person has the skills in his or her repertoire and the performance is blocked due to unrealistic anxiety, then a strategy primarily directed at anxiety reduction is in order. For example, Arkowitz, Lichtenstein, McGovern, and Hines (1975) found that dating-shy men had adequate social skills when they were required to interact with a woman in the laboratory. It appeared that for most of them, however, unrealistic anxiety about their performance inhibited any social initiations with women in the natural environment. Their problem reflected a performance inhibition rather than a skill deficiency. This led to the development of anxiety reduction procedures for dating shyness (e.g., Christensen, Arkowitz, & Anderson, 1975) rather than skill acquisition procedures. A behavioral deficit may indicate either a skill deficit or a performance inhibition. Role play and simulated interactions in the office may assess the skills repertoire of the individual rather than whether they actually use the skills in naturalistic situations. Thus, when we are faced with social avoidance, we should assess how much it reflects an actual social skill deficiency versus a performance inhibition due to anxiety.

The role of physical appearance

The variable of physical appearance is an important one that should be considered as a moderating variable in social skill. The same overt behavior may have very different consequences depending upon an individual's physical appearance. For example, a weak, fragile-looking young man who engages in specified assertive behaviors may be reacted to quite differently from a tall, muscular young man engaging in exactly the same behaviors in the same situation. The importance of physical appearance has already been well-documented in dating interactions (e.g., Berscheid & Walster, 1973; Glasgow & Arkowitz, 1975). It should be noted that physical appearance and physical attractiveness are not fixed characteristics of the individual, but quite modifiable. Arkowitz (1977) suggested greater attention to this variable and the possibility of "appearance training" to modify appearance to enhance effectiveness in the situation. Reese, Arkowitz, and White (1980) demonstrated that physical attractiveness is modifiable, and that varying degrees of physical attractiveness were associated with different reactions from others, given roughly similar behaviors on the part of the individual. When the stimulus person was made to appear physically attractive, she evoked more approval from others than when unattractive. In addition, the potential aversive impact of the stimulus person's depression on others was markedly reduced when the person was physically attractive. Thus, physical appearance and attractiveness are important variables to consider when assessing social skill and may constitute appropriate targets for change as well.

SELECTIVE REVIEW OF ASSESSMENT PROCEDURES

Now that we have considered *what* to measure, *how* to measure social skill and adequacy will be discussed. A number of detailed empirical reviews of assessment procedures for social skill have appeared in the past few years (e.g., Arkowitz, 1977; Bellack, 1979b; Curran & Wessberg, in press; Galassi & Galassi, 1979; Hersen & Bellack, 1977). It would be redundant and beyond the scope of this chapter to provide another detailed review. Instead, I will present a selective review of instruments and procedures that hold the most promise for the practicing clinician, along with some of the strengths and limitations of each. Similar assessment strategies have been employed with problems of minimal dating, sub-assertiveness, and social functioning in socially inadequate psychiatric patients. These include the behavioral interview, self-report, self-monitoring, and role-playing procedures.

Before turning to this review, I should note, as Bellack (1979a) and others have, that we are still far from having psychometrically acceptable procedures for the measurement of social functioning. While we have made significant progress toward the development of reliable and valid instruments, this progress has still been quite limited. The field has been too often characterized by single studies presenting new instruments for the measurement of the same constructs. Thus, we have a large number of self-report instruments for the measurement of social anxiety.

This diversity has not been accompanied by intensive study of the specific instruments; more often investigators have started to develop a new instrument rather than studying the psychometric properties of already existing ones. Thus, there are a large number of instruments and measures for a relatively few constructs, and this has led to confusion in the field.

The Behavioral Interview

For many years, clinicians of all orientations have relied heavily on the interview as a primary method of assessment. This has been true for behavioral clinicians as well. The behavioral interview has certain features distinguishing it from traditional interviewing, including the greater specificity of the questions, the attempt to behaviorally operationalize the patient's constructs, and the functional analysis of problem behaviors in terms of antecedents and consequences. More recently, there has also be an increased interest in the assessment of cognitive factors as well.

Several papers have described behavioral interviewing (e.g., Meyer, Liddell, & Lyons, 1977; Morganstern, 1976), as well as the interviewing chapter in the present volume. Despite the heavy reliance on the behavioral interview as a source of assessment information, there has been surprisingly little research on it. The extent to which behavioral interviews yield reliable and valid information, or serve as the information base for reliable and valid judgments about patients remains to be determined. Haynes and Jensen (1979) have pointed out the need for the behavioral interview to be conceptualized as an assessment instrument and subjected to the same psychometric examination of reliability and validity as other instruments; however, it has yet to be subjected to this kind of scrutiny. Hopefully, this will change in the near future. For now, we are left with primarily clinical descriptions of behavioral interviewing rather than empirical bases to develop such an interview. Eisler (1976) has presented one of the few discussions of the interview for the social skill assessment. In the following section, I will primarily draw from my own clinical experience in using the behavioral interview for assessing social inadequacy. Hopefully, this discussion will be of use to the clinician, as well as providing a starting point for future research.

The interview can provide a rich source of information about the patient that may not be as readily available from other assessment methods. The open-ended nature of interviewing allows for a more idiographic assessment so that the clinician can follow up on potentially interesting leads. By contrast, more structured procedures, like self-report questionnaires, do not allow for such flexibility. In many ways, the interview is potentially one of our most valuable assessment tools. The interview can generate information about the patient's definition of his or her problems, the historical background of the problem, as well as providing a source of behavioral observations of the patient. However, as we discussed earlier, we should be cautious about gen-eralizing from the interview to behavior in other naturalistic social sit-uations.

The interview can also be considered a hypothesis-generating pro-cedure about the patient rather than as a hypothesis-testing procedure. Impressions from the interview should be followed up by more reliable and valid measurement procedures, when such procedures are available. Other procedures will be discussed in subsequent sections. The inter-view can also provide information about areas for which we do not yet have any really reliable and valid assessment procedures, e.g., the pa-tients' evaluations, cognitions, and expectancies regarding their social performance.

Table 9.1, outlines an interview guide I have employed over a number of years of working with socially inadequate patients. It may be used to direct the interviewer to areas of potential importance in the as-sessment of social inadequacy.

One potentially important type of assessment that can be made through an interview concerns whether the social inadequacy is a primary or a secondary problem. The issue is whether the social difficulties are a manifestation of other problems, or are the major problems in them-selves. This point was brought home to me most forcefully while work-ing with a man who was a resident of a halfway house for schizophrenics recently discharged from the state hospital. He was a good-looking and articulate young man who was dreadfully frightened of any kind of

Table 9.1. Interview Guide for Social Inadequacy

I. *Physical description of the patient.* This includes dress and general appearance as well as any noteworthy physical features.

II. *Behavioral observation of the patient during the interview.* This includes a brief description of verbal and nonverbal behaviors including how the patient relates to the interviewer.

III. *Patient's description of presenting problems and treatment goals in his or her own words.*

IV. *Operational definitions of problems and goals.* Operationalizing constructs is one of the hallmarks of behavioral interviewing. Terms reflecting traits, dispositions, and broad constructs are translated into behavioral referents.

V. *Major problems other than social inadequacy.* While there seems to be no consistent association between social inadequacy and other specific forms of psychopathology, it is often the case that socially inadequate patients do have diverse other problems. These may include depression, schizophrenia, alcoholism, sexual deviation, and sexual dysfunction.

VI. *Effects of the social dysfunction on the person's life functioning.* The major question here is the extent to which the social inadequacy may limit the patient in significant areas of their lives. For example, the social dysfunction may limit the patient in certain job opportunities. In my experience, severely inadequate patients seek out jobs which require little or no social contact (e.g., night watchman) in order to avoid dealing with difficult social situations.

VII. *Assessment of social functioning in specific areas.*
  A. Same-sex relationships
  B. Opposite-sex relationships
  C. Casual relationships
  D. Intimate relationships
  E. Ability to express positive feelings toward others
  F. Assertiveness and standing up for one's rights
  G. Interactions with "authority" figures
  H. Interactions with family members
  I. Group situations
  J. Public speaking situations
  K. Initiating social interactions
  L. Maintaining and developing social interactions

VIII. *Estimates of social skill, social anxiety, and self-evaluations in each of the above areas.*

IX. *Cognitions relating to social functioning.* This includes an emphasis on self-talk, irrational assumptions, unrealistic standards, and expectations regarding social encounters.

X. *Sexual knowledge, experiences, and fears.* Many socially inadequate patients have underlying fears relating to sexual failure, homosexual fears, or sexual ignorance. Interview assessment of the area of sexuality is often very significant for social inadequacy.

XI. *Current living situation with particular reference to potential social contacts.*

XII. *Description of a typical day with particular reference to social contacts.*

XIII. *Current employment and educational situation.*

Table 9.1 (con't)

XIV. *Family situation*. Is the patient married, divorced, or single? Is the patient living with family members?

XV. *Interests and pleasurable leisure activities*. These can often form the basis for a program of increasing social contacts.

XVI. *Obstacles to effective social functioning*. These may be any of a number of factors including an isolated living situation, aspects of physical appearance, or health restrictions which may limit social contact.

XVII. *History*.
   A. Description of period of onset of social difficulties (or note if the difficulties have been chronic)
   B. Education
   C. Work history
   D. Family background
   E. Health background
   F. Description of period of "best" social functioning
   G. Description of period of "worst" social functioning

---

social contact with people outside the halfway house. In my assessment of him through various methods, he appeared to quite socially skilled in most situations. Nonetheless, he adamantly refused to leave the halfway house to initiate any social contacts. After several sessions in which we had begun to focus on a desensitization approach, he revealed to me that he still heard voices. He had told the doctors at the hospital that the voices were gone in order to obtain a discharge from the hospital. He believed that the voices were broadcasting highly embarrassing information about him that everybody could hear. It was no wonder that he was socially phobic! In this case, his social dysfunction was more highly determined by his hallucinations than they were by any skills deficit directly relating to social performance, or to any "unrealistic" anxiety. As long as he believed that the voices were broadcasting in this way, his "reality" created a situation which led understandably to social anxiety and avoidance. Other examples of secondary social inadequacy are: 1) dating anxiety associated primarily with fears of sexual failure and dysfunction; 2) fears of contact with members of the same sex due to homosexual fears; and 3) sub-assertiveness in an individual who has had explosive anger outbursts in the past which have gotten him into serious trouble. In cases of secondary social inadequacy, the social difficulties cannot be effectively treated unless the primary problems are also addressed by the treatment.

Self-Report Instruments

There are a large number of self-report instruments to measure different aspects of social functioning. These include measures of social skill, social anxiety, self-statements relating to social performance, initiation, activity, and difficulty. They also cover different areas of social functioning such as dating, assertiveness, public speaking, and friendship. Bellack (1979a) reviewed these instruments and was struck by the similarities in the content of the items across the different questionnaires, although he noted that the response formats often differed considerably. Each new issue of the behavioral journals usually contains at least one article on the development of a new self-report measure for some aspect of social functioning.

Many of the better instruments have been developed for research with college populations. As a result, we are faced with another problem concerning the appropriateness of these questionnaires for more heterogeneous, adult clinical populations.

The self-report measures fall into three main categories. Some relate to general social functioning and include items covering a wide range of types of social situations. These questionnaires may measure different components of social functioning (e.g., skill, anxiety, self-statements), but do try to cover most significant types of social situations. There are others that are more specific to particular areas of social functioning. These include measures designed to tap aspects of dating shyness and assertiveness.

General social functioning

One of the most widely-used general questionnaires is the Social Avoidance and Distress Scale (SADS) originally developed by Watson and Friend (1969). While it was initially developed for a college population, the items are appropriate for the general adult population as well. The items cover same and opposite-sex interactions, group and public speaking situations, and interactions with "authority" figures. The items are stated rather generally (e.g., "I tend to withdraw from people"). One limitation of such a questionnaire is that it does not provide diagnostic information regarding specific areas of dysfunction which would be useful in planning treatment. Instead, the total score seems useful as a general index of the degree of social anxiety and avoidance. A considerable amount of research has accumulated on the reliability and validity of this measure (see reviews by Arkowitz, 1977; Galassi & Galassi, 1979; Hersen & Bellack, 1977), and the research has generally provided some moderate degree of support for this scale.

Other general social anxiety inventories include a modified form of the S-R Inventory of Anxiousness (Arkowitz et al., 1975) and the Social Anxiety Inventory (SAI) developed by Richardson and Tasto (1976). The SAI consists of 100 items, and is of particular interest because they were derived from hierarchies actually used in treatment of socially anxious patients. This inventory lists relevant social situations, and although it was developed for college students, the items are also appropriate to the more general adult population. Richardson and Tasto also conducted a factor analysis of the SAI which yielded seven distinct factors: fear of disapproval or negative evaluation; social assertiveness and visibility; confrontation and anger expression; heterosexual contact; intimacy and interpersonal warmth; conflict with or rejection by parents; and interpersonal loss. Although the factor scores were not validated separately, they can potentially provide information about social problems in different specific areas of social functioning.

Curran, Corriveau, Monti, and Hagerman (1980), constructed an interesting modified version of the SAI where subjects were asked to rate their degree of anxiety and skill in coping with each of the situations listed. Curran et al. (1980) studied the properties of this revised questionnaire with a psychiatric population. Although more research is needed on this revised version of the SAI, it is of particular interest because it yields scores simultaneously on two important dimensions of social functioning: social anxiety and social skill.

Goldsmith and McFall (1975) developed an Interpersonal Situations Inventory for use with a psychiatric population. The items also cover a wide range of social situations and were empirically generated from the functional-analytic model proposed by Goldfried and D'Zurilla (1969). In England, Bryant and Trower (1974) developed a Social Situations Questionnaire subsequently employed by Trower, Bryant, and Argyle (1978). This measure is also appropriate for a general adult patient population and presents a wide range of social situations. The format calls for subjects to respond with self-ratings regarding the difficulty as well as frequency of occurrence of each situation.

Another general social functioning measure developed by Lowe and Cautela (1978) is called the Social Performance Survey Schedule (SPSS). This consists of 100 items, each rated on 5-point scales. The items consist of specific "positive" and "negative" social behaviors that the subject rates for frequency of occurrence. To the extent that these self-reports of specific behavioral frequencies can be considered valid, this measure has the advantage of greater behavioral specificity than most discussed thus far. The information derived from this type of questionnaire can be useful in treatment planning due to its behavioral specificity. By contrast, an instrument like the Social Avoidance and Distress Scale is useful as a general index of distress and lacks the specificity of the SPSS. The SADS may be useful for screening and measuring treatment outcome, but does not yield specific diagnostic information about specific behaviors in specific situations. An instrument like the SPSS is potentially more valuable in this regard.

All of the instruments discussed above have some potential utility. With the exception of the SADS however, there is still relatively little information available on the psychometric properties of these questionnaires. Without further information of this kind, we are still somewhat uncertain what the various instruments are actually measuring.

There are also a number of instruments specifically developed for college students in the area of dating interactions. One is the Situation Questionnaire (SQ) originally developed by Rehm and Marston (1968) for college men. Curran and Gilbert (1975) have developed a modified form for college women. The questionnaire is primarily a measure of discomfort experienced in hierarchically arranged specific dating situations.

One of the more widely used instruments relating to college dating is the Survey of Heterosexual Interactions (SHI) developed by Twentyman and McFall (1975). The original measure was developed for college men, but Williams and Ciminero (1978) developed a version for college women. It is basically a measure of initiation versus avoidance of dating-related situations. The subject is asked to rate his or her ability to carry out specific interactions with members of the opposite sex.

In an interesting study on selection procedures for heterosexual deficits, Wallander, Conger, Mariotto, Curran, and Farrell (1980) administered the SHI along with four other questionnaires (including the SQ and the SADS) to male subjects. They also administered two simulated heterosexual interactions. In general, the results were quite discouraging. Correlations among the questionnaire measures were quite low, and scores on the questionnaires were not particularly good predictors of dating experiences. In addition, the questionnaire scores did not predict self- or judges-ratings particularly well. Of the instruments studied, the SHI did the best, correlating moderately well with other questionnaires (e.g., the SQ and SADS), as well as with dating experience, and self- and judges'-ratings of the stimulated interactions.

In the area of assertiveness, there have also been a number of self-report instruments developed. Some instruments have been specifically developed on college populations: the Rathus Assertiveness Schedule (Rathus, 1973), the College Self-Expression Scale (Galassi, Delo, Galassi, & Bastien, 1974), and the Conflict Resolution Inventory (McFall & Lillesand, 1971). Others have been developed and employed with more general adult populations: the Wolpe-Lazarus Assertiveness Scale (Wolpe & Lazarus, 1966), and the Adult Self-Expression Scale (Gay, Hollandsworth, & Galassi, 1975). While each scale has some associated validational data (see Hersen & Bellack, 1977), none of it seems particularly strong at this time. Most of the assertiveness inventories present statements and measure the degree of endorsement of the statement by the subject. As such, they may be generally less useful for specific treatment planning than are instruments such as the SPSS described above.

Most assertion inventories combine items reflecting "negative" assertiveness (e.g., refusal behavior and standing up for one's rights) with "positive" assertiveness (e.g., expressing tender or positive feelings). These two areas may be quite different and deserve to be measured in their own right.

One promising instrument which has been developed recently for college students by Levenson and Gottman (1978) is the Dating and Assertion Questionnaire, covering dating and assertive items. In the first part, subjects are asked to report the likelihood of engaging in certain behaviors (e.g., standing up for one's rights); in the second part, they are presented with specific situations and asked to rate their comfort and competence in each of them. The questionnaire discriminated between client and normal populations and between individuals with dating versus assertiveness problems. The measure has adequate reliability and was sensitive to changes with treatment. This scale is interesting in its coverage of two specific areas of social functioning, as well as its coverage of the frequency of certain behaviors and the degree of discomfort in different situations. However, the scores have not yet been validated against any form of direct behavioral observation.

As can be seen from this rather cursory review, self-report instruments are diverse in a number of respects. The items differ considerably. In some, subjects are presented with situations; in others with descriptions of feelings or behaviors they are asked to endorse if they apply. In addition to the stimulus items, the response alternatives vary considerably in frequency of occurrence, ratings of discomfort, perceived competence, initiation, etc. Given the diversity of formats and response alternatives, we are faced with a rather confusing array of instruments; nonetheless, some have reasonably established reliability and validity. Others may have some clinical utility in helping plan specific treatment interventions through their inquiries about specific situations.

One recent and interesting development in the focus of self-report instruments reflects the increasing interest in cognitive assessment and therapy. Schwartz and Gottman (1976) developed an inventory of self-statements relating to assertiveness. Glass and Merluzzi (1978) developed a similar self-statement inventory for the area of heterosexual anxiety. Self-report instruments relating to self-statements will probably assume a greater importance with the current increasing interest in cognitive therapies for social dysfunction (e.g., Glass, Gottman, & Shmurak, 1976).

Self-monitoring procedures

Self-monitoring procedures have been used in a number of studies to assess aspects of heterosexual interactions (e.g., frequency of dates and casual heterosexual interactions) as well as same-sex friendship interactions (e.g., Royce & Arkowitz, 1976). However, there has been relatively little use of self-monitoring procedures to assess assertiveness or general social functioning. Self-monitoring procedures are open to criticism based on their reactivity and because of difficulties in firmly establishing their accuracy or reliability (see Ciminero, Nelson, & Lipinski, 1977).

Despite these problems, self-monitoring procedures have certain advantages: they provide access to certain *classes of behavior* which cannot be directly measured in the office. For example, dating-shy subjects have been asked to self-monitor the frequency of date and casual interactions during a one-week period (e.g., Christensen, Arkowitz, & Anderson, 1975). In addition, self-monitoring procedures can provide access to *situational factors* that also cannot be readily measured in the office. In addition to asking patients to record the frequency of certain behaviors, we can also ask them to record the antecedents, consequences, and thoughts which might have occurred during the contact. The patients can also be asked to estimate their anxiety level, as well as their skill and satisfaction with their behaviors. In most cases, self-monitoring has been used to measure the frequency and range (number of different people) of social contacts. However, self-monitoring can also be applied to specific response classes, such as assertive responses or self-disclosures.

In the area of social inadequacy, self-monitoring of the frequency, range, and type of social contacts is particularly useful at a clinical level. In my own experience, the major use has been for evaluating the actual and "potential" social environment of the patient. In clinical work with socially inadequate patients, I typically ask them to self-monitor casual interactions, since these are often the basis for helping the patient establish closer relationships with others. Self-monitoring can also provide a way to assess private events such as cognitions or self-statements, that cannot be assessed in any way other than some form of self-recording.

While there are serious questions about the adequacy of self-monitoring procedures, there are data available which supports the use of these procedures for social activity. For example, Royce and Arkowitz

(1976) found that self-monitoring scores of social interactions correlated significantly with subjects' scores on the Social Avoidance and Distress Scale and with peer-ratings of the subjects' social activity. This latter correlation was reasonably large (r = .65), and is particularly interesting since the peers have the opportunity to observe the subjects' social activities in the natural environment and may be considered to some extent accuracy checks.

Behavioral Measures

Although direct observation in the natural environment is one of the most powerful forms of behavioral assessment. It is not very feasible in the assessment of most social behavior. First, there may not be much to observe; social inadequacy usually involves a low frequency of social contact. Second, the reactive effects of the observer on the situation is likely to be powerful enough to undermine any possible results. Direct observation in the natural environment has been employed in pre-existing social systems such as families, psychiatric wards, and classrooms (Kent & Foster, 1977). Usually, there is a habituation period employed to help the observees adapt to the presence of the observers. With social inadequacy, however, we are not dealing with any particular social system. We are concerned instead with the patient's encounters in a variety of situations with a variety of people. There is usually little opportunity for adaptation, and there is the potential for considerable reactivity, (i.e., consider an observer entering the boss's office with a patient to observe the patient's assertiveness in asking for a raise).

As a result of these considerations, behavioral assessment for social inadequacy has relied very heavily on simulated or role played interactions in the office. There are many variations of the role play procedure. The situations may be enacted and presented on audiotape (e.g., Arkowitz et al., 1975; Goldsmith & McFall, 1975; Perri & Richards, 1979), or they may be role played live using a confederate (e.g., Eisler, Miller, & Hersen, 1973; Melnick, 1973). In addition, discrete situation tests call for a single response (e.g., Eisler, Hersen, Miller, & Blanchard, 1975), while extended interaction tests involve a sequence of interactions between the patient and the confederate (e.g., McFall & Twentyman, 1973). In its most unstructured form, the patient may simply be asked to converse with another person in the laboratory or office in order to assess the patient's performance in a first encounter. The patient may be informed that the other person is a confederate, or there may be some form of deception so that the patient is unaware of this (e.g., McFall & Twentyman, 1973; Melnick, 1973).

One of the earliest discrete situation tests was developed by Rehm and Marston (1968), who presented heterosexual situations to their dating-anxious subjects. The situations were prerecorded and enacted on audiotape; each called for a single response from the subject. For example, one item from Rehm and Marston's Situation Test starts with a male voice describing a situation involving a girl (e.g., "As you are leaving a cafeteria, a girl taps you on the back and says . . ."). A female voice then reads a line of dialogue which the subject is asked to respond aloud to (e.g., "I think you left this book"). Subjects are asked to respond to the situation as they would naturalistically. Their responses are typically rated for skill, anxiety, and adequacy, and scored for such behaviors as latency of response, number of words per response, speech disruptions, and others.

One widely used role-playing task for assertiveness was originally developed by Eisler, Miller, and Hersen (1973). The discrete situation test is known as the Behavioral Assertiveness Test (BAT). In this test, the interaction is with a live confederate. A narrator may describe a situation, such as: "You're in a restaurant with some friends. You order a very rare steak. The waitress brings a steak to the table so well done it looks burned." The confederate says, "I hope you enjoy your dinner, sir." At this point, the subject is expected to respond. The responses are recorded on videotape, which permits the coding of both verbal and nonverbal behaviors. Responses typically scored from such tests include eye contact, smiles, duration of reply, loudness, latency of response, compliance content (i.e., the extent to which the subject complies versus acts assertively), requests for new behavior (e.g., "Get me a new steak cooked the way I ordered it,") and overall assertiveness. The BAT primarily contains items relating to hostile or negative assertiveness. In a revised version of the BAT (the BAT-R) Eisler et al. (1975) added scenes relating to the expression of positive feelings.

More extended forms of role play tests involve either unstructured interactions with live confederates (e.g., Arkowitz et al., 1975; Melnick, 1973) or extended interactions programmed on audiotape. McFall and Twentyman (1973) developed an extended interaction test for assertiveness. More specifically, they studied one aspect of general assertiveness-refusal behavior. In this test, a prerecorded antagonist made an unreasonable request; the subject refused, the antagonist pleaded. If the subject again refused, the antagonist became more insistent. This continued until the subject acquiesced or else refused five times. McFall and Twentyman also had a confederate telephone subjects at home several days after the laboratory assessment. The subjects were unaware who the telephone call was from. The confederate made unreasonable requests of the subject and various aspects of the subject's responses were rated without their awareness.

With only two exceptions, the behavioral tasks described above have been developed and employed primarily with college student populations. The exceptions are the BAT-R (Eisler et al., 1975) and the Interpersonal Behavior Roleplaying Test (Goldsmith & McFall, 1975). There are two recent role-play tests developed specifically for use with adult clinical populations. Curran, Monti, Corriveau, Hay, Hagerman, Zwick, and Farrell (1980) developed a discrete situation test covering a wide range of social situations. The situations are role played with live confederates and involve one prompt after the patient's initial response. Trower et al. (1978) developed a social interaction test in which the patient is asked to interact with a man and woman in a three-way interaction. The man and woman are confederates and the three are given instructions to carry on a conversation and to get to know each other. Trower et al. (1978) have also developed a rather extensive coding system for evaluating the patient's behavior during this social interaction. The coding system involves a 29-item rating scale in which the subject is rated on different aspects of their performance. For example, the rating scale for voice volume ranges from "normal volume" through "abnormally loud and unpleasant or abnormally quiet and often inaudible." This coding system is of interest because it is one of the more exhaustive attempts to specify potentially important dimensions of interpersonal behavior. The coding system includes ratings of voice quality (volume, tone, pitch, clarity, pace, speech disturbances), non-verbal behaviors (proximity, orientation, appearance, face, gaze, posture tonus, posture position, gesture, autistic gesture) and conversation (length, generality, formality, variety, humor, non-verbal grammar, feedback, meshing, turn taking, questions, supportive routines, assertive routines, behavior in public, situation specific routines). More specific definitions of these categories may be found in Trower et al. (1978). In addition, the raters also evaluate the patients by making ratings on such adjectives as: warm, happy, socially anxious, socially skilled, passive, and others.

As you can see, there is enormous variation in the manner in which the situations are presented, the content of the situations, and the behavioral performance dimensions which are coded. In general, ratings of social skill and anxiety from role-play tests have shown good validity when known contrasted groups are employed. In one of the few careful psychometric studies of judges' ratings based on a situation test, Curran et al. (1980) showed that the judges' ratings had adequate psychometric properties. More specifically, judges' ratings from the situation test were found to have good generalizability across judges, good agreement between judges, and good discriminant validity between the attributes of social skill and social anxiety.

Although general performance ratings have shown reasonable validity, the picture is considerably more mixed when it comes to an examination of the specific behavior validity derived from the role-play tests. This is unfortunate, since one of the advantages of these tests is their potential for providing a description of the patient's specific behavior in specific situations which can be useful for treatment planning. In the area of minimal dating, relatively few behavioral differences have been found between active, comfortable daters versus inactive and anxious daters, despite the finding that general ratings of performance often have discriminated between the groups (e.g., Arkowitz et al., 1975).

In the area of assertiveness, more clear behavioral differences have been found. For example, Eisler, et al. (1975) compared high and low assertive psychiatric patients on a number of behavioral measures derived from the BAT-R. Of the 12 behaviors studied, nine significantly discriminated between the groups. The groups differed on number of smiles, affect, duration of reply, speech disturbances, and loudness, compliance content, requests for new behavior, praise, and spontaneous positive behavior. There were no significant differences on duration of eye contact, latency of response, and appreciation.

Trower (1980) used a live, extended role-play test which covered general social functioning in interacting with male and female strangers. He compared psychiatric patients who were rated as socially skilled with another group rated unskilled. Trower found that the skilled patients spoke, looked, smiled, and gestured more than unskilled patients. Another interesting finding of this study was that the skilled group also showed more variability in their behavior in response to situation changes.

One of the real difficulties in evaluating these situation tests is similar to one we encountered in our discussion of self-report measures: there are few "standard" role-play tests that have been employed in more than a few studies. Instead, each study seems to generate a new item pool, mode of presentation, and response alternatives. As a result, it is extremely difficult to make any generalizations about the adequacy of role-play tests for social skill. It is only recently that the psychometric properties of some of these tests have been studied intensively (see Curran et al., 1980) in some form other than a contrasted groups design. We clearly need more intensive study of a few of the more promising tests, rather than the continued development of new ones.

Validational studies using contrasted groups provide one kind of information about the psychometric properties of role-play tests. Another kind of validation relates to external validity and the extent to which observed responses during simulated interactions are an accurate and valid sample of how the patient responds in similar naturalistic situations. This is a particularly important question since the main rationale for these tests is to provide an accurate sample of the patient's performance in the real-life social situations. Recently, Bellack, Hersen, and their associates have conducted an important series of investigations on the external validity of social skill role-play tests. Bellack, Hersen, and Turner (1978) conducted two studies to examine the validity of the BAT-R. In their second study, the performance of psychiatric patients was compared in three settings: including the BAT-R, a structured interview, and a group therapy situation. The main question involved the correspondence of behaviors across situations. If behavior on the role-play tests accurately reflects behavior in other situations, there should be high correlations among similar behavior classes across situations. A patient with a high degree of eye contact on the BAT-R would be expected to show a high degree during the structured interview and group therapy. The results indicated that there was virtually no correspondence across the three situations for the different behaviors under study.

Bellack, Hersen, and Lamparski (1979) compared the behavior of college students in a role play heterosexual interaction test. One week later, the students were surreptitiously observed while they interacted with an opposite-sex student who was actually a confederate. Behaviors during the role-play test and the live interaction were coded using similar categories of behavior. The question of correspondence of behaviors across situations was again examined. For female subjects, behavioral measures in the role-play situation were moderately correlated with those same behaviors in the more naturalistic interactions. However, there were few significant relationships for males. Once again, the external validity of role-play tests was seriously called into question.

The studies discussed above are open to the criticism that role-play situations were not identical to the other situations. This lack of correspondence might have been due to differences among the situations rather than to the poor validity of the role-play measures. What we really need to know is whether we can predict behavior in naturalistic situations from observations of performance in very similar role-played situations. Bellack, Hersen, and Turner (1979) addressed this issue directly in a cleverly designed experiment. In this study, psychiatric inpatients were given the BAT-R role-play test of assertiveness. The subjects were also exposed to some of the same situations from the role-playing test in naturalistic situations on the ward. Subjects were not aware that the ward situations were a part of the experiment or that they were being assessed during these encounters. For example, an item of the BAT-R involved asking the subject to perform an unfair favor. This same situation was also staged by a staff member or research assistant on the ward with the patients. The same behaviors were coded from the role played and naturalistic situations. While there were significant correlations for some behavior categories across the two situations (e.g., latency of response, eye contact, and compliance), these correlations were rather low. In addition, there were not any significant correlations across the situations for several other behaviors.

While these studies raise serious questions about the external validity of role-play tests of social skill, we should not necessarily rule out this method of assessment entirely. One important difference between the role-play and naturalistic samples relates to the potential consequences of the subject's responses. In role-play tests, the subject knows that the social consequences of an inadequate response are relatively minor, while in the naturalistic situation the consequences could have a significant impact on the individual. For example, a subject who is presented with a role-play situation involving asking a girl for a date would not be very concerned about rejection from the girl since he knows that it is a role-played situation. However, concern about rejection in the naturalistic situation would probably be much greater and could influence the subject's performance in the naturalistic situation. It is likely that the closer we can come to replicating the naturalistic situations in the role-play tests, the greater their external validity will be. Thus, surreptitious observations of the subject's behavior with a confederate (with the subject unaware that his/her partner is a confederate) might provide more representative and externally valid samples of behavior. In such situations, the correlations between role play and naturalistic performance might be greater.

Another issue to consider is that role-play situations *require* the subjects to respond, and may be tapping the subject's behavioral repertoire and potential, rather than the way in which they actually handle the situation. For example, the role-play situations may reveal that the subject has adequate skills, while self-monitoring and interview assessment may reveal that subject avoids performance in those situations due to unrealistic anxiety and negative evaluations of his skills. In this sense, role-play tests would not necessarily be expected to correlate with performance in the naturalistic situation, but might provide an index of the skill repertoire of the patient. Nonetheless, these remain only speculations; despite the superficial appeal of role-play tests, the research of Bellack, Hersen, and their associates raises some serious concerns about what generalizations can be drawn from these tests of social skill.

EXAMPLE OF ASSESSMENT IN A CASE OF SOCIAL INADEQUACY

Kathy was a 24-year-old young woman referred to me by the Department of Vocational Rehabilitation. She had sought help in finding employment and schooling, and it was felt that her social difficulties needed attention and would interfere with her employability and schoolwork.

She was a plain but pleasant-looking young woman, who was about 40 pounds overweight. During the initial interview, she was extremely nervous and close to tears most of the time, although she seemed to relax as the interviews progressed.

The interview format outlined in Table 9.1 was followed over the course of several initial assessment interviews. Her own description of her problem was "confusion, depression, and upset." In attempting to operationalize these constructs during the interview, three major areas emerged. The major problem seemed to be social anxiety and isolation with both men and women, although her anxieties were much greater with men. She had very few friends and had not dated at all during the past six years; before then she had dated very little. She had met and married a man when she was 17, and had one child. Her husband was a drug dealer and physically abusive to her. The relationship deteriorated within a year. She left him and entered a transient life involving heavy drug usage, including drugs of all kinds. She reported being "out of it" most of the time, and remembered very little of this period of her life. She recently decided to build a better life for herself, relocated, and enrolled in a community college. She reported that she currently had no close friends and few casual friends. She was very frightened of dating and very fearful of entering into any relationship with a man. She also reported considerable depression, which was the second major problem. She blamed herself for her past confusion and felt she had little to offer to other people. She also believed she was "stupid" and "unattractive." Her third problem area was obesity; she was markedly overweight and this, as well as her inattention to her appearance, were major obstacles to effective social functioning.

The major effects of her problems were social isolation and depressive ruminations. She was relatively unable to initiate any social contacts and had a hard time continuing in school because of her social fears. School was an important area for her in reconstituting her life, but the social anxieties significantly interfered with progress at school.

From the interview, she expressed considerable fears about most areas of social performance and evaluated her abilities in each of the areas quite negatively. The area which seemed most threatening to her concerned casual and intimate contact with men. Kathy's fears of intimacy were also associated with fears of any sexual relationship with a man, but, she did not seem to have any interest in homosexual relationships.

Her current living arrangement was an isolated one. She lived in a small apartment with her daughter and had little to do with other people. Apart from working in a day care center at a local church, she had little interest in leisure activities and had few enjoyable activities in her life. She described a rather chaotic family background with a mother who was severely depressed much of the time and a father who was alcoholic. She had some good years during high school, but after her divorce, she described her life as bleak and as a "blur."

Interview information suggested that Kathy had quite serious and longstanding problems. While she clearly had severe social anxiety in a number of areas and was quite self-critical and depressed, it was not clear from the interview what social skills she possessed.

A summary of the assessment data is presented in Table 9.2. This table also includes pretreatment assessment, as well as the results of posttreatment assessment. The self-report data presented in the table largely confirm many of the interview impressions. She scored considerably above the mean on the Social Avoidance and Distress Scale and on many of the Factor Scales of the Social Anxiety Inventory, particularly on fear of disapproval or negative evaluation and anxiety about heterosexual contact. She was also noticeably sub-assertive, as shown by her scores on the Adult Self-Expression Scale. In addition, she was clinically depressed (as shown by the Beck Depression Inventory).

Self-monitoring data revealed an extreme degree of social isolation. While she had a few contacts with women, her contacts with men were even more limited. Her social range (number of different people with whom she interacted) was similarly restricted.

The behavioral measures were based on two unstructured 10-minute conversations, one with a man and one with a woman. Both partners were confederates, a fact of which Kathy was aware. Observers rated her performance during these interactions, and she was asked to do self-ratings as well. The results from the behavioral performance test showed considerable anxiety and a skill deficit based on both self- and observer ratings. Her anxiety and skill problems were noticeably more severe with men than with women. It is interesting to note that her overly critical set was reflected by the frequent discrepancies between her self-ratings and the observer ratings.

The picture that emerged was of a woman with quite severe social inadequacy associated with depression and sub-assertiveness. Her problems also seemed to be a combination of skill deficit along with anxiety, overly negative evaluations, and fears of rejection. As a result, treatment was multi-faceted including a psychodynamic approach to help

Table 9.2. Summary of Assessment Data for a Socially Inadequate Patient

Measure	Pretreatment Score	Posttreatment Score
Self-Report		
Social Avoidance and Distress Scale[a] (Watson & Friend, 1969)	29	16*
Social Anxiety Inventory[b] (Richardson & Tasto, 1976)		
1. Fears of disapproval or negative evaluation	4.2	3.3*
2. Social assertiveness or visibility	3.5	3.6
3. Confrontation and anger expression	2.8	3.0
4. Heterosexual contact	4.8	3.2*
5. Intimacy and interpersonal warmth	3.8	3.5
6. Conflict with or rejection by parents	2.2	2.2
7. Interpersonal loss	2.5	2.1
Adult Self-Expression Scale (Assertiveness)[c] (Gay, Hollandsworth, & Galassi, 1975)	88	102
Beck Depresion Inventory[d] (Beck, 1967)	24	13*
Diary of Social Activity During 7-Day Period		
1. Total number of social interactions (men + women)	10	37*
2. Number of interactions with men	1	5*
3. Number of interactions with women	9	32*
4. Range of social interactions (Number of different men and women)	8	19*
5. Range of interactions with men	1	4*
6. Range of interactions with women	7	15*
Extended Interaction with Male Confederate[e]		
1. Self-rating of social anxiety	5	3.5*
2. Observer ratings of social anxiety	3.8	3.2*
3. Self-ratings of social skill	2	2.2
4. Observer ratings of social skill	2.7	3.2*
Extended Interaction with Female Confederate		
1. Self-rating of social anxiety	3.5	2*
2. Observer rating of social anxiety	3.3	2.5*
3. Self-rating of social skill	3.0	4*
4. Observer rating of social skill	2.7	3.5*

Notes
[a] The norms for the SAD are a mean of 9, standard deviation of 8
[b] These scores on the SAI reflect item means based on 1–5 ratings with 1 indicating low anxiety and 5 high anxiety
[c] For females, the normative mean was 115 with a standard deviation of 21
[d] Scores over 13 or 14 usually indicate moderate depression according to Beck (1967)
[e] These were ratings based on 1—5 scales. Scores of 1 indicate low degrees of anxiety and skilll while scores of 5 indicate high degrees of anxiety and skill
* Indicates noteworthy change in a positive direction (reduced anxiety, increased skill, increased activity)

her define her problems and reduce her confusion, a supportive approach to help her continue with school and start a new life in her new place of residence, and a combination of behavioral strategies to help increase her skill level, decrease her anxiety and negative self-evaluations, and lose weight. Treatment lasted for 1½ years, varying from once a week to twice a week. Behavioral strategies were social skills training including modeling, behavior rehearsal, feedback, homework, as well as imaginal desensitization. Due to her extreme fear of heterosexual contact, the initial focus was on increasing her skill, comfort, and activity with same-sex friends and with later emphasis on opposite-sex relationships. A weight reduction program was also utilized.

While the results of treatment were generally positive in most areas, the changes that occurred in her heterosexual functioning were minimal. She was somewhat more comfortable with men at the end of treatment, but still did not feel ready to begin dating. She was doing well at school and had formed a few friendships. While she was also more assertive and less depressed, there was still considerable room for progress on all dimensions. This illustrates a point made by Arkowitz, Levine, Grosscup, O'Neal, Youngren, Royce, and Largay (1976), that clinical work with socially inadequate patients is often much slower and has less powerful effects than what is typically seen in analogue studies with mildly distressed college students.

SUMMARY AND FUTURE DIRECTIONS

There have been many advances in the assessment of social inadequacy. Researchers have recently turned their attention away from an exclusive focus on mildly distressed college volunteers to the assessment of social inadequacy in more severely dysfunctional adult populations.

There are many unresolved issues facing researchers and clinicians in the field. At a theoretical level, we need to progress toward a more precise conceptualization of social skill which takes into account a number of parameters. Some suggested parameters include: content versus consequences of social responses; situational specificity; social sensitivity and perception; analyses of behavioral sequences; determination of skills deficits versus performance inhibitions; and the role of physical appearance.

At the level of available assessment instruments, we need to pay considerably more attention to the psychometric properties of our assessment procedures. While there are some very promising starts in the areas of self-report, self-monitoring, and behavioral measures of various

components of social inadequacy, we still have relatively little data on
the psychometric adequacy of these instruments. Although there are a
number of self-report instruments which have reasonably well-demon-
strated reliability and validity, we are still faced with serious questions
about the accuracy and reliability of these procedures. In addition, serious questions remain about the external validity of role-play tests and
the ability of these tests to predict the patient's performance in naturalistic situations. This suggests extreme caution in drawing any inferences about the patient's naturalistic performance from role-play tests.
The continuing proliferation of new instruments is also a problem. A
recurrent theme of this chapter has been the need to more carefully
study the reliability and validity of the more promising existing instruments, rather than racing to develop some "new" measure for similar constructs.

Another issue relates to the diagnosis of social inadequacy. Social
inadequacy does not appear to be a unitary disorder, but one consisting
of a number of different sub-categories. Writers have just begun to
address this issue and the work of Curran and Wessberg (in press) is
a promising start in this direction.

Given the progress we have made in a relatively few years of studying
social inadequacy, I am hopeful that we will have clearer answers to
some of these questions in the near future.

REFERENCES

Argyle, M., Trower, P., & Bryant, B. Explorations in the treatment of personality
disorders and neuroses by social skills training. *British Journal of Medical Psy-
chology,* 1974, *47,* 63–72.
Arkowitz, H. Measurement and modification of minimal dating behavior. In M. Hersen,
R. Eisler, & P. Miller (Eds.), *Progress in behavior modification.* Vol. 5. New York:
Academic Press, 1977.
Arkowitz, H., Lichtenstein, E., McGovern, K., & Hines, P. The behavioral assessment
of social competence in males. *Behavior Therapy,* 1975, *6,* 3–13.
Arkowitz, H., Royce, W. S., Levine, A. G., Largay, D., O'Neill, A., & Youngren,
M. A. *Clinical applications of social skills training: Issues and limitations in gen-
eralization from analogue studies.* Paper presented at the annual meeting of the As-
sociation for the Advancement of Behavior Therapy, New York, 1976.
Bandura, A. *Social learning theory.* Englewood Cliffs, N.J.: Prentice-Hall, 1977.
Beck, A. T. *Depression: Causes and treatment.* Philadelphia: University of Pennsylvania
Press, 1967.
Bellack, A. S. A critical appraisal of strategies for assessing social skill. *Behavioral
Assessment,* 1979, *1,* 157–176. (a)
Bellack, A. S. Behavioral assessment of social skills. In A. S. Bellack & M. Hersen
(Eds.), *Research and practice in social skill training.* New York: Plenum, 1979, p.
75–104. (b)

Bellack, A. S. & Hersen M. (Eds.) *Research and practice in social skills training.* New York: Plenum, 1979.

Bellack, A. S., Hersen, M., & Lamparski, D. Role play tests for assessing social skills: Are they valid? Are they useful? *Journal of Consulting and Clinical Psychology,* 1979, *47,* 335–342.

Bellack, A. S., Hersen, M., & Turner, S. M. Role play tests for assessing social skills: Are they valid? *Behavior Therapy,* 1978, *9,* 448–461.

Bellack, A. S., Hersen, M., & Turner, S. M. The relationship of role playing and knowledge of appropriate behavior to assertion in the natural environment. *Journal of Consulting and Clinical Psychology,* 1979, *47,* 670–678.

Berscheid, E., & Walster, E. Physical attractiveness. In L. Berkowitz (Ed.), *Advances in experimental and social pscychology,* Vol. 7. New York: Academic Press, 1973.

Bryant, B. M., & Trower, P. E. Social difficulty in a student sample. *British Journal of Educational Psychology,* 1974, *44,* 13–21.

Bryant, B. M., Trower, P., Yardley, K., Urbieta, H., & Letemendia, F. A survey of social inadequacy among psychiatric outpatients. *Psychological Medicine,* 1976, *6,* 101–112.

Christensen, A., Arkowitz, H., & Anderson, J. Practice dating as treatment for college dating inhibitions. *Behaviour Research and Therapy,* 1975, *13,* 321–331.

Ciminero, A., Nelson, R. O., & Lipinski, D. Self-monitoring procedures. In A. R. Ciminero, K. R. Calhoun, & H. E. Adams (Eds.), *Handbook of behavioral assessment.* New York: Wiley, 1977.

Clark, J. V., & Arkowitz, H. Social anxiety and self-evaluation of interpersonal performance. *Psychological Reports,* 1975, *36,* 211–221.

Curran, J. P. Skills training as an approach to the treatment of heterosexual-social anxiety. A review. *Psychological Bulletin,* 1977, *84,* 140–157.

Curran, J. P., & Gilbert, F. S. A test of the relative effectiveness of a systematic desensitization program and an interpersonal skills training program with date anxious subjects. *Behavior Therapy,* 1975, *6,* 510–521.

Curran, J. P., & Wessberg, H. The assessment of social inadequacy. In D. H. Barlow (Ed.), *Behavioral assessment of adult disorders.* New York: Guilford Press, in press.

Curran, J. P., Corriveau, D. P., Monti, P. M., & Hagerman, S. Social skill and social anxiety: Self-report measurement in a psychiatric population. *Behavior Modification,* 1980, *4,* 493–512.

Curran, J. P., Miller, I., Zwick, W., Monti, M., & Stout, R. The socially inadequate patient: Incidence rate, demographic features, and hospital and posthospital functioning. *Journal of Consulting and Clinical Psychology,* 1980, *48,* 375–382.

Curran, J., Monti, P., Corriveau, D., Hay, L., Hagerman, S., Zwick, W., & Farrell, A. The generalizability of a procedure for assessing social skills and social anxiety in a psychiatric population. *Behavioral Assessment,* 1980, *4,* 389–402.

Eisler, R. M. Behavioral assessment of social skills. In M. Hersen & A. S. Bellack (Eds.), *Behavioral assessment: A practical handbook.* New York: Pergamon, 1976.

Eisler, R. M., Miller, P. M., & Hersen, M. Components of assertive behavior. *Journal of Clinical Psychology,* 1973, *29,* 295–299.

Eisler, R. M., Hersen, M., Miller, P. M., & Blanchard, E. B. Situational determinants of assertive behavior. *Journal of Consulting and Clinical Psychology,* 1975, *43,* 330–340.

Ekman, P., Friesen, W., & Ellsworth, P. *Emotion in the human face: Guidelines for research and an integration of findings.* New York: Pergamon Press, 1972.

Fischetti, M., Curran, J. P., & Wessberg, H. W. Sense of timing: A skill deficit in heterosexual-socially anxious males. *Behavior Modification,* 1977, *1,* 179–194.

Galassi, J. P., DeLo, J. S., Galassi, M. D., & Bastien, S. The college self-expression scale: A measure of assertiveness. *Behavior Therapy*, 1974, *5*, 165–171.

Galassi, J. P., & Galassi, M. D. Modification of heterosocial skills deficits. In A. S. Bellack & M. Hersen (Eds.), *Research and practice in social skills training*. New York: Plenum, 1979.

Gay, M., Hollandsworth, J., & Galassi, J. An assertiveness inventory for adults. *Journal of Counseling Psychology*, 1975, *22*, 340–344.

Glasgow, R. E., & Arkowitz, H. The behavioral assessment of male and female social competence in dyadic heterosexual interactions. *Behavior Therapy*, 1975, *6*, 488–498.

Glass, C. R., Gottman, J. M., & Shmurak, S. H. Response-acquisition and cognitive self-statement modification approaches to dating-skills training. *Journal of Counseling Psychology*, 1976, *23*, 520–526.

Glass, C. R., & Merluzzi, T. V. *Approaches to the cognitive assessment of social anxiety*. Paper presented at the annual meeting of the Association for the Advancement of Behavior Therapy, Chicago, 1978.

Goldfried, M. R., & D'Zurilla, T. J. A behavioral-analytic model for assessing competence. In C. D. Spielberger (Ed.), *Current topics in clinical psychology*. Vol. 1. New York: Academic Press, 1969.

Goldsmith, J. B., & McFall, R. M. Development and evaluation of an interpersonal skill-training program for psychiatric inpatients. *Journal of Abnormal Psychology*, 1975, *84*, 51–58.

Gottman, J. *Marital interactions: Experimental investigations*. New York: Academic Press, 1979.

Haynes, S., & Jensen, B. The interview as a behavioral assessment instrument. *Behavioral Assessment*, 1979, *1*, 97–106.

Hersen, M., & Bellack, A. S. Assessment of social skills. In A. R. Ciminero, K. R. Calhoun, & H. E. Adams (Eds.), *Handbook of behavioral assessment*. New York: Wiley, 1977.

Himadi, W., Arkowitz, H., Hinton, R., & Perl, J. Minimal dating and its relationship to other social problems and general adjustment. *Behavior Therapy*, 1980, *11*, 345–352.

Kent, R., & Foster, S. Direct observational procedures: Methodological issues in naturalistic settings. In A. R. Ciminero, K. R. Calhoun, & H. E. Adams (Eds.), *Handbook of behavioral assessment*. New York: Wiley, 1977.

Levenson, R. W., & Gottman, J. M. Toward the assessment of social competence. *Journal of Consulting and Clinical Psychology*, 1978, *46*, 453–462.

Libet, J. M., & Lewinsohn, P. M. Concept of social skill with special reference to the behavior of depressed persons. *Journal of Consulting and Clinical Psychology*, 1973, *40*, 304–312.

Lowe, M. R., & Cautela, J. R. A self-report measure of social skill. *Behavior Therapy*, 1978, *9*, 535–544.

McFall, R. M., & Lillesand, D. B. Behavior rehearsal with modeling and coaching in assertion training. *Journal of Abnormal Psychology*, 1971, *77*, 313–323.

McFall, R. M., & Twentyman, C. T. Four experiments on the relative contributions of rehearsal, modeling, and coaching to assertion training. *Journal of Abnormal Psychology*, 1973, *81*, 199–218.

Melnick, J. A comparison of replication techniques in the modification of minimal dating behavior. *Journal of Abnormal Psychology*, 1973, *81*, 51–59.

Meyer, V., Liddell, A., & Lyons, M. Behavioral interviews. In A. R. Ciminero, K. R. Calhoun, & H. R. Adams (Eds.), *Handbook of behavioral assessment*. New York: Wiley, 1977.

Morganstern, K. Behavioral interviewing: The initial stages of assessment. In M. Hersen & A. S. Bellack (Eds.), *Behavioral assessment: A practical handbook.* New York: Pergamon, 1976.

Morrison, R. L., & Bellack, A. The role of social perception in social skills. *Behavior Therapy,* in press.

Perri, M. G., & Richards, C. S. Assessment of heterosocial skills in male college students: Empirical development of a behavior role-playing test. *Behavior Modification,* 1979, *3,* 337–354.

Phibbs, J., & Arkowitz, H. Minimal dating, assertiveness, and depression. *Behavioral Counseling Quarterly,* in press.

Rathus, S. A. A 30-item schedule for assessing assertive behavior. *Behavior Therapy,* 1973, *4,* 398–406.

Reese, S., Arkowitz, H., & White, G. *Depression, physical appearance, and interpersonal attraction.* Unpublished manuscript, University of Arizona, 1980.

Rehm, L. P., & Marston, A. R. Reduction of social anxiety through modification of self-reinforcement: An instigation therapy technique. *Journal of Consulting and Clinical Psychology,* 1968, *32,* 565–574.

Richardson, F. C., & Tasto, D. L. Development and factor analysis of a social anxiety inventory. *Behavior Therapy,* 1976, *7,* 453–462.

Rosenthal, R., Hall, J. A., DiMatteo, M., Rogers, P., & Archer, D. *Sensitivity to nonverbal communications: the PONS test.* Baltimore: The Johns Hopkins University Press, 1979.

Royce, W. S., & Arkowitz, H. Multimodal evaluation of practice interactions as treatment for social isolation. *Journal of Consulting and Clinical Psychology,* 1978, *46,* 239–245.

Schwartz, R. M., & Gottman, J. M. Toward a task analysis of assertive behavior. *Journal of Consulting and Clinical Psychology,* 1976, *44,* 910–920.

Trower, P. Situational analysis of the components and processes of behavior of socially skilled and unskilled patients. *Journal of Consulting and Clinical Psychology,* 1980, *48,* 327–339.

Trower, P., Bryant, B., & Argyle, M. *Social skills and mental health.* London: Methuen, 1978.

Twentyman, C. T., & McFall, R. M. Behavioral training of social skills in shy males. *Journal of Consulting and Clinical Psychology,* 1975, *43,* 384–395.

Twentyman, C. T., & Zimering, R. T. Behavioral training of social skills: A critical review. In M. Hersen, R. Eisler, & P. Miller (Eds.), *Progress in behavior modification.* New York: Academic Press, 1979.

Wallander, J., Conger, A., Mariotto, M., Curran, J., & Farrell, A. Comparability of selection instruments in studies of heterosexual-social problem behaviors. *Behavior Therapy,* 1980, *11,* 548–560.

Watson, D., & Friend, R. Measurement of social-evaluative anxiety. *Journal of Consulting and Clinical Psychology,* 1969, *33,* 448–457.

Williams, C. L., & Ciminero, A. R. Development and validation of a heterosocial skills inventory: The Survey of Heterosexual Interactions for Females. *Journal of Consulting and Clinical Psychology,* 1978, *46,* 1547–1548.

Wolpe, J., & Lazarus, A. A. *Behavior therapy techniques.* New York: Pergamon, 1966.

Chapter 10

Assessment of Psychotic Behavior

Charles J. Wallace

INTRODUCTION

The title of this chapter paradoxically implies too much and too little about its scope. The chapter will *not* survey the plethora of methods to assess thought disorder, the one class of behavior that is indeed the hallmark of schizophrenic psychopathology. Just thumbing through a few years of the *Schizophrenia Bulletin,* the *Journal of Abnormal Psychology,* and the *Archives of General Psychiatry* turns up scores of studies that measure thought disorder in scores of ways, ranging from laboratory-based measures of attention, through ratings of patients' responses, to Rorschach cards, and psychiatrists' ratings of incoherence. Since the focus of this book is on behavioral assessment with the emphasis on practical methods that have relevance for treatment, such measures seem irrelevant. The reader interested in these measures should consult reviews by Neale and Cromwell (1970), Cromwell (1975), Nuechterlein (1977), and Chapman (1979).

This chapter will survey the methods of assessment used in the behavioral treatment of psychotic individuals. Specifically, the "behavioral literature" (*Behavior Therapy, Behavior Modification, Journal of Applied Behavior Analysis, Journal of Behavior Therapy and Experimental Psychiatry, Behaviour Research and Therapy, Journal of Consulting and Clinical Psychology, Journal of Behavioral Assessment, Behavioral Assessment*) was scoured to identify reports of the treatment of various excesses and deficits of psychotic individuals; the assessment methods were abstracted and will be reviewed.

This chapter is organized in terms of the relevance of the assessment information for treatment decisions. The prototypical intervention involves specification and continual assessment of a behavior that is the "target" of the intervention; the assessment provides information that is directly relevant to the decision to continue, change, or terminate treatment. One section of this chapter will summarize the methods of measuring and recording various targeted excesses and deficits. Another class of assessment procedures involves direct observation and recording of behaviors that are not the targets of the intervention. The assessment provides information either about a large scale "unit," such as an inpatient ward or a day hospital facility, or about the generalization of treatment effects to different behaviors, settings, or times. Another section will summarize these assessment methods. Finally, assessment methods that use rating scales will be summarized. Although rating scales have not always been looked upon favorably in the behavioral literature, they have proven sensitive to treatment effects and are relatively inexpensive to administer.

It should be noted that interventions and their effects will not be discussed here. Rather, measurement and recording procedures will be summarized to aid the reader in consulting the relevant studies before implementing his/her own assessment strategy. However, the measurement and recording procedures used with one class of treatment techniques need to be summarized separately. The reports of token economies often barely mention the targeted excesses and deficits and give more space to discussing outcomes measured by the distribution of tokens, the percentages of patients discharged, decreases in "psychotism," etc. This literature will be summarized first.

TOKEN ECONOMIES

Token economies are generally used in settings such as inpatient wards and day hospital facilities to organize staff and patients into a manageable and measurable treatment program. Given the behavioral emphasis, the goals of the program are often stated in terms of the desired levels of performance of various behaviors grouped into classes, such as self-care, interpersonal, and vocational skills. Since both the desired levels of performance and the means to achieve them are applicable to all patients, most of the reports of token economies focus on the outcomes of the program as a whole. The outcomes are often operationalized as the number of tokens distributed, the percentage of patients achieving the desired level of performance, mean increases in "positive" and decreases in "negative" subscales of a rating scale, the num-

ber of patients discharged, etc. Rarely is report space devoted to describing the methods of measuring and recording the many specific
behaviors that are the targets of the token economy and that constitute
a given class of behavior. Hence, this section will review the methods
that have been used to assess the outcomes of token economies.

There are some notable exceptions to the skimpy descriptions of targeted excesses and deficits (Ayllon & Azrin, 1965, 1968a; Nelson &
Cone, 1979; Paul & Lentz, 1977); the reader is urged to consult these
reports, and they will be reviewed in later sections of this chapter. There
are also several comprehensive summaries of the token economy literature that the reader might wish to consult (Carlson, Hersen, & Eisler,
1972; Gripp & Magaro, 1974; Hersen, 1976; Kazdin, 1975, 1977, 1978;
Kazdin & Bootzin, 1972; Patterson, 1976; Stahl & Leitenberg, 1976).

Tokens Distributed

The day-to-day operation of a token economy provides the opportunity
to record information along five dimensions: time, patient, behavior,
staff member, and "back-up" items. A specific staff member at a specific time and day can distribute tokens to patients for performing a
desired or an undesired behavior (earnings and fines). A patient can
exchange tokens with a specific staff member to obtain a desired "back-
up" item (purchases). All of this information can be recorded and then
collapsed to yield summary measures of the effectiveness of the token
economy. The information can be collapsed across staff members and
tasks to obtain the number of tokens earned by a specific patient on
a certain day; a mean can be calculated across a block of days to obtain
a rate of token earnings, a convenient index of a patient's performance
of desired behaviors. The information can be further collapsed across
patients to obtain an index of the performance of desired behaviors for
the program as a whole. Comparisons of rate of earnings across different
time periods can provide estimates of the progress of the patient or of
the program. Similar indices can be calculated for fines, purchases, or
any combination of earnings, fines, and purchases (e.g., savings, proportion of fines to earnings, etc.).

Table 10.1 lists the token economies that have used the distribution
of tokens as a measure of outcome. For example, Doty, McInnis, and
Paul (1974) used fines, payment of fines, and purchases averaged across
the 28 patients participating in their token economy to evaluate the
effects of a new procedure to pay off fines. As expected, payment of
fines and purchases were favorably affected. Upper (1973) evaluated
a fining procedure by monitoring weekly fines averaged across the 30

Table 10.1. Classification of Outcome Measures Used by Various Token Economy Studies

STUDY	Tokens Distribution	Percent Completion	Patient Movement	Direct Behavioral Observation	Scales and Tests[1]
				CLASS OF OUTCOME MEASURE	
Atthowe & Krasner	X		X		
Lloyd & Garlington	X				
Feingold & Migler	X				
Henderson & Scoles	X				
Hersen et al.	X				
Hall et al.	X	X			Numerous (see text)
Pickens et al.	X				MMPI
Cohen et al.	X				
Upper	X				
Doty et al.	X	X			
Ayllon & Azrin		X			
Heap et al.		X	X		
Hollander et al.		X			
Winkler		X			
Shean & Zeidberg		X	X		MACC-II; key
Glickman et al.		X			press
Gershone et al.		X			Menninger; NOSIE-30 HSRS; BPRS
Arann & Horner		X			
McReynolds & Coleman		X	X		
Paul & Lentz		X	X	TSBC SRIC	NOSIE-30; ISMF MSBS; OMI; TOS
Grzesiak & Locke		X			MACC; Locus of Control; Barron's; IES; NOSIE-30
Nelson & Cone		X	X	BOI	
Olson & Greenberg		X		PAC	SABRS
Greenberg et al.			X		
Pomerleau et al.			X		WBI
Steffy et al.			X		PRP; MSBS
Miller & Dermer			X		
Fullerton et al.			X		
Lloyd & Abel			X		
Hollingsworth & Foreyt			X		
Rybolt			X		NOSIE-30
Rostow & Smith				BOWS	MACC
Schaefer & Martin				BSF	
Gripp & Magaro	X			No name given	NOSIE-30; PRP; WAS; MSBS: Elgin

Table 10.1. (continued)

Maley et al.	MACC-II; 5 tasks
Schwartz & Bellack	NOSIE-30
Elliott et al.	NOSIE-30; PRP; Wing & Brown Scales
Marks et al.	Numerous (see text)
Kowalski et al.	NOSIE-30
Milby et al.	COPES
Hartlage	HAS

[1] Full names of scales:
MMPI = Minnesota Multiphasic Personalty Inventory
MACC = Mood, Affect, Cooperation, Communication Scale
NOSIE-30 = Nurses Observation Scale for Inpatient Evaluation-30
HSRS = Health Sickness Rating Scale
BPRS = Brief Psychiatric Rating Scale
ISMF = Inpatient Scale of Minimal Functioning
MSBS = Minimal Social Behavior Scale
OMI = Opinions About Mental Illness
IES = Impulse — Ego — Superego Test
Barron's = Barron's Ego-Strength Scale
PRP = Psychotic Reaction Profile
WAS = Ward Atmosphere Scale
TOS = Therapist Orientation Sheet
SABRS = Social Adjustment Behavior Scale
WBI = Ward Behavior Inventory
COPES = Community Oriented Psychiatric Environment Scale
HAS = Hospital Adjustment Scale
TSBC = Time Sample Behavior Checklist
SRIC = Staff Resident Interaction Chronograph
BOI = Behavioral Observation Instrument
PAC = Patient Activity Checklist
BOWS = Behavior on the Ward Scale
BSF = Behavior Study Form

patients participating in this study. He found that fines reduced across the 8 weeks of treatment compared to 2 weeks of baseline.

Of course, a measure that involves collapsing across information "loses" the information for further analysis. It is not possible to identify which of the 16 behaviors fined by Upper (1973) actually declined and which did not. The Doty et al. (1974) measure does not allow identification of the patients who paid their fines and those who did not. In contrast, Pickens, Errickson, Thompson, Heston, and Eckert (1979) collapsed across staff and days (and probably across some behaviors) to calculate: tokens earned for attending meals, cleaning rooms, completing self-care tasks and ward jobs, and attending classes; points lost (collapsed across fined behaviors); points spent (collapsed across items purchased); and the proportion of tokens spent to tokens earned.

To use the distribution of tokens as a reliable measure of outcome requires that each token transaction be accurately recorded. It is not easy to meet this requirement since the distribution and recording procedures are often distinctly different events, separated in both time and place. For example, Milby, Willicutt, Hawk, McDonald, and Whitfield (1973) required staff members to record token earnings and purchases on a card that patients carried in their shirt pocket, plus noting on paper pads the target behaviors that were reinforced. This information was transferred to a master sheet at either meal time or a shift change. The accuracy of the system depended upon the staff members' diligence in both noting the target behavior and transferring the information to the master sheet. Several articles have discussed different methods of combining delivery and recording procedures. Coleman and Boren (1969) recorded earnings, fines, and purchases on a daily "data matrix" that was visible to both staff and patients; tokens were not actually distributed. Lehrer, Schiff, and Kris (1970) gave patients plastic credit cards embossed with their names that were used to record transactions on credit card slips. Each slip had a single carbon copy that was retained and used to calculate weekly summaries; the original was given to the patient to use for purchases. Logan (1972) printed paper money in different denominations and colors that included spaces for entering the names of the patient and staff involved in the exchange, the date, and the behavior. Data summarization took place after the money was used to purchase back-up items. The accuracy of this system could be unfavorably affected by anything that kept the money "out of circulation" (savings, loss). Aitchison (1972) designed a data collection system that required staff to record earnings on one of eight cards using punches with heads of various complex shapes. Purchases were recorded by overpunching the earned tokens with another punch that used a simple, round head. The patients carried the cards and turned them in at scheduled times so that transactions could be summarized. Tanner, Parrino, and Daniels (1975) used a system similar to Aitchison's (1972), except that there were only two cards: one for earnings and one for purchases. The cards were collected weekly, keypunched, and then analyzed by computer to provide summaries of activity per patient and per hospital unit. Harris (1977) also used a system similar to Aitchison's (1972), but only one card was used; it was collected daily for summarization of transactions.

A difficulty with measures of earnings is that they are subject to the influence of economic variables such as savings, relative rates of pay for various tasks, and relative costs of back-up items (Fethke, 1972;

Fisher, Winkler, & Krasner, 1978; Hayden, Osborne, Hall, & Hall, 1974; Kagel & Winkler, 1972; Milby, Clarke, Charles, & Willicutt, 1977; Winkler, 1971, 1972). As a patient's savings of tokens tends to accumulate, task performance tends to deteriorate. An interpretation of such results in terms of the declining effectiveness of the contingencies would be incorrect since economic variables would be "at fault." Adjustment of the savings balance should increase performance.

Percent Successful

Table 10.1 lists the token economies that have used the percentage of completions of a task as a measure of outcome. In terms of recording the time, patients, behavior, staff, and back-up item involved in a token transaction, this measure transforms the number of tokens distributed into a dichotomous variable: completion or noncompletion of a task. The information can then be collapsed across staff members and patients to obtain the proportion of patients completing a task on a specific day; a mean can then be calculated across a block of days to obtain an average proportion of patients completing a task, a convenient measure of the effectiveness of the program for increasing the performance of a desired behavior. Comparisons of the mean proportions across different time periods can provide estimates of the progress of the program. The information can also be collapsed across days and staff members to obtain the proportion of times that a specific patient performs a task, a convenient measure of a patient's progress. Similar indices can be calculated for undesired behaviors.

For example, Olson and Greenberg (1972) used each patient's attendance at therapeutic activities "as the most important measure of adjustment within the hospital [page 380]." Patients received signed appointment slips whenever they attended a scheduled therapeutic activity. The slips were turned in to the program staff who later summarized the information by collapsing across staff, days, and therapeutic activities. Nelson and Cone (1979) targeted 12 deficits for increase in their token economy. They recorded the completion and noncompletion of each task and then collapsed across patients to obtain the proportion of completions per day per task. They also collapsed across behaviors to obtain the proportion of completions per day in four classes of behavior: personal management, personal hygiene, ward work, and social skills.

To use the proportion of completions as a measure of outcome requires that each token transaction be accurately recorded. Thus, the studies reviewed earlier that discussed methods of combining token delivery and recording procedures are equally relevant here. However, Hall, Baker, and Hutchinson (1977) and Elliott, Barlow, Hooper, and Kingerlee (1979) completely bypassed the token exchange-recording process to obtain their data. They directly observed patients and rated them as acceptable and not acceptable (equivalent to completion and noncompletion) of seven behaviors, at least five of which were the targets of the token economy. Data from these five were collapsed across days, collapsed across staff, patients, time, and tasks to obtain the mean percentage of patients rated acceptable per behavior. Similarly, Gershone, Errickson, Mitchell, and Paulson (1977) had nursing staff observe each of 25 patients at 12 randomly scheduled times per day, and note the presence or absence (equivalent to completion and noncompletion) of seven behaviors, at least five of which were the targets of the token economy. Data from these five were collapsed across days, staff, and patients to obtain the weekly percentage of patients who emitted each of the behaviors.

A difficulty with percentage completion measures that sum across patients is that they mask variations in inter-patient responsiveness to the contingencies. This may be important information in modifying the token economy to achieve maximum success with all patients. Allen and Magaro (1971) addressed themselves to this issue in a study of the effects of being paid versus paying tokens on attendance at occupational therapy. The results for the entire group of 26 patients indicated a relatively constant rate of attendance, which decreased considerably when patients were asked to pay to attend. However, inspection of individual patient records indicated that only nine patients showed the effect. Since the other patients attended at a very low rate, irrespective of the variations in the contingencies, the effects of the nine responsive patients greatly influenced the summated measure. Some token economies do report individual data (e.g., Lloyd & Garlington, 1968), which also indicate the wide range of individual differences in patient responsiveness to treatment.

Patient Movement

Davison (1969) has argued that token economies ought to be evaluated on the basis of "how effective the procedure is in changing the individual so that he can function as a 'normal' person in the outside world [p. 278]." Table 10.1 lists the token economies that have used the movement of patients in and out of the hospital and/or treatment program as a measure of outcome. For example, Paul and Lentz (1977) tallied the number of "significant releases" from their social learning, milieu, and traditional hospital treatment groups. They defined a significant release as one that "required that a resident not only be released from the mental institution (center or hospital) but remain continuously in the community without return to psychiatric or correctional facilities for a minimum of 90 consecutive days [p. 126]." They found that of the original 84 patients matched on several variables who were assigned to the three groups, 96.4 percent of the social learning, 67.9 percent of the milieu, and 46.4 percent of the traditional treatment group achieved a significant release. Paul and Lentz (1977) also calculated the number of "project weeks" in the institution as a measure of the treatments' efficiency of achieving significant releases. This measure was defined as the number of weeks per patient from placement in one of the treatment groups to either: a) achievement of a significant release, or b) transfer to a group for those who were not released. The results indicated that both the social learning and the milieu groups achieved a greater number of significant releases in fewer project weeks than the traditional treatment group. Nelson and Cone (1979) categorized the movement of patients from their token economy as either positive (to the community or to an open ward) or negative (to a more restrictive ward).

However, the decision to discharge is subject to variables beyond the scope of most programs, and it has been argued that discharge is not an appropriate measure of effectiveness (Ayllon & Azrin, 1968a). Paul and Lentz (1977) note that the absolute value of the rate of release is meaningless because of the "ease with which simple administrative decisions and a variety of other factors can influence the act of institutional release [page 439]." They do note that the comparison of release rates across different programs may be a valuable measure of outcome if the types of placements and the quality and quantity of aftercare services are the same. Olson and Greenberg (1972) developed a measure of patient movement that was somewhat less subject to administrative whims and other uncontrolled variables. They measured the number of "days out," defined as the "days spent outside the hospital on trial visits, absences without leave, or following discharge, whether the discharge was with or against medical advice [page 380]." They also tallied the number of passes given for trips into town. Similarly, Greenberg, Scott, Pisa, and Friesen (1975) reported an "out-hospital" measure that was a combination of the number of days spent on a community job before discharge, the number of days spent on home visits, and the number of days spent in the community after discharge.

Several follow-up studies have been conducted to determine the longer term effects of token economies. Paul and Lentz continued to administer several of their measures to discharged patients. Fullerton, Cayner, and McLaughlin-Reidel (1978) contacted patients who had been discharged from their token economy for an average of 3 years and determined their type of living arrangements, their employment, sources of income, and presence or absence of "bizarre" behavior. Hollingsworth and

Foreyt (1975) sent a questionnaire to discharged patients to determine their type of living arrangements, their occupational adjustment, their use of community services, and their adjustment to the community.

Direct Behavioral Observation

Table 10.1 lists the token economies that have used direct behavioral observations as a measure of outcome. Of course, observing a patient to determine if a target behavior has occurred is direct behavioral observation. In this case, however, the term is meant to indicate a well-defined technique of observing each of a group of patients for specified samples of time in order to describe the relative frequency of various classes of behavior, such as: stereotyped motor behavior, solitary active behavior, smiling, gazing, standing, awake, grooming, and unusual verbal behavior.

Several token economies have used these as the major measure of outcome. For example, Paul and Lentz (1977) used the Time Sample Behavior Checklist (TSBC) as a principal measure of monitoring changes in patient behavior across the years the program was in operation. They also used the Staff-Resident Interaction Chronograph (SRIC) as the means of monitoring staff compliance with the procedures of the program. Nelson and Cone (1979) used the Behavioral Observation Instrument (BOI) to measure changes in patients' behavior on and off the ward. Olson and Greenberg (1972) recorded patients' behavior on the Patient Activity Checklist (PAC) during two daily periods of unstructured social activity. Rostow and Smith (1973) measured overall functioning of their ward by observing several characteristics of patients, staff, and the physical environment. Schaefer and Martin (1966, 1969) used the Behavior Study Form (BSF) to evaluate the effects of their token economy on patient "apathy." Each of these measures will be reviewed in a later section.

Rating Scales

Table 10.1 lists the studies that have used various rating scales as measures of outcome. By far the most popular scales have been the NOSIE-30, MACC-II, and MSBS. These plus several others are reviewed in a later section. Additionally, Pickens et al. (1979) correlated MMPI scores with token earnings and found that low scores on scales F and 8 (schizophrenia) and high scores on scale 2 (depression) were associated with the best outcome in the sense of high token earnings for adaptive behaviors. Marks, Sonoda, and Schalock (1968) administered a battery of tests to patients before and after they participated in a token economy and then in relationship therapy. The battery consisted of: the Hospital Adjustment Scale, the Shipley Institute of Living Scale, the Wechsler Memory Scale (a word association test of 24 words from the Kent-Rosanoff list), the Symbolic-Literal Meaning Test (a test of the speed of cancelling letters), the Aiming Test from the Repetitive Psychological Measures, the Stroop Color-Word Test, the Social Memory Test (a test of word fluency), the Gough Adjective Checklist, and the Draw-A-Person Test. Also included were three special Guttman scales designed to measure interpersonal skills, self-care skills, and participation in specified activities each consisting of 11 to 13 hierarchically arranged steps. The results indicated significant improvement over time with no difference between the treatments.

Hall et al. (1977) also administered a battery of tests to patients before, during, and after they participated in either token economy or a "control" treatment. The battery included three measures of intelligence, three psychiatric rating scales, the Wing Ward Behavioral Scales (completed by nursing staff and yielded scores on socially embarrassing and social withdrawal factors), an Occupational Therapy rating scale, a test of verbal conditioning, and the conversation test developed by Baker (1971). There were no significant differences between either of the treatment groups.

Maley, Feldman, and Ruskin (1973) compared token economy and control patients on a test battery consisting of five tasks: orientation (17 questions), spending (purchasing items and making change), discrimination (circles, squares, and triangles of different colors and sizes), commands (perform two actions per command without repetition of command), and a timed walk (80 yards). Token economy patients were superior to control patients on all measures except the timed walk. A similar measure was used by Shean and Zeidberg (1971). They had token economy and control patients tap a telegraph key for 5 minutes as an indicator of "motivation." Token economy patients improved significantly over the course of three testings.

Perhaps the historical basis for the use of such motor tasks is the work of Lindsley and his colleagues (Lindsley, 1956, 1960, 1963; Lindsley & Skinner, 1954). Lindsley had extremely chronic, regressed patients participate in as many as 500 daily, 1-hour sessions in which lever-pulling was reinforced with candy, cigarettes, etc. (1-minute VI schedule). He found that the rate of pulling varied as a function of such events as being given ground privileges, changes in medication, and the presence or absence of a therapist. He also found that the patients paused more in their responding than normals, and that this variability in the absence of external events could be labeled as psychotic incidents (short pauses), episodes (moderate length pauses), or cycles (long-term variations in rate). Psychotic incidents were often accompanied by vocal hallucinatory symptoms. Based on correlations with two rating scales (Mednick & Lindsley, 1958), Lindsely concluded that low rates of pulling reflected a high degree of pathology. Hutchinson and Azrin (1961), and King, Merrill, Loevinger, and Denny (1957) used FR schedules and did not find the same results.

Lindsley and his colleagues then applied similar methodology to analyze social interactions. Using "conjugate reinforcement," each dyadic partner's rate of looking, listening, and talking could be measured. In two studies with chronic (Lindsley, 1962) and acute (Nathan, Schneller, & Lindsley, 1964) psychotics, the rates of patients' looking, listening, and talking were affected by the content of the conversation, the type of partner (psychologist or fellow patient), and severity of psychopathology.

TARGETED DEFICITS

Table 10.2 lists the classes of behaviors that have been targeted for increases in various nontoken economy studies. These studies have focused on only a few patients at most, and have set as a goal the increase of generally desirable behaviors. The remainder of this discussion, however, will include both token economy and nontoken economy studies.

Self-care Skills

There is general agreement among studies about the behaviors that constitute self-care skills, although there is less agreement about the labels that apply to each behavior. Ayllon & Azrin (1965, 1968a) defined the self-care skills of their female patients as: grooming (hair combed, wearing of dress, slip, panties, bra, stockings, and shoes), bathing at the designated time, participating in exercises, making beds, and cleaning around bed areas. Of course, each of these behaviors required further specification, but this was not reported. Nelson and Cone (1979) defined self-care skills as a combination of personal hygiene behaviors (washing face, combing hair, shaving, brushing teeth) and personal management behaviors (dressing neatly, making bed, cleaning bed drawer, and exercising). The thorough specifications for each of these behaviors are listed in their report. Frederiksen and Williams (1977) targeted a patient's cleaning of his own room and dressing neatly; the former was defined in terms of a series of steps that are not specified in the report. Cohen, Florin, Grushce, Meyer-Osterkamp, and Sell (1972) monitored five behaviors at lunch time: entering the dining room within 1 minute

Table 10.2. Classes of Behaviors Assessed by Nontoken Economy Studies

Study	Target Deficits				Target Excesses					Generalization	Rating Scales
	Self Care	Work Skills	Therapy Activities	Inter-personal	Self Care	Delu-sional	Hallucin-ation	Verbal Physical Abuse	Motor		
Frederiksen & Williams (1977)	X¹	X¹		X¹						3, 4, 6, 8, 10 3, 4, 6, 8, 10	
Linscheid et al. (1974)		X		X				X		3, 5, 7, 9, 11	
Calhoun (1974)		X									
Mitchell & Stofelmayer (1973)		X									
Curran et al. (1973)			X								
McInnis et al. (1973)			X								
Ayllon & Azrin (1968,b)			X								
Allen & Magaro (1971)			X								
Sobell et al. (1970)			X							2, 4, 7, 8, 10	
Wallace et al. (1973)			X¹								
Wilson & Walters (1966)				X¹						3, 4, 6, 9, 11	Own "talkativeness"
Bennett & Maley (1973)				X¹						3, 4, 6, 9, 11	MACC-II, PRP
Tracey et al. (1974)				X¹						3, 4, 6, 9, 10	
Wallace & Davis (1974)				X¹						3, 4, 6, 9, 10	
King et al. (1960)				X							EMIS
Liberman (1972)				X¹						3, 5, 6, 9, 11	

Table 10.2. (continued)

Study	Target Deficits				Target Excesses					Generalization	Rating Scales
	Self Care	Work Skills	Therapy Activities	Inter-personal	Self Care	Delu-sional	Hallucin-ation	Verbal Physical Abuse	Motor		
Sabatasso & Jacobson (1970)				X						3, 4, 6, 8, 10	
Sherman (1968; 1965)				X						3, 5, 6, 9, 10	
Isaacs et al. (1960)				X						2, 4, 7, 8, 10	
O'Brien et al. (1969)				X[1]							
Kale et al. (1968)				X[1]						2, 5, 6, 8, 10	
Milby (1970)				X[1]						2, 4, 7, 8, 10	
Stahl et al. (1974)				X[1]							Own; self-care and interpersonal
Roberts (1969)				X							
Fichter et al. (1976)				X[1]						2, 5, 7, 8, 10	
Hollander & Glickman (1976)				X						2, 5, 7, 8, 11	
Schraa et al. (1979)				X						3, 4, 6, 9, 11	
Baker (1971)				X[1]						3, 4, 7, 9, 11	
Sterling (1980)				X							
Jaffe & Carlson (1976)				X[1]						3, 5, 7, 9, 11; 3, 5, 7, 9, 11	PIP; MSBS

341

Table 10.2. (continued)

Study	Target Deficits — Self Care	Work Skills	Therapy Activities	Inter-personal	Target Excesses — Self Care	Delu-sional	Hallucin-ation	Verbal Physical Abuse	Motor	Generalization	Rating Scales
Thomson et al. (1974)				X						2, 4, 7, 9, 10	
Liberman et al. (1974)		X			X	X	X	X			
Ayllon & Michael (1959)					X	X		X			
Ayllon & Haughton (1962)					X						
Ayllon (1963)					X						
Paden et al. (1974)					X						
Upper & Newton (1971)					X						
Moore & Crum (1969)					X						Own; Semantic Differential
Harmatz & Lapuc (1968)					X						
Atthowe (1972)					X						
Wagner & Paul (1972)					X						MSBS
Anderson & Alpert (1974)					X		X		X	3, 5, 6, 9, 11 / 3, 5, 7, 9, 11	
Green (1978)					X						
Parrino et al. (1971)					X						
Rickard et al. (1960)						X					
Patterson & Teigen (1973)						X				2, 5, 7, 8, 10	

Table 10.2. (continued)

Study	Target Deficits					Target Excesses					Rating Scales
	Self Care	Work Skills	Therapy Activities	Inter-personal	Self Care	Delu-sional	Hallucin-ation	Verbal Physical Abuse	Motor	Generalization	
Rickard & Dinoff (1962)						X					
Bartlett et al. (1971)						X¹					
Ullmann et al. (1965)						X¹				3, 4, 6, 9, 11 3, 4, 6, 9, 11	Welsh A&R
Meichenbaum (1969)						X¹				3, 4, 6, 9, 11 3, 4, 6, 9, 11	
Meichenbaum & Cameron (1973)						X¹				3, 4, 6, 9, 11 3, 4, 6, 9, 11	
Ayllon & Haughton (1964)						X					
Wincze et al. (1972)						X¹				3, 5, 6, 9, 11 3, 5, 6, 9, 11	Own; psychiatric interview
Liberman et al. (1973)						X¹				2, 5, 6, 9, 11 2, 5, 6, 9, 11	
Richardson et al. (1972)						X					
Sanders (1971)						X¹					
Kennedy (1964)						X				2, 5, 6, 8, 10 3, 5, 6, 8, 10 2, 5, 7, 8, 10	
Meyers et al. (1976)						X				2, 5, 7, 8, 10 2, 5, 7, 8, 10 2, 5, 7, 8, 10	

Table 10.2. (continued)

Study	Target Deficits					Target Excesses				Generalization	Rating Scales
	Self Care	Work Skills	Therapy Activities	Inter-personal	Self Care	Delu-sional	Hallucin-ation	Verbal Physical Abuse	Motor		
										2, 4, 7, 8, 10	
										2, 4, 7, 8, 10	
Cayner & Kiland (1974)						X		X		2, 4, 7, 8, 10	
Schraa et al. (1978)						X[1]				2, 4, 7, 8, 10	
Williams (1976)						X				2, 4, 7, 8, 10	
										3, 4, 7, 9, 11	
Davis et al. (1976)						X[1]	X[1]			2, 5, 7, 9, 11	
Haynes & Geddy (1973)							X[1]				
Bucher & Fabricatore (1970)							X				
Nydegger (1972)							X			2, 5, 7, 8, 10	
Rutner & Bugle (1969)							X			3, 4, 6, 9, 11	
Moser (1974)							X			3, 4, 6, 9, 11	
Lindsley (1959, 1963)							X			2, 5, 7, 9, 10	
Weingaertner (1970)							X				BPRS, IMPS
Erricksen et al. (1978)							X			2, 4, 7, 8, 10	NOSIE, BPRS, HSRS
Siegel (1975)							X			2, 4, 7, 8, 10	

Table 10.2. (continued)

Study	Target Deficits					Target Excesses				Generalization	Rating Scales
	Self Care	Work Skills	Therapy Activities	Inter-personal	Self Care	Delu-sional	Hallucin-ation	Verbal Physical Abuse	Motor		
Alford & Turner (1976)							X			2, 5, 6, 9, 11	
Turner et al. (1977)							X¹			3, 5, 6, 9, 11	
Weidner (1970)							X			3, 5, 6, 9, 11	
Cautela & Baron (1973)								X		3, 5, 7, 9, 11	
Cox (1976)								X		2, 5, 7, 9, 11	
Bergman (1975)								X		2, 4, 7, 8, 10	
Matson & Stephens (1977)								X¹		2, 4, 7, 8, 10	
Klinge et al. (1975)								X		2, 4, 7, 8, 10	
O'Brien & Azrin (1972)								X		2, 4, 7, 8, 10	
Taylor et al. (1979)									X¹	2, 4, 7, 8, 10 / 2, 5, 6, 8, 10 / 2, 4, 7, 8, 10	
Erriksen & Huber (1975)									X	2, 5, 6, 8, 10 / 2, 4, 7, 8, 10	
Carroccio et al. (1976)									X¹	2, 5, 6, 8, 10 / 2, 4, 7, 8, 10	
Bernhardt et al. (1972)									X¹		

Table 10.2. (continued)

	Target Deficits				Target Excesses						
Study	Self Care	Work Skills	Therapy Activities	Inter-personal	Self Care	Delu-sional	Hallucin-ation	Verbal Physical Abuse	Motor	Generalization	Rating Scales

1 = interrater reliability reported
2 = same response for both generalization and treatment assessment
3 = different response
4 = same setting for both generalization and treatment assessment
5 = different setting
6 = same time for both generalization and treatment assessment
7 = different time
8 = same assessment technique for both
9 = different assessment technique
10 = same response measure (duration, frequency, etc.)
11 = different response

The number of rows in the "generalization" column corresponds to either the number of cases or the number of generalization measures used in the study.

of the announcement that lunch was served, removal of soup plate, replacing soup spoon on the plate, busing dishes, and busing cutlery.

The recording technique usually involved observing the behavior at a specified time and place to make assessment and reinforcement relatively convenient and hopefully more consistent. Ayllon and Azrin (1965, 1968a) provide a relatively complete description of their recording process. Grooming was checked three times per day, bathing was checked at one designated time per week, tooth brushing at one designated time per day, exercises twice a day, and bed-making once per day. Attendants apparently supervised the tasks and recorded patients' performance while distributing tokens.

Work Skills

Work skills have been a targeted class of behaviors in almost all token economies and in several nontoken economy studies. However, there have been wide variations in the behaviors that constitute work skills, and not enough details are reported to resolve these differences. In fairness, most reports do indicate that extensive criteria were developed for each job (e.g., Hersen et al., 1972) and were posted either at some central location or at the job site (e.g., Gripp & Magaro, 1971). For example, Allyon and Azrin (1965, 1968a) established 10 categories of on-ward work (e.g., grooming assistant, laundry assistant, and dietary assistant), with from three to eight jobs per category. Each job was defined in terms of the specific steps necessary for correct completion. The job of oral hygiene assistant consisted of the following steps: "Assembles toothpaste, toothbrushes, gargle solution and paper cups. Pours gargle into cups and dispenses toothpaste or gargle to all patients [1965, page 372]." Other jobs were defined in a similarly thorough fashion. The time and place for the jobs were specified, and attendants supervised the tasks, recorded performance, and distributed tokens.

Nelson and Cone (1979) defined work as an "activity of 2 minutes or more duration that would be helpful to housekeeping or ward staff in maintaining or managing the ward [page 258]." Frederiksen and Williams (1977) targeted a patient's cleaning the bathroom and emptying the trash as part of a contingency contract between the patient and his sister. Each task was defined in terms of a set of behaviors arranged in stepwise fashion. The sister recorded the behaviors; interrater reliability was determined by asking the patient to record his own behavior independently of the sister's recording (reliability was high).

One of the most thoroughly specified definitions of work was provided by Mitchell and Stoffelmayer (1973). They assessed the effects of sitting as a reinforcer for work output in two extremely inactive schizophrenics.

Work was defined as coil-stripping, or "holding the coil in one hand while pulling off the wire from the coil with the other hand [p. 420]." Patients were observed for 30-minute sessions divided into 60, 30-second intervals. "An instance of work was any occurrence of the defined behavior during a 30-second period [p. 420]."

Although not truly classifiable as work, Linscheid, Maloksy, and Zimmerman (1974) attempted to increase the academic skills of a 21-year old female patient. They constructed five tests each for spelling and arithmetic that were presumably equal in difficulty. Staff administered one test of each type daily and noted the number correct. Calhoun (1974) also attempted to increase six academic skills of chronic inpatients. Academic skills were assessed with tests of vocabulary, arithmetic, and analogies (the remaining three skills are not mentioned); the number correct was the measure of the skill.

Attendance at Therapeutic Activities

Many of the token economies have attempted to increase patient attendance at therapeutic activities. Therapeutic activities have included scheduled classes such as occupational therapy, gym class, homemaking class, automotive workshop, and art clinic, plus unscheduled activities such as piano playing, basketball playing, and taking medication. Paul and Lentz (1977), for example, scheduled three, 45-minute class periods for each of their step 1 and 2 patients of 5 days per week. Classes were no larger than 10 patients and included instruction in reading, elementary arithmetic, speaking, writing, grooming, and home economics. Step 1 patients were also scheduled for two, 50-minute activity periods that involved them in crafts, gym, and shopping trips. All patients, irrespective of their step, were scheduled for twice weekly, 14 member group meetings plus a weekly meeting of the entire unit.

Most of the token economies did not specify the definition of attendance; it could have meant various combinations of appearing at the site of the activity, staying for a certain length of time, or "actively" participating. Paul and Lentz (1977), however, thoroughly specified attendance: patients received one token for coming to the place where the activity was announced (they were later escorted to the site of the activity). They also received a token for participating; if necessary, they were given special tokens ("shaping chips") for behaviors that only approximated full participation; these were then exchanged for a token.

Another set of studies, specifically concerned with increasing patient use of therapeutic activities through reinforcer sampling and exposure procedures, defined attendance in terms of a very specific patient be-

havior, which was easily observed and recorded. Curran, Lentz, and
Paul (1973) and McInnis, Himelstein, Doty, and Paul (1974) defined
attendance at evening activities as the asking for or purchase of a pass
available for a limited period of time in the evening, which allowed
entrance to the activity area. Ayllon and Azrin (1968b) defined participation as the paying of a token to go for a walk, listen to music, or
view a movie. Wallace, Davis, Liberman, and Baker (1973) defined both
staff and patient attendance at therapeutic activities as the number of
individuals present at the activity site during each of four surreptitious
checks.

Interpersonal Skills

Several reports of token economies have indicated that interpersonal
skills have been included among the behaviors for which tokens were
disbursed. However, the behaviors constituting these skills have generally not been reported. Exceptions to this are Paul and Lentz (1977)
and Nelson and Cone (1979). Paul and Lentz (1977) used informal interactions to assess and reinforce interpersonal skills defined as "responding to requests, responding courteously and appropriately to conversation, initiating courteous and appropriate conversation, cooperative
interaction . . . and helping another resident [page 90]." The behaviors
were monitored during scheduled times when informal interactions
were likely to occur. Nelson and Cone (1979) defined interpersonal
skills as greeting staff, answering awareness questions correctly, and
participating in group discussions. A thorough definition, which is given
in the report, was constructed for each of these behaviors.

A number of non-token economy studies have thoroughly defined
interpersonal skills. The most consistent element in all of these studies
has been the inclusion of speech as part of the definition of interpersonal
skills. There has been some disagreement, however, about the quantity
and quality of speech that constitutes an interpersonal skill. Some studies have targeted an increase of any sound or speech, irrespective of
content (Liberman, 1972; Jaffe & Carlson, 1976; Stahl, Thompson,
Leitenberg, & Hasazi, 1974; Thomson, Fraser, & McDougall, 1974;
Wilson & Walters, 1966). Others have defined speech in terms of a
very specific response, such as "hello" or "food" (Isaacs, Thomas,
& Goldiamond, 1960; Kale, Kaye, Whelan, & Hopkins, 1968; Sabatasso
& Jacobson, 1970; Sherman, 1965). Still others have defined speech
in terms of one or more response categories (Bennett & Maley, 1973;
Jaffe & Carlson, 1976; Linscheid et al., 1974; O'Brien, Azrin, & Hen-
son, 1969, Roberts, 1969; Sterling, 1980, Tracey, Briddell, & Wilson,
1974; Wallace, & Davis, 1974).

The recording and reinforcement process is relatively straightforward when content is not part of the definition of speech. An observer can tally the number of words or sounds during a session (Hall et al., 1977; Jaffe & Carlson, 1976; Liberman, 1972; Stahl et al., 1974; Wilson & Walters, 1966), automatic devices can be used, particularly when the rate of speech is high enough to make hand tallying difficult (Wilson & Walters, 1966), or the speech can be recorded for later analysis (Jaffe & Carlson, 1976; Thomson et al., 1974).

The recording process is similarly straightforward when a specific response is the target. This is particularly evident in the shaping of speech in mute psychotics (Isaac et al., 1960; Jacobson, 1970; Sherman, 1963, 1965). Assessment consists of matching the patient's response to the behaviors defined in the various steps of the shaping procedure. Kale et al. (1968) similarly provided an easily assessed behavior; the target response was "Hi" or "Hello, Mr. Jones," which was recorded based on scheduled, on-ward contacts.

The recording process is more difficult when speech is defined in terms of a class of responses. The observer has to decide that the patient's response is one of many which can be placed in the targeted categories. Several studies have been performed in relatively controlled sessions, often with one or more observers using partially automated recording or reinforcement devices (Bennett & Maley, 1973; O'Brien et al., 1969; Tracey et al., 1974; Wallace & Davis, 1974). Other studies have observed speech in naturalistic or quasi-naturalistic situations and have rated it in terms of one or more classes of response (Linscheid et al., 1974; Jaffe & Carlson, 1976; Sterling, 1980). Still other studies have used an interview format with standardized questions to elicit answers which have then been categorized in terms of appropriateness (Baker, 1971; Hall et al., 1977; Nelson & Cone, 1979).

In contrast to the use of speech as part of the definition of interpersonal skills, Milby (1970) and Frederiksen and Williams (1977) defined interpersonal skills in terms of social interaction. Milby (1970) further defined interaction as "talking to, working with, or playing with another patient or staff member," and assessed it in 12 daily, 3-minute observations.

Fichter, Wallace, Liberman, and Davis (1976) defined interpersonal skills in terms of three components: voice volume, duration of speech, and placement of hands on the armrests of a chair during conversation. The behaviors were measured during four structured interactions conducted by each staff member.

In a completely different approach, King, Armitage and Tilton (1960) increased "cooperation" among patients using the Multiple Operant

Problem Solving Apparatus (MOPSA). Cooperation was defined as complex patterns of lever pulling which had to be coordinated between patients in order to earn reinforcement. Similarly, Hollander and Glickman (1976) measured cooperation between two female patients, defined as interdependent manipulation of a cigarette-making machine.

TARGETED EXCESSES

This section reviews studies that targeted behavioral excesses that generally are regarded as symptomatic.

Self-care

A relatively small number of token economies have targeted specific excesses such as frequent clothes changing (Winkler, 1970), urinating on the floor (Pomerleau, Bobrove, & Harris, 1972; Upper, 1973), wearing hospital clothes during the daytime (Hersen, Eisler, Smith, & Agras, 1972), overeating (Rybolt, 1973), spitting on the walls or floor (Upper, 1973), and violating smoking rules (Upper, 1973). Several, nontoken economy studies have targeted the reduction of classes of behavior such as inappropriate meal behaviors, incontinence, inappropriate wearing of clothes, hoarding of various objects, and excessive requests for medication. Because these studies have little in common and are often reported in scant detail, their presentation, study-by-study, would be rather disjointed. Hence, the reader interested in targeting mealtime excesses is referred to studies by Ayllon and Michael (1959, two cases of refusal to eat); Ayllon and Haughton (1962, refusal to go to the dining room and refusal to leave); Ayllon (1963, food stealing); Ayllon and Azrin (1968a, refusal to eat, decreased by a shaping program which is particularly well defined); Sobell, Schaefer, Sobell, and Kremer (1970, chronic missing of meals); Harmatz and Lapuc (1968, obesity); Paden, Himelstein and Paul (1974, assessment of correct behaviors); Green (1978, a schizophrenic diabetic's eating inappropriate foods). Enuresis was targeted by Atthowe and Krasner (1968), Atthowe (1972); and Wagner and Paul (1970, also daytime incontinence). Ayllon (1963) and Liberman, Wallace, Teigen, and Davis (1974, two cases) targeted inappropriate use of clothing. Ayllon and Michael (1959) and Ayllon (1963) reported five cases where hoarding was reduced. Parrino, George, and Daniels reduced patients' requests for PRN medication. Anderson and Alpert (1974) targeted the excessive length of time required by their hallucinating patient to complete various self-care tasks.

Delusions

Because of its importance in diagnosing patients and its impact on community adjustment, delusional speech has received a good deal of attention in the behavioral literature.

Delusions have been generally defined as speech at variance with reality. Since the content of delusions varies from patient to patient, most studies have gone through the process of listening to patients and making a catalogue of delusional statements (e.g., Ayllon & Haughton, 1964; Cayner & Kiland, 1974, Case 1; Davis, Wallace, Liberman, & Finch, 1976; Kennedy, 1964; Liberman, Teigen, Patterson, & Baker, 1973; Liberman, et al., 1974; Wincze, Leitenberg, & Agras, 1972). In an unusual variation of this, Williams (1976) asked a patient to record her own delusions defined as ''unwarranted assumptions for which no basis in fact could be ascertained [page 562].'' However, many if not most patients can point to ''facts'' that verify their delusions.

Once defined, several investigators have then simply recorded the number or duration of delusional comments made by the patient during spontaneous interchanges (Davis et al., 1976; Richardson, Karklas, & Lal, 1972; Sanders, 1971). This assumes, of course, that the patient interacts at a high rate and will continue to do so during all of the treatment phases.

The majority of investigators, however, have chosen to approach the patient and assess delusional speech during the scheduled approaches. Liberman et al. (1974), Ayllon and Michael (1969), and Ayllon and Haughton (1964), for example, had nursing staff approach and interact with patients once every half-hour for 1 to 5 minutes. Numerous others have scheduled longer but less frequent approaches (Bartlett, Ora, Brown, & Butler, 1971; Davis et al., 1976; Kennedy, 1964; Liberman et al., 1973, 1974; Meyers, Mercatoris, & Sirota, 1976; Patterson & Teigen, 1973; Rickard, Dignam, & Horner, 1960; Richard & Dinoff, 1962; Schraa, Lautmann, Luzi, & Screven, 1978).

Wincze et al. (1973), Patterson and Teigen (1973), Schraa et al. (1978), and Meyers et al. (1976), then specified that the interviewers ask patients predetermined, ''delusion-eliciting'' questions. This made observation fairly simple since any response to a question other than the correct one was recorded as delusional. Wincze et al's (1972) procedure was particularly involved; interviewers randomly selected 15 questions from a pool of 105 that had been separately constructed for each patient, and the measure of treatment effectiveness was the number of delusional answers. Meyers et al. (1976) used a similar procedure (randomly selecting 11 questions per session from a pool of 55) and thoroughly specified the interviewer's behavior in response to each answer. The interviewer was to maintain eye contact, nod after each sentence, allow 5 seconds of silence after a correct answer, and cut off lengthy answers after 1 minute.

The other studies using scheduled approaches and sessions have described the interviewer as being either "neutral" or "non-directive." In contrast to asking questions, this made recording more difficult since the observer had to decide that a particular verbalization fit one or more categories of delusions rather than merely recording the correctness of an answer to a specific question. These studies also showed a good deal of variation in their measures of treatment effectiveness. Ayllon and Michael (1959), Ayllon and Haughton (1964), and Liberman et al. (1974) used the number of delusional intervals as the measure of treatment effectiveness. Bartlett et al. (1971) and Liberman et al. (1974, case JP) divided sessions into intervals of arbitrary length and used the number of intervals with delusional speech as the measure of treatment effects. Rickard, Dignam, and Horner (1960, experiment 2) and Rickard and Dinoff (1962) recorded the duration of rational speech during 10-minute intervals of a 30-minute interview. Liberman et al. (1973) and Davis et al. (1976) recorded the duration of time during an interview to the onset of the first delusional statement.

Several studies have targeted categories of "sick" and "healthy" talk rather than patient-specific delusions (Meichenbaum, 1969; Meichenbaum & Cameron, 1973; Ullmann, Forsman, Kenny, McInnis, Unikel, & Zeisset, 1965). Instances of health talk, defined as verbalization of comfort, liking, good physical and mental health, and personal assets, were counted on tape recordings of highly structured interviews.

Hallucinations

Haynes and Geddy (1973) have defined hallucinations as "verbal, facial and/or gestural responses to an unobservable stimulus [page 123]." A difficulty with the measurement of hallucinations is the identification of a stimulus that cannot be observed. This difficulty has been resolved in three ways. The patient has frequently been asked to report when he is aware of this stimulus (Alford & Turner, 1976; Anderson & Alpert, 1974; Bucher & Fabricatore, 1970; Erricksen, Darnell, & Labeck, 1978; Liberman et al., 1974 [Case BR]; Moser, 1974; Nydegger, 1972; Rutner & Bugle, 1969; Siegel, 1975; Turner, Hersen, & Bellack, 1977; Weingaertner, 1971). Less frequently, the patient has been observed, and behaviors presumably correlated with hallucinations have been noted

(Anderson & Alpert, 1974; Liberman et al., 1974; Weidner, 1970), or the observational situation has been modified, or the patient behavior so restricted that any response can be considered an indication of hallucinations (Haynes & Geddy, 1973; Lindsley, 1959, 1963).

Three techniques have been used to record self-reported hallucinations. Patients have been asked to note each occurrence of the unobservable stimulus (usually voices and occasionally visions) in a diary or on a wrist counter (e.g., Erricksen, et al., 1978; Moser, 1974; Nydegger, 1972). Patients have been asked during structured interviews about the quality and quantity of their hallucinations (Siegel, 1975; Weingaertner, 1970). This information has then been rated on psychiatric scales such as the Brief Psychiatric Rating Scale or the Inpatient Multidimensional Psychiatric Scale (Erricksen et al., 1978; Weingaertner, 1970). Finally, patients have reported hallucinations during time-limited sessions by either pressing a button (Alford & Turner, 1976; Anderson & Alpert, 1974) or by raising a finger that cued an observer to press a button (Turner et al., 1977) whenever a hallucination occurred.

Three studies observed behaviors that were correlated with hallucinations. Liberman et al. (1974) tallied the behaviors during scheduled interviews; Anderson and Alpert (1974) rated the amount of hallucination-correlated behavior during breakfast and lunch and recorded the amount of time to perform self-care tasks where completion was often delayed by the hallucinations; Weidner (1970) noted the amount of time spent away from the hospital because of auditory hallucination associated with passing strangers.

The patient in the Haynes and Geddy (1973) study was so withdrawn that almost any verbal behavior was considered an indication of hallucinations. Lindsley (1959, 1963) observed patients in experimental rooms where no one but the patient was present. Thus, any vocalization was defined as a "vocal hallucinatory symptom."

Physical and Verbal Abuse

Physical and verbal abuse have been included as targets in several token economies (Gershone et al., 1977; Gripp & Magaro, 1971; Miller & Dermer, 1979; Olson & Greenberg, 1972; Paul & Lentz, 1977; Pickens et al., 1979; Pomerleau et al., 1972; Roback et al., 1972; Steffy et al., 1969; Upper, 1973; Winkler, 1970). The reports included few details about the behaviors that constituted abuse; the recording procedures are similarly described in scant detail, although the behaviors were noted on data sheets or in nursing notes when they occurred.

Surprisingly, only a few more details are given in reports of studies focusing exclusively on the reduction of physical and verbal abuse. Liberman et al. (1974) describe seven cases of verbal abuse, six cases of assault, and five cases of property destruction. O'Brien and Azrin (1972), Linscheid et al. (1974), Klinge, Thrasher, and Myers (1975), Cayner and Kiland (1974), and Bergman (1975, Case 2) targeted some forms of verbal abuse, such as screaming, shouting obsenities, yelling at the "voices" of an auditory hallucination or the "sights" of a visual hallucination, and threatening to injure someone else or destroy property. Klinge et al. (1975), Matson and Stephens (1977), and Cayner and Kiland (1974) targeted some forms of physical abuse such as throwing objects, punching and kicking others, and destroying property. In all but the Klinge et al. (1975) study, the behaviors were recorded whenever they occurred, and it was the count of occurrences that was used as the measure of effectiveness of the procedures. The Klinge et al. (1975) study recorded the duration of each behavior.

Several studies have targeted self-mutilative behavior (Bergman, 1975, Case I; Cautela & Baron, 1973; Cayner & Kiland, 1974, Case 3; Cox, 1975). The recording procedures consisted of either noting the behavior when it occurred (Cautela & Baron, 1973; Cayner & Kiland, 1974), periodically inspecting the permanent products of the behavior (e.g., Bergman, 1974, cuts on arms), or noting the patients' report of the behavior (Cox, 1976).

Motor Movements

Several studies have focused on unusual motor behaviors. Carriccio, Latham, and Carriccio (1976) used contingent rental of a guitar to reduce a patient's repetitive touching of his head and face counted during 3-to 10-minute observation periods. Erriksen and Huber (1975) and Bernhardt, Hersen, and Barlow (1972) modified spasmodic torticollis, a "disorder characterized by contraction of the neck muscles causing deviation of the head." Bernhardt et al. (1972) measured the deviation by seating the patient perpendicular to a closed circuit video camera that transmitted his profile to a monitor over which a grid of black tape had been placed. Whenever the patient's nostril extended into an area that defined the distorted posture characteristic of the disorder, an observer depressed a switch that activated a timer. Erricksen and Huber (1975) had their patient move his gaze between two stimuli (6-inch strips of tape) in time with a metronome set at 40 beats per minute. The gap between the visual stimuli was gradually increased over the course of the treatment. Taylor, Zlutnick, and Hoehle (1979) reported the reduction of tardive dyskinesias with two patients. The movements of both patients were observed during individual sessions from behind a one-way mirror. The observation and recording procedures consisted of alternating 5-second periods of observation and 5-second periods of recording. The specific movements observed were different for each patient. Gardos, Cole, and La Brie (1977) thoroughly critique the currently available methods for assessing tardive dyskinesias.

OBSERVED, NON-TARGETED BEHAVIORS

This section reviews methods of observing and recording behaviors that have not been targeted for modification but have been used to develop a "picture" of the living environment or to determine the generalization of treatment effects to various combinations of non-targeted behaviors, settings, and times.

Environment

Those instruments that have assessed psychiatric environments have had several elements in common. They have all used observers to periodically record an instantaneous picture of the environment using a pre-determined set of categories to code the observed behaviors. The premier examples are the Staff-Resident Interaction Chronograph (SRIC) and the Time Sample Behavior Checklist (TSBC) developed by Paul and his colleagues. The SRIC was designed to observe staff-patient interactions in order to monitor staff's implementation of the treatment procedures in the Paul and Lentz (1977) study. The SRIC has since been used to monitor staff behavior in a variety of programs treating a variety of patient populations (Light, 1980). Each staff member is continually observed for 10 minutes divided into 1-minute segments. The staff member's behavior is coded in terms of 21 categories of interaction, including 13 categories of verbal behavior (e.g., positive verbal, suggest alternatives), eight categories of nonverbal behavior (e.g., positive nonverbal, doing-for), and two categories not involving interaction with patients. The patient's behavior that preceded the interaction is coded in terms of five categories, such as appropriate behavior, inappropriate crazy, and neutral. Thus, each staff-patient interaction is coded in terms of a 5×21 matrix, one for each 1-minute segment of the 10-minute observation period. The information is then analyzed by computer to provide a weekly summary of each staff member's performance.

The TSBC, an expansion of Schaefer and Martin's (1966) Behavior Study Form, was designed as a primary measure of outcome in the Paul and Lentz (1977) study. Like the SRIC, the TSBC has since been used with various patient populations and treatment programs (Power, 1980). Each patient's behavior is coded in terms of seven categories: location (e.g., activity area, sitting room), position (e.g., sitting, running), awake-asleep (eyes open, eyes closed), facial expression (e.g., smiling and/or laughing with stimulus), social orientation (e.g., alone, with staff), concurrent activities (e.g., eating, watching TV), and crazy behaviors (e.g., swearing, rocking, pacing). Observation and recording consists of first finding the patient, noting his location, observing his behavior for 2 seconds, and then recording his behavior in terms of position, eyes open or closed, facial expression, and as many social orientation behaviors, concurrent activities, and crazy behaviors as applies. The information is then analyzed across at least ten observations to provide summary information about each category and a set of higher order scores, including: schizophrenic disorganization, cognitive distortion, hostile-belligerence, total inappropriate behavior, interpersonal interaction, self-maintenance, instrumental activity, individual entertainment, and total appropriate behavior. The TSBC has also been used to evaluate the elimination of psychotropic medication (Paul, Tobias, & Holly, 1972), and to validate a set of measures of patient functioning (Mariotto & Paul, 1974).

Most of the other direct behavioral observation systems are similar to the SRIC and the TSBC. Table 10.3 lists the major dimensions, sampling frequencies, duration of observations, and the method of calculating interrater reliability for each of these systems. Each has yielded valuable information for assessment and evaluation in many different situations. For example, Schaefer and Martin (1966) used the BSF to determine if their token economy reduced apathy, defined as an observation without concomitant behaviors (e.g., watch TV, eat). Nelson and Cone (1979) used the BOI, and Olson and Greenberg (1972) used the PAC to examine the effects of their token economies on behaviors such as social interaction observed both on and off the ward. The BOI has also been used to measure the differences in patient behaviors across various psychiatric settings (Alevizos, De Risi, Liberman, Eckman, & Callahan, 1978), and in response to changing the administration of medication from several times to once per day (Callahan, Alevizos, Teigen, Neuman, & Campbell, 1975). McGuire, Polsky, and their colleagues have observed patients during their first weeks of hospitalization and by the second week found differences in behaviors that discriminate between those who eventually improve and those who do not (Fairbanks, McGuire, Cole, Sbordone, Silvers, Richards, & Akers, 1977; McGuire

Table 10.3. Characteristics of Several Direct Behavioral Observation Instruments

Name and Relevant Studies	Dimensions and Categories	Sampling Frequency	Duration of Observation	Method of Calculating Reliability
Behavior Study Form (BSF) Schaefer & Martin (1966)	(a) mutually exclusive (5 categories) (b) concomitant (13 categories) (c) location	Once every ½ hour	Instantaneous	None indicated
Behavior Mapping Ittelson et al. (1970)	18 categories grouped into 6 "analytic," activity dimensions and location	Varies but generally once every 15 minutes	Instantaneous	(a) % agreement (b) split half
No name given Holahan (1972)	(a) social (3 categories) (b) non-social (3 categories)	Once every 75 seconds during a 45 minute session	Instantaneous	% agreement
No name given Holahan & Saegert (1973)	(a) social (3 categories) (b) non-social active (3 categories) (b) isolated passive (2 categories)	Once every 5 minutes for 75 minutes in morning and afternoon	Instantaneous	Method not indicated but reported as 0.94 to 0.98
Staff-resident interaction chronograph (SRIC) Paul et al. (1973) Paul & Lentz (1977); Light (1980)	(a) patient behavior (5 categories) (b) staff behavior (21 categories)	Not indicated	Each staff member for 10 minutes divided into 10, 1-minute intervals	(a) Intraclass correlation coefficient (b) % agreement
Time sample Behavior checklist (TSBC) Paul et al. (1972) Mariotto & Paul (1974) Paul & Lentz (1977) Power (1980)	25 codes grouped into 7 categories grouped into higher order scores	One every hour	2 seconds	Intraclass correlation coefficient

Table 10.3 (continued)

Name and Relevant Studies	Dimensions and Categories	Sampling Frequency	Duration of Observation	Method of Calculating Reliability
Behavior Observation Instrument (BOI) Callahan et al. (1975) Alevizos et al. (1978) Nelson & Cone (1979)	a) mutually exclusive (5 categories) b) concomitant (16 categories) c) location	Variable; depending upon application	5 seconds	a) intraclass correlation coefficient b) % agreement c) Kappa
No name given Ayllon & Michael (1959) Ayllon & Haughton (1962) (1964) Ayllon (1963)	a) appropriate b) inappropriate c) neutral	Once every ½ hour	1 to 3 minutes	None indicated
No name given Moos (1968)	16 categories of social behavior	Not indicated	Instantaneous	Interobserver r
Location-activity Inventory (LAI) Hunter et al. (1962)	a) location b) position c) posture d) activity	Once every hour	10 seconds	a) contingency coefficient b) split half
No name given Katz et al. (1972)	a) patient behavior (2 categories) b) aide behavior (3 categories)	Every third minute during a 30-minute session; each minute divided into 15 second periods	15 seconds (4 consecutively to total 1 minute)	% agreement
No name given Gelfand et al. (1967) Trudel et al. (1974) Steinbook et al. (1977)	a) 5 degrees of appropriateness of patient behavior b) Environmental response (3 categories)	Observe during activities	Not indicated	a) % agreement in recording of patient-environment sequences b) % agreement for coding c) Spearman rho (Trudel)
No name given Sanson-Fisher et al. (1979)	a) Solitary Behavior (3 categories) b) Interactive Behavior (4 categories) c) Personnel (5 categories)	Twice per hour between 9:00 a.m. and 9:00 p.m.	Instantaneous	% agreement

Table 10.3 (continued)

Name and Relevant Studies	Dimensions and Categories	Sampling Frequency	Duration of Observation	Method of Calculating Reliability
No name given Martindale et al. (1978)	Interaction (positive or negative)	10 per day	Not indicated	a) % agreement b) test-retest
Patient Activity Checklist (PAC) Aumack (1969) Higgs (1970) De Vries (1968) Olson & Greenberg (1972)	Behavior of patients in a dayroom (24 categories)	Not indicated	Instantaneous	a) interobserver r b) split half
Behavior on Ward Scale (BOWS) Rostow & Smith (1975)	General unit atmosphere (5 categories)	Once per day	Not indicated	Method not indicated but reported to be .84
No name given Finch et al. (1976)	7 categories (16 behaviors total)	15-minute period after brief isolation (time out)	10 seconds observe; 20 seconds record; total of 30 per 15-minute period	% agreement
No name given McGuire & Polsky (1979) Polsky & McGuire (1980) Fairbanks et al. (1977)	a) instantaneous observation (8 categories) b) continuous observation (2 categories)	Eight, 30-minute observations per week	a) Instantaneous (1.5 seconds) b) Continuous (80 seconds)	% occurrence agreement

& Polsky, 1979; Polsky & McGuire, 1980). Finch, Wallace, and Davis (1976) found significant intra-patient differences in the frequencies of various behaviors before, during, and after placement in brief isolation (time-out); the behaviors that reflected the effects of the brief isolation were different from patient to patient. Holahan and Saegert (1973) found changes in patients' behaviors as a result of remodeling their ward. De Vries (1968) and Higgs (1970) found temporary increases in appropriate patient behaviors, as measured by the PAC, when patients were moved from an old to a new ward. Moos (1968) observed 16 interaction behaviors and found that wearing a wireless microphone did not significantly affect the frequencies of behaviors of the group as a whole, although the more disturbed patients were affected.

Several studies have focused on staff behavior. Sanson-Fisher, Poole, and Thompson (1979) found that staff members spent most of their time in solitary activity or in interaction with their colleagues (see Alevizos, et al., 1978). Interestingly, the authors used the same scale with patients and found much the same pattern of behaviors. This pattern was then replicated 2 weeks later, even though the patient population had almost completely changed. Three studies used a scale developed by Gelfand, Gelfand, and Dobson (1967) that coded the responses to patient's behaviors as either positive attention, negative attention, or ignores. Patients' behaviors were also coded. Gelfand et al. (1967) found that staff were more inconsistent reinforcers of patients' behavior than other patients. Trudel, Boisvert, Maruca, and Leroux (1974) found that staff on a token economy ward more often attended positively to appropriate patient behavior than staff on a nontoken economy ward. Steinbrook, Jacobson, Moser, and Davies (1977) found that introduction of Goal Attainment Scaling for monitoring patients' programs increased staff's positive attention to appropriate patient behavior. However, improvement in patient behavior, as measured by the NOSIE-30, was not significant. Katz, Johnson, and Gelfand (1972) used a modification of the Gelfand et al. (1967) scale, and found that monetary incentives were more effective than either instructions or verbal prompts in increasing staff's positive interaction.

Generalization

Table 10.2 lists the studies that evaluated how the effects of treatment generalized to behaviors, settings, and/or times not included in the direct intervention. Perhaps the simplest measure of generalization is one in which all elements of the assessment situation are readministered at a later point in time. For example, Wallace et al. (1973) reassessed patient and staff attendance at therapeutic activities 6 weeks after discontinuing the treatment (code 2, 4, 7, 8, 10 in Table 10.2). Rickard and Dinoff (1962) observed the same patient's delusional speech using the same assessment technique as in the original study conducted 2½ years earlier (Rickard et al., 1960). Schraa et al. (1978) reassessed a patient's nondelusional responses to questions by administering the same questions as used in treatment 9, 10, and 12 months after the intervention was discontinued.

Another measure of generalization involves assessment of the target behavior in a different setting (e.g., aftercare) and at a different time than that of treatment. Patterson and Teigen (1973) had an observer ask their patient the same questions in an aftercare facility as were originally asked in the inpatient setting (code 2, 5, 7, 8, 10 in Table

10.2). Fichter et al. (1976) asked observers in two aftercare facilities to assess their patient's interpersonal skills after his discharge from an inpatient treatment program. The observers, who were different than the staff members involved in the inpatient program, used both the same and different topics for the interactions as used in the inpatient phase. Several other studies that include a follow-up assessment do so in a rather anecdotal fashion, simply indicating that the effects of treatment persisted after its termination (e.g., Bergman, 1975; Cautela & Baron, 1973; Kennedy, 1964; Linscheid et al., 1974; Moser, 1974; Nydegger, 1972; Seigel, 1975).

Yet another measure of generalization involves assessment concomitant with treatment of different behaviors and/or settings. Tracey et al. (1974), for example, kept all elements the same between generalization and treatment except the response and, necessarily, the assessment technique (code 3, 4, 6, 9, 10 in Table 10.2). They determined whether the increase in patients' positive statements about the activities generalized to an increase in the actual use of the activities. They examined records ("escort slips") of patients who participated in off ward activities, and found a correlation between the increase in the number of positive statements and the increase in the number of patients using the activities. Alford and Turner (1976) assessed the effects of several interventions on delusions and hallucinations reported by the patient outside of the treatment sessions.

Kale et al. (1968) assessed generalization of greeting responses from the "experimenter" to several other staff members (code, 2, 5, 6, 8, 10 in Table 10.2). No generalization was found until the staff members used the treatment procedures. Kale et al. also mentioned the "generalization" of treatment effects when a contingency is deliberately removed as part of a reversal or withdrawal experimental design. This is, in a sense, generalization across time. However, since this is an issue concerned with the procedures for demonstrating treatment effects and not with procedures for assessment, it will not be discussed here. The reader is referred to Hersen and Barlow (1976) for discussion of various experimental designs, and to Hartmann and Atkinson (1973) for a discussion of difficulties in evaluating this type of generalization.

Most studies have assessed generalization effects using a combination of different settings, responses, etc. For example, Bennett and Maley (1973) initially increased the time duration that patients spent during sessions engaged in four interpersonal behaviors: talking and attending to another person, asking and answering questions, and working cooperatively. Generalization was assessed in two ways. Records of token earnings were examined to determine if there had been an increase in behaviors such as grooming. Generalization thus involved behaviors different than the targets, assessed in a different manner, and with a different response measure (duration versus number of tokens) than treatment (code 3, 4, 6, 9, 11 in Table 10.2). Second, 20 daily, randomly scheduled, 1-minute observations were conducted to determine if patients increased their audible verbalization to other patients; again, this was a different response from three of the four targets with a different assessment technique and response measure. Both assessment procedures indicated improvement, the several differences between generalization and treatment adding confidence in the power of the treatment techniques.

RATING SCALES

Although rating scales have not always been favorably received within the behavioral literature, several have proven to be sensitive to the effects of behavioral interventions, particularly token economies. This section will review those scales, discussing first those that assess multiple levels of functioning, and then those made for the assessment of more specific areas. For general reviews of rating scales for use with chronic mental patients, the reader is referred to Goldberg (1974).

Multiple Areas

Table 10.4 lists some of the characteristics of scales that have been used in studies of behavioral interventions with chronic mental patients. Paul and his colleagues have conducted extensive studies to determine the reliability and validity of the Inpatient Multi Dimensional Psychiatric Scale (IMPS), Nurses Observation Scale for Inpatient Evaluation-30 (NOISE-30), and the Inpatient Scale of Minimal Functioning (ISMF) (a variation of the Social Breakdown Syndrome Gradient Index, SBSGI; Gruenberg, Brandon, & Kasius, 1966). Paul et al. (1972) used the Social Breakdown Syndrome Gradient Index (SBSGI), NOISE-30, IMPS, Minimal Social Behavior Scale (MSBS) (see below), and Time Sample Behavior Checklist (TSBC) to evaluate changes in functioning as a result of the withdrawal of maintenance doses of psychotropic medication. No medication-related changes were found on any of the measures. Correlations among the measures "supported the validity of the assessment instruments in measuring a common factor, but indicated that additional information is added by each instrument [p. 112]." Lentz, Paul, and Calhoun (1971) used the SBSGI, NOISE-30, and MSBS with 137 chronic patients who had been rejected for placement in the community. They found that all three scales were quite reliable and that

Table 10.4. Characteristics of Rating Scales

Characteristics	Scales							
	Multiple Areas of Functioning					Specific Areas		
Name and Authors	Nurses Observations Scale for Inpatients (NOSIE: NOSIE-30) Honingfeld et al. (1966)	Inpatient Scale of Minimal Functioning (ISMF) Paul et al. (1976)	Psychotic Reaction Profile (PRP) Lorr et al. (1960)	Inpatient Multi Dimensional Psychiatric Scale (IMPS) Lorr & Klett (1966)	Mood, Affect, Communication Cooperation (MACC-II) Ellsworth (1962)	Ward Atmosphere Scale (WAS) Moos & Houts (1968)	Minimal Social Behavior Scale (MSBS) Farina et al. (1957)	Community Oriented Environment Scale, Form C (COPES) Moos (1972)
No. Items	30 or 65	23	85	75	16	120	32	102
Rated by	Ward Staff	Ward Staff	Ward Staff	Interviewer	Ward Staff	Staff and Patients	Interviewer	Staff and Patients
Rating Period	3 days before rating	7 days before rating	3 days before rating	After interview	Retrospective	Retrospective	After Interview	Retrospective
Scores	Total assets; Social competence; Social interest Personal Neatness; Irritability Manifest psychosis; Retardation	Total	Thinking Disorganization; Withdrawal; Paranoid belligerence; Agitated depression	Excitement vs. retardation; Schiz. disorganization; Cognitive distortion; Anxious intro-punitiveness; Total morbidity	Mood; Affect; Communication; Cooperation	12 subscales such as: order, variety, clarity, + "Halo" scale	Total only	10 subscales such as: involvement, support, control

the "significant correlations between total scores of all three instruments show that a common 'level of functioning' factor is assessed over raters, behaviors, situations, and instruments; however, the level of intercorrelations further indicates that each of the three instruments, contributes additional information on patient functioning as well [p. 73]."

Mariotto and Paul (1974) then assessed the validity of the IMPS through a multitrait-multimethod study using the NOSIE-30, SBSGI, MSBS, and TSBC, each administered at two points in time, 6 months apart. They again found that the IMPS was highly correlated with the other measures, and they concluded that the IMPS has excellent concurrent validity. However, the IMPS was not a very good predictor of changes. Interestingly, the authors concluded that this was most likely due to the more abstract and judgmental items of the IMPS, which made the scale susceptible to rater bias; they suggest that the IMPS be restricted to cases in which the desired information is an ordinal ranking rather than an absolute level of functioning.

Other studies have generally found that the NOSIE-30 reflects the effect of behavioral interventions (Elliott et al., 1979; Erricksen et al., 1978; Gripp & Magaro, 1971; Nelson & Cone, 1979; Rybolt, 1975; Schwartz & Bellack, 1975). Kowalski et al. (1976), however, found that nonpsychotics did not show an improvement in the NOSIE-30 during their participation in a token economy, but remained at a fairly high level of functioning throughout. Psychotic patients did show an improvement from an initially low level of functioning. The MACC-II has also been found to reflect the effects of behavioral interventions (Bennett & Maley, 1973; Grzesiak & Locke, 1975; Maley et al., 1973; Rostow & Smith, 1975; Schean & Zeidberg, 1971), as has the PRP (Bennett & Maley, 1973; Elliott et al., 1979). Weingaertner (1971), like Mariotto and Paul (1974), found the IMPS to be an insensitive measure of change.

Specific Areas

Several rating scales have been developed to assess the social skills of psychotic patients. Baker (1971) and Hall et al. (1977) used a simple scale to rate mute patients' replies to a verbally presented, 60-item questionnaire; 0 for no reply, 1 for a grunt, 2 for an inappropriate or imperfect reply, 3 for a perfect reply, and 4 for a perfect reply plus some extra speech. Wilson and Walters (1966) assessed ward-ward generalization of a laboratory-generated increase in the speech of near-mute psychotics by having ward staff indicate the "talkativeness" of each patient on a 7-point scale.

By far the most frequently used scale for assessing social skills in lower functioning patients is the MSBS. The MSBS is not so much a rating scale as a rigidly structured interview in which the patient is presented with standard questions and "social situations." The situations include items such as the interviewer's offering to shake hands and offering the patient a cigarette, and then searching for matches to light his own cigarette (the matches are deliberately placed close to the patient). Of the eight studies that have used the MSBS, all but one (Gripp & Margaro, 1971) have found it to reflect improvement with behavioral interventions and to be highly correlated with the ISMF, NOSIE-30, IMPS, and other scales. Additionally, Lentz (1975) found that the MSBS was not affected by instructions and contingencies given to patients to "fake good" (i.e., impression management).

A number of social skills scales have been developed primarily to assess the effects of assertion training with higher functioning patients. These involve both self-report items and behavioral, role-played tasks. The latter are usually audio or video tape-recorded and later rated for behaviors such as eye contact, fluency, and latency. Because these scales have been recently reviewed, they will not be discussed here. The reader is referred to Hersen and Bellack (1976), Bellack and Hersen (1978), and Bellack (1979).

In a rather different vein, Moos and his colleagues (e.g., Moos & Houts, 1968) have developed a rating scale to assess patient and staff perception of ward "atmosphere." An initial version of the scale used a semantic differential technique which was revised to the true-false format of the Ward Atmosphere Scale (WAS), Form B. Gripp and Magaro (1971) used the WAS, Form B in their comparison of a token economy with three control wards; they found a considerable number of positive changes for the token economy program compared to the control wards.

Moos (1972) revised the WAS, Form B and renamed it the Community Oriented Environment Scale (COPES). Milby, Pendergrass, and Clarke (1975) used the COPES to evaluate differences in ward atmosphere between token economy and control wards. They found that token economy patients saw themselves as more involved and encouraged than control patients.

DISCUSSION

The reader should be alerted to several potential problems before starting to develop his/her own assessment strategy. These problems make the assessment information either unreliable (i.e., a high proportion of the information is error) or invalid (i.e., the information does not reflect the variables the assessor presumes it does).

Definition of the Behavior

The definition of the behavior to be recorded or rated should be as specific and precise as possible. Ayllon and Azrin (1968a) state this succinctly in their Dimensions of Behavior Rule: "Describe the behavior in specific terms that require a minimum of interpretation [page 36]." In effect, the less the observer has to interpret, the less error from observation to observation and observer to observer. Behaviors as seemingly straight-forward as, "clean dress, hair combed, and clean nails," can be extremely difficult to define and may lead to disagreement between observers (Feingold & Migler, 1972). Ayllon and Azrin (1968a) present four cases in which an imprecise definition of a simple work behavior led to disagreement between observers about when the behavior had been performed. Error added to the assessment process makes the detection of a treatment effect more difficult. Sherman (1965) reported that he was unable to systematically increase voice volume in one patient because he could not accurately measure and consistently reinforce very small but increasing changes in volume.

Fortunately, there are several ways to sharpen the definition of a behavior, each ultimately reducing the difficulty of the observer's discriminations (interpretations that the behavior has or has not occurred). One way is to simply remove the observer from the entire assessment process by using completely automated assessment devices. This was, of course, the tack taken by Wilson and Walters (1966) with their speech rate meter, and by Lindsley in both his work with chronic schizophrenics (Lindsley 1959, 1960, 1963) and in his assessment of social situations (Nathan et al., 1964).

A second way is to focus on the "permanent products" of the behavior (i.e., permanent changes in the environment that occur as a result of the behavior). Ayllon and Azrin (1968a) state this in their Behavior Effect Rule: "Arrange the situation so that the behavior produces some enduring changes in the physical environment [page 127]." Examples are the weight criterion of the obesity studies of Upper and Newton (1971), Moore and Crum (1969), and Harmatz and Lapuc (1968); the weight criterion of excessive clothes (Ayllon, 1963); the wetness criterion of enuresis (Atthowe, 1972; Wagner & Paul, 1970); the job criteria of Ayllon and Azrin (1965); the monitoring of sugar in the urine to assess inappropriate eating (Green, 1978).

A third way is to include in the definition such a narrow range of behavior that discrimination is relatively easy. This was the approach taken by Patterson and Teigen (1973), Wincze et al. (1972), Schraa et al. (1978), and Meyers et al. (1976) in their use of delusion-eliciting questions. All but the correct answers were labeled delusional, with the correct answers consisting of only a few words. The observer's task was simply to match the patient's answer to the few words of the "standard." Bernhardt et al.'s (1972) use of a grid placed over the TV monitor made it much easier for the observer to record normal and abnormal head posture. The observer had only to watch the position of the patient's nostril; its position relative to the grid defined normal and abnormal posture. Nelson and Cone (1979) noted that the recording of personal hygiene behaviors in their token economy required the observers to judge only that the behaviors had occurred, not that they had resulted in a particular quality of outcome (e.g., washing face = "application of water to at least two-thirds of facial area followed by drying with a towel [p. 258]." Cohen et al. (1972) sidestepped the problem by selecting for observation and modification only those behaviors that they believed easy to discriminate.

A fourth way is, paradoxically, the opposite: define the response so broadly that the discrimination is easy. This was the approach taken by Wilson and Walters (1966), Liberman (1972), Jaffe and Carlson (1976), and Thomson et al. (1974) in defining speech as any audible verbalizations.

Observer

There are several problems associated with the observer that may invalidate the assessment information. These have been reviewed in detail by Johnson and Bolstad (1973), who also suggest several solutions to these problems. The reader is referred to their article since their discussion and suggestions will only be briefly summarized here.

Bias. Almost all of the studies cited in this review have used observers who were aware of the various phases and likely results of the treatment process. Such knowledge (experimenter bias) may lead to distortions in the assessment process, even to the point of blatant faking of the data (Azrin, Holz, Ulrich, & Goldiamond, 1961). Bias may also affect the treatment process through verbal and non-verbal communication to the patient of the manner in which he is expected to behave. In this case, it may not be the actual treatment that is effective; it may rather be the combination of the expectancy and the treatment, similar to the sensitizing manner of a pretest in attitude research.

Johnson and Bolstad (1973) give several suggestions for reducing bias: (a) give as little information to the observer as possible about the

treatment phases or about the assignment of patients to various conditions (e.g., Bartlett et al., 1971; Bennett & Maley, 1973; Jaffe &
Carlson, 1976; Tracey et al., 1974); (b) continually check the observer
(e.g., Tracey et al., 1974); (c) provide no payoff to the observers for
obtaining particular patterns of results. It should also be noted that the
more ambiguous the response definition, the more likely the effects of
bias (Kent, O'Leary, Diament, & Dietz, 1974).

Reactivity. Reactivity refers to the possibility that the observation process itself, apart from the effects of treatment procedures, may be responsible for changes in the observed behavior. This, of course, makes
questionable the generalization of information from assessed to non-
assessed times. Studies of reactivity have yielded somewhat contradictory results (see Johnson & Bolstad [1973] for a review). More recent
studies have continued this contradictory "trend." Johnson and Bolstad
(1975) found that families did not behave differently when observers
were present than when observers were absent.

Hagen, Craighead, and Paul (1975) similarly took surreptitious audio
recordings of staff behavior during a lunch routine; they found that the
presence or absence of an observer did not significantly affect the quality or quantity of staff behavior. In contrast, Mariotto (1980) notes,
anecdotally, that staff being observed in programs not part of the Paul
and Lentz (1977) unit were reactive to the SRIC, with some staff apparently not adapting during 10 continuous days of observation. Moos
(1968) found that patients wearing a wireless microphone did not, in
general, lead to marked reactivity effects defined in terms of 16 interaction behaviors such as looking, smiling, and talking.

However, this was true only for the group as a whole; individual
patients showed large reactivity effects, with the more disturbed patients
showing larger effects. Unfortunately, the design of the experiment
allows an alternate interpretation: individual reactivity effects may have
simply reflected the greater variability of the more disturbed patients
(no comparison was given of the same patients in the same setting and
condition at different times).

Johnson and Bolstad (1973) suggest several ways to reduce reactivity,
should it be a problem. The observation process should be as unobtrusive as possible (e.g., Hagen et al.'s [1975] tape recorder; Paul et al.'s
[1973] having observers act as "pieces of furniture" with no eye contact
to staff or patients). At the very least, a period of adaptation to the
observer's presence should be allowed before information is gathered
(e.g., Hunter et al., 1962).

Certain types of observers may be associated with higher degrees of
reactivity. For example, the presence of a "doctor" may elicit more

somatic complaints and/or delusional statements than other types of observers (Zarlock, 1966).

Perhaps the lowest degree of reactivity is obtained with measures focusing on the "outcomes" or products of the treatment process. For example, Palmer and McGuire (1973) developed a scale of 50 "unobtrusive" items that they believed potentially related to patient rehabilitation on a state hospital ward. Those items included observations of the working condition of the washer and dryer, the number of pieces of incoming mail, and the number of referrals to vocational rehabilitation services. Holahan (1972), in addition to the time sampling measure of social interaction, recorded the number of cigarette butts left in the experimental dayroom after the sessions, the number of ounces of coffee consumed, and the number of minutes spent in the room after the anounced end of the session. Interestingly, all three measures were positively correlated with the amount of social interaction.

Accuracy. There are two general procedures for determining the accuracy (reliability) of observations: (a) the observer's recordings can be compared to a criterion set of recordings developed from known stimulus material; (b) the observer can be joined in the recording process by another observer with later comparison between the two recordings. The latter is the more typical way of assessing accuracy, and is most often labeled interrater reliability or interrater agreement. It is obviously essential to determine the accuracy of the assessment information; inaccurate information is worthless. Indeed, Paul and his colleagues train their TSBC and SRIC observers to 100 percent agreement on each and every instance of observation. As Fiske (1980) points out, this is an extraordinarily high level of interrater agreement and is the foundation for the demonstrated usefulness of the TSBC and SRIC for patient assessment and/or program evaluation.

The most widely reported index of agreement simply divides the number of agreements by the sum of agreements plus disagreements, and then multiplies the result by 100 to achieve a percent agreement figure (Frederiksen &, Williams, 1977; Holahan, 1972; Jaffe & Carlson, 1976; Tracey et al., 1974; Wincze et al., 1972). The use of this formula with behaviors that have either a very high or very low rate of occurrence, however, may lead to spuriously inflated agreement estimates. Hawkins and Dotson (1975) suggest corrective alterations of the index. If a behavior occurs at a very low rate, then only occasions when either observer scored the behavior should be included in calculating the index (e.g., Wallace & Davis, 1974). If a behavior occurs at a high rate, then only the occasions when either observer did not score the behavior should be included in the calculations. Other corrective alterations have been suggested, and the reader can consult Wallace and Elder (1980) for a summary. Interrater agreement can be calculated in several other ways (also summarized in Wallace & Elder, 1980): Pearson correlation coefficient (e.g., Fichter et al., 1976; Martindale et al., 1978; Turner et al., 1978), intraclass correlation coefficient (Alevizos et al., 1978; Paul et al., 1973), contingency coefficient (Hunter et al., 1962), phi coefficient (Winkler, 1970), kappa (Winkler, 1970), or weighted kappa (Alevizos et al., 1978).

A difficulty in the measurement of interrater agreement is the reactivity of the agreement process. Several laboratory-based studies (Kent et al., 1974; O'Leary & Kent, 1973) have indicated that agreement may increase when the observer is aware that his agreement with an independent observer is being assessed. The implication is that data are different when the observer is being assessed than when he or she is not. To reduce this effect, it is possible to either use continuous agreement monitoring (Tracey et al., 1974), or randomly schedule frequent checks.

Methods of Observation and Recording

Perhaps the most convenient observation (as well as the lowest in reactivity) is the recording of the permanent products of a behavior. Assuming that the products last long enough, observations can be scheduled to suit the time and place of the observer.

Many behaviors, however, are not easily defined in terms of enduring environmental changes (e.g., delusions). These behaviors have to be directly observed and are usually recorded each time they occur (e.g., Richardson et al., 1972; Winkler's [1970] recording of noise and violence). If, however, the behavior occurs at either a very high or low rate, the observer may "miss" instances of the behavior. A solution to this is to schedule the time and place for the occurrence of the behavior, counting only during the scheduled observations (e.g., Ayllon & Haughton, 1964; Fichter et al., 1976; Wincze et al., 1972). Another solution is to divide the observation period into intervals and then record the occurrence or non-occurrence of the behavior during each interval, rather than counting the number of instances of it (e.g., Mitchell & Stoeffelmayer, 1973). Still another solution is to schedule brief observation periods as samples of a larger time block such as a day, noting the occurrence or non-occurrence of the behavior during each period (e.g., Hunter et al., 1962; Schaefer & Martin, 1966; Taylor et al., 1979).

Validity

The question of the validity of behavioral measures has rarely been considered. Johnson and Bolstad (1973) have a cogent discussion of the issues involved, and the reader is urged to consult their article. Briefly, construct validity refers to the generalization of information from one method of measuring a construct to another method of measuring the same construct. This implies that behavior assessments are concerned with constructs rather than discrete, unitary behaviors. As seemingly simple a label as self-care skills encompasses a large array of discrete behaviors and is best considered a construct rather than a "behavior." This is even more the case for labels such as interpersonal skills or delusional speech.

Studies by Paul and his colleagues (e.g., Mariotto, 1980; Mariotto & Paul, 1974; Power, 1980) have extensively investigated the construct validities of their instruments. In the Mariotto and Paul (1974) study, several methods (interview-based rating scales, ward rating scales, and observational measures) were used to assess a set of traits defined by the IMPS. As indicated previously, concurrent validity of the IMPS was good, although it was not a valid measure of change. Unfortunately, besides the studies conducted by Paul and his colleagues and the studies of the validity of various methods of assessing social skills (see Bellack, 1979; Hersen & Bellack, 1978), scant attention has been paid to assessing the content, criterion-related, or construct validities of behavioral assessment methods used with chronic psychiatric patients.

CASE EXAMPLE

A case treated on the Clinical Research Unit (CRU) at Camarillo State Hospital will be described as a means of illustrating several of the observation and recording procedures reviewed.

Patient

BR was a 20-year-old caucasian male who had been hospitalized for 5 months before he was transferred to the CRU. His DSM-II diagnosis, given by the admitting physician, was simple schizophrenia. He had been hospitalized with the same diagnosis for a 3-week period approximately 6 months prior to the current hospitalization. He was referred to the CRU because of his aggressive behavior at home, incoherent speech, and difficulty in performing simple self-care and personal hygiene behaviors.

Setting

The CRU has been described in detail in another publication (Liberman et al., 1974). However, to briefly review, the CRU is a 12-bed inpatient unit designed to provide intensive behavioral treatment for a variety of disorders. The unit is relatively "richly" staffed by 14 nurses and psychiatric technicians (for 24-hour coverage), and a psychiatrist, psychologist, and social worker (all full time). Each patient participates in both standardized and individualized treatment programs. The standardized programs are organized into a token economy and apply to all patients on the unit. Included as targets are self-care and personal hygiene skills (grooming, showering, eating behaviors, room maintenance), physical assault, and work skills (on- and off-unit jobs). The individualized programs are, of course, unique to each patient and allow almost complete flexibility in the selection of target behaviors, assessment, and the use of contingencies.

Assessment and Treatment

Based on the reasons for BR's referral to the CRU and on observations by all staff members during his first week on the unit, several behaviors were targeted for change. Among them were the following:

Voice Volume. It became apparent from just a few hours observation that BR's speech was not so much incoherent as so low in volume that it was unintelligible. There was no evidence of incoherence in the sense of thought disorder (e.g., thought insertion, thought stopping), delusions, or hallucinations. Since the extremely low volume made interaction with BR difficult and unpleasant, a decision was made to design an individualized program to increase his volume.

The first step in designing the program was to decide on a general approach to treatment. Voice volume could have simply been increased by not attending to BR's requests until he spoke at a "normal" volume. However, the determination of "normal" volume was quite likely to vary considerably from staff member to staff member and to depend, at least to some extent, on the amount of noise present when the request was made. Additionally, this approach would not have allowed "shaping" of volume since the levels intermediate to the initially low level and the final "normal" level would have been very difficult to reliably discriminate and reinforce, particularly as BR was making requests in the midst of the usual hubbub of the unit. Hence, the general approach to treatment was to train voice volume in scheduled sessions, using an assessment procedure that would reliably discriminate small shifts in volume.

The second step was to design the assessment procedures. One option was to have staff members assess relative loudness levels; however, this would have required laboriously training all 17 to accurately detect differences between BR's volume and some arbitrary standard. A far easier and more accurate procedure was to use an automatic device, such as a voice actuated relay or the db meter of a tape recorder. A voice actuated relay was selected since it could easily be connected to a feedback stimulus, such as lights. (A voice actuated relay closes when the volume of ambient noise exceeds a criterion level that can be adjusted by the user. The relay can be used to operate lights, times, reinforcement dispensers, etc.) The feedback would train both BR and staff members present during the scheduled session to discriminate among various volume levels.

Two different types of sessions were planned with the voice actuated relay. Both sessions were to be conducted in a small, somewhat sound attenuated room on the CRU. The first type of session, used at the beginning of treatment program, involved asking BR questions about the names of the staff members who fulfilled various roles on the unit (e.g., who is the unit charge?). The staff member conducting the session looked at the lights operated by the voice actuated relay only when BR answered. If the lights came on when BR pronounced just the last name of the staff member, a "1" was tallied on a data sheet. If the lights did not come on, the volume was not loud enough and a "0" was tallied. The data sheet was kept on a clipboard in the nursing office along with clipboards for each of the other CRU patients. BR's clipboard was carried to each of the two daily sessions. The data from each session were summarized and graphed by the staff on the graveyard shift.

It was apparent from the beginning of the program that increasing the volume with which BR spoke one word of a two or three word reply was not the terminal goal of treatment. Rather, the terminal goal was to increase volume in day-to-day conversations with interpersonal partners with whom BR might eventually form friendships. Thus, the second type of session, used during the later part of the program, changed the focus from answering questions to participating in conversations. This also required a change in the method of assessing volume from a frequency count of discrete "trials" exceeding a criterion level, to the duration of time that BR's speech exceeded the criterion. However, to actually carry on a conversation would have meant a natural ebb and flow in BR's speech that would have differed from conversation to conversation and would have affected the duration measure (adding to error). Hence, the assessment procedures for the second type of session consisted of giving BR a newspaper and asking him to read selected articles for 5 minutes (timed by a stopwatch). The relay was connected to a timer, so that it turned on and stayed on as long as the volume exceeded the criterion.

The third step was to specify the contingencies. BR received one "special" token during the first type of session whenever a "1" was recorded on the data sheet. Three special tokens were then exchanged for one regular token. For the second type of session, BR received one regular token for each 20 seconds that his speech exceeded the criterion.

Grooming. BR's rather unkempt appearance also seemed to be an obstacle to his forming friendships and being "accepted" into the community. Thus, BR's grooming was targeted for improvement in a two-part program. The first part was designed to ensure that BR groomed correctly after arising in the morning. This was assessed as part of the standardized personal hygiene program. BR was observed with three other patients in a morning session in which he was expected to comb his hair, brush his teeth, wash his face and hands, shave, tuck in his shirt, and have on matching socks and matching shoes with the laces tied. When BR thought that he had completed his grooming, he asked the supervising staff member to check his appearance. If he had not been observed performing a behavior (e.g., brush teeth), or his appearance was not appropriate (e.g., hair not neatly combed), he was prompted to correct the deficiencies. The number of prompts was the measure of grooming for this part.

The second part of the program was designed to ensure that BR's appropriate grooming was maintained throughout the day. BR's appearance was checked at 10:00 a.m., 12:15 p.m., 4:30 p.m., 6:00 p.m., and 8:00 p.m., with each of the following noted as being appropriate or inappropriate: matching shoes on and tied, matching socks on, shirt on and fully buttoned and tucked in, pants on and zipped, face clean (no obvious dirt smudges), and hands clean (no obvious smudges or dirt under the finger nails). With the parents' cooperation, home visits were made contingent upon at least 3 out of 7 days with no prompts during the morning grooming session, plus 4 days with at least four of the five checks completely appropriate.

Results

Figure 10.1 presents the results for the first type of session to increase BR's voice volume. To demonstrate that the contingency was responsible for the increase in volume, it was discontinued for 2 days, at which point his performance deteriorated. Reinstating the contingency resulted in an immediate increase in volume.

Figure 10.2 presents the results for the second type of session. During this period, the parents requested that his medication be discontinued since they thought it was unnecessary and may even have interferred with his social responsiveness. The medication was discontinued and, after an initial increase, his volume deteriorated markedly. Rather than

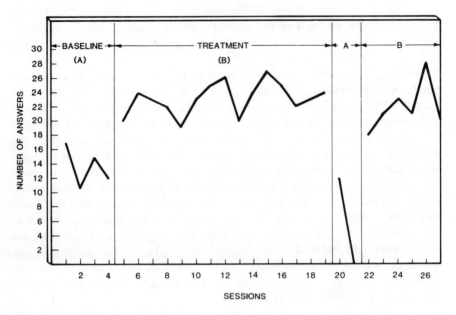

Fig. 10.1. Number of answers per session in which the volume of the last word met or exceeded the criterion level.

read, BR would simply stand and stare blankly at the newspaper. Medication was readministered with a concomitant increase in performance.

The prompts to groom appropriately during the morning session reduced from an average of nine prompts per session during the first eight baseline sessions to only one in the last eight sessions of the program. The number of grooming items noted as inappropriate during the five daily checks reduced from an average of 5.9 per day during the first 8 days to 1.375 during the last 8 days. Both measures of grooming showed a substantial deterioration during the withdrawal of medication.

The parents, who were BR's conservators, informed the unit during the middle of the treatment program that they wanted to remove him from the hospital and keep him at home. In spite of the evidence, they believed that he should not receive medication and that he would do much better at home.

SUMMARY

This chapter surveys the methods of assessments used in the behavioral treatment of psychotic individuals. The chapter is organized into 4 sections. The first reviews the methods of assessing outcome in token

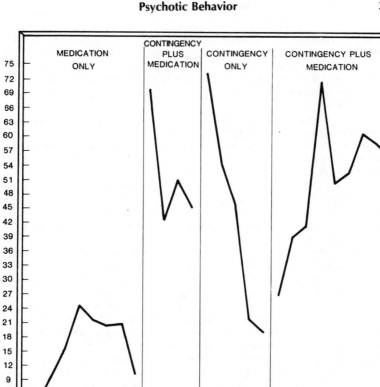

Fig. 10.2. Number of seconds per block of 2 sessions in which BR's volume met or exceeded the criterion level.

economy studies. The second reviews methods of assessing various classes of excesses and deficits that have been the targets of the behavioral interventions. The third section reviews methods of assessing behaviors that have not been the targets of the interventions, but whose data have been used to develop a "picture" of a large scale environment (e.g., a ward or a day hospital) or to evaluate the generalization of treatment effects. The fourth section reviews various rating scales that have been frequently used in studies of behavioral interventions.

REFERENCES

Aitchison, R. A. A low-cost, rapid delivery point system with "automatic" recording. *Journal of Applied Behavior Analysis*, 1972, 5, 527–528.

Alevizos, P., DeRisi, W., Liberman, R., Eckman, T., & Callahan, E. The Behavior Observation Instrument: A method of observation for program evaluation. *Journal of Applied Behavior Analysis*, 1978, *11*, 243–257.

Alford, G. S., & Turner, S. M. Stimulus interference and conditioned inhibition of auditory hallucinations. *Journal of Behavior Therapy and Experimental Psychiatry*, 1976, *7*, 155–160.

Allen, D. J., & Magaro, P. A. Measures of change in token economy programs. *Behaviour Research and Therapy*, 1971, *9*, 311–318.

Anderson, L. T., & Alpert, M. Operant analysis of hallucination frequency in a hospitalized schizophrenic. *Journal of Behavior Therapy and Experimental Psychiatry*, 1974, *5*, 13–19.

Atthowe, J. M. Controlling nocturnal enuresis in severely disabled and chronic patients. *Behavior Therapy*, 1972, *3*, 232–240.

Atthowe, J. M., & Krasner, L. Preliminary report on the application of contingent reinforcement procedures (token economy) on a "chronic" psychiatric ward. *Journal of Abnormal Psychology*, 1968, *73*, 37–43.

Arann, L., & Horner, V. M. Contingency management in an open psychiatric ward. *Journal of Behavior Therapy and Experimental Psychiatry*, 1972, *3*, 31–37.

Ayllon, T. Intensive treatment of psychotic behaviour by stimulus satiation and food reinforcement. *Behaviour Research and Therapy*, 1963, *1*, 53–61.

Ayllon, T., & Azrin, N. H. The measurement and reinforcement of behavior of psychotics. *Journal of the Experimental Analysis of Behavior*, 1965, *8*, 357–383.

Ayllon, T., & Azrin, N. H. *The token economy: A motivational system for therapy and rehabilitation*. New York: Appleton-Century-Crofts, 1968a.

Ayllon, T., & Azrin, N. H. Reinforcer sampling: A technique for increasing the behavior of mental patients. *Journal of Applied Behavior Analysis*, 1968b, *1*, 13–20.

Ayllon, T., & Haughton, E. Control of the behavior of schizophrenic patients by food. *Journal of the Experimental Analysis of Behavior*, 1962, *5*, 343–352.

Ayllon, T., & Haughton, E. Modification of symptomatic verbal behaviour of mental patients. *Behaviour Research and Therapy*, 1964, *2*, 87–97.

Ayllon, T., & Michael, J. The psychiatric nurse as a behavioral engineer. *Journal of Experimental Analysis of Behavior*, 1959, *2*, 323–334.

Azrin, N. H., Holy, W., Ulrich, R., & Goldiamond, I. The control of the content of conversation through reinforcement. *Journal of the Experimental Analysis of Behavior*, 1961, *4*, 25–30.

Aumack, L. The patient activity checklist: An instrument and an approach for measuring behavior. *Journal of Clinical Psychology*, 1969, *25*, 134–137.

Baker, R. The use of operant conditioning to reinstate speech in mute schizophrenics. *Behaviour Research and Therapy*, 1971, *9*, 329–336.

Bartlett, D., Ora, J. P., Brown, E., & Butler, J. The effects of reinforcement on psychotic speech in a case of early infantile autism, age 12. *Journal of Behavior Therapy and Experimental Psychiatry*, 1971, *2*, 145–149.

Bellack, A. S. A critical appraisal of strategies for assessing social skills. *Behavioral Assessment*, 1979, *1*, 157–177.

Bellack, A. S., & Hersen, M. Chronic psychiatric patients: Social skills training. In M. Hersen & A. S. Bellack (Eds.), *Behavior therapy in the psychiatric setting*. Baltimore, Md.: Williams & Wilkins, 1978.

Bennett, P. S., & Maley, R. F. Modification of interactive behaviors in chronic mental patients. *Journal of Applied Behavior Analysis*, 1973, *6*, 609–620.

Bergman, R. L. Behavioral contracting with chronic schizophrenics. *Journal of Behavior Therapy and Experimental Psychiatry*, 1975, *6*, 355–356.

Bernhardt, A. J., Hersen, M., & Barlow, D. H. Measurement and Modification of spasmodic torticollis: An experimental analysis. *Behavior Therapy*, 1972, *3*, 294–297.

Birky, H. J., Chambliss, J. E., & Wasden, R. A comparison of residents discharged from a token economy and two traditional psychiatric programs. *Behavior Therapy*, 1971, *2*, 46–51.

Bucher, B., & Fabricatore, J. Use of patient-administered shock to suppress hallucinations. *Behavior Therapy*, 1970, *1*, 382–385.

Calhoun, J. F. Modifying the academic performance of the chronic psychiatric inpatient. *Journal of Consulting and Clinical Psychology*, 1974, *42*, 621.

Callahan, E. J., Alevizos, P., Teigen, J., Neuman, H., & Campbell, M. Behavioral effects of reducing the daily frequency of phenothiazine administration. *Archives of General Psychiatry*, 1975, *32*, 1285–1290.

Carlson, C. G., Hersen, M., & Eisler, R. M. Token economy programs in the treatment of hospitalized adult psychiatric patients. *Journal of Nervous and Mental Diseases*, 1972, *155*, 192–204.

Carroccio, D. F., Latham, S., & Carroccio, B. B. Rate-contingent guitar rental to decelerate stereotyped head/face touching of an adult male psychiatric patient. *Behavior Therapy*, 1976, *6*, 104–109.

Cautela, J. R., & Baron, M. G. Multifaceted behavior therapy of self-injurious behavior. *Journal of Behavior Therapy and Experimental Psychiatry*, 1973, *4*, 125–131.

Cayner, J. J., & Kiland, J. R. Use of brief time out with three schizophrenic patients. *Journal of Behavior Therapy and Experimental Psychiatry*, 1974, *5*, 141–145.

Chapman, L. J. Recent advances in the study of schizophrenic cognition. *Schizophrenia Bulletin*, 1979, *5*, 568–581.

Coleman, A. D., & Boren, J. J. An information system for measuring patient behavior and its use by staff. *Journal of Applied Behavior Analysis*, 1969, *2*, 207–214.

Cox, M. D. Treatment and management of a case of self-burning. *Behaviour Research and Therapy*, 1976, *14*, 382–385.

Cromwell, R. L. Assessment of schizophrenia. *Annual Review of Psychology*, 1975, *26*, 593–621.

Curran, J. P., Lentz, R. J., & Paul, G. L. Effectiveness of sampling-exposure procedures on facilities utilization by psychiatric hard-core chronic patients. *Journal of Behavior Therapy and Experimental Psychiatry*, 1973, *4*, 201–207.

Davis, J. R., Wallace, C. J., Liberman, R. P., & Finch, B. E. The use of brief isolation to suppress delusional and hallucinatory speech. *Journal of Behavior Therapy and Experimental Psychiatry*, 1976, *7*, 269–275.

Davison, G. C. Appraisal of behavior modification techniques with adults in institutional settings. In C. M. Franks (Ed.), *Behavior therapy: Appraisal and status*. New York: McGraw-Hill, 1969.

DeVries, D. L. Effects of environmental change and of participation on the behavior of mental patients. *Journal of Consulting and Clinical Psychology*, 1968, *32*, 532–536.

Doty, D. W., McInnis, T., & Paul, G. L. Remediation of negative side effects of an ongoing response-cost system with chronic mental patients. *Journal of Applied Behavior Analysis*, 1974, *7*, 191–198.

Elliott, P. A., Barlow, F., Hooper, A., & Kingerlee, P. E. Maintaining patients' improvements in a token economy. *Behaviour Research and Therapy*, 1979, *17*, 355–367.

Ellsworth, R. B. The MACC behavioral adjustment scale, Form II. Beverly Hills, California: Western Psychological Services, 1962.

Ericksen, R. A., & Huber, H. Elimination of hysterial torticollis through the use of a metronome in an operant conditioning paradigm. *Behavior Therapy*, 1975, *6*, 405–406.

Errickson, E., Darnell, M. H., & Labeck, L. Brief treatment of hallucinatory behavior with behavioral techniques. *Behavior Therapy*, 1978, *9*, 663–665.

Fairbanks, L. A., McGuire, M. T., Cole, S. R., Sbordone, R., Silvers, F. M., Richards, M., & Akers, I. The ethological study of four psychiatric wards: Patient, staff, and system behaviours. *Journal of Psychiatric Research*, 1977, *13*, 193–209.

Farina, A., Arenberg, D., & Guskin, S. A scale for measuring minimal social behavior. *Journal of Consulting Psychology*, 1957, *21*, 265–268.

Feingold, L., & Migler, B. The use of experimental dependency relationships as a motivating procedure on a token economy ward. In R. D. Rubin, H. Fensterheim, J. D. Henderson, & L. P. Ullmann (Eds.), *Advances in behavior therapy*. New York: Academic Press, 1972.

Fethke, G. C. The relevance of economic theory and technology to token reinforcement systems. *Behaviour Research and Therapy*, 1972, *10*, 191–192.

Fichter, M. M., Wallace, C. J., Liberman, R. P., & Davis, J. R. Improving social interaction in a chronic psychotic using discriminated avoidance ("nagging"): Experimental analysis and generalization. *Journal of Applied Behavior Analysis*, 1976, *9*, 377–386.

Finch, B. E., Wallace, C. J., & Davis, J. R. Behavioral observations before, during, and after brief isolation (time-out). *The Journal of Nervous and Mental Diseases*, 1976, *163*, 408–413.

Fisher, E. B., Winkler, R. C., & Krauser, L. Economic perspectives in behavior therapy: Complex interdependencies in token economies. *Behavior Therapy*, *9*, 391–403.

Fiske, D. W. A demonstration of the value of interchangeable observers. *Journal of Behavior Assessment*, 1980, in press.

Frederiksen, L. W., & Williams, I. G. Individualized point systems with a chronic schizophrenic: Component analysis and management in the natural environment. *Journal of Behavior Therapy and Experimental Psychiatry*, 1977, *8*, 205–209.

Fullerton, D. T., Cayner, J. J., & McLaughlin-Reidel, T. Results of a token economy. *Archives of General Psychiatry*, 1978, *35*, 1451–1453.

Gardos, G., Cole, I. O., & LaBrie, R. The assessment of tardive dyskinesia. *Archives of General Psychiatry*, 1977, *34*, 1206–1212.

Gelfand, D. M., Gelfand, S., & Dobson, N. R. Unprogrammed reinforcement of patients' behavior in a mental hospital. *Behaviour Research and Therapy*, 1967, *5*, 201–207.

Gershone, J. R., Errickson, E. A., Mitchell, J. E., & Paulson, D. A. Behavioral comparison of a token economy and a standard psychiatric treatment ward. *Journal of Behavior Therapy and Experimental Psychiatry*, 1977, *8*, 381–385.

Glickman, H., Plutchik, R., & Landau, H. Social and biological reinforcement in an open psychiatric ward. *Journal of Behavior Therapy and Experimental Psychiatry*, 1973, *4*, 121–124.

Goldberg, L. R. Objective diagnostic tests and measures. *Annual Review of Psychology*. 1974, *25*, 343–367.

Green, R. W. Self-regulated eating behaviors in a diabetic mental patient. *Behavior Therapy*, 1978, *9*, 521–525.

Greenberg, D. J., Scott, S. B., Pisa, A., & Friesen, D. D. Beyond the token economy: A comparison of two contingency programs. *Journal of Consulting and Clinical Psychology*, 1975, *43*, 498–503.

Gripp, R. F., & Magaro, P. A. A token economy program evaluation with untreated ward comparisons. *Behaviour Research and Therapy*, 1971, *9*, 137–149.

Gripp, R. F., & Magaro, P. A. The token economy program in the psychiatric hospital: A review and analysis. *Behaviour Research and Therapy*, 1974, *12*, 205–228.

Gruenberg, E. M., Brandon, S., & Kasius, R. D. Identifying cases of the social breakdown syndrome. In E. M. Gruenberg (Ed.), *Evaluating the effectiveness of community mental health services*. New York: Milbank, 1966.

Grzesiak, R. C., & Locke, B. J. Cognitive and behavioral correlates to overt behavior change within a token economy. *Journal of Consulting and Clinical Psychology*, 1975, *43*, 272.

Hagen, R. L., Craighead, W. E., & Paul, G. L. Staff reactivity to evaluative behavioral observations. *Behavior Therapy*, 1975, *6*, 201–206.

Hall. I. N., Baker, R. D., & Hutchinson, K. A controlled evaluation of token economy procedures with chronic schizophrenic patients. *Behaviour Research and Therapy*, 1977, *15*, 261–283.

Harmatz, M. G., & Lapuc, R. Behavior modification of over-eating in a psychiatric population. *Journal of Consulting and Clinical Psychology*, 1968, *32*, 583–587.

Harris, C. S. A non-automated, but practical rapid delivery point card system for token economies. *Behavior Therapy*, 1977, *8*, 495–498.

Hartlage, L. C. Subprofessional therapists' use of reinforcement versus traditional psychotherapeutic techniques with schizophrenics. *Journal of Consulting and Clinical Psychology*, 1970, *34*, 181–183.

Hartmann, D. P., & Atkinson, C. Having your cake and eating it too: A note on some apparent contradictions between therapeutic achievements and design requirements in N = 1 studies. *Behavior Therapy*, 1973, *4*, 589–591.

Hawkins, R. P., & Dotson, V. A. Reliability scores that delude. In E. Ramp, & G. Semb (Eds.), *Behavior analysis: Areas of research and application*. Englewood Cliffs, New Jersey: Prentice-Hall, 1975.

Hayden, T., Osborne, A. E., Hall. S. M., & Hall, R. R. Behavioral effects of price changes in a token economy. *Journal of Abnormal Psychology*, 1974, *83*, 432–439.

Haynes, S. N., & Geddy, P. Suppression of psychotic hallucinations through time-out. *Behavior Therapy*, 1973, *4*, 123–127.

Heap, R. T., Boblitt, W. E., Moore, C. H., & Hord, J. E. Behavior-milieu therapy with chronic neuropsychiatric patients. *Journal of Abnormal Psychology*. 1970, *76*, 349–354.

Henderson, J. D., & Scoles, P. E., Jr. Conditioning techniques in a community-based operant environment for psychotic men. *Behavior Therapy*, 1970, *1*, 245–251.

Hersen, M. Token economies in institutional settings: Historical, political, deprivation, ethical, and generalization issues. *Journal of Nervous and Mental Disease*, 1976, *162*, 206–211.

Hersen, M., & Barlow, D. H. *Single case experimental designs: Strategies for studying behavior change*. New York: Pergamon Press, 1976.

Hersen, M., Eisler, R. M., Smith, B. S., & Agras, W. S. A token reinforcement ward for young psychiatric patients. *American Journal of Psychiatry*, 1972, *129*, 228–233.

Higgs, W. J. Effects of gross environmental changes upon behavior of schizophrenics: A cautionary note. *Journal of Abnormal Psychology*, 1970, *76*, 421–422.

Holahan, C. J. Seating patterns and patient behavior in an experimental dayroom. *Journal of Abnormal Psychology*, 1972, *80*, 115–124.

Holahan, C. J., & Saegert, S. Behavioral and attitudinal effects of large-scale variation in the physical environment of psychiatric wards. *Journal of Abnormal Psychology*, 1973, *82*, 454–462.

Hollander, M., & Glickman, H. Cooperating training in schizophrenics. *Behavior Therapy*, 1976, *7*, 696–697.

Hollander, M., Plutchik, R., & Horner, V. Interaction of patient and attendant reinforcement programs: The "piggyback" effect. *Journal of Consulting and Clinical
Psychology*, 1973, *41*, 43–47.

Hollingsworth, R., & Foreyt, J. P. Community adjustment of released token economy
patients. *Journal of Behavior Therapy and Experimental Psychiatry*, 1975, *6*, 271–
274.

Honigfeld, G., Gillis, R. O., & Klett, C. J. NOSIE – 30: A treatment-sensitive ward
behavior scale, *Psychological Reports*, 1966, *19*, 180–182.

Hunter, M., Schooler, C., & Spohn, H. E. The measurement of characteristic patterns
of ward behaviors in chronic schizophrenics. *Journal of Consulting Psychology*, 1962,
26, 69–73.

Hutchinson, R. R., & Azrin, N. H. Conditioning of mental-hospital patients. *Journal
of the Experimental Analysis of Behavior*, 1961, *4*, 87–93.

Issacs, W., Thomas, J., & Goldiamond, I. Application of operant conditioning to reinstate verbal behavior in psychotics. *Journal of Speech and Hearing Disorders*, 1960,
25, 8–12.

Ittelson, W. H., Rivlin, L. G., & Proshansky, H. M. The use of behavioral maps in
environmental psychology. In H. M. Proshansky, W. H. Ittelson, & L. G. Rivlin
(Eds.), *Environmental Psychology*. New York: Holt, Rinehart & Winston, 1970.

Jaffe, P. G., & Carlson, P. M. Relative efficacy of modeling and instructions in eliciting
social behavior from chronic psychiatric patients. *Journal of Consulting and Clinical
Psychology*, 1976, *44*, 200–207.

Johnson, S. M., & Bolstad, O. D. Methodological issues in naturalistic observation:
Some problems and solutions for field research. In L. A. Hamerlynck, L. C. Handy,
& E. J. Mash (Eds.), *Behavior Change: Methodology, Concepts, and Practice*. Cham-
paign, Ill.: Research Press, 1973.

Johnson, S. M., & Bolstad, O. D. Reactivity to home observation: A comparison of
audio recorded behavior with observers present or absent. *Journal of Applied Behavioral Analysis*, 1975, *8*, 181–187.

Kagel, J. H., & Winkler, R. C. Behavioral economics: Areas of cooperative research
between economics and applied behavior analysis. *Journal of Applied Behavior Analysis*, 1972, *5*, 335–342.

Kale, R. J., Kaye, J. H., Whelan, P. A., & Hopkins, B. L. The effects of reinforcement
on the modification, maintenance, and generalization of social responses of mental
patients. *Journal of Applied Behavior Analysis*, 1968, *1*, 307–314.

Katz, R. C., Johnson, C. A., & Gelfand, S. Modifying the dispensing of reinforcers:
Some implications for behavior modification with hospitalized patients. *Behavior
Therapy*, 1972, *3*, 579–588.

Kazdin, A. E. Recent advances in token economy research. In M. Hersen, R. M. Eisler,
& P. M. Miller (Eds.), *Progress in behavior modification*. Vol. I. New York: Academic Press, 1975.

Kazdin, A. E. *The token economy*. New York: Plenum Press, 1977.

Kazdin, A. E. Chronic psychiatric patients: Wardwide reinforcement programs. In M. Hersen
& A. S. Bellack (Eds.), *Behavior therapy in the psychiatric setting*. Baltimore, Md.: Williams & Wilkins, 1978.

Kazdin, A. E., & Bootzin, R. R. The token economy: An evaluative review. *Journal
of Applied Behavior Analysis*, 1972, *5*, 343–372.

Kennedy, T. Treatment of chronic schizophrenia by behaviour therapy: Case reports.
Behaviour Research and Therapy, 1964, *2*, 1–5.

Kent, R. N., O'Leary, K. D., Diament, C., & Dietz, A. Expectation biases in observational evaluation of therapeutic change. *Journal of Consulting and Clinical Psychology*, 1974, *42*, 774–781.

King, G. F., Armitage, S. G., & Tilton, J. R. A therapeutic approach to schizophrenics of extreme pathology: An operant-interpersonal method. *Journal of Abnormal and Social Psychology,* 1960, *61,* 276–286.

King, G. F., Merrell, D. W., Lovinger, E., & Denny, M. R. Operant motor behavior in acute schizophrenia. *Journal of Personality,* 1957, *25,* 317–326.

Klinge, V., Thrasher, P., & Meyers, S. Use of bedrest overcorrection in a chronic schizophrenia. *Journal of Behavior Therapy and Experimental Psychiatry,* 1975, *6,* 69–73.

Kowalski, P. A., Daley, G. D., & Gripp, R. F. Token economy: Who responds how? *Behaviour Research and Therapy,* 1976, *14,* 372–374.

Lehrer, P., Schiff, L., & Kris, A. The use of a credit card in a token economy. *Journal of Applied Behavior Analysis,* 1970, *3,* 289–291.

Lentz, R. J. Changes in chronic mental patients' interview behavior: Effects of differential treatment and management. *Journal of Behavior Therapy and Experimental Psychiatry,* 1975, *6,* 192–199.

Lentz, R. J., Paul, G. L., & Calhoun, J. F. Reliability and validity of three measures of functioning with "hard core" chronic mental patients. *Journal of Abnormal Psychology,* 1971, *78,* 69–76.

Liberman, R. P. Reinforcement of social interaction in a group of chronic mental patients. In R. D. Rubin, H. Fensterheim, J. D. Henderson, & L. P. Ullmann (Eds.), *Advances in behavior therapy.* New York: Academic Press, 1972.

Liberman, R. P., Teigen, J., Patterson, R., & Baker, V. Reducing delusional speech in chronic, paranoid schizophrenics. *Journal of Applied Behavior Analysis,* 1973, *6,* 57–64.

Liberman, R. P., Wallace, C. J., Teigen, J., & Davis, J. R. Interventions with psychotic behaviors. In K. S. Calhoun, H. E. Adams, & K. M. Mitchell (Eds.), *Innovative treatment methods in psychopathology.* New York: Wiley, 1974.

Light, M. H. The staff resident interaction chronograph: Observational assessment of staff performance. *Journal of Behavior Assessment,* 1980, in press.

Lindsley, O. R. Operant conditioning methods applied to research in chronic schizophrenia. *Psychiatric Research Reports,* 1956, *5,* 118–139.

Lindsley, O. R. Reduction in rate of vocal psychotic symptoms by differential positive reinforcement. *Journal of the Experimental Analysis of Behavior,* 1959, *2,* 269.

Lindsley, O. R. Characteristics of the behavior of chronic psychotics as revealed by free-operant conditioning methods. *Diseases of the Nervous System,* 1960, *21,* 66–78.

Lindsley, O. R. Direct behavioral analysis of psychotherapy session by conjugately programmed closed-circuit television. Paper read at the Annual Meeting of the American Psychological Association, St. Louis, 1962.

Lindsley, O. R. Direct measurement and functional definition of vocal hallucinatory symptoms. *Journal of Nervous and Mental Disease,* 1963, *136,* 293–297.

Lindsley, O. R., & Skinner, B. F. A method for the experimental analysis of the behavior of psychotic patients. *American Psychologist,* 1954, *9,* 419–420.

Linscheid, T. R., Malosky, P., & Zimmerman, I. Discharge as the major consequence in a hospitalized patient's behavior management program: A case study. *Behavior Therapy,* 1974, 559–564.

Lloyd, K. E., & Abel, L., Performance on a token economy psychiatric ward: A two year summary. *Behaviour Research and Therapy,* 1970, *8,* 1–9.

Lloyd, K. E., & Garlington, W. K. Weekly variations in performance on a token economy psychiatric ward. *Behaviour Research and Therapy,* 1968, *6,* 407–410.

Logan, D. L. A "paper money" token system as a recording aid in institutional settings. *Journal of Applied Behavior Analysis,* 1970, *3,* 183–184.

Lorr, M., & Klett, C. J. *Inpatient multidimensional psychiatric scale*. Palo Alto, California: Consulting Psychologists Press, 1966.

- Lorr, M., O'Connor, J. P., & Stafford, J. W. The psychotic reactions profile. *Journal of Clinical Psychology*, 1960, *16*, 241–245.

McInnis, T., Himelstein, H. C., Doty, D. W., & Paul, G. L. Modification of sampling-exposure procedures for facilities utilization by chronic mental patients. *Journal of Behavior Therapy and Experimental Psychiatry*, 1974, *5*, 119–129.

McReynolds, W. T., & Coleman, J. Token economy: Patient and staff changes. *Behaviour Research and Therapy*, 1972, *10*, 29–35.

Mednick, M. T., & Lindsley, O. R. Some clinical correlates of operant behavior. *Journal of Abnormal and Social Psychology*, 1958, *57*, 13–16.

Meichenbaum, D. H. The effects of instructions and reinforcement on thinking and language behavior of schizophrenics. *Behaviour Research and Therapy*, 1969, *7*, 101–114.

Meichenbaum, D. H., & Cameron, R. Training schizophrenics to talk to themselves: A means of developing attentional controls. *Behavior Therapy*, 1973, *4*, 515–534.

Meyers, A., Mercatoris, M., & Sirota, A. Use of covert self-instruction for the elimination of psychotic speech. *Journal of Consulting and Clinical Psychology*, 1976, *44*, 480–482.

Milby, J. B. Modification of extreme social isolation by contingent social reinforcement. *Journal of Applied Behavior Analysis*, 1970, *3*, 149–152.

Milby, J. B., Clarke, C., Charles, E., & Willicutt, H. C. Token economy process variables: Effects of increasing and decreasing the critical range of savings. *Behavior Therapy*, 1977, *8*, 137–145.

Milby, J. B., Pendergrass, P. E., & Clarke, C. J. Token economy versus control ward: A comparison of staff and patient attitudes toward ward environment. *Behavior Therapy*, 1975, *6*, 22–30.

Milby, J. B., Willicutt, H. C., Hawk, J., MacDonald, M., & Whitfield, K. A system for efficiently recording individualized behavioral measures. *Journal of Applied Behavior Analysis*, 1973, *6*, 333–338.

Miller, H. R., & Dermer, S. W. Quasi-experimental follow-up of token economy and conventional treatment graduates. *Journal of Consulting and Clinical Psychology*, 1979, *47*, 625–627.

Mitchell, W. S., & Stoffelmayer, B. C. Application of the Premack principle of the behavioral control of extremely inactive schizophrenics. *Journal of Applied Behavioral Analysis*, 1973, *6*, 419–425.

Moore, C. W., & Crum, B. C. Weight reduction of a chronic schizophrenic by means of operant conditioning procedures: A case study. *Behaviour Research and Therapy*, *7*, 129–131.

Moos, R. H. Behavioral effects of being observed: Reactions to a wireless radio transmitter. *Journal of Consulting and Clinical Psychology*, 1968, *32*, 383–388.

Moos, R. H. Assessment of the environments of community-oriented psychiatric treatment programs. *Journal of Abnormal Psychology*, 1972, *79*, 9–18.

Moos, R. H., & Houts, P. S. Assessment of the social atmospheres of psychiatric wards. *Journal of Abnormal Psychology*, 1968, *73*, 595–604.

Moser, A. J. Covert punishment of hallucinatory behavior in a psychotic male. *Journal of Behavior Therapy and Experimental Psychiatry*, 1974, *5*, 297–301.

Nathan, P. E., Schneller, P., & Lindsley, O. R. Direct measurement of communication during psychiatric admission interviews. *Behaviour Research and Therapy*, 1964, *2*, 49–57.

Neale, J. M., & Cromwell, R. L. Attention and schizophrenia. In B. A. Maher (Ed.), *Progress in experimental personality research*. New York: Academic Press, 1970.

Nelson, G. L., & Cone, J. D. Multiple baseline analysis of a token economy for psychiatric in-patients. *Journal of Applied Behavior Analysis,* 1979, *12,* 255–271.

Nuechterlein, K. H. Reaction time and attention in schizophrenia: A critical evaluation of the data and theories. *Schizophrenia Bulletin,* 1977, *3,* 373–428.

Nydegger, R. V. The elimination of hallucinatory and delusional behavior by verbal conditioning and assertive training: A case study. *Journal of Behavior Therapy and Experimental Psychiatry,* 1972, *3,* 225–227.

O'Brien, F., & Azrin, N. H. Symptom reduction by functional displacement in a token economy: A case study. *Journal of Behavior Therapy & Experimental Psychiatry,* 1972, *3,* 205–207.

O'Brien, F., Azrin, N. H., & Henson, K. Increased communications of chronic mental patients by reinforcement and response priming. *Journal of Applied Behavior Analysis,* 1969, *2,* 23–31.

Olson, R. P., & Greenberg, D. J. Effects of contingency-contracting and decision making groups with chronic mental patients. *Journal of Consulting and Clinical Psychology,* 1972, *38,* 376–383.

Paden, R. C., Himelstein, H. C. & Paul, G. L. Videotape versus verbal feedback in the modification of meal behavior of chronic mental patients. *Journal of Consulting and Clinical Psychology,* 1974, *42,* 623–624.

Palmer, J., & McGuire, F. L. The use of unobtrusive measures in mental health research. *Journal of Consulting and Clinical Psychology,* 1973, *40,* 431–436.

Parrino, J. J., George, L., & Daniels, A. C. Token control of pill-taking behavior in a psychiatric ward. *Journal of Behavior Therapy and Experimental Psychiatry,* 1971, *2,* 181–185.

Patterson, R. L. *Maintaining effective token economies.* Springfield, Ill.: Charles C. Thomas, 1976.

Patterson, R. L., & Teigen, J. R. Conditioning and post-hospital generalization of nondelusional responses in a chronic psychotic patient. *Journal of Applied Behavior Analysis,* 1973, *6,* 65–70.

Paul, G. L., & Lentz, R. J. *Psychosocial treatment of mental patients.* Cambridge, Mass.: Harvard University Press, 1977.

Paul, G. L., McInnis, T. L., & Mariotto, M. J. Objective performance outcomes associated with two approaches to training mental health technicians in milieu and social-learning programs. *Journal of Abnormal Psychology,* 1973, *82,* 523–532.

Paul, G. L., Redfield, J. P., & Lentz, R. J. The inpatient scale of minimal functioning: A revision of the social breakdown syndrome gradient index. *Journal of Consulting and Clinical Psychology,* 1976, *44,* 1021–1022.

Paul, G. L., Tobias, L. L., & Holly, B. L. Maintenance psychotropic drugs in the presence of active treatment programs. *Archives of General Psychiatry,* 1972, *27,* 106–115.

Pickens, R., Errickson, E., Thompson, T., Heston, L., & Eckert, E. D. MMPI correlates of performance on a behavior therapy ward. *Behaviour Research and Therapy,* 1979, *17,* 17–24.

Polsky, R. H., & McGuire, M. T. Observational assessment of behavioral changes accompanying clinical improvement in hospitalized psychiatric patients. *Journal of Behavioral Assessment,* 1980, in press.

Pomerleau, O. F., Bobrove, P. H., & Harris, L. C. Some observations on a controlled social environment for psychiatric patients. *Journal of Behavior Therapy and Experimental Psychiatry,* 1972, *3,* 15–21.

Power, C. T. The time-sample behavior checklist: Observational assessment of patient functioning. *Journal of Behavior Assessment,* 1980, in press.

Richardson, R., Karkalas, Y., & Lal, H. Application of operant procedures in treatment of hallucinations in chronic psychotics. In R. D. Rubin, H. Fensterheim, J. D. Henderson, & L. P. Ullmann (Eds.), *Advances in behavior therapy.* New York: Academic Press, 1972.

Rickard, H. C., Dignam, P. J., & Horner, R. F. Verbal manipulation in a psychotherapeutic relationship. *Journal of Clinical Psychology,* 1960, *16,* 364–367.

Rickard, H. C. & Dinoff, M. A. A follow-up note on "verbal manipulation in a psychotherapeutic relationship." *Psychological Reports,* 1962, *11,* 506.

Roback, H., Frayn, D., Gumby, L., & Tuters, K. A multifactorial approach to the treatment and ward management of a self-mutilating patient. *Journal of Behavior Therapy and Experimental Psychiatry,* 1972, *3,* 189–193.

Roberts, A. E. Development of self-control using Premack's differential rate hypothesis: A case study. *Behaviour Research and Therapy,* 1969, *7,* 341–344.

Rostow, C. D., & Smith, C. E. Effects of contingency management of chronic patients on ward control and behavioral adjustment. *Journal of Behavior Therapy and Experimental Psychiatry,* 1975, *6,* 1–4.

Rutner, I. T., & Bugle, C. An experimental procedure for the modification of psychotic behavior. *Journal of Consulting and Clinical Psychology,* 1969, *33,* 651–653.

Rybolt, G. A. Token reinforcement therapy with chronic psychiatric patients: A three year evaluation, *Journal of Behavior Therapy and Experimental Psychiatry.* 1975, *6,* 188–191.

Sabatasso, A. P., & Jacobson, L. I. Use of behavioral therapy in the reinstatement of verbal behavior in a mute psychotic with chronic brain syndrome. *Journal of Abnormal Psychology,* 1970, *76,* 322–324.

Sanders, R. M. Time-out procedure for the modification of speech content—A case study. *Journal of Behavior Therapy and Experimental Psychiatry,* 1971, *2,* 199–202.

Sanson-Fisher, R. W., Poole, A. D., & Thompson, V. Behaviour patterns within a general hospital psychiatric unit: An observational study. *Behaviour Research and Therapy,* 1979, *17,* 317–332.

Schaefer, H. H., & Martin, P. L. Behavioral therapy for "apathy" of hospitalized schizophrenics. *Psychological Reports,* 1966, *19,* 1147–1158.

Schaefer, H. H., & Martin, P. L. *Behavioral therapy.* New York: McGraw Hill, 1969.

Schraa, J. C., Lautmann, L., Luzi, M. K., & Screven, C. G. Establishment of non-delusional responses in a socially withdrawn chronic schizophrenic. *Journal of Applied Behavior Analysis,* 1978, *11,* 433–434.

Schraa, J. C., Lautmann, L., & Screven, C. G. Increasing appropriate speech in a chronic schizophrenic. *Journal of Applied Behavior Analysis,* 1979, *12,* 302.

Schwartz, J., & Bellack, A. S. A comparison of a token economy with standard inpatient treatment. *Journal of Consulting and Clinical Psychology,* 1975, *43,* 107–109.

Shean, G. D., & Zeidberg, Z. Token reinforcement therapy: A comparison of matched groups, *Journal of Behavior Therapy and Experimental Psychiatry,* 1971, *2,* 94–105.

Sherman, J. A. Reinstatement of verbal behavior in a psychotic by reinforcement methods. *Journal of Speech and Hearing Disorders,* 1963, *28,* 398–401.

Sherman, J. A. Use of reinforcement and imitation to reinstate verbal behavior in mute psychotics. *Journal of Abnormal Psychology,* 1965, *70,* 155–164.

Siegel, J. M. Successful systematic desensitization in a chronic schizophrenic patient. *Journal of Behavior Therapy and Experimental Psychiatry,* 1975, *6,* 345–346.

Sobell, L. C., Schaefer, H. H., Sobell, M. B., & Kremer, M. E. Food priming: A therapeutic tool to increase the percentage of meals bought by chronic mental patients. *Behaviour Research and Therapy,* 1970, *8,* 339–345.

Stahl, J. R., & Leitenberg, H. Behavioral treatment of the chronic mental hospital patient. In H. Leitenberg (Ed.), *Handbook of behavior modification and behavior therapy.* Englewood Cliffs, New Jersey: Prentice-Hall, 1976.

Stahl, J. R., Thomson, L. E., Leitenberg, H., & Hasazi, J. E. Establishment of praise as a conditioned reinforcer in socially unresponsive psychiatric patients. *Journal of Abnormal Psychology,* 1974, *83,* 488–496.

Steffy, R. A., Hart, J., Craw, M., Torney, D., & Marlett, N. Operant behavior modification techniques applied to a ward of severely regressed and aggressive patients. *Canadian Psychiatric Association Journal,* 1969, *14,* 59–67.

Steinbook, R. M., Jacobson, A. F., Mosher, J. C., & Davies, D. L. The Goal Attainment Scale: An instructional guide for the delivery of social reinforcement. *Archives of General Psychiatry,* 1977, *34,* 923–926.

Sterling, F. E. Net positive social approaches of young psychiatric inpatients as influenced by nurse's attire. *Journal of Consulting and Clinical Psychology,* 1980, *48,* 58–62.

Tanner, B. A., Parrino, J. J., & Daniels, A. C. A token economy with "automated" data collection. *Behavior Therapy,* 1975, *6,* 111–118.

Taylor, C. B., Zlutnick, S. I., & Hoehle, W. The effects of behavioral procedures on Tardive Dyskinesias. *Behavior Therapy,* 1979, *10,* 37–45.

Thomson, N., Fraser, D., & McDougall, A. The reinstatment of speech in near-mute chronic schizophrenics by instructions, imitative prompts and reinforcement. *Journal of Behavior Therapy and Experimental Psychiatry,* 1974, *5,* 83–89.

Tracey, D. A., Briddell, D. W., & Wilson, G. T. Generalization of verbal conditioning to verbal and nonverbal behavior: Group therapy with chronic psychiatric patient dyads. *Journal of Applied Behavioral Analysis,* 1974, *7,* 391–402.

Trudel, G., & Boisvert, J. M. Unprogrammed reinforcement of patients' behaviors in wards with and without a token economy. *Journal of Behavior Therapy and Experimental Psychiatry,* 1974, *5,* 147–149.

Turner, S. M., Hersen, M., & Bellack, A. S. Effects of social disruption, stimulus interference, and aversive conditioning in auditory hallucinations. *Behavior Modification,* 1977, *1,* 249–258.

Ullmann, L. P., Forsman, R. G., Kenny, J. W., McInnis, T. L., Unikel, I. P., & Zeisset, R. M. Selective reinforcement of schizophrenics' interview responses. *Behaviour Research and Therapy,* 1965, *2,* 205–212.

Upper, D. "Ticket" system for reducing ward rules violations on a token economy program. *Journal of Behavior Therapy and Experimental Psychiatry,* 1973, *4,* 137–140.

Upper, D., & Newton, J. G. A weight reduction program for schizophrenic patients on a token economy unit: Two case studies. *Journal of Behavior Therapy and Experimental Psychiatry,* 1971, *2,* 113–115.

Wagner, B. R., & Paul, G. L. Reduction of incontinence in chronic patients: A pilot project. *Journal of Behavior Therapy and Experimental Psychiatry,* 1970, *1,* 29–38.

Wallace, C. J., & Davis, J. R. The effects of information and reinforcement on the conversational behavior of chronic psychiatric patient dyads. *Journal of Consulting and Clinical Psychology,* 1974, *42,* 656–662.

Wallace, C. J., Davis, J. R., Liberman, R. P., & Baker, V. Modeling and staff behavior. *Journal of Consulting and Clinical Psychology,* 1973, *41,* 422–426.

Wallace, C. J., & Elder, J. P. Statistics to evaluate measurement accuracy and treatment effects in single subject research designs. In M. Hersen, R. M. Eisler, & P. M. Miller (Eds.), *Progress in behavior modification.* Vol. 10. New York: Academic Press, 1980.

Weidner, F. In vivo desensitization of a paranoid schizophrenic. *Journal of Behavior Therapy and Experimental Psychiatry,* 1970, *1,* 79–81.

Weingaertner, A. H. Self-administered aversive stimulation with hallucinating hospitalized schizophrenics. *Journal of Consulting and Clinical Psychology,* 1971, *36,* 422–429.

Williams, J. E. Self-monitoring of paranoid behavior. *Behavior Therapy,* 1976, *7,* 562.

Wilson, F. S., & Walters, R. H. Modification of speech output of near mute schizophrenics through social learning procedures. *Behaviour Research and Therapy*, 1966,
4, 59–67.

Wincze, J. P., Leitenberg, H., & Agras, W. S. The effects of token reinforcement and
feedback on the delusional verbal behavior of chronic paranoid schizophrenics. *Journal of Applied Behavior Analysis*, 1972, *5*, 247–262.

Winkler, R. C. Management of chronic psychiatric patients by a token reinforcement
system. *Journal of Applied Behavior Analysis*, 1970, *3*, 47–55.

Winkler, R. C. The relevance of economic theory and technology to token reinforcement
systems. *Behaviour Research and Therapy*, 1971, *9*, 81–88.

Winkler, R. C. A theory of equilibrium in token economies. *Journal of Abnormal Psychology*, 1972, *79*, 169–173.

Zarlock, S. P. Social expectations, language, and schizophrenia. *Journal of Humanistic
Psychology*, 1966, *6*, 68–75.

Chapter 11
Assessment of Marital Dysfunction

Gayla Margolin
and
Neil S. Jacobson

INTRODUCTION

The assessment of marital dysfunction presents a rather unique challenge
to behaviorists since it requires examination of an ever-changing, idiosyncratic system linking two individuals in what is referred to as a
"relationship." As other chapters in this volume describe, behavioral
assessment typically directs attention to an individual's responses to
specific environmental situations. Applying this model of behavioral
assessment to dyadic systems has led to the view that marital relationships are the sum total of behaviors emitted by the two participants,
with each partner's behavior providing stimulus and reinforcing control
for the other. In this chapter, we will examine developments in marital
assessment that have grown out of the behavioral model, and the interface between the "traditional" objectives of behavioral assessment
and the assessment of marital systems. We will also explore a broad-
based assessment approach that ventures beyond the level of the individual and considers subjective as well as behavioral targets.

A historical review of the behavioral marital movement reveals a
simultaneous burgeoning of assessment instruments and therapy procedures during the past decade. Many of the important contributions
to the behavioral assessment of marriage came from the creative collaboration between the Oregon Research Institute and what is now the
Oregon Marital Studies Program (Patterson, 1976; Weiss, Hops, &

Patterson, 1973; Weiss & Margolin, 1977). Marking the beginning of a new era in the assessment of couples, these investigators explored a variety of new areas such as: (1) participant observation by spouses of the events in their marriage; (2) examination of the multitude of events that comprise spouses' day-to-day interactions; and (3) sequential coding of couples' problem-solving conversations.

Several comprehensive reviews offer detailed descriptions of instruments developed by the Oregon group as well as by other investigators (Jacob, 1976; Jacobson, Elwood, & Dallas, 1981; Weiss & Margolin, 1977). According to these reviews, the objectives of behavior marital instruments converge with the objectives that generally characterize behavioral assessment: (1) to aid the clinician in selecting appropriate therapeutic interventions; (2) to monitor and evaluate the efficacy of therapeutic interventions; and (3) to describe couples who are being treated. The atheoretical stance suggested by these objectives belies the theoretical parentage that actually spawned behavioral marital instruments.

The most pervasive theoretical basis for behavioral marital therapy and assessment comes from *behavior exchange theory*, which is essentially an integration of social exchange theory and operant learning principles (Jacobson & Moore, in press). As applied to marital relationships, this theory suggests that happy marriages are characterized by the maximization of mutual rewards and the minimization of costs. Unhappy marriages, in contrast, are characterized by a relative scarcity of positive reinforcers in partners' behavioral exchange (Rappaport & Harrell, 1971; Stuart, 1969). This integration of theories gave rise to the term *reciprocity*, which defines spouses' tendencies to reward one another at approximately equal rates (Patterson & Reid, 1970). It was further hypothesized that marital dissatisfaction is a function of couples' exchange of punishers, and that the ratio of rewards/punishments will provide the most accurate index of marital distress.

Not surprisingly, the assessment strategy that evolved from behavior exchange theory attempts to emphasize the exchange of positive and negative behaviors in the natural environment. The most widely used approach for assessing day-to-day exchanges of behavior is the *Spouse Observation Checklist* (SOC) (Patterson, 1976; Weiss & Perry, 1979), a lengthy list of pleasing and displeasing relationship behaviors. In a nomothetic approach, the individual items were designated as pleases or displeases by the originators of the checklist. Idiographic procedures for specifying the frequency and topography of rewarding and punishing exchanges include the behavioral interview and couples' self-monitoring of specific behaviors. (see Jacobson, Waldron, & Moore, 1980; Margolin, 1981).

The second major theoretical influence comes from *coercion theory* (Patterson & Reid, 1970), which suggests that marital conflict is the result of dysfunctional behavior change skills on the part of spouses (Patterson & Hops, 1972; Patterson, Hops, & Weiss, 1974; Weiss, Hops, & Patterson, 1973). Coercive behaviors are a subclass of aversive behaviors, used contingently to "turn off" attacks and/or elicit attention from the partner. The earmark of the coercive process is that one person is reinforced for behaving unpleasantly while the other is reinforced for complying. Although coercion may begin as a one-sided process, it is hypothesized that, over time, the victim learns to reciprocate these aversive control strategies with a net increase in intensity of aversive exchanges in both directions.

Coercion theory led to the assessment of couples' problem-solving capabilities through behavioral coding systems such as the *Marital Interaction Coding System* (MICS) by Hops, Wills, Patterson, and Weiss (1972), and the *Couples' Interaction Coding System* (CISS) by Gottman (1979). Although the coercion hypothesis describes changes that develop over a long period of time, it is presumed that coercive processes could be evidenced in certain behavioral outcomes, i.e., increased levels of blaming and threatening communications as well as decreased levels of constructive problem solving statements and positive affect.

A third input only recently integrated with behavior theory comes from the *systems* perspective: the notion that a relationship is more than the sum of its individual parts (Lederer & Jackson, 1968). To assess a marriage, it is not sufficient to assess the behavior, cognitions, and affective responses of each individual. It is also necessary to analyze and define characteristics of the relationship as a system. The study of interpersonal relationships requires examination of the types of interactional sequences which take place between people (Peterson, 1977). The understanding of ongoing overlapping chains of events led to the following formulation:

> A given item of A's behavior is a stimulus insofar as it is followed by an item contributed by B and that by another item contributed by A. But insofar as A's item is sandwiched between two items contributed by B, it is a response. Similarly A's item is a reinforcement insofar as it follows an item contributed by B. The ongoing interchanges, then which we are here discussing, constitute a chain of overlapping triadic links . . . [Bateson & Jackson, 1964, p. 273–274].

By viewing interactions as the basic unit, relationships can be characterized by their recurrent sequences.

Exploration of relationship variables is made possible by assessing reciprocal influences between spouses, with interactional sequences the target of observation. The predominant assessment procedure has been the sequential analysis of communication samples. Distressed and non-distressed couples, for example, have been differentiated by the extent to which their interactions are reciprocal, i.e., whether one person's behavior changes the probability of a similar behavior by the partner (Gottman, Markman, & Notarius, 1977; Margolin & Wampold, 1981). Gottman et al. further differentiated between the two sets of couples on the basis of their differential likelihood of engaging in certain recurrent interaction sequences of recognizable topography. More molar relationship patterns that occur in the natural environment (e.g., whether fights serve as antecedents for the high level of intimacy or withdrawal) may be assessed informally through the clinical interview.

The social learning variant of behavior theory provides the fourth major input into the development of behavioral marital assessment. Behavioral researchers may debate the relative emphasis on cognitions, but for marital therapy, the exclusion of cognitions is untenable. It is often the conclusion that spouses draw from the partner's behavior, rather than the behavior itself, which constitutes the primary problem.

The recent emphasis on internal processes has led behavioral marital therapists to employ a variety of fairly traditional assessment instruments. Most typically, efforts have been directed at the measurement of overall marital satisfaction through global self-report questionnaires. Self-report inventories more consistent with the behavioral approach introduce behavioral referents for the global construct of marital satisfaction, and assess perceived strengths and weaknesses of more precisely defined areas of relationship competency.

Additional strategies for assessing cognitions come in response to the need to define the interface between overt and covert behavior. What behaviors increase or decrease marital satisfaction? (Jacobson & Margolin, 1979; Weiss & Margolin, 1977). This question has resulted in attempts to identify the types of relationship events that have an impact on global marital satisfaction (Jacobson, et al., 1980; Margolin, 1981; Wills, Weiss, & Patterson, 1974). It has also led to procedures for measuring spouses' covert perceptions during direct interactions (Gottman, Notarius, Markman, Bank, Yoppi, & Rubin, 1976). With couples, any examination of mutually reciprocal overt-covert events is further complicated by the fact that spouses are constantly processing and appraising their own as well as the partner's behavior.

Additional cognitive dimensions to be assessed by the behavioral marital therapist are spouses' longstanding cognitions and expectations that give structure to the relationship in the form of rules (Birchler & Spinks, 1980; Weiss, 1978). Whether implicit or explicit, these rules govern spouses' reactions and behaviors across a variety of situations. Despite recognition of the important function served by these rules, they have been relegated to informal and sporadic assessment.

In the sections that follow, it is our intention to offer a relatively critical appraisal of behavioral marital assessment. In the first section, we outline some basic issues in behavioral marital assessment that provide a context for the empirical findings that follow. The empirical review describes and critically examines the most commonly used behavioral marital instruments. A final section, on directions for future research, addresses questions of ecological validity, the utilization of these instruments for clinical and theoretical prediction, and implications of cognitive and systems perspectives for behavioral marital assessment. A case description is offered to illustrate the types of data that can be obtained from a behavioral marital assessment.

ISSUES

Content versus process focus

The majority of instruments used to assess marriages fall into two categories: (1) those used to identify and measure specific content areas that spouses complain about (e.g., finances, sex, in-laws), and (2) those used to evaluate how spouses resolve their differences or affirm their emotional commitment to one another. The focus on couples' specific complaints represents an idiographic approach. Spouses identify the criterion behaviors that are believed, by their presence or absence, related to marital dissatisfaction. Careful assessment of the criterion behavior takes the form of a functional analysis to reliably describe characteristics such as frequency, intensity, and duration, and also to identify the environmental conditions that elicit and maintain those behaviors. From a clinical standpoint, the primary objective of this functional analysis is the selection of an intervention that will alter the frequency, intensity, or duration of the criterion behaviors in such a way that increased marital satisfaction is fostered.

The exploration of process dimensions is based upon the belief that marital distress is more a function of communication deficits than the specific content issues about which spouses are communicating. The relevance of instruments designed to measure communication process depends upon the validity of this belief (Jacobson et al., 1981 [b].

Recommendations for a comprehensive assessment include the measurement of both process and content dimensions of marital discord. It is expected that improvement in communication processes will be accompanied by desired changes in the specific content to which the new process skills are applied. It is also predicted that such improvement is crucial for maintaining the therapeutic gains that have been obtained in specific content areas. Process skills, therefore, are viewed as long-range strategies to handle a relationship more effectively—skills to apply when a relationship begins to falter (Jacobson & Margolin, 1979).

Insider versus outsider perceptions

The insider versus outsider distinction refers to whose definition of reality is most important: the self-reports of participant spouses or the observations of trained observers (Olson, 1977). This distinction applies to two facets of assessment: a) Who chooses the behaviors that are assessed, and b) who monitors the frequency or adequacy with which those behaviors are performed. Applying the insider-outsider dichotomy to each of these questions results in a 2 × 2 matrix of assessment options: Either insiders or outsiders can report on self-determined or outsider-determined assessment targets. In reality, these alternatives have not received equal attention. Spouses typically collect data on spouse-determined targets and occasionally collect data on outsider-specified behaviors. Thus far, observers have been trained to collect data solely on targets determined by outsiders.

The insider versus outsider distinction, as it applies to the *identification* of assessment targets, reflects the *substantive* issue of what behaviors are to be assessed. Having spouses identify which specific content areas they perceive to be the sources of marital stress is, of course, crucial for understanding each spouse's position. However, since couples tend to have difficulty specifying the sources of tension in their marriage, it is recommended that therapists also be guided by their own formulations of marital distress and collect information that goes beyond the couple's presentation of concerns (Jacobson & Margolin, 1979). Based on a behavioral conceptualization of marital distress, a wide array of topics are explored, including problem-solving skills, shared interests, relationship rules, etc. It is rare for these topics to be spontaneously introduced by the couple; yet, with probing by the therapist, the topics appear relevant to the experiences of many couples.

The insider versus outsider distinction pertaining to *mode* of data collection reflects a methodological consideration. Reports based on spouse observation reflect the phenomenological realities of the relationship. Since the ''psychological realities'' of one spouse may be markedly different from those of the partner, this subjective approach cannot be overlooked. Outsiders' observations, in contrast, offer a more objective, consistent, and reliable measurement of a reality that is perhaps less relevant to the participants. As the empirical section will indicate, there has been minimal exploration of the relationship between insider and outsider perceptions.

Sign versus sample approaches to assessment

The sign versus sample distinction in assessment has often been viewed as one of the primary factors differentiating traditional personality testing from behavioral assessment. As summarized by Goldfried and Kent (1972):

> The sign approach assumes that the response may best be construed as an indirect manifestation of some underlying personality characteristic. The sample approach assumes that the test behavior constitutes a subset of the actual behavior of interest. Whereas traditional personality tests have typically taken the sign approach to interpretation, behavioral procedures approach test intepretation with the sample orientation. [p. 413].

To a view a behavior as a sample, it must bear similarity to the behavior being predicted. In viewing an observed behavior as a sign, it is assumed to be an indicant of some criterion behavior, which may be topographically quite dissimilar (Wiggins, 1974). Thus, an assessment that is directed towards the observation of behavior rather than the identification of traits is not necessarily indicative of a sample approach.

While behavioral marital assessment is based to a large degree on the observation of behavior, it cannot be construed as a sample approach. To adequately assess the vast number of diverse dimensions that comprise marital functioning, assessors have typically relied on signs, used either singly or in combination, to evaluate the criterion of marital adjustment. Most statements about marital functioning are simply generalizations from a subset of overt or covert behaviors. Even when there are attempts to assess large numbers of relationship behaviors (e.g., through the SOC), data on individual behaviors are collapsed into general pleasing and displeasing categories, with the ratio between the two categories taken as an index of marital adjustment. Individual behaviors tend to hold only limited interest. Similarly, categories of behavior from laboratory observation (e.g., agreement, paraphrase, not tracking) rarely receive attention as criterion behaviors per se but are perceived as part of an overall index of constructive or destructive communication.

Another factor limiting the sample approach in marital assessment is that the behaviors presumed to be highly significant for marital satisfaction are seldomly directly observed or even potentially observable. For example, samples of spouse interaction in social situations with other couples are difficult to obtain. Other behaviors, such as sexual intimacies or physical abusiveness, are unlikely to transpire in the presence of a third party. Moreover, those behaviors are accompanied by such high emotional involvement that participant observation by the spouses is rendered difficult. Once the interactions are scaled down to a level more amenable to observation (i.e., bringing the couple into the laboratory for structured communication tasks), it no longer can be presumed that the observed behaviors are either topographically or functionally similar to the criterion behaviors of interest.

Assessment for clinical versus research purposes

The choice of assessment instruments depends both upon the assessor's goals and the resources that the assessor can command. Since the resources that are accessible to the research investigator often exceed those provided for the practicing marital therapist, and the goals of research often diverge from the goals of a clinical assessment, clinicians tend to utilize different assessment instruments than do researchers. Determining how to intervene in a distressed marriage tends to be the highest assessment priority for the clinicians. Researchers tend to be more interested in describing differences between distressed and non-distressed couples, uncovering the characteristics that predict future marital distress, and measuring the effects of therapy in a precise manner. The following questions point to issues that differentiate the clinician from the researcher.

Can we separate assessment from therapy? Behavioral marital therapists typically recommend a well-planned pretreatment assessment package that requires 2 to 3 weeks to administer (Jacobson & Margolin, 1979; Weiss et al., 1973). The potential reactivity of this assessment package has not been systematically studied. Certainly there may be some effects of having spouses carefully evaluate and monitor their relationship. From the clinician's standpoint, any positive effects that accrue from these assessment procedures are highly desirable. In fact, Jacobson and Margolin (1979) recommend that the behavioral marital therapist strive to engender a collaborative, optimistic spirit during the assessment phase. While refraining from specific skills training or direct injunctions to interact differently, the therapist tries to demonstrate empathy for the spouses' anger and pain, defuse their animosities, and reframe behavior in a more positive light (Jacobson & Margolin, 1979). "Being a good therapist" during the assessment phase is crucial for maintaining the distraught couples' involvement prior to the onset of any intervention. For the researcher, of course, the therapeutic effects of a pretreatment assessment are likely to be regarded as a nuisance.

How useful are behavioral observations in marital assessment? For the most part, behavioral observations have been utilized only by researchers. These procedures are not a practical choice for the clinician (Jacobson et al., in press; Weiss & Margolin, 1977). Behavioral observations are extremely costly, sometimes requiring up to 30 hours to transcribe and code every hour of actual interaction (Gottman, 1979). With this time demand, therapy is well underway before coded observational data even cross the clinician's desk. The essential question is whether the information from these data justify the expense. Answers to this question reside in the reliability and validity of the coding systems, as well as their incremental utility above and beyond the less structured observations that the clinician routinely obtains in the course of his/her interaction with the couple.

What types of interpretations are of interest to the clinician and researcher? Descriptions of behavioral marital assessment tend to stress the multiple uses of each instrument. For example, the researchers' primary interest in self-report indices is in terms of the couple's overall score, which is interpreted as an indicant of marital dissatisfaction and used to categorize a couple as distressed or nondistressed. The clinician, in contrast, is attuned toward a more impressionistic interpretation of data, examining spouses' responses to individual items and making predictions (a priori) about which behaviors are the sources of the couple's dissatisfaction. The clinician typically embarks on a much more subjective interpretation of test data, taking note of patterns across different inventories (both self-report and behavioral) and between individual responses of the two partners. In a striking parallel to traditional assessment, the behavioral marital therapist relies on clinical judgments to analyze and combine various types of data. In the empirical review, we examine how warranted this type of of interpretation is.

To some degree our dichotomy between the goals of clinician and researcher may be a false one. Perhaps if researchers had already established a set of empirically-based criteria from which to base clinical judgments, this gap would be closed. However, even in a utopian world of well-validated assessment techniques and actuarial bases for clinical judgments, clinicians and researchers will continue to hold different goals and command different resources for achieving them. The relevance of behavioral marital assessment research for the behavioral marital therapist remains to be determined.

EMPIRICAL REVIEW

Interactional Coding Systems

Although communication training is the sine qua non of most marital therapists, behavioral marital therapy has distinguished itself in the development of highly sophisticated interactional coding systems for assessing communication patterns. The early research on communication samples required family members to achieve consensus over a revealed difference conflict resolution task (Olson & Ryder, 1970; Strodbeck, 1951). Investigators examined these discussions for outcomes (i.e., "agreement" or "win" scores), as well as for process dimensions of conflict, dominance, affect, and communication clarity (Jacob, 1976).

The behavioral approach to the assessment of communication, as exemplified by the Oregon group and Gottman's group, contains several significant modifications in both the collection and evaluation of the data. Rather than creating an artificial conflict situation, couples discuss topics that are indeed troublesome in their relationship. The therapist assists the couple in defining an area of conflict but then leaves the room so that the couple can engage in an undisturbed discussion. Discussions are usually limited to 10 minutes, with the therapist telling the couple when to begin and end each discussion. Specific instructions for these discussions have not been standardized and include, "Attempt to resolve this problem to the best of your ability," "Discuss this topic as you would at home," or simply, "Discuss this topic," with no mention of reaching resolution.

Systems for coding marital interaction evolved in response to several objectives (Jacobson et al., 1981; Jones, Reid, & Patterson, 1975). First, it was necessary to uncover the critical behavioral events during marital communication in order to design treatment programs which would focus on modifying appropriate behaviors. Second, the systems were needed to provide behavioral data for evaluating treatment outcomes. Third, based on the assumption that faulty communication, specifically inadequate problem-solving skills, may be a precursor to and/or outcome of marital distress, information from these systems would contribute to a theoretical understanding of marital distress.

Two systems have been developed for coding these problem-solving discussions. The *MICS* (Hops et al., 1972), after undergoing one minor revision, currently consists of 30 behavioral categories. For most data analysis purposes, these 30 codes are combined into six summary categories: *Problem Solving* (Accept Responsibility, Compromise, Problem-Solution); *Verbal Positive* (Agree, Approval, Humor, Paraphrase/Reflection); *Nonverbal Positive* (Assent, Attention, Compliance, Physical Positive, Smile/Laugh); *Nonverbal Negative* (No Response, Not Tracking, Turn off); *Verbal Negative* (Command, Criticism, Put-down, Deny Responsibility, Excuse, Disagree, Interrupt, Noncomply, Negative Solution); and *Neutral* (Normative, Problem Description, Question, and Talk). Definitions of specific codes take into account a variety of class-defining characteristics including verbal content, semantics, and affect (Jacobson et al., 1981). Observers sequentially code in 30-second intervals, indicating each new speaker and listener behavior.

Gottman and his colleagues (Gottman et al., 1976) developed the CISS for coding patterns of couples' communication. The CISS was formulated on the premise that each response must be coded separately for affect (nonverbal behavior by the speaker) and content (verbal behavior) (Gottman, 1979; Watzlawick, Beavin & Jackson, 1967). Each behavior is assigned one of eight content codes (Agreement, Disagreement, Communication Talk, Mindreading, Proposing a Solution, Summarizing Other, Summarizing Self, Problem Information or Feeling). In a separate coding, the same behavioral units are assigned positive, negative, or neutral affect and content codes based upon a hierarchical scanning of voice tone, facial cues, and body posture. Thus, any CISS content code can be paired with any affect code, contrary to the MICS in which codes are based on both content and affect.

Reliability. The standard index for computing observer reliability has been percentage of interobserver agreement reported as the ratio of agreement (numerator) to agreements plus disagreements (denominator). Using this index, investigators typically train their observers to a criterion of 70-80 percent agreement. Reliability figures reported in the literature generally fall in the 80-90 percent range (Gottman, 1979; Weider & Weiss, 1980), with some investigators recoding any samples that are below the 70 percent criterion. In coding sequential data, as provided by the MICS and CISS, agreement must be tied to specific codes on specific units of behavior (Gottman, 1979). Not only is it important that observers report a particular code the same number of times, they must also agree on when that code was observed. Thus, the interobserver ratios reflect point-by-point agreement rather than overall frequencies.

Even with these relatively stringent criteria, the interobserver agreement ratio has been criticized as an insufficient index (Gottman, 1979; Jacobson et al., 1981 [a]; Hartmann, 1977; Hollenbeck, 1978). First, an overall agreement figure obscures the fact that some categories can be coded with high accuracy while others may be coded with virtually no agreement. Second, this ratio does not take into account observer drift, unless agreement is assessed across multiple pairs of observers.

Some recent recommendations for computing reliability for observational coding systems call upon Chronbach's generalizability theory (Gottman, 1979; Jones et al., 1975). Generalizability across observers is to be computed with observers as the source of variance. Gottman's data (1979) indicated generalizability coefficients of .84 to 1.00 for content codes and .78 to .99 for affect and context codes. Vincent, Friedman, Nugent, and Messerly (1979) reported generalizability coefficients for MICS summary categories which ranged from .41 to .90. In attempting to isolate different components of variance in MICS coding, Wieder and Wiess (1980) found that coder biases only accounted for between 1 percent and 9 percent of variance in MICS summary categories. These figures are negligible compared to between 61 percent and 82 percent of the variance accounted by couple differences and situational differences.

Stability from one observational occasion to another provides an alternate measure of reliability. Data on the MICS indicate that summary categories are stable across the time span of one week (Wieder & Weiss, 1980) and across two divergent topics that were discussed in succession (Margolin, 1978a).

Reactivity. A widely acknowledged difficulty in the use of observational coding systems is that the data collection procedures may produce artificial responding. The data may be affected by the constraints provided by the observational procedures. During laboratory observations, unlike naturalistic encounters, the couple cannot readily terminate the discussion or leave the room. Spouses are also aware that they are being observed and/or videotaped, a factor which may affect their performance. Finally, they may believe that their performance on this task will influence the therapist's decision to accept them into therapy. Couples' estimates of their own perceived reactivity indicate that the observation sessions are mildly disruptive, but that their behavior is minimally influenced (Haynes, Follingstad, & Sullivan, 1979). Obviously, those estimates are also subject to demand characteristics.

In a clever test of reactivity, Vincent et al. (1979) sought to measure couples' abilities to "fake good" or "fake bad" in standardized problem-solving discussions by instructing them to present either "a happy, blissful, contented couple" or "an unhappy, conflicted and distressed couple." While there was only limited evidence for differential responsiveness to faking instructions between distressed and nondistressed couples, this study indicated that both sets of couples significantly altered their verbal behaviors according to instructions. Nonverbal behaviors, in contrast, were much less susceptible to the faking instructions. Cohen and Christensen (1980) examined a similar question by having couples provide samples of their own "effective" and "ineffective" communications while discussing conflict areas in their relationship. Based on verbal codes only, this study revealed no differences between the effective and ineffective conditions. Findings from these two studies lead to the conclusion that coded interaction data are not immune to demand characteristics, but that certain behavior in conjunction with certain instructions are more susceptible than others.

Validity. The application of traditional distinctions between content, criterion, and construct validity is somewhat inappropriate in evaluations of interactional coding systems. The relevance of those distinctions is limited by a lack of clarity regarding the construct that coding systems actually measure in light of the multiple purposes for which they were designed.

Content validity has been built into the MICS and CISS. Marital investigators speculated (as in the MICS) or empirically determined (as in the CISS) what interactional behaviors are important in couples' problem-solving discussions and then developed systems to encompass those behaviors. Whether or not the content validity of these instruments extends beyond the notions of their creators is less clear. When undergraduates have been asked to identify behaviors that differentiated the interactions of distressed and nondistressed couples, they listed some of the same behaviors contained in the MICS (Resnick, Sweet, Kieffer, Bart & Rubin, 1977; Royce & Weiss, 1975). But the essential question is whether MICS or CISS categories hold significance for the couples themselves. Margolin's (1978a) examinations of MICS coding and distressed couples' own ratings of communication positiveness revealed little agreement between trained observers and the spouses themselves regarding quality of communication. Yet, these data are far from conclusive in terms of individual categories. Still to be answered are the following questions: Do spouses concur with investigators about the relevance of MICS or CISS categories? Do spouses agree with the valence assigned to observational codes?

Concurrent validity as applied to coding systems translates into two questions: Do the systems differentiate between couples identified as distressed or nondistressed by another measure? Is there an association between couples' interaction data and their scores on other measures? Based on MICS summary codes, it has been shown, that compared to nondistressed couples, distressed couples employ a greater frequency of negative behaviors and a reduced frequency of positive behavior (Vincent, Weiss, & Birchler, 1975; Vincent et al. 1979). Margolin and Wampold (1981) found similar results on positive behaviors. While there were no significant differences between distressed and nondistressed couples on summary negative cagetories, wives were more likely than husbands to emit verbal negatives. Results from comparisons between distressed and nondistressed couples on various subsamples of MICS codes have offered tentative support for the discriminative validity of several specific behaviors. However, as a group these studies provide inconsistent and sometimes unexpected findings (Haynes et al., 1979; Klier & Rothberg, 1977; Resick et al., 1977).

Between-group comparisons on the CISS reveal that, with the exception of the category agreement, content codes alone do not discriminate between distressed and nondistressed couples; however, there were significant differences for certain content codes (Feeling Expression, Mindreading, and Disagreement) in combination with negative affect. Additionally, nonverbal behaviors alone generally discriminated between distressed and nondistressed couples. The nonverbal behavior of distressed couples was less positive and more negative than that of satisfied couples. Gottman's results offer strong support for the importance of nonverbal, as opposed to verbal, behavior in discriminating between distressed and nondistressed couples.

Attention has recently been directed to the identification of communication sequences that differentiate distressed from nondistressed couples. Sequential analyses provide a way to analyze whether one person's behavior is affected by preceding events emitted by another (Gottman & Bakeman, 1979). Examination of behavioral chains that have been coded with the MICS or CISS reveal that distressed, compared to nondistressed, couples are more likely to reciprocate negative behavior (Gottman, 1979; Gottman et al., 1977; Margolin & Wampold, 1981). Gottman's data further suggest that clinic couples are likely to enter a "cross-complaining" loop at the beginning of a discussion and a "negative exchange loop" at a subsequent time. Nonclinic couples, in contrast, are likely to begin the discussion with a "validation" sequence, avoid negative exchanges, and end the discussion with a contract agreement. These studies indicate that sequential patterns are more powerful discriminators of marital distress than frequency data alone.

Concurrent validity has also been examined in studies that measure the extent to which MICS codes are related to scores on global measures of marital satisfaction, such as the Locke-Wallace Marital Adjustment Scale (MAS; Locke & Wallace, 1959). These studies have not demonstrated a strong correlation between specific behaviors coded by an outside observer and global impressions of marital satisfaction (Heath,

Kerns, Myskowski & Haynes, 1977; Haynes, 1979; Margolin, 1978b; Robinson & Price, 1980). However, the meaning of these results is obscured by the fact that the global measures of marital satisfaction may include dimensions far beyond what the MICS purports to measure. Additionally, these correlational analyses confound variance due to different observers, varying time frames, and different data collection methods (Cone, 1977).

Attempts to evaluate the *construct validity* of these coding systems have varied. At the most general level, these systems have been viewed as measuring the construct: "marital adjustment." As previously mentioned, the relationship between coded behavior and other indices of marital adjustment has been examined through correlational studies. An alternate interpretation regards the MICS as a reflection of the overall exchange of reinforcement and punishment between spouses. However, as Jacobson et al. (1981) point out, it is by no means obvious that the frequency of positive and negative behaviors that occur in laboratory interactions are representative of the multitude of ways that spouses exchange rewards and punishments. Instead, Margolin and Wampold (1981) found that laboratory interactional data account for very little of the variance in frequency of "pleases" and displeases" as reported by spouses in the natural environment.

"Problem-solving skills" is probably the most applicable construct for interactional coding systems. But how does one evaluate whether the MICS is sensitive to changes in problem-solving effectiveness? According to behavioral marital therapists (Jacobson, 1977; Jacobson & Margolin, 1979), effective problem solving means overcoming a conflict by agreeing upon and implementing a change for the relationship. Currently there are no data on the outcome of problem-solving sessions, such as whether a relationship exists between coded behavior and the degree to which spouses experience a resolution of conflict, i.e., behavioral changes that are actually implemented at home, or greater satisfaction regarding the topic that was discussed (Jacobson et al., 1979). The finding that the MICS is a sensitive measure of preintervention to postintervention change is often reported as evidence of construct validity. However, the circularity in this definition, as Jacobson et al. (1981) argue, cannot go unnoticed.

How do we know that couples were successfully treated? Because they evidenced change on an observation coding system. But how do we know that the observational coding system is a valid measure of change? Because couples manifested change on it after the completion of therapy. It should be clear that independent evidence for the construct validity of the MICS as a measure of problem-solving skill must be provided before changes in therapy can be said to provide such support.

Predictive validity, which has received the least attention, holds tremendous importance for theoretical underpinnings of behavioral marital therapy. Based on the above definition of problem-solving skills, high rates of negative MICS or CISS behaviors and low rates of positive behaviors should predict deficits in ability to handle marital conflict and long-range accumulation of unresolved conflicting issues. This concept has preliminary support from Vincent and his colleagues (Vincent, Cook, & Brady, 1979), who examined whether couples' scores on the MICS predict how they accommodate to the stress of having a child. A prenatal assessment of communication skillfulness on the MICS was predictive of spouses' levels of consideration, companionship, and helpfulness in household tasks, as measured 2 months after childbirth.

Generalizability to the home setting. The interpretation of laboratory interaction data rests, to a large degree, on its generalizability to other settings, particularly the home. Gottman (1979) provided very interesting data on this question. Couples asked to complete a problem-solving discussion at home with an audio cassette recorder were compared to those video-taped in the laboratory. Results indicate that the interaction of couples at home was more negative than couples' interactions in the laboratory on the following dimensions: agreement to disagreement ratios, frequency of negative affect, and reciprocity of negative affect. Since the differences between distressed and nondistressed couples were generally greater at home than in the laboratory, Gottman tentatively concluded that laboratory data *underestimate* the discriminant validity of these measures.

Other investigators who have sent observers into couples' homes report very different findings. Observing couples in relatively unstructured interactions and coding a restricted sample of behaviors, these investigators do not report powerful discriminations between distressed and nondistressed couples (Haynes et al., 1979; Robinson & Price, 1980). Factors that differentiate these studies from Gottman's study include: (1) the presence of live observers (Haynes et al., 1979; Robinson & Price, 1980) rather than audio tape recordings (Gottman, 1979), (2) the lack of a specific problem-solving task, and (3) the reliance on content rather than affective codes in the Haynes et al. (1979) and Robinson & Price (1980) studies.

Summary. Based on the current state of findings, interactional coding systems produce a mixed picture. Since problem-solving skills play a central role in both behavioral marital theory and intervention, there certainly needs to be a vehicle for evaluating these skills. Yet it is important that data from the currently used system not be overinterpreted. First, data collected for MICS and CISS coding are not necessarily representative samples of couple interaction. They are the product of the specific setting, instructions, and time limits, along with couples' own interpretations of what is expected. Gottman's home data are a promising break from previous tradition in this regard. Second, no relationship has yet been demonstrated between these data and a couples' eventual handling of conflictual issues. Hopefully, more data will be forthcoming to explore the potential of these instruments for the prediction of future marital problems, for recommending specific treatment approaches, and unraveling complex patterns in marital interactions.

Returning to the question of the clinical utility of observational systems, we conclude that the necessary resources in coder personnel and equipment make them highly impractical for the clinician. However, we reiterate a message stated elsewhere (Jacobson & Margolin, 1979; Weiss & Margolin, 1977) that direct observation of couples' communication can be available to the clinician without resorting to complex coding systems such as the MICS or CISS. Problem-solving discussions can be audiotaped for later playback or can occur as the therapist directly observes the couple in his/her office. By reading the MICS and CISS coding manuals and becoming informed about what behaviors various investigators have chosen to observe, the clinician can attempt to observe those same behaviors or any others she/he deems important.

Spouses as Participant Observers

The same types of problem-solving discussions coded by trained observers have also been rated by spouses themselves. The usefulness of outside observers depends on their ability to be highly objective and utilize consistent definitions and criteria in coding all couples. The purpose of spouse observation is to assess the nuances of personalized meanings unavailable to outside observers. As observers of their own interactions, spouses provide a metacommunicative perspective on what they subjectively experience during their discussion by indicating "how I see myself," and "how I see you in relation to me" (Knudson, Sommers, & Golding, 1980; Watzlawick, Beavin, & Jackson, 1967).

Gottman and his associates (Gottman, Notarius, Markman, Bank, Yoppi, & Rubin, 1976) utilized a "talk table" which allowed couples to code ongoing communication along a 5-point Likert Scale (1=supernegative; 5=superpositive). As each spouse finished speaking, the listener rated the *impact* of the message received while the speaker rated the *intent* of the message sent. Impact, but not intent, ratings successfully discriminated distressed from nondistressed couples; the behavior of distressed spouses was coded as less positive by the partner than their intention. For nondistressed spouses, there was concordance between intent and impact of behavior.

Markman (1979) utilized the "talk table" to assess whether impact ratings would predict marital satisfaction when measured at one year and 2-1/2 year follow-ups. Impact ratings were strongly predictive of relationship satisfaction at the second but not the first follow-up period. Interestingly, while impact ratings alone were good predictors of later marital satisfaction, the intent-impact discrepancy between spouses was a poor predictor. This study offers preliminary support for the notion that spouses' perceptions of unrewarding communications precede the development of relationship distress.

There is relatively little to report on the psychometric properties of participant observation by spouses. Data from Gottman et al. (1976) provide evidence for discriminant validity while Markman's data are suggestive of predictive validity. With systems designed to elicit subjective impressions, interobserver agreement is no longer a psychometric priority but remains an interesting substantive question. The Gottman et al. (1976) study plus additional data from Margolin's (1978) sample of distressed couples indicated that a lack of agreement between the sender's and the receiver's perceptions is particularly characteristic of distressed couples. Gottman (1979) also provided evidence for a low correspondence between spouse impact ratings and outside-observer coding, but in this case the low agreements were more characteristic of nondistressed couples. Observers' "hit rates" for predicting talk-table impact scores indicated that nonclinic spouses are more likely to read their partners' behaviors differently than the observers do: e.g., of all behaviors that CISS observers coded as negative for nonclinic wives, nonclinic husbands coded .44 as neutral, .33 as positive and only .22 as negative. Gottman interpreted these data as evidence for private message systems in nondistressed couples.

An alternative type of participant observation involves training spouses to count frequencies of specifically defined behaviors rather than simply rating a behavioral segment. With this approach, Robinson and Price (1980) found similarities between spouses and outside observers on a score that combined all pleasurable behaviors. Still there was little agreement between spouses and observers in their rates of specific behavioral codes. These investigators concluded that spouse tracking, even when couples are trained to code a small number of specific behaviors, is subject to "cognitive elaboration."

Spouse observation is an assessment strategy that deserves more attention. Although thus far restricted to research applications, these procedures could assist the clinician in: (1) identifying cognitive filters which influence spouses' views of their own interactions, and (2) prompting spouses to take a close look at their roles in marital interaction. Spouse observation is susceptible to demand characteristics but would provide interesting outcome data if viewed in relation to data from outside observers.

Self-Report Questionnaires

Despite the emphasis on direct observation in behavioral assessment, self-report questionnaires play an important role in the assessment of marital dysfunction. Each of the instruments described below reveals some aspect of spouses' personalized appraisals of their marital situation. Of these instruments, the Spouse Observation Checklist is by far the most compatible with the objectives of behavioral assessment.

Spouse Observation Checklist (SOC). The SOC represents the behavioral marital therapist's commitment to ferreting out the details of spouses' lives together. The sociological literature of the 1960s (Hicks & Platt, 1970; Tharp, 1963) repeatedly identified the following important domains of marital interaction: (1) instrumental behaviors that are necessary for a relationship to survive as a socioeconomic unit; (2) expressive behaviors which convey caring, intimacy, appreciation, and approval; and (3) companionship events which encompass various aspects of shared recreational time. Working from these general dimensions, the Oregon group (Patterson, 1976) devised the SOC, an eight-page listing of pleasing and displeasing relationship behaviors. The most recent revision of the SOC (Weiss & Perry, 1979) contains approximately 400 items that represent 12 relationship categories: Companionship, Affection, Consideration, Sex, Communication Process, Coupling Activities, Household Management, Financial Decision-Making, Employment-Education, Childrearing, Personal Habits, Self and Spouse Independence.

The SOC was designed to obtain repeated recordings of a couple's day-by-day interactions. Spouses are to complete the SOC before retiring each night, reading through the entire inventory and placing a checkmark to indicate what items occurred during the previous 24 hours. For couples in therapy, it is recommended that the SOC be utilized weekly throughout the duration of therapy as feedback on the efficacy of each intervention stage. Spouses are also instructed to indicate their satisfaction with the relationship for that day by marking a 9-point scale from 1 (totally dissatisfied) to 9 (totally satisfied).

Reliability. There has been much controversy over whether the SOC is a behavioral observation measure or a self-report instrument. The SOC requires each spouse to report what the other has done or what the two partners did together as a couple. Thus, spouses are observers of one another. Yet, rather than providing the objective reports of an outside observer, SOC data are highly subject to the vicissitudes of spouses' emotional involvement. A particularly resentful spouse, looking for "evidence" against the partner, may be sensitized to displeasing events and oblivious to pleasing events. One type of SOC instruction actually builds in a subjective response set by telling spouses to record only those events which were experienced as either "pleasing" or "displeasing." The alternate, more objective set of instructions calls for spouses to record all behaviors that occur, without attention to the valence. However, there is no evidence that any instruction eliminates the variability in SOC recording due to selective tracking. Even with an instruction to record all behaviors that occur, the accuracy of recording may be hampered by the fact that spouses are to remember behaviors (sometimes momentary interactions) over the duration of an entire day and to make judgments about the occurrence or nonoccurrence of hundreds of items.

Recent data on interspouse agreement suggest that SOC is best viewed as a self-report instrument rather than a vehicle of behavioral observation. Data on interrater agreement between spouses on the complete SOC or a modified version of the SOC indicate significant correlations between giving and receiving spouses for composite scores of behaviors. However, percentage agreement on individual items was much lower, rarely reaching acceptable levels (Christensen & Nies, 1980; Jacobson & Moore, in press). both sets of investigators found that agreements were particularly low for distressed, as compared to nondistressed, couples. Jacobson and Moore report significantly different interrater scores of 42 percent for distressed and 52 percent for nondistressed couples, illustrating that even nondistressed couples disagree as often as they agree. Both studies further revealed that displeasing items elicited lower agreement scores than pleasing items.

Reactivity and Stability. Due to the nature of the SOC as well as the fact that is is administered week after week, questions arise regarding its reactivity and stability. There are several ways in which the SOC might be reactive. First, simply reading items on the form alerts spouses to a variety of activities to which they have not paid much attention. Awareness of these items may encourage spouses to engage in new behaviors or take notice of behaviors that, in fact, are already occurring but have not received attention. On the other hand, this awareness may cause discouragement over the vast number of possibilities overlooked in the couple's current relationship. Second, knowledge that the partner will be using the same list may foster various forms of impression management, i.e., emitting new behaviors to receive credit for more pleases. Third, repeated exposure to SOC data provides spouses with feedback regarding the relative frequencies of pleases and displeases, the frequency with which specific behaviors occur, and relative frequencies between the two spouses. These type of data may provide couples with a new perspective on their relationship.

In light of these potential sources of reactivity, there is surprisingly little evidence for reactivity effects. It is, of course, impossible to assess the SOC's immediate reactivity since there is no suitable baseline against which to compare these data (Jacobson et al., 1981 [a]). Over a 2-week period, Wills et al. (1974) and Robinson and Price (1980) found no changes in please and displease frequencies. Yet, when involved in SOC data collection over a 4-week period, nondistressed couples showed declines in reported frequencies of pleases (Margolin, 1981), and distressed couples showed declines in displeases (Margolin & Weiss, 1978). Since these reductions were only partially in a socially desirable direction, instrument decay is offered as an explanation, i.e., observer fatigue and reduced motivation.

Similar to reactivity reported in the self-monitoring literature (e.g., Ciminero, Nelson, & Lipinski, 1977), reactivity on the SOC would not necessarily be unwelcome. In fact, in another context we recommend that the SOC be utilized as an intervention aid (Jacobson & Margolin, 1979). At the very least, SOC data must be discussed regularly and integrated into the therapy program to enhance the probability that spouses continue to collect SOC data over the course of the intervention.

Validity. Content validity of the SOC can be examined in terms of summary categories and individual items. The 12 summary categories tend to have high content validity, since they are explicitly chosen to represent the types of concerns couples bring to therapy. Although much is still unknown about the content validity of individual items, Christensen and Nies (1981) shed some light on this issue. A majority of the items on their modified 179-item SOC were endorsed by less than 20 percent of the respondents, raising questions about the relevance of many items. They also reported that spouses do not necessarily attach the same valence to SOC items as researchers have. Although a majority of spouses rated most items in the predicted direction, there was unanimous agreement on less than one-third of the pleases and on only one displease. When disagreements occurred, items were typically rated as neutral by spouses, rather than in the pleasing or displeasing direction defined by researchers.

The contrasted groups method provides another index of validity for the SOC. According to expectation, distressed compared to nondistressed spouses report fewer pleases and more displeases. Please: displease ratios are approximately 4:1 for distressed and 12:1 to 30:1 for nondistressed couples (Bircher, Weiss, & Vincent, 1975; Margolin, 1981). While composite please and displease scores discriminated between groups, not all of the content categories differentiated distressed and nondistressed couples. Frequency of Instrumental Displeases, weighted by valence, was a powerful discriminator in the Barnett and Nietzel (1979) sample, but Instrumental Pleases, Affectional Pleases, and Displeases were not. Based on frequency alone, Margolin (1981) also found significant differences between distressed and nondistressed samples on Instrumental Displeases, as well as Affectional Pleases, Communication Pleases and Displeases. The Margolin study further explored how stage of life cycle affects the behavioral exchange between marital partners. The curvilinear relationship between marital satisfaction and family cycle reported in the sociological literature (e.g., Rollins & Feldman, 1970, Schraum, (1979) was similarly evidenced for SOC pleases and displeases. For both distressed and nondistressed couples, the highest rates of pleasing behaviors, particularly Communication Pleases and Companionship Activities, were reported in young preparenting couples; lower rates were reported for families with either young or adolescent children. In the postparenting stage, pleases are lower still for distressed couples but show a slight reversal of this pattern for nondistressed couples.

Since the SOC has been viewed as a measure of marital adjustment, construct validity has been examined by measuring the degree of association between SOC scores and: (1) daily ratings of marital satisfaction, and (2) one-time measures of marital satisfaction. Wills et al. (1974), the first to examine the relationship between behavioral events and daily satisfaction ratings, based their regression analyses on 12 consecutive days of data from seven nondistressed couples. Five predictor variables (Affectional Pleasing and Displeasing events, Instrumental Pleasing and Displeasing events and Quality of Outside Interaction) collectively accounted for 25 percent of the variance in spouses' daily satisfaction ratings.

Several recent studies further explored these relationships between behaviors and daily satisfaction. Jacobson et al. (1981) found negative behaviors, particularly Negative Verbal Interactions, to be strongly associated with fluctuations in daily satisfaction for both distressed husbands and wives. In contrast, positive behaviors, particularly Shared Recreational Activities for husbands and Positive Communication for wives, were most predictive of daily satisfaction ratings for nondistressed couples. Directly comparing distressed and nondistressed couples, Margolin (1981) also found that distressed couples were negatively influenced by the occurrence of displeases, in particular, Instrumental Displeases. However, the two samples revealed no between-groups differences in the association of pleasing behaviors and satisfaction. Each of these three studies employed somewhat different procedures for data collection, reduction, and analysis. In light of the methodological differences and striking substantive discrepancies, the relationship between behavioral events and daily satisfaction demands further exploration.

Correlations between SOC data and one-time measurement of marital satisfaction indicate overlap between what the SOC measures and the global construct of marital satisfaction. Margolin and Wampold (1981) reported that scores on the Locke-Wallace Marital Adjustment Scale (MAS) correlated positively with mean daily SOC pleases and negatively with SOC displeases. Displeases, but not pleases, also correlated in the predicted direction with Areas of Change scores. Examining category totals, Barnett and Nietzel (1979) found significant relationships between MAS scores and Companionship Activities, Sexual Activities, and Instrumental Pleases.

Utility of the SOC. The SOC may be the most versatile instrument in the armamentarium of the behavioral marital therapist and researcher. As a clinical instrument, the SOC can be employed for a variety of purposes. Baseline SOC data can be compared to normative ratios to derive perspective on the extent of a couple's distress. The SOC assists the therapist in treatment planning by highlighting perceptions about the absence of desirable behaviors and the presence of undesirable behaviors. Through correlations between category frequencies and satisfaction ratings, it is possible to pinpoint the behaviors most salient to fluctuations in daily satisfaction for individual spouses; these behaviors can then be targeted for intervention and maintenance planning to insure a positive impact on marital satisfaction. Furthermore, SOC data collected over several weeks may reveal cyclical patterns in couples' behavioral exchange. Careful examination of the behavioral antecedents to these cycles can be used to demystify what couples tend to perceive as baffling and troublesome relationship shifts.

Interest in the SOC's utility as an outcome measure is shared by both the clinician and researcher. Frequently used as a therapy outcome measure, the SOC has been shown to be a sensitive index of pretherapy to posttherapy change (Margolin & Weiss, 1978; Patterson et al., 1974; Weiss et al., 1973). Given the strong focus in behavioral marital therapy on altering the behavior exchange of couples, positive change on the SOC is difficult to interpret. As mentioned previously, the SOC sometimes even serves as the foundation for such an intervention with the therapist explicitly instructing the clients to increase SOC pleases that appear to be related to marital satisfaction (Jacobson & Margolin, 1979). As the SOC becomes a tool of intervention, its utility as an outcome measure is obviously compromised. Furthermore, when improvement is shown on the SOC, it is impossible to sort out whether: (1) the behavioral frequencies have actually changed, (2) the reporter's criteria for reporting behavior have been altered, or (3) the reporter is responding to demand characteristics of the situation. An alternate application of the SOC that has received little attention is the use of ongoing SOC data in multiple baseline designs. Comparisons between targeted and nontargeted categories of responses would help determine the efficacy of specific interventions at specific points in time.

From the standpoint of a data collection instrument, the demonstrated utility of the SOC lies in its two summary scores of Total Pleases and Total Displeases, for which there exists data related to reliability and validity. Comparatively little is known about the category subtotals or the individual items. Other important but unexplored psychometric concerns about the SOC include length, item overlap, and representativeness of items, particularly for special populations such as older adults.

Overall, the SOC has several important strengths. Although time-consuming for couples, it is inexpensive and readily interpreted. It offers the therapist a tremendous amount of data on which to launch and evaluate interventions. It also introduces couples to the behavioral approach, encouraging them to operationalize vague impressions and to become more aware of their impact on one another. Additionally, the SOC offers a vehicle for examining a variety of the premises of the social learning theory explanation of marital exchange, e.g., reciprocity. However, in light of the unresolved methodological issues surrounding this instrument, it is necessary to exercise extreme caution in interpreting SOC data. The SOC must be viewed as a measurement of the subjective, rather than objective, reality of the couples' world.

Areas of Change Questionnaire (AC). From among the array of brief, easily administered self-report measures of marital adjustment, the AC (Patterson, 1976; Weiss & Perry, 1979) stands out for its precision in examining specific behaviors. The AC assesses the amount of change spouses desire from one another in 34 specific areas of interaction (e.g., decision-making about finances, time spent with relatives, frequency of sex). Each respondent first indicates whether she/he wants the partner to increase, decrease, or not change the rate of each behavior. Repeating the same set of items, the respondent then indicates his/her impressions of how much change the spouses wants in each area. The scoring rules offered by Weiss and Birchler (1975) provide a range of scores from 0 (no change desired) to 68 (change desired for each spouse in each area). Birchler and Webb (1977) reported total change scores of 28.0 and 6.9, respectively, for distressed and nondistressed couples.

Although originally hailed for its behavioral specificity, the data currently available for the AC do not go beyond supporting its utility as a global index of marital satisfaction. Its repeatedly high correlations with the MAS ($r = -.70$ to $-.75$) (Margolin & Wampold, 1981; Weiss et al. 1973) indicate significant overlap in dimensions of marital satisfaction tapped by these instruments. Yet important questions regarding external validity of this instrument remain unanswered: whether noted items are indeed occurring at excessive or deficient frequencies, and whether attention to these items during therapy improves spouses' scores on the AC. In the absence of this information, it is premature to conclude that the AC indeed conveys information about behavioral frequencies.

Other multidimensional self-report indices. Self-report measurements of global marital satisfaction are still the most commonly used instruments in marital assessment. Two widely used measures are the Marital Adjustment Scale (MAS; Locke & Wallace, 1959) and the more recent Dyadic Adjustment Scale (DAS; Spanier, 1976), which elicit spouses' individual perceptions about the degree of happiness in their relationship. Reliability and validity studies have shown that these two instruments are internally consistent and accurate discriminators between satisfied and dissatisfied couples. Based on these psychometric properties, these instruments have become popular choices in the marital literature for screening marital distress versus adjustment. These inventories secondarily offer hints about the areas of interaction that spouses view as most problematic, but this objective is better accomplished in a behaviorally oriented interview. A major drawback to these instruments is their susceptibility to social desirability factors (Edmonds, Withers, & Dibatista, 1972; Murstein & Beck, 1972).

Several other instruments designed to aid in the task of behavioral assessment lack adequate normative data but still contribute to overall understanding of a couple's marital adjustment. A particularly comprehensive instrument is the Marital Pre-Counseling Inventory (MPI; Stuart & Stuart, 1972) which contains 13 sections that direct the therapist's attention to behavior change goals, resources for change, and the degree

of mutual understanding between spouses. Beginning with the family
locator to provide an overview of the topography of the couple's lives
in terms of times and types of contact, this inventory also examines
positive aspects of spouses' behaviors, behavioral goals, and areas of
satisfaction and dissatisfaction. While this inventory is an example of
multidimensional assessment, data are reported for only two of the 13
scales. Second, the Marital Activities Inventory (MAITAI; Birchler et
al., 1975; Weiss et al., 1973) elicits information about how spouses
distribute their time (alone, together, or with others outside the relationship) and how they would like to see the time distributions change.
Finally, the Marital Status Inventory (MSI; Weiss & Cerreto, 1975)
measures the degree to which spouses engage in thoughts and actions
directed towards separation and divorce.

Summary. The self-report questionnaires offer efficient, low-cost methods for gathering information on spouses' personalized, subjective perceptions of their marital situation. Although they sometimes purport to
provide information on specific behaviors, their utility lies in their ability to discriminate marital satisfaction from dissatisfaction. None of
these instruments can be considered a valid index of behavior without
additional data on external validity. Additionally, they are all susceptible to demand characteristics and social desirability factors. Since they
are often viewed as the leading currently available measurements of the
construct of marital "satisfaction" or "adjustment," self-report inventories are widely used as outcome measurements and as criterion
measures for examining the validity of other instruments.

FUTURE DIRECTIONS

Ecological Validity

All previous reviews on behavioral marital assessment have called for
more data on the reliability and validity of the procedures described
above (Jacob, 1976; Margolin & Weiss, 1977). We concur, but want
to emphasize that particular attention must be paid to the ecological
validity of the instruments, i.e., "the extent to which the environment
experienced by the subjects in a scientific investigation has the properties it is supposed or assumed to have by the investigator [Bron-
fennbrenner, 1977, p. 516]." Although observations of couple interactions in the laboratory and at home have occasionally been referred
to as "naturalistic," there is little reason to presume that the tasks we
assign couples and the behaviors they emit in the presence of an observer
or videotape camera in any way resemble what occurs in their natural

environment. With the development of relatively unobtrusive, nonreactive recording devices (e.g., Christensen, 1979), more naturalistic data have been procured. However, the trade-off is that these data are more difficult to code reliably with the same amount of detail as is obtained in the laboratory.

Although ethical and practical considerations constrain access to many dimensions of intimate adult behavior, information can be obtained on ecological validity of behavioral marital instruments. Attempts must be made to discern: (1) how data from laboratory communication exercises relate to interactions at home; and (2) whether items on self-report measures are indicative of actual relationship events. Examining the relationships among different procedures would help to determine their ecological validity. However, rather than correlating summary scores (e.g., MICS positive behaviors and SOC Total pleases), we recommend exploring indices presumed to measure similar dimensions (e.g., correlating the frequency of helpful listening behaviors in the laboratory with those same behaviors from home interaction or with SOC items related to listening and supportiveness). These types of analyses will indicate the extent to which data that are readily obtained through laboratory procedures and self-report measures generalize to couple's home interactions.

Data Combination and Prediction

Decision-making and prediction are the primary reasons for conducting any assessment: to decide upon an intervention strategy, to predict what couples will experience marital distress. The recommended assessment package, including a variety of the previously described procedures, offers a substantial amount of data. Yet, there has been very little attention paid to the question of how to interpret this multitude of information. We can assume that clinicians, researchers, and spouses all formulate their impressions of a relationship by attending to and combining various bits of information from the assessment procedures or from additional personal observations. However, there are no empirical data currently available about which components are important to consider and how they should be differentially weighted.

The clinician's task in data combination and decision-making is to make the transition from assessment data to an effective intervention strategy. Data interpretation simply on the basis of one instrument is not particularly clear-cut; although the MICS, CISS, AC, and SOC have been valued for their utility in informing the clinician of behavioral excesses and deficits, we previously argued that the validity of individual items or category scores is unknown. Thus, there is little empirical basis to guide the clinician's judgment about which behaviors are indeed problematic. Combining data across different instruments is even more complicated. How does one combine MICS data and SOC data to determine the essential treatment components as well as an effective ordering of these components?

Developing a basis for these clinical predictions is a top priority for behavioral marital therapy. Given the general superiority of actuarial over judgmental synthesis of data (Sawyer, 1966; Meehl, 1965), empirical models are needed to generate predictions regarding couple responsiveness to different therapeutic interventions. As part of this process, clinical judgment should be considered as a possible predictor variable. Thus, it is important to study the decision-making process of "successful" marital therapists. Predictions to the criterion in question could then be formulated on the basis of a variety of input data, including raw scores on assessment measures, weighted or combined scores, and clinical interpretation of these scores. In the continued absence of such a prediction model, the clinician's options are limited to relying on feedback from his/her own clinical experience (however effective or ineffective), implementing a standardized therapy package that overlooks individual couple differences, or random matching of couples to intervention strategies.

The researcher must also rely on *a priori* decisions about data combination. The decision, for example, about how to classify couples as distressed or nondistressed has not been systematized. Individual investigators set their own cut-off scores and establish their own rules for combining data from more than one source. More generally, the researcher is concerned with long-term prediction questions. Testing any of the hypotheses about which factors serve as antecedents to marital distress requires the formulation of predictions based on longitudinal data. Correlations between specific data inputs and a criterion, such as the decision to seek therapy or divorce, would help identify which assessment options contribute to accurate decision making. These data would also help determine the validity of the theoretical model from which the assessment instruments have been developed.

Finally, it is presumed that spouses also observe and combine data in the process of appraising their marital relationship. It is unknown to what extent there is overlap between factors that couples attend to and variables that researchers have *a priori* determined to be of interest. To partial out the variance in daily satisfaction ratings due to outsider-determined variables, there still remains a good deal of unaccounted variance (Jacobson et al., 1980; Margolin, 1981; Wills et al., 1974). Since outsider-determined factors will continue to play an important role in the assessment of couples, we recommend finding out the value (both in direction and magnitude) that couples place upon these variables. Decision-making about couples might be more accurate if based on couples' own ratings rather than on *a priori* labels. Furthermore, since the perception of marital satisfaction has been singled out as a particularly important criterion, further exploration should be directed to the study of additional factors that spouses believe have an impact on their satisfaction.

A Cognitive-Affective Model

Behavioral marital and family assessment has been criticized for paying insufficient attention to cognitions and affect (Gurman & Knudson, 1978; Parke, 1978). Indeed, given that one of the ultimate objectives in behavioral marital therapy is the alteration of couples' perceptions about their marriages as well as the intensification or diffusion of certain emotions, there has been relatively little effort to systematize the assessment of these dimensions. With the exception of Gottman's (1979) work with the "talk table," the assessment of cognitions has been relegated to global self-report indices. Gottman (1979) has also highlighted the importance of affect by separately coding this dimension with the CISS. One other attempt to assess affect is found in the Anger Checklist (Margolin, Olkin, & Baum, 1977), where spouses track their physiological, affective, cognitive, and motoric components of anger.

Obviously, the assessment of cognitions, and to a lesser degree, affect, depends on spouses' reports of their own subjective experiences. A particular advantage of the "talk table" procedure is that it identifies ongoing rather than cumulative perceptions, thereby permitting the matching of internal perceptions with external behavior. Although the "talk table" has only been described for research purposes, it certainly appears to hold equal promise for therapy planning. Assessing the meaning that spouses attach to behavior exposes the spouses' individual phenomenologies about what is reinforcing and punishing. This information can be used to identify meaningful behavioral and cognitive targets for change. Additionally, spouses themselves may acquire greater awareness about how they contribute to problematic communications.

It is recommended that spouses' subjective impressions be assessed at both the level of: (1) longstanding attitudes and expectations about the relationship; and (2) immediate cognitive-affective-behavioral sequences. Social learning theorists (Birchler & Spinks, 1980; Jacobson & Margolin, 1979; Weiss, 1978) have recently begun acknowledging what family systems theorists have long maintained—that spouses' rules about their relationship play a role in governing their behavior. In the absence of standardized procedures for examining these important covert processes, the interview is available for exploring spouses' expectations

of each other and themselves, their assumptions about what makes relationships work, and their attributions about causality in relationship
problems. Exploring the second level of immediate cognitive-affective-
behavioral sequences requires the monitoring of moment-by-moment
reactions, either during an ongoing behavioral exchange or while watching a videotaped or audiotaped playback. Based on the assumption that
for each action there is a cognitive construal of the action as well as
an emotional response (Peterson, 1977), the objective is to slow down
the communciation process to a point where all three dimensions can
be understood. Without access to the formal procedures for spouse tracking that are described in the literature (Gottman, 1979; Margolin &
Weiss, 1978a), an alternate option is simply to use audiotape or videotape playback with frequent interruptions to obtain and discuss both
spouses' reactions.

The Couple as a Unit

Neither behavioral nor traditional assessment provides much direction
about how to assess a two-person system as opposed to an individual.
The application of the traditional trait approach to the assessment of
couples results in a label for the couple that is still based upon the
characteristics of individuals, e.g., the hysterical-obsessive marriage.
Behavioral marital therapists, for the most part, have also based their
assessment on the individual, rather than the system, as the unit of
observation. For example, a couple score on self-report instruments
simply translates into the sum or mean of the two partners' scores,
ignoring differences between couples who report similar levels of marital satisfaction versus those who report vastly different levels. Perhaps
a thorough understanding of the couple requires examining individual
scores vis à vis one another, as in the perceptual accuracy measure of
the AC.

Observational assessment, which was developed to examine interactional processes, is only beginning to depart from its reliance upon
the individual as the basis of measurement. The examination of behaviors displayed by two individuals when they are together does not
fully explore interactive processes (Gottman, 1979; Parke, 1978). Recent use of sequential analysis is a far superior approach for providing
a truly interactive picture of how spouses respond to one another. By
examining shifts in the probability that certain behaviors will occur,
sequential analyses begin to describe patterns of behavior that evolve
across time. Interaction sequences, rather than individual behaviors,
then become the fundamental unit of analysis (Gottman, 1979; Peterson,
1977).

Further work through sequential analysis is needed to examine the major theoretical underpinnings of behavioral marital therapy, i.e., that spouses influence each other's behavior through processes such as reciprocity and coercion. Sequential analyses also could provide outcome data to determine whether spouses actually change the nature of their interaction. Although sequential analyses have been limited thus far to couples' moment-by-moment communications, they can also be applied on a molar level. Certainly the time frame can be expanded to examine questions that concern larger units of behavior than what is captured in the MICS or CISS. Furthermore, these procedures can be used to examine how the couple as a unit responds to external stimuli, such as the actions of other persons or shifts in setting characteristics. We view further application of sequential analysis as a challenging future direction for identifying and altering recurrent dysfunctional interactional sequences.

CASE EXAMPLE

Description of Couple

Bob and Bonnie S., aged 25 and 27, had been married 5 years at the time they sought therapy. Both spouses had completed high school and currently were working for different branches of the same chain department store. They had previously been in therapy together but quit after five sessions, when they felt that their conflicts were intensifying. The content issues they presented during the intake session included the following:

1. *Jealousy:* Bonnie enjoyed the attention of men, particularly Bob's friends. When Bob worked into the evening, Bonnie sometimes invited other men over to their home. Until recently Bob had steadfastly remained trusting of Bonnie, even in the face of hints from friends and relatives that he had better "keep an eye" on his wife.
2. *Anger:* Although Bonnie and Bob had a history of getting angry with one another, a recent argument was the first to involve physical violence. Neither was seriously injured but the incident was frightening enough that they decided to end their relationship if this situation reoccurred.
3. *In-law relationships:* Bob expressed annoyance at the extent to which Bonnie was involved with her parents. Her once-daily phone calls to her mother were a source of irritation, particularly when she called first thing in the morning. At the same time, Bob wished that they spent more time with his family.

4. *Household management:* Bonnie complained that Bob delayed in completing tasks he had agreed to do (fixing up their home and yard).
5. *Lack of appreciation:* Both partners felt that they contributed to the relationship in a positive way. However, they felt they received little acknowledgment of those efforts from one another.

Data Summary

Bob and Bonnie attained the following scores during their 12-day preintervention assessment that included the SOC, AC, DAS, and Verbal Interaction Coding System for Couples (VICSC; Margolin, 1978), which is a hybrid combination of the MICS and CISS comprised of nine verbal codes.

Table 11.1

	Bonnie	Bob
VICSC (rate/Minute)		
Positive	1.16	1.10
Negative	.16	.80
SOC (rate/day)		
Pleases	20.33	20.33
Displeases	5.50	2.92
AC	8.00	10.00
DAS	93.00	100.00

Data Interpretation

The most notable features of the VISCS data was the high rate of negative behaviors for Bob and the high rates of mind-reading for both spouses. While communication skills such as Emotional Clarification, Accept Responsibility, and Agree were occurring at moderate rates, Problem Solution was particularly low, indicating this couple's inability to generate specific suggestions to their problems.

Examination of the self-report data indicate a moderate degree of marital distress. The SOC data translate into please:displease ratios of 3.7:1 for Bonnie and 7:1 for Bob. Bonnie's SOC data revealed low to average ratings of daily satisfaction while Bob's were generally above average. The DAS and AC indicate only mild marital satisfaction.

These data portray only part of the interaction patterns contributing to this couple's distress. Based on these data, Bob's behavior appeared to be more destructive to the marital relationship, (e.g., emitting more displeases and negative communications). However, Bonnie's contributions to the relationship problem (i.e. her flirting and partying with other men), was a low frequency event that carried extremely negative impact over a long period of time. Although that particular behavior did not occur during the baseline period and is thus not recorded anywhere in these scores, much of Bob's behavior reflects a cumulative reaction to Bonnie's past behavior.

Secondly, since this couple's difficulty with anger was not adequately assessed by these measures, they were instructed to monitor angry episodes on the Anger Checklist, a self-report measure of the somatic, affective, behavioral and cognitive components of anger (Margolin et al., 1977). This couple averaged three incidents of anger per week, ranging from minimal anger to intense anger. Although there were occasional threats of violence, expressions of anger during the assessment period were primarily limited to verbal behavior, such as blaming and criticism, with withdrawal from one another as the outcome. Spouses were asked to complete the checklist for both themselves and the partner. Matching between spouses revealed little understanding or recognition of the partner's feelings or experiences during these incidents.

Treatment Planning:

The composite picture of this couple based on pretherapy assessment plus ongoing feedback from the SOC and Anger Checklist during therapy led to the following intervention strategies:

1. Formulating an agreement that physical violence was totally unacceptable in this relationship.
2. Encouraging the couple to: (a) express the variety of feelings (e.g., hurt, helplessness, frustration, anxiety) that typically were obscured by angry actions.
3. Training in listening to and reflecting the partner's feelings.
4. Having spouses practice showing appreciation during sessions and at home.
5. Formulating and writing a relationship contract outlining what they agreed is acceptable or unacceptable regarding outside heterosexual relationships.
6. Training in problem-solving that could be applied to issues regarding household management, inlaws, etc.

This brief summary is offered to illustrate how preassessment data are translated into treatment strategies. The reader is referred to Jacobson and Margolin (1979) for more details on the clinically complex issues of getting beyond the spouses' hurt and hopelessness, raising positive expectancies, and preparing the couple for making behavior changes.

SUMMARY

This chapter reviews the current status of behavioral marital assessment, with attention to issues that tend to set couple assessment apart from other types of behavioral assessment: the need to assess a relationship system as opposed to two individuals, the multidimensional nature of relationships, and the importance of subjective, impressionistic criteria of marital adjustment. Currently, the major modalities for assessing couples include interactional coding systems, participant observation by spouses, and self-report questionnaires. Although there is an expanding data base for reliability and validity of major assessment instruments, interpretations based on these instruments are still constrained by questions of ecological validity. With the social learning formulation of marital distress broadening to include facets of systems theory and cognitive theory, behavioral marital assessment should follow suit. Future directions toward this objective include the application of sequential analyses, ongoing assessment of spouses' perceptions, and the empirical validation of predictions related to marital therapy and adjustment.

REFERENCES

Barnett, L. R., & Nietzel, M. T. Relationship of instrumental and affectional behaviors and self-esteem to marital satisfaction in distressed and nondistressed couples. *Journal of Consulting and Clinical Psychology*, 1979, *47*, 946–957.

Bateson, G., & Jackson, D. D. Some varieties of pathogenic organization. *Journal for Research in Nervous and Mental Disease*, 1964, *42*, 207–283.

Birchler, G. R., & Spinks, S. Behavioral systems marital and family therapy: Integration and clinical application. *American Journal of Family Therapy*, 1980, *8*, 6–28.

Birchler, G. R., & Webb, L. J. Discriminating interaction in behavior in happy and unhappy marriages. *Journal of Consulting and Clinical Psychology*, 1977, *45*, 494–495.

Birchler, G. R. Weiss, R. L., & Vincent, J. P. Multimethod analysis of social reinforcement exchange between maritally distressed and nondistressed spouse and stranger dyads. *Journal of Personality and Social Psychology*, 1975, *31*, 349–360.

Bronfenbrenner, V. Toward an experimental ecology of human development. *American Psychologist*, 1977, *32*, 513–531.

Christensen, A., & Nies, D. C. The spouse observation checklist: Empirical analysis and critique, *American Journal of Family Therapy*, 1980, *8*, 69–79.

Ciminero, A. R., Nelson, R. O., & Lipinski, D. P. Self-monitoring procedures in behavioral assessment. In A. R. Ciminero, K. S. Calhoun, & H. E. Adams (Eds.), *Handbook of behavioral assessment*. New York: Wiley, 1977.

Christensen, A. Naturalistic observation of families: A system for random audio recordings in the home. *Behavior Therapy, 1979, 10,* 418–422.

Cohen, R. S., & Christensen, A. Further examination of demand characteristics in marital interaction. *Journal of Consulting and Clinical Psychology, 1980, 48,* 121–123.

Cone, J. D. The relevance of reliability and validity for behavioral assessment. *Behavior Therapy, 1977, 8,* 411–426.

Edmonds, V. M., Withers, G., & Dibatista, B. Adjustment, conservatism, and marital conventionalization. *Journal of Marriage and the Family, 1972, 34,* 96–103.

Goldfried, M. R., & Kent, R. N. Traditional versus behavioral personality assessment: A comparison of methodological and theoretical assumptions. *Psychological Bulletin, 1972, 77,* 409–420.

Gottman, J. M. *Marital interaction: Experimental investigations.* New York: Academic Press, 1979.

Gottman, J. M., & Bakeman, R. The sequential analysis of observational data. In M. Lamb, S. Suomi, & G. Stephenson (Eds.), *Social interaction methodology*. Madison: University of Wisconsin Press, 1979.

Gottman, J., Markman, H., & Notarius, C. The topography of marital conflict: A sequential analysis of verbal and nonverbal behavior. *Journal of Marriage and the Family, 1977, 39,* 461–477.

Gottman, J., Notarius, C., Markman, H., Bank, S., Yoppi, B., & Rubin, M. E. Behavior exchange theory and marital decision making. *Journal of Personality and Social Psychology, 1976, 34,* 14–23.

Gurman, A. S., & Knudson, R. M. Behavior marriage therapy: I. A psychodynamic systems analysis and critique. *Family Process, 1978, 17,* 121–138.

Hartmann, D. P. Considerations in the choice of interobserver reliability estimates. *Journal of Applied Behavior Analysis, 1977, 10,* 103–116.

Haynes, S. N., Follingstad, D. R., & Sullivan, J. C. Assessment of marital satisfaction and interaction. *Journal of Consulting and Clinical Psychology, 1979, 47,* 789–791.

Heath, S., Kerns, R., Myskowski, M., & Haynes, S. N. *The assessment of marital interaction in structured observation situations: Criterion-related validity and internal consistency.* Paper presented at the Eleventh Annual Convention of the Association for the Advancement of Behavior Therapy, Atlanta, December 1977.

Hicks, M. W., & Platt, M. Marital happiness and stability: A review of the research in the sixties. *Journal of Marriage and the Family, 1970, 32,* 553–574.

Hollenbeck, A. R. Problems of reliability in observational research. In B. P. Sackett (Ed.), *Observing behavior*. Vol. II. Baltimore: University Park Press, 1978.

Hops, H., Wills, T. A., Patterson, G. R., & Weiss, R. L. *Marital interaction coding system*. Eugene, Oregon: University of Oregon and Oregon Research Institute, 1972.

Jacob, T. Family interaction in disturbed and normal families: A methodological and substantive review. *Psychological Bulletin, 1975, 82,* 33–65.

Jacob, T. Assessment of marital dysfunction. In M. Hersen, & A. S. Bellack (Eds.), *Behavioral assessment: A practical handbook*. New York: Pergamon, 1976.

Jacobson, N. S. Training couples to solve their marital problems: A behavioral approach to relationship discord. Part I: Problem-solving skills. *International Journal of Family Counseling, 1977, 5,* 22–31.

Jacobson, N. S., & Moore, D. *Spouses as observers of the events in their relationship. Journal of Consulting and Clinical Psychology*, in press.

Jacobson, N. S., & Margolin G. *Marital therapy: Strategies based on social learning and behavior exchange principles.* New York: Brunner/Mazel, 1979.
Jacobson, N. S., Ellwood, R., & Dallas, M. The behavioral assessment of marital dysfunction. In D. H. Barlow (Ed.), *Behavioral assessment of adult disorder.* New York: Guilford Press, 1981.
Jacobson, J. S., Waldron, H., & Moore, D. Toward a behavioral profile of marital distress. *Journal of Consulting and Clinical Psychology,* 1980, *48,* 696–703.
Jones, R. R., Reid, J. B., & Patterson, G. R. Naturalistic observations in a clinical assessment. In P. McReynolds, (Ed.), *Advances in psychological assessment.* Vol. 3. San Francisco: Jossey-Bass, 1975.
Klier, J. L., & Rothberg, M. *Characteristics of conflict resolution in couples.* Paper presented at the Eleventh Annual Convention of the Association for the Advancement of Behavior Therapy, Atlanta, December 1977.
Knudson, R. M., Sommers, A. A., & Golding, S. L. Interpersonal perception and mode of resolution in marital conflict. *Journal of Personality and Social Psychology,* 1980, *38,* 751–763.
Lederer, W. J., & Jackson, D. D. *Mirages of marriage.* New York: Norton, 1968.
Locke, H. J., & Wallace, K. M. Short-term marital adjustment and prediction tests: Their reliability and validity. *Journal of Marriage and Family Living,* 1959, *21,* 251–255.
Margolin, G. A multilevel approach to the assessment of communication positiveness in distressed marital couples. *International Journal of Family Counseling,* 1978, *6,* 81–89.(a)
Margolin, G. The relationship among marital assessment procedures: A correlational study. *Journal of Consulting and Clinical Psychology,* 1978, *46,* 1556–1558. (b)
Margolin, G. *Verbal interaction coding system for couples (VICSC).* Unpublished manuscript, University of Southern California, 1978. (c)
Margolin, G., Behavior exchange in happy and unhappy marriages: A family cycle perspective. *Behavior Therapy,* 1981, in press.
Margolin, G., Olkin, R. E., & Baum, M. *The Anger Checklist.* Unpublished inventory, University of California, Santa Barbara, 1977.
Margolin, G. & Wampold, B. E. *A sequential analysis of conflict and accord in distressed and nondistressed marital pairs.* Journal of Consulting and Clinical Psychology, 1981, in press.
Margolin, G., & Weiss, R. L. Communication training and assessment: A case of behavioral marital enrichment. *Behavior Therapy,* 1978, *9,* 508–520. (a)
Margolin, G., & Weiss, R. L. Comparative evaluation of therapeutic components associated with behavioral marital treatment. *Journal of Consulting and Clinical Psychology,* 1978, *46,* 1476–1486. (b)
Markman, H. J. Application of a behavioral model of marriage in predicting relationship satisfaction of couples planning marriage. *Journal of Consulting and Clinical Psychology,* 1979, *47,* 743–749.
Meehl, P. E. Seer over sign: The first good example. *Journal of Experimental Reseach in Personality,* 1965, *1,* 27–32.
Murstein, B. I., & Beck, G. D. Person perception, marriage adjustment, and social desirability. *Journal of Consulting and Clinical Psychology,* 1972, *39,* 396–403.
Olson, D. H. Insiders' and outsiders' views of relationships: Research studies. In G. Levinger, & H. L. Raush (Eds.), *Close relationships: Perspectives on the meaning of intimacy.* Amhurst: University of Massachusetts Press, 1977.
Olson, D. H., & Ryder, R. G. Inventory of marital conflicts (IMC): An experimental interaction procedure. *Journal of Marriage and the Family,* 1970, *32,* 443–448.

Parke, R. Parent-infant interaction: Progress, paradigms, and problems. In G. Sackett (Ed.), *Observing behavior: Vol. 1. Theory and applications in mental retardation.* Baltimore, Md.: University Park Press, 1978.

Patterson, G. R. Some procedures for assessing changes in marital interaction patterns. *Oregon Research Institute Bulletin,* 1976, Whole No. 16.

Patterson, G. R., & Hops, H. Coercion, a game for two: Intervention techniques for marital conflict. In R. E. Ulrich, & P. Mountjoy (Eds.), *The experimental analysis of social behavior.* New York: Appleton-Century-Crofts, 1972.

Patterson, G. R., Hops, H., & Weiss, R. L. A social learning approach to reducing rates of marital conflict. In R. Stuart, R. Liberman, & S. Wilder (Eds.), *Advances in behavior therapy.* New York: Academic Press, 1974.

Patterson, G. R., & Reid, J. B. Reciprocity and coercion: Two facets of social systems. In C. Neuringer, & J. L. Michael (Eds.), *Behavior modification in clinical psychology.* New York: Appleton-Century-Crofts, 1970.

Peterson, D. R. A functional approach to the study of person-person interactions. In D. Magnusson, & N. S. Endler (Eds.), *Personality at the crossroads: Current issues in interactional psychology.* Hillsdale, N. J.: Lawrence Erlbaum Associates, 1977.

Rappaport, A. F., & Harrell, J. A behavioral exchange model for marital counseling. *The Family Coordinator,* 1972, *22,* 203–212.

Resick, P. A., Sweet, J. J., Kieffer, D. M., Barr, P. K., & Ruby, N. L. *Perceived and actual discriminations of conflict and accord in marital communication.* Paper presented at the Eleventh Annual Convention of the Association for Advancement of Behavior Therapy, Atlanta, December 1977.

Robinson, E. A., & Price, M. G. Pleasurable behavior in marital interaction: An observational study. *Journal of Consulting and Clinical Psychology,* 1980 *48,* 117–118.

Rollins, B. C., & Feldman, H. Marital satisfaction over the family life cycle. *Journal of Marriage and the Family,* 1970, *26,* 20–28.

Royce, W. S., & Weiss, R. L. Behavioral cues in the judgment of marital satisfaction: A linear regression analysis. *Journal of Consulting and Clinical Psychology,* 1975, *43,* 816–824.

Sawyer, J. Measurement and prediction, clinical and statistical. *Psychological Bulletin,* 1966, *66,* 178–200.

Schram, R. W. Marital satisfaction over the family life cycle: A critique and proposal. *Journal of Marriage and the Family,* 1979, *41,* 7–12.

Spanier, G. B. Measuring dyadic adjustment: New scales for assessing the quality of marriage and similar dyads. *Journal of Marriage and the Family,* 1976, *38,* 15–28.

Strodbeck, F. L. Husband-wife interaction over revealed differences. *American Sociological Review,* 1951, *16,* 468–473.

Stuart, R. B. Operant-interpersonal treatment for marital discord. *Journal of Consulting and Clinical Psychology,* 1969, *33,* 675–682.

Stuart, R. B., & Stuart, F. *Marital Pre-Counseling Inventory.* Champaign: Research Press, 1972.

Tharp, R. G. Psychological patterning in marriage. *Psychological Bulletin,* 1963, *60,* 97–117.

Vincent, J. P., Cook, N. I., & Brady, C. P. *Accommodation to birth of the first child: Contribution of marital skills, satisfaction and infant temperament.* Paper presented at the Western Psychological Association Convention, San Diego, April 1979.

Vincent, J. P., Friedman, L. C., Nugent, J., & Messerly, L. Demand characteristics in observations of marital interaction. *Journal of Consulting and Clinical Psychology,* 1979, *47,* 557–566.

Vincent, J. P., Weiss, R. L., & Birchler, G. R. A behavioral analysis of problem solving in distressed and nondistressed married and stranger dyads. *Behavior Therapy,* 1975, *6,* 475–487.

Watzlawick, P., Beavin, J. H., & Jackson, D. D. *Pragmatics of human communication.* New York: Norton, 1967.

Weiss, R. L. The conceptualization of marriage from a behavioral perspective. In T. J. Paolino & B. S. McCrady (Eds.), *Marriage and marital therapy: Psychoanalytic behavioral and systems theory perspectives.* New York: Brunner/Mazel, 1978.

Weiss, R. L., & Birchler, G. R. *Areas of change.* Unpublished manuscript, University of Oregon, 1975.

Weiss, R. L., & Cerreto, M. *Marital status inventory.* Unpublished manuscript, University of Oregon, 1975.

Weiss, R. L., Hops, H., & Patterson, G. R. A framework for conceptualizing marital conflict, a technology for altering it, some data for evaluating it. In L. A. Hamerlynck, L. C. Handy, & E. J. Mash (Eds.), *Behavior change: Methodology, concepts, and practice.* Champaign, Il.: Research Press, 1973.

Weiss, R. L., & Margolin, G. Marital conflict and accord. In A. R. Ciminero, K. S. Calhoun, & H. E. Adams (Eds.), *Handbook for behavioral assessment.* New York: Wiley, 1977.

Weiss, R. L., & Perry, B. A. *Assessment and treatment of marital dysfunction.* Eugene, Oregon: Oregon Marital Studies Program, 1979.

Wieder, G. B., & Weiss, R. L. Generalizability theory and the coding of marital interactions. *Journal of Consulting and Clinical Psychology*, 1980, *48*, 469–477.

Wiggins, J. S., *Personality and prediction: Principles of personality assessment.* Reading, MA.: Addison-Wesley, 1973.

Wills, T. A., Weiss, R. L., & Patterson, G. R. A behavioral analysis of the determinants of marital satisfaction. *Journal of Consulting and Clinical Psychology*, 1974, *42*, 802–811.

Chapter 12

Assessment of Sexual Dysfunction and Deviation

Kurt Freund

and

Ray Blanchard

INTRODUCTION

The realm of behavioral sexology branches off into two main sections: one concerned with *precoital* the other with *coital* sexual behavior. There is a corresponding division in the study of the pathology of sexual behavior, namely the study of anomalous erotic preferences and that of sexual dysfunction. The present chapter is divided correspondingly. (In the following, *pre*coital behavior in humans will be referred to as "erotic" rather than "sexual.")

Assessment of Anomalous Erotic Preferences

In this section: (1) the realm of anomalous erotic preferences will be delineated, (2) the assessment of these anomalies by interview and verbal scales will be introduced, (3) the phallometric method will be discussed, and (4) the possibilities of therapeutic intervention will be briefly reviewed.

The realm of anomalous erotic preferences. The impact of a potentially erotic or sexual stimulus pattern on a vertebrate organism can be defined as a change that this stimulus pattern effects in the organism's preparedness to act or interact sexually. We will call this preparedness the organism's erotic or sexual *arousal level*. This term signifies an intervening variable, which is a function both of concurrent external stimuli and internal constellations. These include an organism's past experience, as well as biochemical (e.g., hormonal) patterns. Let us further call the extent of the stimulus impact its erotic or sexual *arousal value*. We will define erotic activity as those components of a person's behavior which vary as a function of his or her erotic arousal level. The arousal level necessary to trigger a particular erotic activity will be defined as this activity's *erotic threshold value*.

After an individual has reached full physical maturity, the hierarchical orders of erotic stimulus values and activity thresholds remain basically constant. (This also holds for the subtle cyclical changes in these hierarchies which regularly occur within the progression of erotic interaction.) A person's *preferences* in respect to subjects of erotic or sexual fantasy and actual behavior depend largely on these hierarchies of stimulus values and of thresholds for own erotic activities. (There is, however, always some interference, particularly with behavior, from past experience, including a person's upbringing, and from concurrent social pressure.)

Little systematic work has been carried out in establishing norms for the hierarchies of erotic preferences. Nonetheless, there is wide consensus on what constitutes a gross deviation from these norms. These gross deviations are the *anomalous erotic preferences*. Let us stress at this point that these are anomalies in hierarchies which exhibit, in the grossly normal population, fairly wide ranges of erotically rewarding ideation and behavior patterns.

The anomalous erotic preferences are usually classified according to that behavioral aspect where the deviation from the norm is most conspicuous. According to this criterion, they can be divided into anomalies in partner (or object) preference versus anomalies in preferences regarding the subject's own erotic activity. In many individual cases, combinations of these two types of disturbances are encountered. Basic classifcation and definitions are to be found in Freund and Steiner (1980). In the following, only brief characteristics will be given of those anomalies most commonly requiring diagnosis.

Common anomalies in *partner* or *object choice* are homosexuality, pedophilia and/or hebephilia (an anomalous erotic preference for children and/or pubescent youths), and fetishism (where certain parts of the body or inanimate objects have an unusually high erotic arousal value).

Among the anomalies in respect to own erotic activity, two main groups of disturbances can be differentiated. The first has been designated by Krafft-Ebing (1886/1950) as sadism and masochism. This group also includes those disturbances which can be characterized as an abnormally strong preference for erotic dominance or submission.

The second group is characterized by a conspicuous distortion of the phase sequence of precoital or courtship behavior. The typical sequence can be understood as proceeding in four phases: (1) location and/or choice of a suitable partner; (2) pretactile interaction—in humans, looking, smiling, posturing, and talking to a prospective partner, (3) tactile interaction; and (4) effecting genital union (Freund and Kolářský, 1965). The distortion is a disproportionate intensification or exaggeration of one of the four phases, with the remaining phases present only vestigially or missing altogether.

The most common distortions of phasing of courtship behavior, or simply *courtship distortions,* are voyeurism, exhibitionism, toucheurism (and frotteurism), and the pathological rape pattern. Voyeurism is characterized by a strong inclination to watch stealthily a member of the opposite sex in the nude or some stage of undress, having intercourse, or urinating, etc. This anomaly can be understood as an exaggerated and distorted phase of partner location and (initial) appraisal, the first phase of courtship behavior, with the remaining phases only abortively present or nonexistent altogether.

Exhibitionism (Lasègue, 1877) is a similar erotic preference for exposing the penis—or less frequently, other parts of the body—from a distance, and can be understood as an exaggeration of pretactile interaction, the second phase in courtship behavior.

An analogous exaggeration of the phase of tactile interaction of courtship behavior is toucheurism, an anomalously strong inclination for touching the breasts or the genital area of previously unknown females, without their expectation (in contrast to the normal preference for such intimacies as part of mutual erotic interaction). A different mode of such distortion of the third phase is frotteurism, an anomalously strong inclination to press the penis against the buttocks of an unknown and unsuspecting female.

A related disturbance is the erotic preference for effecting genital, or oral genital, union (in the case of the pathological rape pattern [Freund, 1976]) or for other physical sexual interaction (in the case of the pathological rape-*like* patterns), with a female unknown or hardly known to the patient, by threats or using physical force (but without the intention to harm). These two kinds of patterns can be understood as exaggerations of the fourth phase of courtship behavior—transition to coital interaction.

In almost every case, an anomalous erotic preference as to partner (or object) is accompanied by some anomalous modification of the generally preferred *ways* of erotic interaction, and vice versa. For instance, it would appear that the most preferred erotic interaction of heterosexual pedophilic males differs somewhat from the interaction normally sought by males who prefer physically mature females. A converse example is the type of female partner preferred by males whose interaction preferences are masochistic. She has to boss her male partner around, give him commands, and her physique has to suggest the capability to dominate.

A very conspicuous combination of anomalies in preferred category of partner (or object) *and* type of preferred erotic interaction is gross cross-gender identity. This is a sustained or intermittently occurring wishful fantasy about being a member of the opposite sex. Such gender identity inversion may occur only when the individual is sexually aroused (in transvestism), when he is aroused and occasionally when he is not ("borderline transsexualism"), or may be there all the time (transsexualism). In transvestism, borderline transsexualism, or "type B" transsexualism, there is virtually always fetishism for attire or other objects representative of the opposite sex; in "type A" transsexualism, there is virtually always homosexuality (Freund, Steiner, & Chan, 1981).

There is a great difference between what is known about anomalous preferences in males and what is known in this respect about females. We do not know as yet whether or where this is so because female eroticism has been so little explored or because it might be less prone to disturbances. That there can be basic differences between the sexes in respect to vulnerability of sexual development is known from animal studies, such as Harlow's (1965) work with social isolation of infant Rhesus monkeys, and from Schutz's (1975) series of elegant experiments on ducks, the results of which are described in the following.

When newly hatched male ducklings were raised by mothers who belonged to another species, they later formed pairs and copulated with females of this other species and not with those of their own. When raised without a mother and with only other male ducklings of their own species, male ducks later formed homosexual pairs. These were actually quite unsuccessful pairs because both partners continued for years to copulate in the male fashion—neither of the partners assumed the female role. In contrast, it was generally impossible to mold in this way the later partner choice of female ducklings. In further experiments, however, Schutz found that imprinting of the alien partner species actually had occurred in females as well, though less strongly, but had remained latent. It was only apparent after these females were treated in adulthood with testosterone.

Schutz had previously found that testosterone treatment of adult female ducks rendered their partner choice temporarily homosexual, although their courtship and copulatory patterns remained female. When female ducks raised by mothers of another species were homosexualized later in adulthood by treatment with testosterone, they paired up with females belonging to this stepmother species.

Let us now return to what is known about differences in anomalous erotic preferences between human females and males. Kinsey, Pomeroy, and Martin (1948) and Kinsey, Pomeroy, Martin, and Gebhard (1953) thought that more males than females are homosexual. However, these authors based their conclusion on the subject's self-reports, and there may still exist a stronger inhibition in females than in males against disclosing existing sexual anomalies. Clinical practice also appears to show that there may not be any difference in the prevalence of male and female homosexuality. Masochism and fetishism might also not be rarer in females than in males. In contrast, this is not likely to be true for sadism, at least in respect to heterosexual females. The sadistic (heterosexual) woman seems to exist only in the fantasy of masochistic males, although there might be rare exceptions to this rule. It is also uncertain whether true pedophilia or hebephilia exists in females. Moreover, with one not very reliable exception, no case has been published of a *heterosexual* female with gross cross-gender identity (and cross-gender fetishism) although the incidence and prevalence of (homosexual) transsexualism would appear to be about equal in females and males.

The problem of differences between the sexes in anomalies of courtship phasing is even more complicated. There has never been a case published of male-like voyeurism or of a pattern corresponding to male exhibitionism in a nonmentally retarded or grossly deteriorated woman. This would seem to suggest that distortions of phasing of courtship behavior do not exist in women. However, such distortions may be present in females as well, but appear in a less obtrusive way, remaining without the social and, in particular, legal consequences males with these disorders often have to face.

From an analysis of courtship behavior of normal females, it might be possible to deduce the specific forms that distortions of phasing of female courtship behavior could be expected to take. If a woman derived unusually strong arousal by being touched or raped by a previously unknown man, for example, she might lure a male into doing so. This would not have any legal implications for her. Clinically, such females might be misdiagnosed as "sexually inadequate" in normal partner interaction. All of this is still conjecture and will have to be validated by research, and the researchers will have to be women.

Assessment by interview and verbal scales. A detailed sex history is to be taken including gender identity in childhood, first sexual interests, first occurrence of fantasies which resemble later sexual fantasies or behavior, "crushes" in childhood and adolescence, erotic or sexual interactions, and close friendships during the teens. There is no better advice in respect to interviewing in this realm than the rules given by Kinsey et al. (1948), which should be looked up in the original.

It is necessary to communicate to the patient a non-moralistic attitude toward her or his disclosures, and one should try particularly hard to make sure the interviewed person understood the question. The following is an example of a quite frequent misunderstanding: A young man who complained about being impotent when trying to have intercourse with women said that his sexual fantasies were about intercourse with physically mature girls he met at work or at other occasions who seemed appealing to him. However, for this patient "sexual fantasies" meant any imagery with sexual content, whether he willed these images or whether they appeared spontaneously in situations of high sexual arousal. When asked about masturbation fantasies he said that he tried hard to think of females, occasionally with little success, and that usually at the peak of arousal images of males appeared.

With females who are seen because they want to know whether they are hetero-or homosexual, verbal investigation of erotic preferences is often even more difficult, particularly if masturbation fantasies are denied. One patient, for instance, indicated she had intensely tender feelings for a particular female and had never had such feelings for males, though she did not long for any sexual interaction with this woman. Later she conceded she wished to hold this woman in her arms and that there had been previous "crushes" of this kind. However, at the same time she indicated she sometimes enjoyed intercourse with males and was capable of reaching orgasm on such occasions. Whether true bisexuality (i.e., equal erotic arousability by male and female body shape) exists among persons who prefer physically mature partners is beyond the scope of the present chapter. In the authors' opinion, true bisexuality is found only in pedophiles, and even there only in a minority of persons (Freund & Langevin, 1976; Mohr, Turner, & Jerry, 1964).

In these and similar situations, differential diagnoses should still be possible on the basis of verbal exploration alone, if the examiner is sufficiently experienced in the usual self-deceptions of patients who dread giving up a marriage or being rejected by their family or society at large because of their anomalous erotic preference.

The various known syndromes of erotic anomalies can be understood as types, which correspond to clusters localized in n-dimensional space. Measurement along these dimensions started with the masculinity versus femininity scale developed by Terman and Miles (1936). Since then a great number of similar masculinity-femininity scales have been devised (see Freund, Langevin, Satterberg, & Steiner, 1977). The most recent and widely employed is Bem's (1974) Androgyny Scale which, in contrast to the earlier instruments, measures femininity and masculinity separately. Bem's and earlier scales were validated mainly on differentiating between females and males. One instrument, the Gender Identity Scale for Males (Freund et al., 1977) departed from this procedure. The majority of its items are the traditional questions employed by clinicians for the past 50 years when exploring whether a male patient's gender-identity feelings or behavior are, or ever have been, in gross contradiction to what is largely expected from a male. Item analysis and principal components analysis were carried out on male samples only, and the scale was tested by assessing its differentiation among heterosexual, homosexual nontranssexual, and homosexual transsexual males. All the mentioned scales are self-administered questionnaires.

Two pertinent verbal instruments are not self-administered. One is Richard Green's (1974) gender-identity test battery for male children, and the other is the already classic Kinsey scale (Kinsey et al., 1948). The latter is based on an examiner's evaluation of a subject's self-report on sexual responses to members of the same and opposite sexes. For this purpose, sexual response was defined as "erotic arousal or orgasm through physical contact and/or psychic reaction [p. 641]." Obviously, this scale was very well suited for the purposes of the monumental pioneering investigations of Kinsey and his associates; however, its value is less evident in more individual-oriented studies using much smaller numbers of subjects. With the exception of degrees 0 and 6 of the scale, which represent totally heterosexual and totally homosexual orientation, the confounding of arousal brought about by body contact and that elicited by real or imagined visual (or auditory) stimulus configurations makes it difficult to understand what this scale really measures. Such body contact might be just surrogate activity (e.g., homosexual interaction among heterosexual persons in boarding schools, prisons, etc., or heterosexual activity sought by homosexual persons for other than erotic reasons [Freund, 1974]). Kinsey et al. mention such possibilities. The provision taken by Kinsey et al. of giving priority to "psychic reactions" in contrast to responses with a different kind of antecedent, appears to bias the scale toward measuring erotic preference, but poses difficulties by increasing the ambiguity of the basic data.

All the instruments discussed so far are based on a patient's self-report and are employed under the supposition that she or he has the necessary information, is able to remember it reliably, and is truthful in communications. There is, however, a substantial proportion of cases where a patient's seemingly genuine request for diagnosis, advice, or therapy is actually demanded by a third party, and the patient tries to get the examiner's help his own way. This was the case of a young man who came to seek help for "impotence caused by performance anxiety." His wife, many years older than he, was a well-paid university teacher. The patient, however, had never been able to hold a regular job for a reasonable period of time. In the end it turned out that the patient's seeing a psychiatrist had been the condition under which his wife had agreed to refrain from divorce. She complained that the patient had intercourse with her only during the first year of their marriage, and that not long ago she had found out about a long-term relationship between her husband and another man.

Diagnosis may become very difficult in cases of those erotic anomalies (e.g., pedophilia) which tend to lead to socially unacceptable sexual activities. A forensic patient might face more serious consequences of the same offense (e.g., approaching a child sexually) if he is found to erotically *prefer* children to physically mature females, and a diagnosis of dangerous sadism may have grave implications for a patient who scratched a child's throat "playfully" with a pocket knife.

While the patient's predicament is rarely that grave, the demand situation under which the examination is recommended should always be assessed along with the extent of the client's openness or reluctance in admitting an anomalous erotic preference. This is particularly necessary when selecting patients for *research*. For this purpose, two verbal "admitter" scales for use with male patients have been developed: one for pedophilia, the other for hebephilia. For both scales, item analysis was carried out on the responses of 152 males whose history indicated very probable pedo- or hebephilia. The "Pedo Admitter" scale is composed of 12 items, the "Hebe Admitter" scale has five items. The alpha reliability index for the "Pedo Admitter" scale was alpha = 0.92; that for the "Hebe Admitter" scale was alpha = 0.74 (Freund, Chan, & Coulthard, 1979).

The frequency distribution of each of these two scales showed two clear peaks. The Pedo Admitter scale showed one peak at score 0, the other at a score of 10 and 11, and a steep start of this latter peak between scores 7 and 8. Therefore, score 8 is presently taken as the cutting score for classifying the subject as an "admitter" of strong erotic attraction to children. In a similar way, hebephilic Admitters are differentiated from Nonadmitters. (The scales appear in Freund, 1981.) The two indicated Admitter scales differ from the usual Lie scales in that they are tailored to fit the specific problem in question, instead of assessing a person's *general* tendency to appear socially appealing to the examiner.

The phallometric method. The large proportion of invalid self-reports encountered initially instigated the search for nonverbal—in this case, physiological—measures of the erotic arousal produced by various stimulus configurations. It was hoped that measurements of a subject's physiological response to different categories of potentially erotic stimuli, when ordered according to amplitude, would reveal the subject's erotic stimulus hierarchy.

According to Baldwin (1901), the presence or absence of "appetites" is most sensitively reflected by those physiological structures that are most directly involved in satiation of those appetites. Thus, one would expect that penile tumescence would vary more systematically with changes in erotic arousal level than those physiological activities indicative of general arousal (e.g., heart rate, respiratory waveform, galvanic skin response, etc.). The empirical evidence has confirmed this expectation (Freund, 1981; Zuckerman, 1971).

The first to use penile changes, though *not* volume change, as an indicator of erotic arousal was Hynie (1934). His main interest was objective assessment of erectile difficulties and the pharmacological effect of various chemical compounds. Hynie focused on penile and scrotal motility and employed a technique derived from Weitz and Vollers (1926), who had investigated the motility of the smooth musculature of various organs, including the penis. Strings which led to pens of a writing device were attached to various sites on the penis and scrotum.

In the presently discussed phallometric test of erotic preferences (Freund, 1957, 1963, 1980), penile tumescence is monitored during and after discrete presentations of potentially erotic stimuli. For many years, the stimuli used were all photographs or movie clips of potential partner categories (nude males and females of various ages). More recently, attempts have also been made to assess (indirectly) anomalies in a subject's own erotic activities by measuring the erotic arousal value of situations created by such activities. In this way, a patient's erotic preference for exposing as compared with normal pretactile interaction, for example, can be assessed. For this and similar purposes, verbal descriptions of such activities are employed (Abel, Blanchard, Barlow, & Mavissakalian, 1975; Freund, Langevin, Chamberlayne, Deosaran, & Zajac, 1974). In the phallometric test each stimulus category is represented by several separately presented stimuli, usually a standard set. Abel et al. (1975) introduced a more individualized method with optimalization of stimuli by tailoring them to the more idiosyncratic needs of the subject under examination.

There are two types of sensors for monitoring penile tumescence: one volumetric (Freund, 1981; Freund, Sedlácek, and Knob, 1965; McConaghy, 1967); the other circumferential. The volumetric sensor transmits penile volume change through an air-filled tube to a measuring

or recording device. There is in Freund (1981) a short description of
an utterly inexpensive, virtually trouble-free, very sensitive (though
ridiculously archaic) measuring device. A drawing of this device is in
Freund, 1965. With a polygraph, the volumetric sensor is used in conjunction with a pressure coupler, and an air cushion (a small flask) is
interposed to buffer large volume and pressure changes (Freund, Langevin, & Barlow, 1974) because of the limited range of pressure these
couplers can tolerate.

Various strain gauges are used for measurement of penile circumference (see Flanagan, 1978; Laws, 1977; Rosen & Keefe, 1978). The
most convenient would appear to be a mercury strain gauge originally
devised by Whitney (1949) for measurement of other circumferences,
and first employed by Fisher, Gross, and Zuch (1965) for monitoring
penile tumescence in sleep. This transducer can easily be employed with
all the usual recording devices.

Comparisons of volumetric and circumferential transducers in the
diagnosis of erotic sex-age preference have shown the superiority of
the volumetric method (Freund, Langevin, & Barlow, 1974; Mc-
Conaghy, 1974). The difficulty with the circumferential method is not
in the sensitivity of the available strain gauges, but with circumference
itself as an index of penile tumescence. For many subjects, tumescence,
at its start produces penile elongation together with a *decrease* in circumference (which shows on the circumferential curve as an initial
negative wave). Thus, circumferential devices are not well suited for
measuring *very small* penile volume changes. This necessitates much
longer stimulus presentations than customarily employed with the volumetric method. Long stimulus presentations are a disadvantage, particularly in diagnosing "Nonadmitters" (Freund et al., 1979), because
they allow a greater time for the recruitment of fantasy, which the subject may use covertly to "replace" the external stimulus presented by
the examiner. The interested reader may find a more detailed discussion
on phallometry in a recent comprehensive report (Freund, 1981), which
also contains information about attempts to use indicators of *general*
arousal for assessing erotic preferences, for instance, pupillary width
(Hess & Polt, 1960; Hess, Seltzer, & Shlien, 1965), breathing, heart
rate, galvanic skin response, etc.

Attempts have been made to design a transducer for the female genital, that could be used in procedures analogous to male phallometry.
Zuckerman (1971) reviewed the first attempts in this direction, and in
Hoon (1978) there is a comprehensive review of further progress. The
most promising device to date would appear to be that of Sintchak and
Geer (1975). However, these devices tend to detect genital changes only
after prolonged exposure to strong stimuli. This may indicate that the
female sexual response threshold is much higher than male's, or that

the physiological variables tapped by these instruments in the female are not the most appropriate ones, or that the instruments themselves are not yet good enough.

From the start, the phallometric test of erotic preference was intended as a research tool, specifically as a means for reducing syndromes of anomalous erotic preference to more elementary "underlying" components. In this respect it has proved to be dependable. As a diagnostic tool, more specifically as an instrument for diagnosing erotic preferences the subject does *not* want to admit, it was and has remained less reliable.

Experiments assessing the extent to which responses could be suppressed or feigned showed, from the start (Freund, 1961, 1963) that a substantial proportion of subjects were able to "beat the machine." These experiments have been replicated many times, with similar results (see Freund, 1981). "Nonadmitter" tests are (and have been) developed which make response suppression or feigning difficult. We have been working for some time with such nonadmitter forms for diagnosing pedophilia and hebephilia. In these Nonadmitter forms, the "crucial" stimulus (a 14-second film clip of a nude child, or a pubertal or physically mature person) is presented as soon as the subject attains a minute, criterion-level erectile response in the presence of a socially acceptable "prearousal" stimulus (a projected still photograph of a nude adult female). The criterion response to the prearousal stimulus might reflect some mild erotic value of this stimulus itself, or it might result from the subject's attempt to deceive the diagnostician by fantasizing his (anomalous) preferred erotic stimulus in the presence of the socially acceptable prearousal stimulus. In any case, at least some classes of prearoused subjects appear less able to inhibit their responses to immediately following anomalous crucial stimuli (Freund et al., 1979). The main difference between Nonadmitter and the standard modes of the test is that the standard mode does not include prearousal procedures.

In contrast to Nonadmitters, the phallometric assessment of erotic preferences is very accurate with persons who do not hide their preferences; who can quite often tell us (though often much less precisely than the test can) what their erotic preferences are (Freund et al., 1979). An example of such imprecision is the quite frequent claim by *cooperative* pedophilic males that, although they are troubled by feeling erotically attracted to children, their erotic inclination toward physically mature females is even greater. However, in such cases, phallometric testing usually shows a much smaller response to physically mature females than to female children.

A further avenue to be taken in developing phallometric diagnosis involves determining the extent to which a person is able and willing to feign or suppress his erotic responses, when repeatedly undergoing the

test. This and similar methods, together with the earlier mentioned
Nonadmitter scales, could also very much increase our ability to specify
the demand situation the patient is confronted with, and to select appropriate research subjects.

The use of phallometry in assessing therapeutic outcome. It has been generally accepted for several decades that anomalous erotic preferences
can be substantially normalized by traditional psychotherapy or behavior
therapy (Freund, 1980). We are presently witnessing the emergence of
a tacit agreement that this may not be so. Traditional psychotherapy
was first challenged by the behavior therapists, who claimed to have
achieved cures where many years of preceding traditional treatment had
failed. The effectiveness of behavior therapy has been challenged, in
turn, by a small number of clinical workers who concluded that not
even this method is capable of changing erotic preferences (Freund,
1965b). However, psychotherapy or counseling, either alone or as an
ancillary procedure to pharmacological or other sex drive reducing measures (Freund, 1980), and in particular behavior therapy, may well be
of value in helping an individual refrain from *acting* in accordance with
a socially unacceptable erotic preference.

When attempting to evaluate therapeutic success or failure, one should
be familiar with the extent of variability in erotic behavior, and with
the (earlier mentioned) great capability of many patients to deceive
themselves about their erotic anomalies. The senior author has seen
numerous homosexual males who had always been very open in their
communication and had no apparent reason for lying about therapeutic
outcome, who, nonetheless, overjoyed at having learned to achieve intercourse with females whenever necessary, maintained for a long time
that they ceased to desire sexual interaction with males. None of them
remained "cured" (Freund, 1965b, 1977).

Patients with distortions of courtship behavior often indicate, after
going through the embarrassment of being caught exposing, etc., that
they were "cured" for several months. A distortion of courtship behavior occasionally seems to totally disappear for one or two years,
particularly when the patient falls in love or marries. A further example
of a relatively frequent type of self-report on cure without therapy is
the spontaneous fluctuation of the patient's feminine or masculine identification in heterosexual cases of gross cross-gender identity.

Behavior therapists embraced the phallometric test of erotic preference in the hope that it would be a more valid indicator of therapeutic
outcome than a patient's self-report. However, because of the already
mentioned possibility of response suppression or feigning, this is presently only true to a small extent. To make feigning of therapeutic success as difficult as possible, the standard mode of the test should only

be administered prior to therapy. In follow-ups, Nonadmitter modes will have to be employed and no single mode should be used more than once. As mentioned earlier, however, it would appear that there is presently no therapy capable of effecting a substantial long-term change, or possibly any substantial change at all in erotic preferences. The best we can do for a patient who is drawn to socially unacceptable sexual activities, is to employ sex-drive reducing measures (see review by Freund, 1980) combined with long-term counseling.

Assessment of Sexual Dysfunctions

In this section, (1) the various forms of sexual dysfunction are described, (2) differential diagnostic procedures for erectile insufficiency are outlined, (3) psychological causes of sexual dysfunction are briefly discussed, (4) objectives and techniques of psychological assessment are reviewed, and (5) current treatment interventions are introduced.

The term sexual response *disorder* implies that some organic or psychological condition that impairs a particular sexual response is present in an individual. *Sexual inadequacy* refers to the dissatisfaction of one or both partners in a specific sexual relationship. *Sexual dysfunction* has been used to refer both to sexual inadequacy and sexual disorders. The labeling of an individual as sexually inadequate in a particular relationship does not necessarily imply the presence of a gross disorder in sexual response, although such disorders naturally tend to result in sexual inadequacy.

Sexual dysfunctions may be primary, referring to the condition of individuals who have never been competent, or secondary, referring to incompetence which develops subsequent to a period of competence. Secondary dysfunctions may be of acute or insidious onset. Selective or situational dysfunctions occur under one set of circumstances, but not under another.

Specific sexual dysfunctions. There are three main types of male sexual disorders. *Erectile insufficiency* is the persistent inability to obtain or maintain an erection sufficient for vaginal penetration. The requisite degree of penile rigidity may be objectively specified in terms of buckling pressure, thus allowing erectile insufficiency to be identically defined for automasturbation, fellatio, etc. *Premature ejaculation* is the persistent occurrence of orgasm and ejaculation before or immediately following the application of tactile stimulation to the erect (or flaccid) penis. *Ejaculatory incompetence* (retarded ejaculation, ejaculatio retardata, or impotentia ejaculandi) is the persistent difficulty or inability to ejaculate, despite the presence of adequate sexual desire, erection, and stimulation.

Following Kaplan (1974a, 1974b), we shall distinguish three main types of female sexual disorders. *General sexual unresponsiveness* is a disorder in which the female lacks erotic feelings and responses; she is sometimes virtually anesthetic on the clitoris and vaginal entrance. She does not respond significantly to erotic stimuli with vaginal lubrication or with genital vasocongestion (swelling), the female reactions comparable to erection in the male. Such women may or may not be averse to sexual contact. *Orgastic dysfunction* is the complaint of females who respond with lubrication and vasocongestion, but who find it difficult or impossible to achieve orgasm despite adequate desire and effective stimulation. Orgastic dysfunction is analogous in some respects to ejaculatory incompetence.

Vaginismus is an involuntary spasm of the muscles surrounding the vaginal entrance, which occurs in response to introduction of the penis or some other body into the vagina, thus preventing it. Females with vaginismus are usually also phobic of coitus and vaginal penetration. Vaginismus may be associated with general sexual unresponsiveness or orgastic dysfunction, but some females may be sexually responsive and reach orgasm through clitoral stimulation (Kaplan 1974b). The diagnosis of vaginismus requires a pelvic examination (Kaplan, 1974b; Masters & Johnson, 1970). The spastic contraction of the perivaginal muscles is generally viewed as a protective reflex, elicited by the anticipation of pain or fear associated with intromission.

Dyspareunia generally refers to painful coitus experienced by females, but there are certain medical conditions that result in pain during coitus for males also. Masters and Johnson (1970) discuss organic causes of male and female dyspareunia, and Abarbanel (1970) presents the etiological possibilities for female dyspareunia in tabular form.

Organogenic etiology. Any male or female who seeks treatment of a sexual dysfunction must undergo a thorough medical examination. A great number of medical conditions may impair sexual response, including prescription medications, alcohol, and illicit drugs. Lists of such conditions and drugs may be found in Kaplan (1974b), Masters and Johnson (1970), and Karacan, Salis, and Williams (1978). In this section, we will discuss erectile insufficiency, the sexual disorder with the most advanced differential diagnostic techniques.

It is commonly believed that certain patterns of erectile failure are symptomatic of psychological causality; these are acute onset, selective occurrence (with one partner but not another), transient occurrence (during certain periods but not others), and the occurrence of some erection outside of partnership interaction (spontaneous, masturbatory, or morning) (Karacan et al., 1978). Both Schumacher and Lloyd (1976) and Karacan et al. (1978) comment on the lack of empirical evidence for this notion, and point out that some of these symptoms, such as transient occurrence, may just as well characterize certain forms or stages in the development of organogenic impotence.

Keeping the above caveat in mind, the clinician may still use diagnostic signs, such as selective occurrence in combination with other evidence, in establishing the psychological origin of a male's sexual inadequacy. In cases where a male experiences no erectile insufficiency in automasturbation, but is impotent in heterosexual coitus, an anomalous erotic preference is sometimes present. The patient might be better able to fantasize the preferred type of partner or interaction during automasturbation than during intercourse.

A second belief frequently found in the literature is that 90 percent of erectile insufficiency is psychogenic. In practice, psychogenic insufficiency is typically diagnosed when organic pathology cannot be found, even when no positive indicators of psychogenic etiology are identified (Karacan et al., 1978). Thus, the 90 percent figure really depends partly upon the adequacy of current medical diagnostic practice. However, Karacan et al. point out that, not only is the present lack of adequate information on the basic mechanisms of erectile dysfunction sure to result in many failures to identify organic pathology, but so is the common failure of physicians to perform a fully adequate examination. Karacan et al., employing a relatively new diagnostic technique described below, found probable organic involvement in 60 percent of cases. Data reviewed by Schumacher and Lloyd (1976) also suggest that the asserted high rates of psychogenic etiology are inflated by undiagnosed cases of organic involvement. There is one final point regarding any percentage of organogenic or psychogenic etiology that may be reported: the clinical setting determines in part the characteristics of the population who will present for treatment (Schumacher & Lloyd, 1976). The high proportion of organic involvement reported by Karacan et al., for example, may reflect the fact that the radical treatment offered by his team (implantation of a penile prosthesis) is sought by men whose erectile insufficiency has been refractory to other forms of treatment because of organic deficits (Karacan et al., 1978).

A sexual dysfunction clinic should include the facilities for carrying out certain specialized diagnostic procedures. In cases of erectile insufficiency, a comprehensive procedure for determining the presence or absence of organic involvement is now available (Fisher, Schiavi, Lear, Edwards, Davis, & Witkin, 1975; Karacan, Scott, Salis, Attia, Ware, Altinel, & Williams, 1977). This procedure involves the monitoring of nocturnal penile tumescence (NPT). NPT occurs in all healthy boys and men. In adults, NPT episodes, which are closely associated with REM sleep, typically occur every 90–100 minutes during sleep and last an average of 20–40 minutes. There is no evidence that NPT is consistently related to erotic dreams. Certain negative affects in REM dreams (e.g., anxiety) may produce a transient reduction in NPT, but they do not completely suppress NPT if the male is physiologically capable of erection. The working hypothesis for the use of NPT in differential diagnosis is that abnormal NPT patterns indicate organic involvement in erectile insufficiency. If a man complains of erectile insufficiency but exhibits normal NPT (indicating that he is physiologically capable of full erection), the potency disorder is diagnosed as psychogenic.

In assessing whether a man is physiologically capable of an erection sufficient for vaginal penetration, the real variable of interest is penile rigidity, measured as buckling pressure in mm Hg. The available techniques for measuring rigidity cannot be used for continuous recording, so penile circumference is monitored instead, using a mercury in rubber strain gauge. Penile circumference is monitored over a two-night period to determine the maximum erection (largest circumference change) exhibited by the patient. On the third night the patient is awakened when the circumference record shows him to be in a period of maximum erection, and the measurement of buckling pressure is made immediately. The device used by Karacan et al. for this purpose is essentially a large syringe with a rubber cap on one end and a sphygmomanometer on the other. This is pressed against the glans of the penis toward the penis base. The pressure applied at the time the penis first buckles is recorded. A penis insufficiently rigid for vaginal penetration buckles with pressures up to 60 mm Hg.; one that is definitely of sufficient rigidity buckles with pressures greater than 100 mm Hg. Other NPT variables used in differential diagnosis are the total minutes of full episodes (episodes in which full erection is attained) and the number of full episodes during a night's sleep. These data are compared to age norms for normal subjects.

So far, one exception has been identified to the general rule that normal NPT eliminates organic involvement in erectile insufficiency. Males whose organic deficit is a loss in penile sensation may experience erectile difficulties during coitus in consequence, and yet show normal NPT (Karacan et al., 1978). It should also be noted that a positive finding of organic involvement does not rule out contributory psychological factors. A man whose physical condition diminishes his erectile capability may develop coital anxiety in response, which then functions as a superadded inhibitor of erection. Moreover, there is nothing to prevent the coincidental presence of organogenic and psychogenic factors.

Karacan has been quoted as estimating that 10 percent of impotent males have chronically low penile blood pressure caused by a circulatory deficit ("Low Penile Blood Pressure," 1979). The measurement of penile blood pressure requires special techniques. The simplest available is the ultrasonic Doppler method (Abelson, 1975; Engel, Burnham, & Carter, 1978), which could easily be carried out by any member of a sex therapy team. Karacan et al. (1978) measured pressure at various locations on the penis. In normal males, these penile pressures are rather uniform and slightly higher than brachial pressure. When penile pressures are lower, vascular deficits are suggested.

If general medical and penile circulation findings are negative, but NPT is abnormal, the patient should be referred to a neurological laboratory for assessment of conductance of the pertinent peripheral nerves. When circulatory problems are suggested, the patient may be referred for arteriography. In cases of local gross circulatory disorder, an arterial bypass operation may be performed (Michal, Kramár, & Pospíchal, 1974; Sabri & Cotton, 1971), or a penile prosthesis implanted (this method may also be chosen when the erectile disorder is of other, e.g., neuropathic origin).

There are two types of prostheses in use, one inflatable (thus mimicking normal erection), and the other of fixed size and firmness. A comparison of the two types by Smith, Lange, and Fraley (1979) shows a high degree of satisfaction of presumably pre-operatively well-screened patients with both types.

Non-organic etiology. A variety of causes have been hypothesized to account for impaired or absent sexual response in individuals who do not appear to be suffering from any gross organic disease. Most of these hypothesized causes can be grouped under two main headings: current causes, which have an immediate effect upon sexual response, and remote causes, whose influence on sexual response is mediated by current causes. Current causes may be subdivided into three categories: inadequate physical stimulation, inadequate erotic stimulation, and interfering affect.

Inadequate *physical* stimulation has been ascertained as a cause of female orgastic dysfunction. This may result from poor sexual technique on the part of the male partner or from a failure of the female to communicate to her partner the modes of physical stimulation that she finds most arousing.

The affective constellation most often invoked to explain male sexual dysfunction in particular is performance anxiety, a fear of failure in sexual interaction. Hostility and resentment between mates is also believed to contribute to the arousal and orgastic disorders, as well as to vaginismus.

The most commonly diagnosed *remote* causes of sexual dysfunction are sexual trauma, restrictive upbringing, ignorance and misinformation, and neurotic conflict. Many writers believe that a traumatic coital failure produced by fatigue or alcohol intoxication, for example, may engender performance anxiety which then produces erectile insufficiency. Psychological or physical sexual trauma (e.g., rape or dyspareunia) may lead to coital anxiety and then to female unresponsiveness or vaginismus.

It is widely accepted that situational as well as endogenous depressions are associated with sexual dysfunction, though the interpretation of this relationship is uncertain. In manic-depressive illness, the decreased sexual appetite of the depressive phase or the hypersexuality of the manic phase may be mediated by the depressed or manic mood, or may result more directly from the underlying physiologic disorder.

The best established nonorganic causes of sexual dysfunction are anomalous erotic preference, marital discord, and inadequate physical stimulation (female). There is little empirical support from methodologically sound survey studies for most of the remaining causes asserted (see reviews by Cooper, 1969; Morokoff, 1978). One problem with existing survey data is interpretational; one cannot establish causal relationships on the sole basis of even impeccable correlational data. Anxiety, hostility, etc., may often be the consequences of a sexual dysfunction rather than its cause.

Objectives of psychological assessment. The first purpose of assessment is to establish whether psychological causes contribute to a sexual dysfunction, either primarily or secondarily to physical factors. The second purpose is to decide whether sex therapy or some other psychological intervention is the treatment of choice, or whether other psychotherapy or behavior therapy should precede, accompany, or follow it.

Hostility and resentment between marital partners indicates that marital counseling should be conducted prior to sex therapy or in place of it. Major psychiatric illness is considered by some, though not all, practitioners to automatically counterindicate specific treatment for sexual dysfunction. In any case, the clinician must be aware of the potential effects of antipsychotic medication upon sexual response, and it may be necessary to supply reassurance and counseling in this regard to the client. Contributory or coincidental neurotic disorder in a sexually dysfunctional individual must also be assessed. Lobitz and Lobitz (1978) report that if a sexual dysfunction is adjudged to be the result of other psychological problems, they will not accept a couple for treatment until the other problems have been treated. Their decision to provide sex therapy to clients with observed psychopathology rests on two criteria: (a) The problem should not interfere greatly with everyday functioning, and (b) the problem should not be likely to interfere with sex therapy.

Assessment techniques. Most or all information may be obtained by clinical interview. If a couple rather than an individual is to be treated, both partners are interviewed, separately as well as together.

An exact description and history of the problem should be obtained. A male who complains of "impotence," for example, may actually be suffering from premature ejaculation, erectile insufficiency, ejaculatory incompetence, or some combination of these disorders. The history should include whether the dysfunction is primary or secondary, of insidious or acute onset, and if acute, whether the patient can relate its onset to some particular circumstance. If the dysfunction is selective, in what situations does it appear?

The search for non-organic factors contributing to the dysfunction may include, for example, inquiry into whether the dysfunctional individual communicates her (or his) sexual likes and dislikes to her/his partner, whether she finds her partner physically attractive, or whether she feels insecure about her own physical appeal. More cognitive areas, such as the current level of sexual knowledge, are also probed. The developmental history typically includes questions about menarche, beginning of nocturnal emissions, masturbation, early sexual and traumatic sexual experiences, restrictiveness of upbringing, and so on. Suggested outlines for structured sexual history interviews may be found in Masters and Johnson (1970) and LoPiccolo and Heiman (1978).

Formal psychometric instruments have been employed for three purposes: (a) To discriminate psychogenic from organogenic sexual dysfunction, or to investigate psychological contribution when some organic involvement has already been established; (b) to collect specific factual information as a short-cut to interviewing; and (c) to provide a standardized outcome measure for studies of treatment effectiveness. An annotated list of such instruments has been provided by Schiavi, Derogatis, Kuriansky, O'Connor, and Sharpe (1979).

The Male Impotence Test (MIT) (El Senoussi, 1964) was claimed to differentiate psychogenic from organogenic erectile insufficiency. This claim did not survive cross-validation (Beutler, Karacan, Anch, Salis, Scott, & Williams, 1975). Beutler et al. reported that the combined application of two rules derived from MMPI profiles appropriately classified 90 percent of their sample, and Derogatis, Meyer and Dupkin (1976) reported that one subscale of the Derogatis Sexual Functioning Inventory correctly classified 89 percent of cases. Unfortunately, both studies used small sample sizes, and the need for cross-validation in different clinical settings is illustrated by the fact that the personality profiles of the psychogenic groups in the two studies seem more opposite than similar.

The previously mentioned Derogatis Sexual Functioning Inventory (DSFI) was designed as an "omnibus" test of sexual functioning, sampling the major components essential to adequate heterosexual behavior (Derogatis & Melisaratos, 1979). The DSFI consists of ten subtests (e.g., Information, Experience, Gender Role Definition, Body Image), with the weighted scores combined for a global measurement of sexual functioning. We shall consider three possible uses of the DSFI: (1) to make a diagnosis of sexually dysfunctional or not dysfunctional, (2) to save time and effort in clinical assessment, and (3) to provide quantitative information for decisions regarding treatment.

Derogatis and Melisaratos reported in one sample that the DSFI correctly classified 77 percent of males and 75 percent of females as normal or sexually dysfunctional. They argue that since chance alone would result in 50 percent correct assignments in this study, there was about a 25 percent increase in predictive efficiency. However, to evaluate the clinical usefulness of the DSFI for this purpose one would need to know what the base rates of sexual dysfunction and normalcy are among persons presenting at a clinic for treatment of a sexual dysfunction. Does the use of the DSFI result in significantly more correct classifications than through the simple assumption that every person who presents for treatment of a sexual dysfunction in fact suffers from one?

A second argument advanced for using the DSFI is that it provides sufficient amounts of information in a short period of time and reduces the need for long clinical reports. This argument is not a cogent one for all sex therapists; Masters and Johnson, for example, place great emphasis on their very elaborate and lengthy interview procedures.

The greatest use of the DSFI may be in quantifying certain information for clinical decision making. In evaluating a client's sexual knowledge by interview, for example, the clinician implicitly compares a client's knowledge with some subjective criterion carried in his head. The DSFI, on the other hand, provides a standardized score for this dimension.

The most difficult tasks in measuring therapeutic improvement of a sexual dysfunction are formulating a quantitative operational definition of *dysfunction* and obtaining dependable quantitative measurements of the targeted response. The most widely cited instrument designed for pre- and posttest measurement of sex therapeutic change, the Sexual

Interaction Inventory (LoPiccolo & Steger, 1974), sidesteps these problems and attempts rather to assess the sexual *satisfaction* of (heterosexual) couples. But even with this, there are problems. Test-retest reliability correlations (two-week interval) were not particularly high; LoPiccolo and Steger speculated that the first administration of the test might have prompted partners to discuss and improve their sexual interaction. At any rate, it is unlikely that any global measure of sexual satisfaction or personality adjustment will correlate highly enough with change in a specific sexual response to serve as an acceptable indirect measure.

Treatment. The techniques popularized and/or developed by Masters and Johnson (1970) and their followers are the present treatments of choice. Premature ejaculation is treated by a modification of Seman's (1956) technique. The female repeatedly stimulates the erect penis to a point premonitory to ejaculation, then squeezes the glans until erection subsides.

Treatment of erectile insufficiency includes the "teasing technique," exercises where periods of manipulative play and cessation of penile stimulation (allowing erection to subside) are alternated. The goal is to achieve a situation in which the "demand component" is held as low as possible, by the therapist "forbidding" intercourse in order to reduce the man's performance anxiety (the Frankl, 1958, technique).

In ejaculatory incompetence and orgastic dysfunction, the general strategy includes increasing the physical stimulation. In ejaculatory incompetence, the first goal is for the female to force the man's ejaculation manually. Similarly, inorgastic women may be told to first try achieving orgasm by any means (Kaplan, 1974b). If manual or oral stimulation of the vulva by the partner does not produce orgasm, automasturbation is then recommended by applying a vibrator if necessary or having the partner do so.

Vaginismus is treated by the insertion of a graduated series of Hegar dilators. This technique is assumed to extinguish the female's phobia of vaginal penetration.

The large number of cases treated by Masters and Johnson and their encouraging treatment outcome statistics prompted their widespread acceptance. Unfortunately, comparisons among Masters and Johnson's cases and those treated in offshoot programs, by classical behavior modification methods, and untreated sexually dysfunctional persons, are virtually impossible. Different practitioners or clinics use different criteria for accepting individuals into treatment, define normal and dysfunctional sexual response differently and employ variable or inadequate methods for evaluating results. Formal outcome studies generally have used small and sometimes hetergeneous treatment groups. Comparison to untreated controls is virtually nonexistent. Reviews of outcome studies on the effectiveness of sex therapy procedures have been provided by Segraves (1976), Kinder and Blakeney (1977), Reynolds (1977), Sotile and Kilmann (1977), Wright, Perrault, and Mathieu (1977), Hogan (1978), Kilmann and Auerbach (1979), and Munjack and Kanno (1979).

The most commonly employed behavioral technique not specifically designed for sex therapy is systematic desensitization. The clinical indication for this procedure in treating a sexual disorder is the presence of a clear phobia. For present purposes, "performance anxiety" should not be regarded as a phobia. This vaguely-defined phenomenon may consist more of misdirected attention (the *spectator role*), or of feelings of frustration and tension, than of feelings of *fear*.

CASE HISTORIES

Patient A was a 48-year-old man, never indicted for a sexual offence, who had been intimately touching his 10-year-old stepdaughter over a period of 3 years. The girl, who had always resisted this fondling to some extent, complained to her mother, who after consultation with a social worker friend went to the police. The patient obtained a good lawyer, and since he had a good work and family record, was merely interrogated and put on a list of child abusers rather than charged. The patient's wife remained close to him through all these repercussions. A photograph of the girl requested from A showed her to be a particularly attractive child.

The patient was alert, polite, and well groomed. There was no depression, undue elation, or thought disorder. He was college-educated and probably of above-average intelligence.

A was raised by his natural parents in a financially comfortable home. There was one older brother and one older sister. Apart from the usual childhood diseases, A was healthy throughout his life. Throughout school and college, A was an above-average student, active in sports, and liked by his peers.

The patient's first ejaculation was at approximately age 14. He reported that since then he had always been erotically attracted to physically mature females, never to children, and denied sexual involvement with any children other than this particular stepdaughter. A was married at age 20 to a woman of 19. This marriage, which produced four children, dissolved after 16 years. According to A, this was mainly because of his first wife's infidelity. Six years later, he met a 37-year-old widow with three adopted children; they were married after two years. According to A, their marital life was harmonious, with intercourse occurring approximately two to three times a week.

Sexual approaches to children occurring in the context of a social incest situation present a particularly difficult diagnostic problem. In contrast to the case of nonincestuous pedo- or hebephilic males who have frequently approached two or more children, males involved in incest commonly have approached only one (related) child. This difference in recidivism raises the possibility that in such cases some particular relationship has developed between a child and this adult whose partner preference is otherwise for physically mature individuals.

Patient A was given the "nonadmitter" mode of the phallometric test for heterosexual pedo- or hebephilia. In this test, the subject views six stimuli in each of five categories: brief movie clips of nude female adults, pubescents, and two age groups of prepubescent girls, as well as landscapes (neutral stimuli). The patient was prearoused with still photographs of nude adult females. The results showed heterosexual pedophilia.

Patient B was a 25-year-old man with a 10 year history of conviction and incarceration on charges of exposing, various property and narcotics offences, various alcohol-related offences such as being drunk and disorderly and impaired driving, and miscellaneous offenses such as parole violation, driving with a suspended licence, mischief, etc. At examination, B was fully oriented in all spheres with no gross thought disorder. His intelligence was average. Although he admitted to a serious adolescent suicidal attempt (by hanging), there was no current suicidal ideation.

The patient was the youngest of three sons raised by natural parents. The parents got along fairly well; B felt closer to his mother. There was no family history of mental illness or epilepsy. There was no favoritism in the family, and the parents were not excessively strict. They attended church regularly.

Birth and early development were normal. As a child, B was very shy, stuttered frequently, and bit his nails. He attended school from age 5 to 14, completing grade nine. He was then expelled on suspicion of using and selling drugs as well as stealing, and was generally unruly. From the age of 14 on, he lived without direction, periods of sporadic employment alternating with unemployment and incarceration. He remained shy and introverted, given to periods of depression.

The patient began drinking at the age of ten. Alcohol abuse became serious at about 19 years, with B taking about a dozen beers and 20 ounces of whiskey daily. He reported numerous blackouts. Drug abuse began at age 13, and included belladona, marijuana, hashish, LSD, and methamphetamine (injected). Drugs were a factor in ending his school career and in some of his criminal activities.

The patient's longest relationship with a girl lasted 6 months. Exposing (which was only to physically mature females) started at about the same time that his drinking problem became severe. There was also some voyeuristic activity and one episode of frotteurism.

The question in this case was whether B's exposing (and voyeuristic and frotteuristic activities) resulted from a distortion in phasing of courtship behavior, or whether his actions were a result of chronic drug and alcohol abuse upon an inadequate and impulsive individual with below-average heterosexual skills. B was administered the diagnostic test for courtship distortions. This test consists of a series of verbal descriptions of exhibitionistic, voyeuristic, and toucheuristic activities, plus descriptions of normal erotic tactile interaction and genital union as well as erotically neutral activities. The test results showed an erotic preference for exposing.

SUMMARY AND FUTURE CONSIDERATIONS

A brief introduction into the realm of anomalous erotic preferences shows that this field is still in its fetal stage, particularly in respect to the female. This also pertains to normal, i.e., usual, erotic preferences. A multifaceted procedure of assessment of erotic preferences has been outlined. The development of these procedures has been, and should be, based on continual empirical validation. Our main effort up to this point has been developing the phallometric method, which can serve with males as a reasonably reliable indicator of arousal value of potentially erotic stimulus patterns. Although this method is primarily a research tool, it can be used for diagnostic purposes also. However, in both phallometric research and phallometric diagnosis, ancillary methods capable of indicating the examined person's attitude toward the assessment of his erotic preferences should be employed. Such additional information makes possible a rough estimate of the likelihood that he will refrain from voluntary attempts to distort the outcome of the phallometric procedure.

In the realm of research, the use of such ancillary methods makes possible the selection of subjects who are least likely to attempt feigning results. (Nonvoluntary biases have to be taken into account by means of experimental design.) At present, three such verbal "Admitter" scales are in use in research on pedophilia.

In diagnostic work, a choice can be made between using a more general phallometric test mode which gives a broader range of information, but has virtually no safeguards against voluntary feigning, and special

"Nonadmitter" tests that make response feigning very difficult, but give more limited information on erotic preferences. Apart from making possible such a choice, the score on the ancillary verbal scales can provide a useful basis for realistic evaluation of diagnostic phallometric results.

It now appears that a sizeable proportion of erectile insufficiency cases previously believed to be psychogenic are really caused by some organic deficit. The same may be true for at least some of the remaining arousal and orgastic (or ejaculatory) disorders.

Because an individual's sexual response may be simultaneously impaired by psychological and organic factors, one cannot rule out psychological contribution when organic causes have been positively identified, and vice versa. Thus, one needs to be able to separately assess the presence versus absence of organic and psychological contributing factors. So far, a comprehensive procedure for determining the presence or absence of organic involvement has been worked out for only one of the sexual response disorders. No comparably valid procedure for determining the presence or absence of psychological involvement has been worked out for any of these disorders.

The recent development of more effective therapeutic techniques than previously available for treating sexual dysfunctions should not obscure the fact that there is virtually no hard evidence on the psychological causes of sexual dysfunction and that there are considerable gaps in our physiological knowledge of the reproductive system (including relevant brain structures). We do not yet even know where to draw the line between normal and disordered sexual response, particularly with regard to ejaculatory control and orgastic responsiveness.

It is likely that serious research interest in etiology will be rekindled when a sufficient amount of data on sex therapeutic failures has been amassed to make possible the observation of regularities among them. It is also possible that identifying clusters of treatment failures will stimulate a further search for physiologic causes of the common disorder. This endeavor will require a shift in research emphasis from the sexual satisfaction of couples (i.e., sexual adequacy or inadequacy) to detailed and preferably quantitative descriptions of the disordered sexual responses of individuals.

REFERENCES

Abarbanel, A. R. Diagnosis and treatment of coital discomfort. In J. LoPiccolo & L. LoPiccolo (Eds.), *Handbook of sex therapy.* New York: Plenum Press, 1978.

Abel, G. G., Blanchard, E. B., Barlow, D. H., & Mavissakalian, M. Identifying specific erotic cues in sexual deviations by audiotaped descriptions. *Journal of Applied Behavior Analysis,* 1975, *8,* 247–260.

Abelson, D. Diagnostic value of the penile pulse and blood pressure: A Doppler study of impotence in diabetics. *Journal of Urology*, 1975, *113*, 636–639.

Baldwin, J. M. Appetite. In *Dictionary of philosophy and psychology*, 1901. According to W. Craig, Appetites and aversions as constituents of instincts. *Biological Bulletin*, 1918, *34*, 91–107.

Bem. S. L. The measurement of psychological androgyny. *Journal of Consulting and Clinical Psychology*, 1974, *42*, 155–162.

Beutler, L. E., Karacan, I., Anch, A. M., Salis, P. J., Scott, F. B., & Williams, R. L. MMPI and MIT discriminators of biogenic and psychogenic impotence. *Journal of Consulting and Clinical Psychology*, 1975, *43*, 899–903.

Cooper, A. J. Factors in male sexual inadequacy: A review. *Journal of Nervous and Mental Disease*, 1969, *149*, 337–349.

Derogatis, L. R., & Melisaratos, N. The DSFI: A multidimensional measure of sexual functioning. *Journal of Sex & Marital Therapy*, 1979, *5*, 244–281.

Derogatis, L. R., Meyer, J. K., & Dupkin, C. N. Discrimination of organic versus psychogenic impotence with the DSFI. *Journal of Sex & Marital Therapy*, 1976, *2*, 229–240.

El Senoussi. *The Male Impotence Test.* Los Angeles: Western Psychological Services, 1964.

Engel, G., Burnham, S. J., & Carter, M. F. Penile blood pressure in the evaluation of erectile impotence. *Fertility and Sterility*, 1978, *30*, 687–690.

Fisher, C., Gross, J., & Zuch, J. Cycle of penile erection synchronous with dreaming (REM) sleep. *Archives of General Psychiatry*, 1965, *12*, 29–45.

Fisher, C., Schiavi, R., Lear, H., Edwards, A., Davis, D. M., & Witkin, A. P. The assessment of nocturnal REM erection in the differential diagnosis of sexual impotence. *Journal of Sex and Marital Therapy*, 1975, *1*, 277–289.

Flanagan, B. Metal gauge vs. mercury-filled gauge. *TSA News*, June 1978, *2*, 4.

Frankl, V. E. Psychogene Potenzstörungen. *Wiener Medizinische Wochenschrift*, 1958, *108*, 477–481.

Freund, K. Diagnostika homosexuality u mužů (Diagnosing homosexuality in men). *Československá Psychiatrie*, 1957, *53*, 382–393.

Freund, K. Laboratory differential diagnosis of homo- and heterosexuality—an experiment with faking. *Review of Czechoslovac Medicine*, 1961, *7*, 20–31.

Freund, K. A laboratory method for diagnosing predominance of homo- or hetero-erotic interest in the male. *Behaviour Research and Therapy*, 1963, *1*, 85–93.

Freund K. Jednoduchý přistroj k meřeni volumových změn mužského genitálu (A simple de vice for measuring the volume changes of the male genital). *Československá Psychiatrie*, 1965, *61*, 164-168. (a)

Freund, K. *Die Homosexualitat beim Mann (Homosexuality in man)*. Leipzig: S. Hirzel Verlag, 1965. (b)

Freund, K. Male homosexuality: An analysis of the pattern. In J. A. Loraine (Ed.), *Understanding homosexuality: Its biological and psychological bases.* Lancaster, Eng.: Medical and Technical Publishing Co., Ltd., 1974.

Freund, K. Diagnosis and treatment of forensically significant anomalous erotic preferences. *Canadian Journal of Criminology & Corrections*, 1976, *18*, 181–189.

Freund, K. Psychophysiological assessment of change in erotic preferences. *Behaviour Research and Therapy*, 1977, *15*, 197–301.

Freund, K. Assessment of pedophilia. In M. Cook & K. Howells (Eds.), *Adult sexual interest in children.* London: Academic Press, 1981.

Freund, K. Therapeutic sex drive reduction. Acta Psychiatrica Scandinavica Supplementum, *287*, 1980, *62*.

Feund, K., Chan, S., & Coulthard, R. Phallometric diagnosis with ''nonadmitters.'' *Behaviour Research and Therapy*, 1979, *17*, 451–457.

Freund, K., & Kolařský, A. Grundzüge eines einfachen Bezugsystems fur die Analyse sexueller Deviationen (Basic features of a reference system for considering anomalous erotic preferences). *Psychiatrie, Neurologie, und medizinische Psychologie,* 1965, *17,* 221–225.

Freund, K., & Langevin, R. Bisexuality in homosexual pedophilia. *Archives of Sexual Behavior,* 1976, *5,* 415–423.

Freund, K., Langevin, R., & Barlow, D. Comparison of two penile measures of erotic arousal. *Behaviour Research and Therapy,* 1974, *12,* 355–359.

Freund, K., Langevin, R., Chamberlayne, R., Deosaran, A., & Zajac, Y. The phobic theory of male homosexuality. *Archives of General Psychiatry,* 1974, *31,* 495–499.

Freund, K., Langevin, R., Satterberg, J., & Steiner, B. Extension of the gender identity scale for males. *Archives of Sexual Behavior,* 1977, *6,* 507–519.

Freund, K., Sedláĉek, F., & Knob, K. A simple transducer for mechanical plethysmography of the male genital. *Journal of the Experimental Analysis of Behavior,* 1965, *8,* 169–170.

Freund, K., & Steiner, B. W. Disorders of sexual behavior. In S. Greben, R. Pos, V. Rakoff, A. Bonkalo, F. Lowy, & G. Voineskos (Eds.), *A method of psychiatry.* Toronto: Macmillan of Canada, 1980.

Freund, K., Steiner, B. W., & Chan, S. Two types of cross gender identity. *Archives of Sexual Behavior,* in press.

Green, R. *Sexual identity conflict in children and adults.* New York: Basic Books, 1974.

Harlow, H. F. Sexual behavior in the Rhesus monkey. In F. A. Beach (Ed.), *Sex and behavior.* New York: Wiley, 1955.

Hess, E. H., & Polt, J. M. Pupil size as related to interest value of visual stimuli. *Science,* 1960, *132,* 349–350.

Hess, E. H., Seltzer, A. L., & Shlien, J. M. Pupil response of hetero- and homosexual males to pictures of men and women: A pilot study. *Journal of Abnormal Psychology,* 1965, *70,* 165–168.

Hogan, D. R. The effectiveness of sex therapy: A review of the literature. In J. LoPiccolo & L. LoPiccolo (Eds.), *Handbook of sex therapy.* New York: Plenum Press, 1978.

Hoon, P. W. The assessment of sexual arousal in women. In M. Hersen, R. M. Eisler, & P. M. Miller (Eds.), *Progress in behavior modification.* Vol. 7, New York: Academic Press, 1978.

Hynie, J. Nová objektivní metoda vyšetřování mužske sexuální potence (A new objective method of examining male sexual potency). *Časopis Lékařů Českých,* 1934, *73,* 34–39, 70–73, 96–98, 127–131, 153–155, 185–188.

Kaplan, H. S. A new classification of the female sexual dysfunctions. International Congress of Medical Sexology, Paris, 1974. (a)

Kaplan, H. S. *The new sex therapy: Active treatment of sexual dysfunctions.* New York: Bruner/Mazel, 1974. (b)

Karacan, I., Salis, P. J., & Williams, R. L. The role of the sleep laboratory in diagnosis and treatment of impotence. In R. L. Williams & I. Karacan (Eds.), *Sleep disorders: Diagnosis and treatment.* New York: Wiley, 1978.

Karacan, I., Scott, F. B., Salis, P. J., Attia, S. L., Ware, J. C., Altinel, A., & Williams, R. L. Nocturnal erections, differential diagnosis of impotence, and diabetes. *Biological Psychiatry,* 1977, *12,* 373–380.

Kilmann, P. R., & Auerbach, R. Treatments of premature ejaculation and psychogenic impotence: A critical review of the literature. *Archives of Sexual Behavior,* 1979, *8,* 81–100.

Kinder, B. N., & Blakeney, P. Treatment of sexual dysfunction: A review of outcome studies. *Journal of Clinical Psychology,* 1977, *33,* 523–530.

Kinsey, A. C., Pomeroy, W. B., & Martin, C. E. *Sexual behavior in the human male.* Philadelphia: W. B. Saunders Co., 1948.

Kinsey, A. C., Pomeroy, W. B., Martin, C. E., & Gebhard, P. H. *Sexual behavior in the human female.* Philadelphia: W. B. Saunders Co., 1953.

Krafft-Ebing, R. *Psychopathia sexualis: A medico-forensic study.* New York: Pioneer Publications, Inc., 1950 (orig. 1886).

Lasègue, C. Les Exhibitionistes. *L'Union Medicale,* May 1887, *23,* 709.

Laws, D. R. A comparison of the measurement characteristics of two circumferential penile transducers. *Archives of Sexual Behavior,* 1977, *6,* 45–51.

Lobitz, W. C., & Lobitz, G. K. Clinical assessment in the treatment of sexual dysfunctions. In J. LoPiccolo & L. LoPiccolo (Eds.), *Handbook of sex therapy.* New York: Plenum Press, 1978.

LoPiccolo, L., & Heiman, J. R. Sexual assessment and history interview. In J. LoPiccolo & L. LoPiccolo (Eds.), *Handbook of sex therapy.* New York: Plenum Press, 1978.

LoPiccolo, J., & Steger, J. C. The Sexual Interaction Inventory: A new instrument for assessment of sexual dysfunction. *Archives of Sexual Behavior,* 1974, *3,* 585–595.

Low penile blood pressure found in impotent men. *Medical Post* (Toronto: Maclean-Hunter), May 22, 1979, 46.

Masters, W. H., & Johnson, V. E. *Human sexual inadequacy.* Boston: Little, Brown, and Co., 1970.

McConaghy, N. Penile volume change to moving pictures of male and female nudes in heterosexual and homosexual males. *Behaviour Research and Therapy,* 1967, *5,* 43–48.

McConaghy, N. Measurements of change in penile dimensions. *Archives of Sexual Behavior,* 1974, *3,* 381–388.

Michal, V., Kramár, R., & Pospíchal, J. Femoro-pudendal bypass, internal iliac thrombo-endarterectomy and direct arterial anastomosis to the cavernous body in the treatment of erectile impotence. *Bulletin de la Societe Internationale de Chirurgie,* *33,* 343–350.

Mohr, J. W., Turner, R. E., & Jerry, M. B. *Pedophilia and exhibitionism.* Toronto: University of Toronto Press, 1964.

Morokoff, P. Determinants of female orgasm. In J. LoPiccolo & L. LoPiccolo (Eds.), *Handbook of sex therapy.* New York: Plenum Press, 1978.

Munjack, D. J., & Kanno, P. H. Retarded ejaculation: A review. *Archives of Sexual Behavior,* 1979, *8,* 139–150.

Reynolds, B. S. Psychological treatment models and outcome results for erectile dysfunction: A critical review. *Psychological Bulletin,* 1977, *84,* 1218–1238.

Rosen, R. C., & Keefe, F. J. The measurement of human penile tumescence. *Psychophysiology,* 1978, *15,* 366–376.

Sabri, S., & Cotton, L. T. Sexual function following aortoiliac reconstruction. *Lancet,* 1971, *2,* 1218–1219.

Schiavi, R. C., Derogatis, L. R., Kuriansky, J., O'Connor, D., & Sharpe, L. The assessment of sexual function and marital interaction. *Journal of Sex and Marital Therapy,* 1979, *5,* 169–224.

Schumacher, S., & Lloyd, C. W. Assessment of sexual dysfunction. In M. Hersen & A. S. Bellack (Eds.), *Behavioral assessment: A practical handbook.* New York: Pergamon Press, 1976.

Schutz, F. Der Einfluss von Testosteron auf die Partnerwahl bei gepragt aufgezogenen Stockentenweibchen: Nachweis latenter Sexualpragung (Latent sexual imprinting in female mallards made evident by testosterone). *Verhandlungen der Deutschen Zoologischen Gesellschaft,* 1975, *67,* 339–344.

Segraves, R. T. Primary orgasmic dysfunction: Essential treatment components. *Journal of Sex and Marital Therapy*, 1976, *2*, 115–123.

Semans, J. H. Premature ejaculation: A new approach. *Southern Medical Journal*, 1956, *49*, 353–357.

Sintchak, G., & Geer, J. H. A vaginal plethysmograph system. *Psychophysiology*, 1975, *12*, 113–115.

Smith, A. D., Lange, P. H., & Fraley, E. E. A comparison of the Small-Carrion and Scott-Bradly penile prostheses. *Journal of Urology*, 1979, *121*, 609–611.

Sotile, W. M., & Kilmann, P. R. Treatments of psychogenic female sexual dysfunctions. *Psychological Bulletin*, 1977, *84*, 619–633.

Terman, L. M., & Miles, C. *Sex and personality: Studies in masculinity and femininity*. New York: McGraw-Hill, 1936.

Weitz, W., & Vollers, W. Über rhythmische Kontraktionen der glatten Muskulatur an verschiedenen Organen (On the rhythmic contraction of the smooth musculature of various organs) *Zeitschrift für die gesamte experimentelle Medizin*, 1926, *52*, 723–726.

Whitney, R. J. The measurement of changes in human limb-volume by means of a mercury-in-rubber strain gauge. *Journal of Physiology*, 1949, *109*, 5–6.

Wright, J., Perreault, R., & Mathieu, M. The treatment of sexual dysfunction. *Archives of General Psychiatry*, 1977, *34*, 881–890.

Zuckerman, M. Physiological measures of sexual arousal in the human. *Psychological Bulletin*, 1971, 297–329.

Chapter 13
Assessment of Appetitive Disorders

David W. Foy, Robert G. Rychtarik, and Donald M. Prue

INTRODUCTION

Substance abuse constitutes one of the most serious socio-medical problems among adolescents and adults in society today. Alcohol abuse takes its annual toll in highway accident fatalities and serious injuries. Cigarette smoking produces increased health risks for smokers and non-smokers alike. Inappropriate caloric and nutritional management contributes to both cosmetic and health difficulties. And normalized abuse of prescription, patent and, illicit drugs presents vocational and social disruption. Apart from the millions spent annually by consumers, the financial and personal costs paid by society to deal with the negative health and social consequences of substance abuse are staggering.

While the magnitude of appetitive problems does not yet appear to be decreasing, public awareness of the potential negative effects of substance abuse is increasing. Concurrently, the need for improving present capabilities for clinical assessment and treatment of appetitive disorders is highlighted. State and federal funding agencies provide priority support for basic and applied research in substance abuse, making it an attractive area for behavioral scientists to apply their clinical and research talents.

Along with increased public awareness of substance abuse health risks, the market for methods of curbing out-of-control appetites has grown dramatically. Self-help ''how to'' books, readily available at any bookstore, tell the consumer how to control particular appetitive problems, such as eating, drinking or smoking. In most communities, an individual with a substance abuse problem can choose a treatment program from among several offered by lay or professional helpers. Regrettably, increased public awareness and demand for clinical services has not been paralleled by improved efficacy of assessment and treatment. In fact, it will become apparent from the other sections of this chapter that improvements in substance abuse treatment efficacy cannot be made until appropriate empirical assessment methods are developed.

The purpose of this chapter is to present a current state of the art with respect to assessment of appetitive disorders. Because our experiences and expertise are in alcohol and smoking, we will focus primarily on empirical assessment related to these substances. Separate sections on smoking and alcohol are designed to provide critical examinations of: (a) self-reported rate measures; (b) objective rate and topography assessment methods; and (c) recent innovations in physiological and biochemical indices of smoking, alcohol use, and related health risk. The practical goal is to provide guidelines for the empirical clinician or substance abuse researcher in designing assessment strategies and selecting appropriate dependent measures. A case study demonstrating multimodal assessment with cigarette smoking treatment is included, and critical issues are identified for future consideration.

Issues and Questions

The question confronting the empirical clinician or substance abuse researcher is: Which set of dependent measures can I select which will: (a) be acceptable to the client or subject, (b) accurately detect changes in substance use, (c) assess degree of health risk, (d) be within budget and equipment limits of clinic or laboratory, and (e) be comparable to measures used in previous and future studies with this substance? On each dimension there are several options available, each with its own advantages and limitations. In neither alcohol nor smoking is there a single measure available which adequately covers all dimensions. Accordingly, *multimodal* assessment techniques must be selected.

Self-report measures of rate of consumption remain essential because existing literature in alcohol and smoking is based on them. Since problems with respect to validity, reliability, compliance, and reactivity plague the use of self-report measures, their selection is a critical issue in assessment of appetitive disorders. Also, the degree to which consumption impairs an individual's current physical functioning or places him/her at risk for future health problems is an emerging issue in substance abuse. Thus, physiological or biochemical measures of liver, lung, and cardiovascular functions as related to substance abuse are receiving increased attention. Unfortunately, laboratory equipment and supplies necessary for physiological measures are costly, and some methods require technological sophistication which places them beyond certain clinical applications. Accordingly, compromises must be reached considering the advantages and limitations of the various assessment modalities.

The above issues, practical problems associated with them, and suggestions for solving these problems are presented for alcohol and smoking in the sections which follow.

ALCOHOL ASSESSMENT

It is becoming increasingly apparent that assessment of alcohol abuse requires attention to variables other than simply rate or amount of alcohol consumption. Evidence indicates that a change in drinking status is not necessarily correlated with improvements in other areas of life functioning (e.g., Emrick, 1974). Appropriate clinical assessment for the problem of alcohol abuse therefore requires behavioral assessment with respect to social skills, marital adjustment, vocational stability, and intrapersonal adjustment, in addition to alcohol consumption. Assessment of many of these areas are presented elsewhere in the present volume, and therefore will not be covered here. The present discussion will be limited to assessment of the actual drinking response or physiological indicants of it. In this respect, the following assessment modalities will be presented: (a) self-report, (b) analogue laboratory procedures, (c) topographical drinking measures, and (d) biochemical drinking indices.

Self-Report Measures of Drinking

Self-reported drinking is clearly the most frequently used outcome measure in research and the clinical evaluation of client status during aftercare, though it has long been assumed that client reports of drinking are of questionable validity. Recent evidence would suggest, however, that the actual validity of reported drinking may be dependent on the type of drinking information obtained. For example, alcoholics' self-reports of life history and drinking history have generally been found to be quite reliable and valid (Sobell & Sobell, 1978). Similarly, when clients have not been drinking, their reports are accurate (Polich, Armor, & Braiker, 1980; Sobell, Sobell, & VanderSpek, 1979). Self-reports of very recent drinking (i.e., in the last 24 hours), however, have been found to provide less than accurate information on client intoxication (Sobell et al., 1979). Studies find that approximately 44 percent of clients reporting recent drinking underestimate their alcohol intake when compared to breathalyzer measures (Polich et al., 1980; Sobell et al., 1979). It appears that only approximately half of this 44 percent also under report their typical drinking pattern for the past month. In other words, 25 percent of those reporting recent drinking under report *both* recent and typical (past month) drinking behavior (Polich et al., 1980).

To overcome the potential problems of sole reliance on self-reports, relatives and/or acquaintances who have some knowledge of the clients' drinking behavior have been used as collaterals to corroborate client-reported drinking. While the agreement between client self-report and collateral information has been described as high, few actual quantitative comparisons exist. Miller, Crawford, and Taylor (1979) reported overall significant correlations of client self-report with collateral reports of alcohol consumption of .48, .66, and .79 over the course of study from intake, treatment and aftercare respectively. Unfortunately, the validity of the actual collateral reports has not been addressed. A recent study found high rates of uncertainty among collaterals regarding clients' drinking and symptoms of drinking. Furthermore, as much, or more, under reporting was found for collaterals as for clients' self-reports (Polich et al., 1980). Overall, findings suggest that when measures are clearly observable (i.e., complete abstention, days in jail, etc.), collateral reports appear quite accurate. Less noticeable measures (i.e., alcohol consumption, impairment), however, appear less easily validated by collaterals due to their uncertainty and underreporting.

As a result of potential problems with self-report drinking measures and the difficulty of validating them, attention has turned toward development of more objective, observable measures of drinking behavior.

Analogue Assessment Procedures

The earliest behavioral methods of assessing alcohol consumption were operant in nature. The subject was required to make a response (e.g., lever pressing) according to a certain reinforcement schedule in order to obtain fixed amounts of alcoholic beverage. The approach is considered somewhat analogous to the natural setting where a person must work to pay for drinks. Thus, the operant assessment method provides a means of assessing motivation to drink by quantifying how much and how frequently the subject will "work" for alcohol. Operant techniques such as these have been successfully employed to obtain a descriptive analysis of alcoholic drinking (Mello & Mendelson, 1971), to distinguish drinking behavior of alcoholics from social drinkers (Nathan &

O'Brien, 1971), and to evaluate the influence of interpersonal stress on alcohol consumption (Miller, Hersen, Eisler, & Hilsman, 1974).

Despite the apparent internal validity of such operant approaches, their obtrusiveness and susceptibility to experimental demand make external validity questionable. In response to these validity problems, Marlatt, Demming and Reid (1973), and Miller and Hersen (1972a) independently developed an alcohol assessment technique presented under the guise of a taste-rating task. In the taste-rating task the subject is placed at a table and presented with a number of glasses containing either alcoholic or nonalcoholic beverages. Unaware that consumption is being monitored, the subject is asked to rate each beverage along a variety of dimensions (e.g., strong-weak). The subject is then allowed to drink as much or as little as needed while sip rate and amount of alcohol consumption are monitored. This unobtrusive taste-test measure has successfully been employed in research on the influence of stress (Higgins & Marlatt, 1973), sexual arousal (Gabel, Noel, Keane, & Lisman, 1979), modeling (Caudill & Marlatt, 1975; Hendricks, Sobell, & Cooper, 1978), and expectancy (Marlatt et al., 1973) on alcohol consumption.

Though there are many advantages to analogue drink assessment procedures (i.e., good reliability, experimental control, unobtrusiveness), other problems remain. Specifically, the extent that drinking in such disguised situations under laboratory conditions is representative of drinking in the natural environment remains to be investigated. Moreover, while such methods have greatly contributed to our knowledge of the determinants of alcohol consumption in the laboratory, they appear to be of little practical utility for developing treatment planning in the clinical setting. One retrospective study suggests that alcoholics' consumption of alcohol during either operant tasks or taste-tests may be predictive of drinking disposition upon completion of treatment (Miller, Hersen, Eisler, & Elkin, 1974), and Miller and Hersen (1972b) reported measures on the taste-test to be sensitive to treatment changes during and following aversive conditioning treatment. However, until further research on these measures as predictors or indicators of treatment outcome is conducted, their clinical utility is undetermined and their use will likely remain confined to the laboratory setting.

Drink Topography Assessment

The notion that, "in the behavioral approach the behaviors evaluated during the course of assessment are the very ones subjected to modification procedures in treatment [Hersen, 1976, p. 10]'' becomes most apparent in the assessment of alcoholic drinking topography. In this procedure, the client is placed in either a simulated bar setting (Sobell & Sobell, 1973) or a casual living room environment (Miller, Becker, Foy, & Wooten, 1976) and provided with his/her favorite alcoholic beverage. Instructions are given to drink as usual. The client's drinking is then videotaped from an adjoining room. Upon completion of the session, the amount of alcohol consumed is determined and videotapes subsequently rated to obtain measures of number of sips, length of intersip interval, and mix ratio.

Assessment of drink topography grew out of attempts by investigators to observe drinking behavior in settings more closely resembling those in the natural environment. Sobell, Schaefer, and Mills (1972) systematically observed the drinking behavior of 26 male alcoholics and 23 male normal drinkers in a simulated cocktail bar. Results indicated that alcoholics consumed significantly more, preferred straight drinks, when compared with normal drinkers, and drank faster, and consumed larger amounts per sip. These results have generally been replicated elsewhere (Schaefer, Sobell, & Mills, 1971; Williams & Brown, 1974). Such quantitative differences in drinking behaviors between alcoholics and normal drinkers suggested an operational definition of alcohol abuse. Furthermore, it implied that alcoholics might actually be capable of learning to develop the drinking style (topography) of normal drinkers. In this regard, Miller et al. (1976) assessed and trained specific drinking skills (i.e., sip rate, etc.) in an alcoholic by employing a simulated drink setting. Other outcome research has shown that training of drinking skills, in addition to comprehensive broad-spectrum treatment, may be highly effective with respect to treatment outcome (e.g., Sobell & Sobell, 1973).

Clearly, assessment of drinking topography in simulated settings offers advantages over other analogue procedures reviewed above. First, the assessment setting simulates more closely actual natural drinking environments. Second, results of the drinking assessment procedure provide direct information for treatment intervention with nonabstinent oriented clients. However, it again remains unclear how representative the drinking measures obtained in simulated settings are of those in the natural environment. Some support for the validity of simulated drinking environments is found in evidence that natural drinking rates (i.e., number of drinks per hour) observed in the general population are quite similar to those obtained for nonalcoholics in the simulated setting (Reid, 1978). Moreover, modeling influences obtained in simulated settings (Garlington & Dericco, 1977) have recently received some external validation in a pilot investigation of modeling and naturalistic drinking behavior in the general population (Reid, 1978). On the other hand, a recent comparison of *ad lib* drinking topography among college males in a regular laboratory with drinking in the barroom, revealed that barroom drinking was characterized by significantly greater alcohol intake and faster rates of consumption (Strickler, Dobbs, & Maxwell, 1979). As these findings indicate, drinking behavior appears to be somewhat more complex than initially construed. Research suggests that drinking in nonalcoholics may be influenced by such factors as sex (Hunter, Hannon, & Marchin, 1979; Rosenbluth, Nathan, & Lawson), socioeconomic status (Hunter, Hannon, & Marchi, 1979), and the social context of drinking (Cutter & Storm, 1975; Rosenbluth et al., 1978; Sommer, 1965). With respect to this latter point, it is interesting to note that naturalistic studies have found that nonalcoholics consume more when drinking in a social versus solitary context. Solitary versus group social environment, however, does not appear to affect the drinking of alcoholics in the simulated lab (Foy & Simon, 1978). Unfortunately, investigations of drink topography have typically employed nonalcoholic populations; thus, additional information is required on the natural and laboratory drinking of both normal and alcoholic drinkers.

Two additional problems remain with drink topography assessment procedures. First, the methods employed to date typically have been too long (3–4 hours), require considerable staff time, and present notable patient risk (i.e., consumption of large amounts of alcohol) to be of practical utility in the clinical setting. In response to this problem, Foy, Rychtarik, Nunn, and Webster (1980) have presented normative information on the drinking styles of alcoholics in a brief 30-minute drinking assessment paradigm. This shortened procedure appears sensitive to abusive drinking patterns in alcoholics, and yet circumvents practical problems associated with lengthier methods. Finally, if the external validity of simulated drinking environments is firmly documented, the issue of whether the assessment information obtained is necessary or relevant for treatment requires attention. Though investigation has shown the efficacy of drink training programs (e.g., Sobell & Sobell, 1973), the active components of these multicomponent treatment packages still have to be identified.

Biochemical Measures

Assessment procedures reviewed thus far have relied primarily on observation of actual drinking in analogue or simulated environments. Though evidence suggests that measures such as these may be used for purposes of evaluating treatment outcome, their use appears to be only appropriate for those clients choosing a goal of controlled/responsible drinking. Requiring individuals who have a goal of total abstinence to engage in drinking for the purpose of obtaining outcome measures poses potential ethical and clinical problems. When offered the choice of abstinence or controlled drinking goals, the majority of alcoholics still continue to choose abstinence (Foy, Rychtarik, O'Brien, & Nunn, 1979; Kilpatrick, Roitzsch, Best, McAlbany, Sturgis, & Miller, 1978; Pachman, Foy, & VanErd, 1978). Observational drinking outcome measures, therefore, appear to be of practical utility with only a relatively small proportion (less than 20%) of the alcoholic population. Attention will now be given to biochemical indices of drinking, which may be more widely applicable with respect to treatment goal and outcome.

Blood alcohol level. In the breath analysis procedure, a small sample of alveolar air is collected and analyzed for alcohol content via various chemical or electrochemical methods (Cravey & Jain, 1974; Jain & Cravey, 1974). The procedure provides a direct indication of blood alcohol level (BAL) and is typically presented as a percentage of ethyl alcohol to blood volume (e.g., .10 percent BAL = 100 mg/100 ml). Recently, breath analysis instruments have become considerably more sophisticated. Instruments are now available ranging from inexpensive portable (though less accurate) models, to larger machines that are accurate to ± .01 percent. Overall, the breathalyzer provides a highly reliable, valid measure of recent drinking behavior.

Blood alcohol levels obtained via breath analysis have been employed as therapeutic outcome measures (Sobell & Sobell, 1973), as criteria for determining consequences for drinking (Miller, Hersen, Eisler, & Watts, 1974), and as a means of training alcoholics to discriminate varying blood alcohol levels (Lovibond & Caddy, 1970). Despite advantages of breath analysis, however, certain problems exist. Since alcohol is metabolized by the body at the rate of approximately one ounce per hour, breath analysis is sensitive to detecting consumption of large amounts of alcohol for only a period of 24 hours. Abusive drinking occurring 3–4 days prior to breath analysis would not be identified. A client may therefore pace his/her drinking so that a breath test administered at a regularly scheduled appointment would not register drinking. Outcome studies have employed unannounced probe breath tests or tests with little advance warning to overcome this reactive problem (Sobell & Sobell, 1973; Miller et al., 1974). But random breathalyzer probes may also discourage drinking, so results obtained in outcome research may actually be attributable to the assessment procedure itself, as opposed to the treatment program being evaluated. Random probes also require considerable staff time and therefore may not be practical in the typical treatment program. Pacing of drinking episodes so as to avoid detection by regularly scheduled breath tests remains an empirical question. Evidence suggests, at least, that regularly scheduled breathalyzer tests during aftercare do not appear to negatively influence aftercare attendance rates in chronic alcoholics (Nunn, Foy, & Rychtarik, 1980).

Gamma-glutamyl transpeptidase. The limitation of breath analysis for identifying abusive drinking only within 24 hours of occurrence has led investigators to consider other biochemical indicants of abusive drinking. Within the past several years attention has been given to the possible use of blood serum enzymes to supplement self-reports and BAL indications of alcohol consumption. Particular attention has been paid to gamma-glutamyl transpeptidase (GGT), a liver enzyme normally found at low levels in the blood stream. Investigations suggest that elevated levels of GGT may be indicative of abusive drinking and require several weeks to return to normal (Lamy, Baglin, Weill, & Aron, 1975), thus providing an index of drinking in the recent past. Reports in the literature of GGT's accuracy in identifying abusive drinkers have been as high as 81 percent (Boone, Tietz, & Weinstock, 1977). Unfortunately, GGT levels also appear to be elevated by various physical conditions (e.g., liver disease, pancreatitis) and other drug use (e.g., barbiturates, opiates, Dilantin). In fact, recent research with both non-alcoholics (Robinson, Monk, & Bailey, 1979) and abusive drinkers (Garvin, Foy, & Alford, 1980) indicates that after subject samples are screened for concurrent illness and drug usage, GGT elevation correctly identifies only 55 percent of subjects reporting recent alcohol abuse. This finding would bring into serious question the use of GGT as a singular indicator of alcohol abuse. GGT and other potential biochemical markers of alcohol abuse require further investigation. The identification of a means for detecting abusive drinking beyond the 24-hour limit of breath analysis appears to be a priority area for future study. Such measures would hopefully decrease the likelihood that patients could pace drinking to avoid detection. Measures such as GGT, however, have the disadvantage of: (a) requiring sophisticated laboratory techniques for analysis, and (b) having considerable lag time between sample collection and final results.

Carbon disulfide. Up to this point, discussion has centered primarily on biochemical indicants of drinking behavior. Another approach that appears promising is the assessment of antabuse intake, which would presumably be related to abstinence. Antabuse is a drug used in conjunction with alcohol treatment programs that results in flushing, headache, nausea, etc., when followed by the consumption of alcohol. Antabuse consumption may, therefore, serve as a deterrent to drinking.

Assessment of antabuse compliance, however, appears to be a major problem, and an area of promising research and clinical utility. A recent report indicated that self-report and clinical judgments of antabuse compliance were often inaccurate (Paulson, Krause, & Iber, 1977). To overcome this compliance problem, various strategies have employed supervised administration of antabuse on an outpatient basis (Bigelow, Strickler, Liebson, & Griffiths, 1976). Such methods, however, require considerable staff time and high client response cost. Monitoring of the number of antabuse prescriptions filled by the client also has been employed (Keane, Foy, Nunn, & Rychtarik, 1980). This method avoids problems associated with daily monitoring of antabuse intake, yet provides only an indirect measure of compliance.

Another approach to assessing compliance has been to detect antabuse or its metabolites in blood, urine, and/or breath samples. To date, blood and urine sample tests have not been highly successful in providing a practical, reliable measure. However, a breath test for carbon disulfide (CS_2), a metabolite of antabuse, shows considerably more promise. In this procedure, the subject is required to exhale into containers holding various prepared chemical solutions. If CS_2 is present a chemical reaction ensues, yielding an immediate yellow color in the liquid. For more accurate continuous measures, the solution can then be analyzed via spectrophotometry. The advantage of such an assessment procedure is its ability to provide immediate, valid results. Paulson et al. (1977) found this test to be valid within 20–30 hours of antabuse ingestion and therefore useful in the clinical assessment of antabuse compliance. Furthermore, the test does not appear to be influenced by physical illness or ingestion of other substances. It would appear that this technique deserves added attention with respect to reliability and validity considerations. At present, however, it remains in a relatively primitive, not widely applicable stage and may suffer from potential problems similar to those of the breathalyzer. Clients may pace drinking and antabuse consumption so as to obtain a positive CS_2 test at regularly scheduled appointments only.

Summary

Objective procedures for the assessment of alcohol abuse have advanced considerably over the past decade. Moving from sole reliance on self-reported alcohol consumption, direct observational and biochemical indices have received mounting interest. As noted, however, these latter assessment methods are not without their limitations. Specifically, the external validity of analogue procedures and simulated drink settings has yet to be demonstrated. Biochemical indices are limited by either their insensitivity to all but recent drinking (i.e., BAL) or by the limited attention given validity and reliability considerations. It would appear that limitations in assessment are partly the result of a general reluctance to incorporate treatment measures other than self-report in assessment. This reluctance primarily stems from differing treatment philosophies (i.e., abstinence versus responsible drinking) as well as simple practical problems in implementing these new procedures. Hopefully, with further investigation of parameters influencing self-report, and with the incorporation of observational and biochemical indices in treatment programs, problems outlined in this chapter will be obviated.

SMOKING ASSESSMENT

The assessment of cigarette smoking, as well as other tobacco substances, has recently undergone rapid development. These developments stem from limitations of traditional rate measures of cigarette smoking (Benfari, McIntyre, Benfari, Baldwin, & Ockene, 1977; Brockway, 1978; McFall, 1978). Numerous authors have called for more objective or direct measures of cigarette consumption to supplement the past reliance on rate as the sole measure of smoking exposure (Densen, Davidow, Bass, & Jones, 1967; Frederiksen & Simon, 1979; Vogt, 1977). New methods for assessing smoking can be generally classified as more sophisticated analyses of smoking behavior *per se* or the assessment of biochemical changes following smoking. Specific measures in these two categories will be discussed and evaluated for their potential contribution to smoking assessment.

This section will initially review the advantages and disadvantages of rate measures, and a number of suggestions will be made to increase their validity. Two other categories of smoking behavior, substance and topography, will then be reviewed and the advantages and disadvantages of these two measures considered. Finally, three biochemical measures, nicotine, carbon monoxide, and thiocyanate will be examined. Separate sections will cover the relationship of each measure to cigarette smoking, their advantages and disadvantages, and the future role of each measure. A concluding section will briefly introduce additional areas for investigation, as well as summarize important issues in smoking assessment for the practicing clinician.

Self-report Measures

Rate. Rate measures have constituted the primary dependent variable in smoking research and treatment because of the not totally inaccurate assumption that it reflects smoking exposure and accompanying health risks. Rate measures have been obtained by retrospective self-report on questionnaires or by having smokers self-monitor number of cigarettes smoked. (For a comprehensive review of smoking rate measurement, see Frederiksen, Martin, & Webster, 1979.)

A voluminous literature (USPHS 1979) on the dose-response relationship between these self-reports of cigarette consumption and numerous diseases substantiates historical reliance on this variable. Additional reasons for the frequent utilization of rate measures include their ease of collection and low response cost. The possible treatment effect of self-monitoring on subsequent rates of consumption, primarily related to the reactivity of self-monitoring, also constitutes a presumed advantage and may account for its widespread use in applied research (Frederiksen & Simon, 1979).

Despite the many advantages of rate measures, there are a number of serious disadvantages that tend to limit their value; these have plagued rate measures regardless of how they were obtained. The first disadvantage concerns the questionable accuracy of smokers' self-reports of rate (McFall, 1970). Although attempts (e.g., corroboration of significant others) have been made to make self-reports more reliable, they may be intrusive or subject to collusion (Pechacek, 1979). Another major limitation of rate, when collected via self-report or self-monitoring, has been smoker distortion of reported rate. Although always a problem in self-monitoring, distortion has played a particularly important role when self-report measures of smoking have been used to evaluate smoking treatment. Research indicates that from 20 percent (Delarue, 1973) to 48 percent (Ohlin, Lundh, & Westling, 1976; Sillett, Wilson, Malcolm, & Ball, 1978) of smokers continue to smoke despite reporting abstinence following completion of treatment programs. The primary implication of these data is that much of the past research in smoking treatment may be misleading because of the unreliability of its data base.

Another limitation, and one that directly questions the validity of even accurate measurement of rate, is that rate has been considered an invalid index of the health risks of smoking (Benfari et al., 1977; Densen, Davidow, Bass, & Jones, 1967; Vogt, 1977). The importance of substance and topography variables in determining levels of smoking exposure often make simple rate measures misleading indices of smoking. The final disadvantage of smoking rate involves the response cost of self-monitoring to the smoker. Unfortunately, there has been very little work on the effects of having smokers monitor their rate of cigarette consumption. However, a recent report (Moss, Lomax, Martin, & Prue, 1980) indicates that when smokers are required to record cigarette consumption, clinic dropout rates range from 30 percent to 60 percent. When self-monitoring is not required of smokers, the dropout rate is less than 10 percent.

Future rate measurement may be improved by addressing the identified problems. For instance, rate can be corroborated by more objective biochemical indices of smoking exposure, as opposed to the more intrusive methods typically used. In fact, future research and empirically-based treatment reports need to provide supplemental biochemical measures because of the high rate of distortion in past reports. Another way to improve smokers' recording of rate is to make the procedure less reactive. Methods of obtaining rate, such as daily phone checks or having smokers keep their empty cigarette packs, may have less response cost for smokers (Frederiksen, Epstein, & Kosevsky, 1975) and also lead to decreased drop-out rates. Accuracy of self-monitoring may also be improved by requiring or setting the occasion for timely recording of cigarette consumption. Mechanical devices for self-monitoring (Azrin & Powell, 1968) or daily mailing of rate data to the clinic (Prue, Krapfl, & Martin, in press) could improve the accuracy of rate measurement. Finally, when treatment programs are evaluated, treatment differences should be reported in terms of number of subjects who abstained from smoking following treatment, in addition to mean daily rate of cigarette consumption per group (McFall, 1978). The reason for this latter suggestion is that the validity of smokers' self-reports of abstinence can be easily verified by employing biochemical indices. Verification of particular rates of cigarette consumption are more difficult.

In spite of the limitations of present rate measures, past reliance on rate suggests that if comparisons of future research with past reports are to be made, it will be necessary to continue to obtain rate measures.

Substance. Reports of the type or brand of tobacco consumed have been virtually ignored in smoking research, despite their significant role in smoking-related health risks. Differences between types of cigarettes have not been considered as important as rate of cigarette consumption. Yet, epidemiological data (Gori, 1972, 1976) and machine testing (Ross, 1976a, 1976b) indicate that cigarettes differ widely in their potential health effects because of differences in levels of tar and poison gases. In fact, differences in brand may account for more variance in health effects than differences in rates of cigarette consumption (Jaffee, Kanzler, Cohen, & Kaplan, 1978; Prue et al., in press; Turner, Sillett, & Ball, 1974). Future research should consider this very significant, but neglected variable. Also, substance should be easy to assess via direct observation at clinic sessions or by the collection of empty cigarette packs. Both these methods are likely to be reactive, yet the importance of substance variables indicates that they should be monitored in future research.

Smoking Topography Assessment

Another smoking behavior of present concern is smoking topography (Frederiksen, Miller, & Peterson, 1977). Topography is a summary term that refers to variables related to how people smoke, including: number of puffs, puff volume, puff length, inter-puff interval, amount of cigarette consumed, etc. Topography variables have been monitored because much of the health risk associated with smoking is presumably related to how a person smokes. As Frederiksen et al. noted, if two smokers are consuming equal numbers of the same brand of cigarette, then any differences in exposure would be related to topography variables. Topography measurement also allows a much more detailed analysis of a smokers' idiosyncratic patterns of smoking (Frederiksen et al., 1979; Henningfield & Griffiths, 1979). Finally, since changes in a smokers' topography represents an alternative treatment goal for risk reduction (Frederiksen, 1977; Royal College of Physicians, 1971), the use of pre- and posttreatment measures of topography would be helpful in evaluating treatments with noncessation goals.

There are a number of disadvantages with topography as presently measured which have limited its usefulness to smoking researchers and clinicians. First, topography, like rate, is typically assessed via self-report, and there is reason to believe that smokers cannot accurately report their behavior on at least some topography variables (Vogt, 1977; Wald, Idle, & Bailey, 1978). A second disadvantage deals with the mode of topography assessment. Topography measures have traditionally been made in the experimental laboratory by direct observation or by mechanical recording equipment. Topography measures obtained in this fashion are of known reliablility (Henningfield & Griffiths, 1979), but the procedures are expensive to obtain and very reactive. In fact, a recent report has provided data questioning the generalizability of laboratory measures of topography (Comer & Creighton, 1978). Finally, topography variables have not correlated well with measures of biochemical exposure in humans (Henningfield & Griffiths, in press; Turner, Sillett, & Ball, 1974). This may be attributable to the complex interrelations among the topography variables (Dunn & Freiesleben, 1978), as well as interdependencies between smoking topography, substances consumed, and rate of cigarette consumption when assessing smoking exposure.

In summary, the technology of present topography measurement is intrusive, costly, and of questionable generalizability to more natural situations. Also, the relationship between topography variables and more direct, biochemical measures of smoking exposure has not been well documented in humans. Future research must thus examine the basic mechanisms of topography variables, correlations between topography variables, and the relation between topography and increased health risk. On a more positive note, researchers are developing a mouthpiece that electronically monitors topography variables without requiring direct connection to recording devices such as the polygraph. Future research with this instrument should determine its reactivity and whether or not the device can circumvent problems that have plagued the laboratory measurement of topography variables.

Biochemical Measures

Nicotine and cotinine. Nicotine, one of the pharmacologically addicting agents in tobacco, has been monitored because of the agent's importance in continued smoking (Armitage, 1978; Jarvik, Popek, Schneider, Baer-Weiss, & Gritz, 1978; Russell, 1978; Schachter, 1977). Nicotine has been monitored in the blood (Zeidenberg, Jaffe, Kanzler, Levitt, Langone, & Van Vunakis, 1977) and urine (Paxton & Bernacca, 1979). Both these measures have specific advantages, but urine nicotine sampling has not proven to be accurate because of variations in body fluid levels. Blood nicotine sampling is the preferable method of measuring nicotine levels at this time.

The accurate assessment of nicotine would allow health service providers to objectively evaluate tobacco consumption and thereby assess the presence of nicotine as well as level of addiction. However, nicotine is rapidly metabolized by the body, giving it a short half-life of 30 minutes (Langone & Van Vunakis, 1975; Zeidenberg et al., 1977), which in turn makes nicotine levels extremely sensitive to the amount of time elapsed since a smoker's last cigarette (Armitage, 1978; Paxton & Bernacca, 1979). These factors could lead to errors in assessing cigarette exposure based on nicotine monitoring. The fact that even heavy smokers can abstain from smoking for a couple of hours could lead to distortion of their nicotine levels.

A more promising strategy is cotinine assessment. Cotinine is the primary metabolite of nicotine and can be monitored in the blood, urine, or saliva of smokers (Hengen & Hengen, 1978; Langone & Van Vunakis, 1975; Zeidenberg et al., 1977). Cotinine is considerably more stable than nicotine with a half-life of 30 hours (Zeidenberg et al., 1977), making it less affected by diurnal variability and elapsed time since last cigarette (Lader, 1978). Though present research has not yet fully identified the relationship between cotinine levels and rate of cigarette consumption or level of nicotine in smokers' cigarettes, cotinine measurement appears promising. Future research will surely define more closely the parameters of smoking that produce variations in cotinine levels. Cotinine is presently most useful in discriminating smokers from nonsmokers, and when repeated single subject measures are obtained, as an index of changes in tobacco exposure.

Carbon monoxide. The second biochemical measure that has received attention in smoking research is carbon monoxide. Carbon monoxide (CO) is consumed during cigarette smoking and is monitored in blood samples (carboxy-hemoglobin) or in expired air samples (alveolar carbon monoxide). Carbon monoxide levels are important because of their documented relation to rate of cigarette consumption (Frederiksen & Martin, 1979; Vogt, 1977), topography variables (Robinson & Forbes, 1975), and substance smoked (Prue et al., in press). Additionally, CO has been identified as critical in the etiology of numerous smoking related diseases (e.g., chronic obstructive pulmonary disease, chronic heart disease). The primary advantage of CO measurement is that this variable provides an objective measure of exposure and associated health risk. Another advantage is that once the initial equipment to measure CO has been purchased (approximate cost = $1200), the assessment of carbon monoxide is simple, quick, and does not involve any additional expense. Further, in the case of alveolar CO, the results of CO assessments are available within minutes after sampling and can be used to provide immediate feedback to smokers on their health risk.

The disadvantages of using carbon monoxide parallel those of nicotine assessment because carbon monoxide also has a short half-life in the body (2–4 hours). This short half-life leads to diurnal variability and sensitivity to amount of time since a smoker's last cigarette. Such sensitivity can lead to subject distortion of carbon monoxide checks through short periods of abstinence prior to CO sampling. Variations in CO have also occurred because of ambient CO levels and smoker's activity level (Wald & Howard, 1975). Both of these factors can lead to the inadvertent distortion of assessments.

Despite these drawbacks, CO assessment is a promising measure that provides a reliable and direct measure of biochemical exposure to cigarette smoking. Although future research will delineate the utility of this measure, CO assessment has already been widely used in both basic and applied research. (For a comprehensive review, see Frederiksen & Martin, 1979.)

Hydrogen cyanide. The third and final biochemical index of smoking exposure is the measurement of hydrogen cyanide gas consumed during smoking. Measures of hydrogen cyanide intake are obtained by assessing its metabolite, thiocyanate (SCN), in the blood, urine, saliva, or perspiration of smokers. Comparisons of the four fluids indicate that saliva and blood levels of SCN appear to be the most reliable and valid methods of sampling this metabolite.

Thiocyanate assessment is important because of its relationship to rate of cigarette consumption (Butts, Keuhneman, & Widdowson, 1974; Courant, 1974; Tenovuo & Makinen, 1976; Vogt, 1977), topography (Barylko-Pikielna & Pangborn, 1968), and substance smoked (Prue et al., in press). Additionally, hydrogen cyanide gas has been implicated in the etiology of stomach cancer (Boyland & Walker, 1974; Lederer, 1976) and certain respiratory disabilities (Ross, 1976b; USPHS, 1979).

The major advantage of SCN assessment, like carbon monoxide assessment, is that it can be used as an objective measure of smoking exposure. Another advantage of SCN is its extended half-life in the body (10–14 days), which makes it less sensitive to recent rate variations and subject distortion. Finally, the well-documented relationship between smoking parameters and SCN levels makes SCN a useful screening device. Unfortunately, since SCN measures have not seen wide-spread use in research, the ultimate value of this variable has yet to be determined.

There are also a number of disadvantages of SCN assessment. First, research has noted a great deal of intra-subject variability in single subject repeated measures of SCN. This variability has been particularly notable in multiple daily measures. Although the reasons for this variability have not been determined, a number of possible contributing factors have been suggested (Prue, Martin, & Hume, in press; Rue, Martin, Hume, & Davis, in press). Future research will presumably isolate the relevant factors. Second, variations in diet can have an impact on SCN levels because certain foods (e.g., broccoli, cabbage) contain naturally occurring thiocyanate (Densen et al., 1967). Dietetic influences can lead to inadvertent distortions in SCN levels. As in the case of carbon monoxide, there is always the remote possibility that ambient levels of hydrogen cyanide gas can lead to elevated levels. Finally, SCN assessment requires relatively sophisticated laboratory equipment (Levinson & MacFate, 1969). Initial costs for SCN analysis would be around $3000, and individual saliva samples would cost between $4 and $5 per sample after the laboratory has been set up. Despite these disadvantages, SCN offers some promise for the future assessment of smoking exposure, especially as a measure of long-term abstinence, because of its extended half-life in the body.

Summary

The assessment of smoking has recently become more sophisticated as researchers move away from a sole reliance on rate measures. Rate measures are being supplemented by the measurement of new dependent variables. Importantly, these new measures provide a much more sophisticated analysis of smoking. In the case of biochemical measures, the variables are also a more direct measure of exposure and health risk. The treatment of smoking has been constrained by primitive, often unreliable, and perhaps invalid measurement procedures. Hopefully, the development of new approaches to assessment will result in new developments in smoking treatment.

There are also a number of additional measures or areas that deserve the attention of smoking researchers. First, measurement of physiological activity, such as respiratory fitness, via pulmonary function tests (Cosio, Ghezzo, Hogg, Corbin, Loveland, Dosman, & MacKlem, 1978) deserve greater attention. This is especially true because initial differences in pulmonary function have been noted for smokers and nonsmokers (Walter, Nancy, & Collier, 1979; Wynder, Kaufman, & Lesser, 1967) and in smokers following reductions in smoking (McCarthy, Craig & Cherniack, 1976). Second, other physical measures including blood pressure and body weight should be obtained, since their relation to smoking is unclear. Third, measures of physical fitness (Williams, 1972) should be monitored following smoking treatment. For instance, treadmill running (Gutin & Cayce, 1973), step-tests (Miyamura, Kudora, Hirata, & Honda, 1975), and exercise tests (Doolittle & Bigbee, 1968) could be measured prior to and following treatment of cigarette smoking. Ultimately, health variables are the reason for concern with smoking; yet, treatments have not been evaluated on health or fitness measures. Finally, other measures that deserve attention are parameters associated with successful quitting (Frederiksen & Simon, 1979), withdrawal (Myrsten, Elgerot, & Edgren, 1977; Shiffman & Jarvik, 1976), and maintenance of abstinence (Marlatt & Gordon, 1979).

Case Study

History. The client was a 47-year-old female referred to the smoking clinic by her local doctor. The client had respiratory problems (emphysema) and a history of chronic heart disease in her family. She had begun smoking at age 18 and had smoked approximately 26 cigarettes per day since that time. At clinic screening the client reported that she

was consuming Winston cigarettes at a rate of approximately 35 cigarettes per day. Winston cigarettes have been machine tested by the
Federal Trade Commission (1977) and reported to have 19 mg of tar
and 1.2 mg of nicotine per cigarette. Additionally, Ross (1976a; 1976b)
reported that Winston cigarettes have comparatively high amounts of
carbon monoxide and hydrogen cyanide gas based upon smoking machine tests. The tar, nicotine, carbon monoxide, and hydrogen cyanide
gas values indicate that Winstons are in the upper range of toxicity as
compared with other brands. One additional point that must be made
is that the client had attempted abstinence on three different occasions.
The longest successful period of abstinence was 13 days. The client
reported that she became very agitated when attempting cessation and
had difficulty getting along with others during prior attempts at abstinence.

Baseline. The client was screened for treatment and asked to provide
saliva samples for thiocyanate analysis and expired air samples for carbon monoxide assessment. These tests were repeated three times during
the baseline period. The results of these tests are portrayed in figure
13.1, which also shows the daily rate of cigarette consumption based
upon this client's self-monitoring of daily rate. Self-monitoring records
were maintained on 17 cm by 5 cm self-monitoring forms, which were

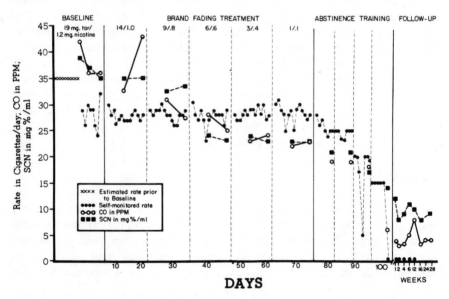

Fig. 13.1. Single subject analysis of smoking risk reduction

designed to slip into the cellophane wrapper of a cigarette pack. The client was given stamped envelopes and asked to mail the forms to the clinic daily. The latter procedure was designed to produce more accurate reports, since daily submission of forms would presumably lead to more timely recording than weekly ones that could not be checked for timeliness. Along with the self-monitoring forms, the smoker mailed in her empty cigarette packs as she finished the cigarettes in each pack. The latter procedure was designed to assess the substance consumed during the treatment program. As figure 13.1 indicates, self-monitoring seemed to have a reactive effect in decreased levels of biochemical exposure and rate. The client's mean daily rate during baseline was approximately 28 cigarettes per day as compared with an estimated prior rate of 35 cigarettes per day.

Brand fading. Following the completion of baseline, the smoker went through a brand fading treatment program (Prue et al., in press) designed to reduce her tar and nicotine consumption. The procedure involves gradual reductions in the tar and nicotine consumption by changing brands of cigarettes. Brand changes were made every two weeks and each brand change represented a decrease of approximately .2 mg nicotine. The client monitored her rate during brand changes and weekly assessments were made of carbon monoxide and saliva thiocyanate. The values for these dependent variables during brand fading are also portrayed in figure 13.1. As can be seen in this figure, biochemical levels are falling as the client changes from Winston to lower tar and nicotine cigarettes. Levels are lowest when the client is consuming cigarettes with 1 mg tar and .1 mg nicotine. Only once during brand fading, while the client consumed cigarettes with 14 mg tar and 1.0 mg nicotine, were levels of biochemical exposure greater than levels of these gases. Rate showed no consistent changes until the smoker began her cessation program.

Abstinence training. A cessation program was designed similar to that described by Pomerleau and Pomerleau (1977) and instituted after the smoker was consuming cigarettes with 1.0 mg tar and .1 mg nicotine. The treatment primarily involved stimulus control procedures, systematic rate reductions, and urge control training. As figure 13.1 indicates, the client successfully reduced her rate of cigarette consumption during abstinence training and parallel decreases occurred in levels of biochemical exposure. By the fourth week of abstinence training, the client's rate was reduced to 15 cigarettes per day and her levels of biochemical exposure approached nonsmokers' levels. At her target date for abstinence, four weeks postbrand fading, the client's consumption dropped to 0 cigarettes per day. This rate was reflected in her carbon monoxide level during the first day of abstinence. Thiocyanate levels, already at a low level, dropped more slowly to nonsmokers' levels. The decreases in biochemical levels followed the pattern expected on the basis of their different metabolic rates in the body.

Follow-up. The active treatment was discontinued two weeks after abstinence training. The client was then scheduled for biweekly follow-ups for one month, a follow-up visit at three months postabstinence, and visits at six months and 12 months postabstinence training. At all follow-up visits the client was assessed on the biochemical levels of smoking exposure. Self-monitoring forms were not requested at follow-up visits because the client reported complete abstinence. As figure 13.1 indicates, the client's carbon monoxide and thiocyanate levels verify these self-reports with the exception of slightly elevated carbon monoxide levels at the three month follow-up visit. The client reaffirmed that she was not smoking, which was verified by low thiocyanate levels. Therefore, it was assumed that the smoker either had a very low rate of cigarette consumption immediately prior to clinic attendance or that she had been in an environment with high ambient carbon monoxide levels.

The above case study illustrates a multi-modal approach to the assessment of an appetitive disorder. Measures of substance, rate, carbon monoxide, and thiocyanate provided important information on tobacco exposure to the clinician. The documented interrelationships between the four measures led to their mutual verification and allowed the clinician to more accurately evaluate the treatment process and final treatment outcome.

SUMMARY AND FUTURE CONSIDERATIONS

In both alcohol and smoking, self-reported measures of rate of consumption must be included in clinical and research assessment procedures. For smoking applications, these measures may be improved by incorporating daily phone checks and having subjects keep their empty cigarette packages. Collateral sources can be used to verify self-reports for both smoking and drinking behavior. For both substances, collaterals need to be selected on the basis of *daily contact* with the subject so that continuous observation of the targeted behavior is possible. Collaterals who do not have daily contact cannot be expected to provide valid independent data, nor will their sporadic checks on the subject appreciably improve the validity of his/her own self-reported data. More often these collaterals produce reports of "I don't know" or "not observed." Unfortunately, for some subjects there is simply no acceptable collateral source available.

Laboratory-based direct observation of smoking and drinking behaviors appear to offer acceptable validity and reliability within that setting. However, the external validity with respect to natural environmental settings cannot be assumed. This limitation renders analogue assessment methods most appropriate for basic studies conducted in laboratory settings. In alcohol applications, laboratory-based observations present an additional ethical consideration. Alcoholic clients for whom the treatment goal is abstinence may be reluctant to participate in any procedure requiring consumption of alcoholic beverages, even for evaluation purposes. Possible countertherapeutic effects and the client's right to refuse participation must be considered.

The latest development among behavioral scientists working with appetitive disorders is the addition of physiological or biochemical techniques in multi-modal assessment approaches. In smoking, monitoring of nicotine, carbon monoxide, and thiocyanate levels is now possible. Methods to determine blood alcohol level, liver function, and alcohol consumption via GGT, and an objective test to determine antabuse compliance are now available for alcohol assessment. While issues of validity, reliability, cost, and complexity remain with most of these measures, they represent important advances beyond self-report and laboratory-based analogue procedures in several respects. First, these measures relate actual substance use to physical impairment and health risk. Second, physiological indicants probably produce less reactivity and are less susceptible to subject distortion. The need for individuals other than the subject to serve as collateral data providers is also reduced. Finally, further development of these more objective physiological methods may provide a consistent set of dependent measures for use in future studies. At this time, direct behavioral observations in the laboratory or clinic, reports of the target behavior in the natural environment by the subject and selected collaterals with daily contact, and newer physiological/biochemical measures need to be included to provide a balanced, comprehensive assessment approach.

REFERENCES

Armitage, A. K. The role of nicotine in the tobacco smoking habit. In R. E. Thornton (Ed.), *Smoking behavior: Physiological and psychological influences.* New York: Churchill Livingstone, 1978.

Azrin, N. H., & Powell, J. Behavioral engineering: The reduction of smoking with a conditioning apparatus and procedure. *Journal of Applied Behavior Analysis,* 1968, *1*, 193–200.

Barylko-Pikielna, N., & Pangborn, R. M. Effect of cigarette smoking on urinary and saliva thiocyanates. *Archives of Environmental Health*, 1968, *17*, 739–745.

Benfari, R. C., McIntyre, K., Benfari, M. J. F., Baldwin, A., & Ockene, J. The use of thiocyanate determination for indication of cigarette smoking status. *Evaluation Quarterly*, 1977, *1*, 629–638.

Bigelow, G., Strickler, D., Liebson, I., & Griffiths, R. Maintaining disulfiram among outpatient alcoholics: A security-deposit contingency contracting procedure. *Behaviour Research and Therapy*, 1976, *14*, 378–381.

Boone, D. J., Tietz, N. W., & Weinstock, A. Significance of gamma-glutamyl Transferace (GGT) activity measurements in alcohol-induced hepatic injury. *Annals of Clinical and Laboratory Science*, 1977, *7*, 25–27.

Boyland, E., & Walker, S. A. Effect of thiocyanate on nitrosation of amines. *Nature*, 1974, *248*, 601–602.

Brockway, B. S. Chemical validation of self-reported smoking rates. *Behavior Therapy*, 1978, *9*, 685–686.

Butts, W. C., Kuehneman, J., & Widdowson, G. M. Automated method for determining serum thiocyanate to distinguish smokers from non-smokers. *Clinical Chemistry*, 1974, *20*, 1344–1348.

Caudill, B. D., & Marlatt, G. A. Modeling influences in social drinking: An experimental analogue. *Journal of Consulting and Clinical Psychology*, 1975. *43*, 405–415.

Comer, A. K., & Creighton, D. E. The effect of experimental conditions on smoking behavior. In R. E. Thornton (Ed.), *Smoking behavior: Physiological and psychological influences*. New York: Churchill Livingstone, 1978.

Cosio, M., Ghezzo, H., Hogg, J. C., Corbin, R., Loveland, M., Dosman, J., & Macklem, P. T. *New England Journal of Medicine*, 1978, *298*, 1277–1281.

Courant, P. The effects of smoking on the antilactobacillus system in saliva. *Odontology Review*, 1967, *18*, 251–267.

Cravey, R. H., & Jain, N. C. Current status of blood alcohol methods. *Journal of Chromatographic Science*, 1974, *12*, 209–213.

Cutter, R. E., & Storm, T. Observational study of alcohol consumption in natural settings; the Vancouver beer parlor. *Journal of Studies on Alcohol*, 1975, *36*, 1173–1183.

Delarue, N. C. The anti-smoking clinic: Is it a potential community service? *Canadian Medical Association Journal*, 1973, *108*, 1164–1165.

Densen, P. M., Davidow, B., Bass, H. E., & Jones, E. W. A chemical test for smoking exposure. *Archives of Environmental Health*, 1967, *14*, 865–874.

Doolittle, T. L., & Bigbee, R. The twelve minute run-walk: A test of cardio-respiratory fitness of adolescent boys. *Research Quarterly*, 1968, *39*, 491–495.

Dunn, P. J., & Freiesleben, E. R. The effects of nicotine enhanced cigarettes on human smoking parameters and alveolar carbon monoxide levels. In R. E. Thornton, (Ed.), *Smoking behavior: Physiological and psychological influences*. New York: Churchill Livingstone, 1978.

Emrick, C. D. A review of psychologically oriented treatment of alcoholism I. The use and interrelationships of outcome criteria and drinking behavior following treatment. *Quarterly Journal of Studies on Alcohol*, 1974, *35*, 523–549.

Federal Trade Commission. *Tar and nicotine content of cigarettes*. DHEW Publication No. (CDC) 78–8703. Washington, D.C.: U.S. Department of Health, Education and Welfare/Public Health Service, 1977.

Foy, D. W., Rychtarik, R. G., Nunn, L. B., & Webster, J. *Objective assessment of drinking behavior in alcoholic veterans*. Paper presented at the New Mexico Conference on Behavior Modification, September 1979.

Foy, D. W., Rychtarik, R. G., O'Brien, T. P., & Nunn, L. B. Goal choice of alcoholics: Effects of training controlled drinking skills. *Behavioural Psychotherapy,* 1979, *7,* 101–110.

Foy, D. W., & Simon, S. J. Alcoholic drinking topography as a function of solitary versus social context. *Addictive Behaviors,* 1978, *3,* 39–41.

Frederiksen, L. W. *But I don't want to quit smoking: Alternatives to abstinence.* Paper presented at the meeting of the Association for Advancement of Behavior Therapy, Atlanta, December 1977.

Frederiksen, L. W., Epstein, L. H., & Kosevsky, B. P. Reliability and controlling effects of three procedures for self-monitoring smoking. *Psychological Record,* 1975, *25,* 255–264.

Frederiksen, L. W., & Martin, J. E. Carbon monoxide and smoking behavior. *Addictive Behaviors,* 1979, *4,* 21–30.

Frederiksen, L. W., Martin, J. E., & Webster, J. S. Assessment of smoking behavior. *Journal of Applied Behavior Analysis,* 1979, *12,* 653–664.

Frederiksen, L. W., Miller, P. M., & Peterson, G. L. Topographical components of smoking behavior. *Addictive Behaviors,* 1977, *2,* 55–61.

Frederiksen, L. W., & Simon, S. J. Modification of smoking behavior. In R. S. Davidson (Ed.), *Modification of pathological behavior.* New York: Gardner Press, 1979.

Gabel, P. C., Noel, N. E., Keane, T. M., & Lisman, S. A. *Effects of sexual versus fear arousal on alcohol consumption in college males.* Unpublished manuscript, State University of New York at Binghamton, 1979.

Garlington, W. K., & Dericco, D. A. The effect of modeling on drinking rate. *Journal of Applied Behavior Analysis,* 1977, *10,* 207–211.

Garvin, R. G., Foy, D. W., & Alford, G. S. *A critical examination of gamma-glutamyl transpeptidase as a biochemical marker for alcohol abuse.* Manuscript submitted for publication, 1980.

Gerrein, J. R., Rosenberg, C. M., & Manohar, V. Disulfiram maintenance in outpatient treatment of alcoholism. *Archives of General Psychiatry,* 1973, *28,* 798–802.

Gori, G. B. Low risk cigarettes: A prescription. *Science,* 1976, 19, 1243–1245.

Gori, G. B. Research in smoking and health at the National Cancer Institute. *Journal of the National Cancer Institute,* 1972, *48,* 1759–1762.

Gutin, B., & Cayce, C. A. The use of submaximal measures to predict all-out treadmill running in college women. *American Corrective Therapy Journal,* 1973, *27,* 151–154.

Hendricks, R. D., Sobell, M. B., & Cooper, A. M. Social influences on human ethanol consumption in an analogue situation. *Addictive Behaviors,* 1978, *3,* 253–259.

Hengen, N., & Hengen, M. Gas-liquid chromatographic determination of nicotine and continine in plasma. *Clinical Chemistry,* 1978, *24,* 50–53.

Henningfield, J. E., & Griffiths, R. R. A preparation for the experimental analysis of human cigarette smoking behavior. *Behavior Research Methods and Instrumentation,* 1979, *11,* 538–544.

Henningfield, J. E., & Griffiths, R. R. Effects of ventilated cigarette holders on cigarette smoking by humans. *Psychopharmacology,* in press.

Hersen, M. Historical perspectives in behavioral assessment. In M. Hersen & A. S. Bellack (Eds.), *Behavioral assessment: A practical handbook.* New York: Pergamon Press, 1976.

Higgins, R. L., & Marlatt, G. A. The effects anxiety arousal upon the consumption of alcohol by alcoholics and social drinkers. *Journal of Consulting and Clinical Psychology,* 1973, *41,* 426–433.

Hunter, P. A., Hannon, R., & Marchi, D. *Observation of drinking behavior in a natural setting.* Paper presented at the meeting of the Association for Advancement of Behavior Therapy, San Francisco, December 1979.

Jaffe, J. H., Kanzler, M., Cohen, M., & Kaplan, T. Inducing low tar/nicotine cigarette smoking in women. *British Journal of Addiction,* 1978, *73,* 271–278.

Jain, N. C., & Cravey, R. H. A review of breath alcohol methods. *Journal of Chromatographic Science,* 1974, *12,* 214–218.

Jarvik, M. E., Popek, P., Schneider, N. G., Baer-Weiss, V., & Gritz, E. R. Can cigarette size and nicotine content influence smoking and puffing rates? *Psychopharmacology,* 1978, *58,* 303–306.

Keane, T. M., Foy, D. W., Nunn, L. B., & Rychtarik, R. G. *Improving antabuse compliance in alcoholic patients.* Manuscript submitted for publication, 1980.

Kilpatrick, D. G., Roitzsch, J. C., Best, C. L., McAlbany, D. A., Sturgis, E. T., & Miller, W. C. Treatment goal preference and problem perception of chronic alcoholics: Behavioral and personality correlates. *Addictive Behaviors,* 1978, *3,* 107–116.

Lader, M. Nicotine and smoking behaviour. *British Journal of Clinical Pharmacology,* 1978, *5,* 289–292.

Lamy, J., Baglin, M. C., Weill, J., & Aron, E. Gamma-glutamyl transpeptidase. *Nonvelle Presse Medicale,* 1975, *4,* 487–490.

Langone, J. J., & Van Vunakis, V. Quantitation of cotinine in sera of smokers. *Research Communications in Chemical Pathology and Pharmacology,* 1975, *10,* 21–28.

Lederer, J. Nitrosamines: A serious problem in alimentary hygiene. *Louvain Medical Journal,* 1976, *95,* 135–143.

Levinson, S., & MacFate, R. T. *Clinical Laboratory Diagnosis.* Philadelphia: Lea Febiger Publishing Company, 1969.

Lovibond, S. H., & Caddy, G. Discriminated aversive control in the moderation of alcoholics' drinking behavior. *Behavior Therapy,* 1970, *1,* 437–444.

Marlatt, G. A., Demming, B., & Reid, J. B. Loss of control drinking in alcoholics: an experimental analogue. *Journal of Abnormal Psychology,* 1973, *81,* 214–233.

Marlatt, G. A., & Gordon, J. R. Determinants of relapse: Implications for the maintenance of behavior change. In P. Davidson (Ed.), *Behavioral medicine: Changing health lifestyles.* New York: Brunner/Mazel, 1979.

McCarthy, D. S., Craig, D. H., & Cherniak, R. M. Effect of modification of the smoking habit on lung function. *American Review of Respiratory Diseases,* 1976, *114,* 103–113.

McFall, R. M. Effects of self-monitoring on normal smoking behavior. *Journal of Consulting and Clinical Psychology,* 1970, *35,* 135–142.

McFall, R. M. Smoking cessation research. *Journal of Consulting and Clinical Psychology,* 1978, *46,* 703–712.

Mello, N. K., & Mendelson, J. H. A quantitative analysis of drinking patterns in alcoholics. *Archives of General Psychiatry,* 1971, *6,* 527–539.

Miller, P. M., Becker, J. V., Foy, D. W., & Wooten, L. S. Instructional control of the components of alcoholic drinking behavior. *Behavior Therapy,* 1976, *7,* 472–480.

Miller, P. M., & Hersen, M. *A quantitative measurement system for alcoholism and treatment.* Paper presented at the annual meeting of the Association for Advancement of Behavior Therapy, New York, 1972. (a)

Miller, P. M., & Hersen, M. Quantitative changes in alcohol consumption as a function of electrical aversive conditioning. *Journal of Clinical Psychology,* 1972, *28,* 590–593. (b)

Miller, P. M., Hersen, M., Eisler, R. M., & Elkin, T. E. A retrospective analysis of alcohol consumption on laboratory tasks as related to therapeutic outcome. *Behaviour Research and Therapy,* 1974, *12,* 73–76.

Miller, P. M., Hersen, M., Eisler, R. M., & Hilsman, G. Effects of social stress on operant drinking of alcoholics and social drinkers. *Behaviour Research and Therapy,* 1974, *12,* 67–72.

Miller, P. M., Hersen, M., Eisler, R. M., & Watts, J. G. Contingent reinforcement of lowered blood/alcohol levels in an outpatient chronic alcoholic. *Behaviour Research and Therapy,* 1974, *12,* 261–263.

Miller, W. R., Crawford, V. L., & Taylor, C. A. Significant others as corroborative sources for problem drinkers. *Addictive Behaviors,* 1979, *4,* 67–70.

Miyamura, M., Kuroda, K., Hirata, K., & Honda, Y. Evaluations of the step test scores based on the measurement of maximal aerobic powers. *Journal of Sports Medicine,* 1975, *15,* 316–322.

Moss, R. A., Lomax, D., Martin, J. E., & Prue, D. M. The effects of self-monitoring on attrition rates in a smoking cessation program. Unpublished manuscript available from the authors, 1980.

Myrsten, A., Elgerot, A., & Edgren, B. Effects of abstinence from tobacco smoking on physiological and psychological arousal levels in habitual smokers. *Psychosomatic Medicine,* 1977, *39,* 25–38.

Nathan, P. E., & O'Brien, J. S. An experimental analysis of the behavior of alcoholics and non-alcoholics during prolonged experimental drinking. *Behavior Therapy,* 1971, *2,* 455–476.

Nunn, L. B., Foy, D. W., & Rychtarik, R. G. *Measuring blood alcohol levels in alcoholics: Influences on alcoholics' aftercare attendance.* Manuscript submitted for publication, 1980.

Ohlin, P., Lundh, B., & Westling, H. Carbon monoxide blood levels and reported cessation of smoking. *Psychopharmacology,* 1976, *49,* 263–265.

Pachman, J. S., Foy, D. W., & Van Erd, M. Goal choice of alcoholics: A comparison of those who choose total abstinence versus those who choose responsible controlled drinking. *Journal of Clinical Psychology,* 1978, *34,* 781–783.

Paulson, S. M., Krause, S., & Iber, F. L. Development and evaluation of a compliance test for patients taking disulfiram. *John Hopkins Medical Journal,* 1977, *141,* 119–125.

Paxton, R., & Bernacca, G. Urinary nicotine concentration as a function of time since last cigarette: Implications for detecting faking in smoking clinics. *Behavior Therapy,* 1979, *10,* 523–528.

Pechacek, T. F. Modification of smoking behavior. USPHS, *Surgeon General's Report on Smoking and Health: 1979.* USDHEW, DHEW Publication No. 79–50066, 1979.

Polich, J. M., Armor, D. J., & Braiker, H. B. *The course of alcoholism: Four years after treatment* (R–2433–NIAAA). Santa Monica, Ca.: Rand Corporation, 1980.

Pomerleau, O. F., & Pomerleau, C. S. *Break the smoking habit: A behavior program for giving up cigarettes.* Champaign, Illinois: Research Press, 1977.

Prue, D. M., Krapfl, J. E., & Martin, J. E. Biochemical exposure following changes to low tar and nicotine cigarettes. *Behavior Therapy,* in press.

Prue, D. M., Martin, J. E., & Hume, A. S. A critical evaluaion of thiocyanate as a biochemical index of smoking exposure. *Behavior Therapy,* in press.

Prue, D. M., Martin, J. E., Hume, A. S., & Davis, N. S. The reliability of thiocyanate measurement of smoking exposure. *Addictive Behaviors,* in press.

Reid, J. B. Study of drinking in natural settings. In G. A. Marlatt & P. E. Nathan (Eds.), *Behavioral approaches to alcoholism.* New Jersey: Rutgers Center on Alcohol Studies, 1978.

Robichand, C., Strickler, D., Bigelow, G., & Liebson, I. Disulfiram maintenance employee alcoholism treatment: A three-phase evaluation. *Behaviour Research and Therapy,* 1979, *17,* 618–621.

Robinson, D., & Forbes, W. F. The role of carbon monoxide in cigarette smoking. *Environmental Health*, 1975, *30*, 425–433.

Robinson, D., Monk, C., & Bailey, A. The relationship between serum gamma-glutamyl transpeptidase level and reported alcohol consumption in healthy men. *Journal of Studies on Alcohol*, 1979, *40*, 896–901.

Rosenbluth, J., Nathan, P. E., & Lawson, D. M. Environmental influences on drinking by college students in a college pub: Behavioral observation in the natural environment. *Addictive Behaviors*, 1978, *3*, 117–121.

Ross, W. S. Poison gases in your cigarettes: Carbon monoxide. *Readers Digest*, 1976, *109*, 114–118. (a)

Ross, W. S. Poison gases in your cigarettes—Part II: Hydrogen cyanide and nitrogen oxides. *Readers Digest*, 1976, *109*, 92–98. (b)

Royal College of Physicians, *Smoking or Health Now*. London: Pitman, 1971.

Russell, M. A. H. Self-regulation of nicotine by smokers. In K. Battig (Ed.), *Behavioral effects of nicotine*. Basel: S. Karger, 1978.

Schachter, S. Nicotine regulation in heavy and light smokers. *Journal of Experimental Psychology: General*, 1977, *106*, 5–12.

Schaefer, H. H., Sobell, M. B., & Mills, K. C. Baseline drinking behaviors in alcoholics and social drinkers, kinds of drinks and sip magnitude. *Behaviour Research and Therapy*, 1971, *9*, 23–27.

Shiffman, S. M., & Jarvik, M. E. Smoking withdrawal symptoms in two weeks of abstinence. *Psychopharmacology*, 1976, *50*, 35–39.

Sillett, R. W., Wilson, M. B., Malcolm, R. E., & Ball, K. P. Deception among smokers. *British Medical Journal*, 1978, *28*, 1185–1186.

Sobell, M. B., Schaefer, H. H., & Mills, K. C. Differences in baseline drinking behavior between alcoholics and normal drinkers. *Behaviour Research and Therapy*, 1972, *10*, 257–267.

Sobell, L. C., & Sobell, M. B. Validity of self-reports in three populations of alcoholics. *Journal of Consulting and Clinical Psychology*, 1978, *46*, 901–907.

Sobell, M. B., & Sobell, L. C. Individualized behavior therapy for alcoholics. *Behavior Therapy*, 1973, *4*, 49–72.

Sobell, M. B., Sobell, L. C., & VanderSpek, R. Relationships among clinical judgment, self-report, and breath analysis measures of intoxication in alcoholics. *Journal of Consulting and Clinical Psychology*, 1979, *47*, 204–206.

Sommer, R. The isolated drinker in the Edmonton beer parlor. *Quarterly Journal of Studies on Alcohol*, 1965, *26*, 26, 95–110.

Strickler, D. P., Dobbs, S. D., & Maxwell, W. A. The influence of setting on drinking behaviors: The laboratory versus the barroom. *Addictive Behaviors*, 1979, *4*, 339–344.

Tenovuo, J., & Makinen, K. K. Concentration of thiocyanate and ionizable iodine in saliva of smokers and non-smokers. *Journal of Dental Research*, 1976, *55*, 661–663.

Turner, J. A., Sillett, R. W., & Ball, K. P. Some effects of changing to low tar and low nicotine cigarettes. *Lancet*, 1974, *2*, 737–739.

U.S. Public Health Service. *Smoking and Health: A report of the Surgeon General: 1979*. Washington, D.C., USDHEW, DHEW Publication No. 79–50066, 1979.

Vogt, T. M. Smoking behavioral factors as predictors of risk. In M. Jarvik, J. Cullen, E. Gritz, T. Vogt, & L. West (Eds.), *Research on smoking behavior*. NIDA Research Monograph No. 17, DHEW Publication No. (ADM) 78–581, 1977.

Wald, N., & Howard S. Smoking, carbon monoxide and arterial disease. *Annals of Occupational Hygiene*, 1975, *18*, 1–14.

Wald, N., Idle, M., & Bailey A. Carboxyhaemoglobin levels and inhaling habits in cigarette smokers. *Thorax*, 1978, *33*, 201–206.

Walter, S., Nancy, N. R., & Collier, C. R. Changes in the forced expiratory spirogram in young male smokers. *American Review of Respiratory Disease,* 1979, *119,* 717–724.

Williams, M. H. Fitness evaluation techniques with emphasis on submaximal and maximal methods of assessing aerobic capacity. *American Corrective Therapy Journal,* 1972, *26,* 85–89.

Williams, R. J., & Brown, R. A. Differences in baseline drinking behavior between New Zealand alcoholics and normal drinkers. *Behaviour Research and Therapy,* 1974, *12,* 287–294.

Wynder, E. L., Kaufman, P. L., & Lesser, R. L. A short-term follow-up study on ex-cigarette smokers. *American Review of Respiratory Diseases,* 1967, *96,* 645–655.

Zeidenberg, P., Jaffe, J. H., Kanzler, M., Levitt, M. D., Langone, J. J., & Van Vunakis, H. Nicotine: Cotinine levels in blood during cessation of smoking. *Comprehensive Psychiatry,* 1977, *18,* 93–101.

Chapter 14

Assessment of Children in Outpatient Settings

Karen C. Wells

INTRODUCTION

This chapter is concerned with the concepts and techniques involved in the behavioral assessment of children who are referred for evaluation and treatment to outpatient clinical settings. In the process of reviewing this area, several questions will be considered. Foremost is the question of the population under consideration: Who are the children referred for outpatient treatment? What problems do they present, and how do they differ from nonreferred or normal children? A second question, which often has a direct bearing on the first, involves referral. What are the factors involved in the referral process which result in a child's presentation to a clinic for evaluation? Once the child is referred there are a number of questions to be posed. What areas should assessment of different categories or "syndromes" of abnormal child behavior cover? And how is information within each of these areas gathered? Finally, once relevant information is obtained, how is this information used? Providing an answer to each of these questions is the initial task of the clinician in the child outpatient setting, since each has a bearing on the ultimate therapeutic process.

As might be implied by these prefatory comments, behavioral assessment of children in outpatient settings has several purposes. One function of assessment is to identify the behavioral dimension(s) that best describes the child's current problems and differentiates him from normal or nonreferred children. Although behaviorists traditionally have rejected this type of "classification," the author will later argue that empirical classification may serve an important purpose in the behavioral assessment and therapy process. A second function of assessment is to provide information that is directly relevant to selection of the most appropriate treatment strategy. This information has to do with identification of target behaviors of primary concern, as well as the antecedent and consequent events currently maintaining these behaviors. A third function of assessment, and one too often forgotten or ignored in clinical settings, is the constant monitoring of progress (or lack of it) during and at termination of therapy. Assessment does not end when therapy begins but rather occurs repeatedly throughout the therapy process, providing feedback to the clinician as to the accuracy of his or her working hypotheses and forcing a reevaluation of the therapeutic plan if progress is not forthcoming. Without repeated and objective assessment, nonproductive treatments are often continued indefinitely due to absence of corrective feedback.

A final function of assessment that is becoming more important in recent years is providing administrative data on the outcome of psychotherapeutic services to large populations of individuals. Clinical professionals working within the behavioral sciences have been too long exempt from the demands placed on medical science professionals to provide objective documentation of the effectiveness of their therapeutic interventions. Medical professionals are forbidden to promote the use of a particular drug before it has been subjected to scientific studies of its efficacy and safety; yet, providers of mental health services have been allowed until recently to charge millions of dollars annually for therapeutic approaches whose efficacy is based almost entirely on promises, theoretical or rational arguments, or testimonials (Doke, 1976). As we move into the "age of accountability" in the mental health field, increased pressure is being placed on mental health service providers by legislators, third party payers, and administrators at every level to document the effectiveness of expensive psychotherapeutic programs and approaches. Clearly, clinical programs that place a premium on the third and fourth assessment functions outlined above will have a distinct advantage over more traditional approaches which do not emphasize repeated measurement. As this pressure increases, it is anticipated that we will see a commensurate increase in the use of behavioral assessment models and strategies in child clinical settings.

CHILD OUTPATIENT POPULATIONS

Behavior therapists have characteristically eschewed traditional assessment approaches aimed at arriving at a diagnostic label of the child (Ciminero & Drabman, 1977). The reasons for this have been outlined

in detail elsewhere, but include: (1) the failure of most existing diagnostic systems to adhere to consistent classification principles, (2)
failure to base diagnostic categories on meaningful and observable behavior, (3) the questionable reliability and validity of the diagnostic
categories currently in use, and (4) the reluctance of clinicians to stig-
matize children with labels that may follow them through life (Hobbs,
1975; Quay, 1979; Zigler & Phillips, 1961). In addition, diagnostic
labels, particularly those used for children, have traditionally provided
very little information relevant to selection of the most appropriate treatment procedures, course of treatment, or treatment outcome.

In spite of the fact that problems exist with traditional diagnostic
systems such as the American Psychiatric Association's DSM series,
they are nevertheless administrative necessities in most child outpatient
settings. Consequently, the early literature describing children who are
referred to outpatient clinical settings reported the distribution of diagnostic labels given to children in these settings. An examination of
this literature indicates that our more traditional colleagues have had
as many pragmatic difficulties with the DSM system as we have had
theoretical and empirical ones. In one of the first studies of this kind
using the DSM-I, Rosen, Bahn, and Kramer (1964) found that children
aged 10–14 have the maximum clinic usage rate in U.S. outpatient
clinics. In spite of this fact, 30 percent of children received no diagnosis, and an additional 40 percent were diagnosed as "adjustment reaction not further delineated." A more recent study (Cerreto & Tuma,
1977), which looked at distributions of DSM-II diagnoses in child clinical facilities, found that 38 percent of children were diagnosed as
"adjustment reaction" and another 30 percent fell under the various
forms of behavior disorder. Thus, with the advent of the DSM-II, it
appeared that while more children received diagnoses, the majority still
received the relatively nonspecific and uninformative "adjustment reaction of childhood or adolescence" (Harris, 1979). As Dreger et al.
(1964) have stated "What this means is that after the elaborate procedures used in most clinics are completed, the child is placed in a
category which says exactly what we knew about him in the first place,
that he has a problem [p. 1]."

Turning from diagnostic studies to those examining the actual behavioral characteristics or presenting problems of children in outpatient
clinics may prove more informative. Wolff (1967) examined the presenting problem of 43 consecutive first-time referrals to a London child
guidance clinic. Of these children, 47 percent presented problems of
uncontrollable or unmanageable behavior (tantrums, aggressiveness,
noncompliance, overactivity). Fourteen percent displayed anxiety, fearfulness, specific fears, and night terrors. Another 12 percent displayed

habit disorders such as bedwetting, encopresis, and head banging, and 12 children displayed speech and other miscellaneous disorders. The most common presenting problem across all children was temper tantrums; next most common was specific fears. Although Wolff (1967) did not attempt an empirical analysis of behavioral clusters presented in her samples, arbitrary groupings were constituted based on behaviors that seemed to be correlated with one another and uncorrelated with other behaviors. Three groupings were obtained using this intuitive method including Phobic Symptoms, Aggressive Symptoms, and Habit Disorders. For the Phobic (anxiety) Symptoms category, girls outnumbered boys five to one. For the Aggressive symptoms category, boys outnumbered girls almost two to one, and for Habit Disorders boys also outnumbered girls four to one.

In a follow-up to this early study, Wolff (1971) examined behavioral characteristics of a larger sample (100 children) of referred primary school age children and, in addition, compared these children to age, sex, and SES matched nonreferred children who attended the same school. Results indicated that behaviors primarily in the aggressive/antisocial category occurred *very rarely* in the control sample (less than 10 percent of the sample) and significantly discriminated between the referred and nonreferred groups. Behaviors in this category included lying, stealing, fighting, destructiveness, enuresis and encopresis. Behaviors *rarely* occurring in the control sample (11–25 percent of the cases) that significantly discriminated between referred and nonreferred children included, being highly strung, disobedience, poor attention, over-activity, sad moods, poor peer relationships, difficulty falling asleep, and school refusal. Behaviors which occurred frequently in the control group (greater than 25 percent of the control sample), but nevertheless discriminated between referred and control children were anxiety, temper tantrums, poor sibling relationships, specific fears, and restless sleep. Interestingly, a number of problems failed to distinguish between the two groups of children. These included psychosomatic complaints, nightmares, nail biting, over-compliance, and bad dreams. Other findings in the Wolff studies included the sex differences in distribution of behavioral complaints. Clinic and control boys were more likely to have disturbances of conduct than girls; girls were more likely to have anxiety and phobic disturbances than boys.

The results of these early studies conducted by Wolff have been largely replicated by those conducted in other countries on the incidence and prevalence of child behavior disorders in clinic and nonclinic populations. The most common referral to a child mental health facility or child guidance clinic is a boy displaying some form of conduct disturbance, who can generally be described as "out of control" of his parents or the community. Younger boys are likely to display disordered behavior in the home, such as opposition to parental authority. Older boys (over eight years of age) often display disordered behavior and learning problems in the home and school, as well as community rule violations (e.g., stealing, truancy, etc.). Girls are seen less frequently than boys for evaluation and treatment and are more likely to display anxiety-related behavior patterns. As we shall see later, Wolff's early results are remarkably consistent with more recent factor analytic studies of psychopathology in children.

It is impossible to completely understand the problems of children referred to outpatient settings without considering the process of referral. Unlike the adult client who typically refers himself to an outpatient clinic for treatment, children and adolescents very seldom self-refer. Initial complaints usually come from parents, teachers or some other caregiver instead of the child. However, as we have already seen, the presenting problems displayed by many children brought by their parents for treatment are also displayed by normal (nonreferred) children. Likewise, a small proportion of children who have never been referred for treatment display behavioral disturbances comparable to those of referred deviant children (Wolff, 1971). Clearly, there is not a one-to-one relationship between behavioral or emotional disturbance in children and referral to a clinic for evaluation. Thus, in order to gain a complete understanding of why the child has been brought for evaluation, the assessment process must also focus on the child's social context, particularly those adults who are closest to the child and are worried about his behavior.

Rather than defining disordered behavior in children (and therefore referral for treatment) as a deviation from an absolute standard of normalcy, Ross (1974) has pointed to the interaction between the child's behavior and the tolerance of significant adults in his environment as one factor responsible for the perception of abnormality. For example, in the case of aggressive or oppositional behavior, parents may have a low tolerance for behavior that is highly disturbing to other family or community members (e.g., fighting with siblings, stealing) and quickly refer when these behaviors occur. On the other hand, anxiety or phobic reactions suffered by the child that do not directly impinge on others may be tolerated to a much greater extent by adults. In addition, young children often do not have the cognitive or linguistic facility to express their subjectively experienced distress, and parents may not recognize their child's difficulties. These differences in awareness and tolerance on the part of parents may partly account for the greater referral rate of conduct disorders than anxiety disorders to child guidance clinics, and for the relatively larger proportion of children in the "normal" population who suffer from anxiety-related symptoms.

Other authors have also pointed out that the reason for referral of children may lie in the parents or family in addition to/rather than the child himself (Rutter & Hersov, 1976), and several studies have recently lent empirical evidence to this hypothesis (Delfini, Bernal, & Rosen, 1976; Griest, Forehand, Wells, & McMahon, 1980; Lobitz & Johnson, 1975). Each of these studies compared clinic-referred, conduct disordered children to nonreferred normal children on numerous measures of child adjustment, including objective, independent behavioral observations in the home, and questionnaires assessing parental perception of child adjustment. Each study demonstrated empirically that some children's parents *perceived* them as deviant even though *behaviorally* they could not be differentiated from normal children. Methodological factors could partially account for this lack of convergence between behavioral and parent perception measures. Nevertheless, Lobitz and Johnson (1975) and Wells and Forehand (in press) have argued that these studies provide empirical demonstration that, in many cases, factors other than child behavior contribute to negative parental *perceptions* and subsequent referral.

Several studies have aimed at specifically identifying those variables which may be related to negative parental perceptions of child behavior and subsequent referral. In an early epidemiological survey of 500 children, Shepherd, Oppenheim, and Mitchell (1971) found that mothers of referred children were more likely to have experienced various emotional problems themselves, have less tolerance for stress, and less ability to cope with their children than mothers of nonreferred children. In another study of behavior problem children, Richman, Stevenson, and Graham (1975) found that, problem children differed significantly in terms of a higher rate of depression in their mothers, when compared to a matched normal control group.

Recent experimental studies corroborate these early epidemiological findings. In the first study of this series (Griest, Wells, & Forehand, 1979), several measures of independently assessed child behavior, maternal *perception* of child behavior, and maternal adjustment were obtained in 22 conduct disordered children and their families. Using multiple regression analyses, it was found that maternal depression was a better predictor of *perceptions* of the child than was the child's actual behavior. These findings were essentially replicated in a second, more complex study of referred and nonreferred children. It demonstrated that in the referred group, maternal perceptions of child adjustment were best predicted by an interaction of the child's behavior and the mother's emotional adjustment. Interestingly, the prediction equations for the referred and nonreferred groups were not the same; in the nonreferred (normal) group, maternal perception of child adjustment was best predicted by the child's actual behavior (Griest et al., 1980). These results suggest that in normal families there is a direct relationship between the child's behavior and the parent's perception of his behavior, whereas in conduct-disordered families parental perceptions of the child are likely to be influenced by the child's behavior as well as the parent's own emotional adjustment.

The final study in this series directly addressed the question of differences in normal, clinic-referred behaviorally deviant, and clinic-referred behaviorally nondeviant children and their families (Rickard, Forehand, Wells, Griest, & McMahon, 1980). In this study, a nonreferred (normal) sample of mothers and children was compared to two groups of clinic-referred children and their mothers. In one of the clinic groups, independent home observations of child behavior indicated that the children were significantly more behaviorally deviant than the normal group. In the second clinic-referred group, the children could not be differentiated from normal on *behavioral* measures. As might be anticipated from our discussions above, parents in both clinic referred groups *perceived* their children as maladjusted. However, parents of children in the clinic-referred, behaviorally nondeviant group were significantly more depressed than parents in the clinic-referred deviant group, as well as parents in the normal group. These results lend further evidence to the fact that it is equally important to assess parental emotional and behavioral adjustment (particularly depression), in addition to the child's reported problem whenever children are referred for treatment.

Turning to other extra-child factors that may influence parental perception and child referral, the quality of the parents' marital relationship has frequently been examined in epidemiological and correlational studies. For example, Richman, Stevenson, and Graham (1975) found that referred behavior problem children differed significantly from a matched normal control group in terms of the poorer quality of the parental marital relationship in the referred group. Johnson and Lobitz (1974) found significant negative correlations between marital satisfaction measured by the Locke-Wallace Marital Inventory and observed levels of child deviance. In addition, these authors found a significant correlation between marital dissatisfaction and the level of observed parental "negativeness" to the child. Experimental studies have generally confirmed the relationship between marital satisfaction and deviant child behavior (e.g., Oltmanns, Broderick, & O'Leary, 1977), although this relationship has not been consistently demonstrated in all samples (Wells, Forehand, & Griest, 1979).

The body of literature reviewed above has enhanced our knowledge about the complex reasons for referral and the problems displayed by children in families who present to outpatient settings for treatment. As we have seen, presence of behavioral or emotional deviations in children is seldom a sufficient or even a necessary condition for referral. It appears that referrals to child outpatient clinics may be comprised of three groups: (1) behaviorally and emotionally deviant children whose parents' perceptions are accurately based on their child's actual behavior, (2) children who are behaviorally or emotionally deviant but whose parents' perceptions also are influenced by their own maladjustment, and (3) relatively normal children whose parents' perceptions are inaccurate and are based on their own personal maladjustment, low tolerance for stress, or high standards of acceptability, rather than on their child's actual behavior. Support for existence of this latter group comes from a study which found that nine percent of children referred to a child guidance clinic received a "diagnosis" of normal adjustment (Bemporad, Pfeifer, & Bloom, 1970).

The implications of the data obtained in these studies for clinicians faced with behavioral assessment of children should be clear. The clinician must not assume that because the child was referred for treatment, he necessarily has a behavioral or emotional disturbance. Since perceptions of children are in many cases skewed by the parents own personal or marital distress, multiple sources of information should be tapped whenever possible (e.g., grandparents, other caregivers who live with the child) and agreement across informants assessed. Whenever possible, independent observations of the child should be made in the settings where the problem behaviors primarily occur. As we shall see later, this not only results in independent validation of the child's reported problems, but also provides important information about the events controlling the child's behavior. Finally, it is increasingly clear that behavioral assessment of children must include an evaluation of the parents' or caregivers' personal and marital adjustment since these factors appear to be directly related to the parents' perceptions of the child or to observed child deviance in many cases. In other cases, parents may bring the child to the clinic as an entrée into treatment for themselves. In either case, failure to assess all the variables contributing to perceptions of child deviance may result in failure to achieve clinically meaningful treatment effects in the short run, and/or generalization of therapeutic effects over time. We will now turn to an examination of literature identifying the dimensions of childhood psychopathology and the techniques of assessment for each of these areas.

CLASSIFICATION OF CHILDHOOD DISORDERS

In the early days of childhood behavior therapy there was little need for discussion of behavioral classification since most early studies involved intervention for single, isolated target behaviors with univariate treatment approaches. However, as behavior therapy has grown, so has the recognition that children's behavior problems do not always occur in isolation, but often as part of a complex or class. Moreover, a greater number of studies have appeared that investigate "functional covariations" among several behaviors that cluster together (Koegel, Firestone, Kramme, & Dunlap, 1974; Wahler, 1975; Wells, Forehand, Hickey, & Green, 1977). In addition, there has been a veritable explosion of research identifying effective behavior therapy strategies with children. As the number of therapeutic interventions has increased, the decision about which treatment to use for the presenting problem has become increasingly complicated (Ciminero & Drabman, 1977).

Thus, the need for an empirically-based classification system for children's disorders is becoming more and more apparent. Such a classification system could serve several purposes. First, it would identify the essential dimensions of childhood psychopathology and allow a statistical statement of a particular child's position along each dimension and his relationship to normal children on these dimensions. Second, it would stimulate research aimed at identifying differential etiologic and prognostic variables associated with different dimensions of child behavior. Third, it would stimulate research aimed at identifying the most efficacious treatments for different dimensions of child behavior. Finally, clearer identification of behavioral dimensions or "syndromes" would promote research on behavioral assessment strategies within each dimension. As knowledge within each of these areas accumulates, classification of a given child's presenting problems would provide the clinician with empirically-based information directly relevant to a clearer description of the child's problems, possible etiologic variables contributing to these problems, and selection of the most appropriate treatment strategy.

In spite of the obvious advantages of an empirically-based classification system behaviorally oriented clinicians have traditionally avoided diagnosis. As Ciminero and Drabman (1977) have pointed out, this may be due to the recognition that the disease model of abnormal behavior upon which most existing classification systems are based may be an inappropriate approach to the study of human behavior (O'Leary & Wilson, 1975; Stuart, 1970). In addition, there was an early recognition among empirical clinicians and researchers that the existing taxonomies of childhood disorders violate all the scientific criteria for an acceptable classification system (Quay, 1979; Zigler & Phillips, 1961). When one recalls that the existing childhood taxonomies (GAP, DSM) were created by committees of psychiatrists who established their respective categories through discussion, opinion polling, and votes, it is not surprising that these systems have no reliability or validity, and little clinical utility.

Unfortunately, in their zeal to point out the problems with existing systems, empirical clinicians developed a general avoidance of classification *per se*. However, there is increasing concern among empirical researchers and clinicians alike that we may have been too quick to "throw out the baby with the bath water," and more and more frequently we are seeing a call for research aimed at developing classification systems based on empirically derived categories of child behavior and high scientific standards (Achenbach, 1974; Ciminero & Drabman, 1977; Ross, 1974). As Achenbach (1974) has so succinctly stated, "The question is not *whether* to classify but *how* to classify." Once we overcome our conditioned avoidance of classification (as it now appears we are beginning to do) we will be free to conduct research studies aimed at empirically identifying clusters of behavioral covariation (which may be differentially associated with etiology, prognosis, outcome, and selection of the most appropriate treatment strategy). In addition, clearer identification of behavioral "syndromes" will stimulate more research on behavioral assessment strategies for each syndrome. We will now turn to a brief description of research that has attempted to empirically identify behavioral syndromes that could serve as a basis for classification of child psychopathology. Also considered will be the assessment strategies currently available within each major area.

In spite of the general avoidance among behaviorally oriented clinicians of diagnosis and classification, several studies were conducted in the 1960s and 1970s by empirical psychologists working in clinical and research settings which laid the foundation for this type of work. The general approach shared by these investigators was an attempt to identify the full range of behavior problems displayed by outpatient clinic-referred as well as nonclinic children, and to determine empirically what behaviors tend to occur together (i.e., covary). This essentially represents a dimensional as opposed to a categorical approach to classification of childhood psychopathology (Quay, 1979), which assumes that children vary along a finite number of behavioral dimensions. Each dimension is assumed to be relatively independent and to consist of a cluster of behaviors that tend to covary with one another, but not with behaviors from other dimensions. In this dimensional model, a "syndrome" is not viewed in the medical model sense of something the client *has*, but as a group of behaviors found to be statistically associated with one another. A clinic-referred child is not characterized best by a single diagnostic label which attempts to type him as an individual, but in terms of his position along each possible behavioral dimension as compared to children in the normal population.

Because of the complexity of examining the interrelationships among all the behavioral variables measured in these studies, sophisticated, multivariate, statistical methods have been used to aid in the search for independent dimensions of child behavior. The methodology that has been followed involves having parents, teachers, or therapists of a large number of clinic and/or nonclinic children fill out checklists sampling a wide range of behaviors displayed by children. These data are then entered into a factor analysis or cluster analysis. In a thorough and comprehensive review of this literature, Achenbach and Edelbrock (1978) have pointed out that despite great diversity across studies with respect to assessment instruments, type of population, and type of respondent, two broad-band behavioral dimensions have been reliably obtained across studies. These two broad-band dimensions usually represent the first principal component obtained in the factor analytic studies. Although different labels have been used by different authors, Achenbach (1966, 1978) has chosen the terms *externalizing* and *internalizing* to describe these two general dimensions. The *externalizing* dimension refers to a behavioral tendency toward acting out, aggression, and coercive behavior. The *internalizing* dimension subsumes behaviors such as anxiety, inhibition, shyness, immaturity, and social withdrawal.

In addition to the two general or broad-band behavioral dimensions, most studies also apply additional statistical manipulations that allow an examination of more specific or narrow-band factors in the data. Although more diversity across studies is obtained when data are analyzed for narrow-band factors, certain patterns emerge nevertheless. In Quay's (1979) recent review of studies examining narrow-band syndromes, he concluded that four major orthogonal factors account for the largest percentage of the variance. These four dimensions included: conduct disorders, socialized aggressive disorders, anxiety/withdrawal, and immaturity. A recent factor analytic study of 14,000 school children (Trites, 1980) indicated that the behaviors Quay (1979) subsumed under immaturity actually comprised two factors: hyperactivity and inattentive-withdrawn.

Besides identification of clusters of child psychopathology, Achenbach's (1966) study also examined the hierarchical relationships between the broad-band and narrow-band syndromes. As might be anticipated, the specific narrow-band factors of hyperactivity, conduct disorder, and socialized aggressive disorder appeared to be subtypes of the broad-band *externalizing* syndrome; the narrow-band factors of anxiety and withdrawal, depression, and somatic complaints appeared to be subtypes of the broad-band *internalizing* syndrome.

The factor and cluster analytic studies reviewed by Quay (1979) and Achebach and Edelbrock (1978) set the foundation for future research on behavioral classification of childhood disorders. Because these studies used empirical methodology to discover the interrelationships among observable behaviors, the reliability and validity of a classification system based on this research should be superior to systems based on the clinical approach. As this research advances, studies will undoubtedly be sampling wider ranges of displayed behavior by more diverse populations of children in multiple settings. In addition, efforts to remove sources of bias from studies of children's behavior may lead to factor and cluster analytic studies of data obtained from direct observations of child behavior by trained independent observers using reliable coding systems. Since direct observational procedures have been the hallmark of behavioral assessment, behaviorally oriented researchers may have a great deal to contribute to this important area of research in the future.

Aggressive Disorders (conduct disorder; socialized aggressive disorder)

The behavioral dimensions of "conduct disorder" and "socialized aggressive disorder" can both be generally described as behaviors that are "out of control" of the parents or community. Chief complaints of the parents of children with aggressive disorders who are brought to outpatient clinics for treatment most often include problems of aggression towards others (hitting, kicking, fighting), physical destructiveness, disobedience to adult authorities, lying, temper tantrums, high rate annoying behaviors (yelling, whining, threatening others), and to a lesser extent (and more often in older children), community rule violations such as stealing or fire setting (see Wells & Forehand, 1981).

Conduct and socialized aggressive disorders represent the dimensions of child psychopathology that have been subject to intensive behavioral assessment using independent observers trained in the use of complex coding systems in the environments of children referred for these problems (Delfini, Bernal, & Rosen, 1976; Forehand, King, Peed, & Yoder, 1975; Lobitz & Johnson, 1975; Patterson, 1976). These behavioral studies have demonstrated that aggressive children display significantly higher rates of "coercive behavior," such as negative commands, disapproval, noncompliance, negativism, physically negative acts, and yelling than normal children, thus confirming data obtained via parent report. In addition, parents of conduct disordered children have been found to display a significantly higher rate of threatening, angry or nagging commands, and criticisms than parents of normal children.

The validity of this behavioral pattern in families with aggressive children is evident since similar results have been obtained in four different laboratories using different coding systems, subjects, and operational definitions. Furthermore, the factor (conduct disorders), isolated in factor analytic studies of data obtained from behavioral checklists, is most frequently composed of items very similar to the behaviors found to differentiate conduct disordered from normal children. Items most frequently found to load on the conduct disorders factor across studies include: fighting, hitting, temper tantrums, disobedience, defiance, destructiveness of property, impertinance, and uncooperative, resistive, and inconsiderate behavior (Quay, 1979).

Conduct disorders and socialized aggressive disorders are discussed together since, superficially, these two behavioral dimensions are often comprised of similar behaviors. In addition, all factor analytic studies do not obtain a separate orthogonal "socialized aggressive" factor. However, those that do are usually studies including adjudicated juvenile delinquents in the sample or are conducted in large urban areas. In the studies in which two separate factors are obtained, items discriminating the two factors relate to group or gang delinquency. These behaviors (has "bad companions," steals in company with others, loyal to delinquent friends, truant, etc.) may be considered deviant by society at large, but may not be considered maladaptive or abnormal in the urban subculture where these children live (Quay, 1979). Evidence is accumulating that differentiating "conduct disorder" from "socialized aggressive disorder" may have important implications from a treatment outcome point of view. Moore, Chamberlain, and Mukai (1979) recently found, in a sample of children who had all initially been classified as "aggressive," that prognosis was much poorer for the subset of children who engaged in stealing outside of the home or as part of a group, as compared to children whose conduct disorders were displayed mainly in the home and school. This study by Moore et al. (1979) illustrates the importance of research to investigate the interaction between classification, treatment selection, and outcome in childhood psychopathology.

Hyperactivity; Inattentive—Passive

All of the clinically derived classification systems of childhood disorders have a diagnostic category labeled hyperactivity or hyperkinetic reaction, and many of the factor analytic studies obtain a separate orthogonal factor labeled hyperactivity. The cardinal features of this cluster of behavior problems include excessive activity level in situations requiring motor inhibition, short attention span, and impulsive behavior.

Although many parents of hyperkinetic children recognize that their child has been extremely active and inattentive from an early age, most hyperactive children are not referred for treatment until they enter school. Such an increase in referral rate at school age is due to the fact that hyperactivity is most clearly a problem in the classroom where the child may face his first real demands to attend and sit still. Because of the hyperactive child's difficulty with motor inhibition and attention, his teacher's most frequent complaints include behaviors such as constantly being out of seat, walking around the classroom without permission, excessive off-task behavior, frequent changing of activity, and restlessness and fidgetiness. The child's impulsivity is reflected in behaviors such as speaking out of turn, frequently getting into fights, or disturbing other children. In addition to these problems, about one-third of hyperactive children have a specific learning impairment, usually in reading or spelling, in spite of an overall average IQ (Safer & Allen, 1976). Also, a large percentage of hyperactive children display disturbances in conduct similar to those seen in aggressive children. About 75 percent of hyperactive children fight or have other disturbances of conduct, and about 38 percent of children who show such misconduct are hyperactive (Safer & Allen, 1976).

A recent attempt has been made to construct and validate an observational code for hyperactive children similar to that used in behavioral assessment studies of aggressive children, and to examine objectively defined and independently-observed behaviors differentiating hyperactive from normal children in the school setting (Abikoff, Gittleman-Klein, & Klein, 1977). Using this code, several behaviors and behavioral dyads were found to discriminate hyperactive from normal children in the school setting. These included interfering with others, off task, minor motor movements, gross motor movements, noncompliance, and out of seat behavior. Thus, data appeared to confirm that hyperactive children indeed display higher levels of behaviors most frequently cited by teachers than normal children.

As the reader may have noticed, hyperactivity and inattentive-passive behavioral dimensions are being discussed in the same section. At first glance the reason for this may be unclear, since hyperactivity seems to fit under the broad-band *externalizing* dimension, whereas inattentive-passive appears to fit under the broad-band *internalizing* dimension. However, it is increasingly clear that the underlying physiological mechanism of these two behavioral dimensions is disturbance in attention associated processes. The basic attentional disturbance in hyperactivity is also associated with disturbances in motor behavior, whereas in the inattentive-passive behavioral dimension, the basic attentional disturbance is not associated with disturbed motor behavior. The constructors of the childhood disorders section of the DSM-III were reflecting this thinking in creating two new categories to replace the old "hyperkinetic reaction of childhood" (DSM-II). These two DSM-III categories are called "attention deficit disorder with hyperactivity" and "attention deficit disorder without hyperactivity." They roughly correspond to the "hyperactivity" and "inattentive-passive" behavioral dimensions, respectively, which are identified in the factor analytic studies.

Because children who predominately display the inattentive-passive behavioral dimension disturb the environment to a much lesser extent than either aggressive or hyperactive children, they are a much less visible and less studied group. A perusal of the factor analytic studies indicates that behaviors most frequently associated with this dimension include short attention span, poor concentration, day-dreaming, staring into space, lack of interest, and lack of perseverance (Quay, 1979). Teachers complaining about these children usually describe an unobtrusive child who stares dreamily out of the window rather than working on his assignment. It has been suggested that these children also display a poorly developed behavioral repertoire of social, problem-solving, and/or coping skills (Quay, 1979).

Before leaving this section it must be noted that some researchers have expressed doubts about the existence of hyperactivity as a dimension independent of all other patterns, particularly conduct disorders (Lahey, Green, & Forehand, 1980; O'Leary & Johnson, 1979; Quay, 1979). Critics frequently cite the high correlation often found between the factors "hyperactivity" and "conduct disorders," and the fact that a behavioral item, hyperactivity, often clusters with the "conduct disorder" factor. Proponents of this view suggest that because the two factors are correlated, they are therefore reflecting the same behavioral dimension, rather than two orthogonal dimensions. However, it must be remembered that in the dimensional approach to classification, dimensions of behavior, not types of individuals, are being studied. Any given individual can vary along several behavioral dimensions. Thus, as we have seen, a high percentage (75 percent) of children who display a cluster of behaviors reflecting deficits in attentional processes and hyperactivity, also show disturbances of conduct (Safer & Allen, 1976). Other children with attentional difficulties do not. Conners and Blouin (1980), in a recent cluster analytic study of dimensions of childhood psychopathology, demonstrated empirically that the behavioral dimension (factor) hyperactivity appears in two distinctive clusters; one cluster also contains the conduct disorder behavioral dimension and the other does not. Thus, the correlation often found between hyperactivity and conduct disorders may reflect the high percentage of children who display both behavioral dimensions. To suggest that because two factors are correlated they are therefore the same seems a basic misinterpretation of results of the factor and cluster analytic studies.

Further evidence for the existence of two separate factors of hyperactivity and conduct disorders comes from factor analytic studies of children's behavior conducted in New Zealand (Werry et al., 1975), the midwestern United States (Sprague et al., 1974), and New York (Kupietz et al., 1972). Each of these studies obtained two separate orthogonal factors of hyperactivity and conduct disorders. A more recent factor analytic study of over 14,000 Canadian school children, the largest sample ever studied, also obtained two orthogonal factors of hyperactivity (accounting for 35.9 percent of the variance) and conduct disorder (accounting for 10.5 percent of the variance) (Trites, 1980). It would appear that evidence is mounting for the existence of separate conduct and hyperactivity dimensions in childhood psychopathology. Nevertheless, the issues involved in this question are very complex and will undoubtedly continue to be a focus of debate and research. The reader is referred to Lahey et al. (1980) and Shaffer and Greenhill (1979) for a presentation of issues involved in this controversy.

Anxiety and Withdrawal

The major behavioral dimension in the broad-band internalizing category can be labeled "anxious-passive" or "anxiety-withdrawn." Although children displaying problems relating to anxiety are less frequently seen in outpatient clinics than those with conduct disorders, these problems occur more frequently than conduct disorders (but less frequently than hyperactivity) in school population studies. Thus, as we have seen in an earlier section, although many children experience problems of anxiety and withdrawal, they tend not to be referred as readily as conduct disordered children.

The behaviors characteristic of the anxious child require more inference on the part of adults who observe them. On behavioral checklists, items endorsed in this category include fearful, tense, shy, bashful, withdrawn, friendless, and hypersensitive among others (Quay, 1979). Although all children display fears throughout the course of normal development, anxious children may display more intense or more long-lasting phobic reactions. For example, I recently interviewed the parents of a 6-year-old boy who two years earlier had become extremely frightened watching the Cookie Monster on Sesame Street and had not been able to watch the television program alone since that time. Teachers often describe these children as easily hurt or upset by others, easily moved to tears, and reticent at involvement in activities with other children (social avoidance). Interestingly, anxious children may also display

motor restlessness, "nervous" fidgetiness, difficulty concentrating on
school work, and poor achievement, and may consequently bear a superficial resemblance to hyperactive children. However, in the case of
the anxious child, these behaviors are the result of high levels of tension
and autonomic arousal, rather than the more fundamental disturbances
of motility and attention found in hyperactive children. This superficial
similarity makes it mandatory to differentiate the anxious from the hyperactive child in the initial assessment, since treatment will be radically
different for the two types of disorders.

BEHAVIORAL ASSESSMENT METHODS

Having described the major dimensions of childhood psychopathology
likely to be seen in outpatient settings, we can now turn our attention
to methods of behavioral assessment that can be employed in evaluating
children who display one or more of these dimensions. The general
methods to be described include direct observational procedures, behavior problem checklists, interviewing, and physiological measurement. Whenever possible, specific instruments or measurement tools
designed to assess each of the dimensions of pathology we have identified will be presented.

Behavioral Interviews

It is fitting that the interview should be the first method of behavioral
assessment discussed here. The traditional clinical interview is one of
the two most extensively used methods for gathering information in
child and adult clinical settings. In spite of an emphasis on objective
assessment, the interview may be the most frequently used instrument
in behavioral assessment as well (Haynes & Jensen, 1979). Recent surveys of practicing behavior therapists have indicated that the interview
is heavily relied upon as an assessment device in applied clinical settings
due to practical and administrative problems accompanying other forms
of behavioral assessment (i.e., naturalistic observation) (Swan & Mc-
Donald, 1978; Wade & Hartmann, 1979).

In view of the extent to which reliance is placed on the interview
in clinical settings, it is surprising to consider the relative paucity of
research on the utility and psychometric properties of this method of
assessment. This may be partly due to the rejection of verbal report
measures by early behaviorists as being subject to myriad sources of
bias and therefore invalid in accurately describing behavior and its functional components. Such attitudes appeared to have been substantiated
by reports from developmental psychologists on the inaccuracy of parental retrospective recall of child behavior (Chess, Thomas, & Birch,

1966; Yarrow, Campbell, & Burton, 1970). These studies showed that maternal perceptions and memories elicited in interviews were more a function of dominant cultural attitudes and theories of child rearing, and of social desirability (the need to appear normal) than of the child's actual developmental accomplishments (Evans & Nelson, 1977). On the other hand, it should be pointed out that in these early studies, results were based on responses of mothers in open ended interviews to questions about their child's behavior three to thirty years earlier! Such reliance on long-term memory is not usually required in behavioral interviews with children and parents, as such interviews are heavily focused on current target problems. This type of factual information was recalled with a greater degree of accuracy than personality or developmental assessments. Lapouse and Monk (1958) verified that behavioral items are recalled by mothers with much greater reliability than more loosely defined problems. These studies illustrate that lack of reliability and validity is not *necessarily* inherent in the interview. The relationship of topographic features of the interview to reliability and validity bears further investigation.

In spite of the slow start, there has been increasing interest recently in conceptualizing the interview as an assessment instrument and subjecting it to the same demands for adequate description, reliability, and validity as other assessment devices (Haynes, 1978; Haynes & Jensen, 1979; Linehan, 1977). This interest has come with the recognition that behavioral researchers and clinicians are using the interview for a variety of purposes. Before reviewing interviewing methods for children and parents, it would be worthwhile to review these purposes from the behavioral perspective (see also Chapter 3). The interview has been used most frequently for purposes of screening and diagnosis (Haynes & Jensen, 1979). Indeed, this may be another reason why behaviorists have had little interest in the interview as an assessment method until recently. However, with the revival of interest in empirical classification of childhood disorders (Quay, 1979), the interview may become increasingly important as a method for assigning clients to behavioral dimensions. As pointed out earlier, research is beginning to occur identifying the most appropriate methods of treatment for dimensions of child pathology; it can be anticipated that in the future behavioral classification activities will have increasing importance for treatment selection, outcome, and prognosis. As such, the interview may assume a new importance in behavioral assessment activity.

A second purpose of the behavioral interview is to gain information relevant to the identification and functional analysis of target behaviors (see Ciminero, 1977). This has direct implications for treatment selection, since in clinical behavior therapy the environmental, physiological, and cognitive events that elicit and maintain target behaviors are presumed to vary from individual to individual. Such events must be taken into account in designing any treatment plan. Along with direct observation (by self or others), the interview is the only method for soliciting information on the cognitive and environmental maintaining factors of behavior.

Finally, the behavioral interview can be used as one measure of outcome in intervention programs. Until recently, interview data have been discounted as a measure of treatment outcome by behaviorists, since self-report measures often do not change in concordance with behavioral measures (Forehand, Griest, & Wells, 1979). From a strict methodological point of view, it may be appropriate to place greater emphasis on objective behavioral measures of improvement since a variety of extraneous factors may influence *perceptions* of behavior change. However, from a clinical point of view, it seems absurd not to ask the child and his parents whether they think his problems have improved, even if the behavioral data indicate that they have. This is tantamount to saying to the child ''I know you've improved—the fact that you don't think you have is irrelevant.'' In the final analysis, if the client does not believe he has improved, the therapy has been a failure from his point of view. The lack of concordance between behavior change and the child or parents' perceptions of that change may be one of the factors contributing to failure in achieving generalization of clinically meaningful effects in some treatment programs. If parents and children do not perceive the change, they stop using the strategy they learned when the therapist withdraws. The child and parents' reports gathered in the interview should be considered equally important as behavioral and physiological measures when assessing treatment outcome in clinical settings.

With increasing recognition of the potential utility of the interview, several standardized interviews for children and parents have been recently developed in research settings. Some of these interviews have been designed to elicit more severe forms of child psychopathology most frequently seen in inpatient settings (Kiddie-SADS, Kovacs Interview Schedule for Children), and they will, therefore, not be discussed here. However, Herjanic and her colleagues have been working for the past several years on a set of child and parent structured interviews designed to elicit information relevant to DSM-III diagnostic categories. In these interviews, the child is administered a set of structured questions regarding his/her current behavioral and emotional status, and school and social adjustment. The child's responses are recorded as the interview proceeds. A second structured interview is independently administered to the child's parents and consists of questions similar to those on the child interview. Using these interviews, Herjanic and Campbell (1977) demonstrated that psychiatric clinic-referred children were clearly distinguished from a matched-normal pediatric control group on a number of their interview responses. Evidence for the validity of these findings on interview data comes from the similarity of these results to studies using behavioral checklists as the source of data: disturbances of conduct more clearly distinguished between psychiatric and normal pediatric clinic children than neurotic and somatic symptoms, which were the poorest discriminators. In another study, Herjanic, Herjanic, Brown, and Wheatt (1975) found an 80 percent average agreement between children and mothers on the structured interviews. Higher agreement was found on questions relating to factual information. Other evidence for the reliability and validity of child and parent interviews has been provided by Rutter and Graham (1968) and Graham and Rutter (1968).

Structured interviews of the type discussed above have descriptive and diagnostic utility. However, as with behavior checklists, interviews that are aimed solely at deriving a ''diagnosis'' do not elicit additional information important in behavioral assessment (i.e., information relevant to the eliciting and maintaining variables of behavior). To address this question, Wahler and Cormier (1970) have described an ecological interview for use in child outpatient settings. Recognizing that deviant children display problem behaviors in a variety of settings, this type of interview elicits target behaviors in each of several settings (i.e., home, community, and school), as well as information relevant to controlling antecedent and consequent events. Although the ecological interview is particularly suited to child behavior therapy, Wahler and Cormier (1970) unfortunately present no data on the reliability and validity of this type of interview.

As described by Wahler and Cormier, as well as other behavior therapists, behavioral interviews should include questions designed to elicit information such as: What is the problem(s) of most concern at the present time? In what situation(s) does the child display the problem(s)? In each situation, what happens just before the child's behavior problem(s) occurs? What does the parent, teacher, or caregiver do in response to the problem behavior? How does the child react to that intervention? What methods have the parents tried in the past for dealing with the target problems? Other information relevant to the topographic features of the target problems in each situation should also be obtained (i.e., frequency, duration and intensity). As pointed out in other sections of this chapter, it is important to assess information relative to the parents' perceptions, and personal and marital adjustment in child outpatient settings.

As attested by the brevity of this review, research on child and parent interviews is only beginning to occur. The revival of interest in study of the functions, utility, and psychometric properties of the interview is welcomed. Only through research in this area can advantages and limitations of the interview be clearly understood. Once the limitations are clearly identified, we may begin to see development of techniques aimed at improving the reliability and validity of the interview, since this approach to assessment will most assuredly continue to be used in outpatient clinical settings.

Behavior Problem Checklists

Behavior problem checklists and rating scales represent a major tactic in child behavioral assessment. Along with interviewing, checklists and rating scales traditionally have been the primary means of gathering information in the *initial* assessment phase in outpatient settings. As seen in an earlier section of this chapter, checklists and rating scales also have been the primary tools used by researchers investigating the dimensional approach to classification of childhood disorders. As typically employed, the child's caregivers are asked to assign a rating to one or more traits or behaviors displayed by their child. The child then receives a score on one or more dimensions based on the items endorsed by the person filling out the checklist.

Behavior checklists and rating scales vary with respect to the number of items included and the range of behaviors or traits sampled. Checklists may contain as few as five or as many as two hundred items. Shorter checklists often are designed to sample one particular dimension of child pathology (e.g., hyperactivity), whereas longer checklists often sample the full range of childhood disorders. Examples of short unidimensional checklists are the Abbreviated Teacher Questionnaire (Conners, 1973) and the Rating Scales for Hyperkinesis (Davids, 1971), both commonly used as screening devices and/or to provide repeated measurement of hyperkinesis in clinical and research settings. Examples of multidimensional behavior checklists include the Conners Parent and Teacher Questionnaires (Conners, 1969, 1970) with eight (Conners & Blouin, 1980) and six factors respectively, and the Behavior Problem Checklist (Quay, 1977; Quay & Peterson, 1967) which measures four primary dimensions.

Checklists also vary with respect to the informant who fills out the rating scales and the specificity and objectivity of the items included in the scale. Scales are designed to be filled out by clinicians, parents, and teachers, but rarely the child himself. They may range from a single rating of global improvement (e.g., the 7-point Clinical Global Impressions Scale, ECDEU, 1976), to items requiring inference or judgment on the part of the informant (e.g., "feels inadequate," "has too few friends''), to very specific behavioral items (e.g., ''smokes cigarettes,'' ''wets bed''). Generally speaking, increasing the number and specificity of items included in checklists will increase reliability; however, many of the empirically derived abbreviated rating scales have adequate reliability (Zentall & Barack, 1979).

The popularity of rating scales and behavioral checklists as assessment tools in child psychopathology can be attributed to several factors. They are economical and easy to administer and score in contrast to behavioral coding systems, which are expensive and require specialized training for administration and scoring. Furthermore, multidimensional checklists survey a wide range of behaviors, thus identifying problem areas that may be missed in an interview. Finally, many checklists have been found sensitive to treatment effects and can therefore serve as a measure for evaluating therapy outcome (Ciminero & Drabman, 1977). On the other hand, a number of problems and questions can be raised regarding the use of behavior checklists and scales. As we saw earlier, a variety of factors other than the child's actual behavior can influence the perceptions of caregivers about children. Thus, rating scales and checklists filled out by caregivers are subject to the situational and contextual biases and potential misperceptions of these individuals and may not accurately reflect the child's actual behavioral characteristics and tendencies. The effects of such bias and misperception show up in less than adequate reliability and validity. For example, Whalen and Henker (1976) have indicated that there is a poor correlation between rated and observed behaviors and have documented poor interrater reliability in many of the commonly used rating scales. With respect to validity, Ciminero and Drabman (1977) have correctly pointed out that while many studies have provided data on the discriminative validity of checklists, the most important demonstration may be in the area of predictive validity (i.e., the extent to which scores on checklists help predict response to various forms of treatment). Very few studies exist on the predictive validity of behavioral checklists. Finally, from a behavioral assessment point of view, checklists and rating scales provide no information relevant to a functional analysis of target behaviors (see Ciminero, 1977); while rating scales may aid in the descriptive identification of problem behaviors, information relevant to antecedent and consequent environmental, cognitive, or organismic variables that elicit and maintain target problems is not assessed. Thus, behavioral assessment should include, but not be restricted to, the use of behavioral checklists and rating scales. When these are used, the choice of a checklist should be based on research indicating adequate reliability, validity, and normative data. To this end, three of the more extensively researched multidimensional checklists will be briefly reviewed.

The Behavior Problem Checklist is perhaps the most extensively researched of the behavioral checklists and rating scales. Items for the BPCL were first derived in an examination of the referral problems of 427 cases at a child guidance clinic (Peterson, 1961). A factor analysis of the original checklist revealed two principal factors: "conduct disorder" and "personality disorder." The scale has since been adapted by Quay and Peterson (1967) and currently consists of 55 items. Depending on the population being studied, two additional factors also have been extracted using this checklist: "subcultural (socialized) delinquency" (Quay & Peterson, 1967) when delinquent children are studied, and "inadequacy-immaturity," when school classes containing emotionally disturbed children are studied (Quay, Morse, & Cutler, 1966). As we saw earlier, Quay's "inadequacy-immaturity" factor may actually comprise two factors: "inattentive-withdrawn" and "hyperactivity" (Trites, 1980).

Using the BPCL, Mack (1969) reported split-half reliabilities of .92 for conduct disorders, .81 for anxiety withdrawal, and .26 for immaturity. Interrater reliabilities of .77 for conduct disorders and .75 for anxiety-withdrawal have been reported for kindergarten children (Peterson, 1961). However, interrater reliability appears to decrease for older children (Quay & Quay, 1965). Quay (1979) has indicated that this may be due to the decreased contact junior high school teachers have with their pupils as compared to kindergarten teachers.

Other characteristics of the BPCL recommend its use in clinical settings. With respect to validity, data have been reported indicating the discriminant (McCarthy & Paraskevopoulos, 1969; Speer, 1971) and predictive validity (Proger, Mann, Green, Bayuk, & Burger, 1975) of the BPCL. Extensive normative data also have been collected (Speer, 1971; Touliatos & Lindholm, 1976; Werry & Quay, 1971). This checklist can be filled out by teachers or by parents. One disadvantage of the checklist is that it is focused on assessment of deviancy. No items assessing pro-social behavior are included in the checklist and, therefore, no factors reflecting appropriate behavior or adjustment emerge.

Another set of checklists was developed by Conners (1969, 1970) to measure outcome of drug and psychotherapy treatment on various dimensions of child psychopathology. These include the *Conners Parent Rating Scale* (CPRS) (Conners, 1970), the *Conners Teacher Rating Scale* (CTRS) (Conners, 1969), and the *Abbreviated Teacher Questionnaire* (ATQ) (Conners, 1973). The Conners questionnaires have been used extensively in treatment outcome (particularly pharmacological) research by scores of investigators. The CTRS was adopted by the NIMH Early Clinical Drug Evaluation Unit (ECDEU, Assessment

Manual, 1976), which encourages its use in any drug research with children funded by the NIMH.

The CPRS is a 93-item checklist of behaviors rated on a 4-point scale by parents. It has recently been reanalyzed (Conners & Blouin, 1980) to reveal eight primary factors: conduct disorder, fearful-anxious, restless-disorganized, learning problem—immature, psychosomatic, obsessional, antisocial, hyperactive-immature. The CTRS is a 39-item checklist of behaviors rated by the child's teachers. This checklist contains five primary factors: conduct disorder, passive-inattentive, anxiety, hyperactive, and social/cooperative. The factor structure of the CTRS has been replicated in several diverse populations of children (Werry, Sprague, & Cohen, 1975). The Abbreviated Teacher Questionnaire is a brief 10-item checklist consisting of those behaviors most frequently checked on the CTRS and the CPRS. Scores on this scale have been found to reflect positive changes in behavior occurring as a function of drug treatment (Conners & Werry, 1979; Sprague & Sleator, 1973) and behavior modification (O'Leary, Pelham, Rosenbaum, & Price, 1976; O'Leary & Pelham, 1978). Because of its brevity and sensitivity to treatment effects, this scale is often used when frequent reports from parents or teachers are needed during the course of a research study or clinical evaluation.

On the CTRS, test-retest factor reliabilities have ranged from .70 to .90 (Conners, 1973); no data on test-retest reliability for the CPRS are available, although these have been assumed similar to those for teachers. As might be expected, interrater reliabilities (mother vs. father; parent vs. teacher) are somewhat lower, but significant (Goyette, Conners, & Ulrich, 1978). The scales have been shown to discriminate normal and deviant children (Conners, 1970; Kupietz, Bialer, & Winsberg, 1972). Extensive normative data for the CTRS and the CPRS are available (Conners, 1970; Goyette, Conners, & Ulrich, 1978; Werry et al., 1975; Werry & Hawthorne, 1976). In addition, the CTRS contains one factor measuring appropriate prosocial behavior.

The final behavior checklist to be discussed in detail has recently been developed by Achenbach (Achenbach, 1978; Achenbach & Edelbrock, 1979). Known as the *Child Behavior Checklist,* this scale records a diverse array of behavior problems as well as adaptive competencies of children aged 4 to 16 as reported by their parents. Scores derived from the checklist are entered onto the Child Behavior Profile, which allows a quick visual assessment of the relationship of the target child's scores to norms for his sex and age. Separate additions of the profile have been standardized for each sex at ages 4 to 5, 6 to 11, and 12 to 16. The scales are based on factor analyses within sex and age groups of outpatient clinic-referred children. Norms also are available for most of the age and sex groups.

Because Achenbach chose to factor analyze the Behavior Problem Checklist within age/sex categories, the factors vary slightly across the different age and sex groupings. Each profile contains approximately eight behavioral problem factors and three social competency scales. As an example of the behavior problem scales, factor analyses of the data for boys age 6 to 11 revealed the following scales: schizoid, depressed, uncommunicative obessive-compulsive, somatic complaints, social withdrawal, hyperactive, aggressive, and delinquent. The three social competency scales were entitled *activities, social,* and *school success.* Achenbach has reported test-retest reliabilities of .87 to .89 and interrater reliabilities of .67 to .74. The checklist has been shown to discriminate clinic and non-clinic samples on all behavior problem and social competency scales.

The three behavior problem checklists described above are among those subjected to the most extensive research and are most frequently used. The Conners and the Achenbach scales have more factors than the Quay-Peterson scale and thus may be useful when a more fine-grained assessment is needed. Achenbach has taken a developmental approach in attempting to describe child psychopathology, and his scale can be recommended when comparisons within or across age categories are of particular interest. The profile approach of Achenbach also allows for easy inspection of how the child's problems and competencies cluster and how the child compares with normal children of similar age and sex. In addition to these advantages, Achenbach has provided computerized and hand scored versions of his profiles. For these reasons, it is predicted that the Achenbach scale will be used with increasing frequency in child outpatient settings in the future.

Several other checklists are available for assessment of children (see Humphreys & Ciminero, 1979; Spivak & Swift, 1973). These include the Louisville Behavior Checklist (Miller, 1967 a,b) and the Pittsburgh Adjustment Survey Scale (Ross, Lacey, & Parton, 1965) which measure both behavior problems and prosocial adjustment, and the Devereux Elementary School Behavior Rating Scale (Spivak & Swift, 1966) which measures behaviors specifically related to classroom performance. The Quay, Conners, and Achenbach checklists are discussed because they are extensively researched and include factors describing the major types of child psychopathology we have been discussing in this chapter.

As employed in behavioral assessment, behavioral checklists and rating scales can be used as screening devices to quickly identify potential target behaviors and evaluate a particular child's position along the various dimensions of childhood psychopathology as compared to children in the normal population. As such, they may be useful in narrowing the range of treatment approaches and predicting treatment outcome. Factor scores on checklists also can be obtained pre- and posttreatment as a measure of treatment effectiveness. Checklists should never be used as the only method of assessment, since they do not provide a functional analysis of target behaviors and are subject to interpretive and contextual biases of the informants who filled them out.

Direct Observational Assessment

Direct observation has come to be the basis of behavioral assessment. In this approach, target behaviors of the individual child are operationally defined, observed by a trained observer, and recorded according to a specified set of rules (Doke, 1976; Roberts & Forehand, 1978). Observations may occur in an analogue setting, such as a clinic or laboratory, or in the environment where the behaviors have been identified as the problem (home, school, etc.). As we have seen repeatedly throughout this chapter, child behavior is often influenced by the actions of significant adults in the child's environment. Consequently, many behavioral coding systems also provide for recording of the behavior of these significant adults (e.g., parents, teachers). As such, coding systems provide the only objective assessment of the functional relationship between the target child's behavior and antecedent and consequent variables that may be maintaining their occurrence.

Early behaviorists turned to direct observational procedures due to their disenchantment with more traditional methods of psychological assessment, which primarily measured attitudes, constructs, or personality traits rather than actual behavior (Patterson, 1977). It was thought that data derived from direct observations would provide a more reliable and valid representation of problem behavior as it occurs naturally, since such systems rely on operational definitions of target behaviors observed by highly trained independent observers who are presumed to be free of the interpretive biases of parents and teachers. Nevertheless, direct observation procedures have problems of their own, including the time and expense involved in obtaining and training observers, and in guarding against other processes that can negatively affect reliability and validity (e.g., observer bias, observer reactivity, observer drift, and instrument decay). Furthermore, although behavioral coding systems have a great deal of face validity, they are not exempt by virtue of being ''behavioral'' from research demonstrating their content, concurrent, and predictive validity, and such research is only beginning to occur (Ciminero & Drabman, 1977). As each of these issues has been discussed in detailed reviews by Ciminero and Drabman (1977), Johnson and Bolstad (1973), Kent and Foster (1977), as well as Chapter 4 of this volume, they will not be dwelled on here. Suffice it to say that despite the problems involved in direct observational procedures, they will remain an important component of the behavioral assessment armamentarium and should be employed in clinical practice as much as possible.

Conduct Disorders. There are four well recognized coding systems for measurement of conduct disorders in use today. The first and most widely employed and researched system was developed by Patterson and his colleagues at the Oregon Research Institute, when they first began designing assessment and treatment studies of families with aggressive children. Since then a manual describing the construction and use of this coding system has been published (Reid, 1978). The coding system is designed primarily for use in home settings, although it can and has been extended to laboratory analogue (Lobitz & Johnson, 1975) and school settings (Patterson, Cobb & Ray, 1973) as well. As described most recently by Reid (1978), this system has a total of 29 behavioral codes divided into first order codes (22 behaviors) and second order codes (7 behaviors). First order code behaviors are presumed to have greater relation to a theory of social learning (see Patterson, 1976) and greater relevance for evaluating outcome of treatment than second order codes. Using this coding system, sequences of behavior between the target child and other family members can be recorded.

The Patterson coding system and adaptations of it have been used extensively by Patterson's group as well as by other researchers. Jones, Reid, and Patterson (1975) and Patterson, Reid, and Maerov (1978) have presented analyses indicating adequate test-retest and interobserver reliability, and several studies support the discriminant and construct validity of this coding system (Patterson, 1974, 1977; Reid & Hendricks, 1973).

Patterson's coding system was designed to assess family interactions and is therefore used primarily in home settings. Two other coding systems have been developed for use in home, school, and laboratory settings, thus allowing for analyses of child behavior across multiple settings. Wahler, House, and Stambaugh (1976) developed a system containing 19 child behavioral codes subsumed under five classes of behavior (compliance/opposition, autistic, play, work, and social behaviors). In addition, five categories of aversive and nonaversive adult stimulus events are available, allowing for recording of adult/child interactional chains. While Wahler et al. (1976) have presented reliability data indicating high interobserver agreement for this coding system, their single case design approach has not encouraged validity studies of this coding system.

The second system designed for use across settings was adapted by Forehand and his colleagues from the original work of C. Hanf. This system is more restricted in its utility since it was designed primarily to measure one particular class of child behavior: compliance and noncompliance. Other forms of conduct disordered behavior are subsumed by a catch-all category: "other deviant behavior." In addition to these child behaviors, six antecedent and consequent parent behaviors are coded. Thus, the Forehand coding system also allows for recording of interactive sequences of parent/child behavior. As mentioned earlier, this coding system is most appropriate when noncompliance or oppositional behavior is the primary target child behavior of interest, and has been used in home, laboratory (Peed, Roberts, & Forehand, 1977; Wells, Griest, & Forehand, 1980) and school settings (Forehand, Sturgis, Aguar, McMahon, Green, Wells, & Breiner, 1979).

Forehand, Peed, Roberts, McMahon, Griest, and Humphreys (1979) developed a manual for training observers in use of the Forehand coding system, although the manual has not been published for widespread dissemination as have the Wahler and Patterson systems. Using this coding system, Forehand and Peed (1979) have reported an average interobserver agreement of 75 percent across a series of studies. The system has been found to have adequate discriminant validity (Forehand et al., 1975) and is sensitive to changes in behavior occurring as a function of treatment (Peed, Roberts, & Forehand, 1977; Wells et al., 1980).

A final coding system which should be mentioned was developed by O'Leary and his colleagues (O'Leary et al., 1971). This coding system was initially designed for research on conduct disordered children in classroom settings; thus, it primarily samples behaviors which may be defined as inappropriate due to the demands of that particular setting (e.g., out-of-seat behavior, off-task behavior, inappropriate or unpermitted vocalizations). Kent and O'Leary (1976) have reported average reliability coefficients for the observational codes ranging from .44 to 1.00. Limited validity data are available (see Kent & Foster, 1977). However, because this is the only coding system designed specifically for assessment of conduct disordered children in school settings, further investigations of its utility are warranted.

Hyperactivity. As mentioned in an earlier section of this chapter, there has been a recent attempt to construct and validate an observational code specifically for use with hyperactive children in classroom settings (Abikoff et al., 1977). This observational code is a modified version of an earlier one developed by Tonick, Friehling, and Warhit (1973) for studying behavior problem children and includes items considered to be more specific to the hyperactive behavioral dimension. The system samples 13 disruptive or inappropriate behaviors and has a 14th category for absence of inappropriate behavior. Using this system, Abikoff et al. (1977) found that several behaviors and behavioral dyads typically associated clinically with the hyperactive behavioral dimension, in fact discriminated hyperactive from normal children in the school setting. In addition, adequate reliability, calculated as Phi coefficients, was reported for most of the behavioral codes. Therefore, this coding system would appear to represent an important step toward an acceptable behavioral code specifically for measurement of the hyperactive dimension. On the other hand, because hyperactive children share many behaviors in common with conduct-disordered children, any code purporting to measure hyperactivity must be shown to discriminate between these two groups, at least on certain critical items. In addition, methodological problems with the Abikoff et al. (1977) study preclude our ability to accept unqualifiedly this coding system and its results as a measure of hyperactivity (Haynes & Kerns, 1979). Nevertheless, this study represents the best attempt to date toward developing and validating a coding system for measuring hyperactivity.

Two additional coding systems designed to evaluate hyperactive children in classroom settings should be mentioned here. O'Leary, Pelham, Rosenbaum, and Price (1976) employed a relatively simple three code system for measuring the effects of behavior therapy for hyperkinetic children. The three behaviors included in this system are locomotion, fidgeting, and not attending to tasks. O'Leary et al. (1976) reported that scores based on the *average* of these three behaviors significantly discriminated between hyperactive and normal children in a classroom setting. No data on reliability of this simple coding system were presented, other than the statement that observers were trained to a reliability criterion of .85 before beginning their observations. A second study by O'Leary and his colleagues (Jacob, O'Leary, & Rosenblad, 1978) employed a coding system called the Hyperactive Behavior Code which included six behaviors clinically deemed to reflect the low frustration tolerance, motor restlessness, and short attention span of hyperactive children. Results of this study indicated that a composite hyperactivity score based on all six behaviors significantly discriminated between hyperactive and normal children in a formal classroom setting. High correlations between composite hyperactivity scores and teacher ratings on the Conners Teacher Rating Scale (CTRS) provided further evidence for the validity of this code. Pooled reliability for the coding system determined by Cohen's Kappa was .86, with adequate reliabilities reported for most of the individual behavioral codes. Although neither of the O'Leary codes has been submitted to extensive evaluation at the present time, preliminary data are encouraging. In addition, the fact that both of these codes are relatively simple indicates that further investigations of their use as assessment devices by clinicians are warranted. The Abikoff system contains many more code categories and is relatively more difficult to use in terms of the time and effort required to train and maintain observers to a high level of reliability. It may therefore prove more useful in research settings.

Anxiety and Withdrawal. Less work has occurred on development of coding systems designed to measure the *internalizing* behavioral dimensions than for conduct disorders and hyperactivity. This may be due to the fact that anxious, withdrawn children are less frequently seen in child outpatient settings than are aggressive or hyperactive ones. In addition, researchers and clinicians have relied on self-report and physiological measures of anxiety to a greater extent, since overt manifestations of anxiety are less discriminable to the observer than are disorders of conduct. Nevertheless, at least one observational coding system has been developed to measure behaviors presumed to be associated with anxiety. The Observer Rating Scale of Anxiety (ORSA) was developed by Melamed and Siegel (1975) and consists of 29 categories of verbal and skeletal motor behavior. Behaviors such as "trembling hands," "stutters," "talks about fears" are scored by a trained observer using a time-sampling procedure. Using this coding system, Melamed and Siegel (1975) reported average interrater agreements of 94 percent. Although the ORSA has discriminated between treated and untreated children (Melamed & Siegel, 1975), no other validity data are available. This scale was developed for use in hospital settings. However, with minor adaptations it could be used in other settings as well.

Assessment of behaviors associated with social withdrawal in children has received increasing attention in the literature. Many withdrawn children suffer primarily from interpersonal anxiety which inhibits performance of social behavior in appropriate situations. In these cases anxiety becomes the primary focus of assessment and treatment. However, it is increasingly apparent that in addition to a primary problem of *anxiety,* other withdrawn children display behavioral deficiencies in age-appropriate social skills (Combs & Slaby, 1977). Basically, these children do not interact with others because they are afraid, but because they do not know how. Of course, once a child experiences social failure and rejection from his peers, reactive anxiety to social situations may develop. In these cases, however, anxiety is viewed as secondary to the primary social skill deficit.

Concurrent with the interest in treatment approaches aimed at remediating social deficiencies in children, assessment technologies for measurement of social skills are being developed. Two forms of observational assessment have been used in this regard: naturalistic observation and role-play tests.

Naturalistic Observational Codes. One of the first and most frequently used observational codes was developed by Charlesworth and Hartup (1967), and has been adapted by other researchers (e.g., Gottman, Gonzo, & Rasmussen, 1975). In this coding system, three global categories of social behavior are coded, each subsuming several discrete behaviors. The three global categories are "negative interaction" (noncompliance, interference, threats, etc.), "positive interaction" (attention, approval, affection, etc.) as well. In spite of its widespread use, this coding system has several limitations, including the fact that the categories were defined clinically rather than empirically, the grouping of several potentially unrelated behaviors under one global category, and the failure to specify situational or antecedent factors (Michelson, Foster, & Ritchey, in press).

A second observational coding system, developed by Strain and his colleagues for use in classroom settings, allows for a slightly more fine-grained analysis of social behaviors and antecedent stimulus events (Strain, Shores, & Kerr, 1976). In this system, two general classes of interactive behavior (motor-gestural and vocal-verbal) along with their positive and negative topographic features are scored. In addition, two categories of teacher behavior (prompting and reinforcement) are coded. In contrast to the original Charlesworth and Hartrup (1967) system, the Strain system distinguishes between child initiations and responses and codes the person with whom the child interacted. Using this system, Strain and his colleagues have reported high interobserver reliability for all code categories. The coding system is sensitive to changes in social behavior induced by treatment procedures that are aimed at improving social skills and interaction of isolative children and their peers.

Although standard coding systems such as those described above may be useful for large scale studies of children's social behavior, Strain, Shores, and Timm (1977) have argued that in clinical settings, systems for assessment of social behavior need to be specifically tailored to the needs of the individual child. Examples of individually derived coding systems of this sort have been developed by Allen et al. (1964), Kirby and Toler (1970), and Beck, Forehand, Wells, and Quante (1978).

Role-Play Tests. Observational coding systems are useful for assessing relatively high frequency responses or global response categories in the natural environment. However, many aspects of social skills may be of low frequency or occur only in response to specific stimulus events, requiring hours of observation time to collect a representative sample of behavior (Michelson et al., in press). As pointed out earlier, naturalistic observations can also be expensive and time consuming. To address these problems, role-play tests have been developed for assessment of specific components of social skills and have become an integral aspect of analogue measurement. Since Rehm and Martson (1968) developed the original role-play test, this technology has been developed and refined for use in adult populations (Eisler, Hersen, Miller, & Blanchard, 1975; Wells, Hersen, Bellack, & Himmelhoch, 1979), and has recently been extended to child populations (Bornstein, Bellack, & Hersen, 1977, 1980). Specifically, two role-play tests, the Behavioral Assertiveness Test for Children (BAT-C) (Bornstein, et al., 1977, 1980) and the Behavioral Assertiveness Test for Boys (BAT-B) (Reardon, Hersen, Bellack, & Foley, 1979) have been developed. The BAT-C has been used for assessment of withdrawn school children as well as aggressive 8 to 12-year-old inpatient boys and girls. The BAT-B has been used to assess social skills in high and low assertive third to eighth grade boys. Each role-play test (BAT-C and BAT-B) consists of a series of scenes designed to elicit positive and negative assertive responses. Children are presented with a description of each scene and respond to an opening statement delivered by a role model prompt. Role-played scenes are videotaped and rated retrospectively for a variety of verbal and nonverbal measures of social skill (see Eisler, Miller, & Hersen, 1973; Eisler et al., 1975; Reardon et al., 1979; Wells et al., 1979). Bornstein et al. (1977, 1980) and Reardon et al. (1979) have reported adequate reliabilities for behaviors scored in role-play tests. Furthermore, Reardon et al. (1979) demonstrated that low assertive and high assertive boys differed significantly on six of the behavioral response components scored in role-play tests. On the other hand, recent studies (e.g., Bellack, Hersen, & Lamparski, 1979) have called into question the validity of these tests in measuring social skills in adults. These studies indicate that further investigations of the validity of role-play tests for measuring social skill in children are needed. Nevertheless, in clinical settings where naturalistic observation may be difficult or impossible to obtain, role-play tests may represent the only means of assessing molecular components of social behavior in children. To date, most studies of social skills, in children which use role-play tests have focused on inpatient or school populations. Empirical clinicians working in outpatient clinical settings should be encouraged to investigate the psychometric properties and generalizability of results of role-play tests with children presenting with difficulties of anxiety, social withdrawal, and aggressiveness, and to examine methods for enhancing validity of these assessment techniques.

Observation by Significant Others. An alternative to the use of observers trained in complex coding systems is to have the child's caregivers observe and record certain types of child behaviors in the home or school. This procedure has most frequently been employed with conduct disordered children whose behaviors are readily discernible by adults. Parental recording of child behavior can provide the therapist with valuable assessment information on baseline and treatment phase rates of target behaviors; in addition, it is often used for therapeutic purposes. Patterson, Reid, Jones, and Conger (1975) taught parents to pinpoint, track, and observe two prosocial and two deviant behaviors for the first three weeks of treatment in order to adjust parents' misperceptions of the child's positive and negative behaviors. Wells et al. (1980) incorporated parental monitoring of their own and their child's behaviors as part of a program aimed at enhancing temporal generalization.

As described in most studies employing this methodology (Forehand et al., 1979; Patterson et al., 1975; Wahler et al., 1976), parents identify the two or three target behaviors of most concern to them in the initial interview. They are then asked to observe and record the frequency of these behaviors for several days. In addition, Wahler et al. (1976) and Wells et al. (1980) had parents record classes of events antecedent and consequent to the child's targeted behaviors, thus providing information relevant to a functional analysis of the target behavior. Parental recording may occur continually throughout the baseline and treatment process, or probes may occur at select points before, during, or after treatment.

Though significant-other behavioral recording might appear especially promising for use in clinical settings, the reliability and validity of this methodology must be demonstrated, and research undertaken. Kubany and Sloggett (1973) demonstrated that teacher records during spot checks within 20-minute observational sessions produced a behavioral profile similar to that of more fine-grained time sampling procedures. However,

Wells et al. (1980) reported only very moderate correlations between independent observer ratings and parental recorded behavior (range: .47 to .64). Although a high degree of accuracy in parental monitoring may not be necessary to obtain a beneficial *treatment* effect (Broden, Hall, & Mitts, 1971), accuracy of recording is necessary if significant-other collected data is to be used for *assessment* purposes. Empirical clinicians may need to develop techniques for training significant-others to be accurate observers if parent and teacher-collected data is to be used as a measure of treatment effectiveness in clinical settings.

Psychophysiological Assessment

Physiological assessment of adult disorders currently enjoys some prominence in the clinical research literature. While some generalization of these technologies to childhood disorders is beginning to occur, physiological assessment of children in behavior therapy has received considerably less attention. Thus, there have been no systematic research programs aimed at developing and evaluating psychophysiological assessment approaches for various dimensions of childhood psychopathology as has occurred for behavioral coding systems and behavior problem checklists. However, at least three reasons can be offered for encouraging research of this type. First, considerable evidence exists in the adult literature that correlations between overt behavior, verbal report, and physiological measures are frequently moderate to low (see Hersen, 1973), and we have reason to believe that similar imperfect relationships are seen in children (Johnson & Melamed, 1979). These data indicate that physiological changes in treatment cannot be inferred from behavioral data but must be measured directly. Second, many childhood disorders involve a primary psychophysiological component (e.g., asthma, headaches, chronic rumination in infants), and measurement of the physiological response system involved may have direct treatment implications. Third, evidence is accumulating that certain disorders of conduct or performance (e.g., attention deficit disorders, learning disabilities) may have underlying pathophysiologic etiologies. Until recently, treatment was most frequently aimed at the behavioral manifestation of these disorders. However, there is some evidence to suggest that direct modification of the pathophysiological response system may represent one important approach to treatment. For example, Conners (1971) and Preston and Guthrie (1974) found a striking attenuation of visual cortical-evoked response in the left parietal area of the brain in subjects with severe reading disability (dyslexia). Based on research indicating that evoked responses are larger in the presence of abundant alpha rhythms, Conners (1979) subsequently reported direct modification of visual evoked response in a severely dyslexic child using biofeedback for increases in production of alpha. Studies such as this suggest that biofeedback combined with direct educational training may be more effective than educational training alone in treatment of these performance deficits. In a study of EEG biofeedback for training of visual attention in children, Mulholland (1974) concluded that it is time to incorporate hardware into the classroom.

For the reasons outlined above, it is predicted that we will see an exponential increase in use of physiological assessment with children. Examples of this type of assessment in child behavior therapy are already scattered throughout the literature. Van Hasselt, Hersen, Bellack, Rosenblum, and Lamparski (1979) recently illustrated tripartite assessment (measurement of motoric, cognitive, and physiological response systems) of the effects of relaxation training and systematic desensitization in an 11-year-old multiphobic child. Physiological measures of heart rate and finger pulse volume were monitored before and throughout treatment. As might be predicted from the adult literature, physiological measures did not change in direct concordance with motoric avoidance and cognitive measures. The implications for this lack of correlation are discussed by the authors.

In the area of hyperactivity and learning disabilities, several studies have recently appeared. Braud, Lupin, and Braud (1975) used EMG assessment and feedback in treatment of a 6½-year-old hyperactive boy. Biofeedback induced reductions of muscular activity were associated with improvements in behavior, test scores, achievement tests, self-esteem, and a reduction in psychosomatic symptomatology. In a more recent study which may serve as a model of behavioral assessment of hyperactivity in psychiatric settings, Wells, Conners, Imber, and Delamater (in press) demonstrated that behavioral and physiological measures can be used to evaluate differential clinical response to two stimulant medications. In this study, physiological measures of electromyographic activity and peripheral vasoconstriction were correlated with behavioral measures of improvement in response to one stimulant medication, but not another. Collection of physiologic measures enhanced the validity of the judgment of clinical improvement in this study, and is illustrative of the way they can be added to the behavioral assessment routine in clinical settings.

These studies illustrate the use of physiological assessment for dimensions of childhood disorder most often seen in outpatient settings. As with behavioral coding systems and rating scales, research is needed to establish the reliability and validity of physiological assessment methods in children. Although the expense of such methodology has been prohibitive for all but specialized research settings in the past, recent technological advances are resulting in reductions in the cost of equipment necessary for physiological assessment. Furthermore, operation of physiological recording equipment has been simplified so that one no longer has to be an electronics wizard in order to obtain this type of measurement. On the other hand, basic knowledge of physiological response systems is necessary for the intelligent use of physiological measurement. Nevertheless, physiological measurement appears to be a very promising addition to the behavioral assessment armamentarium with children. We will undoubtedly be seeing more frequent use of this type of assessment with children in the future.

BEHAVIORAL ASSESSMENT OF A SAMPLE CASE

In the introduction to this chapter, five different functions of behavioral assessment with children in outpatient settings were discussed: 1) to identify the child's position along the behavioral dimensions which describe childhood psychopathology and distinguish him from normal children, 2) to identify specific target problems and their functional components within each dimension, 3) to provide information relevant to selection of the most appropriate treatment procedures, 4) to evaluate progress during treatment, and 5) to evaluate the ultimate outcome of treatment. Throughout the remainder of this chapter, various methods included in the behavioral assessor's armamentarium have been outlined. It should be clear at this point that different methods (i.e., observations, checklists, interviews, etc.) may be best suited for different functions of assessment. For example, interviews and behavioral problem checklists are most useful for initial description and classification of the child's behavioral tendencies and specific target problems. Such description should aid in selection of the most appropriate available treatment procedures. Physiological measurement and direct observational procedures (by trained observers or the child's caregivers) are most useful for establishing pretreatment rates or levels of target problems, and monitoring progress throughout treatment. Finally, all four classes of behavioral assessment (interviews, observations, physiologic measures, behavioral problem checklists) can be repeated at treatment termination and at follow-up to provide information relevant to program evaluation. In addition to the straightforward assessment techniques themselves, the importance of assessing the process by which the child was referred for evaluation, who is concerned about his problems, the psychological status of the child's caregivers, and the need for multiple sources of information whenever possible have also been emphasized.

The following case example may illustrate the process of behavioral assessment in child outpatient settings. Obviously, certain limitations impinge upon any description of this type. For example, the importance of a complete developmental and social history is definitely acknowledged within the behavioral assessment paradigm, since such information can have implications for treatment. Likewise, intellectual, neuropsychological, or achievement testing may be indicated for some outpatient cases. These areas of assessment will not be discussed here since each deserves a separate chapter; the reader should not view this deletion as minimizing the importance of these assessment areas. Behavioral assessment is compatible with each of these areas of assessment, and behavior therapy is often influenced by information gathered not only in the behavioral assessment, but in developmental, social, or intellectual assessments as well.

Case Example

Doug is a 7-year, 4-month-old Caucasian male child brought to the Outpatient Clinic by his mother, Mrs. S. When the initial appointment was scheduled, Mrs. S. had been asked to come one hour early so that she could register and fill out some questionnaires. Doug did not come for the first appointment. Upon arrival, Mrs. S. was given the Conners Parents Rating Scale, a developmental history questionnaire, and a form asking for description of the family structure. Mrs. S. was asked to fill out these questionnaires in the waiting room. Afterwards, she was escorted to the therapist's office. In response to questions regarding the reasons for bringing Doug to the clinic, Mrs. S. talked about the problem of most concern to her—namely, Doug's increasing defiance and belligerence and his obdurate refusal to do anything she asked him to do, whether his everyday chores or a simple favor like helping with the dishes. He became angry whenever she asked anything of him and was beginning to "back talk" and "sass," her. In addition, Doug was beginning to bully his little brother by taking toys from him and making him cry. When asked why she was bringing Doug to the clinic at this particular time, Mrs. S. stated that Doug was getting too big to handle. In addition, she had received a note from the second grade teacher that Doug was not obeying classroom rules and had gotten into two fights at the playground. At that point the therapist explained that she would like to ask Mrs. S. some very specific questions about Doug so that she could have a clear understanding of all the problems he was displaying. The Herjanic parent interview was then administered, requiring about one hour to complete. At the end of the interview it was explained to Mrs. S. that there would be a few more sessions of gathering information, followed by a feedback session about the nature of Doug's problems and the proposed treatment plan. Written consent was obtained from her to contact Doug's school principal and teacher. Mrs. S. was given two more copies of the Conners Parent Questionnaire to take home—one for her husband to fill out and one for Doug's grandmother, who lived with the family. It was stressed that these questionnaires should be filled out independently by Mr. S. and the grandmother.

In the second session the therapist interviewed Doug. When asked why he thought he and his Mom were coming to the clinic he said that he wasn't sure but thought it might be because he had taken some money from his Mom's purse to buy candy and she had gotten real mad at him. (Mrs. S. had not mentioned this in her initial list of problems, but it had come out in the Herjanic interview.) Other than that, Doug said that he and his Mom got along just fine. After the interview with Doug, the therapist explained that he would like to observe Mrs. S. and Doug from behind a one-way mirror. Mrs. S. was asked to play with Doug for 15 minutes. When she heard a knock on the window, she was to begin giving him some commands to play with certain toys or clean up the room. During this time, the therapist observed and coded the mother-child interaction. The Forehand coding system was chosen for use since Mrs. S.'s primary complaint was defiance and noncompliance. At the end of the session, Mrs. S. was given four index cards and asked to record the frequency of two behaviors on four consecutive days from the time Doug returned home from school till bedtime. The two behaviors were noncompliance and bullying. Mrs. S. was also asked to describe briefly how each incident was handled or not handled by her.

Before the next clinic interview, the therapist scored each of the Conners questionnaires obtained from Doug's primary caregivers (Mr. and Mrs. S. and grandmother), as well as the Conners Teacher Questionnaire which had been obtained from the teacher. On the questionnaire filled out by Mrs. S., Doug fell two standard deviations from the mean for a normal sample on Conduct Problems I and II (Goyette, Conners, & Ulrich, 1978). His score on the Impulsive-Hyperactive factor was also elevated, but was not as deviant as the Conduct Disorders factors. Doug's scores on the questionnaire filled out by his grandmother were very similar to his mother's scores. However, scores from the father's questionnaire were very dissimilar. None of the factor scores fell outside one standard deviation.

Although the Conners Teacher Questionnaire has somewhat different items and factor structure than the Parent Questionnaire, results were largely predicted by the parent questionnaire responses of Mrs. S. and grandmother. Doug scored close to the second standard deviation on the Conduct Disorders factor and between the first and second standard deviation on the Hyperactivity factor.

The Herjanic parent interview and the clinic observational data were also scored by the therapist. On the Herjanic interview, items primarily endorsed by Mrs. S. had to do with home behavior problems of the type already mentioned. In addition, several items were endorsed having to do with peer relationships. Most of these items referred to picking fights or bullying peers. Data from the behavioral coding system indicated that Doug was clearly in control of his mother in the more structured command situation. Mrs. S.'s request to "play with the dog" or "put the toy away now" were often completely ignored by Doug or met with verbal refusals to comply. On most occasions, Mrs. S. repeated her request as many as seven or eight times before Doug grudgingly complied; on other occasions, Mrs. S. withdrew her request. Very little positive interaction, scored as attending or rewarding, occurred between Doug and Mrs. S. during either the structured or the unstructured situation.

During the next clinic session, Mrs. S. brought in the index cards containing records of the two behaviors of most concern to her and her responses to these behaviors. The cards indicated a range of 15 to 22 instances of noncompliance across the four days and one to three instances of bullying his sibling. The record of her behavior in response to Doug indicated that Mrs. S. withdrew the request on many occasions. Three episodes were recorded as angry repetition of commands, followed ultimately by a spanking for continued noncompliance. Review of the index cards led to further discussion of other methods Mrs. S. had tried for managing Doug's behavior in the past, as well as other settings in which his behavior was problematic (i.e., visiting friends, shopping, in a restaurant). In addition, the discrepancy between Mr. and Mrs. S.'s questionnaire data was brought up. Mrs. S. became tearful while explaining that her husband, a long-distance truck driver, was frequently away from home and did not see the frequency or severity of the behavioral problems that she observed on a daily basis. Furthermore, he was critical of Mrs. S. for seeking treatment for Doug, stating that there was nothing wrong wth Doug that a good spanking every now and then would not cure. Indeed, Mrs. S. reported that Doug's behavior always improved when his father was home, as Doug "knew what would happen if he didn't mind Mr. S." However, as soon as his father left, Mom lost all control.

On the basis of this assessment it was clear that Doug was displaying a cluster of behaviors which could be classified primarily on the conduct disorders behavioral dimension. Because Doug's behavior was most

problematic in the home, it was decided to institute treatment in that
setting first. Treatment in this case consisted of 18 sessions of parent
training for Mrs. S., focused on improving her methods of managing
Doug's behavior in the home. Many of the discussions with Mrs. S.
were aimed at reversing some of her behaviors revealed in the assessment process (i.e., repeating commands, withdrawing commands) and
increasing positive interactions with her son. Every three weeks during
therapy, Mrs. S. recorded noncompliance and bullying on index cards
as she had during the pretreatment baseline phase. These data revealed
a gradual decrease to an acceptable level of noncompliance and bullying
at the end of 15 weeks. Although treatment was not introduced in the
school at first, the teacher was asked to monitor fighting in school. The
therapist called the teacher once a week to obtain information on the
frequency of fighting for the week. After 12 weeks of treatment with
Mrs. S., the teacher questionnaire was repeated, indicating only slight
improvement in Doug's position on the conduct disorders factor. In
addition, fighting continued to occur in school. Therefore, a home-based
daily report system was introduced for three of Doug's school behaviors:
following instructions, completing assignments, and not fighting with
other children. The teacher's daily report cards provided a record of
the frequency of these problems over the next six weeks, and indicated
elimination of fighting and improvement to an acceptable level of following instructions and completing assignments. At this point, the therapist began fading out contacts with Mrs. S. and Doug in the clinic
to every two weeks and then once a month. Six months after the first
contact all assessment devices were readministered (i.e., parent questionnaires, teacher questionnaire, clinic observation, Herjanic interview,
parent recording in the home). Questionnaire data revealed that Doug's
position on the conduct disorder factors had decreased to within the
first standard deviation in both home and school settings. Fewer problems were reported by Mrs. S. on the Herjanic interview as compared
to pretreatment. Parent recorded data indicated slight increases in noncompliance as compared to the last week of recording during the treatment program. Mrs. S. was therefore encouraged to reinstitute her use
of procedures learned during treatment in order to prevent further relapse. Telephone contacts were made monthly for the next six months
to support Mrs. S.'s treatment gains and trouble-shoot minor problems
that arose.

This case represents a rather ideal example of a child with no significant learning or developmental problems and a parent who was
motivated not only to administer treatment, but to participate in the
assessment process before and throughout treatment. Such cooperation
may not be elicited in every case. However, whenever possible, the

process illustrated above should be implemented in outpatient clinical settings.

As can be seen, use of behavioral checklists and structured interviews allowed for classification of Doug's position along the conduct disorders behavioral dimension and a statistical statement of his relation to non-clinic children before treatment and at a follow-up. Initial classification had direct implications for treatment, since research has demonstrated that behavior therapy approaches, particularly parent training, are the treatment of choice for disorders of conduct. One-to-one psychotherapy has no demonstrated effectiveness for this target population (Rutter & Hersov, 1976). Once the general problem area had been identified, the interview, home recorded data, and clinic observations provided information directly relevant to the specific strategies employed during treatment. In the interview, Mrs. S. identified the two problems of most concern to her. Clinic observational data and home-collected data confirmed that defiant behavior indeed was a problem. It provided information about Mrs. S.'s behavior vis à vis Doug that was incorporated directly into the parent training program. Reassessment of Doug's behavior in school with the teacher questionnaire and telephone interviews provided the therapist with the feedback that, although Doug's home behavior was improving, problems were still occurring in school. This feedback prompted the therapist to institute treatment in the school setting, while continuation of parent and teacher behavior monitoring allowed for repeated assessment of progress. Repeat of the entire assessment package after treatment termination provided pre-post data relevant to program evaluation (i.e., Doug's pre-post questionnaire scores, as well as parent collected and clinic observational data were entered into the child guidance center's computer). Similar data collected from all cases seen in the clinic for the year would provide administrative information relevant to evaluation of the center's effectiveness in providing services to children and families.

SUMMARY

In the introduction to this chapter, several critical questions related to behavioral assessment of children in outpatient settings were outlined. In the remainder of the chapter, the empirical literature relevant to each of these questions was selectively reviewed, and the current state of knowledge was presented. It is clear that we have come a long way toward answering many of these critical questions. Advances in the area of behavioral classification have enhanced our knowledge of the "behavioral syndromes" displayed by outpatient child populations. Recent research addressing the factors influencing parental perceptions of children and the referral process has alerted us to the importance of assessing particular parent and family variables. As the number of behavioral assessment techniques and behavior therapy procedures increases, there is greater awareness of the need for research directly relating assessment to selection of the most appropriate treatment strategy, understanding of etiologic variables, and prediction of outcome.

It is clear, however, that many of the theoretical as well as practical problems in behavioral assessment of children have not been adequately addressed. One important area that has too long been ignored is the area of normal child development. Behaviorists have typically displayed very little appreciation of normal variations in behavioral and emotional responding that reliably occur at different ages in children. Such knowledge is imperative, since it can appreciably influence the behavioral assessment and therapy process. For example, because of the normal increase in anxiety and specific fears that occurs in three to four-year-old children (O'Leary & Wilson, 1975), it is much more likely that encopresis in the younger child is related to phobic avoidance of the toileting situation (e.g., fears of the flushing noise, fears of being swept away) than in the eight or nine-year-old encopretic who is more likely to have conquered these fears. While older children can certainly retain phobic avoidance patterns, it is more likely that motivational or skills deficits are the salient maintaining factors. Obviously, an understanding of relevant behavioral or emotional variations in children at different ages can influence the assessment and therapy process, and research is needed to define empirically these normal developmental variations in children using instruments and techniques described in this chapter.

Other critical questions have to do with the relationship of assessment to treatment. At the present time, insufficient data exist defining the decision rules relating information gathered in the assessment process to treatment selection and planning. While behavioral classification and assessment may narrow the range of acceptable available treatment alternatives, the final choice of a particular technique, and how, where, and by whom it is carried out, largely depends on clinical judgment and impressions (Ciminero & Drabman, 1977). While the critical decisions about treatment must ultimately rest with the therapist and client, it is clear that the therapist's treatment recommendations should be based on objective criteria derived from empirical research investigating the interaction of assessment and treatment outcome for various techniques and populations of children. Such research is only beginning to occur. Clearly, behavioral assessment of children in outpatient settings will be a rich area of research in the future.

REFERENCES

Abikoff, H., Gittleman-Klein, R., & Klein, D. F. Validation of a classroom observation code for hyperactive children. *Journal of Consulting and Clinical Psychology*, 1977, *45*, 772–783.

Achenbach, T. M. The classification of children's psychiatric symptoms: A factor-analytic study. *Psychological Monographs*, 1966, *80* (whole no. 615).

Achenbach, T. M. *Developmental psychopathology*. New York: Ronald Press, 1974.

Achenbach, T. M. The Child Behavior Profile: I. Boys aged 6 through 11. *Journal of Consulting and Clinical Psychology*, 1978, *46*, 478–488.

Achenbach, T. M., & Edelbrock, C. S. The classification of child psychopathology: A review and analysis of empirical efforts. *Psychological Bulletin*, 1978, *85*, 1275–1301.

Achenbach, T. M., & Edelbrock, C. S. The Child Behavior Profile: II. Boys aged 12-16 and girls aged 6-11 and 12-16. *Journal of Consulting and Clinical Psychology*, 1979, *47*, 223–233.

Allen, K. E., Hart, B., Buell, J. S., Harris, F. R., & Wolf, M. M. Effects of social reinforcement on isolate behavior of a nursery school child. *Child Development*, 1964, *35*, 511–518.

Beck, S., Forehand, R., Wells, K. C., & Quante, A. Social skills training with children: An examination of generalization from analogue to natural settings. Unpublished manuscript, University of Georgia, 1978.

Bellack, A. S., Hersen, M., & Lamparski, D. Role-play tests for assessing social skills: Are they valid? Are they useful? *Journal of Consulting and Clinical Psychology*, 1979, *47*, 335–342.

Bemporad, J. R., Pfeifer, C. M., & Bloom, W. Twelve months experience with the GAP classification of childhood disorders. *American Journal of Psychiatry*, 1970, *127*, 658–664.

Bornstein, M. R., Bellack, A. S., & Hersen, M. Social-skills training for unassertive children: A multiple-baseline analysis. *Journal of Applied Behavior Analysis*, 1977, *10*, 183–195.

Bornstein, M. R., Bellack, A. S., & Hersen, M. Social skills training for highly aggressive children: Treatment in an inpatient psychiatric setting. *Behavior Modification*, 1980, *4*, 173–186.

Braud, L. W., Lupin, M. N., & Braud, W. G. The use of electromyographic biofeedback in the control of hyperactivity. *Journal of Learning Disabilities*, 1975, *8*, 21–26.

Broden, M., Hall, R. V., & Mitts, B. The effect of self-recording on the classroom behavior of two eighth-grade students. *Journal of Applied Behavior Analysis*, 1971, *4*, 191–199.

Cerreto, M. C., & Tuma, J. M. Distribution of DSM-II diagnosis in a child psychiatric setting. *Journal of Abnormal Child Psychology*, 1977, *5*, 147–153.

Charlesworth, R., & Hartrup, W. W. Positive social reinforcement in the nursery school peer group. *Child Development*, 1967, *38*, 993–1003.

Chess, S., Thomas, A., & Birch, H. G. Distortions in developmental reporting made by parents of behaviorally disturbed children. *Journal of the American Academy of Child Psychiatry*, 1966, *5*, 226–231.

Ciminero, A. R. Behavioral assessment: An overview. In A. R. Ciminero, K. S. Calhoun, & H. E. Adams (Eds.), *Handbook of behavioral assessment*. New York: Wiley, 1977.

Ciminero, A. R., & Drabman, R. S. Current developments in the behavioral assessment of children. In B. B. Lahey & A. E. Kazdin (Eds.), *Advances in clinical child psychology*. Vol. I. New York: Plenum, 1977.

Combs, M. L., & Slaby, D. A. Social skills training with children. In B. B. Lahey & A. E. Kazdin (Eds.), *Advances in clinical child psychology*. Vol. 1. New York: Plenum, 1977.

Conners, C. K. A teacher rating scale for use in drug studies with children. *American Journal of Psychiatry*, 1969, *126*, 152–156.

Conners, C. K. Symptom patterns in hyperactive, neurotic and normal children. *Child Development*, 1970, *41*, 667–682.

Conners, C. K. Cortical visual evoked response in children with learning disorders. *Psychophysiology*, 1971, *7*, 418–428.

Conners, C. K. Psychological effects of stimulant drugs in children with minimal brain dysfunction. *Pediatrics*, 1972, *49*, 702–708.

Conners, C. K. Rating scales for use in drug studies with children. *Psychopharmacology Bulletin* (Special Issue, Pharmacotherapy of Children), 1973, 24–29.

Conners, C. K. Application of biofeedback to treatment of children. *Journal of the American Academy of Child Psychiatry*, 1979, *18*, 143–153.

Conners, C. K., & Blouin, A. Hyperkinetic syndrome and psychopathology in children. Paper presented at the Annual Meeting of the American Psychological Association, Montreal, Canada, 1980.

Conners, C. K., & Werry, J. S. Pharmacotherapy. In H. C. Quay & J. S. Werry (Eds.), *Psychopathological disorders of childhood*. (2nd ed.) New York: Wiley, 1979.

Davids, A. An objective instrument for assessing hyperkinesis in children. *Journal of Learning Disabilities*, 1971, *4*, 35–37.

Delfini, L. F., Bernal, M. E., & Rosen, P. M. Comparison of deviant and normal boys in home settings. In E. J. Mash, L. A. Hamerlynck, & L. C. Handy (Eds.), *Behavior modification and families*. New York: Brunner/Mazel, 1976.

Doke, L. A. Assessment of children's behavioral deficits. In M. Hersen & A. S. Bellack (Eds.), *Behavioral assessment: A practical handbook*. Elmsford, NY: Pergamon, 1976.

Dreger, R. M., Lewis, P. M., Rich, T. A., Miller, K. S., Reid, M. P., Overlake, D. C., Taffer, C., & Fleming, E. L. Behavioral classification project. *Journal of Consulting Psychology*, 1964, *28*, 1–13.

ECDEU assessment manual for psychopharmacology. U.S. Department of HEW, ADAMHA, 1976.

Eisler, R. M., Hersen, M., Miller, P. M., & Blanchard, E. B. Situational determinants of assertive behaviors. *Journal of Consulting and Clinical Psychology*, 1975, *43*, 330–340.

Eisler, R. M., Miller, P. M., & Hersen, M. Components of assertive behavior. *Journal of Clinical Psychology*, 1973, *29*, 295–299.

Evans, I. M., & Nelson, R. O. Assessment of child behavior problems. In A. R. Ciminero, K. S. Calhoun, & H. E. Adams (Eds.), *Handbook of behavioral assessment*. New York: Wiley, 1977.

Forehand, R., Griest, D. L., & Wells, K. C. Parent behavioral training: An analysis of the relationship among multiple outcome measures. *Journal of Abnormal Child Psychology,* 1979, *7,* 229–242.

Forehand, R., King, H. E., Peed, S., & Yoder, P. Mother-child interactions. Comparison of a non-compliant clinic group and a non-clinic group. *Behaviour Research and Therapy,* 1975, *13,* 79–84.

Forehand, R., & Peed, S. Training parents to modify the noncompliant behavior of their children. In A. J. Finch & P. C. Kendall (Eds.), *Clinical treatment and research in child psychopathology.* New York: Spectrum, 1979.

Forehand, R., Peed, S., Roberts, M., McMahon, R., Griest, D. L., & Humphreys, L. Coding manual for scoring mother-child interaction. (3rd ed.) Unpublished manuscript, University of Georgia, 1979.

Forehand, R., Sturgis, E. T., McMahon, R. J., Aguar, D., Green, K., Wells, K. C., & Breiner, J. Parent behavioral training to modify child noncompliance. *Behavior Modification,* 1979, *3,* 3–25.

Forehand, R., Wells, K. C., & Griest, D. L. An examination of the social validity of a parent training program. *Behavior Therapy,* 1980, *11,* 488–502.

Gottman, J., Gonzo, J., & Rasmussen, B. Social interaction, social competence, and friendship in children. *Child Development,* 1975, *46,* 709–718.

Goyette, C. H., Conners, C. K., & Ulrich, R. F. Normative data on revised Conners parent and teacher rating scales. *Journal of Abnormal Child Psychology,* 1978, *6,* 221–236.

Graham, P., & Rutter, M. The reliability and validity of the psychiatric assessment of the child. II. Interview with the parent. *British Journal of Psychiatry,* 1968, *114,* 581–592.

Griest, D. L., Wells, K. C., & Forehand, R. An examination of predictors of maternal perceptions of maladjustment in clinic-referred children. *Journal of Abnormal Psychology,* 1979, *88,* 277–281.

Griest, D. L., Forehand, R., Wells, K. C., & McMahon, R. J. An examination of differences between nonclinic and behavior problem clinic-referred children and their mothers. *Journal of Abnormal Psychology,* 1980, *89,* 497–500.

Harris, S. L., DSM-III—Its implications for children. *Child Behavior Therapy,* 1979, *1,* 37–46.

Haynes, S. N. *Principles of behavioral assessment.* New York: Gardner Press, 1978.

Haynes, S. N., & Kerns, R. D. Validation of a behavioral observation system. *Journal of Consulting and Clinical Psychology,* 1979, *47,* 397–400.

Haynes, S. N., & Jensen, B. J. The interview as a behavioral assessment instrument. *Behavioral Assessment,* 1979, *1,* 97–106.

Herjanic, B., & Campbell, W. Differentiating psychiatrically disturbed children on the basis of a structured interview. *Journal of Abnormal Child Psychology,* 1977, *5,* 127–133.

Herjanic, B., Herjanic, M., Brown, F., & Wheatt, T. Are children reliable reporters? *Journal of Abnormal Child Psychology,* 1975, *3,* 41–48.

Hersen, M. Self-assessment of fear. *Behavior Therapy,* 1973, *4,* 241–257.

Hobbs, N. *The futures of children: Categories, labels, and their consequences.* San Francisco: Jossey-Bass, 1975.

Humphreys, L. E., & Ciminero, A. R. Parent report measures of child behavior: A review, *Journal of Clinical Child Psychology,* 1979, 56–63.

Jacob, R. G., O'Leary, K. D., & Rosenblad, C. Formal and informal classroom settings: Effects on hyperactivity. *Journal of Abnormal Child Psychology,* 1978, *6,* 47–59.

Johnson, S. B., & Melamed, B. G. The assessment and treatment of children's fears. In B. B. Lahey & A. E. Kazdin (Eds.), *Advances in clinical child psychology.* Vol. 2. New York: Plenum, 1979.

Johnson, S. M., & Bolstad, O. D. Methodological issues in naturalistic observation: Some problems and solutions for field research. In L. A. Hamerlynck, L. C. Handy, & E. J. Mash (Eds.), *Behavior change methodology, concepts, and practice.* Champaign, Illinois: Research Press, 1973.

Johnson, S. M., & Lobitz, G. K. The personal and marital adjustment of parents as related to observed child deviance and parenting behaviors. *Journal of Abnormal Child Psychology* 1974, *2,* 192–207.

Jones, R. R., Reid, J. B., & Patterson, G. R. Naturalistic observations in clinical assessment. In P. McReynolds (Ed.), *Advances in psychological assessment.* Vol. 3. San Francisco: Jossey-Bass, 1975.

Kent, R. N., & Foster, S. L. Direct observational procedures: Methodological issues in naturalistic settings. In A. R. Ciminero, K. S. Calhoun, & H. E. Adams (Eds.), *Handbook of behavioral assessment.* New York: Wiley, 1977.

Kent, R. N., & O'Leary, K. D. A controlled evaluation of behavior modification with conduct problem children. *Journal of Consulting and Clinical Psychology,* 1976, *44,* 586–596.

Kirby, F. D., & Toler, H. C. Modification of preschool isolate behavior: A case study. *Journal of Applied Behavior Analysis,* 1970, *3,* 309–314.

Koegel, R. L., Firestone, P. B., Kramme, K. W., & Dunlap, G. Increasing spontaneous play by suppressing self-stimulation in autistic children. *Journal of Applied Behavior Analysis,* 1974, *7,* 521–528.

Kubany, E. S., & Sloggett, B. B. A coding procedure for teachers. *Journal of Applied Behavior Analysis,* 1973, *6,* 339–344.

Kupietz, S., Bialer, I., & Winsberg, B. A behavior rating scale for assessing improvement in behaviorally deviant children: A preliminary investigation. *American Journal of Psychiatry,* 1972, *128,* 1432–1436.

Lahey, B. B., Green, K. D., & Forehand, R. On the independence of ratings of hyperactivity, conduct problems, and attention deficits in children: A multiple regression analysis. *Journal of Consulting and Clinical Psychology,* 1980, *48,* 566–574.

Lapouse, R., & Monk, M. A. An epidemiologic study of behavior characteristics in children. *American Journal of Public Health,* 1958, *48,* 170–179.

Linehan, M. Issues in behavioral interviewing. In J. D. Cone & R. P. Hawkins (Eds.), *Behavioral assessment.* New York: Brunner/Mazel, 1977.

Lobitz, G. K., & Johnson, S. M. Normal versus deviant children: A multimethod comparison. *Journal of Abnormal Child Psychology,* 1975, *3,* 353–374.

Mack, J. L. Behavior ratings of recidivist and nonrecidivist delinquent males. *Psychological Reports,* 1969, *25,* 260.

McCarthy, J. M., & Paraskevopoulos, J. Behavior patterns of learning disabled, emotionally disturbed, and average children. *Exceptional Children,* 1969, *36,* 69–74.

Melamed, B., & Siegel, L. Reduction of anxiety in children facing hospitalization and surgery by use of filmed modeling. *Journal of Consulting and Clinical Psychology,* 1975, *43,* 511–521.

Michelson, L., Foster, S. L., & Ritchey, W. L. Social skills assessment of children. In B. B. Lahey & A. E. Kazdin (Eds.), *Advances in clinical child psychology.* New York: Plenum, in press.

Miller, L. C. Dimensions of psychopathology in middle childhood, *Psychological Reports,* 1967, *21,* 897–903. (a)

Miller, L. C. Louisville Behavior Checklist for males 6-12 years of age. *Psychological Reports,* 1967, *21,* 885–896. (b)

Moore, D. R., Chamberlain, P., & Mukai, L. H. Children at risk for delinquency: A follow-up comparison of aggressive children and children who steal. *Journal of Abnormal Child Psychology,* 1979, *7,* 345–355.

Mulholland, T. B. Training visual attention. *Academic Therapy,* 1974, *10,* 5–17.

O'Leary, K. D., & Johnson, S. B. Psychological assessment. In H. C. Quay & J. S. Werry (Eds.), *Psychopathological disorders of childhood*. (2nd ed.) New York: Wiley, 1979.

O'Leary, K. D., & Pelham, W. E. Behavior therapy and withdrawal of stimulant medication with hyperactive children. *Pediatrics*, 1978, *61*, 211–217.

O'Leary, K. D., Pelham, W. E., Rosenbaum, A., & Price, G. H. Behavioral treatment of hyperkinetic children. *Clinical Pediatrics*, 1976, *15*, 510–515.

O'Leary, K. D., Romanczyk, R. G., Kass, R. E., Dietz, A., & Santagrossi, D. Procedures for classroom observations of teachers and children. Unpublished manuscript, State University of New York at Stony Brook, 1971.

O'Leary, K. D., & Wilson, G. T. *Behavior therapy: Application and outcome*. Englewood Cliffs, New Jersey: Prentice Hall, 1975.

Oltmanns, T. F., Broderick, J. E., & O'Leary, K. D. Marital adjustment and the efficacy of behavior therapy with children. *Journal of Consulting and Clinical Psychology*, 1977, *45*, 724–729.

Patterson, G. R. Interventions for boys with conduct problems: Multiple settings, treatments, and criteria. *Journal of Consulting and Clinical Psychology*, 1974, *42*, 471–481.

Patterson, G. R. The aggressive child: Victim and architect of a coercive system. In E. J. Mash, L. A. Hamerlynck, & L. C. Handy (Eds.), *Behavior modification and families*. New York: Brunner/Mazel, 1976.

Patterson, G. R. Naturalistic observation in clinical assessment. *Journal of Abnormal Child Psychology*, 1977, *5*, 309–321.

Patterson, G. R., Cobb, J. A., & Ray, R. S. A social engineering technology for retraining the families of aggressive boys. In H. E. Adams & I. P. Unikel (Eds.), *Issues and trends in behavior therapy*. Springfield, Ill.: Charles C. Thomas, 1973.

Patterson, G. R., Reid, J. B., Jones, R. R., & Conger, R. E. *A social learning approach to family intervention. Volume 1: Families with aggressive children*. Eugene, Oregon: Castalia Press, 1975.

Patterson, G. R., Reid, J. B., & Maerov, S. L. Development of the family interaction coding system (FICS). In J. B. Reid (Ed.), *A social learning approach to family intervention. Volume 2: Observation in home settings*. Eugene, Oregon: Castalia Press, 1978.

Peed, S. F., Roberts, M., & Forehand, R. Evaluations of the effectiveness of a standardized parent training program in altering the interaction of mothers and their noncompliant children. *Behavior Modification*, 1977, *3*, 323–350.

Peterson, D. R. Behavioral problems of middle childhood. *Journal of Consulting Psychology*, 1961, *25*, 205–209.

Preston, M., & Guthrie, J. Visual evoked responses (VERs) in normal and disabled readers. *Psychophysiology*, 1974, *11*, 452–457.

Proger, B. B., Mann, L., Green, P. A., Bayuk, R. J., & Burger, R. M. Discriminators of clinically defined emotional maladjustment: Predictive validity of the Behavior Problem Checklist and the Devereux scales. *Journal of Abnormal Child Psychology*, 1975, *3*, 71–82.

Quay, H. C. Measuring dimensions of deviant behavior: The Behavior Problem Checklist. *Journal of Abnormal Child Psychology*, 1977, *5*, 277–289.

Quay, H. C. Classification. In H. C. Quay & J. S. Werry (Eds.), *Psychopathological disorders of childhood*. (2nd ed.) New York: Wiley, 1979.

Quay, H. C., Morse, W. C., & Cutler, R. L. Personality patterns of pupils in special classes for the emotionally disturbed. *Exceptional Children*, 1966, *32*, 297–301.

Quay, H. C., & Peterson, D. R. *Manual for the Behavior Problem Checklist*. Champaign: University of Illinois, Children's Research Center, 1967.

Quay, H. C., & Quay, L. C. Behavior problems in early adolescence. *Child Development*, 1965, *36*, 215–220.

Reardon, R. C., Hersen, M., Bellack, A. S., & Foley, J. M. Measuring social skill in grade school boys. *Journal of Behavioral Assessment*, 1979, *1*, 87–105.

Rehm, L. P., & Marston, A. R. Reduction of social anxiety through modification of self-reinforcement: An instigation therapy technique. *Journal of Consulting and Clinical Psychology*, 1968, *32*, 565–574.

Reid, J. B. *A social learning approach to family intervention. II. Observation in home settings*. Eugene, Oregon: Castalia, 1978.

Reid, J. B., & Hendricks, A. F. C. J. A preliminary analysis of the effectiveness of direct home intervention for treatment of predelinquent boys who steal. In L. A. Hamerlynck, L. C. Handy, & E. J. Mash (Eds.), *Behavior therapy: Methodology, concepts, and practice*. Champaign, Illinois: Research Press, 1973.

Richman, N., Stevenson, J., & Graham, P. Prevalence of behavior problems in 3-year-old children: An epidemiological study in a London borough. *Journal of Child Psychology and Psychiatry*, 1975, *16*, 272–287.

Rickard, K. M., Forehand, R., Wells, K. C., Griest, D. L., & McMahon, R. J. A comparison of mothers of clinic-referred deviant, clinic-referred nondeviant, and nonclinic children. Unpublished manuscript, University of Georgia, 1980.

Roberts, M. W., & Forehand, R. The assessment of maladaptive parent-child interaction by direct observation: An analysis of methods. *Journal of Abnormal Child Psychology*, 1978, *6*, 257–270.

Rosen, B. M., Bahn, A. K., & Kramer, M. Demographic and diagnostic characteristics of psychiatric clinic outpatients in the U.S.A., 1961. *American Journal of Orthopsychiatry*, 1964, *34*, 455–468.

Ross, A. O. *Psychological disorders of children: A behavioral approach to theory, research, and therapy*. New York: McGraw-Hill, 1974.

Ross, A. O., Lacey, H. M., & Parton, D. A. The development of a behavior checklist for boys. *Child Development*, 1965, *36*, 1013–1027.

Rutter, M., & Graham, P. The reliability and validity of the psychiatric assessment of the child. *British Journal of Psychiatry*, 1968, *114*, 563–579.

Rutter, M., & Hersov, L. *Child psychiatry: Modern approaches*. Philadelphia: Lippincott, 1976.

Safer, D. J., & Allen, R. P. *Hyperactive children: Diagnosis and management*. Baltimore: University Park Press, 1976.

Shaffer, D., & Greenhill, L. A crucial note on the predictive validity of "the hyperkinetic syndrome." *Journal of Child Psychology and Psychiatry*, 1979, *20*, 61–72.

Shepherd, M., Oppenheim, A. N., & Mitchell, S. *Childhood behaviour and mental health*. London: University of London Press, 1971.

Speer, D. C. The Behavior Problem Checklist (Peterson-Quay): Baseline data from parents of child guidance and nonclinic children. *Journal of Consulting and Clinical Psychology*, 1971, *36*, 221–228.

Spivak, J., & Swift, M. The Devereux Elementary School Behavior Rating Scales: A study of the nature and organization of achievement related disturbed classroom behavior. *Journal of Special Education*, 1966, *1*, 71–90.

Spivak, G., & Swift, M. The classroom behavior of children: A critical review of teacher-administered rating scales. *Journal of Special Education*, 1973, *7*, 55–89.

Sprague, R. L., Christensen, D. E., & Werry, J. S. Experimental psychology and stimulant drugs. In C. K. Conners (Ed.), *Clinical use of stimulant drugs in children*. The Hague: Exerpta Medica, 1974.

Sprague, R. L., & Sleator, E. K. Effects of psychopharmacological agents on learning disorders. *Pediatric Clinics of North America*, 1973, *20*, 719–735.

Strain, P. S., Shores, R. E., & Kerr, M. M. An experimental analysis of "spillover" effects on the social interaction of behaviorally handicapped preschool children. *Journal of Applied Behavior Analysis*, 1976, *9*, 31–40.

Strain, P. S., Shores, R. E., & Timm, M. A. Effects of peer social initiations on the behavior of withdrawn preschool children. *Journal of Applied Behavior Analysis*, 1977, *10*, 289–298.

Stuart, R. B. *Trick or treatment: How and when psychotherapy fails.* Champaign, Ill.: Research Press, 1970.

Swan, G. E., & McDonald, M. L. Behavior therapy in practice: A national survey of behavior therapists. *Behavior Therapy*, 1978, *9*, 799–807.

Tonick, I., Friehling, J., & Warhit, J. *Classroom observational code.* Unpublished manuscript, Point of Woods Laboratory School, State University of New York at Stony Brook, 1973.

Touliatos, J., & Lindholm, B. W. Behavior problems of Anglo and Mexican-American children. *Journal of Abnormal Child Psychology*, 1976, *4*, 299–304.

Trites, R. Unpublished manuscript, Royal Ottawa Hospital, University of Ottawa, 1980.

Van Hassalt, V. B., Hersen, M., Bellack, A. S., Rosenblum, N. D., & Lamparski, D. Tripartite assessment of the effects of systematic desensitization in a multi-phobic child: An experimental analysis. *Journal of Behavior Therapy and Experimental Psychiatry*, 1979, *10*, 51–55.

Wade, T. C., & Hartmann, D. P. Behavior therapists self-reported views and practices. *The Behavior Therapist*, 1979, *2*, 3–6.

Wahler, R. G. Some structural aspects of deviant child behavior. *Journal of Applied Behavior Analysis*, 1975, *8*, 27–42.

Wahler, R. G., & Cormier, W. H. The ecological interview: A first step in outpatient child behavior therapy. *Journal of Behavior Therapy and Experimental Psychiatry*, 1970, *1*, 279–289.

Wahler, R. G., House, A. E., & Stambaugh, E. E. *Ecological assessment of child problem behavior.* New York: Pergamon Press, 1976.

Wells, K. C., Conners, C. K., Imber, S., & Delamater, A. Use of single case methodology in clinical decision-making with hyperactive children on the psychiatric in-patient unit. *Behavioral Assessment*, in press.

Wells, K. C., & Forehand, R. Childhood behavior problems in the home. In S. M. Turner, K. S. Calhoun, & H. E. Adams (Eds.), *Handbook of clinical behavior therapy.* New York: Wiley, 1981.

Wells, K. C., Forehand, R., & Griest, D. L. Marital adjustment: Relationship to child noncompliance and effects on the outcome of parent training. Unpublished manuscript, University of Georgia, 1979.

Wells, K. C., Forehand, R., Hickey, K., & Green, K. D. Effects of a procedure derived from the overcorrection principle on manipulated and nonmanipulated behaviors. *Journal of Applied Behavior Analysis*, 1977, *10*, 679–687.

Wells, K. C., Griest, D. L., & Forehand, R. The use of a self-control package to enhance temporal generality of a parent training program. *Behaviour Research and Therapy*, 1980, *18*, 347–353.

Wells, K. C., Hersen, M., Bellack, A. S., & Himmelhoch, J. Social skills training in unipolar nonpsychotic depression. *American Journal of Psychiatry*, 1979, *136*, 1331–1332.

Werry, J. S., & Hawthorne, D. Conners' teacher questionnaire—norms and validity. *Australian and New Zealand Journal of Psychiatry*, 1976, *10*, 257–262.

Werry, J. S., & Quay, H. C. The prevalence of behavior symptoms in younger elementary school children. *American Journal of Orthopsychiatry*, 1971, *41*, 136–143.

Werry, J. S., Sprague, R. G., & Cohen, M. N. Conners' Teacher Rating Scale for use in drug studies with children—An empirical study. *Journal of Abnormal Child Psychology*, 1975, *3*, 217–229.

Whaler, C. K., & Henker, B. Psychostimulants and children: A review and analysis. *Psychological Bulletin*, 1976, *83*, 1113–1130.

Wolff, S. Behavioural characteristics of primary school children referred to a psychiatric department. *British Journal of Psychiatry*, 1967, *113*, 885–893.

Wolff, S. Dimensions and clusters of symptoms in disturbed children. *British Journal of Psychiatry*, 1971, *118*, 421–427.

Yarrow, M. R., Campbell, J. D., & Burton, R. V. Recollections of childhood: A study of the retrospective method. *Monographs of the Society for Research in Child Development*, 1970, *35*, (5, Serial No. 138).

Zentall, S. S., & Barack, R. S. Rating scales for hyperactivity. Concurrent validity, reliability and decisions to label for the Conners and Davids abbreviated scales. *Journal of Abnormal Child Psychology*, 1979, *7*, 179–190.

Zigler, E., & Phillips, L. Psychiatric diagnosis: A critique. *Journal of Abnormal and Social Psychology*, 1961, *63*, 607–618.

Chapter 15
Assessment of Children in Inpatient Settings

Johnny L. Matson
and
Steven Beck

INTRODUCTION

Inpatient assessment and treatment of children often are viewed by care providers as a drastic procedure since, among other issues, institutional placement can be upsetting for the child and traumatic for the parents. Besides stress associated with family separation and the stigma of such placements, other factors seem to argue against placing children in residential programs. Historically, children's residential centers have served primarily as custodial care providers instead of treatment facilities, leading many to consider such placements as "dumping grounds," poorly designed, marginally furnished, and minimally staffed (American Psychological Association, 1980). This state of affairs had led many professionals to assert that institutionalization of any kind has a disruptive effect on a child's emotional and intellectual development. At best, such placements have often been viewed as merely giving the parents and community respite from the child. Unfortunately, too often the child is returned to his/her home, where rapid deterioration of appropriate behavior occurs. Proponents against full hospitalization for children also point out the staggering cost of an inpatient program, due to facilities and staff required to operate a 24-hour-a-day service.

There are other apparent disadvantages to inpatient settings. First, behavior problems that are obvious in the child's natural environment often fail to be exhibited under the highly controlled conditions frequently in force in ward settings. As an example, children who are school phobic usually attend classes with little difficulty on an inpatient ward; similarly, children with a history of noncompliance or antisocial behaviors are frequently compliant while hospitalized. Another disadvantage of inpatient settings is that the ward or group-living structure can elicit new behavior problems unrelated to deviant behaviors the child displayed prior to hospitalization. For example, a child may become enuretic or encopretic once hospitalized. Children with minimal responsibilities at home may find it difficult to carry out ward chores, such as making their beds, putting their clothes away, or cleaning up after meals. Thus, the current inpatient program model of care for children seems frought with difficulties.

Despite these problems, full hospitalization or inpatient programs can provide needed services to the child and his or her family. Hospitalization often occurs when children exhibit behavioral excesses or deficits to such an extent that their actions are threatening to self, family, school, or the community at large. Such behavior can be manifested in numerous ways. Suicidal and self-injurious behaviors, high levels of aggression, or severe withdrawal are types of behaviors which typically prompt professionals to recommend inpatient placement. Inpatient programs take these exceptional children who typically exhaust alternative, less restrictive treatment options. Such settings can provide extensive assessment and treatment for children who display severe emotional problems. For example, since continuous 24-hour evaluations can be conducted otherwise, difficult assessments, such as a child's interactions with others or sleep disturbances can be closely monitored. For children admitted to psychiatric hospitals, laboratory studies (such as serum chemistries, urinalysis, thyroid function studies, and electroencephalographs [EEG's]), in addition to physical and dental examinations, can also be performed.

It has been noted that hospitalization is occasionally due to variables other than a change in a child's behavior, related instead to a combination of family and/or community stresses (Hagamen, 1977). Factors necessitating child placement are exhaustion or psychiatric difficulties of the parents. When this occurs, 24-hour-a-day treatment settings provide needed relief to stressed families and often remove the child from a maladaptive environment. This is most important since it provides the necessary support for the child and his/her family and helps avoid potential neglect resulting from inadequate paternal care.

In summary, there are a number of advantages to full time institutional placement for children. The purpose of this chapter is to familiarize the reader with assessment methods available to professionals concerned with children's inpatient care. A presentation of a typical child inpatient assessment under normal clinical circumstances will be contrasted to an assessment under optimal inpatient conditions. Finally, suggestions concerning the future of assessment in these settings where additional development is needed will be outlined. While this chapter is devoted to assessment techniques, the authors are aware that the primary concern and orientation of inpatient staff is upon treatment. Nonetheless, the lack of comprehensive assessment methods leads to incomplete or at best ineffective treatment. Until comprehensive assessment and concomitant treatment become primary activities, institutional settings will not be able to counteract the notion that these facilities are merely ''holding centers.''

ASSESSMENT GOALS OF AN INPATIENT PROGRAM

Inpatient or short-term residential programs need to be time-limited and specific due to spiraling institutional costs and the general philosophy of returning children to the community. The authors believe that assessment, treatment, and proper placements are elements that deserve to be stressed during a child's inpatient stay. However, treatment strategies and decisions about future placements cannot be formulated until assessment has been undertaken. Two primary assessment goals are identifying target behaviors that require modification and accurately diagnosing the child. Diagnosis is important because it may elucidate the etiology of the problem and indicate how successful treatment may be. Specific behaviors requiring change must be identified, however, before treatment and placement plans are developed.

Identifying Target Behaviors

One of the formidable tasks facing any mental health professional is specifying behaviors for assessment (Hawkins, 1975) particularly with children since their self-reports are typically not reliable (Evans & Nelson, 1977). To complicate matters, children placed in a residential setting may not exhibit their more problematic behaviors. Contingencies and cues that may affect a child's behavior in the natural environment may not be present in an inpatient setting. To further compound the situation, children may begin to display behaviors on the ward that were not problematic prior to placement. Nonetheless, an attempt to identify relevant target behaviors in children with severe behavior problems in an outpatient setting may prove even more difficult. In an outpatient setting comprehensive assessment can be difficult since a continuous sample of the child's behavior cannot be made. As a result, mental health professionals must make clinical judgments of exceptional children based upon interviews, parent and teacher reports, standardized tests, and so forth. In short, one is left with the unpleasant task of making critical treatment decisions based almost solely on indirect samples of behavior. From a behavior therapist's point of view, this is an unfortunate state of affairs.

Inpatient evaluation allows for a direct sample of the child's behavior across a range of situations and types of assessment modes, including self-report, direct behavioral observations, and rating of the child's behavior by parents and professionals knowledgeable about the problem. In this way, proper diagnostic, treatment, and prognostic formulations can readily be made.

Unfortunately, little information is available in the literature describing the general classes of behavior that need to be targeted for a child hospitalized in a psychiatric ward. Drabman, Jarvie, and Hammer (1978) state that treatment goals should focus upon the elimination of responses which cause the child to appear bizarre or interfere with interactions toward peers and adults. (According to these authors, the child's behavior should be improved to the extent that he/she may be placed in the home. As we will later note in this chapter, this may prove to be a deceiving criterion.) They further recommend that a critical component of the total treatment plan is to train parents to use more consistent and effective management skills so that the successful transition from ward to home occurs. Treatment goals are based on the premise of eliminating bizarre, disruptive behavior, replacing such behavior with more pro-social skills, and assisting parents in the development of skills allowing them to better manage their child. Their view of an inpatient program is that of a brief intensive skills training center, in contrast to our contention that assessment and placement decisions should be an equal, if not greater priority.

In short, although little information in the literature specifies what behaviors require targeting for children placed in institutional settings, there are central areas that deserve evaluation. These assessment priorities affect the child's total functioning and include the patient's family system, the child's social competence, and the child's academic skills. The following section briefly outlines why we believe these areas deserve attention.

The Child's Family. It is difficult to contemplate assessing a child without evaluating his/her family. Appropriate development in this social context is essential. Critical aspects of the family evaluation are expectations and possible misconceptions regarding the identified child's hospitalization. It is important to keep in mind that most families (and the child in question) have experienced outpatient treatment which has generally been marginally successful. In addition, families may not understand the requisite psychological terminology. For example, they may have a difficult time expressing or knowing what to expect from short-term hospitalization or residential programs, and it may be necessary to minimize fears and clarify expectations about the stay. Information about parent interviews and observations between parent and child will be discussed later in the chapter.

Social Competence. The ability to interact in a successful, rewarding fashion with peers is another vital assessment area for children. Poor social adjustment is a common complaint of parents, teachers, and peers of children with behavior problems. The ability of children to interact successfully with peers has received considerable recent attention (Beck & Forehand, in press; Combs & Slaby, 1977; Van Hasselt, Hersen, Bellack, & Whitehill, 1979). All of these reviews note retrospective studies which have shown that poor social skills have been associated with juvenile delinquency (Roff, Sells, & Golden, 1972) and later adult mental health problems (Cowen, Pederson, Babigan, Izzo, & Trost, 1973). Children who manifest social deficits may also suffer other related dysfunctions, including poor academic achievement (Green, Forehand, Beck, & Vosk, in press), deficient cognitive and emotional development (Patterson, 1964), and social withdrawal in later childhood. In addition, unpopular children may also experience more immediate consequences in their unsuccessful social attempts. Investigators have theorized that a vicious circle may be established for the ignored or rejected child who often becomes unwittingly reinforced by peers and adults for resorting to negative behaviors, such as aggressiveness, in order to gain control, recognition, and attention (Combs & Slaby, 1977).

Academic Skills. Another area requiring thorough evaluation is the child's academic functioning. Zigler and Trickett (1978) have argued that in order to accurately assess social competency among school age children a measure of academic achievement must be included. While instrumental role behavior (e.g., work performance) is an important criterion for assessing adult psychopathology, it is apparent that age-appropriate role performance for a child is school performance. In addition, teachers (except for parents) have more opportunity than anyone to observe the behavior of children, particularly in their interactions with other children. Standardized intelligence and achievement tests, school grades, teacher interview and checklists, and behavioral observations of children in the classroom are methods of assessing academic and social competence. An academic area of interest in recent years has been the diagnostic category of learning disabilities (Gearheart, 1973). Children placed in short-term residential programs often fit the criteria for learning disabled if they are of average or dull-normal intelligence. These children typically have deficits in one or more academic areas, due in part to interference in either a combination of motor, linguistic, perceptual, or auditory modalities (Lahey, 1976). Numerous paper and pencil tests are available to assess learning disabilities. Individualized and structured programs typically need to be established to remediate such deficits.

Classification of Childhood Psychopathology

As previously mentioned, the other primary assessment goal of an inpatient program is to make proper diagnoses. The purpose of this section is to introduce the controversy around and rationale for classifying child psychopathology. This section will also present diagnostic categories of severe behavior problems, since the children placed in inpatient settings often are labeled schizophrenic, autistic, or mentally retarded. As already noted, diagnoses can dictate what type of placement alternatives are available for a child once short-term placement is terminated. For example, those diagnosed autistic are likely to be resistant to brief treatment and subsequently require placement in an intermediate residential facility which specializes in treatment of such children. Of course, there are no steadfast criteria for placing children after full hospitalization. Children with marked behavioral deficits (e.g., high frequent self-stimulatory behavior) can return home after a brief hospitalization if parents are determined to provide the requisite treatment (Lovaas, Koegel, Simmons, & Long, 1973). On the other hand, less severe behavior problems, such as children with conduct problems which have been successfully treated (Kent & O'Leary, 1976), can be placed in intermediate or long-term placements if their parents are viewed incapable of managing them.

Rationale for Classification

Unfortunately, with the exception of the general categories of "psychotic" or "neurotic," diagnoses typically fail to convey precise information about etiology or prognosis. In particular, the diagnostic categories of childhood psychopathology are not agreed upon by mental health professionals (American Psychological Association, 1980). The controversy centers around organizing a classification system on dimensional behavioral criteria versus a categorical, disease model represented in the new Diagnostic and Statistical Manual of Mental Disorders (DSM-III) (American Psychiatric Association, 1980). (The interested reader is referred to Schacht and Nathan's [1977] article for a discussion of the advantages and disadvantages of the DSM III, along with Quay [1979] for a review of the several classification systems presently available for childhood psychopathology.)

For years, traditional diagnostic methods and classification systems (e.g., American Psychiatric Association, 1968; Group for Advancement of Psychiatry, 1966) have been ignored by behaviorists for two basic reasons. First, standard classification systems typically have poor reliability and validity. Second, behaviorists have been critical of the actual methods used to collect data, the types of data collected, and the interpretations of the putative causes (Ciminero & Drabman, 1977). It is important, however, to recognize that behaviorists have not been arguing against diagnosis *per se,* but the methods used to arrive at the conclusions. Most professionals working with children understand the need for a reliable and valid classification system. Besides scientific credibility, a systematic childhood classification system has other advantages. As Hobbs (1975) explains, a coherent and orderly childhood taxonomy has the potential for improving communication among professionals. In addition, a uniform classification of childhood psychopathology would promote pharmacological and psychological treatment with specific, homogeneous samples of children. Until such categorization occurs, significant advances in the treatment of childhood disorders will be impeded.

Regardless of these problems, present childhood classification systems are widespread and will undoubtedly continue to be used. It is our impression that classification systems should be used when professionals discuss children exhibiting severe forms of aberrant behaviors, since there is general agreement among professionals in identifying them (Zubin, 1967). However, professionals need to be aware of possible iatrogenic effects of labeling children with severe forms of psychopathology. Prognosis is poor for many of these problems, and this can affect the way professionals view treatment, as well as the type of children with whom the person is grouped. It is essential that a specific diagnosis not preclude further assessment and treatment. The following section will briefly describe generally agreed-upon severe forms of childhood psychopathology, since many children placed in short-term or residential programs are assigned these labels. Childhood depression will also be discussed since this diagnostic category is currently being used frequently for children placed in inpatient settings (Petti, 1978).

Childhood Schizophrenia. According to DSM-III, childhood schizophrenia has the following characteristics: evidence of a thought disorder or characteristic delusions or hallucinations that are not related to a known organic factor and that have lasted at least six months. In short, childhood schizophrenia is characterized by marked pervasive deviations from the normal developmental sequence. This diagnosis differs at various developmental levels of expectancy in relation to age. The earliest behavioral manifestations do not usually occur until after the child's second year. At this time, the young child often shows intense fear of being separated from his or her mother. This is accompanied by clinging behavior; the child frequently gives up communicative speech. The picture is usually one of gradual withdrawal, emotional aloofness, and distorted perception of reality.

Later childhood schizophrenia is not seen until the age period between 6 and 12–13 years. Onset may be gradual, with more anxiety-related symptoms first appearing, followed by looseness of association in thought processes. Later development may include marked withdrawal, involvement in fantasy, emotional aloofness, and disorder in thinking and reality. In some instances, more acute and sudden eruptions during this age period may involve intense anxiety and uncontrollable phobias. Some children show sudden and wild outbursts of either aggressive behavior or self-mutilation, inappropriate mood swings, and suicidal threats and attempts.

Childhood schizophrenia is thought to be influenced by a combination of genetic and psychogenic factors. Twin studies show a high degree of concordance between monozypotic twins (86 percent), but a significantly power concordance rate in dizygotic twins (15 percent) (Rosenthal, 1970), strongly suggesting a genetic component influencing childhood schizophrenia. If it is possible to summarize the wealth of material regarding this diagnosis, psychogenic theories usually depict these children coming from extremely dysfunctional families with a history of schizophrenia, who have dominant mothers and weak ineffectual fathers who engage in contradictory communications with their children. Outcome studies in childhood schizophrenia are generally poor. The best predictor of eventual adjustment is the child's IQ; approximately 50 percent of children labeled as schizophrenic will have serious psychological impairment in adulthood (Werry, 1971). Prevalence of childhood schizophrenia varies, but approximately six to seven per 10,000 children are believed to have this disorder (O'Leary & Wilson, 1975).

A battery of assessment methods can identify this disorder. Information collected from parents and extreme scores derived from specific checklists (see assessment method section) begin to alert clinicians to this diagnosis. Behavioral observations, particularly marked withdrawal or unusual thinking and behavior, often confirm a diagnosis of childhood schizophrenia. Standardized tests of cognitive ability typically are difficult to interpret, since the child's actual intellectual capacities may be difficult to determine if his/her behavior has regressed. However, intellectual functioning assessment is critical given the finding that IQ is an important prognostic indicator.

Autism. Autism is another severe childhood disorder with an extremely poor prognosis for recovery (Ritvo, 1976). It was first believed that autism was a form of schizophrenia, although the autism/schizophrenia dichotomy now appears to be fairly well established (Werry, 1979). According to DSM III, infantile autism has several critical characteristics (onset usually prior to 30 months, but up to 42 months; lack of responsiveness to others; self-isolation; gross deficits in language development; if langauge is present, peculiar speech patterns [e.g., echolalia]; and the excessive and/or inappropriate interest or attachment to animals or inanimate objects). As can be seen from these characteristics, early infantile autism appears to have its onset during the first few months in the first year of life, with failure on the part of the infant to develop an attachment to the mother. The infant remains aloof, showing little apparent awareness of human contact, and is preoccupied with inanimate objects. Speech development is delayed or absent; when it appears, speech is generally not used for the purpose of communication. The child often shows a strong need for the maintenance of sameness and tends to resist change, responding with marked outbursts of temper or intense anxiety when routines are altered. Sleeping and feeding problems are often severe. Stereotyped motor patterns, often bizarre (for example, flapping arms), are frequent. Intellectual development may be normal, advanced, or retarded. In many cases, the incapacity to perceive reality correctly and to communicate through speech may render most intellectual functions impaired.

Prognosis for autistic children is more bleak than children diagnosed schizophrenic. In an 8 year study of 120 children diagnosed autistic, only two percent were considered functioning normally at follow-up (DeMyer, Barton, DeMyer, Norton, Allen, & Steel, 1973). Since such children's prognosis is poor, intermediate or long-term placement is usually required. Estimates of prevalence of autism also vary, with figures of approximately 2 to 4.5 per 10,000 children (Graham, 1979), with boys outnumbering girls three to one.

Differentiation between schizophrenia and autism is important given the bleak prognosis and customary institutional placement for autistic children. Thorough inpatient assessment should distinguish these two disorders. If a child evinces autistic or schizophrenic-like behaviors, developmental information collected from interviews with parents should assess if the child appeared detached and unresponsive during infancy or if deviant behaviors appeared later in his/her development. Since parental information can be unreliable (see assessment methods section), behavioral observations in an inpatient setting can confirm or disprove an autistic or schizophrenic diagnosis. Observations would show that autistic children self-isolate, perform stereotypic behaviors, and demonstrate excessive and inappropriate attachments to objects. On the other hand, schizophrenic children would typically have communicative abilities and engage in interactions though often in a bizarre or odd manner. In conclusion, as the prevalence rates point out, these two conditions are relatively rare disorders. Nonetheless, many children exhibiting extremely deviant behavior will be placed in inpatient or short-term residential programs. This will be done to rule out or confirm a schizophrenic or autistic diagnosis, since these diagnoses have serious treatment and prognostic implications.

Childhood Depression. Although not as severe as schizophrenia or autism, the diagnosis of childhood depression has recently received wide attention (Lefkowitz & Burton, 1978; Lefkowitz & Tesiny, 1980; Schulterbrandt & Raskin, 1977). Consequently, children presently seen by mental health professionals may likely receive a diagnosis of primary or secondary depression (Carlson & Cantwell, 1980). This diagnosis has also become one of the most prevalent for children in inpatient settings (Petti, 1978). Nonetheless, the ability of this syndrome to stand as an independent clinical entity is presently debated. Achenbach and Edlebrock (1979) found depression in children, but not independently from other more salient clinical dimensions. However, many experienced mental health professionals and researchers who have treated children in an inpatient or outpatient basis have encountered those who have displayed symptoms of subjective sadness, apathy (e.g., rapid school failure or disinterest), and disturbance of sleep and appetite. This latter group of professionals view depression in childhood as a separate clinical entity. It is considered acceptable in some professional circles to treat children displaying symptoms associated with depression with tricyclic antidepressants (Schulterbrandt & Raskin, 1977), although this form of treatment has not been subjected to experimental evaluation (Conners & Werry, 1979).

Proponents taking a more cautious approach toward identifying childhood depression as an independent constellation of symptoms, argue that depressive behavior or variables found in children are not a distinct clinical entity, but a phenomena of normal childhood development that is transitory in nature and not necessitating clinical intervention. They also argue that the use of pharmacotherapy as a primary treatment intervention could produce possible iatrogenic and unwanted effects for children who would otherwise spontaneously remit their symptoms if left untreated.

It is clear that a reliable and valid measure of childhood depression needs to be conducted on a representative sample of children to determine the existence and prevalence of such a syndrome. Such research is now beginning. Lefkowitz and Tesiny (1980) assessed the constellation of features normally associated with depression in a sample of approximately 1,000 children in 61 fourth and fifth grade classrooms from various New York City elementary schools. This cross-validational study used peer nominations, self-ratings, teacher ratings, and unobtrusive measures, such as days absent from school. Presumed symptoms of childhood depression were found in this sample. Three factors, labeled loneliness, inadequacy, and dejection could be translated into observable behaviors and reliably and validly assessed by a peer nomination procedure. Given the acceptable psychometric properties of this study, epidemiological studies that plot and monitor the prevalence and fate of depressed children can now be undertaken.

Inpatient evaluations may prove useful in identifying and treating depressed children. Parental information, specific checklists that identify depression, and several behavioral observations such as sleep patterns, peer interactions, and classroom performance can all be collected simultaneously in an inpatient setting to provide concurrent validity for this disputed disorder.

Mental Retardation. Although this disorder is not a form of psychopathology, mentally retarded children often demonstrate behavioral excesses, such as aggression, classroom disruption, self-injury, and stereotyped movements (Forehand & Baumeister, 1976), which result in hospitalization. Furthermore, the prevalence of these disorders is high. Estimates of the prevalence of mental retardation range from one percent (DSM III, 1980), to 3, to 5 percent of the population (Birnbrauer, 1976).

Mental retardation can best be classified according to traditional psychological and behavioral assessment methods as endorsed by the American Association on Mental Deficiency (Grossman, 1977). According to this definition, mental retardation refers to significantly subaverage intellectual functioning existing concurrently with deficits in adaptive behavior manifested during the developmental period (before the age of 18). Subaverage intellectual functioning represents two or more standard deviations below the mean on a test of general intelligence, such as a score of 68 on the Standford-Binet or a score of 69 on the

Wechsler Intelligence Scale for Children. Deficits in adaptic behavior are lags in motor skills, self-help skills, communication, and social or academic skills, depending upon the age of the child. As a result of the high incidence rate and probability of behavioral excesses or deficits, mentally retarded children are often placed in inpatient or short-term, residential settings.

There are four subtypes of mental retardation reflecting the degree of intellectual impairment. Children with mild mental retardation have IQ's between 55 and 69 (based on WISC-R) and are considered "educable." These children usually develop social and communication skills, need minimal supervision, and typically function adequately as adults with minimal guidance. The majority of children with mental retardation fall into this subtype. Children with moderate mental retardation have IQ's between 40 and 54. These children generally have communication skills, but require moderate supervision and perform unskilled or semi-skilled work under close supervision in sheltered workshops as adults. The final two subtypes, severe and profound mental retardation, have IQ's below 39 and only comprise approximately eight percent of individuals with mental retardation. These children display little, if any, speech and self-care skills, and require constant supervision in a highly structured environment.

Retardation, therefore, is defined using a dual behavioral definition, consisting of deficits both in standardized intelligence and adaptive behavior. This latter assessment strategy is tantamount to the use of behavioral assessment for diagnosing a highly prevalent disorder. In an inpatient or short-term residential setting, mental retardation is diagnosed using intelligence tests and adaptive behavior scales to assess everyday living skills. However, as already mentioned, most mentally retarded children referred to inpatient settings have primary deviant behavior problems. In this case, multiple assessment methods are used to identify these problematic behaviors.

Review and Rationale for Behavioral Assessment in Inpatient Settings

As was discussed in this section, two primary assessment goals in an inpatient setting are to identify behaviors that require modification and to properly diagnose severely deviant children for treatment and future placement considerations. Behavior modifiers have traditionally minimized the utility of diagnostic categories and focused instead upon behavior samples in specific situations as primary assessment information. We believe traditional diagnostic formulations deserve attention in an inpatient setting, although the method by which they are derived should

be more behavioral than is often the case (e.g., use of direct observations, etc.). State and local laws, third party payers, and institutional
placement require such information. Moreover, until childhood disorders
are reliably and validly categorized, effective treatment for large samples of exceptional children will be obstructed. For example, consider
the attention given to the treatment of autistic children (see Lovaas &
Newsom, 1976) after this disorder was recognized as an independent
clinical entity. Inpatient settings, employing multiple assessment methods, may prove helpful in identifying and treating further subsamples
of severe childhood disorders. For example, the previous section discusses how assessment of inpatients can help identify or reject the controversial clinical entity known as childhood depression.

An emphasis throughout this chapter has been the necessity of thorough assessment of each child placed in an inpatient or short-term residential setting. The authors believe this can best be accomplished using
a behavioral assessment that has been discussed in detail elsewhere
(Ciminero, Calhoun, & Adams, 1977; Hersen & Bellack, 1976). A few
of the features as they relate to the following assessment section will
be outlined. Primary characteristics of behavioral assessment are accurate and complete descriptions of an individual's behavior and the
conditions maintaining it. The definition and quantification of problem
behaviors is essential for selecting relevant target behaviors and subsequent treatment strategies. For ideal assessment, an individual's responses should be sampled in a variety of settings. As was discussed
in the preceding sections, assessment of children in an inpatient setting
is limited since individuals are typically evaluated in the confines of
the hospital. However, behavioral observations discussed in the following
section potentially allow for evaluation with parents and peers in a
classroom setting, and of course, on the ward. Another primary feature
of behavioral assessment is the attempt to gather information on three
response channels: cognitive, motoric, and physiological. With the exception of physiological responses, the following section presents several assessment methods that evaluate cognitive and motoric response
channels.

ASSESSMENT METHODS

This section will review methods which should be included in stan-
darized inpatient assessments for children. The assessment methods are
procedures which allow inpatient personnel to efficiently evaluate the
child's family, social competency, and classroom performance. Methods
reviewed include behavioral interviewing, behavioral observations,

problem checklists, standardized tests of cognitive ability, adaptive behavior scales, and physiological measures. Each category will be reviewed only briefly, with examples of some of the better measures in each of the areas included. More comprehensive reviews of all the measurement systems are available elsewhere (Anastasi, 1976; Matarazzo, 1972; Meyers, Nihira, & Zetlin, 1979). Despite the importance of standard intelligence tests such as the Wechsler and Stanford-Binet scales, and achievement tests such as the Wide Range Achievement test, they will not be reviewed, since they are thoroughly described in a number of texts.

This wide range of measures is described since it is believed that behavioral assessment can and does involve more than behavioral observations and interviewing. It is our opinion that a broad range of assessment instruments, providing data across various situations and persons with whom the child interacts, is vital in constructing learning theory oriented treatment. This is the case since both observable behavior and cognitive ability are important variables in deciding the type and sophistication of the treatment programs used.

Interviews

Interviewing, is considered the universal tool for obtaining information for assessment and treatment. The behavioral interview is differentiated primarily by its content and focus. It is intended to identify problem behaviors of the child and environmental variables that control and maintain them. Another goal is to determine the feasibility of establishing a positive interpersonal relationship with the child and, perhaps more importantly, with the child's parents, since relationships are often crucial to the success of assessment and subsequent treatment (Linehan, 1977). One advantage of an inpatient service is that a series of interviews can be conducted within a short time span so that information can be collected quickly. Energy can then be devoted to using more standardized procedures in the inpatient setting to gather information.

On an outpatient basis, the ability to do comprehensive assessments is usually curtailed due to an over reliance on self-report and traditional assessment procedures to the exclusion of direct behavioral observations to a large degree. This fact was substantiated by two similar surveys conducted with the Association for Advancement of Behavior Therapy (AABT) members (Swan & MacDonald, 1978; Wade & Hartmann, 1979). In these surveys, practical administrative and methodological problems were reported in the utilization of behavioral assessment in applied settings. A decided advantage of an inpatient setting is that assessment pcocedures do not have to be compromised to the same degree, since a child is available for continuous observation and assessment over an extended period of time.

Parent Interviews

When a child is the identified client, the primary source of information about the child's behavior is the parents. However, information collected from parents may not have high validity (parents' memories are not always consistent with known facts about the child), nor good reliability (information from one interview is not consistent with another) (Evans & Nelson, 1977). Mothers tend to be more accurate when detailing factual events. For example, medical information, such as childhood illnesses and developmental landmarks (e.g., age when child began walking and talking), was accurate in a group of mothers anywhere from 3 to 30 years later when given open-ended questions regarding their child's preschool experiences (Yarrow, Campbell, & Burton, 1970). On the other hand, emotionally charged subject matter tends to be less reliable. Examples are parental attitudes and practices regarding specific aspects of child rearing (e.g., describing how child is punished) (Chess, Thomas, & Birch, 1966). Parental inaccuracies are therefore likely to be in the direction of social desirability, placing the parent interviewed in a positive light. Nonetheless, interviewing parents is an expected procedure in an inpatient residential setting. We are not suggesting clinicians no longer attempt to gather information from parents, but that interviewers should be aware of possible inaccuracies parents may make when asked about their children. This problem is particularly salient in cases of residential placement, since these parents are more likely to evince various types of pathology which further compound the difficulties associated with obtaining accurate information. Another important reason for this type of interview is to begin establishing a relationship with the parents. Clear communication and mutual understanding between the clinician and parents is critical if treatment gains are to be transferred from the inpatient setting to the child's home. We suggest interviews with parents conducted in the late afternoon or early evening. Parents often have difficulties leaving work or obtaining babysitters during the day. Flexible scheduling also allows for longer or shorter interviews, depending upon the parents' comfort and ability to share information, and the skill of the interviewer in collecting relevant information.

The following questions should be answered as fully as possible by the parent(s) during assessment interviews. According to the parents' perception, do they believe there is a need for inpatient treatment? Do they agree or disagree with the referral and why? By whom were they referred? What do they believe is the problem? Can they state the problem specifically with the interviewer's help? How often does the specified problem occur? What do they believe caused the problem? What strategies have the parents used to deal with the problem? What strategies did they believe were helpful or not helpful? Was there any significant or dramatic event that occurred at the onset, or immediately before or after the behavior problem, such as a death in the family, separation or divorce, move to another school or city, financial or housing problems, psychiatric problems of the parents, other siblings, or significant external family members? What were the child's reactions to the events?

An attempt should be made to assess how the parents feel about their child, although the interviewer should be aware of the social desirability factor inherent in this question. Many parents may be hesitant to verbalize dislike for the identified child or other children in the family. Other questions asked should be: What do the parents think about the child's social development? Does the child have friends? Have they ever observed the child's play? Does the child assume an active or passive role when playing with peers?

Finally, the parents' expectations and motivation needs to be assessed within an interview format. What are the parents' specific expectations of the intended treatment? What would they accept as successful treatment? What would they view as unsuccessful treatment? Are they able to verbalize, with the interviewer's help, clear behavioral goals? Do the parents require treatment about their own problems independent of their problems with the child? Are the parents willing to be actively involved on a regular basis with parent training or other skills training during and after inpatient treatment? How often will the parents visit the child? Finally, medical and developmental information, along with data regarding the child's extended family history can be obtained by a standardized interview or checklist.

Child Interview

Two types of information should be emphasized during the child's interview. First, the child's perception of him/herself and second, observations of how the child handles him/herself with an unknown adult. The child's perception of many issues, such as his or her view of the reason for hospitalization, allows the clinician to assess the degree that the child can discuss relevant information. At the same time, the skills exhibited in interacting with the clinician provide information about the child's assets and level of dysfunction. It is often difficult to interview a child, particularly a young or nonverbal one, in a fashion typically used with adults. We recommend playing with puppets, toys, or drawings as vehicles which can help elicit clinically relevant information.

Initial assessment interviews with the parent and child together and separately are also recommended. While conducting interviews, clinicians apparently view disturbed children less favorably when the entire family is interviewed than when interviews with the child and parents are conducted separately (Gaines & Stedman, 1979). One explanation for this is that separate interviews allow the identified child to be more relaxed, spontaneous, and verbal, thereby enhancing the interaction with the clinician. Certainly, more data on parameters such as these are needed. However, these tentative findings should be considered while constructing initial interviews.

Behavioral Observations

Although interviewing can be helpful in identifying potential target behaviors, nothing substitutes for the actual observation of such events. The advantage of observation is that the assessor can systematically observe and record the child's behavior. In an inpatient setting, information collected from interviews, checklists, and standardized tests can begin to isolate response classes exhibited by the child in his or her natural environment (e.g., in the home, classroom, and with peers). In other words, response classes, such as noncompliance at home, hyperactivity in the classroom, or aggressiveness with peers can be identified. These response classes can then be targeted and precisely measured using behavioral observations. Besides identifying relevant target behaviors, behavioral observations will also identify antecedent and consequent stimulus events, which may be contributing to the maintenance of inappropriate behavior or limiting the occurrence of appropriate responses.

Ideally, behaviors that occur in the child's natural environment should be observed on the ward. Only in this way can conditions that elicit specific behaviors or response classes be identified. For such behaviors to be observed, however, the assessor may need to employ analogue situations that allow observations of responses that may otherwise be infrequently observed on the ward. An inpatient or residential setting has the access, time, and usually the equipment to perform analogue or role-play situations. For example, children requiring inpatient placement usually have social skill deficits. As a result, analogue situations, or specifically, role-play tests can be employed to assess aspects of these children's social competence.

A recent study by Bornstein, Bellack, and Hersen (1980) describes how social skills were assessed and treated with four children in an inpatient setting. Role-play sessions were conducted in a playroom equipped with a one-way mirror and sound equipment in an adjacent observation room. Structured role-play situations, in which an interpersonal encounter was described, were presented to each child by an adult during assessment. Children were assessed by trained observers in the next room. They were assessed for such molecular behaviors as ratio of eye contact to speech duration, frequency of hostile tone, and number of requests for new behavior. They also were assessed on a measure of overall assertiveness. After baseline was completed, the children were individually trained using instructions, modeling, feedback, and other techniques to provide more appropriate responses in the role-play scenes. Results showed that the four children demonstrated generalization of appropriate responses to other nontreated role play scenes. It also was anecdotally reported that these children stopped making threats to staff on the ward whenever frustrated, but instead calmly expressed dissatisfaction and appropriately requested behavior change. This study serves as a model for children inpatient programs in constructing role-play scenes to assess and treat specific aspects of children's social skills, employing behavioral observations as the primary assessment tool.

In another study, Elder, Edelstein, and Narick (1979) modified four institutionalized adolescents' aggressive behaviors using social skills training. This study is an example of how an inpatient setting can be used to assess children in various ward activities. These authors specifically assessed generalization of treatment to dissimilar situations on the ward where treatment did not occur. Subjects were assessed for social skills during baseline and treatment, for treated and nontreated role play scenes in a similar manner as described in the Bornstein et al. (1980) study. In addition, subjects' ward behavior was observed unobtrusively by recording the number of "fines" levied against each subject for aggressive outbursts. Results indicated that all four subjects, who had histories of verbally and physically aggressive behaviors, decreased their aggressive behaviors significantly. Decreases in the number of fines and time in seclusion offered an externally valid index of generalization of treatment results.

Besides ward behavior, observations of parent-child interactions and classroom behaviors provide important assessment material. Parent-child interactions, in particular, furnish relevant information, since many children requiring psychiatric hospitalization have ineffectual or dysfunctional parents (Hagamen, 1978). Observations in laboratory playrooms have proven excellent vehicles for gathering parent-child interaction patterns (Forehand, King, Peed, & Yoder, 1975). Such playrooms can easily be established in an inpatient setting with toys, chairs, a table and, preferably, a one-way mirror to unobstructively observe the parents and child. Assessments are performed by recording the frequency of commands, questions, appropriate attention, or rewards a parent makes to his or her child. Additionally, children are assessed for the frequency of compliant and noncompliant behaviors.

Instructions can be given to parents in these rooms to play whatever game or activity their child chooses and then to switch instructions so that the child is told to play whatever game the parent chooses. This situation allows one observance of the child's overall compliance rate, the parent's ability to give commands and consequate compliance or noncompliance. Instructing the parents to ask their child to "clean up" the room also assesses their ability to issue clear commands and their response to child compliance or noncompliance.

Other accessible settings for systematic observations in an inpatient setting are classrooms that are usually located in or near the ward. The validity of classroom observational procedures is well documented. Specific observational codes have successfully identified hyperactive children (Abikoff, Gittelman-Klein, & Klein, 1977), conduct problem children (Werry & Quay, 1969), and medication effects on emotionally disturbed children (Sprague, Barnes, & Werry, 1974). It is evident that systematic observations of classroom behaviors, such as time spent out of the chair, inappropriate vocalizations, and on-task behavior can provide helpful diagnostic information. Inpatient settings should take advantage of the nearby classroom setting to observe relevant clinical information.

As with all assessment methods, there are problems associated with behavioral observations. One difficulty is that the presence of an observer may alter the child's behavior such that it is no longer representative of his/her actions. This problem can be partly circumvented by using unobtrusive measures, such as those employed by Elder et al. (1979). Another problem with behavioral observations can be the cost and time involved in such an undertaking. There are often economic and pragmatic restrictions in this assessment approach. Recruiting, training observers, and the logistics of actually observing someone can be a cumbersome and time-consuming task. In an inpatient setting, standardized situations, such as the role-play scenes described earlier, can be performed by specific staff and other personnel (e.g., undergraduate college students, volunteers). Consequently, efficiency and the expertise of the trainers and observers should increase as the assessment scenes are continually performed.

In conclusion, information gathered from observational procedures can begin to target behaviors requiring modification and confirm diagnostic impressions collected from parental and child interviews, paper and pencil tests, and standardized tests. While behavioral observations provide a direct sample of a child's behavior, there are practical difficulties that prohibit relying too heavily on this method for collecting assessment information.

Problem Checklists

The number of checklists available to assess childhood psychopathology are numerous, spanning a wide gamut from homemade in-house scales to highly sophisticated measures with relatively good norms. For those interested in choosing a battery of assessment measures, the latter group of procedures obviously would be preferable under optimal conditions. Two additional conditions should be considered when selecting scales for inpatient assessment, however. These include the length of the scale (the time required to complete it) and how applicable the measure is to a wide range of pathology.

Certainly, there are a number of measures which meet at least some of these criteria. The authors have selected two of the measures which are representative of how behaviors of inpatient hospitalized persons may be effectively measured. Among the most well constructed problem checklists are the Behavior Problem Checklist (Quay & Peterson, 1975) and the Child Behavior Profile (Achenbach, 1978; in press). These measures are briefly described below. We have attempted to point out why they are among the best methods for assessing deficits of hospitalized children.

Behavior Problem Checklist (BPC). The Behavior Problem Checklist (BPC) is a 3-point scale for the rating of problem behavior traits occurring in childhood and adolescence. There are three major subscales that make up this instrument: conduct, personality, and inadequacy-immaturity. These three factors were established by factor analyzing behavior ratings on both deviant and "normal" persons from age six through the teenage years. A fourth scale is composed of items derived from factor analytic studies of case history records. This factor is referred to as socialization-delinquency. The authors have included these behaviors in this latter subscale since the rationale is that such behaviors are often observed in clinical settings.

As noted above, the major assets of this particular scale are that it is useful for measuring a wide range of pathology, and that it is well constructed, relative to the other scales available in most settings for children in psychiatric hospitals.

Child Behavior Profile (CBP). This instrument and the Behavior Problem Checklist are similar in many respects. One difference is the subscale titles. In the case of the CBP, there are a number of overlapping categories such as aggression and withdrawal. However, the greater number of specific diagnostic categories is included with the CBP. Some of these are depression, schizoid personality, and hyperactivity. It seems reasonable that this difference exists since the CBP has been developed much more recently, and the added subscales correspond to the increasing attempts to identify a wide range of pathology in children. On the other hand, the CBP has not been in use nearly as long as the BPC, and the amount of research data demonstrating the value of the CBP is not as impressive. This difference in modes of assessing childhood psychopathology is referred to as a broad versus a narrow band approach (Achenbach, 1978).

Adaptive Behavior Scales

The emphasis on adaptive behavior scales as a method of assessing functioning level initially grew out of a major dissatisfaction with existing measures for assessing the breadth of intellectual functioning of the mentally retarded. While IQ tests were of considerable value, it was felt that there were additional aspects of mental retardation that needed to be evaluated, primarily the everyday living skills that mentally retarded persons possess. This precedent is primarily responsible for the fact that these scales are still used almost exclusively with the mentally retarded. This state of affairs should be considered unfortunate by behavior modifiers, since an emphasis on this type of assessment is based on the observation of discrete behaviors in the environment. Additionally, development of other behavioral scales could benefit from the manner in which traditional psychometric properties are incorporated into test construction.

The emphasis on adaptive behavior scales began in the 1940s, but since that time they have become of increasing importance in the assessment of intelligence. Measures of this sort have benefited greatly from the fact that they often provide the type of information important in the development of behavioral programming. Furthermore, the type of "intelligence" they measure is radically different from what is assessed with IQ tests and, thus, additional highly useful information about a person's adaptive skills is obtained. From that standpoint, these instruments may also prove useful in developing programs for children without major intellectual deficits. To date, however, this has not been the case. Similarly, for at least some of the behaviors that have been measured (particularly the AAMD adaptive behavior scales), these scales have proven sensitive to changes produced by treatment on specific behaviors or behavior clusters. This finding has made adaptive behavior scales useful for measuring treatment outcome, a contention supported by the fact that they have been used in this manner in a number of empirical studies.

As noted, the number of adaptive behavior scales have proliferated in recent years. Along with the increased number of scales, there has been an increase in the number of behaviors that can be evaluated using these assessment tools. Among the skills added recently to the growing list of behaviors that can be evaluated are language skills (Boroskin, 1971), school compliance (Levine, Elzey, Thornahlen, & Cain, 1976), and social and prevocational skills (Halpern, Raffeld, Irwin, & Link, 1975). Comprehensive reviews of these adaptive behavior scales are available elsewhere (Leland, Shellhaas, Nihira, & Foster, 1967; Meyers, Nihira, & Zetlin, 1979).

Due to the nature of the normative groups used to standardize the instrument and the type of questions asked, most are not applicable for an inpatient children's unit. The older more traditional scales, such as the Vineland Social Maturity Scale and American Association on Mental Deficiency Adaptive Behavior Scales, tend to be the most useful. The Balthazar (1971, 1973) scale may be of some value as well, particularly for those who have mental retardation as at least part of their problem. Similarly, children with extreme emotional problems, such as autism or childhood schizophrenia, would benefit from the information derived using an adaptive behavior scale.

The possible uses for adaptive behavior scales are, at least in our opinion, restricted. Traditionally, these measures have been employed almost exclusively with the mentally retarded. However, this does not mean that more extensive uses are impossible if additional scales are developed. It seems that such development would be most advantageous to the behavior modifier, since the focus of assessment is on observable, operationally-defined behaviors.

Physiological Measures

One of the most rapidly expanding areas of assessment in our field in the last 10 years has been the use of physiological measures. Among the methods frequently employed to assess anxiety, fear, and other phychological problems are heart rate, galvanic skin response, gastric motility, electrodermal, and muscular responses (Epstein, 1976). The proliferation of these assessments has been governed by two overriding criteria: the persons assessed are in most cases adults and have been typically referred for a very specific behavior problem. These are considered to be gross measures since it is difficult to state, based on heart rate, for example, specific cut-offs representative of mild versus moderate anxiety. By such criteria, the usefulness of these methods in an inpatient setting for children is limited, since the diagnosis of even some very general behaviors must be made.

Another limitation of this type of measurement is the lack of broad applicability of the assessment instruments. The diversity of problems that children present on an inpatient setting is considerable. Thus, even in the general armamentarium of "standard psychological assessment devices," it is difficult to establish a general test battery with this group. The hardware needed for these assessments is most expensive, and the tester requires specialized training. This makes for a system that is limited, costly, and time consuming to develop and maintain. The problems described are far from insurmountable, but do suggest that physiological assessment measures, despite their potential, have not gained as much widespread acceptance as other behavioral assessment measures reviewed.

Specialty Tests

In addition to the more general measures of cognitive functioning and emotional disturbance, the behavior therapist may also wish to administer tests specifically designed to measure a particular type of problem. An example is the Child Depression Inventory (Kovacs & Beck, 1977), a self-report measure of depression with 27 items. With this particular instrument the child is given three alternative statements from which he/she must select one (e.g., I am bad all the time, I am bad many times, I am bad once in a while). Norms are established and, thus, a criteria for depression is available. Specialized behaviorally-oriented instruments can be of particular value in supporting the findings obtained with the more general measures and observation data systems described in this chapter.

Summary and Extensions

In the preceding sections of this chapter, the emphasis has been on reviewing the types of problems and assessment instruments proven useful in evaluating children receiving inpatient care. We have proposed several measures carried out in inpatient settings for children and some types of assessments, such as the physiological measures, which are infrequently employed. In the ensuing section, an example of a possible assessment package for a hypothetical, hospitalized child will be presented.

SAMPLE ASSESSMENTS

This section will describe what we consider an ideal and typical assessment on a children's inpatient ward, based on our experiences with such evaluations. Obviously, a number of additional possibilities exist in a description of this type. We have, however, tried to emphasize the types of patient characteristics that might be observed in a wide range of inpatient settings. In the first description, we present a child and situation that are, from our perspective, ideal. This case illustrates a variety of problems which have impeded our attempt to provide assessment to children on an inpatient basis.

Description of the Child

This 9-year-old male, Joey, was referred for treatment due to an inability to behave in a socially appropriate manner at school. The child was in a special education classroom for educable mentally retarded children and evinced an unwillingness to participate in educational tasks, often becoming withdrawn. This behavior usually resulted in noncompliance (e.g., talking back to teachers). In addition to this problem, he frequently talked loudly to himself and other children in class, and it was unclear whether he was attempting to gain attention or was evidencing a schizophrenic thought disorder. These behaviors had become more pronounced since kindergarten and eventually resulted in removal from a regular classroom to the special education class where he resided at the time of his admission. Joey had been seen sporadically for approximately 6 months by a therapist at a local mental health agency, but neither the therapist nor Joey's mother believed he had improved as a result of these contacts.

His father had left home while the boy was 3 years of age. He subsequently remarried and had occasional contact with Joey. Mother reported an inability to provide adequate discipline. She had held various jobs as a waitress and grocery store clerk, although she currently was unemployed. When she had gone to Joey's school to discuss his problems, there was evidence to suggest she was intoxicated and had a serious alcohol problem. Additionally, mother had reported being close to committing suicide on at least one occasion in the past, when she considered herself to be having "a nervous breakdown." Due to these problems, she indicated doubt as to her ability to cope with her child, although she professed love for him and an unwillingness to have him placed in a residential setting.

Joey's brother, Tim, who was 12 years of age, had also been in an EMR classroom since first grade. He too had been treated sporadically on an outpatient basis for the last two years due to conduct problems in school. The admission of Joey to the inpatient unit of a psychiatric hospital occurred after an incident in school when he threw a brick at his teacher during recess. Joey indicated to school authorities that he felt justified in this action since the teacher had been "picking on him." This belief, however, was not substantiated by the teacher or other children in his class. Rather, the other children considered him a "troublemaker," and it was reported that he had no friends in school.

The Ideal Assessment

Joey is a 9-year, 4-month-old male referred by his parents for psychological assessment and treatment. Initial interviews were conducted with the parents and with Joey and his brother, Tim. Everyone was cooperative and readily able to understand the questions asked of them and were prompt in both attendance and in attention to questions posed. The mother, at the suggestion of the interviewer, also agreed to begin receiving outpatient therapy. Also, the family was fortunate to have adequate medical coverage, thus obviating the need to curtail needed psychological services.

Following the interview, each parent filled out the behavior problem checklist and the AAMD adaptive behavior scale. The correlation between test scores of the parents, computed separately, was remarkably high (well above 90 percent). From these data, it was determined that the child was perceived to be evidencing considerable aggression, and his level of cognitive functioning with respect to adaptive behavior was in the moderate range of mental retardation.

Joey was evaluated for the first two weeks based on observations of operationally defined target behaviors. Since aggressive behavior had been noted on the parents' reports on the Child Behavior Profile as one prevalent theme, behaviors such as inappropriate vocalizations and threatening verbal and physical behavior were monitored daily in six, 30-minute time sampling periods on the ward and in the classroom. High rates of inappropriate behavior were noted, supporting data obtained on the Child Behavior Profile.

Another measure of social aggressive behavior was made by evaluating how Joey role played situations where conditions were described that might be stressful to him and he was required to provide an answer. An important aspect of this assessment was to determine what antecedent events led to aggressive episodes. These data were of value since they helped identify strategies the staff could employ to teach alternative coping methods useful in curbing aggression.

Joey was given one week to acclimate to the unit and was administered an individual test battery. The first test was the Wechsler Intelligence Scale for Children (WISC), followed by the Wide Range Achievement Test (WRAT). The Child Depression Inventory was also given since the child had been reported withdrawn. Throughout the 1-hour, 20-minute testing session, the child was cooperative and attentive, as evidenced by consistent eye contact while speaking and the willingness to readily answer questions. Additionally, he seemed motivated to do his best. Joey's full scale IQ on the WISC was 49, which placed him in the moderate range of mental retardation, a score consistent with data obtained on the administration of the AAMD adaptive behavior scale. Similarly, on the WRAT, Joey was two years behind grade level, a score corresponding to what would be expected of a child with this level of intellectual functioning. This type of academic performance would make him most suited for a trainable mentally retarded classroom. No evidence of depression was noted on the Child Depression Inventory.

Based on the present evaluation, it is evident that Joey is a moderately mentally retarded child with extreme antisocial behavior, but no apparent psychotic or depressive features. The primary emphasis of the treatment plan should therefore focus on teaching and reinforcing more socially desirable behaviors, teaching the parents to cope adequately with these aggressive behaviors, and stressing to parents and teachers the child's cognitive handicap and the type of behavior they can reasonably expect him to perform. Based upon Joey's diagnosis and identification of target behaviors, it was decided that he could return home after discharge from the inpatient program.

The Typical Assessment

The typical assessment would incorporate all of the steps in the evaluative process described in the ideal assessment. The primary differences, at least from our experience, are that the data are often incomplete and that there is frequently disagreement between data reported by various staff and parents.

It often is the case that all of the family members do not attend the interview. Most frequently, the mother will be present but not the father, and in many cases some of the children will not be present. In addition, we have frequently found that both parents are willing to participate in parent training but not individual therapy. Furthermore, the emphasis is generally on the fact that the problems are caused by the child, frequently in combination with the school, and the parents are unwilling to accept responsibility for at least some of the problems. This does not mean that many parents do not present a much more positive profile; however, most families reaching inpatient care have been unable to cope with the child on their own or with the assistance of various mental health agencies on an outpatient basis. These variables typically add up to a family with considerable interpersonal functioning difficulties and, frequently, serious mental health or drug addiction problems in one or both of the parents. Because of these problems, the parental reports of the child's behavior are often inconsistent with each other and tend to differ markedly from observational and other assessment data obtained while the child is on the unit.

Finally, with respect to the child himself, the "on ward" observations and role-play data tend to be some of the most accurate information. Little individual test time is required, making these data easy to obtain. The individual testing sessions, on the other hand, can differ considerably. This situation is primarily due to attention-span difficulties and loss of at least some cooperation after 20 or 30 minutes of testing.

With a typical assessment of Joey, we would still be able to determine that he was mentally retarded, and that his primary emotional problems centered around aggressive and otherwise unsocialized behavior. However, the primary difference between this and the ideal assessment is that data would not be as consistent; some of the measurements would prove to be invalid. In addition, assessment of mother's parental skill after parent training would be critical in this situation to determine if further extended placement in an intermediate residential facility is required for Joey.

SUMMARY

Some general assumptions can be made based on this limited review of available assessment techniques. First, behavioral interviewing, direct behavioral observation, problem checklists, and standardized tests of IQ and adaptive behavior scales are routinely used, while psychophysiological measurement appears less common. These instruments tend to measure more general functioning rather than discrete behavior; the exception to this rule is direct behavioral measurement.

An important observation is the inevitable finding that observed behavior on the unit tends not to appear as severe to staff as that reported by teachers, parents, and other nonmental health-related staff in the community. Such findings coincide with studies showing that psychologists and psychiatrists tend to rate inappropriate behaviors less severely (Sonis & Costello, 1980). In many inpatient settings, the structure prevents many inappropriate behaviors from occurring. The disadvantage of this method, from a behavioral point of view, is that the staff do not have an ample opportunity to teach coping skills for these responses.

Perhaps the most striking feature of the current review is the relative lack of assessment instruments and systems specifically developed for inpatient evaluation of children and, in conjunction with this, the wide variability in types of assessment systems currently in use. Despite the numerous inadequacies of outpatient assessment, they seem minor in comparison to their inpatient counterparts. This is unfortunate since residential settings provide a highly controlled setting where many assessment techniques not applicable in outpatient settings could be used. Hopefully, behavioral researchers will take stock of this situation and begin to develop the necessary diagnostic tools. The time certainly seems ripe, given the state of the technology and the increasing emphasis on behavioral assessment as evidenced by the two new journals on the topic and the Association for Advancement of Behavior Therapy's declaration that the 1980s will be the period of the scientist/clinician.

Another point the reader should consider is that behavioral assessment has not interfaced well with the most prevalent classification system in mental health—DSM III. In past versions of this diagnostic classification system, it has been easy to reconcile this difference since the diagnostic groupings heavily emphasized psychodynamic formulations of mental health problems. However, a considerable change has occurred in this third revision. Definitions have been made much more objective and have been operationalized to some degree. With this increased emphasis on observable "symptoms," behavior modifiers should attempt to capitalize where possible by relating behavioral systems to these traditional methods. What does this mean? The authors believe if behavior modifiers are to have an even greater impact on the field as a whole, they must be willing to formulate behavioral assessment strategies into the existing diagnostic framework. This will increase the visibility of behavioral assessment methods in the general mental health community and the long-term impact of how assessment and diagnosis are done. Furthermore, if behavior therapists choose to ignore the existing structure, they are likely to lose what influence they have in applied settings; decisions using general psychiatric nomenclature will be made with or without the input of behaviorists.

The general structure of behavioral observations and ratings by self and others are methods likely to be greatly expanded in the areas of specialized assessments, such as in the evaluation of depression. Additionally, it would be of considerable value if behavioral systems of assessment could be used to reliably establish the types of children most likely to respond to various treatments. Given the relatively small amount of behavioral assessment research in general, and inpatient work with children in particular, these goals require a number of years of intensive development. However, the interest in assessment research of this type is at an all-time high; the impetus for answering the questions addressed in this chapter may be at hand.

REFERENCES

Abikoff, H., Gittelmann-Klein, R., & Klein, D. F. Validation of a classroom observation code for hyperactive children. *Journal of Consulting and Clinical Psychology,* 1977, *45,* 772–83.

Achenbach, T. M. The child behavior profile: I. Boys aged 6 through 11. *Journal of Consulting and Clinical Psychology,* 1978, *46,* 478–88.

Achenbach, T. M. The child behavior profile: An empirically based system for assessing children's behavioral problems and competencies. *International Journal of Mental Health,* in press.

Achenbach, T. M., & Edelbrock, C. S. The child behavior profile: II. Boys aged 12–16 and girls aged 6–11 and 12–16. *Journal of Consulting and Clinical Psychology,* 1979, *47,* 223–33.

Achenbach, T. M., & Edelbrock, C. S. The classification of child psychopathology: A review and analysis of empirical efforts. *Psychological Bulletin,* 1978, *85,* 1275–1301.

American Psychological Association. *Monitor.* Washington, DC: Author, May 1979.

American Psychological Association. *Monitor.* Washington, DC: Author, January 1980.

American Psychological Association. *Monitor.* Washington, DC: Author, June 1980.

American Psychiatric Association. *Diagnostic and statistical manual of mental disorders (2nd ed.)* Washington, DC: Author, 1968.

American Psychiatric Association. *Diagnostic and statistical manual of mental disorders (3rd ed.).* Washington, DC: Author, 1980.

Anastasi, A. *Psychological testing.* New York: MacMillan, 1976.

Averill, J. R., & Opton, E. M. Psychophysiological assessment: rationale and problems. In R. McReynolds (Ed.), *Advances in psychological assessment: Volume I.* Palto Alto: Sciences and Behavioral Books, 1968.

Balthazar, E. E. *Balthazar scales of adaptive behavior. I: Scales for functional independence.* Champaign, IL: Research Press, 1971.

Balthazar, E. E. *Balthazar scales of adaptive behavior. II: Scales for social adaptation.* Palto Alto, CA: Consulting Psychologists Press, 1973.

Beck, S., & Forehand, R. Social skills training for children: A review and methodological analysis of behavior modification studies. Unpublished manuscript, 1980.

Birnbrauer, J. S. Mental retardation. In H. Leitenberg (Ed.), *Handbook of behavior modification and behavior therapy.* Englewood Cliffs, NJ: Prentice Hall, 1976.

Bornstein, M., Bellack, A. S., & Hersen, M. Social skills training for highly aggressive children: Treatment in an inpatient psychiatric setting. *Behavior Modification,* 1980, *4,* 173–186.

Boroskin, A. *Fairview language evaluation scale birth to six years.* Costa Mesa, CA: Fairview State Hospital, 1971.

Carlson, G. A., & Cantwell, D. P. Unmasking masked depression in children and adolescents. *American Journal of Psychiatry,* 1980, *137,* 445–449.

Chess, S., Thomas, A., & Birch, H. G. Distortions in developmental recordings made by parents of behaviorally disturbed children. *Journal of the American Academy of Child Psychiatry,* 1966, *5,* 226–31.

Ciminero, A. R., & Drabman, R. S. Current developments in the behavioral assessment of children. In B. B. Lahey & A. E. Kazdin (Eds.), *Advances in child clinical psychology*. Vol. 1. New York: Plenum Press, 1977.

Ciminero, A. R., Calhoun, K. S., & Adams, H. E. (Eds.), *Handbook of behavioral assessment*. New York: Wiley, 1977.

Conners, C. K., & Werry, J. S. Pharmacotherapy. In H. C. Quay & J. S. Werry (Eds.), *Psychopathological disorders of childhood*. (2nd ed.) New York: Wiley, 1979.

Combs, M. L., & Slaby, D. A. Social skills training with children. In B. B. Lahey & A. E. Kazdin (Eds.), *Advances in clinical child psychology*. Vol. 1. New York: Plenum Press, 1977.

Costello, C. S. Childhood depression: Three basic but questionable assumptions in the Lefkowitz and Burton Critique. *Psychological Bulletin*, 1980, *87*, 185–90.

Cowen, E. L., Pederson, A., Babigan, H., Izzo, L. D., & Trost, M. A. Long term follow-up of early detected vulnerable children. *Journal of Consulting and Clinical Psychology*, 1973, *41*, 438–46.

DeMyer, J., Barton, S., DeMyer, W., Norton, J., Allen, J., & Steele, R. Prognosis in autism: A follow-up study. *Journal of Autism and Schizophrenia*, 1973, *3*, 199–246.

Doll, E. A. *Social maturity scale*. Circle Pines, MN: American Guidance Service, 1965.

Drabman, R. S., Jarvie, G. J., & Hammer, D. Residential child treatment. In M. Hersen & A. S. Bellack (Eds.), *Behavior therapy in the psychiatric setting*. Baltimore: Williams & Wilkins, 1978.

Elder, J. P., Edelstein, B. A., & Narick, M. M. Adolescent psychiatric patients: Modifying aggressive behavior with social skills training. *Behavior Modification*, 1979, *3*, 161–78.

Epstein, L. H. Psychophysiological measurement in assessment. In M. Hersen & A. S. Bellack (Eds.), *Behavioral assessment: A practical handbook*. Oxford: Pergamon Press, 1976.

Evans, I. M., & Nelson, R. O. Assessment of child behavior problems. In A. R. Ciminero, K. S. Calhoun & H. E. Adams (Eds.), *Handbook of behavioral assessment*. New York: Wiley, 1977.

Forehand, R., & Baumeister, A. A. Deceleration of aberrant behavior among retarded individuals. In M. Hersen, R. M. Eisler, & P. M. Miller (Eds.), *Progress in behavior modification*. Vol. 2. New York: Academic Press, 1976.

Forehand, R., King, H. E., Peed, S., & Yoder, P. Mother-child interactions: Comparisons of a noncompliant clinic-group and a non-clinic group. *Behavior Research and Therapy*, 1975, *13*, 79–84.

Gaines, T., & Stedman, J. M. Influence of separate interviews on clinician's evaluative perceptions in family therapy. *Journal of Consulting and Clinical Psychology*, 1979, *47*, 1138–39.

Gearhart, B. R. *Learning disabilities: Educational strategies*. St. Louis, MO: Mosby, 1973.

Graham, P. J. Epidemiological studies. In H. C. Quay & J. S. Werry (Eds.), *Psychopathological disorders of childhood*. (2nd ed.) New York: Wiley, 1979.

Green, K. D., Forehand, R., Beck, S., & Vosk, B. An assessment of the relationship among measures of children's social competence and children's academic achievement. *Child Development*, in press.

Grossman, H. J. (Ed.) *Manual on terminology and classification in mental retardation*. Washington, DC: American Association on Mental Deficiency, 1977.

Group for the Advancement of Psychiatry. *Psychopathological disorders in childhood: Theoretical considerations and a proposed classification*. New York: Author, 1966.

Hagamen, M. B. Family support systems: Their effect on long-term psychiatric hospitalization in children. *Journal of the American Academy of Child Psychiatry*, 1977, *16*, 53–66.

Hagamen, M. B. Childhood psychosis: Residential treatment and its alternatives. In B. B. Wolman, J. Egan, & A. O. Ross (Eds.), *Handbook of treatment of mental disorders in childhood and adolescence*. Englewood Cliffs, NJ: Prentice Hall, 1978.

Halpern, A., Raffeld, P., Irvin, L. K., & Link, R. *Textbook for the social and prevocational information battery*. Monterey: CTB/McGraw-Hill, 1975.

Hawkins, R. P. Who decided that was the problem? Two stages of responsibility for applied behavior analysists. In W. S. Wood (Ed.), *Issues in evaluating behavior modification*. Champaign, IL: Research Press, 1975.

Hersen, M., & Bellack, A. S. (Eds.), *Behavioral assessment: A practical handbook*. Oxford: Pergamon Press, 1976.

Hobbs, N. *The futures of children*. San Francisco: Jossey-Bass, 1975.

Kent, R. N., & O'Leary, K. D. A controlled evaluation of behavior modification with conduct problem children. *Journal of Consulting and Clinical Psychology*, 1976, *44*, 586–96.

Kovacs, M., & Beck, A. T. An empirical clinical approach towards a definition of childhood depression. In Schultebrandt, J. G., & Raskin, A. (Eds.), *Depression in Children: Diagnosis, treatment and conceptual models*. New York: Raven Press, 1977.

Lacey, J. I. Psychophysiological approaches to the evaluation of psychotherapeutic process and outcome. In E. A. Rubenstein & M. B. Parloff (Eds.), *Research in psychotherapy*. Vol. I. Washington, DC: American Psychological Association, 1962.

Lahey, B. B. Behavior modification with learning disabilities and related problems. In M. Hersen, R. M. Eisler, & P. M. Miller (Eds.), *Progress in behavior modification*. Vol. 3. New York: Academic Press, 1976.

Lahey, B. B., & Kupfer, D. L. Partial hospitalization programs for children and adolescents. In R. F. Luber (Ed.), *Partial hospitalization: A current perspective*. New York: Plenum Press, 1979.

Lang, P. The application of psychophysiological methods to the study of psychotherapy and behavior modification. In A. E. Bergin & S. L. Garfield (Eds.), *Handbook of psychotherapy and behavior change: An empirical analysis*. New York: Wiley, 1971.

Lefkowitz, M. M., & Burton, N. Childhood depression: A critique of the concept. *Psychological Bulletin*, 1978, *85*, 716–26.

Lefkowitz, M. M., & Tesiny, E. R. Assessment of childhood depression. *Journal of Consulting and Clinical Psychology*, 1980, *48*, 43–50.

Leland, H., Shellhaas, M., Nihira, K., & Foster, R. Adaptive behavior: A new dimension in the qualification of the mentally retarded. *Mental Retardation Abstracts*, 1967, *4*, 359–87.

Levine, S., Elzey, F. F., Thormahlen, P., & Cain, L. F. *The T.M.R. school competency scales*. Palto Alto: Consulting Psychologists Press, 1976.

Linehan, M. M. Issues in behavioral interviewing. In J. D. Cone & L. P. Hawkins (Eds.), *Behavioral assessment: New directions in clinical psychology*. New York: Brunner/Mazel, 1977.

Lovaas, O. I., Koegel, R., Simmons, J. Q., & Long, J. S. Some generalization and follow-up measures on autistic children in behavior therapy. *Journal of Applied Behavior Analysis*, 1973, *6*, 131–66.

Lovaas, O. I., & Newsom, C. D. Behavior modification with psychotic children. In H. Leitenberg (Ed.), *Handbook of behavior modification and behavior therapy*. Englewood Cliffs, NJ: Prentice Hall, 1976.

Matarazzo, J. D. *Wechsler's measurement and appraisal of adult intelligence*. Baltimore: Williams & Wilkins, 1972.

Meyers, C. E., Nihira, K., & Zetlin, A. the measurement of adaptive behavior. In N. Ellis (Ed.), *Handbook of mental deficiency, psychological theory and research*. Hillsdale: Lawrence Erlbaum Associates, 1979.

O'Leary, K. D., & Wilson, G. T. *Behavior therapy: Application and outcome*. Englewood Cliffs, NJ: Prentice Hall, 1975.

Patterson, G. R. An empirical approach to the classification of disturbed children. *Journal of Clinical Psychology*, 1964, *20*, 326–37.

Petti, T. A. Depression in hospitalized child psychiatry patients: Approaches to measuring depression. *American Academy of Child Psychiatry*, 1978, *17*, 49–59.

Proger, B. B. Peabody individual achievement test: A review. *Journal of Special Education*, 1970, *4*, 461–67.

Quay, H. C., & Peterson, D. R. *Manual for the behavior problem checklist*. Unpublished manuscript, 1975.

Quay, H. C. Measuring dimensions of deviant behavior: The behavior problem checklist. *Journal of Abnormal Child Psychology*, 1977, *5*, 277–87.

Quay, H. C. Classification. In H. C. Quay & J. S. Werry (Eds.), *Psychopathological disorders of childhood*. (2nd ed.) New York: Wiley, 1979.

Ritvo, E. (Ed.), *Autism: Diagnosis, current research and management*. New York: Spectrum, 1976.

Roff, M., Sells, B., & Golden, M. *Social adjustment and personality development in children*. Minneapolis: University of Minnesota Press, 1972.

Rosenthal, D. *Genetic theory and abnormal behavior*. New York: McGraw-Hill, 1970.

Schacht, T., & Nathan, P. E. But is it good for psychologists? Appraisal and status of DSM III. *American Psychologist*, 1977, *32*, 1017–25.

Schulterbrandt, J. G., & Raskin, A. (Eds.) *Depression in childhood: Diagnosis, treatment and conceptual models*. New York: Raven Press, 1977.

Sonis, W. A., & Costello, A. J. Evaluation of differential data sources: Application of the diagnostic process in child psychiatry. Unpublished manuscript, University of Pittsburgh School of Medicine, 1980.

Sprague, R. L., Barnes, K. P., & Werry, J. S. Experimental psychology and stimulant drugs. In C. K. Conners (Ed.), *Clinical use of stimulant drugs in children*. Boston: Excerpta Medica, 1974.

Swan, G. E., & MacDonald, M. L. Behavior therapy in practice: A national survey of behavior therapists. *Behavior Therapy*, 1978, *9*, 799–807.

Van Hasselt, V. B., Hersen, M., Bellack, A. S., & Whitehill, M. B. Social skill assessment and training for children: An evaluative review. *Behaviour Research and Therapy*, 1979, *17*, 413–37.

Wade, T. C., & Hartmann, D. P. Behavior therapists self-reported views and practices. *The Behavior Therapist*, 1979, *2*, 3–6.

Waldrop, M. F., & Halverson, C. F. Intensive and extensive peer behaviors: Longitudinal and cross-sectional analyses. *Child Development*, 1975, *46*, 19–26.

Wechsler, D. *Manual for the Weschler Intelligence Scale for Children*. New York: Psychological Corporation, 1974.

Werry, J. S. Childhood psychosis. In H. C. Quay & J. S. Werry (Eds.), *Psychopathological disorders of childhood*. (1st ed.) New York: Wiley, 1972.

Werry, J. S. The childhood psychoses. In H. C. Quay & J. S. Werry (Eds.), *Psychopathological disorders of childhood*. (2nd ed.) New York: Wiley, 1979.

Werry, J. S., & Quay, H. C. Observing the classroom behavior of elementary school children. *Exceptional Children*, 1969, *35*, 461–72.

Yarrow, M. R., Campbell, J. D., & Burton, R. V. Recollections of childhood: A study of the retrospective method. *Monographs of the Society for Research in Child Development*, 1970, 35, 5, (Serial No. 138).

Zigler, E., & Trickett, P. K. IQ, social competence and evaluation of early childhood intervention program. *American Psychologist*, 1978, *33*, 789–98.

Zubin, L. Classification of the behavior disorders. *Annual Review of Psychology*, 1967, *18*, 373–406.

Author Index

Author Index

Subject Index

construct of, 246-248
signs, 251-252
symptom content, 250-251
Depression, childhood, 543-544
Depression scales
clinician ratings, 263-270
self-report, 253-263
Derogatis Sexual Functioning Inventory (DSFI), 446
"Dimensions of Behavior Rule," 367
Dyadic Adjustment Scale (DAS), 413
Dysfunctional Attitude Scale, 159, 160, 163
Dyspareunia, 440

Electromyogram (EMG), 183-184
anxiety measure, 221-222
Electrodermal measures, 184-185
anxiety, 225-226
Electrodes, 177-178
Electrophysiological. See
Psychophysiological
Environment, 356-361
Erectile insufficiency, 439, 440-443, 447
Erotic activity, 428
Erotic threshold value, 428
Exhibitionism, 429
Extended Interaction Test, 231

Fear. See
Anxiety
Fear Survey Schedule (FSS), 232
Fear Thermometer (FT), 233
Feelings and Concerns Checklist, 269-270
Frequency measures, 104-105
Frotteurism, 429

Gender Identity Scales for Males. See
Masculinity-femininity scales
Generalizability theory, 49-51
relevance to behavioral assessment, 51
universes of generalizability, 50-51
Generalization, 361-363

Hamilton Rating Scale, 264-266
Hallucinations, as targeted behavior, 353-354
Heart rate. See
Cardiovascular measures
"Hebe Admitter" scale, 434
Hopelessness Scale, 160, 163
Hyperactive Behavior Code, 512
Hyperactivity. See
Childhood disorders; Physiological measures

Inpatient Multi-Dimensional Psychiatric Scale (IMPS), 363-364
Inter-beat-interval, 181
Interobserver agreement. See
reliability
Interpersonal skills. See
Social skills
Interpersonal Situations Inventory, 310
Interval recording, 107-108
Interview
anxiety, 234-235, 236-237
with children, 500-504
with children inpatients, 547-550
ethical issues, 76-80
goals of, 72-73, 77, 88-89
schema, 73-76
social skills deficits, 305-309
Interviewer-client relationship, 80-82
"ideal therapist," 81
Interviewing, 82-83
closing, 95-96
redefinition of problem, 92-94
specification of problem, 89-92
starting, 83-88
Inventories. See
Questionnaires
"in vivo" assessment, 160
Irrational Beliefs Test, 159, 160, 161

Katz Adjustment Scales, 279-281
Kinsey scale. See
Masculinity-femininity scales

content, 45
convergent, 47
criterion-related, 47
discriminant, 47-48
incremental, 48
relationship to accuracy and
reliability, 59-60
treatment, 48
Variability, interpretation of, 52-53

Vineland Social Maturity Scale. *See*
Adaptive behavior scales
Visual Analog Scale, 262

Work skills, 347-348

Zung Self-Rating Depression Scale
(SDS), 259-260

About the Contributors

Michel Hersen (Ph.D., State University of New York at Buffalo, 1966) is Professor of Psychiatry and Psychology at the University of Pittsburgh. He is the Past President of the Association for Advancement of Behavior Therapy. He has co-authored and co-edited 18 books including: *Single-case experimental designs: Strategies for studying behavior change, Behavior therapy in the psychiatric setting, Behavior modification: An introductory textbook,* and *Introduction to clinical psychology.* With Bellack, he is editor and founder of *Behavior Modification* and *Clinical Psychology Review.* He is Associate Editor of *Addictive Behaviors* and Editor of *Progress in behavior modification.* Dr. Hersen is the recipient of several NIMH research grants.

Alan S. Bellack (Ph.D., Pennsylvania State University, 1970) is Professor of Psychology and Psychiatry and Director of Clinical Psychology Training at the University of Pittsburgh. He is co-author and co-editor of seven books including: *Behavior modification: An introductory textbook, Research and practice in social skills training,* and *Introduction to clinical psychology.* He has published numerous journal articles and has received several NIMH research grants on social skills, behavioral assessment, and weight control. With Hersen, he is editor and founder of the journals *Behavior Modification* and *Clinical Psychology Review.* He has served on the editorial boards of numerous journals and has been a consultant to a number of publishing companies and mental health facilities as well as NIMH.

Hal Arkowitz received his Ph.D. from the University of Pennsylvania and completed a predoctoral internship at Langley Porter Neuropsychiatric Institute and a post-doctoral fellowship in clinical psychology at the State University of New York at Stony Brook. He taught at the Psychology Department at the University of Oregon before moving to the University of Arizona, where he is currently Associate Professor of Psychology and an Associate in the Psychiatry Department at the University of Arizona School of Medicine. He has published articles and chapters in the areas of anxiety, social skills assessment and treatment, and depression. He is on the editorial board of several journals including *Behavior Therapy, Behavior Modification,* and the *Journal of Consulting and Clinical Psychology.*

Steven Beck is a doctoral student in clinical psychology at the University of Georgia. His primary interest areas are the assessment and treatment of psychopathology in children and the use of behavioral medicine strategies.

Kelly M. Bemis is an advanced graduate student in the Department of Psychology of the University of Minnesota. Her major areas of interest include anorexia and cognitive behavioral therapy.

Douglas A. Bernstein received his Ph.D. from Northwestern University in 1968 and is currently Professor and Associate Head of the Department of Psychology at the University of Illinois at Urbana-Champaign. His research interests center on behavioral medicine, particularly the areas of reduction of general tension, elimination of anxiety relating to dental procedures, and prevention of serious diseases through the modification of smoking behavior. He is senior author of *Progressive Relaxation training* (1973) and *Introduction to clinical psychology* (1980).

Ray Blanchard, Ph.D. in psychology from the University of Illinois at Urbana-Champaign, in 1973, worked with sex offenders while a staff psychologist at the Ontario Correctional Institute. In 1980, he took up the position of Senior Research Psychologist, Gender Identity Clinic, Clarke Institute of Psychiatry, Toronto.

John D. Cone received his A.B. degree at Stanford University in 1964 and his Ph.D. in clinical psychology from the University of Washington in 1968. He has been Chief Psychologist, Madigan General Hospital, Tacoma, Washington and a lecturer in psychology at the University of Puget Sound. Since 1970 Dr. Cone has been on the faculty of the child clinical psychology program at West Virginia University. He is co-editor (with R. P. Hawkins) of *Behavioral assessment: New directions in clinical psychology* and is an associate editor of *Behavioral Assessment*.

Dr. David W. Foy, collaborated in substance abuse efforts at V.A. Medical Center, Jackson from 1978–1980. Having received his graduate training from the University of Southern Mississippi, he completed his internship requirements in clinical psychology at the University of Mississippi Medical Center—V.A. Medical Center, Jackson Psychology Training Consortium.

Kurt Freund—M.D. 1937, Medical School, Charles University, Prague, Czechoslovakia. Left Czechoslovakia in 1968, at which time he was "Docent" (Associate Professor) in Psychiatry, the narrower specialization being in Behavioral Sexology. Since 1969 he has been Head, Department of Behavioral Sexology, Clarke Institute of Psychiatry, Toronto, Canada; and at first Assistant, then Associate Professor, and since 1979 (at age 65) Special Lecturer, Department of Psychiatry, University of Toronto.

Dr. Steven C. Hayes is an Assistant Professor of Psychology at the University of North Carolina at Greensboro. He is an associate editor of the *Journal of Applied Behavior Analysis,* and is on the editorial boards of the *Journal of Consulting and Clinical Psychology, Behavior Modification,* and *Behavioral Assessment.* His research has been in self-control, cognitive therapy, single case designs, behavioral assessment, sexual behavior, and environmental problems.

Steven D. Hollon is Associate Professor of Psychology at the University of Minnesota. He obtained his Ph.D. in 1977 from the Florida State University. His major interest is in the area of the affective disorders.

Neil S. Jacobson, Ph.D. is a faculty member in the Department of Psychology, University of Washington, Seattle, Washington. He is coauthor (along with Gayla Margolin) of the book *Marital therapy: Strategies based on social learning and behavior exchange principles.* He has also published a number of articles and book chapters in the areas of marital interaction and therapy from a behavioral perspective, depression, and design considerations in behavior modification research. In addition to his position as the associate editor of *the American Journal of Family Therapy,* he serves as an editorial board member and editorial consultant for a number of other journals.

Alan E. Kazdin is Professor of Psychiatry at Western Psychiatric Institute and Clinic, University of Pittsburgh School of Medicine. He currently is editor of *Behavior Therapy* and has been President of the Association for Advancement of Behavior Therapy and a Fellow at the Center for Advanced Study in the Behavioral Sciences. His present research consists of evaluating assessment and intervention methods with psychiatrically disturbed children.

Gayla Margolin, Ph.D. is an assistant professor of Psychology at the University of Southern California. She is coauthor (with Neil Jacobson) of the book *Marital therapy: Strategies based on social learning and behavior exchange principles.* She has published a number of articles and book chapters on the assessment and treatment of marital and family relationships, and serves on the editorial board of the *American Journal of Family Therapy.*

Johnny L. Matson is a psychologist and assistant professor of child psychiatry at the University of Pittsburgh School of Medicine. His primary research interests include the treatment and assessment of psychopathology and adaptive skills in the full age range of mentally retarded persons and in children without major cognitive impairments.

Kenneth P. Morganstern received his Ph.D. from the Pennsylvania State University and joined the clinical psychology faculty of the University of Oregon. **Helen E. Tevlin** received her Ph.D. from the University of Oregon and completed a post-doctoral training program in sex therapy at Rutgers Medical School. Both are presently psychologists for the Risk Factor Obesity Control Program and are in private clinical practice in Portland.

Dr. Rosemery O. Nelson is Professor of Psychology and Director of Clinical Training at the University of North Carolina at Greensboro. She is President-Elect of the Association for Advancement of Behavior Therapy and editor of *Behavioral Assessment.* Her research and writing have been in the areas of behavioral assessment, self-monitoring, behavioral school psychology, and environmental influences in self control and in cognitive behavior therapy.

Michael T. Nietzel received his Ph.D. from the University of Illinois at Champaign-Urbana in 1973. He currently is Associate Professor of Psychology at the University of Kentucky, where he has been Director of the Clinical Training Program since 1977. Nietzel's research interests are concentrated on evaluation of social learning theory interventions, forensic psychology and applications of psychology to community problems.

Dr. Donald M. Prue collaborated in substance abuse efforts at V.A. Medical Center, Jackson from 1978–1980. Having received his graduate training from West Virginia University, he completed his internship requirements in clinical psychology at the University of Mississippi Medical Center—V.A. Medical Center, Jackson Psychology Training Consortium.

William J. Ray is an Associate Professor of psychology at The Pennsylvania State University. His research interest involves the interface between clinical ˙ psychology and psychophysiology/neuropsychology. Recent books include *Biofeedback: Potential and Limits* (with R. M. Stern); *Psychophysiological Recording* (with R. M. Stern & C. M. Davis); *Evaluation of Clinical Biofeedback* (with J. Raczynski, T. Rogers, & W. Kimball); and *Methods Toward a Science of Behavior and Experience* (with R. Ravizza).

James M. Raczynski received his Ph.D. from The Pennsylvania State University and has recently completed a clinical psychology internship at the University of Mississippi Medical Center. He is a co-author of *Evaluation of clinical biofeedback*. His research interests include psychophysiology and behavioral medicine.

Lynn P. Rehm did his graduate work at the University of Wisconsin-Madison. Since then he has held academic positions at the UCLA Department of Psychiatry and the University of Pittsburgh. Presently, he is Professor and Director of Clinical Training at the University of Houston. Dr. Rehm's research interests are in the areas of self-control and depression. He is the editor of *Behavior therapy for depression: Present status and future directions* published by Academic Press and is author of the forthcoming book *The assessment of depression published by Guilford Press*.

Dr. Robert G. Rychtarik collaborated in substance abuse efforts at V.A. Medical Center, Jackson from 1978–1980. Having received his graduate training from the University of Montana, he completed his internship requirements in clinical psychology at the University of Mississippi Medical Center—V.A. Medical Center, Jackson Psychology Training Consortium.

Charles J. Wallace is co-principal investigator (along with Robert Liberman, M.D.) of the NIMH-funded Mental Health Clinical Research Center for the Study of Schizophrenia and of an NIHR-funded Rehabilitation Research and Training Center (Mental Illness Area). Dr. Wallace is an Associate Clinical Professor of Psychology at the UCLA-Neuropsychiatric Institute and a Visiting Associate Professor at the Fuller Graduate School of Psychology. His primary research and clinical interests are in the assessment and training of social and independent living skills of chronic schizophrenics.

Karen C. Wells, Ph.D. is a faculty member in the Department of Psychiatry at Children's Hospital National Medical Center, Washington, D.C. A graduate of the University of Georgia, her clinical and research interests are in the area of behavior therapy with children in the pediatric and psychiatric settings. She has authored numerous papers on behavioral approaches to assessment and treatment of conduct disordered, hyperkinetic, and developmentally disabled children.

Pergamon General Psychology Series

Editors: Arnold P. Goldstein, Syracuse University
Leonard Krasner, SUNY, Stony Brook